PSYCHOLOGY TODAY
An Introduction

PSYCHOLOGY TODAY
An Introduction

CRM BOOKS
Del Mar, California

PREFACE

Success in presenting a definitive introduction to psychology has eluded the efforts of experts for over a century—whether in a large book or in a single sentence. The problem appears to have been, and appears still to be, one of consensus among psychologists about just what psychology is.

As early as 1890, William James said, "Psychology is the science of mental life." Twenty years later, E. B. Tichener had decided that "definition of the subject-matter of psychology is impossible." In another twenty years, however, J. B. Watson had again defined psychology, this time as "the behavior of human beings," and, on quite a different tack, Sigmund Freud had resumed the pursuit of psychology as the science of mental life. So it has gone: visions and revisions of psychology evolving through many discoveries, many disputes, and little consensus down to this day—in which psychologists are still disputing the basic conception of psychology.

But contradiction and dispute are the life signs of a vital field, and to those who have produced this book, the lack of a universally accepted definition of psychology is, rather than an obstacle, an opportunity. It is not the purpose of *Psychology Today: An Introduction* to foster consensus about the limits of psychology, but fairly and fully to represent the abundance of opinions that prevents it.

David A. Dushkin, Publisher

CONTENTS

PSYCHOLOGY TODAY
An Introduction

UNIT I

INTRODUCTION Psychology derives its name from two Greek words, *psyche*, meaning spirits, and *logos*, meaning speech or sayings. In classical terms, then, psychology is a collection of words about the spirit or mind. The Greeks liked to differentiate between the physical side of man—his corporeal being—and his mental or spiritual side. From this ancient dualism has come the most troublesome specter ever to haunt a science—namely, the mind-body problem. Does the mind affect the body's behavior or vice versa? If the spirit or mind has no physical dimensions, how can it be in touch with corporeal behavior and motivate or affect it? And how do bodily actions affect the mind? Even today, psychology has not completely solved this dualistic dilemma, but it does seem clear to today's psychologists that a study of the mind—or, better said, of mental processes—is not complete without a healthy understanding of behavior as well.

1

PSYCHOLOGY TODAY

PSYCHOLOGY TODAY is best defined as the *scientific study of behavior*. Compared with some interpretations of the term during the past, this definition is somewhat novel and, in its way, rather radical. The definition is new in that most people still think that psychology is primarily concerned with the human psyche, or mind—an approach that would have been taken in an introductory psychology course fifty years ago. In those days, you would have been told that psychology was the scientific study of the mind, for psychologists then tended to focus on man's inner life, his subjective experiences, his stream of consciousness. The noted American psychologist William James wrote in 1896, for example, that *mind* was the sum of a man's experience. Even in 1896, however, psychologists were aware that what goes on inside a person is never really totally perceptible and therefore cannot be examined directly. Mental events can be studied only if the person experiencing those events expresses them, but even then we can study only the person's verbal report, not what goes on inside him. One of the great tragedies of human existence is that we can never really know another person intimately; we can never experience someone else's mental life—what he sees, thinks, feels. All we ever know about another person—no matter how close we are to him—is what he indicates to us by his behavior.

The individuality of our mental world can be illustrated by the way we see things. We all know, for example, that grass in springtime is green, lush green. You look at the grass and say it is green, and so does a friend of yours. But can you prove that the two of you actually see the same color? No, unfortunately you cannot. Moreover, perhaps your friend is among the approximately 10 percent of the men in this world who have considerable difficulty seeing "green" at all—who are partially or completely color blind and to whom green may look exactly the same as red. They know that a rose is red and grass is green because they have been told this all their lives. They may insist that they "see" grass as being a different color than a rose, but when we study their color vision in a laboratory, we discover that they cannot differentiate between red and green very well, if at all. Thus, we might examine your description of grass as being green and *infer* that you see the same color that your friend does, but we cannot prove that our inference is correct. The best we can do is to check you and your friend in a number of situations to see if you consistently report similar experiences when you encounter similar objects. But nevertheless, what you see remains privately yours.

If we return to our definition, then, it becomes clearer that psychology is a *behavioral science* in that its objects of study are the actions and reactions of all animals, including man. The radical part of this definition stems not only from the realization that the only thing we *can* study is behavior but also from the fact that psychologists insist that behavior can be studied *scientifically*. The notion of applying the scientific method to the analysis of behavior is rather new and, to many people, somewhat disturbing. A century ago, most educated people would probably have denied that human behavior either could or should be studied scientifically. Today, at least in the United States and Canada, people accept rather calmly the notion that psychologists can and should study people in laboratories. In other parts of the world, however, the scientific approach to the study of human behavior would be rejected out of hand, without further discussion, for emotional rather than intellectual reasons. Such rejections point up perhaps the single most important variable in determining any person's behavior: the type of emotional learning or conditioning he has acquired during his life.

Likes and dislikes are, almost without exception, learned. If you were invited to someone's house for dinner and were served a meal of succulent roast puppy, fried worms, and raw newborn mice dipped in honey, it is unlikely that you would overeat; indeed, there is a very good chance that you would even refuse to taste anything at all. In many parts of the world, however, these foods that cause American gorges to rise are accepted as *haut cuisine,* as the ultimate delicacies. Had you grown up in some parts of Mexico, for example, you would, rather early in life, have acquired a taste for fried fat white grub worms and would be genuinely distressed if an American friend rejected such a tidbit.

Although it may be easy for you to appreciate that our mealtime habits are learned, it is not so easy to understand that our acceptance or rejection of almost

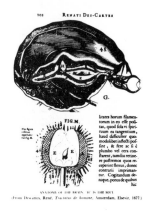

ANATOMY OF THE BRAIN. IT IS THE SOUL
(From Descartes, René, *Tractatus de homine,* Amsterdam, Elsevir, 1677.)

everything is a product of our emotional conditioning. Our morals, our religious tendencies, our political outlook, even our aesthetic appreciation of art and music—the seeds of all these viewpoints are planted in us when we are very young. Later, as young adults, we may defend our morals or politics on rational grounds, but in fact these views are typically not a product of rational decision making on our parts. Whatever we learned at our mother's knee seems natural to us when we grow up; whatever we did not learn seems unnatural, peculiar, something to be rejected out of hand.

Although such emotional conditioning is a powerful determinant in all our lives, the scientist must nevertheless take an unbiased and unemotional view toward whatever he studies; the fact that science is a very recent development in the course of human history suggests how difficult a task this is. For a science to succeed, it must be able to look at its subject matter objectively and dispassionately; the scientist must be able to discard prior ideas as they prove impractical no matter how strongly he was conditioned to accept them when he was young. Physics could not develop as a science as long as the belief that inanimate objects were motivated by spirits of some kind was prevalent. The law of gravity could not be formulated during the Dark Ages because men were not able to look at the physical world objectively, to realize that data gathered during a scientific experiment are somehow more meaningful and trustworthy than reliance on common sense, which itself turns out to be quite uncommon. Astronomy could not come into its own as a scientific discipline until people were willing to admit that astronomical observations were more readily explained and understood if one accepted the sun's central position and made the Earth but one of the sun's many satellites. There are still a few people in the Western world (and large numbers in the East) who believe that the Earth is flat; they tend to dismiss recent astronautical accomplishments as being lies and artifices because they have been conditioned to do so.

One of the major problems that psychology must explain is why, in a contest between emotional conditioning and logic, the emotions almost always seem to win. One possible explanation is that emotions are controlled by parts of the brain that are more primitive and developmentally much older than the part of the brain that appears to mediate logical thinking. Thus, as we shall see in the

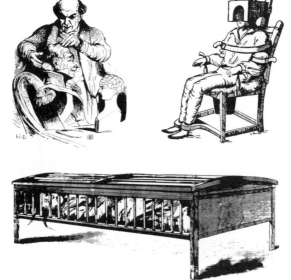

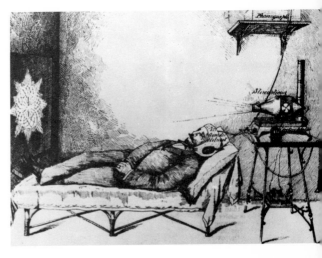

5

next chapter, psychology is a *biological science,* and some knowledge of human neurophysiology is useful in understanding human conduct.

Although physicists and chemists demonstrated centuries ago that objective, unemotional analysis applied to the physical world yielded a rich reward for humanity, not until the 1800s did people begin to realize that the biological and medical sciences could make excellent use of the same scientific methods. For more than 2,000 years, medical science progressed slowly, if at all, on the insights and informal experiments of a few great physicians. Disputes about medical problems were settled by appeal to ancient authorities or common sense. The uncommon sense of the experimental method, applied first to the physical sciences in the 1600s, did not become general practice in the biological sciences until man was willing to admit that his bodily functions followed predictable, analyzable physiological functions. Only when man changed his attitude toward his body could the scientific revolution occur in biology and medicine. The facts that our lifespan has doubled in the past century, that infant mortality rates have decreased enormously, and that we are, on the average, bigger and stronger and healthier than at any previous time in human history are testimony to the benefits of this revolution.

The scientific revolution occurred first in astronomy, physics, and chemistry, in part because these fields are somewhat removed from man's everyday life. The winds of change blew through the biological sciences much later, perhaps because man was slower to accept new viewpoints toward his body than toward the motions of the stars. The scientific revolution is still occurring in psychology, having really gotten started no earlier than World War I. As yet, the revolution is largely confined to the Western world, for Eastern philosophy in general is incompatible with behavioral science.

When we say psychology is a behavioral science, we primarily mean that we assume that behavior is lawful, orderly, and predictable and therefore can be studied using scientific methods. As innocuous as that statement first appears, it contains a point of view as radical as the notion that the Earth moves around the sun was in Newton's time. We can transplant a heart from one person to another because we have learned that one heart is, at a very basic structural and functional level, much the same as another and that differences among hearts are

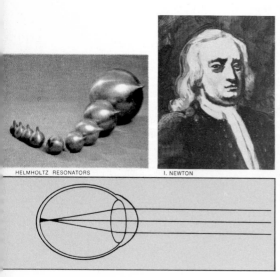

HELMHOLTZ RESONATORS

I. NEWTON

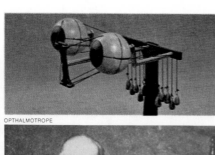

OPTHALMOTROPE

H. von HELMHOLTZ

G. T. FECHNER

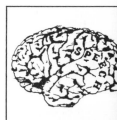

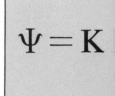

$$\frac{\Delta I}{I}$$

$$\Psi = K$$

fairly predictable and can be controlled. If each person had an entirely unique circulatory system, cardiology could not have become a science and heart transplants would be unthinkable. For many centuries, man thought of himself as a unique being, the master of his individual fate, the captain of his own destiny. Now, because of the psychological revolution, we are beginning to think quite differently. We see that there are tremendous similarities in the way people behave. It is true that you are different from everyone else in the world—but only in relatively minor ways. We therefore can study man's behavior scientifically because of these similarities, because of the regularities in and predictabilities of his actions. Our behaviors are as alike as our hearts.

The scientific revolution in physics, chemistry, and biology was effective for one major reason: science works. Pasteur's idea that nearly invisible organisms called microbes cause disease and sickness seemed ridiculous to most of cultured Europe when he first advanced it. Who could logically believe that tiny little creatures could kill a big, strong man? Nevertheless, when Pasteur showed that heating milk both destroyed the germs and prevented disease, most people were willing to concede the point. Expectant mothers insisted that obstetricians wash their hands before delivering babies because experiments showed that the physician's cleanliness gave the mothers a much better chance of surviving childbirth. The revolution now taking place in psychology will, in like fashion, succeed or fail depending on whether it helps us solve our everyday problems better than do other, older methods.

In the past, man has settled psychological problems through argumentation or even war. If you thought that your race was superior to all others, you settled the issue by shouting louder than or by trying to kill off anyone who disputed you. If you thought that sex education in the schools weakened the moral fiber of young people, you settled the issue by quoting important people who seemed to agree with you or by referring to some young person you knew (or perhaps had only heard of) who had taken such a course and then been ruined. The thought that

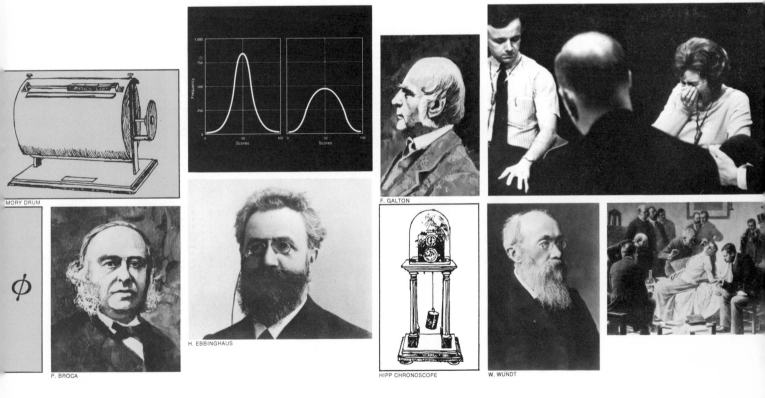

MORY DRUM

F. GALTON

P. BROCA

H. EBBINGHAUS

HIPP CHRONOSCOPE

W. WUNDT

scientific methods can be employed to resolve such disputes still does not occur to many individuals.

Scientific methods work partly because they are free from many of the biases that beset the commonsense approach and partly because most scientific knowledge comes from repeatable experiments. A scientific experiment may be defined as a controlled observation that can be repeated by anyone anywhere who is willing to follow the experimenter's procedures exactly. That definition exposes both the strengths and the weaknesses of scientific methods.

Experimental findings are more trustworthy than casual, commonplace observations because they are made under controlled conditions and because their results are public knowledge, influenced as little as possible by the prejudices of the person conducting the experiment. One reason that the physical sciences developed rapidly is because it is fairly easy for a physicist to control the factors that might influence his experimental results. For example, if you dropped a weight off the tower at Pisa, its speed would be affected by such diverse factors as the size and shape of the object (feathers fall more slowly than does a lead ball), the barometric pressure (the thicker the air, the more slowly the object will fall), and what direction and at what speed the wind is blowing. The physicist can avoid most of these problems by dropping the weight in a vacuum rather than in open air. It is rather difficult for someone working with human subjects to suspend them in a vacuum, however, so the psychologist must usually control extraneous variables in a different way. Before we examine the psychologist's methodology, however, it is instructive to see just what kinds of controls can be applied when one uses the methods of science.

Suppose that you have discovered a new drug you think will cure headaches. Before the advent of the scientific era, you would probably have given it to a few people who said they had a headache and, if they reported being cured, start to

C. DARWIN

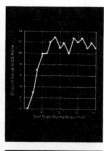

I. PAVLOV

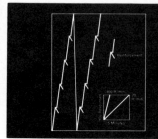

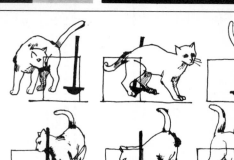

market the drug and make your fortune. Today, the Food and Drug Administration insists that you test it first on animals to show that it is not toxic. (As you will see throughout this book, psychologists often use animals too as research subjects before testing their theories at the human level.) Once the safety of your new drug has been established beyond reasonable doubt, you can try it (perhaps in pill form) on human subjects. But what form would your experiment take? Suppose that you took a hundred or so people with headaches and gave them the drug, then checked with them a week or so later. If you found that all their headaches were gone, would it mean that your drug is effective? No, and the Food and Drug Administration would not accept those data as proving much of anything because most headaches do not last a week. Even if you examined the subjects an hour after administration of the drug and then at frequent intervals thereafter, your results would not impress the FDA, for we know that most headaches go away even if people take no drug at all.

To show that your pill works *better* than not giving the people any medication at all, you must employ a *control group*—that is, a group of people with headaches who are not given the pill. This control group must be treated as closely as possible to the way you treat the *experimental group*, the group that actually gets the pill. But there is one obvious difference between the two groups: the experimental subjects are given something, but the control subjects are not. We know from a large number of experiments that sick people who are given a sugar pill (called a *placebo*) often show better recovery rates than if they are not given anything. Thus, you also need a control group composed of people who have headaches and are given a placebo. If the experimental group shows a significantly greater improvement (see Chapter 3) than either of the control groups, you have some evidence that your pill actually worked. Before you can

W. JAMES

TONE VARIATOR

S. FREUD

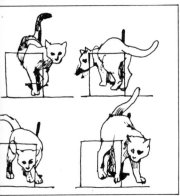

E. THORNDIKE

market the pill, however, you must show additionally that there are no long-term deleterious effects from taking the pill, and other scientists must confirm your preliminary results.

As you can see, scientific methods have a major restriction—they can deal only with that which is public knowledge, that which can be openly examined and agreed upon by an impartial jury. When a scientist performs an experiment, he records exactly what he did and what results he got. If his experimental findings are valid, then anyone else who performs exactly the same manipulations should get exactly the same results. If others attempt to repeat his experiment and fail, either they did not do what he did or there was something wrong with the original experiment. We can best illustrate how this methodology works in psychology by looking at one of the more controversial areas: extrasensory perception, or ESP.

As we shall see in Chapter 14, all the knowledge you have about the world around you comes to you through your sense organs. Scientists have gained at least a rudimentary knowledge of how the sense receptors in the eye and the ear operate: physical energy (light or sound waves) is translated into neurological energy by tiny receptor cells, which flash a message to the brain saying that they have been stimulated by something in the external world. The only known way the brain can receive messages about the surrounding environment is through these sensory receptors. Yet there are many people (scientists included) who believe that humans have a way of perceiving and affecting external events by mental rather than physical means. This extrasensory perception and control are thought to take many forms. *Telepathy* is direct mental contact between two (or more) humans; it is a form of mind reading. *Precognition* is the ability to foresee the future. *Telekinesis* is the ability to manipulate objects in the environment without actually touching them in any way. Scientists who believe in ESP are, in

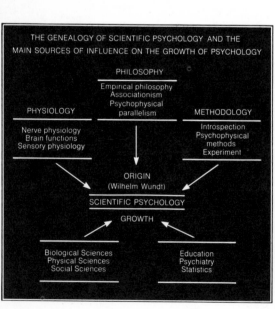

THE GENEALOGY OF SCIENTIFIC PSYCHOLOGY AND THE MAIN SOURCES OF INFLUENCE ON THE GROWTH OF PSYCHOLOGY

A. BINET

C. JUNG

W. McDOUGALL

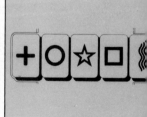

effect, challenging the theories that most physical scientists hold about the world. The confrontation between these two groups provides an interesting example of what scientific methodology is all about.

Suppose that you believe in mental telepathy. How would you go about proving its existence scientifically? Experimenters such as J. B. Rhine at Duke University have struggled with this problem for decades. Rhine's experiments on telepathy have often involved the use of the Zener cards. If we showed 100 of the cards to you, face down, and asked you to guess which symbol appeared on the face of the card just by looking at its back, you would have no way of physically knowing what each card was; therefore, you would be forced to guess. The laws of chance state that, on the average, you will guess correctly about 20 percent of the time. Some of Rhine's experimental subjects have reportedly been able to guess correctly much more of the time than the laws of chance would allow. Rhine believes that these subjects are able to perceive what is on the face of the cards by nonphysical means, but most scientists remain skeptical. These skeptics point out that in Rhine's early (and in some ways most dramatic) experiments, the Zener cards he was using were badly printed so that faint impressions of the symbols could be seen on the back of the cards. In other experiments, it could be shown that the experimenter actually knew which card was correct and was passing along very subtle visual and auditory cues to the subject, who picked the cues up and responded appropriately. As we shall see in Chapter 3, this type of experimenter bias does occur in psychological experi-

A. FREUD

A. ADLER

J. WATSON

M. WERTHEIMER

R. M. YERKES

ments and must constantly be guarded against. In fairness to Rhine and other experimenters in this area, it must be said that not all ESP experiments have been so poorly controlled or so easily explained away.

When Rhine first began his work, many scientists rejected his findings because ESP violates many of the physical laws of the universe as we currently see it. For instance, all physical energy decreases in strength as you move farther away from the source of the energy, and this decrease is absolutely regular and predictable. The farther away you are from a light source, the weaker the light seems to be. Yet telepathy seems to work as well at a distance of 200 miles as it does at 2 feet. But this contradiction is not the primary reason that scientists today, for the most part, remain skeptical of ESP. It is axiomatic in science that a phenomenon be repeatable and predictable. To demonstrate conclusively that ESP exists, a scientist would have to be able to reproduce it whenever he liked. To date, this has proved impossible. Even Rhine's best subjects show but brief flashes of telepathy—their ability to mind-read comes and goes almost whimsically in unpredictable fashion. Many of the most noted psychologists in the world have attempted to repeat Rhine's experiments, but with no success at all. The best that can be said of ESP, then, is that it remains an unproven but

K. LASHLEY

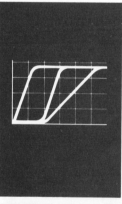

H. S. SULLIVAN

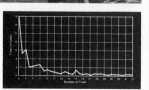

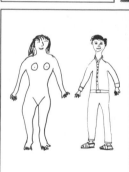

fascinating phenomenon. If and when Rhine (or anyone else) can specify the conditions under which ESP will occur (and equally important, when it will not occur), then and only then will most other scientists be willing to admit that Rhine has successfully challenged the axiom.

In commonsense terms, if one event follows another consistently, then the first event is believed to cause the second. In scientific terms, this is not the case, for scientists have learned that, particularly in regard to human behavior, it is often difficult to determine from mere uncontrolled observation what is causing what. Take hypnosis, for example, an area of psychology that has often been considered as controversial as ESP. No one doubts that hypnosis exists, for it can readily be demonstrated in a laboratory under controlled conditions, but what it is and how it occurs are matters of dispute. A French scientist named Anton Mesmer was the first to study hypnotic trances in a laboratory. In the late 1700s, when Mesmer first began his work, physicists were fascinated by the phenomenon of magnetism. Mesmer wanted to see if he could magnetize human beings,

W. HUNTER

$$_sE_R = {_sH_R} \cdot t \cdot x \cdot D$$

C. HULL

E. TOLMAN

L. L. THURSTONE

E. FROMM

F. ALLPORT

M. PRINCE

so he waved a large magnet in front of their eyes and discovered that they fell into trance states during which they would do very odd things. Mesmer at first believed that it was the magnet that was inducing the trance—after all, each time he waved the magnet, the person seemed to go into a trance. Had he employed the proper control groups in his first studies, he would have discovered immediately what it took scientists more than a hundred years to determine. If he thought that the magnet was responsible for inducing the trance, he should have proved it by waving a piece of wood, or nothing at all, in front of the subjects. Had he done so, he would have found that the magnet was not at all necessary, so magnetism was not involved at all. He might also have tried saying to the subjects everything that he normally said but not waving his hands at all; had he done so, he would have found what another European scientist named

C. HOVLAND

E. R. GUTHRIE

K. BÜHLER

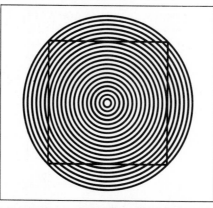

K. LEWIN

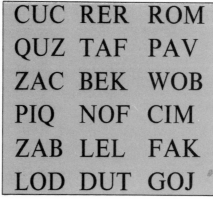

CUC RER ROM
QUZ TAF PAV
ZAC BEK WOB
PIQ NOF CIM
ZAB LEL FAK
LOD DUT GOJ

E. G. BORING

Bernheim found a century later: that hypnosis can be induced by verbal suggestion alone.

The behavior of a hypnotized person can be studied objectively; what he actually experiences when hypnotized cannot be investigated scientifically. Each of us has a private world of experience that is simply not amenable to psychological experimentation. Science is but one aspect of human existence—art, literature, music, religion, and moral judgments belong to quite different domains. To accept the scientific approach to human behavior as being valid in its own right in no way detracts from one's ability to appreciate the many other aspects of human existence. Scientific psychology is a way of answering questions about the

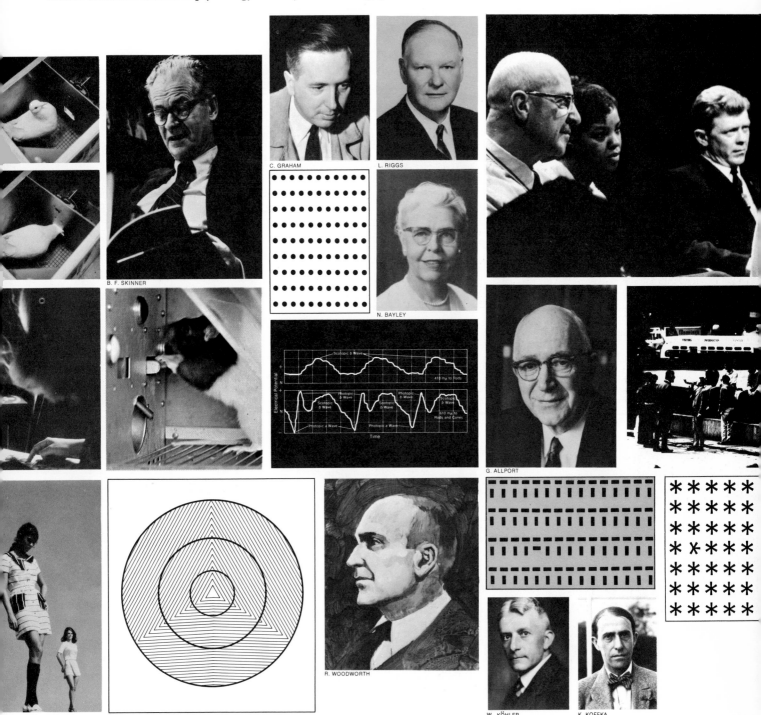

C. GRAHAM

L. RIGGS

B. F. SKINNER

N. BAYLEY

G. ALLPORT

R. WOODWORTH

W. KÖHLER

K. KOFFKA

more public aspects of human and animal behavior; and used properly, it is a very powerful technique indeed. But we must never believe that it is the only valid way of probing human existence.

The behavior of a falling object is influenced by a limited set of physical factors. The behavior of a human being is affected by an enormous range of factors, some biological, some psychological, and some sociological. We are as influenced by the people around us as we are by our genetic make-up. If the people we are with expect us to behave in a certain way and they communicate their expectations to us, we are likely to play the role that they expect us to play. Psychology today is thus a social science as well as a biological science and a behavioral science, and it is beginning to be an applied science. As we shall see

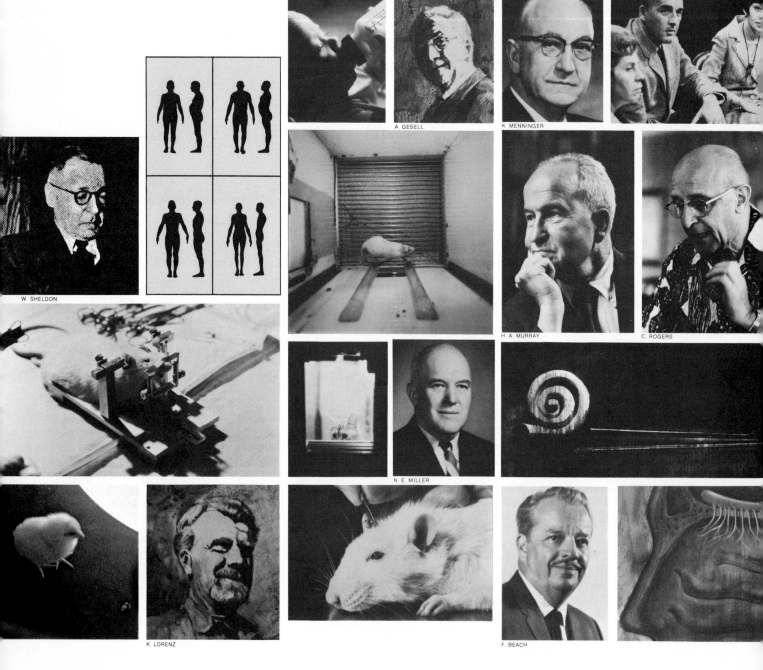

W. SHELDON

A. GESELL

K. MENNINGER

H. A. MURRAY

C. ROGERS

N. E. MILLER

K. LORENZ

F. BEACH

in the next few chapters, what psychologists have learned about the brain has already proved of significant value in helping treat various types of physiological illnesses. What psychologists have learned about the ways in which the human personality develops now aids us in understanding how mental illness may occur and how best it might be prevented and cured. Experiments to determine how

A. KINSEY

OLFACTOMETER

D. O. HEBB

G. von BÉKÉSY

F. ALEXANDER

H. EYSENCK

C. PFAFFMANN

R. GRANIT

animals learn are currently having a revolutionary impact on human education. And, as we shall see in the final chapter of this book, studies of human and animal motivation have led to the use of exciting new techniques for handling such behavioral problems as marital difficulties and juvenile delinquency. Indeed, the application of scientific methods to the solution of behavioral problems promises to change our lives in the future as much as the application to physical and biological problems has in the recent past. This book, then, is an introduction to psychology today and a forecast of psychology tomorrow.

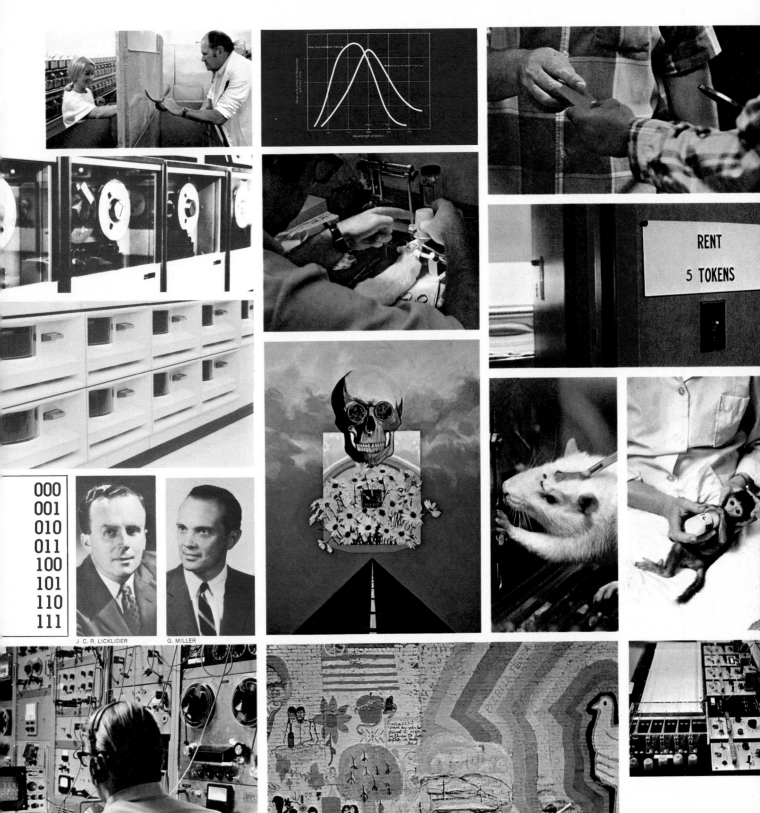

2

THE BIOLOGICAL ORGANISM

YOU ARE A THIRTY-YEAR-OLD HOUSEWIFE who once was cursed with epilepsy. It began when you were a child, for reasons that neither you nor the doctors understand yet. At first, the seizures were mild and quite infrequent, if embarrassing. By using a drug called Dilantin you could, for the most part, keep the seizures under control. But a few years ago, when you were twenty-five and had been married for some time, the seizures started getting worse and worse. Dilantin was no longer effective, and by the time you were twenty-nine, you were experiencing as many as a dozen convulsive fits a day, each one of such severity that you wondered if you could possibly live through the next. It was no longer a matter of embarrassment, but of life or death. The doctors finally recommended a radical new type of surgery in which the left half of your brain was disconnected from the right. They thought it might help, and they insisted that the after-effects would be mild. But they did tell you something strange—they said that you might find that there were two of you living in your body after the operation. You did not know quite what they meant, and it did not matter much to you anyway—anything to get rid of the terrible, devastating seizures. So a year ago you had the operation.

Incredibly enough, your prayers were answered. You have not had a seizure since the operation. For a while you seemed to be partially paralyzed. No, not paralyzed really—it was just that the left half of your body would not respond too readily to the commands that you gave it. It took you a long time to figure out what was wrong, and even when you did, it was pretty hard to believe. You see, there is someone else living in your body along with you, and "she"—the other personality—has control over the left half of your body much of the time. You really do not know who "she" is because you do not seem able to communicate with her, she doesn't seem to bother you too much, and really, the two of you get along quite well. Live and let live, you always used to say. But you do wonder occasionally at the rather odd things that your left hand seems to be doing.

An epileptic seizure typically begins in one hemisphere of the brain but then spreads to the other. To halt the spread of this massive excitation, surgeons can cut the thick tract of nerve fibers that runs from one cortical hemisphere to the other through the corpus callosum. Psychologists at the California Institute of Technology, working under the direction of Roger Sperry, have made an extensive study of what happens to individuals who undergo this operation.

Perhaps the most encouraging change in such a person's behavior is the almost total relief he experiences from epileptic attacks. But from a psychological point of view, there are more interesting effects. When the two halves of the brain are disconnected, two separate and distinct consciousnesses or personalities emerge, one in each hemisphere. For the most part, the left half of the brain controls the right half of the body, and the right half of the brain controls the left half of the body. Because the speech center is located (in right-handed individuals) in the left cortical hemisphere, only the personality "resident" in the left half of the brain is able to speak. But we can communicate independently with the personality in the right half of the brain by speaking into the right ear (and not letting the left ear hear what we say). The right-half personality can likewise communicate with the psychologist by writing with, or pointing with, the left hand or foot (which is under its dominant control). If the psychologist arranges things properly, the "person" can perform two tasks at the same time, one with each hand, a feat that no normal individual can manage. The two personalities tend to go to sleep and to awaken at about the same time (recent experiments suggest that such events may be controlled chemically), but they have independent memory systems and are not in direct contact with each other. If one presents the right-half personality with an erotically stimulating stimulus, the whole person blushes. If one then asks the left-half personality why the blushing has occurred, the left-half personality (which alone can speak) is confused, cannot explain why, and occasionally makes up a story (see Confabulation, Chapter 19). Just why there should be two potentially different personalities in each intact brain is not yet known, nor do we yet have any idea what the limitations of the "silent" personality are. We do know that the person who undergoes this operation does not seem to be particularly disturbed by the fact that two separate consciousnesses share one body; indeed, the two separate personalities seem to get along with each other very well.

Biology and Psychology

Psychology is the scientific study of behavior, but it is *organisms* that behave. And organisms have a biological side to their nature as well as a psychological. In most of this book, we shall be concerned with the observable actions and re-actions of human beings, that is, with human behavior. But we must realize that, in the final analysis, behavior is generated by physiological processes inside our bodies. Unless we knew that there are two halves to the brain, that they are mirror images of each other, and that they are connected by a structure called the *corpus callosum,* how could we hope to understand the behavior of the house-wife who had epilepsy? Unless Sperry and his associates had known that the separated halves of the woman's brain might function independently, would they have bothered to attempt to communicate with the "silent" half of the brain? In the final analysis, a psychologist is as dependent upon knowledge of the biological underpinnings of behavior as he is upon a scientific understanding of behavior itself.

Biology has played two principal roles in the development of modern psychology. The first derives directly from the evolutionary framework that has also served as an orienting concept for much of modern biology; the second role concerns our attempts to explain the processes that intervene between the stimuli impinging upon an organism and the responses made by that organism.

The evolutionary prospect forces us to consider both the biological heritage of the organism and its current ecological niche with respect both to other animals and to its natural environment. From the psychologist's viewpoint, it emphasizes the adaptive aspects of behavior, in the sense that particular behavior patterns are seen as promoting or inhibiting the reproductive success and ultimate survival of a particular species. Thus, observation of a particular behavior pattern—for example, the stereotyped manner in which a cat stalks and pounces upon a rat—leads to explanations of this pattern in terms of the benefit to the organism involved (the cat, not the rat). In contrast, the second biological approach could be used to explain why a cat attacks a rat in a particular way. In this case, the stimulus effects (from the sight of the rat) would be traced through the visual system and into a particular region of the brain (the hypothalamus) concerned with the integration of the stalking-attack sequence, and behavior would thus be explained in terms of the underlying activity of particular cells in the brain.

It should be understood that both of these types of explanation are legitimate interactions between psychology and biology. The impact of evolutionary and genetic explanations will be considered in successive chapters. Here our main concern will be to lay the groundwork for a proper appreciation of the processes in the brain and glandular systems that underlie significant behavior patterns.

The Nervous System

The nervous system of the vertebrate animal is composed of the brain, encased by the protective bony skull; the spinal cord; and a variety of peripheral nerves. The nervous system is composed of a great many individual cells specialized for *excitation* and *conduction*. It has been estimated that the human brain contains some 12 billion individual brain cells. Every nerve cell normally maintains an electric charge between its interior surface and the body fluids just outside its cell membrane. This charge is called the *resting potential* and is maintained by cellular metabolic processes. When appropriately stimulated, this potential breaks down and the nerve cell discharges or *fires*, that is, a wave of electric energy (called a *spike*) sweeps from one end of the cell to another. Under certain conditions, to be explained in a moment, the discharging of one nerve cell may upset the resting potential of any other nerve cell to which it is connected and thus may cause other nerve cells to discharge or fire. In this fashion, a pattern of nervous excitation may be communicated from one part of the body to another.

There has been a traditional division of the nervous system into a *sensory portion,* concerned with the detection and preliminary analysis of environmental stimuli; a *motor portion,* comprising those cells that are clearly involved in the activation of the muscles and the glands; and a broad group of *associative cells* that intervene between sense reception and motor activities. Scientists have been most successful in identifying sensory and motor cells; the class of associative cells is thus largely composed of all the cells that are not in the first two categories. Moreover, it is not always clear where a particular sensory system ends and associative systems begin. Certain cells, for example, originate within the brain but send projections to the peripheral sense organs, such as the auditory receptors, where they presumably modulate the reception of incoming information. The classification of such cells within a simple sensory-motor-associative framework is misleading.

The nervous system is a highly sensitive device for the detection and processing of environmental information and the initiation of appropriate actions. We shall therefore consider the functioning of the nervous system by examining the regulation of those vertebrate behavior patterns that have received particular attention from the psychologist. We shall begin with a brief consideration of the activities of individual nerve cells that form the building blocks of the system, then proceed to a consideration of spinal reflexes—which are important both to survival and as a simplified model for understanding neural interactions. Finally, we shall examine some of the structures in the brain that play a primary role in the regulation of intellectual, drive-related, and emotional activities.

Nerve Cells

There are two basic categories of nerve cell in the vertebrate organism: *neurons* and *neuroglia*. The former are the specialized cells that transmit electric activity from one region of the nervous system to the next and then to the muscles. The functions of the neuroglia are still unclear, although it has been traditional to assign them a supportive or nourishing role. In this section, we shall focus upon the structure and activity of individual neurons. The typical vertebrate neuron, depicted in Figure 2.1, has three basic subdivisions: *dendrites, soma* (or cell body), and *axon*. There are many different types of neurons, and there are numerous ways of classifying them—according to the shape and size of the cell body, the presence or absence of specialized dendrite processes, the length of the axons, and whether or not the axons are covered by the fatty *myelin sheath* depicted in Figure 2.1. However, there are certain characteristics of neurons, relative to their electric and chemical activity, that have considerable generality. These characteristics can be examined by first considering a set of electric responses, then investigating the chemical events that underlie these electric phenomena.

If a glass pipette drawn to a very fine tip and filled with potassium chloride solution as a conducting fluid is inserted inside an axon, it is possible to record an electric potential (energy difference) between the fluids outside the cell and the interior of the axon. Although some of the pioneering research in this area was carried out by Hodgkin and Huxley using the giant axon of the squid (see Figure 2.2), recent developments have extended this type of recording to mammalian cells as well. In a typical spinal cord cell, this potential might be on the order of 70 millivolts, with the outside of the neuron carrying a positive

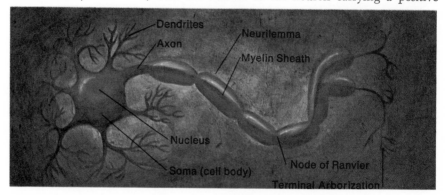

Figure 2.1
A neuron with a myelinated axon.

charge relative to the inside of the neuron (this is a relatively large potential—approximately one-twentieth that generated by a common flashlight battery). This potential is known as the *resting potential*. If the neuron is excited with appropriate chemical or electric stimuli, a change takes place in the resting potential. At first, there is a comparatively slow shift in voltage, which represents an *excitatory potential*. This shift produces a decrease in the potential difference recorded across the cell membrane. When a critical difference in voltage is reached (the *threshold value*), an *action potential* is generated. The action potential or spike (because of its resemblance to a nail in recordings) is a rapid change in voltage that results in a brief reversal of the resting-potential condition; that is, the interior of the membrane briefly becomes positively charged with respect to the outside of the cell before the resting potential is restored. The entire sequence of changes is depicted in Figure 2.3.

There are two key features of action potentials. First, they are *all or none*; that is, if the threshold value is reached and an action potential is generated, the size of the potential is not related to the magnitude of the original stimulus. The second key characteristic is that they are nondecremental: any action potential, once generated in the cell body or axon hillock, will travel to the ends of the axon farthest from the cell body without dying out or fading away regardless of

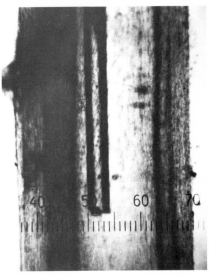

Figure 2.2
Micropipette inserted into a very large axon found in the squid. Each scale division equals thirty-three microns.
(After Hodgkin and Huxley, 1945.)

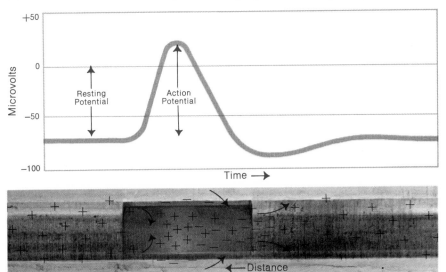

Figure 2.3
(Top) The changes in membrane potential as the spike moves past a particular point on the axon. *(Bottom)* The passage of the action potential, moving to the left along the axon. Voltage change toward the positive is represented by brightening orange.
(After Katz, 1952.)

the length of the axon. The speed with which an axon potential moves along the axon, known as the *conduction velocity*, varies from one neuron to the next, with a minimum velocity of approximately 10 feet per second and a maximum of 390 feet per second.

It should be noted that all-or-none activity and nondecremental conduction are the properties of axons and parts of the cell membrane. The dendrites and other parts of the cell body are not known to generate spike potentials; rather, they respond in a manner directly proportional to stimulus intensity and exhibit a decrement in the magnitude of response related to the distance from the point of stimulation.

The detailed sequence of changes in voltage accompanying the generation of and recovery from an action potential is shown in Figure 2.4. Although this sequence of changes takes place in a matter of milliseconds, within this time there is a set of parallel changes in the excitability of the neuron that affects the ability of any neuron to discharge successive action potentials. Immediately following the generation of an action potential, there is a *relative refractory*

Figure 2.4

Changes in membrane potential and the associated changes in the excitability of the neuron during the generation of and recovery from an action potential.
(After Morgan, 1943.)

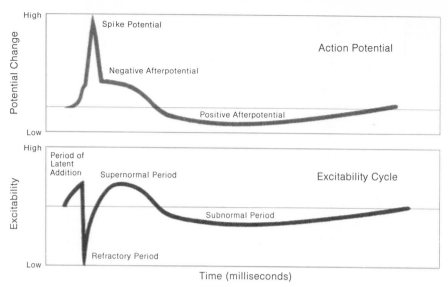

period, in which a stronger than usual stimulus is required to evoke a second spike potential.

The all-or-none characteristic of neurons and the nature of the relative refractory period together affect a very important relation between stimulus intensity and neural discharge: a stronger stimulus produces a more rapid rate of action potentials by successively activating the cell earlier in the relative refractory period. This interaction relates in turn to one of the fundamental problems in the neurology of behavior: how the nervous system transforms information about the environment into a particular pattern of nervous discharge. The process whereby this transformation is accomplished is known as *coding.* The primary factors involved when the nervous system codes information appear to be (1) the rate of discharge of action potentials within individual neurons and (2) which neurons are discharging. As a stimulus grows successively more intense— for example, when a sound becomes louder—two changes tend to occur. First, there would be an increase in the rate of discharge of individual nerve cells. Second, there would be a greater number of neurons involved in discharging action potentials. Because different neurons have different thresholds of excitation, a more intense stimulus will exceed the critical threshold value for a greater percentage of the nerve cells involved. (See the discussion of spontaneous activity, inhibition, and coding later in this chapter.)

■THE ACTIVATION OF NERVE CELLS

In the normal vertebrate neuron, one nerve cell exerts its influence on another neuron through the release of chemical transmitters from the terminal points of axon filaments. These chemicals diffuse across a small fluid-filled space and induce electric changes in the dendrite and cell bodies of the neurons with which they come in contact. The gap between the axonal endings of one cell and the cell membrane of the next neuron is known as the *synaptic junction,* and the unit composed of the presynaptic cell, the postsynaptic cell, and the gap between them are known collectively as the *synapse.* Although evidence indicating the existence of such gaps has been accumulating since the turn of the century, it was only with the development of the electron microscope that the synaptic junction became visible (Figure 2.5).

■EXCITATION AND INHIBITION

Thus far in this chapter, we have been exclusively concerned with the mechanism whereby a neuron is excited and generates an action potential. As indicated

26

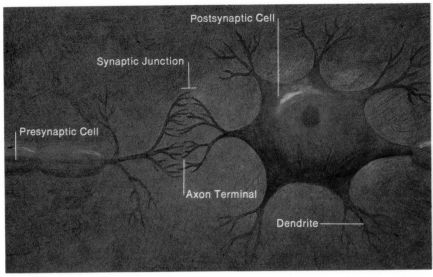

Figure 2.5
The synapse.

above, the release of some chemical transmitter substances will excite a post-synaptic cell and lead to production of action potential in that cell. However, other substances (as yet largely unidentified) *inhibit* the discharge of the post-synaptic cell instead of exciting it. Thus, the rate of discharge is reduced and, if there is sufficient amount of inhibitory transmitter substance present, the post-synaptic cell may become silent for a period of time; that is, it may not discharge any action potentials.

In general, there are a great many axon terminals converging upon individual neurons, each of which can contribute a quantity of transmitter substance to activation or inhibition of the postsynaptic cell. The ultimate frequency of discharge for a particular cell at a particular time is a function of (1) the relative quantities of excitatory and inhibitory transmitter substances acting on the membrane of the postsynaptic cell and (2) the intrinsic excitability of the cell (how recently it had discharged, metabolic status, and so on).

■NEUROCHEMICAL CONSIDERATIONS

Two aspects of cellular chemistry that must be considered in this context are the basis of the resting and action potentials and transmission at synaptic junctions. The resting potential results from the fact that there are unequal amounts of certain chemicals on the two sides of the cell membrane. This type of distribution can occur because when certain chemical compounds are placed in solution, they tend to lose their typical molecular configurations and gain or lose electrons. When common table salt, for example, is placed in solution it divides into sodium and chlorine, the sodium losing an electron in the process and thus acquiring a net positive charge, the chlorine gaining an electron and thus acquiring a net negative charge. These charged particles are known as *ions*. (Pure crystalline sodium and pure chlorine gas are neutral in electric charge; that is, they have as many positive protons in their nuclei as negative electrons in their orbits.)

The main ions involved in the resting and action potentials of nerve cells are sodium, potassium, chlorine, and some large organic molecules that carry a negative charge and are limited to the interior of the cell. The details of the processes that result in an unequal distribution of ions across the cell membrane are beyond the scope of this chapter, but we can briefly summarize these results. In the resting cell, there is a net excess of positively charged ions on the outside of the cell membrane that results in the recorded resting potential (such as that

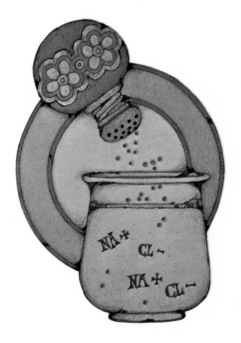

27

shown earlier, in Figure 2.3). During the generation of an action potential, there is a rapid influx of sodium ions, which are positively charged and briefly cause the interior of the membrane to become positively charged with respect to the exterior of the cell. The location of this influx of sodium progresses down the length of the axon and is responsible for propagating the electric action potential along the axon.

Although a variety of transmitter substances function in the activity of the vertebrate nervous system, it is believed that a given neuron releases only a single transmitter substance at all its axonal endings. Perhaps the most studied excitatory transmitter substance is acetylcholine (ACh) which is involved in transmission in the parasympathetic nervous system (see below) and probably within parts of the brain and spinal cord, as well as at neuromuscular junctions. For any transmitter substance released by a neuron, there are also chemical compounds present in the vicinity of the axonal endings that act to inactivate the transmitter by transforming it into a different chemical compound. If such inactivating compounds did not exist, transmitter substances would accumulate indefinitely in the region of the postsynaptic membrane, resulting in the continuous stimulation of the cell and blurring all message transmission. Thus, the combination of a small quantity of transmitter substance being released and the rapid inactivation of the transmitter by local chemical compounds results in the transmission of discrete messages across synaptic junctions.

Two substances known to be involved in the inactivation of ACh are the enzymes acetylcholinesterase and cholinesterase. Most of the common nonprescription sleeping pills now on the market contain the chemical scopolamine, which acts to depress transmission at synaptic junctions where the release of ACh is the critical event. The blurring of vision and increment in heart rate noted on the label as possible side effects of ingesting scopolamine are the direct results of action of the drug on synapses in the parasympathetic nervous system, whereas the sleep-inducing effects presumably result from some action on the central nervous system at an as yet unknown site(s). No inhibitory transmitter substances have been isolated that can unequivocally be shown to be normally released in the course of neuronal activity within the central nervous system of vertebrates, although a substance known as gamma-aminobutyric acid (GABA), which has been extracted from mammalian brains, evidently has many of the properties we would normally associate with the operation of an inhibitory transmitter substance.

Functional Anatomy of the Nervous System

The nervous system is composed of two basic subdivisions: the central nervous system (CNS), comprising those structures encased in the bony protection of the skull and spinal cord, and the peripheral nervous system, containing the remaining neurons that carry sensory information from the periphery of the body to the CNS and, in some cases, convey the neuronal activity necessary for activation of selected glands or muscular groups. Because the anatomy of the nervous system is extraordinarily complicated, we shall restrict our discussion to those structures that are especially relevant to psychological problems.

The Spinal Cord

The spinal cord is of particular interest to us both as a neural substrate for reflex activities critical to the survival of the organism and as a simplified model of a neurological system that receives information, processes information, and then delivers appropriate impulses to the periphery for the initiation and integration of motor sequences. The simplest spinal reflex arc involves just two neurons: an *afferent* sensory neuron, conveying information about stimulation *from* the periphery, and an *efferent* motor neuron, which runs *to* a muscle group. The knee jerk elicited by a tap below the kneecap is the result of the simultaneous activation of a number of such two-neuron reflex arcs (Figure 2.8). However, such two-neuron arcs are in the minority of our functioning spinal reflexes. In most cases there are one or more *interneurons,* which intervene between afferent and efferent neurons and greatly increase the possibilities for complex reflex activity. The complexity is further raised by the role of inhibitory and excitatory fibers in reflex activity. Thus, in the case of the knee jerk, at the same time that the muscles on the dorsal surface of the leg are being excited and are contracting, the motor nerves that innervate the muscles on the ventral surface are being inhibited from discharge of action potentials. This inhibition prevents the simultaneous contraction of the two muscle groups that move the leg around the knee joint and ensure a smooth, coordinated extension of the lower leg (despite its identification as a jerk). (More complicated reflexes are depicted in Figure 2.9.) This coordination of motor movements, involving the excitation of some

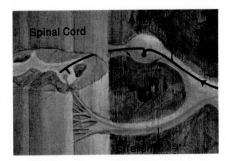

Figure 2.7
The reflex pathways in and out of the spinal cord.

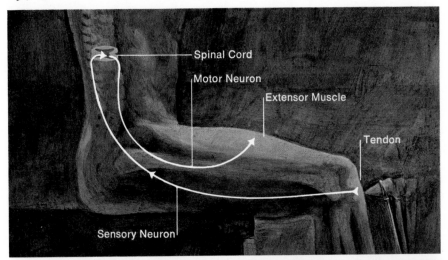

Figure 2.8
The type of reflex arc involved in the elicitation of a knee jerk by a tap below the kneecap.

Figure 2.9
Complicated spinal reflexes: the flexor reflex (A) and the cross-extensor reflex (B).

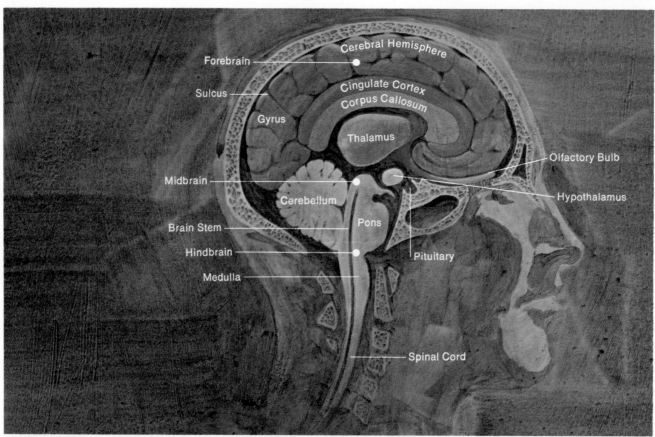

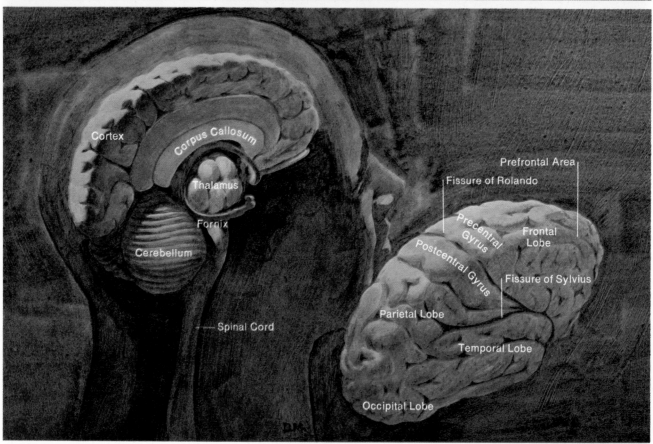

motor neurons and the simultaneous inhibition of other motor neurons, is the key characteristic of spinal reflex regulation of behavior.

The Brain

The vertebrate brain is commonly subdivided into three regions: the forebrain, the midbrain, and the hindbrain, corresponding to the sections of the neural material out of which they are formed during the process of embryonic development. The forebrain consists of the cerebral hemispheres, including such interior structures as the thalamus and hypothalamus; the hindbrain, of the medulla, pons, and cerebellum; and the midbrain, of the intermediate zone where the forebrain is connected to the hindbrain (see Figure 2.10). We have just considered some aspects of function in the spinal cord. Let us now move to the highest levels of the central nervous system, the cerebral hemispheres, then work our way back down toward the spinal cord.

The Cerebral Hemispheres

An examination of the external surface of the cerebral hemispheres of the human brain reveals a set of intricate convolutions, which cover the entire visible extent, with the two hemispheres appearing to be mirror images (see Figures 2.10, 2.11, and 2.13). The indentations, known as fissures, or *sulci*, divide the outer covering, or *cortex,* of the cerebral hemispheres into a complex set of *gyri*. The cortex of all vertebrates is not intensively convoluted. The surface of the rat brain, for example, is virtually smooth, except for the large longitudinal fissure that separates the two hemispheres and the rhinal fissure, which can be seen on the lateral surface (the side) of the cerebral hemispheres. There are actually a variety of different types of cortex, classified according to the particular varieties of cells contained therein and the distribution of these cells. The possession of a highly developed cortex is largely a mammalian characteristic and correlates with the development of intellectual capacity. Fish and amphibia possess only the most primitive indication of cortical tissue, and the reptiles represent a transitional group. In these latter species, the visible part of the forebrain is dominated by nerve cells linked with the olfactory system subserving the sense of smell. Extensive studies in comparative learning ability seem to illustrate the importance of cortical tissue for intellectual behavior, although such tissue is certainly not a requisite for simple learning.

Figure 2.10 *(opposite)*
Lateral view of the human brain in cross section.

Figure 2.11 *(opposite)*
The left and right cerebral hemispheres.

The cortex of man, in conjunction with some underlying interior structures, is divisible into a set of four lobes. The *occipital lobe* is located at the most posterior position of each hemisphere, and the cortex of this region is particularly concerned with the reception and analysis of visual information. In man, injury to these portions of the cortex can produce a blindness for objects in part of the visual field. The *temporal lobes* are located in the lateral surface of the hemispheres and are separated from the remainder of the hemisphere by the lateral fissure of Silvius. The auditory reception areas are located in the temporal cortex, as are certain areas for the processing of visual perceptual information. In a dramatic series of studies with particular types of epileptic patients, the Canadian neurologist Penfield was able to elicit complex auditory or visual illusions and even complete memory sequences through electric stimulation of the cortical tissue in parts of the temporal lobe, and the designation interpretative cortex is consequently sometimes used for this area.

At the anteriormost point in the hemisphere is the *frontal lobe*. This region of the brain consists of tissue in front of the central sulcus, also known as the fissure of Rolando (see Figure 2.11). The area immediately in front of this sulcus is primarily concerned with the regulation of fine voluntary movements

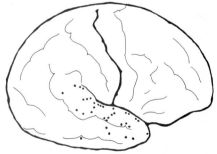

Figure 2.12
Stimulation at the point on the temporal lobe indicated by the colored dot caused a patient to say, "Dream is starting—there are a lot of people in the living room—one of them is my mother."
(After Penfield, 1946.)

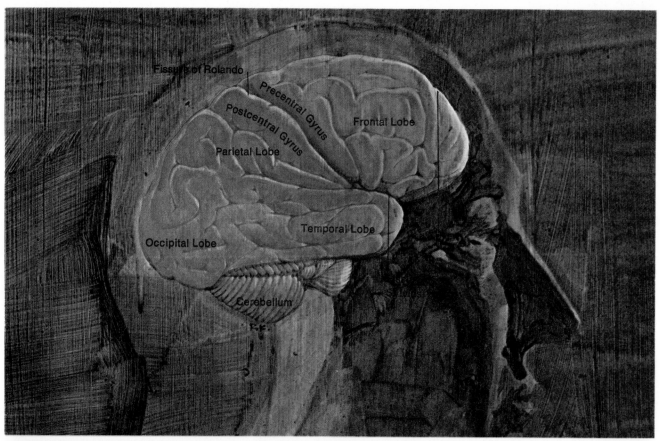

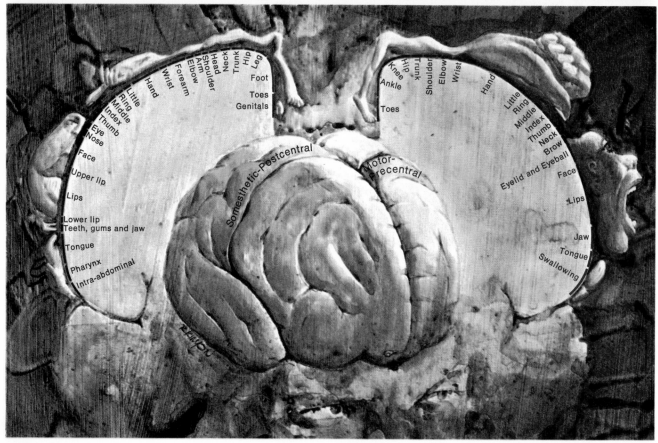

(Figure 2.13). Laterally on the surface of the frontal lobe is Broca's area, first discovered by a French physician as a region having to do with the use of language. Damage to this area can produce severe language disability. However, still further anterior is an extensive region of the frontal lobe known as the prefrontal area. These regions have not been associated with particular sensory or motor functions but at various times have been viewed as the repository of intellectual ability or emotional control. The former belief undoubtedly sprang from the enormous expansion of this region in the course of phylogenetic development and the parallel development of intellectual capacity. However, most modern researchers would not accept this all-encompassing view of frontal lobe regulation of intellectual performance. Intelligence-test performance may be relatively unimpaired even following massive removal of the frontal lobe tissue, and it now appears that the defects in behavior resulting from frontal lobe lesions are of a much more subtle nature, involving the ability to order stimuli and sort out information. The emotional-control view of frontal lobe function led, in part, to the development of an operative procedure known as a prefrontal lobotomy, in which patients with mental problems were sometimes subjected to surgery in which their frontal lobes were disconnected from the remainder of the brain (that is, all the neurons connecting prefrontal and other areas were severed with a surgical knife). Although a Portuguese neurosurgeon named Moniz was actually awarded a Nobel Prize for this work, it never fulfilled its early promise and has been virtually abandoned as a technique of psychological treatment.

Located between the frontal, occipital, and temporal lobes of each hemisphere are the *parietal lobes*. These lobes contain the primary cortical receiving areas for the somesthetic system subserving our sense of bodily position, with the various regions of the body represented in an orderly fashion in the postcentral gyrus (the gyrus behind the central sulcus), as shown in Figure 2.13. The postcentral gyrus is actually known as the primary receiving area for the skin senses, although there are several supplementary areas for both skin reception and motor activity. It should be noted that for both the motor cortex and the somesthetic cortex we have what is known as *contralateral control*; that is, the cortex of the right hemisphere is concerned with activities and reception on the left side of the body, whereas the right side of the body is represented and controlled by the cortical cells of the left hemisphere. An additional parallel between motor and sensory representation should be observed. The magnitude of representation of bodily areas in the cortex is not proportional to their geometric area on the body surface or the mass of the muscle groups that are innervated. Rather, the representation in the cortex reflects either the degree of precise motor control or the sensitivity of the bodily area concerned. Thus, the fingers have much larger representation than the trunk within the motor cortex, and the lips are disproportionately represented within the somesthetic cortex (Figure 2.14).

Lesions of the somesthetic cortex produce deficits in tactile sensibility, and extensive parietal lobe lesions extending beyond the primary sensory area produce unusual difficulty with spatial organization of the environment and distorted self-perceptions of the body image.

■ HEMISPHERIC DOMINANCE

Although the two hemispheres are apparently mirror images of one another, there must be chemical or structural differences between them that account for such phenomena as "handedness" and for the localization of particular functions relating to speech, perception, and intelligence-test performance in one hemisphere. Thus, most people are right-handed, have their primary speech center

Figure 2.13 *(opposite)*
The major divisions of the cortex.
The vertical line shows the scalpel cut made in the performance of a prefrontal lobotomy.

Figure 2.14 *(opposite)*
The proportions of the body's representation in the motor cortex (in front of the central fissure) and in the somesthetic cortex (the postcentral gyrus).
(After Penfield and Rasmussen, 1950.)

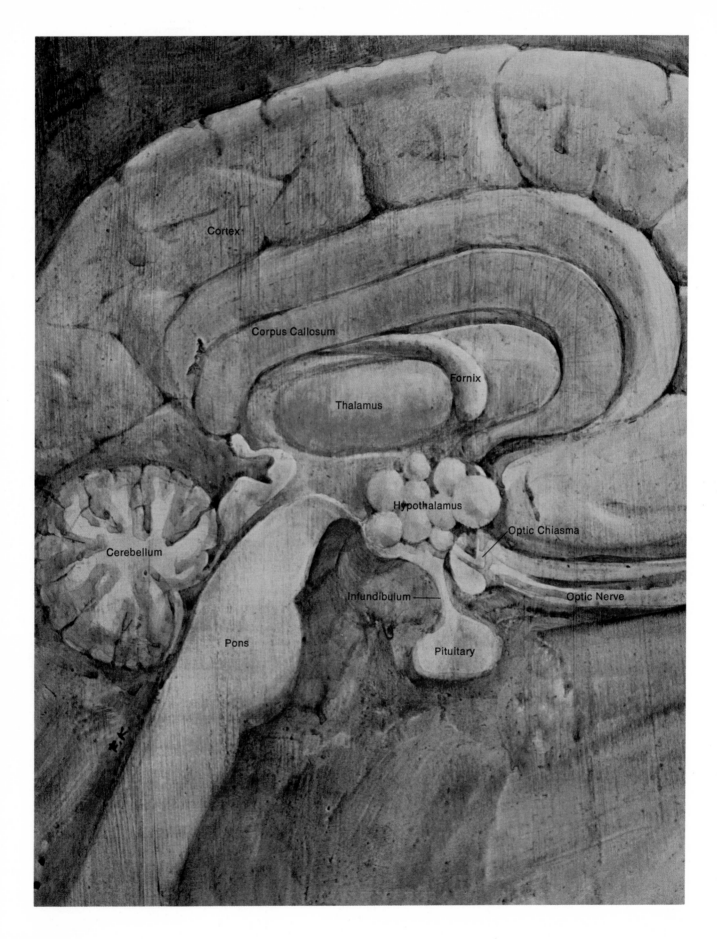

located in the left hemisphere, and show a division in the effects of temporal lobe lesion: lesions of the left temporal lobe impair intelligence-test performance severely while leaving perceptual-test performance intact, but lesions of the right temporal lobe have the opposite syndrome.

■INTERHEMISPHERIC CONNECTION

Although there are many routes of communication between the two hemispheres, the primary band of fibers that connect the cortex of one hemisphere with the equivalent region in the opposite hemisphere is known as the *corpus callosum* (Figure 2.15). Until recently, the functions of the corpus callosum were virtually unknown, but there are some clear indications that this massive group of fibers helps in synchronizing the activity of the two hemispheres. Thus, cats trained to make a visual discrimination on the basis of stimuli that are confined to one hemisphere immediately transfer their discriminatory ability to the opposite hemisphere if the callosum is present at the time of original learning. If the callosum is cut prior to learning, however, the second hemisphere may need total retraining before the cat shows adequate performance on the problem.

The Thalamus

The thalamus consists of a set of nuclei that are developed extensively among the mammalian species. A nucleus is a group of nerve cells, located in close proximity to one another and presumably having common function and connections. Some of the thalamic nuclei are known as relay nuclei because they relay sensory information from the peripheral parts of the sensory system to particular regions of the cortex. Other thalamic nuclei are involved with connections between cortical areas or between cortical and subcortical structures within the brain.

The Hypothalamus

Located near the base of the brain on either side of the midline (Figure 2.15) are the hypothalamic nuclei, which compose the hypothalamus. This relatively small structure (in the human brain) has enormous importance for the regulation of vertebrate behavior. The control of many basic drives (hunger, thirst, and sex), the regulation of secretion from the pituitary gland, and the control of the internal environment of the body (blood pressure, heart rate, temperature regulation, and so on) are all mediated at some point by the activity of particular hypothalamic cells. (The effects of lesions and stimulation on basic drives are discussed in Chapter 7.)

■THE AUTONOMIC NERVOUS SYSTEM

The control of the so-called involuntary functions of the body by the hypothalamus is accomplished through *the autonomic nervous system* (Figure 2.16), which consists of two divisions: the *sympathetic* and the *parasympathetic*. In both divisions, the nerve fibers exerting primary control over the varied involuntary activities leave the brain stem or spinal cord and synapse in ganglia located outside the CNS. (Ganglia are groups of neurons like nuclei, but located outside the CNS.) In the case of the parasympathetic nervous system, the efferent fibers leave either from the region of the cranial nerves or from the sacral division of the spinal cord and synapse in ganglia located near the muscle groups to be innervated. The sympathetic fibers leave the spinal cord in its thoracic and lumbar regions and synapse in ganglia located adjacent to the spinal cord, and the final fibers that innervate the musculature of the internal organs leave from these ganglia.

In general, the sympathetic and parasympathetic systems can be viewed as working antagonistically to one another. The sympathetic system tends to promote energy expenditure, particularly mobilizing the bodily resources to meet

Figure 2.15 *(opposite)*
Lateral view of the human brain. The relative position of the hypothalamic structures are shown schematically.
(After CIBA, 1957.)

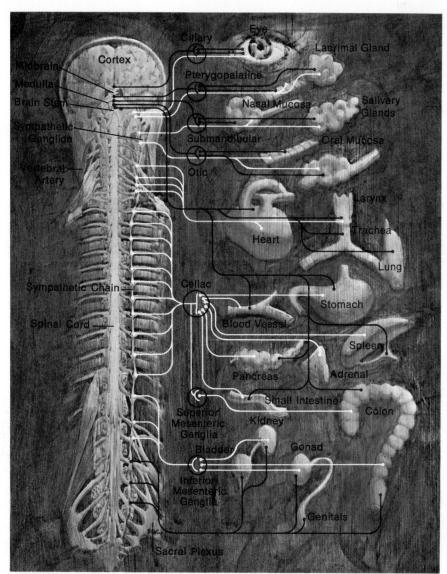

Figure 2.16
The autonomic nervous system and the organs it controls. The sympathetic division (white lines) emerges from the spinal cord through the sympathetic chain of ganglia. The parasympathetic division (black lines) emerges from the brain and the lower spinal cord. Note the reciprocal innervation of most organs by both divisions.

(After Gray, 1966.)

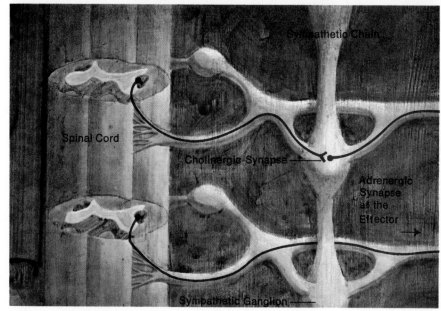

Figure 2.17
Sections of the spinal cord showing the relationship of the sympathetic ganglia to the central nervous system. Stimulation of an adrenergic nerve fiber usually excites an effector organ; stimulation of a cholinergic nerve fiber usually inhibits the organ's activity.

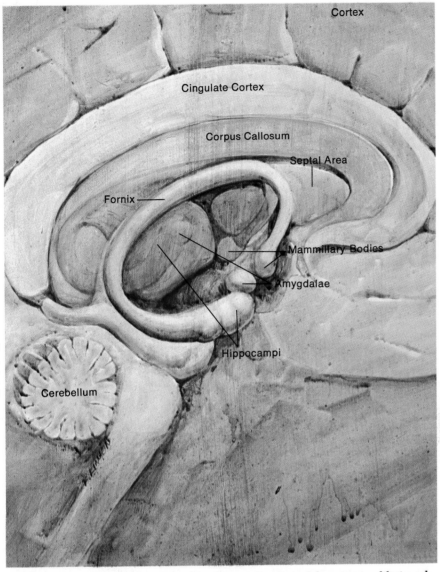

Figure 2.18
The structure of the limbic system.

emergency conditions (increasing blood sugar levels and heart rate, dilating the peripheral blood vessels through which oxygen and nutriments are supplied to the skeletal musculature, and inhibiting digestive processes). The parasympathetic system, as an energy-conserving system, slows heart rate and enhances digestive activity. Finally, the two systems differ with respect to the transmitter substances involved in their innervation; the parasympathetic system is a cholinergic system; the sympathetic, an adrenergic-cholinergic system (Figure 2.17).

■ THE LIMBIC SYSTEM

There are varied groups of interconnected structures in the forebrain that have recently received much attention because of their presumed role in regulating the emotional activity of the organism. The structures involved include the amygdala, cingulate cortex, hippocampus, and septal area. Although their original link was through association with the olfactory system, it is now clear that their major role in the higher mammal is nonolfactory in nature. Lesions in those areas have profound effects on emotional reactivity, turning such highly excitable creatures as monkeys and mountain lions into docile pets and converting highly tame laboratory rats into ferocious prone-to-fight subjects (at least for a limited time). However, it should be noted that these are highly complicated structures

37

Cortex

Thalamus

Visual Impulse

Auditory Impulse

Reticular Formation

Spinal Cord

likely to have diverse functions in addition to the emotional effects just noted. Thus, in man, the hippocampus has been implicated in memory storage processes.

■ THE RETICULAR ACTIVATING SYSTEM

Contained within the central core of the midbrain and upper hindbrain is an intricate latticework of nerve cells known as the reticular formation (see Figure 2.19). Intensive research has disclosed that this primitive system, which exists in the brains of all vertebrate species, plays a primary role in regulating the level of alertness of the organism (see Chapter 18). Thus, lesions in the midbrain reticular system produce an animal that sleeps much of the time and exhibits a cortical brain wave pattern characteristic of stages of deep sleep.

There are three systems that are generally included in any discussion of the generation of behavior: the nervous system, the muscular system, and the glandular system. In this chapter, we shall largely take for granted the muscular system—not because it is any less crucial than the other two but rather because of a psychological tradition that tends to view the muscular system as a passive instrument that merely acts when appropriately instructed by the joint influence of neurons and glandular secretions. If the correct nerves and glands are activated, the correct muscular movement is thought to follow automatically.

Just as nerve cells are specialized for conduction and muscles for contraction, so glandular cells are specialized for secretion of fluids. (Nerve cells also secrete, but the products are usually transmitter substances emitted in minute quantities and presumably have only local influence.) There are two basic classes of glands: those that release their secretions through a duct upon a selected body surface (the *exocrine* glands), and those that release their secretions directly into the blood or lymphatic system (the *endocrine* glands). Both kinds of glandular secretions have assumed a prominent role in psychological work. The salivary glands of the mouth and the sweat glands of the skin are two examples of exocrine glands that have been extensively utilized in psychological research. The salivary glands, for example, provided the primary response measure for Pavlov's classic studies of conditioned reflexes (see Chapter 4), and the sweat glands, secreting under the control of the sympathetic nervous system, provide the basic changes in skin resistance that underlie the galvanic skin response (GSR) widely employed to measure emotional reactivity and a part of most so-called lie-detecting systems. The location of the varied glands that make up the endocrine system are depicted in Figure 2.20. The activities of the major glands are discussed below and of other endocrine glands are summarized in Table 2.1.

The hypophysis, or *pituitary gland*, is sometimes referred to as the master gland of the endocrine system. It is composed of two distinct divisions, which have rather different embryological origin: the posterior pituitary (or neurohypophysis) develops from neural tissue, whereas the anterior pituitary (or adenohypophysis) originates in tissues from the roof of the mouth. The posterior pituitary secretes two hormones: the antidiuretic hormone (ADH) that raises blood pressure and enhances the retention of body water, and oxytocin, which is released at the appropriate time in pregnancy for the induction of uterine contractions in the female mammal. This latter hormone is employed clinically to induce labor when this appears medically desirable. The anterior pituitary secretes a variety of hormones, most of which act upon other endocrine or exocrine glands, including thyroid-stimulating hormone (TSH), adrenocorticotrophic hormone (ACTH), diabetogenic hormone (acting on the pancreas), follicle-stimulating hormone (FSH), and luteinizing hormone (LH), acting on

Figure 2.19 *(opposite)*
The passage of impulses from the sense organs through the reticular system to the cortex.
(After CIBA, 1957.)

The Glandular System

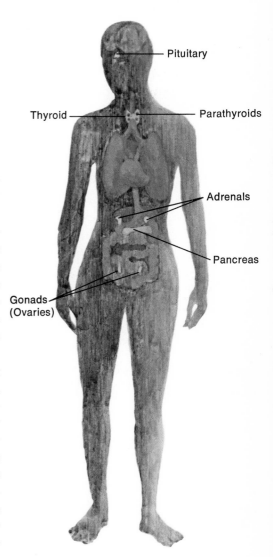

Figure 2.20
The endocrine glands of the female.
(After *The Body* ©1964 Time Inc.)

Table 2.1—The Endocrine System of Vertebrates

Gland	Hormones	Principal Actions
Anterior lobe of hypophysis	growth (somatotropic) gonadotropic thyrotropic corticotropic lactogenic parathyrotropic (?) diabetogenic (?)	stimulates growth stimulates gonads stimulates thyroid stimulates adrenal cortex stimulates secretion by mammary gland stimulates parathyroids influences carbohydrate metabolism
Intermediate lobe of hypophysis	intermedin	dispersion of pigment granules in the lower vertebrates; no known action in man
Neurohypophysis	oxytocin (oxytocic principle) pitressin (vasopressor or antidiuretic principle)	stimulates uterine contractility contraction of blood vessels, prevention of diuresis
Thyroid	iodothyroglobulin (thyroxin)	accelerates the metabolic rate
Parathyroid	parathormone	conditions the metabolism of calcium and phosphorus
Pancreatic islets	insulin lipocaic (?)	regulates the storage and utilization of carbohydrate prevents fatty livers
Duodenal mucosa	secretin cholecystokinin enterogastrone	regulates flow of pancreatic juice controls gallbladder inhibits gastric secretion and motility
Adrenal medulla	epinephrine	produces practically the same effects as stimulation of the sympathetic nerves
Adrenal cortex	cortin (corticosterone, desoxycorticosterone, and other steroid compounds)	carbohydrate metabolism, fluid shifts, and renal function
Ovarian follicle	estrogen (follicular hormone)	stimulates female sex accessory organs, regulates secondary sex characters, influences sexual behavior
Corpus luteum	progesterone (luteal hormone)	cooperates with estrogen in regulating the sex accessories, prepares female for pregnancy and lactation
Testis	male sex hormone (testosterone and related compounds)	maintains functional status of sex accessories and secondary sex characters, influences sexual behavior
Placenta	chorionic gonadotropin estrogen progesterone	important in evolution of viviparity, adjunct to hypophysis and ovary

Source: C. Donnell Turner, *General Endocrinology* (Philadelphia: Saunders, 1948), p. 13.

the ovaries. In addition, there is the hormone prolactin, which induces the secretion of milk by the exocrine mammary glands of the female mammal, and the growth hormone, which, as indicated, affects the rate of growth of the organism.

Each of the target glands—glands to which the pituitary sends activating secretions—in turn produces hormones after appropriate stimulation from the anterior pituitary. For example, under the influence of TSH, the thyroid glands secrete thyroxin, which affects the rate at which bodily metabolic processes proceed. The circulating levels of thyroxin also affect the rate of secretion of TSH by the pituitary gland; and as the levels of thyroxin rise, the secretion of TSH is reduced and this in turn reduces the level of circulating thyroxin to a proper level. This self-regulating circuit acts to ensure those levels of circulating

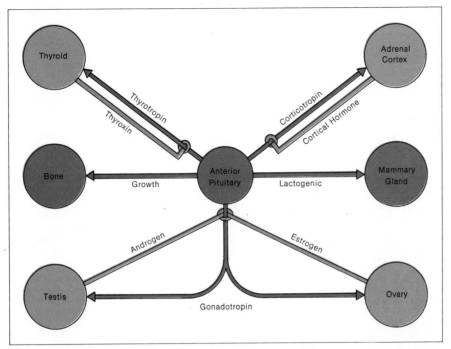

Figure 2.21
Self-regulating circulation of thyroxin.
(After Turner, 1966.)

thyroxin that are optimal for normal bodily function (Figure 2.21). Individuals with too high levels of thyroxin (hyperthyroid people) may seem tense or unable to sleep; individuals with insufficient thyroxin (hypothyroid subjects) may be listless and apathetic. However, in both cases, deviation from the normal circulating levels of the hormones produces behavioral inefficiency.

The *adrenal glands,* located adjacent to the kidneys, consist of two sections: an internal core known as the adrenal medulla and an external covering known as the adrenal cortex. The adrenal medulla secretes the hormones epinephrine (adrenalin) and norepinephrine, which have effects similar to stimulation of the sympathetic nervous system. This similarity is not surprising in view of the fact that epinephrine and norepinephrine are transmitter substances at the sympathetic ganglia. Moreover, the adrenal medulla is stimulated to release epinephrine and norepinephrine by direct neural inflow from the sympathetic system. Thus, we have a positive-feedback circuit in which sympathetic activity facilitates adrenal medullary activity, which in turn facilitates further sympathetic activity.

The cortex of the adrenal gland is stimulated by ACTH instead of the direct neural pathway that runs to the medulla. Under the influence of ACTH, the adrenal cortex releases a variety of steroid hormones that regulate water balance and energy expenditure. A great deal of effort has been expended documenting the role of the adrenal cortex in assisting animals and men to withstand stressful stimuli.

3

MEASUREMENT AND METHODS

PHILOSOPHERS AND PUNDITS, from Socrates and Plato down to the Beatles, have insisted that the solution to most of our problems is a state or condition known as *love*. But what is love? How does anyone know if he's in love or not? Love cannot be seen; it has no existence independent of the person who is doing the loving. Love is a personal experience, something that occurs in an individual's private world. Does that mean that a psychologist cannot study love? No, it merely means that he finds love difficult to investigate because he has no easy way of measuring it other than asking the person involved what he or she feels. Scientists have learned that the more accurately they can measure whatever it is they are studying, the more they can learn about it. But how would you go about measuring love?

In the preceding chapter, we looked at the biological organism. Biological organisms are always busy living and functioning, but it is the behavior of organisms that is the special field of psychology. The psychologist has some interest, for example, in the fact that the pupil of the eye becomes larger when the light becomes dimmer. But he is more interested in the increase in pupil size when a woman sees a man she's in love with, or when a man sees a sports car, a football game, or a pretty woman. To be able to make careful observations, the psychologist studies change in pupil size in the laboratory, using pictures to stimulate the subjects. The increase in pupil size occurs momentarily after the subject first sees the picture. Later, the pupil changes back toward its earlier size. For the psychologist, the problem is to catch the behaving as it occurs. Although he could watch the pupil and observe its fluctuations, he would have trouble estimating accurately the amount of the change. Therefore, he photographs the pupil and

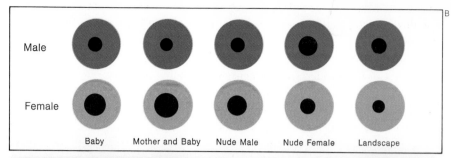

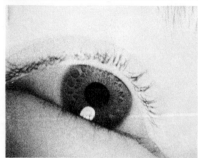

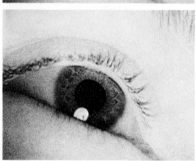

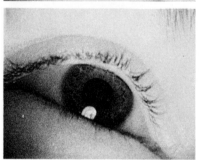

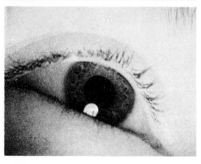

Figure 3.1

(A) The dilating pupil and (B) male and female pupillary responses to several stimuli. (C) The apparatus for stimulating and filming the subject.
(After Hess and Polt, 1960.)

later measures the change as it occurs, frame by frame, on the image projected from the motion picture film.

Notice that only one aspect of the subject's reaction, the amount of change in pupil size from prior level to maximum after seeing the picture, has been considered. The psychologist could also study the speed of increase and of later decrease or determine whether it increases steadily and evenly or in several successive steps. But when a scientist studies a phenomenon or an object, he looks at some characteristics and not at others: he selects or guesses the properties most relevant to his problem and ignores the others. At the same time, he may or may not study other, simultaneous phenomena. If he were studying a young girl falling in love, for example, he might also measure such physiological phenomena as change in heart rate and respiration.

Similarly, when a psychologist testing the intelligence of a very young boy asks the child whether he is a boy or a girl, he records only the content of the reply. He does not record how rapidly the boy replies or even whether he answers uncertainly or with firm assurance of his masculinity. On the other hand, a therapist dealing with an effeminate boy is primarily interested in his masculine assertiveness and not much at all in his intelligence.

Some scientists study fixed properties of organisms or elements and therefore have the advantage of being able to measure such properties several times, to check the accuracy of their measurements. Some properties, however, cannot be studied more than once in the same object. If you want to see how far a rubber band will stretch before it breaks, you can stretch it only once. To make repeated measurements, you have to take several rubber bands made the same way and test each. Similarly, in many parts of psychology, the same characteristic cannot

44

be measured repeatedly in the same organism. The reaction of an organism to a stimulus may change the organism so that it reacts a little more rapidly or a little less strongly the next time the stimulus occurs. Most girls fall in love with a given boy only once. Consequently, to obtain dependable answers, psychologists often have to repeat their measurements on different organisms.

Psychology has another distinctive feature. Like everyone else, the psychologist has been observing human beings and learning about people all his life. The phenomena of psychology are hard to look at objectively because they are so important to everyone; everyone has had a lot of experience with them, and everyone has built up a set of beliefs about people. The psychologist has to keep his great interest in and his personal involvement with people from biasing his observations, and he has to make sure that his thinking about human behavior is not restricted by the intuitive generalizations he has learned from his everyday experience.

Moreover, everyone is his own psychologist. Ask anyone if he understands people, and he will surely reply, "Yes." He has to believe that he does, because he has to interact with people most of his waking time. But the intuitive generalizations that people build up are only partly true, or at best true under particular circumstances. Thus, although such maxims as "Absence makes the heart grow fonder" are often accurate, frequently "Out of sight, out of mind" is a truer statement. The task of the psychologist is to determine what general laws do apply to behavior and under what circumstances each is true or not true.

Some psychological statements hold for everyone or within a given culture. If a gun is fired behind a person, he will tend to assume a certain tensed-up posture. If you are introduced to another adult and hold out your right hand, he will take it. There are some situations in which the behavior of almost everyone is restricted or controlled by the specific stimulus or the total situation, but most behavior is not so obviously determined. Many factors can affect behavior, and several may contribute to one act. For example, a dog may react to a stranger by wagging its tail and barking while slowly backing away. It has been argued that the multiple determination of behavior makes its scientific study more difficult than the study of other phenomena. It may simply be that different kinds of factors can determine a reaction and that psychologists today can isolate and

Figure 3.2
The startle reaction.

45

identify these factors only under very limited conditions and often only in the laboratory, not in everyday life.

Psychological Observations

We might think that the psychologist should have no trouble observing the phenomena he wants to study. They are all around him all the time. Psychologists do use their everyday experience with other people, as well as their experience with themselves, their own inner experiences, as part of the grist for their mill. But observations of such phenomena are unsystematic and frequently biased. These experiences are most useful as a source of hunches to be confirmed by more carefully controlled observations. Similarly, the fiction writer portrays the world of people as he sees it, and his picture may broaden our experience. Literature and art, however, do not ordinarily give us psychological *laws*.

Kinds of Observations

Professional psychologists may observe behavior *under natural conditions*. Some study personal products—autobiographies, compositions, and letters. Some make such systematic observations of behavior under natural conditions as how many drivers stop completely at a "Stop" sign or how many go through without stopping, and at what speeds. The growing field of ethology was initiated by the observations of American, German, and British scientists on the behavior of animals, birds, and insects in nature (see Chapter 5). Nursery school children are observed on the playground.

A common source of data is *ratings*, which may be made by peers or by superiors (teachers, job supervisors). How a person is perceived by others is, rightly or wrongly, of major significance for his vocational career and, more generally, for his happiness. Observations are often made by experts by means of interviews in connection with selection for school admission or for a job.

Other kinds of observations require the subject himself to furnish the data. The psychologist does not necessarily accept the subject's statement as the ultimate truth, but he does take it for what it is, that is, for what the subject says about himself. One such well-known method is the *survey*, as in public opinion polling. In these, a carefully selected sample of people is asked questions, and the responses are considered to be estimates for the population from which the sample was drawn. This method, however, is not always as simple as it initially seems: the data gathered from such polling during presidential elections must be interpreted carefully if the surveyor wants to maximize his accuracy of predicting the election. For example, he gives more weight to responses given by the kind of people who are likely to go to the polls on election day.

Other methods of observation include *inventories* and *tests*. Much can be learned by asking subjects about their past life, about their interests, and about how they see themselves (see Chapter 24). By having a subject solve various problems or perform certain tasks, it is possible to estimate his intelligence and skills (see Chapter 23). Notice that in these tests the psychologist uses the person's actual performance in the testing situation, whereas in self-report inventories, the psychologist uses what the person says now about his prior behavior.

Finally, the psychologist can observe the physiological functioning of people. He can record pupil size, heartbeat, breathing pattern, blood volume in the finger, skin conductance, and electrical activity in the brain.

The Observation, the Index, and the Variable

It is apparent that psychologists do not lack methods of observation. The more critical problem is making something out of their observations. The researcher is

never interested in his observations just for their own sake: he wants to do something with them. He is interested in estimating something, such as the average response of a person or a group of animals. To make a reliable estimate, he has to make a series of observations. If he is estimating an ability in a person, he asks the subject to answer many questions and takes the person's total score as an index of the person's ability. He has learned from past experience that this score is more dependable than the score from any one item (question) in his test. Similarly, the experimenter studying learning in rats will observe a number of rats and take their average performance as his index.

The Observer's Perspective

One of the major problems of psychology is that its phenomena depend more upon the observer than do the phenomena of other scientists. You have undoubtedly heard about the objectivity of the scientist; you have heard about science's requirement that observers agree on what they see and that scientists must be able to repeat their own experiments and those of other scientists before the findings become accepted as part of scientific knowledge. But there are often discrepancies between phenomena as perceived by different people. You may see a friend as less likable than he sees himself as being, or as less so than his wife sees him. Thus, the objectivity of psychologists' observations is of a different sort than that in the physical sciences.

Psychologists seek consensus on phenomena as seen by some designated person or persons. You may see a mother grab her child who is running out into the street. You may think she is trying to protect her child from being hurt. But

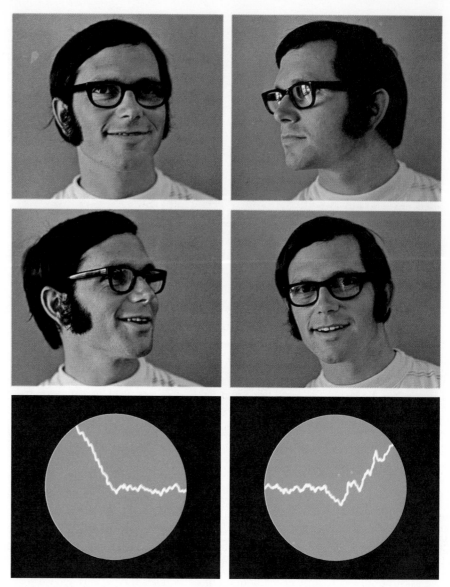

Figure 3.4
A subject's expression may show no change while a record of his skin conductivity indicates that he is relaxing *(bottom left)* or growing uneasy *(bottom right)*.

a moment later you may hear her say as she spanks the child, "Don't you ever hit your little brother again!" and you realize that she was reaching for the child to punish him for something else. Someone else who had observed the incident from the beginning might report that the child had been running into the street simply to escape from his mother. In this event, the essential psychological phenomena are the experiences of the child and of the mother. If we could get into the child's mind, what would we find that he was trying to do? What would a mother tell a close friend that she was doing? The phenomena you observed as a disinterested third party might also be of interest in terms of how people interpret the behavior of others. But for each of these viewpoints—yours, the child's, and the mother's—the psychologist needs to obtain dependable observations on what the phenomena were from that particular perspective. Psychologists seek objectivity in the sense of agreement between competent observers, but the agreement sought is agreement on what the phenomena are from some perspective.

There are, therefore, several perspectives from which the psychologist's data can be produced. The psychologist must treat the data from each perspective as a separate set of phenomena. In some instances, he may find that two different perspectives yield data that agree closely with each other, but until he has such empirical evidence, he must recognize the conceptual independence of each point of view. One of the major sources of disagreement between psychological observations made by different methods is simply a result of utilizing different perspectives, each perspective producing its own specific phenomena.

Finally, there are the stimuli themselves. In tests, the stimuli are the separate questions, problems, or items. A person's score on a vocabulary test will vary a little with the particular test used, that is, with the particular words included in it. A person's score on a questionnaire about proneness to anxiety will also vary with the particular instrument—and may vary a great deal, especially when the different questionnaires have been constructed by different psychologists with somewhat varying ideas about anxiety and its manifestations.

Psychology has many methods for collecting data and many concepts it wants to study. Like any science, it must find methods appropriate for each concept and must make sure that the methods really do produce data relevant to the concept. The discussion above has indicated that the target concepts at which measurement is aimed should be concepts associated with a stated perspective: how a person sees himself, how others see him, and so on. Within each perspective, the methods of measurement must use conditions and stimuli that are congruent with the concept as it has been spelled out. Thus, it is apparent that each global variable, like learning, intelligence, love, or emotionality, takes various forms when seen from different viewpoints; and within each viewpoint, its manifestations may vary with the conditions and with the stimuli. The enormous task faced by psychology is to create a conceptual framework into which all these pieces can be fitted. As things stand today, it is no wonder that different methods for measuring what is thought to be the same variable typically disagree with each other to a major degree.

Problems in Observing

From what has been said above and from his own experience, the reader can readily accept the assertion that psychological observations by laymen are very likely to be biased when compared to those made by a more objective observer. We would not expect a mother's description of her child to agree with a teacher's or with a neighbor's. We would not expect an applicant for a job to describe his deficiencies with utter frankness. It is hardly necessary, then, to warn the reader about the possibilities for strong *observer effects* (effects associated with a particular perspective or particular conditions) in data based on reports by observers who are personally involved or have not been trained in systematic observation.

Errors in Observations

One might think that a trained psychological observer would encounter little difficulty in making observations objectively because he has experience at doing so, but such observations are not easy. First, let us consider a person in an experimental study in which the psychologist is not studying the person himself but rather is trying to draw conclusions about people in general—for example, a study to determine the threshold for hearing a sound, that is, the lowest intensity that a human subject can detect auditorially. The experimenter begins with a sound he is sure the subject can hear and then gradually lowers its intensity, asking each time, "Can you still hear it?" The subject will tend to continue reporting affirmatively even when the intensity is reduced considerably. Next, the experimenter begins at a very low intensity, perhaps telling the subject that he will hear nothing for a while. In this series, the subject is likely to report not hearing the sound even when its intensity has reached the level at which, in the series with descending intensity, he was still reporting that he heard it. This example shows the possible *error of habituation.*

Now suppose that the experimenter again begins with very low intensity but instructs the subject to attend very carefully and to be sure to report the sound just as soon as he hears it, even if it is very faint. This instruction is likely to produce *errors of expectation.* For example, after the subject has been making his reports for a few minutes, perhaps from one series with increasing intensities and then with a decreasing series, the experimenter can make it appear that the next series will be one with ascending intensities but actually not have any sound at all. Under these conditions, many subjects will, sooner or later, report hearing a sound. They may indicate uncertainty, but their report will be positive.

A person is very likely to hear or see something that he is set to hear or see, whether it is there or not. Experimental procedures have to be carefully planned to control such effects or to measure them so that appropriate corrections can be made in the data. Another form of this kind of bias is the *stimulus error.* When an observer knows something about the actual stimulus, his knowledge may influence and distort the report of his experience.

When a person's expectation comes from what someone else says or does, we often refer to it as *suggestion.* When a person with prestige, a person we respect, says something, we tend to believe him. If you go to your doctor for treatment and he gives you a pill and says, "This will make you feel better," you are likely to start feeling better even if the pill contains nothing but a little sugar. Doctors have known about this effect for some time, and researchers studying the effects of drugs have to design their experiments to control such influences. In the typical design, subjects in an experimental group are given the drug and those in the control group are given a placebo, a pill with no effect. The experimenter then determines whether the observed effects in the experimental group are greater than those in the control group.

Experimenter Effects
The subject is not the only person in an experiment influenced by expectations. If a medical researcher knows which subjects are in the experimental group and which in the control, his observations of the subjects or his report of what they say may be influenced by this knowledge. For example, suppose that an experimenter believes he has found the cure for a disease that was formerly untreatable. He wants very much to obtain results demonstrating his cure, and he is likely to see effects whether they are there or not. To guard against this tendency, medical research is often performed using a double-blind design. Not only the subject but also the observer is functionally blinded: neither knows whether the subject got the experimental drug or the placebo. Only a third person, such as the pharmacist preparing the pills, holds the secret. Of course, in such experiments, the pills must be indistinguishable; the experimental drug and the placebo must be prepared in pills of the same size, color, and taste.

Psychologists know that an experimenter can unwittingly affect his empirical data in accordance with his expectations. In a standard demonstration, subjects are asked to judge each of a series of photographs of people as to whether the person has been experiencing success or failure. The subject is told that this is a test of empathy, of how well he is able to put himself into someone else's place. Then the person doing the experiment instructs some assistants (who are really the subjects of most interest in the experiment) that they are repeating a well-known experiment. Some of these assistants are told that their subjects will give an average rating of moderate success; others are told that the average reported

Figure 3.5
By smiling or looking solemn, an experimenter can modify the behavior of his subjects.

will be that of moderate failure. Each assistant administers the test to ten to twenty subjects. The results clearly demonstrate the effect (and the experiment has been done many times): experimenters expecting ratings in one direction obtain just that. It must be noted that the obtained averages do not reach the averages that the assistants have been led to expect, but the effects are unequivocal. Also note that the conditions are such as to facilitate the appearance of such an effect. The subjects are given a task that they cannot do—they cannot judge success or failure from the typical picture found in a news magazine—and it is under such circumstances that outside influences are likely to have the most effect on judgments.

These discoveries are very sobering. Experimenter biases in observations often occur in the physical and biological sciences as well as in the behavioral sciences. Seeing early data in an experiment may produce expectancies affecting data collected later. Even experimenters studying simple animal behavior may get results biased toward their expectations. If the experimenters believe their rats to be particularly bright, their rats will learn faster than those of experimenters with the opposite expectation. The effects are small, as in the experiments with human subjects, but they are obtained consistently and they are sufficiently large to affect the interpretations of experiments.

Remedies for such biasing influence are available. The researcher can use assistants who do not know what he hopes to find out and who do not have any clear expectations or any reason for obtaining results of a given kind. Even better are automated procedures. By recording the instructions on tape, for example, the possibilities for subtle communication can be reduced and the experimenter can make sure that his experimental and control subjects are treated the same way except for whatever critical variable he is studying.

Errors of Measurement

Measurements always contain errors. That is, measurements always are influenced by factors that the experimenter would like to eliminate. There are three major types of error in measurement. One is *observer bias,* which we have considered above. In that category, we can also include many experimenter effects that influence the behavior of the subject. A sophisticated experimenter who is aware of such dangers and has a good knowledge of the experimental literature can devise experimental procedures for minimizing the possible influence of such errors.

Another kind of measurement error, *design error,* occurs when the experimenter measures something that does not exactly coincide with what he wants to measure. A psychologist studying dreams might ask people in the middle of the day to report a dream they had the night before. Such a report is not the same as the original dream. A better procedure would be to ask the person to record his dreams as soon as he wakes in the morning. Unfortunately, this report also is not the original dream. Experimenters have compared reports on first awakening in the morning with reports by subjects who were awakened during the night just after they had a dream and have found that much of the detail has been lost between these two recall points. But note that even the report immediately after the dream is of an experience occurring many minutes earlier. Psychologists have yet to obtain records of dreams while the subject is dreaming them.

The third kind of measurement error, shared by psychologists and all other scientists, is simple *imprecision.* In physics, the speed of light has been measured by many experimenters over the course of several decades. With increasing technical skill and sophistication, the precision of the measurement has increased steadily. Most psychological measurement, however, has nowhere near such precision.

Precision is the degree of agreement among repeated observations; it is the same as the concept of reliability (see Chapter 23). Lack of precision is due to uncontrolled factors that affect the observations. Sometimes the experimenter may know what these factors are; sometimes he may not. After the experimenter has done the best he can in eliminating unwanted factors or in controlling their influence, he assesses the reliability of his observations. If the reliability is still unsatisfactory, he seeks to improve his measuring techniques.

The kind of imprecision considered above is random error of measurement, that is, disagreements between measurements repeated under conditions that are identical as far as we can tell. Another kind of imprecision is systematic, as in measuring weight with a spring balance that always yields too low a value or in measuring length with a yardstick that has expanded from heat and moisture. This kind of error can generally be controlled by checking the calibration against a standard instrument not subject to the same kinds of distortion. But note that we can detect systematic bias only when we have an independent set of measuring operations that we trust more than the one being used and evaluated.

Measuring   Observing is seeing and recording what is seen. Measuring is going from observations to indices; it is assigning numbers to things in accordance with certain rules. The rule for measuring a book may be that if one end of a ruler is lined up with the bottom edge, the height is taken as that inch mark on the ruler that comes closest to the top of the book. The rule for measuring speed of learning may be to assign the number of the trial on which the organism first completes the task successfully. These rules are arbitrary, in that alternative rules are usually available. The experimenter chooses the rule that seems most rational to him, the one that seems best to index the attribute he is studying. In more technical words, measuring is mapping observations into a number system, an abstract model. The resulting values can then be manipulated according to the rules permissible for the system: sometimes we can add, subtract, and multiply them; sometimes we run great risks by even adding them, as we shall see below.

Psychology uses several number systems, or scales. The first, the *nominal,* involves simply assigning numbers for identification purposes, as in assigning license plates to automobiles. Scientifically, such numbers have no utility—it is senseless to subtract or divide them—and we could use letters or any other marks as well.

An excellent example of a nominal scale is the set of numbers assigned to the members of a football team. If the quarterback wears the number 15, is he but a third as big, or strong, or powerful as the end who wears number 45? Can we subtract a center (number 54) from a tackle (number 74) and get a halfback (number 20)? No, these numbers are merely symbols used to help differentiate one player from another. We cannot manipulate these numbers in any really meaningful way.

The next type of scale is the *ordinal,* in which numbers are assigned to people or events in terms of how they rank along a given dimension. For example, even if we did not have a yardstick handy, we could line up the members of a football team in order of their height. We would not be able to say that the fullback was *three inches* shorter than the flanker back, but we could say that one was taller than the other.

When we have an absolute unit of measurement, then and only then can we make absolute comparisons. For example, if we compared the salaries paid to professional football players, we could say that a man who received $20,000 for the season was paid exactly twice what a man paid $10,000 received. Money is an example of a *ratio scale,* the most powerful type of scale a scientist can use. Distance measured in inches or centimeters and weight measured in pounds or grams are examples of other ratio scales. A ratio scale comprises equal units (the difference between $100 and $101 is exactly the same as the difference

Scales

Figure 3.7
These numbers form only a nominal scale.

Figure 3.8
Ranking on the basis of height is measurement of height on an ordinal scale.

between $996 and $997, namely, $1); and, as we all know, it has an absolute zero point, too. Neither an ordinal scale nor a nominal scale has equal units or an absolute zero point.

When we make our measurements with a ratio scale (as scientists almost always prefer to do), we can manipulate the numbers we get in any way we wish—add them, subtract them, or compare them in any way we find meaningful. When we deal with scales other than the ratio, we have to make certain assumptions about the numbers that sometimes are hard to justify. Intelligence and personality tests are often scored like college quizzes—that is, the subject is given one point for each correct answer. But are psychologists justified in such procedures? Do the items in an intelligence test represent equal units of ability, even though some are easy and some are difficult? Does the difference between IQs of 100 and 110 represent just the same difference in ability as the difference between IQs of 90 and 100? No one really knows. All we can say is that some assumptions usually seem to work and that, at worst, they probably do not lead psychologists too far astray.

Research Designs We have considered the kinds of observations made by psychologists and the possible sources of error in them. We have seen that observations are converted into numbers. But what kinds of plans underlie the making of observations and the recording of numbers? There are two major types: the *correlational* and the *experimental.*

A correlation tells us the degree of relatedness between two things. For example, let us take two college students, Mark and Mary. Suppose you happened to notice that, during a certain period of a week or so, almost every time you saw Mark anywhere, you also saw Mary. You saw them together at several parties, at a football game, in the student union, at several meals, and even in a class or two. The appearance of Mark at any given place is obviously correlated with the appearance of Mary; that is, the two events tend to occur together most of the time. If someone told you that he went to a party and saw Mary there, you might be willing to give rather good odds that Mark was there too. Thus, knowing that a correlation exists, you could *predict* the occurrence of one event (seeing Mark) from the occurrence of the other (seeing Mary). In loose terms, a *positive correlation* between two things merely means that they go together, much as we might presume that Mark and Mary were "going together." A correlation tells us nothing about *why* the two events tend to be associated, however.

There are *negative correlations* as well as positive. If Mark and Mary had been engaged but had had a violent argument and broken up with great hostility toward each other, you could predict fairly well that if you went to a party and saw Mary, Mark would not be there. Negative correlations allow you to predict the *nonoccurrence* of events with just as much accuracy as positive correlations allow you to predict their occurrence. We seldom invite our enemies to dinner.

The single most important thing to remember about correlations is that they tell us nothing at all about causality, although most people intuitively believe that they do. Take Mark and Mary, for example. We automatically assume that if we see them together all the time, they must be going steady, that is, they must be mutually attracted. If Mark's mother looked at the situation, she might imply a different causality—namely, that Mary was throwing herself at Mark and thus causing them to be seen together all the time. Mary's mother, of course, might believe just the opposite, that the causality was all Mark's doing. In point

54

of fact, all these assumptions could be false. It might be that both Mark and Mary were cheerleaders and therefore were thrown together a great deal by factors outside their control although neither one particularly liked the other.

It is a psychological truism that "positive traits correlate positively." In his famous study of gifted children, Terman found that high IQs were positively correlated with such other factors as better than average health, larger than average size, good looks, superior adjustment, and success. It is easy for most of us to see that good looks do not cause high intelligence, or vice versa; rather, the same genetic factors that lead to one probably also cause the other. It is not so simple for us to see that the high positive correlation between smoking cigarettes, for example, and getting lung cancer does not in and of itself *prove* that smoking causes the illness—it merely gives us a hypothesis that must then be tested experimentally. With only the correlation to deal with, it is scientifically just as tenable to hypothesize that perhaps incipient lung cancer causes a person to become a heavy smoker (because the nicotine tends to deaden the pain from already-irritated lung tissue). The noted British scientist Hans Eysenck has cogently argued that the correlation between smoking and lung cancer is probably due primarily to genetic factors that predispose a person likely to get the disease also to take up smoking. He points out, too, that the correlation between lung cancer and air pollution is much higher than that between cancer and smoking tobacco, a fact most people tend to forget. Obviously, smoking is an unhealthy habit that for sound physiological reasons should be discouraged. Moreover, experimental evidence may eventually show that smoking is indeed a significant contributing cause of cancer. But the point of the present discussion is that the causal relationship between smoking and various diseases in humans cannot be *proved* by mere correlations.

Mathematically speaking, correlation coefficients run from $+1.0$ to -1.0, the extreme coefficients indicating either a perfect positive or a perfect negative relationship. A correlation of zero implies that there is no relationship at all between the two variables being measured. A positive correlation of .85 denotes a much stronger relationship between the events than, say, a coefficient of $+.35$; that is, if the correlation between seeing Mark and also seeing Mary is .85, you can predict their behavior much more accurately than if the correlation is .35. To discover why the correlation exists, you must make use of the experimental method.

Suppose a psychologist noticed that students who drank a cup of coffee just before taking a long examination seemed to be more alert toward the end of the test than did students who had had nothing to drink. At this point, he merely has noticed a correlation between ingestion of coffee and alertness. If he then performed an experiment in which one group of students (the experimental group) was given coffee while another was given a placebo drink that looked and tasted like coffee (the control group), and subsequently the experimental group was indeed more alert, he would be on the track of a causal connection. He might then assume that it was the caffeine in the coffee that caused the effect and repeat the experiment giving regular coffee to an experimental group and caffeine-free coffee to the control group. If again the experimental students were more alert, he would be relatively sure that the caffeine did cause the alertness, but he still would not know why.

Next, he might inject caffeine solutions into rats to see if their nervous systems reacted differently than when they were injected with a control solution such as a weak salt solution. If he found that caffeine does indeed act as a

Figure 3.9

Scatterplots. To the extent that the position of a point on one axis is a good predictor of position on the other axis, the points tend to be close together on a line. Note that highly related measures *(bottom)* need not be related in a simple way.

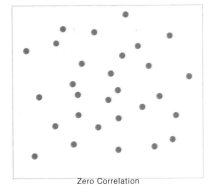

Zero Correlation

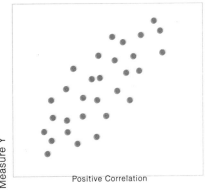

Positive Correlation

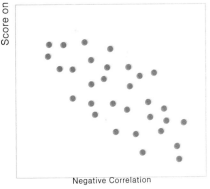

Negative Correlation

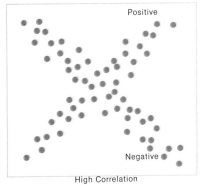

High Correlation

Score on Measure X

Score on Measure Y

neurological excitant, he could safely conclude that coffee causes alertness because the caffeine in it excites the brain in a certain fashion. In all these studies, he would make use of control groups to prove that his results were due to the experimental variable he was manipulating (the coffee or the caffeine) rather than being due to such extraneous variables as the students' knowing they were participating in an experiment or the rats' becoming excited merely because they had been stuck by a needle. No single part of planning an experiment is more important than the wise selection of control groups. The more extraneous variables an experimenter controls for, the greater faith he can have that his experimental variable is doing what he thinks it is doing.

Statistical Analyses   Once the experimenter has gathered his observations on his experimental and his one or more control groups, how does he proceed toward a finding and an interpretation? He uses two kinds of statistics, *descriptive* and *inferential*.

Descriptive Statistics   The psychologist uses descriptive statistics to reduce a mass of data to more manageable terms and to make these data more readily understandable. Suppose we gave a history quiz made up of 100 questions to a class containing 39 students. After grading the quiz, we find that the highest score was 65, the lowest, 40; the *range* of the scores is therefore 25 (65 − 40 = 25). We can now plot a *frequency distribution* of the scores by laying them out as shown in Figure 3.10. We can see that one student made a score of 40, that no one made scores of 41, 42, 43, or 44, that three students made a score of 55, and that only one student scored 65. Now, look at the shape of this frequency distribution. It is clear that most students scored about 55, with relatively few scoring at either extreme. In most tests of this type, the scores do tend to pile up in the middle of the distribution. As will be noted in Chapter 23, for example, roughly two-thirds of the scores on IQ tests fall between 85 and 115, although the range of the test can be as much as 200 points.

Now suppose we want to compare this class' performance on the quiz with that of another class that took the same test. How could we most meaningfully make such a comparison? One simple way is to find out what the average performance by each group was, then compare the averages. By definition, the average performance is always in the middle or center of the distribution, so when we seek an average of some kind, we are really looking for what psycholo-

Figure 3.10
Frequency distribution of scores.

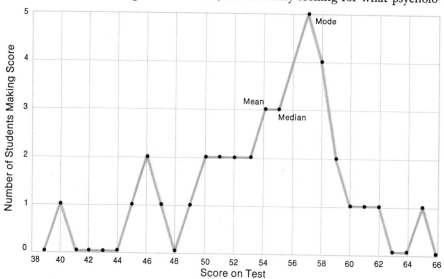

56

gists call a *measure of central tendency*. One such measure of central tendency is the arithmetic *mean;* to find it, you merely add up all the scores and then divide by the number of people who took the test. In the case of the history class, the mean of the distribution is 54. In order to justify calculating a mean on mathematical terms, you must use a measurement scale that has equal intervals.

Sometimes the scores on a given scale are so oddly distributed that a mean would give us a distorted idea of where the center of the distribution actually was. For example, if you went into a large urban ghetto and randomly asked eleven people their annual income, you might accidentally select ten very poor people plus one slum landlord who was in the ghetto to collect rent. The poor people might do well to earn $1,000 a year each; the landlord might easily make $1 million. If we add their incomes together, we would get $1,010,000; if we took the arithmetic mean of this figure, we would find that their average annual income was about $92,000. Mathematically, this is a true statement; socially, it is a gross distortion of the facts. In such cases, psychologists make use of a different statistic, the *median,* which is that score in the exact middle of the distribution. In the case of the history class, the median score was 55; in the case of the ghetto dwellers, it was $1,000. When the data you are gathering come from an ordinal scale, you cannot use the mean; you must make use of the median.

A third measure of central tendency occasionally used by psychologists is the *mode,* which is that score made most frequently in any distribution. In the case of the history class, the modal score was 57. Notice that in the distribution of quiz scores, the mean, median, and mode were all different, although closely related to each other. In a perfectly symmetrical distribution, such as the one shown in Figure 3.12, the mean, median, and mode might be 50. However, compare this distribution with that in Figure 3.13, whose mean, median, and mode are also 50. The range of the two distributions is also the same. Yet what a difference between the two in terms of how the scores are dispersed about the center. In Figure 3.12, the bulk of the scores are packed tightly about the middle; in Figure 3.13, the scores are spread out evenly from one end to the other. It would be misleading to compare these two distributions merely by talking about their similar means or medians; rather, we need some additional descriptive statistic that tells us how the scores vary about the center point. One such statistic is the *variance* of the distribution. To find the variance, we first calculate the mean, then subtract each score from the mean, square this differ-

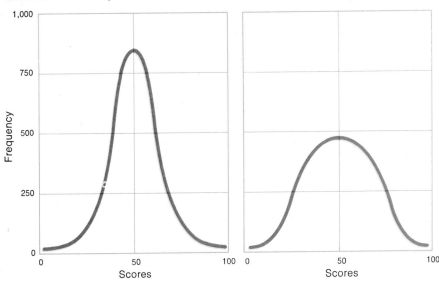

Figure 3.12
A distribution of scores with low variance.

Figure 3.13
A distribution of scores with larger variance.

Scores	Mean = 6	
3	6 − 3 = 3	$3^2 = 9$
4	6 − 4 = 2	$2^2 = 4$
5	6 − 5 = 1	$1^2 = 1$
5	6 − 5 = 1	$1^2 = 1$
6	6 − 6 = 0	$0^2 = 0$
6	6 − 6 = 0	$0^2 = 0$
7	7 − 6 = 1	$1^2 = 1$
7	7 − 6 = 1	$1^2 = 1$
8	8 − 6 = 2	$2^2 = 4$
9	9 − 6 = 3	$3^2 = 9$

Sum of Squares = 30

÷

Number of Scores = 10

= 3 (Variance)

$\sqrt{3}$ (Standard Deviation)

Figure 3.14
The computation of variance.

ence for each score, add all the squares together, then divide by the number of scores we had in the first place. Figure 3.14 shows how this is done with a very small distribution of scores. A more useful statistic for most psychological purposes is the *standard deviation,* which is merely the square root of the variance.

Both the variance and the standard deviation tell us something important about the shape of the distribution. If they are relatively large, the scores are widely spread out (as in Figure 3.13). If they are relatively small (as in Figure 3.12), the scores are closely packed about the center of the distribution. To calculate either the variance or the standard deviation, we must use a measurement scale with equal intervals.

Measures of central tendency and of variation are used to describe a set of observations (such as test scores) for a single variable (the history quiz itself) or to compare two sets of observations (the scores of one history class compared to those of another) on the same variable. If we wish to determine the relationship between two variables (the heights of a team of football players and their test scores on a quiz), we would calculate the mathematical correlation between the two sets of scores. This number, which, as we said above, varies from +1.0 to −1.0, is called the correlation coefficient.

Inferential Statistics

Descriptive statistics are important, but inferential statistics are even more so, for they provide the researcher with ground rules or conventions for determining what conclusion can be drawn from his data. Consider a man tossing a coin high in the air 100 times. If it lands heads up 53 times, is the coin biased? What if it lands heads up 79 times? Statisticians have worked out methods for determining the probability of obtaining any given result with any given number of tosses of an unbiased coin. More exactly, if the probability of heads is .50, there are tables to indicate how often, in (say) 100 tosses, one can expect to obtain 28 heads, 53, 79, or any other number of heads from 0 to 100. Probability is a complex technical topic and our intuitions about it are not always correct. For example, if a coin is really not biased, and if it lands heads 5 times in a row, the chance of its landing heads the next time is still .50; the fact that there has been a run of heads does not affect the best bet on the next trial, provided the toss is honest.

The history of modern probability theory begins in the late 1700s, when a group of French gamblers hired the noted mathematician Pierre Simon, later

Figure 3.15
Frequency distribution of the outcomes of
200 tosses of ten pennies.

Marquis de Laplace, to help them determine what odds they should give on such games of chance as a roulette wheel. The odds on most such devices (as well as on such card games as poker and bridge) have long since been worked out, which is one reason the casinos in Las Vegas continue to make money year after year. Take a roulette wheel, for instance. There are the 36 red and black squares, plus a zero and a double zero that are usually colored green. If you place a dollar bet on the number 3, you would expect to win (on the average) one time in 38. Yet when you win, the casino pays you but $35 (they also give you back the dollar that you bet the time that you won). In short, each 38 turns of the wheel you would pay the casino $38, but you would expect to get back only $36. The odds in favor of the casino are 38 to 36. No matter how much one individual may win on one occasion, if he keeps on playing the game for a sufficiently long time, he will end up losing—provided, of course, that the wheel is honest. In Las Vegas, the gambling houses usually go to considerable lengths to make sure that their games are honest—it is the safest way they have of making sure that they make a profit.

When we say that a roulette wheel is honest, what we are saying is that there are no biasing factors present that make it more likely that the roulette ball will fall into one numbered pocket more than any other. If one of the pockets was substantially larger than all the rest, the wheel would be biased in favor of this number. But suppose the biasing factor were more difficult to detect; for in-

stance, suppose the roulette ball were made of metal and one of the pockets had a tiny magnet hidden beneath it. How could you, as an external observer, detect the presence of this biasing factor?

The detection of such biasing or controlling factors is what the business of inferential statistics is all about. Let us go back to the coin-flipping example. The odds of getting a head on any given toss are 50/50; that is, a head will turn up one-half of the time. To find the odds of getting two heads in a row, we multiply the odds for getting one event (a head) by the odds of getting the second (another head); 1/2 times 1/2 is 1/4. If you got two heads in a row, would you begin to think the coin was biased? No, because such an event occurs about one-fourth of the time. The odds of getting three heads in a row are $1/2 \times 1/2 \times 1/2$, or 1/8, still respectable odds that would not make us suspicious about the coin. If we got four heads in a row, the odds would be 1/16 that such an event occurred by chance alone, and now we might start muttering to ourselves about our luck (if we were betting on tails).

At what point would our suspicions become so aroused that we would insist on inspecting and perhaps analyzing the coin? Such a decision obviously would be arbitrary and would vary from one individual to another. Psychologists, like most other scientists, have adopted an arbitrary convention: If the odds against a given event's occurring are 1 in 20—that is, if we would expect the event to occur by chance alone only 5 percent of the time—then we are willing to admit that there is a significant likelihood that the results cannot be explained merely in terms of chance variation. If the odds against the event's occurring are 100 to 1—that is, if we would expect the event to occur by chance alone only 1 percent of the time—then we are strongly convinced that something other than chance probably accounts for the results.

Suppose that we ran an experiment in which an experimental group of rats was injected with caffeine and the control animals were injected with a weak salt solution, and we found that the experimental animals learned a maze on the average in 30 trials (that is, the mean number of trials to learn the maze was 30), while the control animals on the average took 38 trials. What can we infer from these means? Does the difference between the two means really make a difference? Or could we have obtained these differences by chance alone?

To test our hypothesis that the caffeine injection enabled the experimental animals to learn faster, we would usually make use of an inferential statistic called the *t* test. The *t* test allows us to use the means and standard deviation to calculate the odds that such a difference between two means was due to chance alone. If the odds were 1 in 20, we would know that we would obtain such a difference by chance alone only 5 percent of the time, so we could accept our hypothesis that caffeine increases speed of learning a maze at what psychologists call the *5 percent level of confidence* (sometimes also called the *.05 level of significance*). If the odds were 100 to 1, we could accept the hypothesis at what we call the *1 percent level of confidence* (sometimes also called the *.01 level of significance*). In both cases, what we are saying is that we are reasonably confident that our results have some real psychological significance.

If our results (using the *t* test or perhaps some other more complicated inferential statistic) do not reach the .05 level of significance, then by convention we assume that our hypothesis was not accurate because the odds are too great that the results could be due to chance variation.

As you might guess from the lengthy and rather complicated description we have given of this topic, the proper use of descriptive and inferential statistics is at the heart of many scientific methods, and anyone wishing to do professional work in any of the social, behavioral, biological, or physical sciences must have at least a rudimentary understanding of such matters.

No one experiment ever proves anything. A soundly designed and executed experiment can, at best, change our subjective probability that a statement is correct. When we have studied an experiment and found it convincing because its methodology conforms to acceptable scientific standards, we have more confidence that some relationship holds or that it does not hold. Scientific methods are sophisticated common sense. They are the use of rational thinking derived from basic, generally accepted assumptions.

Findings, Facts, and Theories

There have probably never been, in psychology, truly crucial experiments that provide a clear basis for choosing between propositions derived from two opposed theories. Such experiments are very rare in any science. The final test in science is replication. A scientific finding becomes established when it has been obtained in several experiments (and the more, the better), experiments conducted by different experimenters in different places but with the same basic methods. Psychology has few such firmly established findings or facts. Psychologists, and especially students just beginning in research, do not like to repeat the studies done by others; they naturally prefer to do something original, such as repeating an experiment but with a modification of a basic condition. Hopefully, this situation will change so that psychology can become a more mature science.

Science builds on models. Psychologists use statistical models and measurement models in collecting and processing their data and statistical models in evaluating their findings. Psychologists use conceptual models to guide their research, to determine what data to collect and what to look for in the data after collection. These conceptual models become theories, structures that permit interpretation of natural phenomena. We understand what we observe by referring observations to theories. Working the other way, we make predictions derived from these theoretical models. As long as our observations agree with our predictions, we tend to accept the theory. But when these predictions are not consistent with observations, we must change our theory or seek another one that fits more observations. The true goal of science is not the prediction and control of events but the understanding of them. Prediction is merely the way we test our understanding of the world around us, and control of that world is the practical reward of our efforts.

UNIT II

LEARNING AND MOTIVATION

Life is synonymous with change. Perhaps the major difference between animate and inanimate objects is that living organisms change and adapt rapidly to their environments. A stone survives by being so hard that wind and rain wear it down very slowly. A human being is much more fragile than a stone; humans survive by escaping from wind and rain when they occur or, more importantly, by learning to predict when bad weather is likely to occur and hence avoiding its worst elements. Stones are not motivated to learn—they do not suffer pain or enjoy pleasure as humans do. Perhaps nothing is more important to our understanding of the behavior of organisms than how learning occurs and what motivates it.

63

KINDS AND NATURE OF LEARNING

EVERYONE LEARNS SOMETHING new every day. The experiences and encounters of this day—even if it is only a few hours old—have already made you a different person than you were before the day began. If you have been studying French or practicing the piano, you have learned words or musical phrases that you did not know yesterday. If you have been daydreaming, you can at least say that you have been daydreaming today, a statement you could not have made with certainty yesterday. Learning involves changes in a person's behavior as a result of his experiences. The psychology of learning is concerned with what kinds of changes occur and with what sorts of experiences are effective in bringing about the various kinds of changes in behavior.

Rarely does an individual learn a completely new capability or skill, no part of which could have been performed previously. Usually, learning consists of the maintenance and modification of capabilities or skills already available to the learner. For example, by the time a person learning to play tennis has the physical strength to hold a racket, he has developed his innate eye-hand coordination to the point that he can hit the ball with the racket. To be sure, he learns to hit the ball better with practice—a more effective stroke develops and the player learns to hit the ball from any location on his court to any location on the opponent's court. But simply hitting the ball with the racket is not a part of learning to play tennis. Rather, it is a skill that the player possesses before his first lesson and that is modified during the course of his learning to play the game. It is a matter of refining an already available skill.

Something similar happens when an individual learns to listen to the different instruments playing in a string quartet. His ability to learn to distinguish the musical lines indicates that he can selectively direct his attention and that his ear can make the required discriminations of musical tones. Thus, what is involved in such learning is not the development of these capabilities but rather the use of them to identify music produced by particular instruments.

Learning and Performance

As the preceding examples suggest, learning is inferred from performance. No one actually observes learning taking place but, rather, only a person in the act of learning; from changes in the individual's performance, the process of learning is inferred. The road between learning and performance is a one-way street: changes in performance indicate a change in learning, but changes in performance cannot be inferred from changes in learning because learning cannot be measured or observed directly. Consequently, some psychologists think only in terms of performance (see Chapter 6) and relegate the concept of learning to secondary status. But as we shall see later in this chapter, learning nevertheless retains much of its usefulness as an explanatory concept.

Much of the work discussed in this chapter concerns experiments with such animals as rats, pigeons, and monkeys. The extensive use of animals in psychological experiments offers the psychologist many advantages, including a more scientifically controlled environment and more hazardous experiments than are possible when human beings are used as subjects. However, the use of animals does limit the scope of the experiment. It is, for example, impossible to study speech with animals. Nevertheless, animals and their behavior are intrinsically interesting to some investigators, and it is quite likely that many of the basic psychological principles of learning and motivation worked out with animals under precise experimental control have some application to people, particularly with regard to the biological processes underlying behavior.

In experiments with animals, learning and performance can be clearly distinguished. For example, when an animal that has been taught to respond in a certain way for food reward when it is hungry is allowed to eat as much as it wishes, it usually becomes reluctant to make the learned response. The learning of the animal has not been impaired by the large amount of food, but the performance has. Learning has suffered not at all, as is shown by the animal's lively demonstrations of it when hungry again.

The distinction between learning and performance can be made with humans too, of course. The mere fact that we have learned how to ski does not mean that we will necessarily be motivated to give the best possible performance

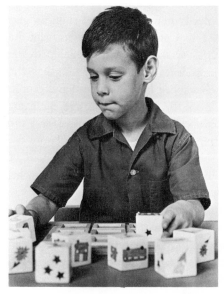

Figure 4.1

The time it takes for a child to categorize sets of pictures can be measured directly. Statements about his ability to learn, however, are only inferences from measurements of this kind.

on the slope if no one is watching. It is also true that a professor cannot tell how much a student has actually learned—he can only measure the student's performance on a written test or during an oral examination.

Two Basic Kinds of Learning

In the jargon of the laboratory, learning is often referred to as conditioning and is usually divided into two types. The first type is called by several names—*Pavlovian conditioning, classical conditioning,* or *respondent conditioning*—and involves the process by which innate reflexes are modified. An example of classical conditioning is afforded by our learning to fear painful stimuli. Touching fire, for example, is painful and causes us to withdraw our hand quickly. We do not have to learn this response to pain—it is innately determined by the structure of our nervous system. But every time we touch fire and are pained by it, we also see the fire. As a result, we come to fear the mere sight of fire because the sight of fire replaces the touching of the hot object as a stimulus for producing fear.

The second type of learning is called *instrumental* or *operant conditioning* and is more typical of what we usually think of when we say that we have "learned something." If some action of ours is instrumental in gaining us a reward, we tend to repeat that action often. We have no innate reflex that causes us to work hard in order to get money, and the first time we see money (as a child) we do not typically show an innate grasping reflex. We have to learn that money buys us many things that are enjoyable and helps us avoid other things that are unenjoyable. Behavior that results in our obtaining money tends to be repeated. Money itself does not produce the behavior that obtains it; rather, the behavior that is instrumental in obtaining money for us tends to persist and to be tried out over and over again.

Before the classical studies of these two kinds of conditioning can be understood in more detail, it is necessary to appreciate something of the elementary biological character of organisms, including man. Organisms inherit three general classes of characteristics relevant to the learning process: reflexes, uncontrolled or voluntary behavior, and innate likes and dislikes, which serve in learning as rewards and punishments.

The *reflexes* are inborn, stimulus-response connections. In each, a particular stimulus *elicits* a particular response because of the nature of the organism. A bright light shined into the eye elicits constriction of the pupil. The mild acid of a pickle elicits the occasionally uncomfortable secretion of the salivary glands. A thorn elicits reflexive withdrawal of the foot it pierces. A tap on the patellar tendon elicits the knee jerk. Each reflex is a tight, stimulus-response connection dictated by the physiological structure of the organism.

But all behavior is not reflexive. Most behavior is seemingly *voluntary* precisely because it is not elicited by any single environmental stimulus. Hand waving to attract attention in school is not elicited by an innate need for attention; rather, it occurs because it is effective in attracting attention. A rat's sniffing and moving about in a cage is not elicited by any particular stimulus, for a rat sniffs and moves about no matter where it is. Such behavior is as natural for a rat as is flying for a bird or swinging from limb to limb for a monkey. The babbling of babies is another example of operant behavior. Babbling is not elicited by external stimuli; it simply occurs. Such behavior is said to be *emitted* by the organism, not elicited, because there is no identifiable stimulus provoking it.

Individuals also have *inherent likes and dislikes,* things or circumstances that they naturally seek or avoid. The sweet taste of sugar, or of saccharin, is liked

Figure 4.2

Fear of a hot burner is classically conditioned, but reward for running to mother is an example of operant conditioning.

innately by most organisms, as is food of any kind if an organism is sufficiently hungry. Startling pain, such as that afforded by electrical shock, is fairly generally disliked. It comes as no surprise, then, that food and pain are the most common rewards and punishments in laboratory experiments in psychology.

Aside from our liking or disliking for them, rewards and punishments are important for the psychology of learning because they influence operant behavior. Generally, any behavior that results in the appearance or attainment of something that is liked probably will be repeated, and any operant behavior that results in something that is disliked probably will not be repeated. There are exceptions to these general rules, but the fact remains that operant or voluntary behavior is effectively manipulated by the consequences of the behavior.

Pavlov's Respondent Conditioning

In the course of a series of studies on the physiology of digestion for which he was awarded the Nobel Prize in 1903, the noted Russian physiologist Ivan Pavlov encountered the type of conditioning that bears his name today. He was originally concerned with the preparatory reflexes of the stomach; that is, how the stomach prepares itself with digestive juices for the morsels of food that are already in the mouth. He found that even the mouth prepares itself for the

Figure 4.3
Twitmyer first obtained a conditional knee jerk quite accidentally.

reception of food that is seen or smelled. The fundamentals that he unraveled of an animal's learning to secrete saliva when it sees food have had an extraordinary influence on nearly every theoretical position in the psychology of learning.

In point of fact, Pavlov did not "discover" the conditioned reflex, for scientists had observed it in farm animals and house pets centuries earlier. Nor was Pavlov the first to study the phenomenon in the laboratory—that honor goes to a little-known American psychologist named Twitmyer.

About the turn of the century, E. B. Twitmyer was a graduate student at the University of Pennsylvania. As his dissertation experiment, he chose to work with the patellar reflex, or knee jerk. Twitmyer rigged up a small hammer that would strike the subject's patellar tendon when he let the hammer fall. As a warning that he was about to release the hammer, he always sounded a bell beforehand. One day while he was testing a subject, he accidentally hit the bell. Although the hammer did not drop, nor was the subject's patellar tendon stimulated, the subject's knee jerked anyway. When Twitmyer asked him, the subject reported that the response was involuntary. Twitmyer immediately recognized that he had stumbled onto something very interesting and abandoned the original plan of his dissertation to study this fascinating new type of learned response.

He reported his findings at the annual meeting of the American Psychological Association in 1904, but none of the world-famous scientists there saw the significance of his work, which was, in fact, the first published description of what we now call classical or respondent conditioning. Twitmyer was disappointed in the reception the scientific world gave his experiments and abandoned them entirely.

Within a year or so, Pavlov made essentially the same discovery working with dogs rather than with humans. The scientific world gave Pavlov little encouragement at first either, but he was an established investigator with the Nobel Prize and with his own well-equipped laboratory. Because Pavlov gave the response an interesting name (conditional reflex) and persevered until finally other scientists saw the tremendous importance of his work, it is Pavlov's name, not Twitmyer's, that is associated with the discovery. And because Pavlov's work was more complete and, in its way, more elegant than Twitmyer's, we shall discuss it in detail.

The salivary reflex, like all other reflexes, consists of a stimulus—food in an organism's mouth—which elicits a response—salivation. Pavlov discovered that any stimulus that regularly precedes food in the mouth gradually comes to elicit the salivation by itself. In Pavlov's terms, the food in the mouth is an *unconditional stimulus,* eliciting the *unconditional response* because it neither depends on nor is conditional on any previous experience of the organism; the reflex is innate. Any stimulus—be it the sight of food (in the more natural case) or the ticking of a metronome or the flash of a light in the more experimental cases— that appears regularly before food is put in the mouth gradually takes on the power to elicit salivation all by itself.

Pavlov's preparation of the dogs with which he worked and the method of measuring the dog's production of saliva are illustrated in Figure 4.5. In front of the dog was a tray, into which food could be placed and from which the dog ate. The unconditional stimulus was food in its mouth. Also available in Pavlov's experiments were a variety of conditional stimuli: a metronome whose ticks were clearly audible, a visible light, and a brush for delivering tactual stimulation to the animal's body. The dog was harnessed to restrict its movements so that the continuous measurement of its salivation was possible. Pavlov could count the drops of saliva coming from the salivary gland at any time by means of a tube

Figure 4.4
Ivan Pavlov.

Figure 4.5
Pavlov's apparatus for conditioning salivation in the dog.
(After Pavlov, 1927.)

leading from the duct of the gland, inside the dog's mouth, to the outside. The drops were counted by an observer, who watched them fall into a vessel that measured the total volume.

Pavlov studied the effect on salivation of a number of procedures. In a typical study, a stimulus—say, the light—was presented for a period of time (usually five seconds), then a piece of food was dropped into the tray. (In some experiments, weak acid, like that from a pickle, was introduced directly into the dog's mouth.) The dog picked up the food and salivated as a result of the food in its mouth: the unconditional reflex. As the pairing of light and food continued trial after trial, the light itself began to elicit salivation. Figure 4.6 shows the results of a test of conditioning. Once every few trials, only the light was presented without food. The number of drops of saliva elicited by presentations of the light without any food at all increases as a function of the number of previous trials.

Figure 4.6

Acquisition of conditional salivation.
(After Pavlov, 1927.)

Figure 4.7

Extinction of the conditional reflex.
(After Pavlov, 1927.)

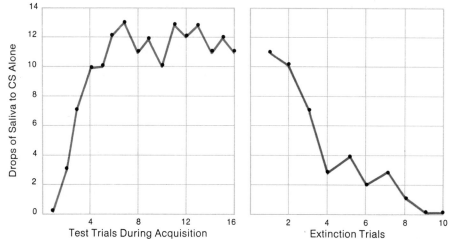

By virtue of having preceded the elicitation of the unconditional reflex (food in the mouth eliciting saliva), the light became a conditional stimulus that itself would elicit salivation. The term "conditional stimulus" is derived from the fact that the light's eliciting salivation is conditional on the previous experience of the organism.

Pavlov and his colleagues before World War I showed that other reflexes besides salivation could be conditioned according to this procedure. Reflexes of withdrawal, for example, were subjected to Pavlovian or respondent conditioning. An electric shock to a dog's forepaw causes reflexive withdrawal of the forelimb even though this withdrawal does not avoid or attenuate the shock (compare avoidance conditioning, to be discussed later). The unconditional reflex in this case consists of the shock to the forepaw as stimulus and withdrawal of the limb as response. If the unconditional stimulus (the shock) is regularly preceded by some other stimulus—for example, the ticking of a metronome—then the mere ticking will itself, over the course of a number of trials, come to elicit limb withdrawal.

■EXPERIMENTAL EXTINCTION

Unconditional reflexes persist for life, but conditional reflexes depend for their continuance on the occasional elicitation of the unconditional reflex in conjunction with the conditional stimulus. Thus, if the light is presented to the organism on a number of successive trials without the unconditional stimulus, the amount of saliva elicited by the light gradually declines until it is zero. Similarly, if the ticking of the metronome is presented to the dog a number of times without being followed by shock to the forelimb, the dog's tendency to lift the limb in response to the ticking declines. In this process, called *experimental extinction* by Pavlov, the conditional reflex built upon the unconditional reflex gradually wanes and is extinguished in the absence of a shoring up (Pavlov called it reinforcement) by elicitations of the unconditional reflex.

Pavlov demonstrated that reflexive responses could become conditional on stimuli other than their innate, naturally occurring ones and that the conditionality was temporary. More important, however, was his specification of the details of an exact procedure for bringing about these changes in the behavior of organisms, from which learning can be validly inferred.

Operant or Instrumental Conditioning

It is clear that only a small part of an organism's behavior is elicited by particular stimuli in the manner of a reflex. There is no known stimulus that will automatically assure that an untrained rat will rise on its hind legs and methodically press a piece of steel extending into its living quarters from the outside of one wall. Nor is there any stimulus that will automatically lead all American children of age two and a half to say, "Balderdash," if they have not been trained to do so. These responses—pressing levers on the part of rats and saying words on the part of children—are not elicited behaviors but rather the emitted operants mentioned previously. They raise the problem of behavioral control. How is it that, of all the things a rat can do, it selects lever pressing as the most attractive? How is it that from all the words a child can utter at a given time, he selects "balderdash" as the most appropriate?

The answer lies in the principle of reward, or reinforcement: in general, those responses of an organism that are rewarded in a particular situation tend to persist in that situation. In general, the most likely response in the presence of a given stimulus or situation is the response that has previously been reinforced or rewarded in the presence of that stimulus.

This principle has always been known, although in less exact terms, by animal trainers, child raisers, and people manipulators. The trainer compels obedience from an animal by making the comfort of the animal dependent on obeying. The parent controls the behavior of his child by making the child's likes and the avoidance of his dislikes dependent on the behavior that passes for good in the culture to which they belong. The businessman accumulates money by making the spending of money a precondition for either comfort or the relief of discomfort on the part of the buyer.

In the laboratory, no one has shown as elegantly—or contributed so extensively both to the demonstration and to the explication of—this principle of reinforcement as has B. F. Skinner. Skinner's training box has become the staple piece of apparatus for the study of the conditioning and learning of operant behavior, not only with animals but also with human beings.

The type of box used for the study of animal behavior is pictured in Figure 4.8. Such boxes consist of a lever or a key, whose depression by the rat or the pigeon is the operant response under study; a series of stimuli, such as lights and musical tones in whose presence pressing the lever (the response) may be reinforced; and provision for making food available to the organism at the will of the experimenter, depending usually on whether or not the animal has pressed the lever.

In order to see what operant conditioning is all about, let us trace the history of a hungry rat's career in this type of apparatus. Assume that the rat has spent so much time in the box that it is no longer uneasy there and that it has been taught (see Chapter 6) to take food from the dispenser when it operates. When

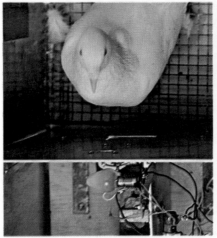 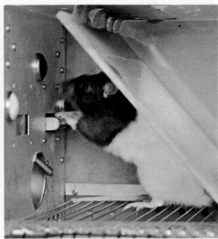

Figure 4.8
Types of training boxes developed
by Skinner.

the food is not available, the hungry, active rat engages in behavior characterized as random, voluntary, uncontrolled, or simply operant. One of the things it will naturally do, perhaps in its attempts to explore the upper reaches of the box, is depress the lever. Suppose that the depression of the lever activates the food mechanism so that food is available for several seconds. The rat will take the food. This constitutes *reinforcement* of lever pressing; the food is a reinforcer for the hungry rat and the lever pressing is the response. The result of reinforcement is that the lever pressing increases in frequency and persists—the rat presses the lever again and again. Figure 4.9 is a cumulative record of the number of lever presses as a function of the time elapsed since the rat was placed in the box on a given day. Food was presented after the first depression of the lever, but there was no reinforcement of lever presses immediately thereafter. After some fifteen unreinforced responses, all owing to the one reinforcement of the one response, reinforcement followed every response that occurred thereafter. The result of the first reinforcement was a vast increase in the frequency of the rat's lever pressing: the operant behavior of lever pressing was selected by reinforcement from all the things the rat was doing. Later, continual reinforcement of the response led the rat to emit responses at a high rate.

There is nothing magical about lever pressing as a response, although it is the one most studied in experiments on rats. If reinforcement were made dependent on another response, such as smelling in the corner, the rat would soon do little else. Whatever response is essential for the occurrence of food is the response that the animals tend to emit—in this simple situation, almost to the total exclusion of other responses. Lever pressing is used simply because it is a well-defined response that rats can perform easily, and because there are easy ways of recording automatically exactly when the animal has responded.

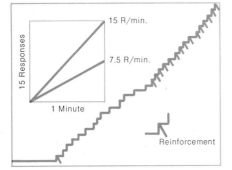

Figure 4.9
A cumulative record of reinforced and unreinforced lever presses in the rat.

■STIMULUS CONTROL

Assume that the rat's chamber has been illuminated during the preceding phase of the experiment. Suppose that we now change the procedure so that periods of several minutes of darkness alternate with periods of illumination and that lever presses that occur in the dark will not be reinforced but those that occur during the periods of illumination will be.

Very quickly, the rat stops pressing the lever during the periods of darkness, because lever presses are not reinforced then. But it continues to press the lever for food during periods of illumination. The light, as stimulus, comes into control over the behavior because pressing the lever is reinforced in the presence of the light. The dark periods control no responding, because responses made in the dark are not reinforced. The nonreinforcement during dark periods is analogous in operant conditioning to the procedure of experimental extinction in Pavlov's conditioning (described above).

Thus, with reinforcement—in this case the presentation of food to a hungry organism—it is possible to select for predominance any behavior and to bring that behavior under the control of specific stimuli.

Several other kinds of apparatus have been in common use for the study of operant behavior. Foremost among these are various kinds of mazes (see Figure 4.10). Mazes accomplish the same sort of conditioning as does Skinner's box, with the exception that the response is usually running or swimming through the labyrinth rather than depressing a lever and that the stimuli are presented spatially rather than alternated in time. The rat's behavior changes under the dependencies between running and the reinforcement it finds at the end of the maze in much the same way as its behavior changes under the dependencies

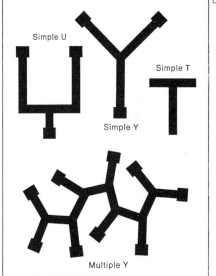

arranged between pressing the lever and reinforcement in Skinner's box. Figure 4.11 shows the increase in the speed of running with successive reinforced trials in the simplest of mazes, a straight alleyway, and the decrease in the number of false turns in a more complicated maze, such as that shown in Figure 4.10D. These pieces of apparatus combine the two processes of reinforcing the response and bringing the response predominantly under the control of particular stimuli,

Figure 4.10

Laboratory mazes: (A) Y maze for rats, (B) the same Y-maze plan set up for goldfish, (C) T maze for rats, (D) floor plans of several types of mazes.

Figure 4.11

Times for a rat to run down a straight alleyway on successive trials. (Reprinted from Woodworth, 1921.)

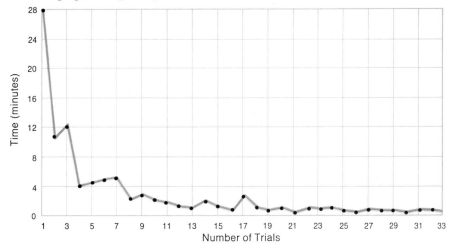

so the changes in performance from which learning is inferred are gradual rather than sudden, as they usually are in Skinner's box. But they apply the same principles to the conditioning of operant behavior.

Another piece of apparatus is the jump stand, invented by Karl Lashley, for generations America's premier physiological psychologist, in order to bring about rapid learning. Figure 4.12 shows the stand from which the rat jumps and the doors—each fitted out with distinctive stimuli—toward and through which the rat jumps. The rat's task is to learn to jump always toward the same stimulus, no matter whether it appears on the right or on the left door. Although it usually takes some pressure—a squeeze of the tail—to get the rat to jump at all, rats learn which stimulus to jump toward relatively quickly as compared with their performance in a maze. The secret is that the door with the wrong stimulus on it is locked, so that when the rat jumps toward it, it bumps its nose and falls into a net. The combination of food for jumping toward one stimulus and punishment for jumping toward the other is very effective in establishing rapid discrimination by the rat.

Just as in Pavlov's procedure reflexes elicited by such painful events as electric shock could be conditioned, so in operant behavior the withdrawal of

aversive events is reinforcing. Organisms naturally escape from or avoid electric shock, much as they work for and approach food when hungry. Learning to escape from electric shock has been studied in a variety of pieces of apparatus, including Skinner's box. Figure 4.13 shows the cumulative record of an animal pressing the bar in the box under avoidance conditions. Every time that the rat allows ten seconds to go by without a press of the bar, a shock occurs. The record shows that although the animal allows this to happen often, it presses very consistently, indicating that the avoidance of shock is a powerful reinforcer.

Avoidance has also been studied in the shuttle box (see Figure 4.14). Here the animal runs or climbs into a separate compartment in order to escape shock rather than pressing a lever, just as in mazes the animal runs for food rather than pressing a lever. Typically a stimulus, such as the light over one side of the shuttle box, appears and the light is followed several seconds later by shock. If the rat tarries too long, it is shocked. If the rat vacates that side of the box during the time between the start of the light and the shock, it avoids the shock, because the other side of the shuttle box is not electrified. On the next trial, the light in that compartment is turned on before shock, and the rat must go back where it

Figure 4.12
In this version of Lashley's jump stand, a puff of air from a tube leading to the platform is used to make the rat jump.

Figure 4.13
Cumulative records of avoidance behavior.

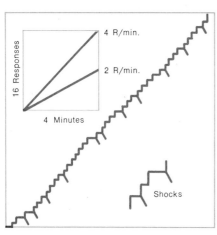

Figure 4.14
The cat hears the signal for shock and makes an avoidance response.

started in order to avoid shock. Thus, in a series of trials the rat avoids shock by shuttling back and forth in response to the light—hence, shuttle box.

The preceding examples cover the important manifestations of the two types of simple learning as they have been studied in the experimental laboratory. Now we turn to more complex forms. These kinds of learning involve the same mechanisms of conditioning already encountered, but they represent sufficiently complex combinations of more basic patterns to warrant separate coverage. It will be instructive for the reader to attempt to reduce these types of learning to the simpler principles of conditioning. When operant conditioning accounts for the learning, discover first what response is followed by what reward or punishment. Then apply the operant principles that rewarded behavior persists and that punished and unrewarded behavior fades away. Sometimes it will be difficult to bridge the gap between the simple mechanisms of operant conditioning and the complex behaviors being discussed, but patient searching for the actual behavioral response that is rewarded or punished by an actual environmental event will always prove illuminating.

Figure 4.15
A type of tracking apparatus similar to the pursuit rotor.

Motor Skills

A motor skill that has been widely studied by experimental psychologists is provided by the pursuit rotor task. The pursuit rotor machine consists of a disc that rotates, sometimes at variable speeds, on the surface of a rectangular box. The subject is required to keep a stylus in contact with the disc; that is, his task is pursuit of the rotating disc (see Figure 4.15). This task is an example of a more general skill—tracking—which has widespread application in industry and in everyday life. For example, a common aspect of driver-education programs involves a type of tracking sequence. The trainee turns a steering wheel in order to keep the visual image of an automobile in the appropriate lane of traffic.

It should be clear that by characterizing behavior as a motor skill even in as simple a task as the pursuit rotor we are guilty of oversimplification. The motor skill also involves sensory and perceptual components as well as a complex gradation of muscular responses.

■ KNOWLEDGE OF RESULTS

Of the factors that influence learning, knowledge of results has relevance for both verbal learning (see Chapter 18) and motor skills. Another way to charac-

Factors Influencing Motor and Verbal Learning

terize knowledge of results is by the more familiar term *feedback*. When we are learning to throw darts, for example, it is beneficial to see the results of one throw before firing the next. An interesting study illustrating the importance of knowledge of results—and one that is also instructive in pinpointing the nature of its contribution—was performed by Bilodeau. He demonstrated that supplying knowledge of results at the end of a series of trials for one group was sufficient to bring performance up to the level of a group that had knowledge of results on all trials (see Figure 4.16). This finding provides very practical insight into the administration of knowledge of results, particularly when supplying feedback is costly or time consuming, for it indicates that it is far more *efficient* to provide knowledge of results on a few selected trials toward the end of training rather than to provide knowledge of results throughout. Unfortunately, this result probably applies to only certain tasks. In all likelihood, the complex behavior

Figure 4.16

The effects of knowledge of results (KR) on the performance of Bilodeau's task. (After Bilodeau, *et al.,* 1959.)

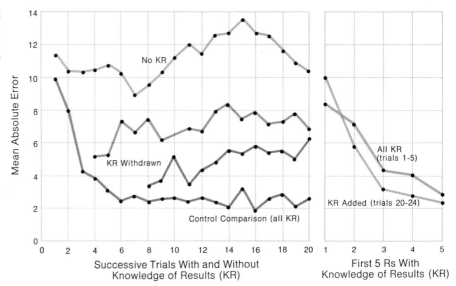

demanded by difficult tasks would benefit by great amounts of feedback. Indeed, there appears to be an interaction between the complexity of a task and the effects of knowledge of results. For example, the relatively simple task of the pursuit rotor does not seem to be aided by knowledge of results, but more complicated tracking tasks are.

■METHOD OF LEARNING

A second factor to be considered is *whole versus part learning*. Thus, a particularly germane question to studies of verbal learning is whether a body of material is better learned if practiced in its entirety or if divided and practiced in parts. Is whole learning or part learning more efficient? Is it more efficient, for example, to memorize a speech from start to finish or to split the speech up into several parts and memorize the parts separately before attempting to commit the entire speech to memory?

The part method has a distinct advantage and a distinct disadvantage relative to the whole method. It is most efficient in the sense that the subject works with a particular part of a speech precisely as long as it takes to reach a certain level of mastery. Thus, a particularly difficult portion of the speech will receive special attention whereas an easy portion will not receive the undue attention that it would receive with the whole method. The disadvantage of the part method is that after the individual parts are learned, they must be put together to constitute the whole. In other words, part learning involves an additional step that is often extremely time consuming. In view of these two considerations, it is not surprising that most human subjects adopt some compromise or combination method. For example, one may generally memorize material as a whole but may single out certain difficult portions for particular emphasis.

As one might expect, as the length of the material to be memorized increases, the part method becomes more advantageous. Consider, for example, the task of memorizing this chapter *verbatim*. Although such a task would be monstrous under any circumstance, the reader would no doubt feel more confident if he could memorize segments or a page or two at a time before trying to put them together. Another important result in this area is that the more intelligent the subject, the more advantageous the whole method. Similarly, the older a subject is, the greater the efficiency of the whole method. These findings suggest that the higher the level of mental development of a subject, the more efficient it will be for him to use the whole method.

■DISTRIBUTION OF PRACTICE

One of the most significant factors influencing verbal learning and the development of motor skills is the distribution of practice, the way in which practice is distributed over time. Consider, for example, a person learning to drive an automobile. If he is to be given fifteen hours of instruction, how should the fifteen hours be distributed in time? Is it more efficient to learn in one or two sessions of extensive practice or to spread the practice out over as long a period as possible?

Fortunately, many experiments have been done on this important problem, including Lorge's pioneer experiment in 1930. Lorge studied learning of a mirror-drawing task under three different conditions of distribution of practice. In mirror drawing, the subject tries to sketch a particular figure while looking at his handiwork in a mirror. First, Lorge used a massed-practice condition, in which each trial started immediately following the conclusion of the previous effort. In another condition, the subject's trials were separated by one-day intervals. Finally, for an intermediate group of subjects, one-minute intervals separated the trials. Figure 4.17 shows that learning was most rapid when the trials were distributed in one-day intervals. Most significantly, massed practice produced the worst results, and the most salient difference was between the group trained with massed practice and the groups trained with distributed practice. In other words, it did not appear that the specific length of the interval between trials was a particularly important determiner of performance in this situation. As a first approximation, this conclusion has survived the test of time. Although some studies have shown that there is an optimal intertrial interval and that this optimal interval depends upon the nature of the task being studied, differences among groups trained with different degrees of distributed practice are generally less impressive than the difference between any of these groups and a massed-practice group.

Although it would seem that this finding is of extreme practical significance for everyday learning situations, there is one problem with the distributed-practice method: it takes more time than massed practice. In other words, if the intertrial time is added to the time actually used in practicing the task, the distributed method appears poorer in terms of total learning time. Thus, from a practical point of view, whether one should use the distributed or the massed method depends upon two considerations: how important it is for the subject to learn the task in as short a (total) time as possible and how important or costly the instructor's time is. In cases where the critical factor is speedy learning by the subject, it would appear that a crash program of massed practice is in order. On the other hand, when it is desirable or practical to use only a fixed amount of an

Figure 4.17

Improvement in performances on a mirror-drawing task under three conditions of trial spacing. (After Lorge, 1930.)

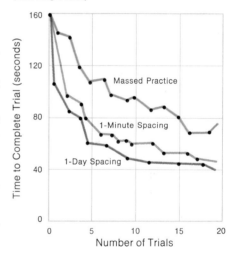

instructor's time (or a fixed number of lessons), the distributed-practice method may be optimal.

A final note on the effects of distributed practice: throughout the above discussion, the effects of distributed practice upon different tasks have not been distinguished. An important and well-documented generalization is that the effect of distributed practice in speeding up learning is greater for motor skills than for verbal learning, which makes good intuitive sense. Suppose that the mechanism that is facilitated by distributed practice involves the dissipation of physical fatigue built up by executing the motor response. The fatigue dissipates during the period of rest provided by distributed practice. Thus, distributed practice enhances motor learning because the subject is rested during each practice period.

■REMINISCENCE

A final factor influencing learning is reminiscence—the interesting and puzzling phenomenon in which a subject often performs better after a long delay than he did on the previous practice trial. For example, a person learning a list of fifty words may be able to remember forty of them after the tenth and final presentation; if he is tested for retention two days later, he may remember *more* than forty words. This improved retention after a rest period can be viewed as a special case of the effects of the distribution of practice (see Figure 4.18).

Figure 4.18

Spontaneous recovery, an increase in performance after a rest period following extinction (see page 111), is a phenomenon that may help to explain reminiscence.

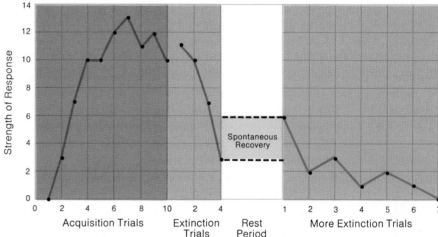

Reminiscence is common for motor skills, which can be understood in terms of the dissipation of fatigue. It is more puzzling when encountered with verbal skills. Indeed, the first study reporting reminiscence used verbal material. Ballard, in 1913, studied children's ability to memorize poetry and nonsense material. At the end of a practice session in which some children were required to memorize poetry and others nonsense material, Ballard conducted a retention test to determine the children's mastery of the required material. The students were not informed that they would be tested again. Some of the students, however, were tested for retention of the material on the following day. Others were tested after two, three, four, five, six, or seven days. In Figure 4.19, which shows the degree of retention for each group, 100 percent retention is taken to be retention equal to that on the test following the practice sessions. Thus, performances over 100 percent reflect reminiscence, which is evident for at least the first few days following the practice session.

Figure 4.19

Retention of verbal material.
(After Ballard, 1913.)

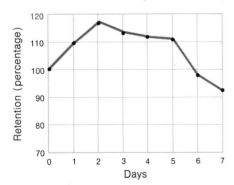

There are two principal problems with interpreting reminiscence. First, the retention trial following the practice session may have constituted further practice for the subjects; reminiscence may merely reflect the beneficial effects upon retention of this additional practice. Second, although the subjects did not know that they were to be tested again, they may have been rehearsing the material during the days between the practice session and the retention test.

Problem Solving

Problem solving involves tasks that require a substantial intellectual contribution from the subject generally beyond that required in motor skills and in the memorization of verbal material. Although this type of learning is more complex than the two basic types considered above, Pavlovian and operant, examples of this research can be illustrated with a rather simple apparatus: jars of water.

In the first type of problem solving we take up, *concept formation,* we shall consider the concept of conservation of volume. A small child is presented with a quantity of water that fills a short beaker. We then pour this water into a tall thin container and refill the short beaker. We now ask the child which jar contains more water. Children below a certain age will reliably point to the tall thin beaker. After a certain age, however, children correctly recognize that both jars contain the same amount of water. Their behavior thus reflects that they appreciate the concept of conservation of volume.

We now take a more elaborate set of jars and discuss a more difficult type of problem: the water-jar problem developed by Luchins. The subjects were given three containers. In one problem, the first container (A) held 21 units of water, the second container (B) held 127 units of water and the third container (C) held 3 units of water. The subjects were asked to use these three measuring containers to obtain a specified amount of water, in this case 100 units. The subjects easily arrived at the following solution: fill container B once and subtract from it the contents of container A once and container C twice. In other words, fill the 127-unit container, then pour out 21 units into container A and twice pour 3 units into container C. The water remaining in container B will be measured at precisely 100 units. This solution can be expressed in abstract terms: $B - A - 2C$ is the requisite amount of water. Subjects were then given a series of additional problems in which the same solution ($B - A - 2C$) applied. Luchins then gave his subjects a problem in which the same solution applied but for which there was a more efficient solution. For example, container A held 23 units, container B 49 units, and container C 3 units. The subjects were required to obtain 20 units of water. Although the solution that had been required in the previous problem still worked here, a better solution was available: fill container A, then from it fill container C ($23 - 3 = 20$). Subsequently, the subjects were faced with the following problem: container A held 28 units, B held 76 units, and C held 3 units; the subjects were required to obtain 25 units. In this case, the old solution was no longer applicable: $76 - 28 - (3 \times 2) = 42$, not 25. The easy solution, of course, is $A - C$ ($28 - 3 = 25$).

To determine meaningfully how well subjects did when it became efficient or necessary to abandon the solution that had enabled them to solve quickly several previous problems, a control group that did not have training with the old solution had to be used as a comparison. Luchins gave these subjects just one problem, in which the old solution was applicable, and then dismissed them for a brief period. They returned to the experimental situation to tackle the problems we have outlined above in which the old solution was not the best one to use. As might be expected, subjects that had solved several problems with the old solution were less likely to utilize the new and more efficient solution when it became optimal than were subjects from the control group. Similarly, the experimental subjects were less able to solve the problem in which the old

Figure 4.20
The conservation of volume.

solution would not work. Thus, these studies show that the subjects had acquired a more or less rigid set to solve the problem in a particular way, and this set interfered with their ability to solve the problem when the nature of the solution was altered (see also Chapter 20). It would seem, then, that in order to train subjects to use a wide variety of innovative solutions in solving problems, it is wise to teach them a variety of problems and a variety of solutions. By varying the subjects' problem-solving experiences, rigidity is reduced and the subjects' potential for demonstrating insight is increased.

Although insight is often considered a separate type of learning, it may be more profitably treated as a phenomenon of problem solving. Perhaps the most intriguing studies of insight have been performed by the Gestalt psychologists. Wolfgang Köhler, for example, studied a fascinating array of problems with apes as subjects. In a typical experiment, food was placed outside a chimpanzee's cage. The chimpanzee had two sticks in his cage, but neither was long enough to reach the food. The sticks could be joined together, however, so that the food could be reached. After extensive trial-and-error behavior, Köhler's chimpanzee suddenly solved the problem. In other words, the animal seemed to see the relation between joining the sticks and obtaining the food. It is this grasping of relations between various aspects of a situation that characterizes insightful behavior.

Another instructive example of insightful behavior is that of the detour or Umweg problem, also devised by Köhler. Imagine a pigeon staring at some food through a wire fence. The pigeon is hungry but must go around the barrier in

Figure 4.21
Everyday examples of the influence of set. People have difficulty, for example, with bottle tops that do not require openers.

Figure 4.22
A pigeon solves the Umweg problem.

order to obtain food. Insight in this situation involves temporarily moving away from the reward in order to circumvent the barrier. Although this is a trivially easy problem for an adult human, very young children find the problem extremely difficult. A chimpanzee may have difficulty at first, employing seemingly random trial-and-error movements characterized, particularly, by futile movements toward the food. Chimpanzees, however, often show sudden solutions to the problem. It is as if they had suddenly gone through an *"Aha* experience."

Incidental Learning

Learning without either being instructed or intending to learn is known as incidental learning; for example, you are asked in a classroom situation to administer a verbal learning test to an experimental subject. You present the subject with a list of verbal material and after each presentation of the list you test the subject for mastery of the list. After the subject has successfully memorized the list, the professor turns and asks you, the administrator, to recall the list. Any learning that you demonstrate is incidental learning. Experiments that have studied incidental learning have demonstrated that it is qualitatively very similar to intentional learning. Quantitatively, however, there is a difference: a greater amount of learning occurs when the learning is intentional than when it is incidental.

A critical variable in determining how much incidental learning will take place is whether or not the subject actually makes the responses that are to be learned. In other words, if the procedure requires the subject to repeat the material being learned by the intentional learner, the degree of incidental learning will exceed that which would be obtained if repetition of the items by the subject were not required in the procedure. Little or no incidental learning would take place if the subject paid no attention to the task. A great deal of incidental learning generally takes place, for example, when we are driven from

81

one part of a new city to another. To the extent that the driver engages in conversation, however, less incidental learning takes place. Finally, in the extreme case, if we close our eyes and sleep, no incidental learning will be possible. Intentional learning produces better results than incidental learning primarily because it forces the subject to concentrate upon the task.

Latent Learning

Latent learning is closely related to incidental learning. When the amount of learning (be it intentional or incidental) is measured, it is found to depend critically upon the subject's motivation to respond, particularly if the response is effortful or elaborate. Consider the performance of rats in a complex maze. Some rats are placed in the start box of a maze and are removed *without receiving food* when they reach the end of the maze. Other rats receive food reward at the end of the maze. Each rat receives one trial per day. The behavior of the rats reinforced with food is more accurate, as is indicated in Figure 4.23. But are the rats that are making frequent errors (the nonreinforced groups) learning more than their performance reveals? The curve for these rats indicates only a slight reduction in errors over successive days. Have they acquired more *knowledge* about the maze than these curves indicate? Because knowledge is *potential behavior,* we need only translate it into observable behavior to demonstrate its existence. This translation is achieved by providing the rats with food on a particular trial (trial 3 for one group, trial 7 for another). As Figure 4.23 shows, on the next trial the number of errors is sharply reduced. Thus, the rats had indeed learned quite a bit about the maze. The learning that had occurred but that had not been translated into performance until the introduction of reward was *latent learning*.

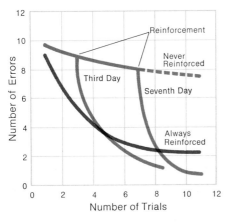

Figure 4.23
The patterns of performance that provide evidence for latent learning.
(After Tolman and Honzik, 1930.)

Cognitive Maps

Our discussion of latent learning and knowledge leads us to Tolman's notion of *cognitive maps.* A cognitive map refers to an animal's cognitive expectations of the consequences of turning one way or another in a maze. It also implies a certain grasp of relationships in the environment and a certain degree of spatial orientation. The latent-learning experiment discussed above supports the notion of a cognitive map. Tolman and his associates also showed that rats can solve many tricky spatial-orientation problems. The main conclusion of this experimental work was to correct the impression that the rat was merely performing specific motor responses in the presence of specific stimuli. Many examples could be given to indicate that the rat is learning more than a specific motor response. For example, Macfarlane trained rats to swim from one part of a chamber to another and then tested them when the chamber was drained so that swimming was impossible. The rat that ran from its starting point to the point containing the food obviously had learned more than a specific chain of motor responses: it had learned something about the location of the food.

An example of a type of learning that is compatible with cognitive maps but incompatible with the notion that the animal learns nothing more than specific motor habits that have been rewarded is called *perceptual learning.* This learning occurs without overt responses; evidence for it comes from studies that have employed curare, a drug that so immobilizes the animal that it cannot perform overt responses. Experiments by Solomon and his associates have demonstrated that learning can take place in curarized animals.

Learning to Learn

Harlow's concept of learning to learn is almost self-explanatory. He taught monkeys a series of two-choice problems and observed that they solved successive

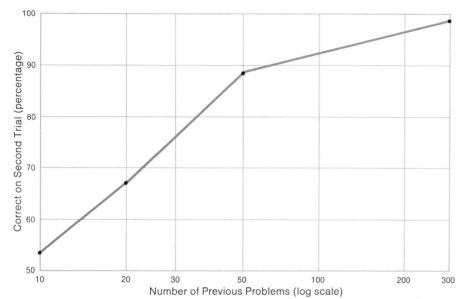

Figure 4.24

As they solved more problems, more and more monkeys made the correct response after the first trial on a new one. (After Harlow, 1949.)

problems faster and faster (see Figure 4.24). They learned how to learn efficiently.

Each problem consisted of two small objects, each covering a depression in the board in front of the monkey. Under only one of the objects was a raisin, the reward. The side on which the correct object appeared varied randomly from trial to trial. On each trial, the monkey was allowed to lift only one object. If he lifted the correct object, he could eat the raisin. If he lifted the incorrect object, there was no raisin. As he learned more and more problems, it took the monkey a smaller and smaller number of trials to learn new problems.

Although this is complex learning, it can be reduced to the principles of operant conditioning discussed at the beginning of this chapter. Obviously the raisin is the reward, and behavioral responses that lead to raisins would be expected to be learned and repeated. What responses does the monkey learn? He learns to pick up the correct object, of course, but he learns more than this over the course of a large number of problems. If he finds a raisin under one object, he learns to select that object on the next trial. If he finds no raisin under the object, he learns to select the other object on the next trial. If the monkey applies this win-stay–lose-shift strategy perfectly, he will solve any two-choice problem with at most only one error. On those problems where he chances to select the wrong object on the first trial, he switches again and hence makes no more errors. What appeared at first to be a complex kind of learning can be reduced to a combination of simpler kinds.

Figure 4.25

The two-choice problem: the cat learns that food is found under the white triangle but not under the black disc.

5

ANIMAL BEHAVIOR AND INSTINCT

EVEN BACK WHEN men were more like animals than like men, they observed (other) animals and recorded their behavior, as the delicate artwork left on the walls of caves in which early man dwelled attests. For primitive man, animals were a source of both food and danger, but they also were a source of wonder and mystery—feelings shared by modern man. Although animals are of economic importance in our daily lives, they also provide us with a broadened framework from which to evaluate human existence. Until recently man's interpretations of animal behavior were anthropomorphic (human-centered and evaluated in terms of human experience), intuitive, symbolic, and even superstitious, but today the mechanisms of animal behavior are explored with the objective observational and analytical techniques of modern science. As a source of fear, wonder, and inspiration, the study of animal behavior is ancient; as a science, it remains an infant.

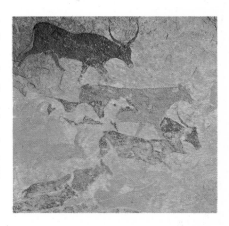

Behavior and Ethology

Ethology is usually defined as the scientific study of animal behavior, which is much the same definition that *comparative psychologists* give to their own field of study. In general, ethologists are zoologists who tend to study animal behavior in natural settings; their interests usually are in innate behavior patterns. The comparative psychologist, on the other hand, often works with animals in laboratory settings and is more experimental than observational in his approach; his chief interest is likely to be in how innate behaviors are modified or changed. Konrad Lorenz stands out as the founder of much current ethological work, but

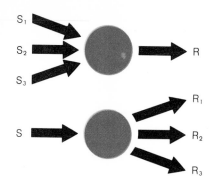

Figure 5.2
A single response is affected by a variety of stimuli, and a single stimulus affects many responses.

its roots go back to Charles Darwin, an early, most perceptive observer of animal behavior.

The first stage of most ethological studies is detailed observation of a particular species of animal in unrestricted conditions in the field. After obtaining a fairly complete record of behavior as it normally occurs, the ethologist can apply analytical procedures. The approach is what Tinbergen and others have called the natural experiment. Various behaviors are observed, catalogued, and subdivided into their component parts, and the interrelationships among these components and between them and the fluctuations in the external environment are determined. The term *ethogram* is often applied to these detailed descriptive studies. It has been found that certain components of behavior, such as relatively stereotyped *fixed action patterns,* and particular features in the environment, or *sign stimuli,* are as characteristic of a given species as many bodily characteristics. These *species-specific* components of behavior have been the basis for many comparative studies between species.

Although the dissection of behaviors into their component parts is an important feature of ethology, it is by no means the only emphasis. Behavior is a process, not an entity. That is, behavior is most properly considered as a sequence of events that occur over time. Thus, ethologists also focus on the rules of temporal organization and behavioral interactions. Although the organism responds to particular features in its environment, the type and probability of responses to specific stimuli are not static but fluctuate. Because the changes in the external environment in themselves cannot account for these fluctuations, it becomes necessary also to take into account events occurring within the organism.

Figure 5.2 is a diagrammatic summary of some of the common features in behavioral control observed by ethologists. The general rules are these: (1) a given motor output may be affected by more than one input (defined both within and external to the organism), and these inputs may combine to varying degrees in their effect; (2) a given input typically influences more than one motor output, and these outputs may be affected simultaneously, alternately, or sequentially. A major task of ethology is to work out the details of these rules for a particular set of organisms and then to compare the data obtained for different animals under different environmental circumstances.

Concept of Instinct

Ethology is a direct descendant of Darwin's evolutionary theory, and, as a result, problems of the inheritance and functional consequences of behavior have been considered in some detail. In the earlier ethological writings, as well as in the early writings of certain branches of psychology, the concept of *instinct* received major attention. Ethologists were impressed by the fact that different species behave differently and that certain behaviors were characteristic (*specific*) for a given species. Furthermore, many of these species-characteristic behaviors were obviously not learned in a direct sense. A young wolf will howl and pounce in a characteristic manner even if it has not had the opportunity to observe other wolves do so. As Lorenz has pointed out, it is striking how many species-characteristic behaviors survive under a variety of environmental and developmental conditions. Many of these behaviors may be parts of quite complex sequences, and unlike simple reflexes, they appear to be largely driven from within. The concept of instinct developed out of an attempt to account for these observations.

In common parlance, instinct is often matched against intelligence; man acts intelligently whereas animals, particularly the lower organisms, are instinctive

Figure 5.3
A young wolf, hand-reared, can howl
and pounce as normally reared wolves do.

automatons. Indeed, we often use the word "instinctive" to apply to automatic behaviors developed in man through long practice—such as the baseball player who instinctively makes the appropriate play or the experienced driver who instinctively steps on the brakes of his car when a young child darts into its path. Here some of the semantic difficulties in the scientific application of everyday language become apparent. By "maternal instinct" do we mean a series of purely automatic (and unconscious) behaviors? No, instead we seem to be saying little more than that love of children is a basic tendency common to human mothers. We do not even discount the possibility that learning may play a role in refining such activities.

If intelligence is contrasted with instinct, will this help us clarify the distinction? The hunting wasp illustrated in Figure 5.4 provides an interesting example. This animal digs a nest, flies once or twice around the nest site, then heads off in search of food. The wasp can find its way back flawlessly, something that many people might not be able to do. The wasp obviously learns the appropriate landmarks extremely rapidly—and learning rate is something we tend to think of as being correlated with intelligence. However, if the pattern of landmarks is displaced a relatively short distance, the wasp becomes hopelessly disoriented, even when the nest is in clear sight. Here we have a behavior whose details are obviously dependent upon learning but that is extremely inflexible once the details are acquired.

As a general although not perfect rule, the farther one moves up the phylogenetic scale, the greater the increase in alternative approaches to a given problem. In one experiment, for example, a rat, a chimp, and a human child

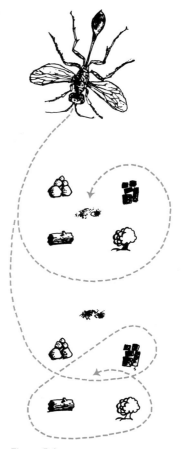

Figure 5.4
The hunting wasp is unable to adjust to
slight changes in the landmarks it has
learned to use to find its nest.

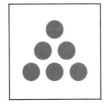

Figure 5.5
The stimuli used to investigate phylogenetic differences in generalization.

were taught a simple discrimination between a circle and a triangle (Figure 5.5). All learned the task, although the rat was slightly faster than the chimp and the child. The two-year-old child was the slowest. However, when the triangle was subsequently rotated, the rat had to relearn the problem, whereas the chimp and the child successfully generalized from the previous solution. And if a triangle was constructed out of circles, the chimp treated this figure as a circle—it failed to discriminate between the two stimulus objects, or failed to abstract the overall triangular form. Again, flexibility of behavior and the ability to reorganize relevant features of the environment appear to be roughly correlated with phylogenetic position. This characteristic, however, is somewhat different from our original instinct versus intelligence dichotomy.

Even within a single organism, concepts such as intelligence may be hard to define with precision, for one's conclusions depend on how well particular aptitudes and behavioral propensities are tapped. For example, it was extremely easy to train a young timber wolf to do the dog trick of shaking hands (three trials), but took many long hours to get the animal to sit upon request (see Figure 5.6). Is the animal "smarter" or "dumber" than dogs? Such questions miss the point, for timber wolves typically make pawing movements during play, and the training session was designed as an extension of the play period. The response was thus already there and simply had to be brought under the control of a voice request. On the other hand, timber wolves, particularly when excited, rarely sit, so this behavior was more difficult to teach.

The problem of the hereditary and experiential contributions in the development of behavior are central to the question of instinct. When a young digger wasp emerges from its pupa in the spring, its parents have already died. Thus, the fundamental instructions for complex wasp behavior cannot be learned from

Figure 5.6
A young wolf can quickly learn to shake hands—a behavior similar to its pawing movements—but does not readily learn to sit upon command.

the parents. In contrast, higher animals usually undergo a long period of tutelage by their parents and siblings.

Female rats will display normal maternal behavior with their first litter even if they have had no opportunity to learn this behavior directly by watching another rat. This can be demonstrated by rearing the female rat in isolation, and thus the case for instinct might seem proved. However, Birch found that placing a wide collar around the neck of a female rat almost at birth prevented the rat from licking itself, which subsequently resulted in its failing to care for its young when it was an adult. Although such data remain somewhat controversial, the logical lesson is clear: even if a given behavior pattern persists in impoverished environments, one cannot rule out all experiential factors.

The basic conclusions from behavioral experiments on animals reared under a variety of conditions are clear. Animals of a given strain may manifest differences in behavior when reared under different conditions. In these cases, we can attribute the *differences* in behavior to environmental factors. Conversely, if animals with different heredities are reared under identical conditions (which can be a tricky proposition), then the *differences* in behavior observed can be attributed to genetic variables. This is simply a variation on the theme that behavior is inseparably tangled with *both* hereditary and learned components.

Behavioral Interactions

Initially, ethologists are more concerned with *how* various subsystems interact with one another in terms of the functional whole, rather than *where* a particular isolated component of behavior is organized in the nervous system. An excellent example of this approach is found in the electrical stimulation studies of Holst and Saint Paul, illustrated in Figure 5.7. Electrodes were lowered into various regions of the brain in chickens until meaningful components of behavior could be elicited. It was found that several loci might elicit a particular behavior and that any given behavior might be affected by more than a single locus. They then sought functional interactions between these loci and were able, for example, to produce behavioral conflicts similar to those occurring in nature. They also determined how separate and combined loci shifted with the animal's behavioral status or "mood" and how stimulation of the nervous system combined with stimuli in the external world. One of their important conclusions was that the brains of vertebrates such as the bird are not organized in discrete and independent *centers* but should be viewed in terms of interlocking systems, each of which has certain unique features but also certain features shared with other (not necessarily anatomically adjacent) systems. Human clinical neurologists are coming to similar conclusions about higher neural functions in man.

In ethology, the term "function" is used in three ways, each of which represents an important aspect of ethological work. The first use is purely descriptive: the ethologist asks how the system functions; that is, what it does. The second use implies a causal analysis: how X varies as a function of Y. For example, does fighting behavior depend on the secretion of a particular hormone such as testosterone or upon a particular feature of the environment (or upon both)? The third use refers to the adaptive significance of the behavior: how the behavior functions to promote the survival of the animal and of the species. For example, to what degree does successful mating in doves depend on courtship displays, and how does the completion of this behavior affect species survival?

An excellent demonstration of the subtleties of behavioral interactions probed by ethologists is found in the concept of *displacement activities*. Consider the situa-

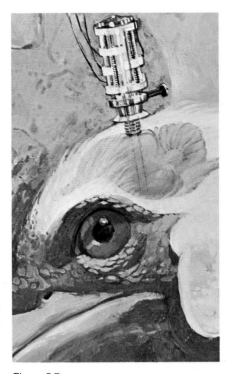

Figure 5.7
Stimulation at some points aroused the chicken, at others caused it to turn its head to the right or to shake it.

Displacement Activities

Figure 5.8
Sea birds grooming. This behavior may suddenly appear in birds that are threatening one another.

tion in which a particular species of bird or rodent is vacillating between approaching and avoiding a particular object or event (such as an intruder into its territory). The animal may quite suddenly stop and begin grooming movements. The environmental situation thus facilitated (although not necessarily directed) a sequence of movements in a behavioral pattern that appears contextually irrelevant in the sense that we did not initially expect it—although ethologists have found such behaviors to be highly predictable upon subsequent analysis. The term "displacement" was initially used to suggest that some type of energy was displaced from the conflicting behaviors into this seemingly irrelevant activity. Although such energy models are really descriptive and are not to be confused with the functioning of underlying neural mechanisms, the observation of these initially unexpected displacement activities does emphasize the subtle behavioral interactions that are a major focus in modern ethology.

The question of behavioral specificity is of some historical interest in ethology, where detailed attention has been paid to the mechanisms that control individual components of behavior as well as their interactions. Based upon the fact that these components may often fluctuate relatively independently of one another, early ethological models stressed the specificity of underlying systems. Psychologists, on the other hand, have concentrated upon higher-order functions in behavior, such as degree of wakefulness or arousal, and thus have stressed general (for example, motivational) processes. One answer to this apparent paradox is that the generality or specificity of behavioral systems is largely dependent upon the types examined and the level of analysis employed.

Motivation The responsiveness of animals to particular stimuli and the types of responses shown in a given environmental context are not constant but shift with the animals' internal states. Birds migrate at particular times of the year, the praying mantis is most receptive to prey after the insect has gone some time without eating, and a major feature of our own daily lives is that we switch from one behavior to another partially as a consequence of changes in the world around us, but also partially as a response to changes in our inner world of moods, emotions, and needs.

Ethologists have been particularly concerned with what makes an animal do what it does at any given instant. An important first approach to this problem is to determine changes in responsiveness to a constant external environment. Such changes reflect alterations in the internal state of the organism and fall within the general heading of motivation. A precise definition of "motivation" is difficult, for internal changes in responsiveness may be found even at the level of the spinal cord. However, the term is most usefully applied to fluctuations in behavior in the intact organism that are not primarily sensory or motor in nature.

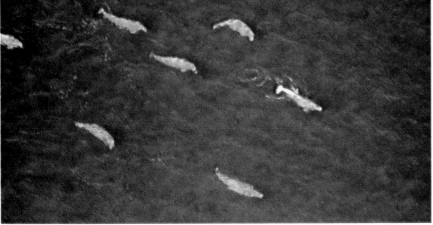

Figure 5.9
Internal states as well as environmental conditions control the migration of birds and butterflies.

Figure 5.10
Migrating whales.

These fluctuations may last for minutes, hours, or even days, but in general they can be separated from permanent behavioral alterations that occur during behavioral development and learning.

A classic example of this operational approach to motivation can be seen in Hinde's detailed studies on the chaffinch. If a chaffinch is presented with a model of a potential predator (such as a dog or owl), it responds with a characteristic *chinking* call. This chinking response, however, is not constant but shows complex patterns of both increases and decreases in strength over time (see Figure 5.11). The maximum rate of chinking occurs after two and a half minutes, after

Figure 5.11

Rate of chinking in the chaffinch as a function of time since a model predator was presented.
(After Hinde, 1954.)

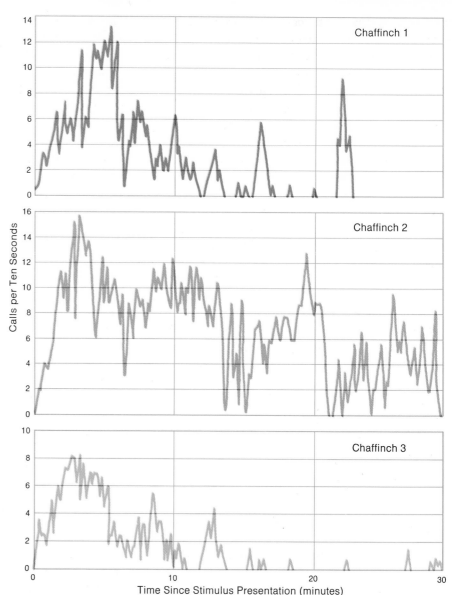

which there is a fluctuating decline in responsiveness. Hinde also found that if the model predator was removed during the period of vigorous responding, the chinking behavior persisted for a relatively long period of time. In other experiments, he was able to determine the degree to which these response changes were specific to a particular stimulus (owl versus dog), as well as to work out the behavioral details of a number of intervening processes. Thus, motivational changes show in a dramatic fashion the subtle interplay between internal and external processes in controlling behavioral responsiveness.

A major lesson in ethology is that one must be aware of limitations in the extent to which it is possible to generalize data obtained with particular behaviors in particular species. However, possible analogies between studies of displacement activities and the control of behavior in man are worth considering. Man often performs simple stereotyped movements such as scratching his head and drumming his fingers on a table when under moderately extreme levels of arousal and conflict. It is possible that such behaviors occur in these situations because they are both relatively simple and stereotyped in nature. There is considerable evidence from both psychological and neurophysiological studies that in states of moderate conflict, behaviors of this type are the least likely to be suppressed. It is also interesting that simple, often repeated, and stereotyped behaviors survive a variety of lesions in higher neural systems that prevent the expression of more complex and unique behavior patterns. Thus, there is the further possibility that conflict behavior and moderately excessive arousal levels may reduce the efficiency of underlying neuronal machinery and that displacement activities occur partially for this reason.

Aggressive behavior is of particular interest in this day and age, and ethologists have found that it is not so common in wild animals as we might suppose. Animals that are confined in small enclosures show much higher levels of aggression, and thus we again see that environmental variables can have many different effects on the same genetic potential.

The balance between endogenous and exogenous factors is a particularly subtle issue in the control of motivational systems in which there are many stages between sensory inputs and motor outputs. Early motivational models in ethology, as in psychology, emphasized the fact that motivated behaviors are driven from within. Thus, sign stimuli were thought to release the internally driven behaviors—and little more. We know today that this hypothesis is an oversimplification, for stimuli may both increase and decrease the strength of the motivation. At present, our knowledge of this dual role of stimuli is incomplete.

Formerly, drives were thought to build up in the organism irrespective of the environmental situation. In extreme cases, this appears to be true. Lorenz has described the behavior of a well-fed starling that has been deprived of the opportunity to catch flies for an extended period of time. The bird would occasionally go through elaborate fly-catching movements even though no appropriate stimuli could be discerned by the observer, a type of behavior called *vacuum activity*. Indeed, it is a striking example of how motivational processes that build up inside an animal can lead to a given behavior even in the absence of normally necessary cues.

In our daily experience, we often speak of the importance of giving children, and even adults, the occasional opportunity to "work off steam." Social philosophers have even suggested that an occasional war may be necessary for similar reasons. However, the public recently has become more aware of the other side of the coin. The build-up of aggression within the organism is not independent of the environment, and it is probable that watching violence on TV can serve as much as a stimulant as it serves as a catharsis for aggressive behavior. There is a two-way interplay in these situations that we do not fully understand.

Models of Behavior

In *The Study of Instinct,* Tinbergen formalized the notion of hierarchically arranged behavior systems in which relatively general processes feed into progressively more specific control mechanisms. Drawing upon the work of earlier investigators, he suggested that during the course of a behavioral sequence, such as searching out and consuming food, the early phases of the sequence were more general or higher in the hierarchy, whereas later phases were more specific in their control (see Figure 5.12). These early phases were called *appetitive behaviors*; the later ones were called *consummatory acts*.

Tinbergen's scheme has undergone revisions. For example, the model suggested that behavioral energy flowed from appetitive behavior to consummatory acts. Such energy models not only are difficult to relate to neuronal processes but appear contradicted by some behavioral data. However, the model succeeded admirably in summarizing a variety of data and suggested many new experiments

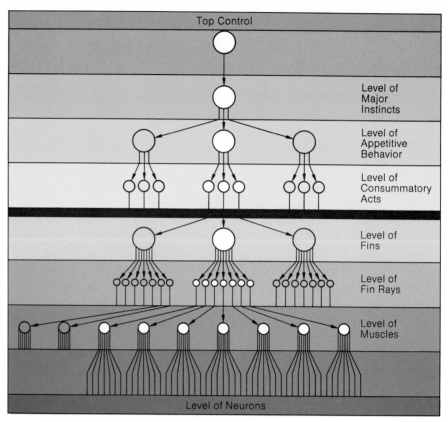

Figure 5.12

Tinbergen's conception of the organization of behavior by a hierarchy of progressively specific control mechanisms.
(After Tinbergen, 1951.)

at various levels of analysis. Today, most workers in ethology as well as psychology and neurophysiology still feel that some type of hierarchical model of behavioral control is the most appropriate, and concerted efforts are being made to fill in the details.

Ethologists are becoming increasingly concerned with formulating behavioral models that can be translated to the physiological level. Lehrman, for example, noticed that a male ring dove exposed to the sight of a female would initiate courtship behavior after some period. This courtship in turn led to ovarian development in the female. Changes in reproductive behavior were found to be hormonally mediated, but the hormonal changes themselves were largely dependent upon previous behavioral experience. This is an elegant example of the subtle interactions between organism and environment referred to above. It is obvious that the search for causal processes is a never-ending one, for each new mechanism soon breaks down into a complex system with its own problems of control.

Processing Sensory Input

We know from our daily lives that the sensory world around us stimulates, releases, and guides much of our behavior. The same is true for the nonhuman animals, but their world of experience may be quite different from our own. The sensory world that produces measurable effects upon behavior is highly selective. The European naturalist Uexküll verbally painted a vivid picture of the mated female tick who would climb into the branches of a tree and wait for many days and weeks until a mammal passed directly beneath her. Until this time she appeared unresponsive to the barrage of sights, sounds, and odors about her. It was the specific smell of butyric acid generated by mammalian skin glands that signaled her approaching meal and led her to drop on her host. The high selectivity of her responses to butyric acid would not be apparent to the casual observer. In Uexküll's words, the tick acts like a gourmet who picks the raisins out of a cake.

Ethologists were quick to realize the importance of such observations on the diverse sensory worlds of different animal species. Indeed, many species can be classified by the stimuli they attend to in much the same way that they can be compared in terms of fixed motor acts. It is because specific stimuli in the external environment so often appear to serve as the signal for a complex sequence of behaviors that the ethologists incorporated their fascinating observations under the heading of *sign stimuli*. Because particular stimuli appear to release highly specific behaviors in a characteristic manner for a given species, the hypothetical construct of an *innate releasing mechanism* was developed. It is now known that developmental variables may play a more important role in various species-characteristic stimulus-response relations than supposed, that the specificity of the stimulus character producing a response is not absolute, that stimuli can excite as well as release behaviors, and that sensory input typically goes through several stages of neural processing rather than serving as a simple key that unlocks a unitary mechanism. But it was the early ethological studies of behavior that first indicated the excitement and significance of probing into the diverse sensory worlds of different species.

Consider the male stickleback, who will attack a crude model of another stickleback if the model has a red belly. Models that to us appear much more fishlike but lack this red belly are often ignored by the fish in a test situation (Figure 5.13). Red breast feathers are the signal most efficient in producing an attack by a male robin who is setting up his territory. The feeding response of young herring gulls is more affected by the presence or absence of a red patch on the lower mandible of a model of the parent than by distortions that to us might make the model appear very unbirdlike (see Figure 5.14).

Such data are fundamental to the understanding of the sensory worlds of animals, and analogies to our own daily lives are not hard to imagine. It is important to recognize that these data do not indicate that a given behavior is elicited by only *one* feature of the environment or that the response to a particular sign stimulus is invariable. The relationship of stimuli with one another can be important. The red patch on a model stickleback is much more effective when placed on the underside than on top. In a sense, the color of the patch summates with its position; there is a degree of convergence of stimulus properties with respect to the probability of aggressive behavior being elicited. Thus, the principle has been called *heterogeneous summation* by ethologists. The combined effects of different stimulus components need not be a simple additive process. The male stickleback does not always show the same strength of response to a given model, for shifts within the internal (for example, motivational) state of the animal can affect response probability, duration, and vigor.

A rather remarkable finding is that some stimuli appear to be *more effective* than naturally occurring stimuli in releasing species-specific reactions. Tinbergen, for example, illustrated that an oystercatcher would attempt to brood a model egg several times the normal size of an oystercatcher's own eggs and would actually choose this *supernormal stimulus* if given a preference test. This preference was shown even when the model egg was so large that the bird was unable to assume a normal brooding position (see Figure 5.15). Thus, *quantitative* as well as *qualitative* aspects of an environmental stimulus appear to be important in determining a given response. How these quantitative and qualitative features interact within the nervous system is not known. Nor is it really understood why

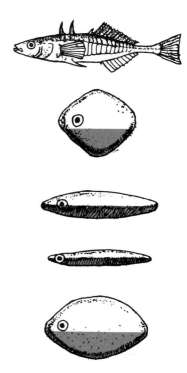

Figure 5.13
The stickleback may ignore the top model but will attack any of the lower ones.
(After Tinbergen, 1951.)

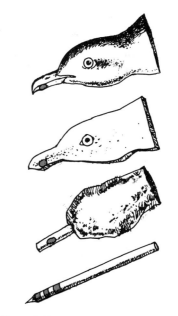

Figure 5.14
Young herring gulls peck at the bottom model most frequently.

95

Figure 5.15
An oystercatcher attempting to brood a supernormal egg.

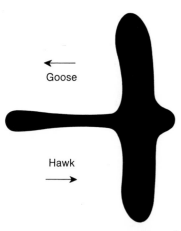

Goose

Hawk

Figure 5.16
This figure resembles a hawk if moved to the right and elicits escape responses in young turkeys. If moved to the left, however, it casts a gooselike shadow and fails to elicit escape.
(After Tinbergen, 1951.)

it is relatively easy to improve upon nature in terms of the effectiveness with which a response is elicited. Again, however, it is not difficult to think of analogies in our own lives, although here the role of cultural variables appears important.

The subtle interactions between quantitative and qualitative aspects of stimulus control, as well as some of the potential difficulties in the study of sign stimuli, are clearly evident in an experiment in which young turkeys were found to give a vigorous escape response to a cardboard model turned so that it had a short neck and a long tail (see Figure 5.16). The shadow cast resembled that of a hawk. If the model was subsequently turned in the opposite direction so that it appeared to have a long neck and short tail (like a flying goose), the young turkeys showed very little escape response. On the basis of such early experiments, it would be very easy to conclude that this is not only a highly specific response to a potential predator but also, because the turkeys had never seen any live hawks, an innate behavior. (Some have suggested that perhaps it was a goose flying backward that was frightening.)

There are limitations in the sensory apparatus of any particular species. Man, for example, cannot tell whether or not light is polarized, but many invertebrates use polarization for orientation. For the female tick, an important stimulus is butyric acid in concentrations the human olfactory system cannot ordinarily detect. The upper limitation of auditory sensitivity in man is about 20,000 cycles per second, but rodents can often hear up to 100,000 cycles per second. It is easy to demonstrate that these high-frequency components are important to mice or rats, who show a definite startle response to hand claps but do not do so if these hand claps are recorded on tape; even good-fidelity tape recorders cut off the high-frequency components to which the rodents are particularly susceptible. Moreover, bats navigate by means of echolocation involving frequencies considerably above what humans can detect.

There is an increasing appreciation among neurophysiologists that to understand the sensory apparatus of a given animal it is important to present the animal with stimuli that are meaningful to it. Lettvin and his colleagues found cells in the retina of frogs that were particularly sensitive to stimuli that resemble a moving bug, a potential source of food for the frog. Hubel and Wiesel have conducted a long series of experiments showing that there are cells in the cat's cortex that are particularly sensitive to certain types of movement in the visual field. Such studies apparently support ethologists' contention that the way in which the brain is innately shaped is highly important to the development of the particular responsiveness of animals to certain attributes of their sensory worlds. However, to what extent neurons can be found that respond specifically to only a single class of very complex stimuli, how these neural connections that underlie complex sensory processing are formed during development, and the mechanics by which responsiveness to a given class of stimuli fluctuates with the internal state of the organism remain mysteries.

In our discussion so far, components of animal behavior have been rather arbitrarily divided into the programming of motor output and the processing of sensory input. The control of movement often involves a delicate interaction with sensory signals (for example, proprioception), and the sensitivity of the organism to particular stimuli can in turn be modulated by outputs from various parts of the nervous system. However, behaviors vary considerably with respect to the degree to which their orientation is guided by environmental stimuli. If we are startled by a loud sound, the initial startle response is not specifically oriented to the source of the sound, although subsequently we may turn in the direction of the disturbance.

Early workers in animal behavior suggested that it is often valuable to distinguish between *kinesis* and *taxis* in the control of behavior sequences. Kinesis comprises those behaviors, or components of a sequence of movements, that are elicited, accelerated, and decelerated by environmental stimuli but are not directly guided by these stimuli. The fact that kinesis can serve to orient the animal is illustrated by the behavior of the wood louse in damp and dry environments. This animal cannot survive in prolonged periods of dryness and responds to dryness by increasing its locomotive behavior. If the animal's journeys lead it to a more moist location, the locomotion slows down and may even come to a complete stop. Similarly, many flatworms reside in dark environments and increase locomotion and rates of change in direction when they are exposed to the light (see Figure 5.17).

Although kinetic changes in overall activity under different environmental conditions can lead to successful orientation in an indirect manner, *taxes* are often more efficient. Taxes are responses oriented in relation to particular features of the environment. They have been divided into many types depending upon the particular manner in which the animal makes use of environmental stimuli. For example, in *klinotaxis* the animal makes *successive comparisons* of the environmental stimulus by moving its receptors from side to side; in *tropotaxis, simultaneous comparison* is made of stimuli falling upon each side of the body (and thus depends upon bilateral symmetry); and in *telotaxis,* the animal moves either toward or away from the source of stimulation without obvious successive or simultaneous comparisons.

The orientation of many animal species is a remarkable display of nature's virtuosity. Particularly dramatic examples involve the migration of animals over vast distances. Alaskan fur seals, for example, breed only on the Pribilof Islands in the Bering Sea. During the winter, the females and young seals swim some

Orientation

Figure 5.17
When a flatworm is exposed to light, its rate of change of direction increases sharply, then slowly returns to its original level.
(After Ullyott, 1936.)

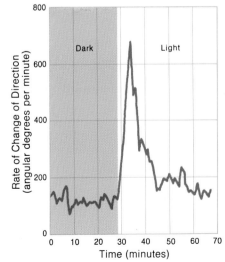

Figure 5.18
Radio has been used in an attempt to track green turtles, which travel thousands of miles to return to their breeding grounds.

3,000 miles to the coast of southern California while the males travel to the southern Aleutian Islands, a much shorter journey. In the spring, both sexes rejoin in the Pribilofs. Similarly, eels born in the Sargasso Sea find their way to the coasts of North America and Europe, salmon return to their home streams to spawn after journeys of hundreds of miles into the ocean, and both the night-hawk and the barn swallow of North America breed in the cold reaches of the Yukon and Alaska after a trip from as far south as Argentina, a distance of some 7,000 miles.

The exact cues used by various species during these remarkable trips have been under active investigation by workers in animal behavior. Birds, the most thoroughly studied, often appear to use both the sun and the stars as guides in addition to various landmarks. Among the most impressive studies are those that indicate that homing and migration in birds are much more than a long flight over a fixed course. Matthews, for example, describes experiments in which birds were transported over large distances and then released. Many species were still able to find their way "home," and they somehow must have calculated their starting point at the beginning of their journey. Such phenomena add the dimension of rather subtle navigation to the problem of animal orientation, and many experiments are being performed to help isolate the relevant cues.

Development of Behavior

The study of behavioral development is a logical extension of the causal explanations discussed in previous sections. The importance of developmental studies for getting beneath such concepts as instinctive behavior has already been mentioned. The analysis of behavioral development can be applied to basic sensory and motor phenomena, as well as to such high-order processes as motivation. The problem of behavioral development is also closely linked with problems of learning, for it has now become apparent that animals typically learn different types of things at different ages.

A young timber wolf reared in isolation from other wolves may show the species-characteristic pouncing behavior at about eight weeks of age when a small object is moved through the grass. This fixed pattern obviously does not depend upon seeing other wolves perform the behavior, nor is long experience with moving objects a prerequisite. On the other hand, the orientation of these early pouncing movements is poor. If the object is moved to the right, the wolf may pounce straight ahead or even to the left. These observations give us a clue that the role of experience may be more important in the orientation of a simple movement than in its elicitation. In a similar manner, Eibl-Eibesfeldt has reported that squirrels show quite early the fixed motor components of gnawing a nut but that considerable practice is needed for these individual movements to be organized into an efficient nut-opening sequence. The orientation component of these motor acts is more dependent upon practice than are the individual movements.

In terms of the basic coordination of simple species-characteristic motor stereotypes, there is thus good reason to believe that environmental variables play a minimal role during development. The same hypotheses seem to be true for many basic sensory processes. For example, Sperry rotated the eyes of frogs and salamanders and found that these animals would persist in striking at prey objects in the inappropriate direction. These results could be obtained by either rotating the eye in its socket or actually severing the optic nerve and then rotating the eye. The nerve regenerates in such a manner that a given nerve cell in the eye still connects with its original location in the brain, but now that the eye is turned upside down, images in the lower visual field project to the part of the brain that normally receives images from the upper visual field. The animal's behavior is disarranged accordingly (Figure 5.19). Jacobson has pursued related studies at the neuronal and biochemical level, and it appears that there is a remarkable degree of specificity of neuronal organization in basic sensory and motor

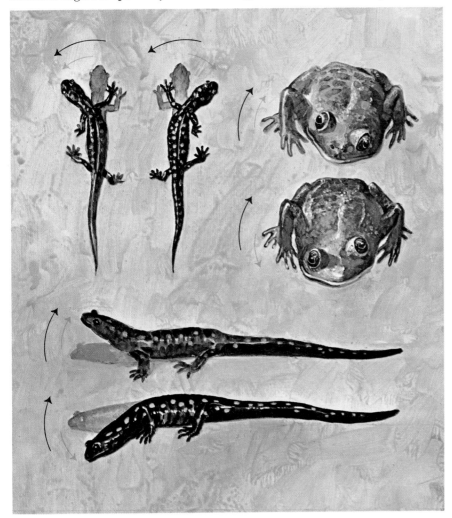

Figure 5.19
The response of Sperry's animals to visual stimuli. Black arrows show the motion of a visual pattern past the animal. Blue arrows show the animal's response. The first animal in each pair is normal. Note that disorientation can be produced in any plane by the appropriate rotation of the eye. (After Sperry, 1951.)

systems, which minimizes the role of experience in the functional development of these systems.

However, one must be careful in generalizing from these studies. Prechtl, for example, has found that the position of the legs during the last week before birth can produce significant alterations in reflex behavior in the human infant. More data on behavioral development in a variety of motor systems are needed.

Bird Songs It is in the development of species-characteristic bird songs that many of the most detailed behavioral analyses have been made. As in the great majority of ethological studies, the relations between genetic and environmental factors in bird song development appear to be multivariate and extremely subtle.

The patterning of avian vocalizations can be studied particularly well with the aid of sound spectrographs, which plot the frequency of sound against time (Figure 5.20). In many passerine birds, individual call notes develop normally in

Figure 5.20

Sound spectrographs of chaffinch song: (A) the normal song, (B) the song of a bird reared from birth in isolation, (C) the song of a bird removed from a group at an early age and reared in isolation, (D) the song of a bird reared in isolation but tutored with a recording spliced so that the ending of the song came in the middle.
(After Thorpe, 1961.)

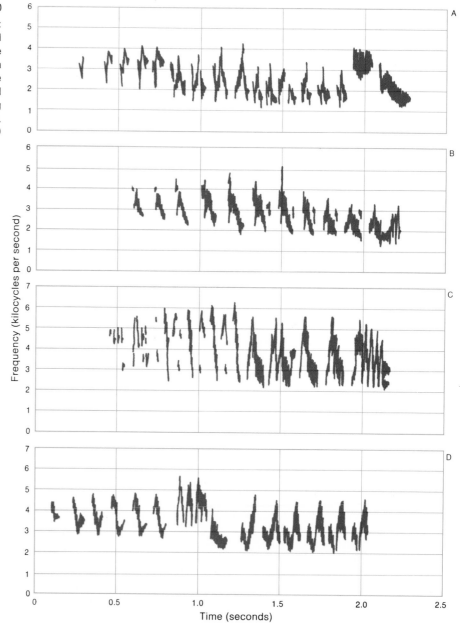

birds reared in isolation, although this is not universally the case. More complex songs are made up of individual call notes. Thorpe has shown that chaffinches hand-reared in isolation developed only very simple types of song (Figure 5.20). If young chaffinches are exposed to the calls of other immature birds, their spring songs are often more complex. Thus, auditory experience other than hearing the fully developed adult song can affect the development of songs in young birds. Chaffinches and other birds are known to imitate the songs of neighboring birds, for local dialects are found that cannot be attributed to genetic differences. However, there are limits to which this imitation can be carried out. Thorpe, for example, found that tape recordings of pure tones did not modify the development of song in isolated chaffinches but that tape recordings containing chaffinch songs did, even if these recordings were played in the reverse direction (giving a backward song). Stevenson has obtained some evidence that chaffinches will work to expose themselves to their species song. She gave birds a choice of two perches. When they jumped on one, they heard the normal chaffinch song; when they jumped on the other, they heard white noise. There is the interesting possibility that part of the genetic program is translated in such a way as to cause the animals to expose themselves to stimuli in the environment necessary for the complete development of a normal song.

Animals reared in isolation can still hear themselves sing. Konishi asked what would happen if birds were experimentally deafened. He found that Oregon juncos deafened at an early age developed many of the normal features of adult song. However, there was also a greater degree of variability in deafened as compared to undeafened birds. It appears that in these birds, which develop normal songs when reared in isolation but without deafening, auditory feedback is an important component in the final crystallization of the species-typical stereotyped song pattern.

Marler and Tamura found that white-crowned sparrows, like chaffinches, develop local dialects through listening to the songs of the local populations of their species. If young sparrows are kept in isolation, they develop a full song, but this song is abnormal in certain important respects and fails to show the local dialect of the area in which the birds were captured. In these birds, there is a period of several months between the time that song patterns are acquired and the time that young birds first sing the song themselves. If the sparrows are deafened shortly after the sensitive period in which they acquire the song, their songs deteriorate, but if the birds are not deafened until they have developed their full song, the consequences of losing auditory feedback are minimal. Thus, there are several facets in the interplay between genetic and experimental variables during the course of song development, and it is necessary not only to break the motor pattern of singing into component parts but to subdivide developmental periods as well.

The study of *imprinting* provides a striking example of interactions between genetic potential and experience during the development of stimulus-response relationships. Lorenz brought to the attention of ethologists the interesting fact that newly hatched ducklings or goslings will at a certain age follow almost any moving object. After a subsequent period of often not more than several hours, novel objects fail to produce the following response. This phenomenon indicates that there are certain stages in the life of these animals during which they are particularly susceptible to forming attachments to moving objects. It is not difficult to imagine the significance of this in the animals' normal adjustment to their

Imprinting

Figure 5.21
Imprinting chicks. The chicks follow the blue ball—the imprinting stimulus—which is rotated slowly around the runway.

environment. Birds of a feather flock together, as the old saying goes, and it is the formation of these early attachments to particular moving objects, which in the wild are most likely to be other birds of their own species, that serves as the glue in the formation of many avian social structures.

The objects that are followed do not have to be particularly good models of the animals' species, and indeed the conspicuousness of the objects may partially determine what is followed. This is another example of the importance of quantitative dimensions in behavior. In his early writings, Lorenz argued that once the social bonds are formed, they are difficult if not impossible to break. Thus, a barnyard goose may not only follow its keeper but upon reaching sexual maturity may actually attempt to mate with him.

Imprinting was considered initially to be a special process in which objects presented during a highly restricted critical period were stamped-in (literally, imprinted) and from that point on were totally resistant to subsequent modification. It is now known that animals can learn certain characteristics of their environment prior to the imprinting period and that subsequent modification of the initial preferences is sometimes possible. There is, however, no doubt that animals are more likely to form attachments to objects presented at certain times in their early development than to objects presented either earlier or later. There are sensitive periods in development for learning a variety of stimulus-response relationships, but the boundaries are not quite as marked as initially thought.

One of the interesting features of behavioral development that has become particularly clear in studies of imprinting is that once animals are familiar with a

Figure 5.22
The period in which a chick may be readily imprinted is delimited by an early inability to run after a stimulus and a later tendency to avoid novel stimuli.
(After Hess, 1959.)

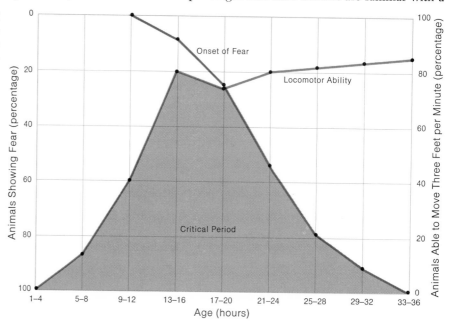

given set of environmental surroundings, they are likely to avoid novel stimuli. Indeed, one of the factors that appears to limit the sensitive period of imprinting is the accumulation of sufficient experience to make novel stimuli apparent. It is as if the animals build up an internal representation of certain features of their environment, then avoid stimuli that do not match this framework. Although on a very different level, it is interesting to note that many wild mammals, such as the young wolf, go through a very shy period after they appear to have mastered their immediate environment. A slight change in the environment (for example, moving an object from one place to another) will often result in extreme avoidance reactions.

It is often possible either to prolong or to shorten the time at which the sensitive period ends. Thus, the developmental processes so well illustrated by the phenomenon of imprinting are not rigidly run off like clockwork but may be modified within limits by environmental stimuli during development.

Socialization and Emotionality

Studies of the socialization of wild mammalian species provide additional information on the interplay between genetic and environmental variables during development. If timber wolves are obtained at a young age (four to six weeks), for example, it is relatively easy to get them not only to accept close human companionship but actually to seek it out. At first, this might appear to be quite a drastic alteration in the behavior of man's long-dreaded enemy, but more probably the wolf is preprogrammed to form strong social attachments with those he is in close contact with during the first few weeks of life. Wolves can be socialized at a later age, but only with much greater difficulty. Wolves that have been socialized also retain much of their timidity in the presence of novel stimuli, and thus there are limitations in the degree to which the animals' behavior is modified by early human handling.

Handling of mammals in early life can produce marked changes in emotionality, however. For example, Levine and Denenberg have found that rats that are handled during infancy often show much reduced timidity and stress reactions when placed in novel environments. These events are mediated both prenatally and postnatally and may even be perpetuated via prenatal effects upon the fetal environment over more than a single generation. This phenomenon adds a new dimension to genetic-environmental interactions, for if nongenetically induced alterations in behavior can affect not only the behavior of the parental animals but also that of the maternal offspring, then the flexibility in the coding of behavioral information is potentially increased. It is not difficult to imagine how such flexibility may, in the proper circumstances, even have survival value.

6

OPERANT CONDITIONING

IF YOU HAVE EVER been to Las Vegas or to one of the other gambling meccas in Nevada, you probably were struck by the sight of thousands of people standing in front of the slot machines, pulling the handles as mechanically as robots, a fixed look machined on their faces as they put in a coin and pull the handle again and again and again. If you are not particularly pleasured by this type of gambling, you may well have wondered what it could possibly be that keeps people slaving in front of a slot machine for hours on end, day after day. They must know that, in the long run, they are going to lose; then why do they keep up this mechanical responding as if it were actually pleasant to them?

If you are a particularly astute observer of human behavior, you may also have noticed that most gamblers have certain little idiosyncrasies about the way in which they place their chips on a roulette table or a characteristic series of motions they make when playing a slot machine. Over and over again, they repeat these self-same movements. You may have noticed too that some gamblers always appear in the same clothes, while others carry a rabbit's foot or a lucky coin. At first blush it might seem that the study of such mechanical, superstitious behavior would be the province of abnormal psychology, but it is not. We do not need to appeal to a study of deep-seated neuroses or childhood fears to understand this aspect of human life; rather, we must look at that part of learning that is called *instrumental* or *operant conditioning.*

When a child first touches a fire and withdraws his hand rapidly because of the pain, a process of learning occurs that we call classical or Pavlovian conditioning (see Chapter 4). In this case, the environment acts on the child, and the painful stimulus elicits an automatic withdrawal of the child's hand. Later, the child responds to the sight of fire by avoiding it. Because the response to fire is automatic and involuntary, hence out of the conscious control of the child, this type of learning is also called *respondent* conditioning. When the child grows up, goes to Las Vegas, and learns that pulling slot machine handles can (very) occasionally lead to winning jackpots, we can hardly say that the same type of automatic learning has occurred. For here the gambler is acting on his environment—he consciously puts in the coin and pulls the lever. The sight of fire can be said to generate or elicit the unconscious withdrawal response; but men go seeking slot machines deliberately. In short, something inside us causes us to emit or generate certain responses (such as gambling) that are instrumental in changing or operating on our environments. The learning of these responses is hence called instrumental or operant conditioning. If our behavior modifies the environment in ways we like, we tend to repeat the behavior; if the behavior leads to environmental modifications we do not like, we tend not to repeat the responses. And this is what operant conditioning—and gambling—is all about.

Reinforcement and Punishment

The environmental consequences of behavior are conveniently divided into two categories, depending on their effect on the behavior. Consequences that result in the repetition of the behavior that produces them are called *reinforcers;* consequences that result in the suppression of the behavior that produces them are called *punishers,* or aversive stimuli. Money, for example, is classed as a reinforcer for people, because behavior that accumulates money tends to be repeated. Loss of friendship and pain are classified as aversive or punishing, because behavior that produces them tends not to be repeated. In fact, if a person is exposed to an aversive situation, any behavior that terminates it tends to be repeated. Thus, the termination of aversive stimulation is itself a reinforcer.

In each case, a response is followed by a consequence, and as a result the organism's tendency to engage in the behavior in the future is modified. Responses that are reinforced tend to be repeated; responses that are punished tend not to be repeated. The fundamental effect of reinforcement is to increase the frequency of occurrence of the behavior that it follows.

Effects of Reinforcement

Reinforcement has another effect of equal importance: it brings the reinforced behavior under the control of stimuli prevailing at the time of reinforcement; that is, behavior tends to occur predominately in the presence of those stimuli that have, in the past, set the occasion for reinforcement of the response. Reinforcement not only affects the frequency of occurrence of behavior but also brings it under stimulus control.

The two effects of reinforcement may be contrasted by considering a small child's learning to talk. Early in the learning of language, parents are content if the child says anything at all. Thus, any sounds that even approximate English words tend to be reinforced. The response here is the audible vocal behavior of the child, and the reinforcer is some part of the behavior of the parents, either their attentive response to vocalization or their approval, and on occasion a concrete reward such as a piece of candy. Reinforcement increases the frequency with which the child vocalizes, particularly the frequency of those vocalizations that happen to occur and are reinforced by the parents. As the child grows older, however, it is not enough for him merely to speak. He is expected to speak distinctly and to use words properly, and parents withhold reinforcement for particular responses (words) used indiscriminately. Thus, "bye-bye," which earlier would have been reinforced no matter how it was used because it is so clearly human speech, is no longer reinforced unless someone is actually leaving. The restriction of reinforcement of the response to particular situations—in the presence of particular stimuli—brings the response under the control of those situations. The child comes to say "bye-bye" only when someone is leaving.

Reinforcement acts not only on the frequency of a response but also on its other parameters as well. Obviously, only audible vocalizations will be reinforced, because parents do not initially react to a child's speech if they cannot hear it. (Later, reinforcement of silent behavior may occur on the supposition that the child is thinking.) This arrangement carries with it a dependency between reinforcement and the loudness of the vocalization. To be sure, there is no upper limit, just the lower one—that the words be loud enough to be heard—but nevertheless only audible words are reinforced. Reinforcement of responses tends to produce responses of that or greater loudness.

This principle can be observed when you speak with a slightly deaf person. If he fails to react to what you say, you speak increasingly louder until he hears and reinforces your behavior. Thereafter, when you encounter that person you will tend to speak more loudly than usual, in keeping with the function of reinforcement to bring behavior under the control of stimuli. In this case, the deaf person is a stimulus controlling louder speaking, because only louder speaking is reinforced by the deaf.

Especially in sports, behaviors persist simply because they happen to precede reinforcement, not because they are essential for reinforceable performance. Styles of putting in golf are particularly influenced in this way. There is no one style of addressing the ball that will guarantee excellent putting, as witnessed by the variety of styles adopted by successful, professional golfers. Yet each golfer has a distinctive style. What happens is that a style happens to be adopted before several excellent putts and tends to remain because it is reinforced. In fact,

players often explicitly alter their style after a sequence of particularly bad putts. When they are again successful, the style that happens to be in use at the time is the one that persists for a while.

Acquisition and Shaping of Behavior

In Chapter 4, we saw how a rat learned to press a lever in Skinner's box. Now it is necessary to provide a slightly more detailed look at the process of operant conditioning in such an apparatus. You will recall that we assumed that the rat had been trained to take food from the dispenser before we began reinforcing the animal's bar presses. This food, in pellet form, drops into the cup or dispenser from a plastic tube (known as a food magazine) outside the box. Teaching the rat to approach the food cup—a procedure called *magazine training*—is necessary to ensure that bar presses are reinforced immediately. If reinforcement were delayed, the rat would have a chance to do something else after pressing the bar, with the result that the other behavior, not the bar pressing, would be immediately reinforced. Because it takes time for an animal to get food into its mouth, food is not a good immediate reinforcer. The purpose of magazine training is to make use of the principle that stimuli that regularly accompany presentations of a reinforcer such as food become themselves (conditioned) reinforcers. When a pellet of food drops from the food magazine into the cup, it makes a distinctive "click" sound. Magazine training turns the sights and sounds that accompany the presentation of food into conditioning reinforcers. Because the sights and sounds reach the animal instantly, they can be presented immediately after behavior such as bar pressing, reinforcing it immediately.

In order to carry out magazine training, food is presented a number of times regardless of what the animal happens to be doing. After several presentations, when the pellet falls into the cup, the rat runs directly to the magazine, seizes the food in its mouth, and eats it. The behavior indicates that the sights

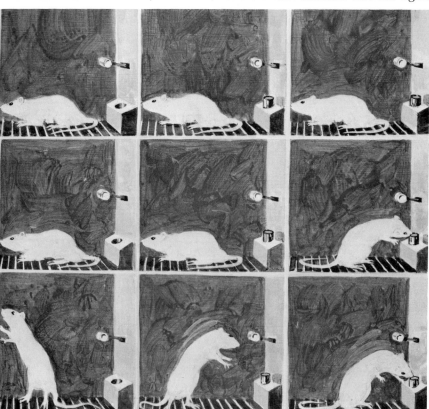

Figure 6.2

Magazine training of a thirsty rat. The rise of the water dipper through the hole is accompanied by a loud click. At first, the animal fails to find the water, but eventually it learns to go to the dipper as soon as the click sounds.

and sounds accompanying the food have become well enough established to act as effective, immediate conditioned reinforcers for lever pressing. It is at this point that bar pressing can be effectively reinforced by food and the conditioned reinforcing stimuli accompanying the presentation of food.

Operant behavior, as we have pointed out, has no eliciting stimulus but is said to be *emitted* by the organism. Because there is no particular stimulus that will force the rat to press a lever, we must wait for a lever press to occur. Such waiting is tedious, and fortunately there is an alternative. Because reinforcement works so well, it is possible to use it to *shape* the animal's behavior into the form of the desired response. In order to press the lever, the rat must approach it, rise up on its hind legs, put its front paws on the lever, and ride down toward the floor carrying the lever with him. The rat has all the behaviors necessary for bar pressing in its behavioral repertoire at the start of the experiment, but they occur in the wrong order. Consequently, in the shaping process, reinforcement is applied to these separate behaviors to mold them into the desired behavior of pressing the bar.

Shaping begins by reinforcing the first response in the desired behavior sequence, in this case approaching the lever. The rat then frequently interrupts its other behavior to approach the lever, because that response is reinforced. Next, reinforcement is withheld until the rat not only approaches the lever but also rises slightly off the floor in front of it. We reinforce a closer approximation to the final form of the behavior than is afforded by simply approaching the lever. At first, we may have to settle for reinforcing the mere lifting of one paw off the floor, but if we then select lifts of greater and greater magnitude for reinforcement, we cannot fail to get the rat to rise up high enough. Then reinforcement is again withheld until the lift from the floor brings the rat into contact with the lever. At that point, lever pressing is practically guaranteed. We

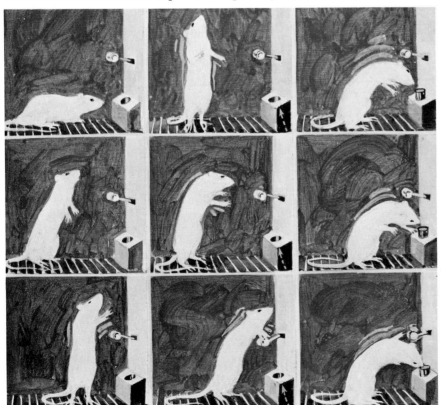

Figure 6.3

Shaping a bar press in the rat. The click of the water dipper (now a conditioned reinforcer) is first used to strengthen the behavior of rising on the hind legs, then dropping forward. Finally, the rat depresses the bar and is rewarded.

Figure 6.4
Reinforcement is used to maintain in porpoises and a killer whale those behaviors that were first emitted after reinforcement of successive approximations.

simply withhold reinforcement until the lever is actually depressed, and we have shaped a bar press.

The process of shaping, then, involves selecting for reinforcement successively closer and closer approximations to the desired behaviors that make up the final response. The *principle of successive approximations* is a powerful one and is at the heart of the shaping procedure. But its proper use often assumes the status of an art rather than a science, for it takes a skilled trainer to know which approximations to reward and which to ignore; and because the approximate responses are emitted rather than elicited, they cannot always be specified in advance. We do know that each successive approximation must be a small step from what the animal was previously doing—if the steps attempted are too large, the whole procedure fails and the animal never reaches the final or terminal response at all. In the long run, shaping is possible because reinforcement really works: The behavior that is reinforced tends to be repeated, furnishing raw behavioral material from which a closer approximation to the final product may be selected for further reinforcement.

Extinction Shaping involves many periods of time during which reinforcement is withheld when the organism fails to emit a response that is a closer approximation to the desired response. Why do we expect a closer approximation to occur? Isn't it more likely that the organism will abandon the response and that we will be back where we started prior to the beginning of the shaping process? The answer to these questions involves an understanding of the effects of extinction.

Extinction is the withdrawal of reinforcement. It has several effects. The first is a decrease in the probability of occurrence of the previously reinforced behavior. Responding that is no longer reinforced gradually ceases to occur. The other effects of extinction occur during the gradual cessation of responding: responding becomes more variable, and individual responses become more force-

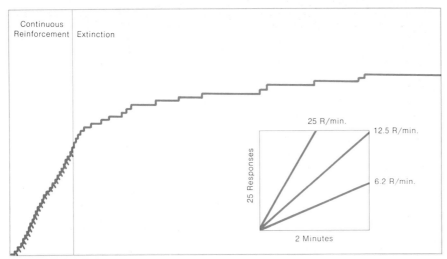

Figure 6.5
Cumulative record of extinction. The cumulative number of responses is plotted as a function of time. Rates represented by different slopes of the cumulative record are shown in the inset.

ful. When, in the course of shaping bar pressing in the rat, we cease reinforcing slight liftings of the forepaws off the floor, the liftings gradually decrease in frequency. But as they do, the lifts become more variable and more forceful. From these more variable and forceful liftings, we select a closer approximation to the desired response of rising high enough off the floor to press the lever.

These effects of extinction occur whenever a previously reinforced response is no longer reinforced. Suppose that for some reason the door to the dining hall will not open. The previously reinforced response of grasping the knob and turning no longer results in the reinforcing consequence of opening the door. Faced with this, an individual's attempts to open the door will become less frequent, and he will abandon trying to get the door open altogether in a matter of a few minutes. But during this time, the responses become more variable and more forceful. The knob is turned harder, perhaps with both hands. The individual may kick the door. He may even run around to another door, an extreme instance of variable responding. If any of these more variable and more forceful responses is successful in opening the door—if any is reinforced—it will tend to persist. If none is successful, all will cease to occur.

Figure 6.5 illustrates a typical *extinction curve*: the gradual decrease of un-reinforced responding over time. Up to the point indicated by the vertical line, responding has been occasionally rewarded with food. Subsequently, however, reinforcement is withheld. Eventually the organism stops responding altogether.

Spontaneous Recovery

If, after extinction, the organism is removed from the experimental chamber for a short while and then placed again in it, responding recurs at a higher rate than prevailed at the end of extinction. This phenomenon is called *spontaneous recovery*, because responding seems to recover from the effects of extinction spontaneously during the rest period outside of the chamber. It is likely, however, that the organism is simply responding to the fact that it has just been placed in the chamber, because this has always been in the past an occasion for the reinforcement of its responses.

Stimulus Control

Consider a pigeon whose key pecking has been reinforced in the presence of a red light. We now present a green light and observe whether or not the pigeon responds. If the pigeon does not respond, we say that he is discriminating between the two colors. If the pigeon does respond, however, we have an instance of *stimulus generalization*. Because both generalization and discrimination relate to the control of behavior by stimuli, a useful term for these processes is *stimulus*

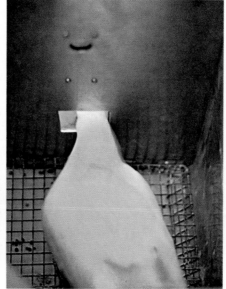

Figure 6.6
The pigeon pecks when the key is red
and is reinforced. The last frame is a view
into the food hopper.

control. When a stimulus has precise control over responding, a slight change in that stimulus may result in lack of response. When the control is not precise, however, it may be possible to alter the stimulus radically and still maintain the appropriate response. It should be obvious that both phenomena are crucial to the maintenance of appropriate behavior.

If discrimination were always perfect, very little learning could take place because stimulus situations are rarely if ever identical from time to time. Thus, behavior learned in the presence of one stimulus complex would not occur in the presence of even a slightly different stimulus complex. The experience of a child who touches fire, for example, would not prevent the behavior from recurring, because the next fire the child sees is certain to look somewhat different. At the other extreme, however, complete generalization would mean that a reinforced response would continue to occur regardless of the stimulus conditions. If a person whose behavior generalized completely somehow managed to survive, his behavior would be grotesque and completely inappropriate for normal functioning.

Usually, neither of these two extremes occurs. Although a pigeon trained to make a particular response to a red light may indeed, under certain circumstances, make the same response to any colored light, it is unlikely that it would make the response to the sound of a bell. Thus, although there may be a great deal of generalization within a stimulus dimension, there will be much less interdimensional generalization. Similarly, there is a limit to the extent of discriminative control that a stimulus can exert. The ultimate limit is reached when the organism cannot possibly make a discrimination between two stimuli—such as tones with frequences of 5,000 and 5,001 cycles per second (see Chapter 14). Such a discrimination would require an acoustic resolving power not possessed by most subjects. Moreover, a stimulus does not generally acquire even as much control as would be permitted by the organism's biological limitations.

If an organism has been reinforced for responding in the presence of a white light, it will generally respond, perhaps with a lowered rate, in the presence of a stimulus that is clearly discriminable from the white light—for example, a green light. Such generalization does not necessarily imply that the animal does not discriminate between the white and green lights, however. We should avoid the pitfall of assuming that a failure to respond differently to two stimuli implies a failure to distinguish between them. What the animal does will depend very much upon what it has learned to attend to. For example, if the organism has learned to respond in the presence of a white light, it may only have learned that responding to a bright light is reinforced. Thus, it will respond to lights on the basis of their brightness, not their color.

In a typical laboratory study of stimulus control, each of two pigeons is intermittently reinforced for responding in the presence of light A. One of the birds receives the following *discrimination training*: light A alternates with a light B, which is associated with nonreinforcement. Figure 6.7 shows that responding in the presence of light B decreases as training progresses on this discrimination procedure. Next, each pigeon is exposed to a generalization test—a series of lights of several different wavelengths, including A and B.

These generalization tests are carried out under extinction; that is, responding is no longer reinforced even when light A is on. Because the animal's responding is now being extinguished, eventually he will stop responding. We are concerned with the number of responses he makes in the presence of each of the various lights before extinction is complete. Figure 6.8 shows the results of a typical experiment of this type. The amount of responding is plotted along the ordinate; the color of the lights is plotted along the abscissa. The resulting curve is called a *generalization gradient*. The peak of the generalization gradient is nearly at the point that corresponds to light A. The more dissimilar the stimulus is from light A, the less the animal responds. The pigeon that did not receive discrimination training produces a flatter generalization gradient than the bird that received discrimination training. This fact points up an important and well-documented finding: the effect of discrimination training is to sharpen stimulus control. Note also that discrimination training shifts the peak of the generalization gradient away from the stimulus associated with nonreinforcement (in this case, light B), a phenomenon called the *peak shift*.

It should be noted that in addition to discrimination training, other variables

Gradients of Generalization

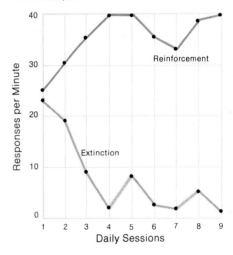

Figure 6.7
The development of discrimination.

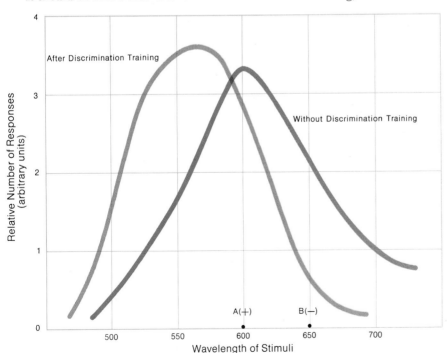

Figure 6.8
Generalization gradients on color, showing peak shift following discrimination training.
(After Hanson, 1959.)

influence the steepness of the generalization gradient, including the degree of training and of deprivation and the schedule of reinforcement, discussed below.

Conditioned Reinforcement The phenomena of generalization and discrimination are ubiquitous and essential for the normal functioning of organisms, but we now turn to an equally important determinant of our behavior, one that enables our behavior to be appropriately variable and sophisticated: conditioned, or secondary, reinforcement. A conditioned reinforcer is one that is reinforcing by virtue of its past association with a primary or innate reinforcer such as food, water, or sex. If it were not for conditioned reinforcers, behavior would occur only when reinforced by primary reinforcers. A moment's reflection will lead you to conclude that most of your behavior is reinforced only indirectly by these primary reinforcers.

Conditioned reinforcers have been studied in three general ways. One technique employs an extinction procedure. Responses during training produce primary reinforcement in the presence of a neutral stimulus. During extinction, when the response no longer produces primary reward, a subject responds more often when the neutral stimulus is produced than when its responses are totally ineffective. This phenomenon has been taken as evidence that the neutral stimulus has become a conditioned reinforcer. Unfortunately, however, it is possible that stimulus generalization, not conditioned reinforcement, may be responsible for the more persistent responding, because the difference between training and extinction is less noticeable when the stimulus occurs occasionally.

The second technique also omits primary reinforcement but requires the subject to learn a new response that produces the stimulus. Unfortunately, conditioned reinforcement is somewhat difficult to demonstrate using this procedure, perhaps because the potency of the conditioned reinforcer is itself waning in extinction and is therefore not sufficient to reinforce the new response. Thus, a third technique has been gaining favor in recent years among scientists studying conditioned reinforcement. This technique uses a chaining procedure to maintain the effectiveness of the conditioned reinforcer by continuing to present the primary reinforcement in its presence. In a two-link chain, for example, responses in the initial link produce a different stimulus, in the presence of which responses produce primary reinforcement. The conditioned reinforcer is the stimulus in whose presence food is obtainable.

Thus, if responding in the presence of a blue light produces a red light and responding in the presence of a red light produces food, the red light will be the conditioned reinforcer. The contention that the red light is a conditioned reinforcer has been proved by demonstrations that responding in the presence of the blue light is controlled by the schedule of (conditioned) reinforcement programming access to the red light. The red light is a conditioned reinforcer maintaining responding in the presence of the blue light, and it also is a discriminative stimulus for responding in its presence to obtain primary reinforcement. Under certain circumstances, it is possible to differentially affect the discriminative and reinforcing functions of the stimulus.

A type of chained schedule has been used in some classic experiments with chimpanzees and token rewards. In one experiment, a chimpanzee learned to work in order to obtain tokens. These tokens could later be exchanged for primary reinforcement by inserting them into a machine called a Chimp-O-Mat. The most important conclusion stemming from this work with the Chimp-O-Mat is that the tokens would bridge very long delays between the performance of a response and the onset of reinforcement. Without the conditioned reinforce-

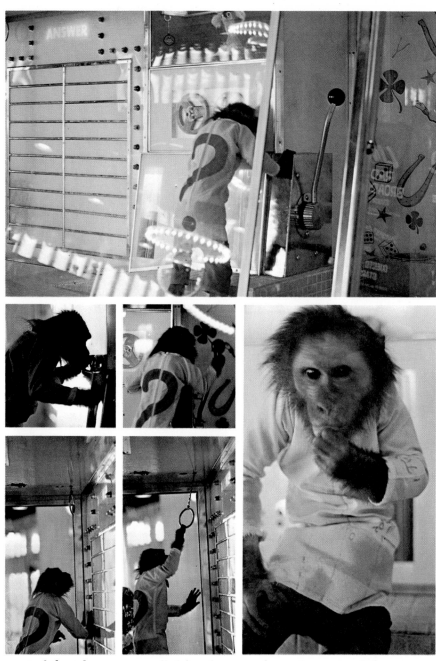

Figure 6.9
Chained schedules of reinforcement maintain the performances of chimps at Las Vegas.

ment of the token, even small delays between the performance of the response and the onset of reinforcement were sufficient to disrupt severely the maintenance of the response.

Generalized Reinforcers

We have been discussing conditioned reinforcers that have gained their strength by virtue of pairings with a particular primary reinforcement. When a stimulus is paired with not one but several different primary reinforcers, it is called a *generalized reinforcer*. A common example of a generalized reinforcer is money. Money can be exchanged for many types of primary and conditioned reinforcers and can also be used to reduce pain and other noxious stimuli. Generalized reinforcers such as money are extremely resistant to extinction. Indeed, behavior reinforced by generalized reinforcers is so resistant to extinction as to appear to be *functionally autonomous* of the conditions that gave rise to it. According to the theory of functional autonomy, behavior that has often led to reinforcement may become reinforcing *in itself,* even though it is no longer a mechanism for obtaining reinforcement. Although this is an appealing theory, there is virtually no evidence for it.

Schedules of Reinforcement

As we have seen, it is by no means necessary to reinforce each occurrence of a response. In fact, such frequent reinforcement almost never occurs in nature and is a rare event even in the laboratory. Results of great value for the psychology of behavior are obtained when only a few of the many occurrences of a given response are followed by reinforcement. In such cases, behavior is reinforced on a *schedule.*

A schedule of reinforcement is simply a rule for choosing from among the many occurrences of a response those few that will be reinforced. In laboratory studies of a rat's bar pressing or a pigeon's key pecking, the schedule is arranged by automatic programming equipment, which arranges for reinforcement according to the rule. Perhaps every fiftieth response is chosen for reinforcement on a regular basis, or the machine might be programmed to reinforce only those responses that follow the previous response by at least ten seconds but no more than twenty seconds. In all cases, there is a rule that unequivocally decides for each response whether or not it will be reinforced.

Four simple schedules of reinforcement have been studied most frequently. The first is called a *fixed-ratio schedule* because the exact response that will yield the organism a reward is determined in a fixed manner. If the rat is rewarded every time it presses the bar, this is the simplest form of fixed-ratio schedule. After the animal has learned this response, it can be shifted easily to a 2:1 ratio—that is, it is now rewarded for every second response. If we say an animal is on a 50:1 fixed-ratio schedule, we mean that the animal is rewarded for its fiftieth response, its hundredth, and so on, no matter how long it takes the animal to press the bar fifty or a hundred times. As you might guess, it does not take the animal very long to know just about how many responses it must make before it next gets the reward. For this reason, experimenters often prefer the second type of schedule, the *variable-ratio schedule.* An animal on a 50:1 variable-ratio schedule gets rewarded *on the average* every fiftieth response, but it cannot ever tell exactly when the next reinforcement is going to come because the number of required responses varies. Sometimes the tenth response will be rewarded, sometimes the eighty-first, and so on, but because the schedule is usually determined in random fashion, all the animal can learn is that it must on the average respond about fifty times to get reinforced.

The other two simple schedules are defined in terms of the time elapsed since the previous reinforced response. The *fixed-interval schedule* reinforces the first response that occurs after a fixed period of time has elapsed since the previous reinforced response; the *variable-interval schedule* reinforces on the basis of a variable period of elapsed time since the last reinforcement and is described in terms of the average of these periods of time.

Each of these simple schedules of reinforcement maintains a different pattern of responding. From an analysis of the variables responsible for these effects of schedules of reinforcement, it is possible to learn a great deal about the control of behavior. Unfortunately, the analysis is not complete because schedules have been intensively investigated in the laboratory for only a relatively short time. But some information is available, and it is instructive to compare how animals behave when confronted with a given schedule with how people behave when

Figure 6.10
The effectiveness of intermittent reinforcement.

confronted with a similar schedule in everyday life. In some simple cases, what has been learned about why animals behave as they do is strikingly applicable to an analysis of human behavior.

The variable-ratio schedule maintains an extremely high rate of responding. If the key pecks of a pigeon are reinforced with food on a variable-ratio schedule, they occur at the fantastically high rate shown in Figure 6.11. Occasionally the bird even pecks on the key during reinforcement, in preference to eating. Why this behavior occurs is not difficult to explain. Responding faster and faster means that reinforcement occurs more and more frequently, because it is the *number* of responses that is directly, although variably, responsible for reinforcement. The variable ratio is the appropriate schedule for generating a high rate of responding.

People are reinforced on variable ratios in a variety of situations, most prominently gambling. It is no accident that this is one of the most preferred activities in which people engage. For example, consider again the slot machine, or one-armed bandit. The response is pulling down the arm of the machine, and reinforcement or nonreinforcement occurs after a short delay, when the whirling in the windows has ceased. Reinforcement on these machines is set to occur on the average after every *n*th play, or pull of the arm. The value of *n* is chosen by the owner of the machine so that the amount paid out in reinforcement is adequately balanced by the amount paid for the privilege of pulling the arm. Of course, the payoff or reinforcement never occurs for precisely the same number of plays (fixed-ratio reinforcement), because that would provoke fights around the machine as the required number of responses was approached and would be a certain giveaway to the fact that it costs more money to play than is taken in the winning. Instead, the numbers involved are variable, the schedule is a

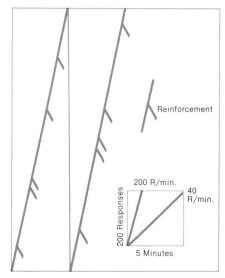

Figure 6.11
Cumulative record of responses reinforced on a variable-ratio schedule.

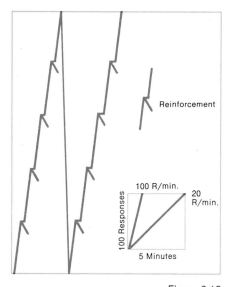

Figure 6.12

Cumulative record of behavior reinforced on a fixed-ratio schedule.

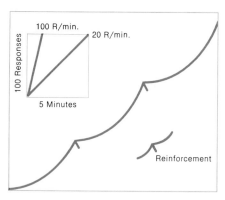

Figure 6.13

The slope of the record (representing rate of responding) increases as the time for the next reinforcement approaches.

variable ratio, and the performance of winners—those who have been reinforced—occurs at the same high rate and with the same dedication of purpose as the pigeon exhibits in pecking for grain on the same schedule. Just as the pigeon occasionally forgoes eating the reinforcer even though it has been earned, there are cases in which a gambler failed to pick up the jackpot because of his eagerness to get on with earning the next.

Fixed-ratio schedules also generate extremely high rates of responding, rivaling those produced by the variable-ratio scale, as Figure 6.12 shows. If fixed ratios are too large, however, the phenomenon called *strain* occurs. Instead of the continuous high rate of responding right from the start of responding up to the reinforced response, there are breaks in the record. Figure 6.12 showed what happened to a pigeon's key pecking when the ratio was increased from a low value of ten to a high value of fifty. Just after the increase in the number of pecks required for reinforcement, the bird was able to emit the fifty responses without a pause. Soon, however, strain developed, and the appearance of pauses during the running off of the ratio. What this means in practice is that the length of the ratio cannot be made too long if it is to remain intact as a performance. Pauses after reinforcement could be tolerated by industrial managers, for example, if the ratios were long enough to make for profit despite the pauses. But lengthening the ratio increases the likelihood of pauses during the performance, and this means less work during the day. Although fixed ratios maintain high levels of output, they are inefficient tools for the industrial control of behavior because they regularly produce pauses after reinforcement.

The interval schedules of reinforcement, defined in terms of the time elapsed since the last reinforced response, are quite a different story. In the first place, they generate much lower rates of responding, overall, than do ratio schedules—in part because rapid responding does not substantially increase the frequency of reinforcement. When the requirement for reinforcement is defined temporally, it makes little or no difference how rapidly responses occur because reinforcement occurs on time anyway.

The fixed-interval schedule of reinforcement produces in pigeons and other animals the regular performance shown in the cumulative record in Figure 6.13. Immediately after reinforcement, very few responses occur. As time passes, responding begins; it is, after all, responding that is reinforced. As the time for reinforcement approaches, responding increases in frequency. The low rate of responding soon after reinforcement is accounted for by the fact that responses are never reinforced at that time. The acceleration in the responding is due to the fact that the organism cannot tell exactly what time it is. Interval after interval, the progress of responding is the same: pause, acceleration, high rate.

Examples of pure fixed-interval schedules are not common in everyday human life. The schedule and performance the fixed interval maintains is interesting to the psychologist because it permits him to examine some variables that are important in controlling behavior and that are not exposed by the ratio schedules. When fixed intervals do occur, their effects on people are all too similar to their effects on pigeons and rats. The best example is drawn from the field of avoidance behavior rather than from studies of positive reinforcement, from which most examples of schedules are typically drawn. Consider the annoying habit of universities to give examinations on a regular temporal basis, the quarter or semester system. In this case, the reinforcement is not the presentation of food or the winning of money, but the avoidance of failure. The response is studying. At the beginning of the quarter, soon after the last avoidance of failure, there is little studying; studying increases in frequency as the quarter or semester continues and reaches a high rate as the time for the next final-examination period approaches.

Variable-interval, in distinction to fixed-interval, schedules reinforce responses after a variable period of time has elapsed since the previous reinforced response. If examinations are given on the average three or four times a year but at unpredictable, variable intervals, the behavior of studying is emitted at a relatively constant rate; the students do their assigned reading on time and write out their homework promptly. On any given day, there may be an examination, and the wary are ill-advised to be unprepared on even one day. Something parallel happens in Skinner's box when pigeons are reinforced on a variable-interval schedule. Instead of pausing and then responding after each reinforcement, as they do on a fixed-interval schedule, they peck the key at a relatively constant rate throughout each variable interval between two successive reinforcements. There is some tendency to respond more slowly just after reinforcement, because very short times between two reinforcements are infrequent, but there are no long pauses in responding. Figure 6.14B shows the typical behavior maintained by the usual variable-interval schedule of food reinforcement.

More elaborate schedules of reinforcement are also the subject of investigation in the psychologist's laboratory. Extremely infrequent responding can be generated by schedules that require infrequent responding for reinforcement. Moreover, rates of responding exceeding even those generated by variable-ratio schedules can be produced if the high rate is an absolute precondition of reinforcement. Some clever tricks can be played on the organism by requiring peculiar combinations of responses before reinforcing one of the responses. The possibilities for schedules of reinforcement are endless; they are just beginning to be investigated, and the technology of behavior based on them is embryonic.

Now that we have discussed the maintenance of behavior under different schedules of reinforcement, we are in a position to consider the effects of scheduling of reinforcement upon subsequent behavior in extinction. Figure 6.15 illustrates extinction after several representative schedules of reinforcement.

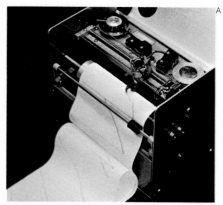

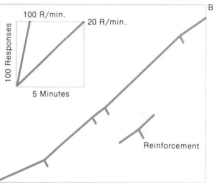

Figure 6.14

(A) The type of machine typically used to make (B) cumulative records of responding.

Figure 6.15

Patterns of responding in extinction after reinforcement on four different schedules. (After Reynolds, 1968.)

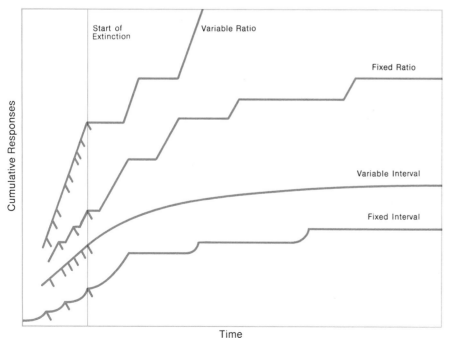

Aversive Control

Up to now we have been concerned with positive reinforcers. We now turn to negative reinforcers, those stimuli whose *withdrawal* reinforces behavior. Such negative reinforcers reduce the rate of the responses that produce them and increase the rate of responses leading to their removal. Three basic types of procedures have generally been employed in the study of aversive control.

Escape

First, in *escape conditioning,* a subject receiving aversive stimulation such as electric shock learns to respond to turn off the stimulation. Escape conditioning proceeds rather rapidly, and less shaping is generally required to establish an escape response than to establish a response with positive reinforcement. It is tempting to attribute this fact to the notion that negative reinforcers are in some sense more potent than positive reinforcers, but such a conclusion would be hard to maintain. Although certain levels of aversive stimulation might be more potent in motivating a response than a certain amount of food, an experimenter could find levels of electric shock, amounts of food reinforcement, and degrees of hunger that would lead to the opposite conclusion.

Moreover, there is an additional explanation to account for the fact that shaping with aversive stimulation is very rapid. Aversive stimulation produces a great amount of activity, thus enhancing the probability of making the correct response in a given period of time. Consider, for example, a rat in a small box whose floor consists of grid bars through which shock is transmitted (see Figure 6.16). When shock is applied through the grid bars, the rat hops up and down and otherwise moves about, thus providing the experimenter with a wide selection of behavior from which to choose a response that closely approximates the desired behavior; the behavior is reinforced by turning off the shock. The maintenance of behavior under an escape procedure appears to be substantially the same as it is with positive reinforcement. It should be noted, however, that much less work has been done exploring schedules of negative reinforcement.

Avoidance

In *avoidance conditioning,* the subject is permitted to avoid the shock by making the appropriate response prior to its onset. The acquisition of avoidance behavior often follows a more tedious course than that of escape conditioning or conditioning with positive reinforcement—for many reasons, some of which are poorly understood. One critical factor is the nature of the response. A running response, for example, is acquired rapidly. On the other hand, a lever-press response is acquired very slowly. Indeed, if an animal must learn to press a lever to avoid shock, its behavior will be greatly facilitated if it is first required to run to the lever. This somewhat surprising result is illustrated in Figure 6.17. The rats

Figure 6.16
A rat being shocked through a grid floor.

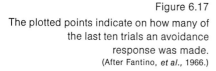

Figure 6.17
The plotted points indicate on how many of the last ten trials an avoidance response was made.
(After Fantino, *et al.*, 1966.)

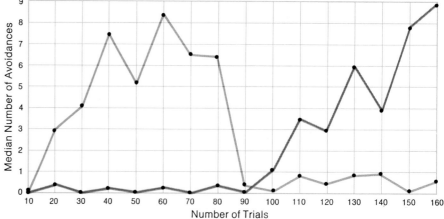

whose data are represented by the orange line have just five seconds to avoid shock; in that time the rat must run from one box to another and press a lever in the second box. The rats whose data are represented by the red line, however, start the trial in the same box with the lever and have five seconds to press it; because they generally stay near the lever at all times, the requirement that they press the lever within five seconds appears to be trivial.

Figure 6.17 shows an additional finding of interest. After the eightieth trial, the two groups were reversed, and the group of rats that was now required to run picked up the response rapidly, as one would have expected from the result of the first part of the experiment. The surprising finding was that the rats that had learned to run and press no longer pressed when the requirement was made simpler. Subjects in this condition showed no trace of their earlier learning when switched to the lever-press-only condition.

A method of producing rapid avoidance learning is the simple technique of picking up the animal and letting him down ten seconds or so prior to an avoidance trial. This procedure greatly increases the likelihood of a successful avoidance response, although why this handling has such a profound effect is poorly understood. Possibly the handling disrupts the behavior of freezing into immobility, which may be responsible for the failure of rats to avoid in the lever-pressing situation. Supporting this notion is the finding that tranquilizing drugs enhance the learning of avoidance in the lever-pressing situation in rats.

Punishment

Punishment, or the presentation of a negative reinforcer, appears to lower the probability of the response producing it in precisely the same manner as a positive reinforcer increases the probability of the response leading to it. Of course, to study punishment in any detail, it is necessary to punish a response that is being maintained by some positive reinforcer. Otherwise, one or two punishments would permanently remove the response from the subject's behavioral repertoire, leaving little for the psychologist to study. Thus, punishment is generally applied to a response that is concomitantly maintained with positive reinforcement. Figure 6.18 shows how varying degrees of punishment affect the maintenance of behavior in such a situation.

Although punishment is successful in eliminating undesirable behavior, or at least in reducing its frequency, it is not often the method of choice because it has undesirable by-products. Because punishment involves aversive stimulation, it is intrinsically unpleasant. In addition, it provides a basis for reinforcement of generalized avoidance responses. An individual who is educated by punishment may avoid the educational institution altogether, rather than undergo the

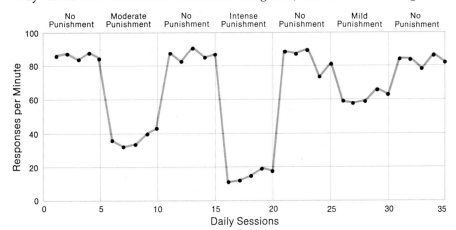

Figure 6.18

Rate of responding for food under various punishment conditions.
(After Reynolds, 1968.)

punishment. There are other methods for eliminating behavior that do not have these undesirable effects. One is to condition other, incompatible responses with positive reinforcement; for example, instead of attempting to eliminate stuttering by punishing it, smooth speech may be reinforced. Other methods try to avoid the necessity of punishing incorrect behavior altogether by ensuring from the start that only correct behavior occurs. These methods have been developed primarily in educational settings (see Chapter 35).

The Physiological Basis of Learning

Whenever an organism acquires a new conditioned response, there must be a change of some kind inside that organism's body that parallels the change in the organism's behavior. Most of us do not usually think about what goes on inside our bodies when we are learning something, any more than we think about the physiological changes that occur when our bodies are healing cuts and bruises we have acquired. We can *see* the behavioral changes that take place when, say, we learn a friend's new telephone number; the internal correlates of learning that phone number are as yet invisible even to the most powerful microscope. Yet they must be there, and the attempts to find them constitute one of the more interesting branches of psychology.

In the early part of this century, a German scientist named Richard Semon theorized that whenever an organism experienced something new, there had to remain within its nervous system a *trace* of the experience. Semon called this trace an *engram,* a term that Sigmund Freud popularized as meaning the physiological representation of a memory. Karl Lashley spent most of his long and productive scientific career searching for the engram, but never could find it. We know a great deal more now about the engram than did Lashley, Freud, and Semon, but we still are not sure what it is. Yet most psychologists believe that we will not really understand what learning is all about—be it operant or respondent conditioning—until we know as much about the physiological storage of memories as we do about how to shape behavior psychologically.

There are two dominant theories as to what the engram is. One group of scientists believes that memories are somehow stored in our nervous systems by some kind of rearrangement of the way one nerve cell excites or stimulates another. Most of these theorists believe that learning is a matter of changing the structural or synaptic connections found in the central nervous system. The other dominant theory holds that the engram is chemical rather than neurophysiological—that whenever an organism is conditioned, highly specific changes take place in giant molecules found inside each nerve cell. These chemical changes are believed to affect cellular functioning in such a fashion that the nervous system reacts quite differently than it did before the chemical changes occurred. Both theories have a long and honorable history; William James was a physiological theorist, while Semon believed the engram was chemical. Although we shall discuss the theories separately, we must keep in mind that neither is entirely satisfactory and that it is quite likely that each theory merely describes one part of a very complex process that includes both chemical and physiological changes.

In general, those scientists who lean toward a physiological explanation of memory have sought a specific locus of the engram somewhere in the brain using the standard tools of electrophysiology.

Localization of Memories

For the most part, it has been impossible to localize the effects produced by experience as they are reflected in memories. Various methods and approaches have been used to find storage sites for memory or for a specific type of memory, but all without success. Two types of research related to such attempts are of interest, however, because of their suggestions as to how the brain is organized. The first represents the evaluation of the contribution of the temporal lobes in man; the second is a general study of association areas in man as well as in the lower animals.

■ TEMPORAL LOBES

Stimulation of the temporal lobes in certain patients with temporal-lobe epilepsy produces experiences that are related to earlier memories. The patient often reports, for example, the reexperiencing of earlier events or déjà vu (feelings that what is going on now has happened before). It should be emphasized that these and other experiences are found only in some patients with certain kinds of temporal-lobe epilepsy and are relatively rare even among this disease class. Nevertheless, the fact that memory-related experiences have been produced in even some patients has led to other investigations and established an association between memory and temporal-lobe systems.

In some other patients, in whom one or both temporal lobes were removed for the relief of seizures, a radical impairment of memory for recent events has been observed. In this case, "recent" refers to events occurring after the surgical procedure and extending up to the present attention span of the patient. In the most extreme case, as soon as the patient's attention is diverted, whoever or whatever the patient was looking at is completely forgotten. Yet the cases in which unilateral or bilateral temporal-lobe damage produces such radical memory impairments are rare. Furthermore, many patients have had temporal lobes

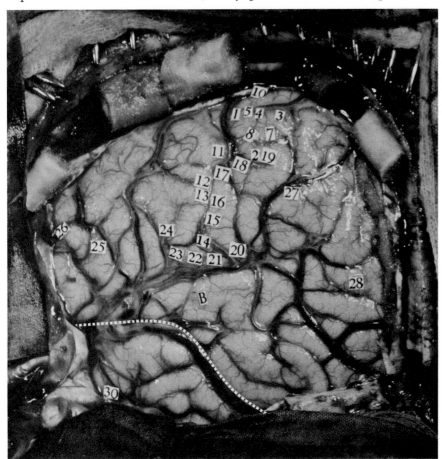

Figure 6.19
Exposure of the cortex during an operation following a brain injury. The numbers indicate points at which electrical stimulation produced reports from the patient. The dotted line follows a major vein across the temporal lobe. The fissure of Silvius runs about halfway across the middle of the brain area exposed.
(After Penfield and Roberts, 1959.)

removed without an associated memory defect. The reasons why some patients have memory disturbances and others do not are not known.

■OTHER ASSOCIATION AREAS

When anatomists and physiologists were first investigating the functions of various parts of the cortex a century or so ago, they found some areas they could clearly label as sensory, some that were clearly motor areas, and a wide expanse of cortical tissue that was neither. These nonsensory, nonmotor areas were called *association areas* because it was presumed that it was in these regions that sensations became associated with motor responses. Early neurophysiologists also believed that thinking and problem solving took place in the association areas. Unfortunately, identification of any of these functions with any association area has not proved possible, at least yet.

Destruction of any of the major association areas—frontal, parietal, occipital, or temporal—does produce effects upon behavior and sometimes upon the learning of specific tasks. These performance changes cannot be adequately explained in terms of losses in learning or memory. For example, destruction of one part of the frontal association area produces a deficit in the ability to learn problems in which an animal must delay its response after the signal is given as to which response should be made. The delayed-response test and the impairment found after frontal-lobe damage have been subjected to extensive analyses, but a definite explanation has not yet resulted. It is clear that neither a generalized nor a specific memory loss results from the destruction of the frontal association areas. The same conclusion can be drawn for the other association areas and for the primary motor and sensory areas of the neocortex as well.

Electrical Correlates of Learning

There have been a large number of studies directed toward understanding the electrical events that can be recorded from the brain during learning and conditioning. The vast majority are studies in which gross electrical events have been recorded from the brain using more or less standard recording techniques. Within this majority of studies, two further types can be distinguished: (1) those in which records of the electroencephalogical correlates of learning were made and (2) those in which attempts were made to follow certain rhythms as they progressed through the brain during the course of conditioning. In this latter type of experiment, rhythms are imposed upon the organism, such as those created by the flickering rate of a bright light, which is conditioned to occur after a stimulus, such as a sound, is presented. A few studies that have investigated the activity of single neurons over their course of conditioning will be discussed separately.

A typical conditioned response of the gross electrical activity of the brain is shown in Figure 6.20. In this experiment, sound comes to elicit the arousal response (*desynchronization*) of the occipital slow-wave activity (alpha rhythm), which previously only occurred to the light stimulus. Conditioned electrical activity of the brain can be reflected in desynchronization or a facilitation of prevailing brain rhythms.

When intermittent stimuli are applied to some sensory modality, rhythmic potentials of a similar frequency can be found in the recorded electroencephalograph (EEG) patterns. Often a flashing light is used to provide the rhythmic source of stimulation, and the response of the brain of the same frequency is called *photic driving*. The aim of such experiments is to determine if the photic driving can be conditioned to occur following sensory stimulation over a different modality. In general, the answer seems to be that photic driving can be condi-

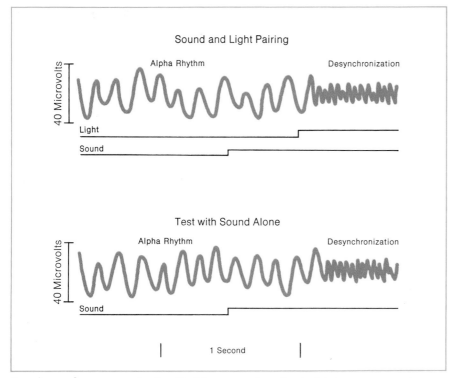

Figure 6.20
Conditioned response of alpha rhythm
elicited by sound.

tioned to other types of stimuli. However, the photic-driving response is not directly and perfectly correlated with the imposed frequency of the light used as the unconditioned stimulus.

In an attempt to determine more precisely the effects of conditioned electrical activity, Morrell undertook the investigation of single-neuron activity during the conditioning of gross EEG activity. Because some cells increased their activity and others decreased activity, it was necessary to establish simple rules to determine whether a given area should be considered as showing an increase or a decrease, as a whole. In general, Morrell found that single units of the reticular formation tended to increase in activity at the initial presentations of sound and the intermittent photic stimulation and that further increases were found during initial stages of learning. Units of the visual cortex increased refirings during initial stages of conditioning but slowed later in a middle range of conditioning only to increase once again in a final stage. Neurons of the hippocampus tended to increase their rates during all but the final stages of learning.

This study illustrates the most adequate justification of using electrical activities to track learning mechanisms. The gross EEG is a poorly understood phenomenon at best, and conclusions based only on it are subject to many interpretations. Morrell attempted to discover regular sequential patterns of change in many brain areas during a particular type of learning. Information of this sort may be quite useful when coupled with data from other types of experiments.

The central nervous system controls and directs the remainder of the body as an animal moves about the environment, beginning certain behavioral episodes, ending others, and seemingly avoiding still others. Both internal factors and external factors play a considerable role in the selection of appropriate episodes, as does the prior history of the animal. The particular goals of behavioral episodes are those selected on the basis of the internal motivational systems, and we now are aware of the important role of the hypothalamus and the associated limbic system with such systems. We have learned, also, of the important role of genetic inheritance in determining the animal's capacities and its predilections for shaping certain types of episodes.

■CHANGES IN NEURONAL SIZE

Sir John Eccles has argued for a very simple principle of nerve reaction related to behavior, namely, that use of a neural pathway strengthens transmission along it but disuse weakens it. In support of this principle one can show that cutting the dorsal root nerves into the cord (peripheral to the ganglion) at later periods both produces a shrinkage in the size of the nerve and weakens the reflexive response evoked by electrical stimulation of the remaining intact nerve (central to the ganglion). The shrinkage of the nerve after cutting may extend into the spinal cord and be associated with diminished synaptic endings in the cord itself. The fact that neurons are alive and do show sizable changes in appearance during their lives should not be ignored. Physical growth at the synapse remains a viable possibility as an explanation of how the brain stores memories.

■SPROUTING

If the input to an area of the spinal cord is removed, fibrils from adjacent neurons grow into the area—the phenomenon of *sprouting,* first observed in the 1920s by Ramón y Cajal, the famous Spanish anatomist. More recently, sprouting has been found in the cerebral cortex in cases where no more than a few layers of brain tissue have been damaged. Of special interest is the sprouting of fibers from the optic tract into the colliculi after the input from cerebral cortex was removed. The sprouting was from the preterminal regions of the axon and represents a possible anatomical correlate of functional plasticity in the central nervous system.

■CELL PROLIFERATION

Although the number of neurons in the central nervous system is generally fixed by genetic factors and neurons continue to be formed through cell division for only a relatively short period after birth, the supportive, neuroglia cells are formed over the life of the individual. Suggestions have been made that greater neuronal activity requires greater levels of support from the glia cells surrounding the neuron. In support of this view is the observation by Friede and Van Houten of a linear relationship between the number of glia cells surrounding the cell body of certain neurons and the length of the cell's axon. Increases in glia cells have been reported in the spinal cord after motor activity and in the neocortex after animals had been raised in enriched as opposed to impoverished environments. Moreover, making rats dehydrated produces a considerable increase in cell division among glia cells in the hypothalamic regions related to control of water intake.

■DENDRITIC SPINES

When neurophysiologists and neuroanatomists first observed the dendrites of nerve cells, they appeared to be smooth and featureless. Later investigations using more powerful microscopic techniques showed that each dendrite was covered with hundreds or even thousands of spines, much like the quills on a porcupine. Until recently, these spines had not been thought of as being involved in the functioning of the nervous system, but recent work suggests that the number of spines in cortical neurons decreases when input to that area of the cortex is reduced.

Such findings suggest that the greater the use of the cortical area (although the same types of changes could occur in other regions of the brain), the greater will be the growth of dendritic spines. Because the spines are thought to be related to the synaptic connections of axons reaching that dendrite, spine growth

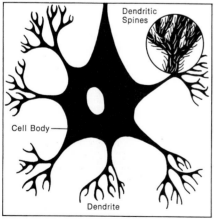

Dendritic
Spines

Cell Body

Dendrite

Figure 6.21
Dendritic spines.

126

could be a mechanism that allows greater synaptic contact to be generated between two cells. This contact would facilitate the control of one cell by another and could be the basis of the changes in behavior represented by learning.

Perhaps the most we can say about the neurophysiological theory of learning and memory is that the nervous system must be involved somewhere, either in storing the engram or in retrieving it from storage. Studies do show that if we make one neuron excite time and again another cell with which it makes synapse, the amount of energy needed to cross the synapse decreases significantly; but this fact is the only real evidence at a functional level that synapses might be involved in learning.

Most of the scientists who lean toward the neurophysiological theory have worked with higher organisms, chiefly with mammals. For a variety of reasons, those theorists who believe that memories may be stored chemically have often worked with much simpler animals, including the invertebrates. And, as we shall see, they have not even restricted their search for the engram to the brain.

Learning in Lower Organisms

Many biological scientists assume rather automatically that learning and memory must occur in the nervous system, chiefly in the brain. And, following this assumption, they have not bothered to look for the engram outside the central nervous system of vertebrates. But at least 95 percent of the animals on earth are invertebrates, and by far the greatest number of organisms now living are the protozoans, highly complicated but single-celled animals. Obviously, an organism whose entire body is made up of but one cell cannot have a central nervous system. Thus, if such lower animals can be shown capable of learning, the standard neurophysiological theory of the engram cannot hold for them. Although there is a fair amount of evidence that learning can indeed occur in such single-celled animals as the paramecium, the work remains controversial (in part, perhaps, because neurophysiological theorists are reluctant to accept evidence that would appear to overthrow their theory). Experiments with planarians and cockroaches are less controversial, however, and so we shall look at these studies in some detail.

The planarian is a simple flatworm, less than an inch in length, found in ponds, streams, and rivers throughout the world. Experiments beginning in the late 1800s and continuing through the 1960s have shown that planarians can be trained in a variety of ways, including classical conditioning, avoidance conditioning, simple mazes, and even a type of operant conditioning in which the worm learns to shut off a noxious stimulus by interrupting a beam of light.

Current interest in planarian learning began in 1959, when it was reported that learning survived the regenerative process in these animals. If the planarian

Figure 6.22

A classical conditioning trial: (A) the planarian is between trials; (B) light is presented and (C) is followed by the unconditional stimulus, electric shock.

A

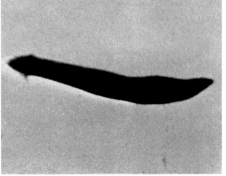

B

C

is cut in half across its midsection, the animal does not die; rather, each half regenerates or regrows its missing parts and becomes an intact, complete animal again. If trained planarians are cut in half, the head section grows a new tail, the tail section grows a new head, and both regenerated sections show excellent retention of the original learning. If the trained worms are cut in several pieces, all the regenerated sections show retention of the original training. The intriguing part of this work is that all but the head sections must grow an entirely new head ganglion, or "brain," so if they subsequently "remember," it must be that the engram is not located just in the head ganglion, but rather is stored throughout the animal's body. We shall have more to say about planarians in a moment.

Cockroaches are much more complicated animals than are flatworms. The central nervous system of cockroaches (and of other insects) consists of a brain and a series of segmented ganglia that extend from the brain along a nerve cord that runs almost the entire length of the animal's body. Cockroaches have three pairs of legs, each leg being controlled by its own ganglion. With surgical techniques, it is possible to isolate one leg and its ganglion from the rest of the nervous system. This leg can then be trained to withdraw itself from water by shocking the leg each time it touches the water. Although there are no more than 150 nerve cells in this leg-ganglion system, it is apparently able to "remember" the avoidance response for at least twenty-four hours. Obviously, in this case at least, learning can occur in a very limited part of the nervous system.

Whether or not engrams can be formed and stored in very limited segments of the nervous systems of higher animals remains to be seen, although there is some evidence even in mammals that learning can occur in the spinal cord if it is isolated from the brain. Perhaps the greatest importance of all this work, however, is the fact that it has led some theorists to suggest that the engram may be chemical rather than neurophysiological.

The Biochemistry of Memory

Let us return to the planarian experiments. The fact that regenerated tails could "remember" suggested to McConnell and his colleagues (who performed the original studies) that memories in flatworms might be stored by chemical changes in cells throughout the worm's body. To test this theory, they trained planarians and then cut up these worms and fed them to untrained, cannibalistic planarians. The cannibals were subsequently trained on the same task as were the "victims." From the very first trials, it was apparent that cannibals that had eaten "educated" worms were significantly superior to cannibals that had eaten untrained animals. This was the first evidence that some part of the memory process might be transferrable from one organism to another. Subsequently these experimenters demonstrated that they could extract ribonucleic acid (RNA) from trained worms, inject it into untrained planarians, and achieve what appeared to be a memory transfer using chemicals.

RNA is a giant molecule found in almost every cell in an animal's body. It is very similar to deoxyribonucleic acid (DNA), the substance that genes are believed to be made of. Those theorists who lean toward the chemical theory of memory point out that the DNA an organism inherits from its parents determines what the organism will look like and what its innate behavior patterns will be. Using very subtle biochemical techniques, geneticists have been able to determine just how the structure of the DNA molecule codes these genetic patterns. DNA can then be said to store "memories" of what the organism's ancestors were like by means of this *genetic code*. DNA is found chiefly in the nucleus of a cell; it controls the metabolism of the cell by manufacturing *messenger* RNA, which migrates from the nucleus out to the sites in the rest of the cell where proteins are synthesized. In general, the messenger RNA determines what types of proteins the cell will manufacture at any given moment in time. The theorists speculate that if DNA carries the genetic code by which an organism "remembers" what its parents were like, perhaps RNA might act as a coding or storage agent for each animal's individual experiences or memories. The theory is, then, that whenever an animal learns something, its RNA somehow "codes" and stores these behavioral changes much as DNA codes and stores the animal's instinctual behavior patterns.

RNA has been implicated in memory storage in several ways. To begin with, the noted Swedish biologist Hydén has shown that there are fairly specific changes in the RNA molecules found in a rat's brain when it is forced to learn to climb a wire to get food or to reach for food with its nonpreferred paw. Various chemicals that inhibit RNA or protein synthesis appear to inhibit remembering if injected into animals during training, whereas chemicals that speed up RNA or protein synthesis appear to facilitate remembering. If planarians are trained in water containing ribonuclease, a chemical that destroys RNA, the worms seem to be incapable of learning or remembering. A number of laboratories have reported that chemicals extracted from the brains of trained rats and injected into untrained animals cause much the same sort of memory-transfer effect as had been reported earlier with planarians. In some of these studies, if the brain material from the trained donors was treated with ribonuclease prior to injection into the recipient animals, no transfer was obtained.

At the moment, much of this work remains controversial, for not everyone who has attempted to repeat it has been successful. Even if the reports of memory transfer prove to be accurate, however, we still do not know what part of the memory process can be shifted chemically from one animal to another or how the injected chemicals actually affect the recipient brains. It does seem fairly clear, however, that chemicals taken from the brains of trained animals and injected into untrained animals do cause rather specific changes in the subsequent behavior of the recipients.

In the long run, it is likely that an amalgamation of the chemical and neurophysiological theories will take place. For even if memories are stored chemically, behavior is always a function of patterns of neural excitation and the chemical theorists must somehow translate their chemical "codes" into changes of firing rates of individual nerve cells; and the neurophysiological theorists are the first to admit that the physiological or synaptic changes they postulate as being involved in the formation of engrams must have a biochemical correlate. Thus, chemicals must somehow be involved in memory storage.

Whatever the case, once we know what the engram really is, we may well be able to use this knowledge to speed up learning. And it is not too much to hope that these investigations into the substrates of memory will some day allow us to increase the functional intelligence of all organisms, including college students.

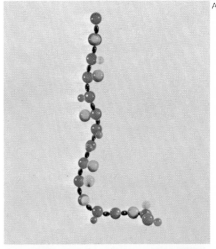

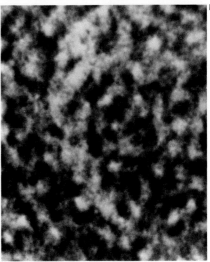

Figure 6.23

(A) A chemical model of a single strand of messenger RNA. (B) An electron micrograph showing DNA's helical structure.

FUNDAMENTALS OF MOTIVATION

SUPPOSE YOU DEPRIVED A RAT of all water for a day or so, then turned it loose. What would you expect the animal to do? Search for something to drink? Of course, but *why* would the rat go looking for water? If you say, "Because it is thirsty," you really have not answered the question at all. For if we now ask you to define thirst, what would you say? That thirst is a condition that occurs in an organism when it has been without water for a while? The circularity of this kind of reasoning should be obvious, for all you have said is that when an animal is deprived of water it gets thirsty so it looks for water because it has been deprived of water. The real question is, of course, what is thirst that it makes an organism get up off its haunches and hunt for something to drink. In short, what does water deprivation do to an organism internally that somehow excites the proper parts of its nervous system that somehow activate the proper muscles that propel the animal to where water is? And once that part of the nervous system has been set to firing, why does it stop firing when the animal actually drinks? To phrase the problem another way, how does the organism know that it is *water* that it needs rather than, say, food or air or sex?

Motivation is a concept used by psychologists to explain why organisms do what they do. Whenever circumstances deprive an animal of a substance necessary for life, we say that the animal has a *need* for that substance. The need exists whether or not the organism is aware of what it lacks or even that something is lacking. Most organisms, including man, are so constituted that whenever a need exists, certain changes take place within them that cause them to seek the missing element or substance. If you had to describe the behavior of a rat that needed water, you would probably say that it seemed that the rat was *driven* by something inside it to find liquid when it needed it. Any time some departure from the organism's ideal state of existence occurs, a need exists and frequently a *drive* is elicited. Drives are extremely important in determining the type of behavior that occurs.

Water deprivation leads to the creation of a drive we call *thirst,* but merely giving it a name does not explain it. In order to understand motivational states, we must look at what changes take place inside an organism when a need occurs and a drive results. Because thirst is one of the motivations that has been most thoroughly studied and is best understood, we shall discuss it first, using this discussion to introduce a number of basic concepts.

Thirst In order to remain alive, the body needs the proper amount of water—either too little or too much is fatal. Therefore, the only land animals that have survived are those that have evolved some way of regulating the amount of water in their bodies. Such regulation is given the name *homeostasis,* which translated from the Greek means "same position."

If an animal is short of water, certain physiological mechanisms start to function in order to conserve it. For example, a hormone (antidiuretic hormone, or ADH) is released that allows the tubules in the kidneys to reabsorb water so that the urine is more concentrated and less water is lost. If the body has too much water, the secretion of ADH is inhibited so that more urine is formed. These physiological mechanisms help to maintain homeostasis.

The Drive Animals adjust to needs at both a physiological and a behavioral level. The release of ADH is a physiological adjustment to the organism's need for water. Of the behavioral adjustments an animal makes when it has the drive of thirst, four are of major importance.

First, the greater the deficit in water, the more of it the animal will consume. Second, when the animal is thirsty, water serves as a reinforcer or reward to produce the learning of those responses that precede drinking and to maintain the performance of those responses that lead to water. If the animal is not thirsty, water is not a reinforcer (see Chapter 6).

Third, the greater the deficit in water, the more successful the response reinforced by water is in overcoming the competition of other responses motivated by other drives. This greater strength of the response reinforced by water has a number of consequences: The animal will be more likely to choose water in competition with food, sex, or other goal objects. It will be more likely to pay attention to stimuli that in the past have been associated with drinking. Aversive stimuli, such as electric shocks, will have to be stronger to keep it away from water; it will be more likely to accept bitter water. In situations where there are competing distractions, it will learn faster how to get water (when there are no competing responses, the strength of a drive does not seem to be as important an influence on learning). Often an animal may have learned a number of different ways to get water, or one way to get water in one situation and another way in another situation. The tendency to perform all these habits previously reinforced with water is strengthened by a deficit in water.

Fourth, the thirstier the animal is, the more signs of frustration and emotional disturbance it will show when a response that has led to water in the past is no longer reinforced.

■DRIVE AND REINFORCEMENT

A reinforcer is an event that strengthens the tendency to perform any immediately preceding response; in other words, it produces learning and maintains performance (see Chapter 4).

Drives determine what events will be reinforcing. In the comfortable circumstances of a middle-class life in an affluent society, it is easy to underestimate the enormous power of certain basic homeostatic drives. But shipwrecked sailors have been known to fight to the death for water and stranded pioneer parties to overcome their taboos against murder and cannibalism.

Sometimes "motivation" is used as a synonym for "drive." Because a drive does not remain effective in maintaining behavior without a suitable reinforcer and a reinforcer (at least, a homeostatic one) is not effective without a suitable drive, the term "motivation" often is used to refer to the joint effect of a suitable drive and a suitable reinforcer. When a drive is present, the promise or hope of a reinforcer frequently is referred to as an *incentive*.

Some reinforcers are more effective than others. When you are slightly thirsty, clean, sparkling, cool water will be a better reinforcer than warm, murky water reeking of chlorine. Similarly, a child does not have to be very hungry to reach for candy. Often the attractiveness of a reinforcer is referred to as its incentive value. Because the ambiguous use of these terms may be confusing, however, we shall usually use only "drive" and "reinforcer."

If thirst were produced in only one way—say, by depriving an animal of water for a number of hours—and we were dealing with only one effect—say, the amount of water drunk—there would be no use for a term like "thirst." It would be simpler to say that the more hours an animal has been deprived of water, the more water it will drink. The situation is diagrammed in Figure 7.1, where it can be seen that the diagram with the single arrow is simpler.

But we can produce thirst in a number of different ways: by depriving an animal of water for a number of hours, by feeding a hungry animal dry food, or, as we shall see, by injecting a salt solution into its veins. Furthermore, thirst produces a cluster of effects, as is shown in Figure 7.2, where it can be seen that using thirst as an intervening variable is simpler than stating separately each of the possible relationships.

Because such treatments as depriving an animal of food produce an analogous

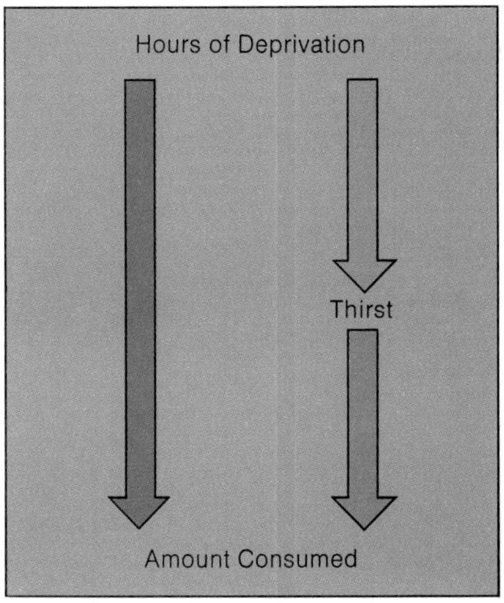

Figure 7.1
The variable thirst is a complication.

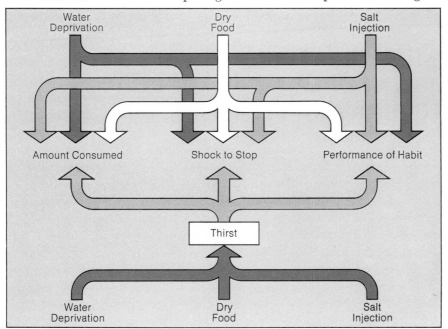

Figure 7.2
The use of the intervening variable thirst simplifies the picture.

cluster of effects functionally similar to those produced by thirst (except that food is substituted for water), we find it useful to speak of hunger. Because there are a number of these similar clusters of effects, we find it useful to use a more general term, "drive."

■DRIVES AND NEED

A *need* is something that an animal requires in order to remain alive and healthy. A number of needs, like the need for water and the need for food, produce drives, but not all needs produce the cluster of behavioral effects that we refer to as a drive. For example, an animal may desperately need to escape from carbon monoxide, but this need does not elicit any drive, so the animal will fail to escape and will die. Similarly, an animal with pernicious anemia may desperately need to eat liver but not be driven to choose it. From the theory of evolution, we can see why needs produce drives in most natural situations, but needs do not always produce drives, especially in unusual situations. Furthermore, as we shall see, there are nonhomeostatic drives that do not seem to be based on obvious bodily needs. Therefore, we have to distinguish between needs and drives.

The Mechanisms of Thirst

Most of us take for granted that a thirsty animal works for water, drinks, and stops before it is waterlogged. But what mechanisms cause it to do this? Considering this question gives us a deeper appreciation for the way our body adapts to its environment. It also shows us how scientists go about discovering the mechanisms involved in adaptive behavior.

Normally, the blood and other body fluids contain approximately 0.9 percent salt. As the body loses water, the percentage of salt, and hence the tendency of the body fluids to attract water (their osmotic pressure), goes up. When Verney made the blood in the brain slightly saltier by slowly injecting a salt solution into the carotid artery that feeds the brain, he found that this injection caused ADH to be secreted so that the kidneys formed less urine in order to keep more water in the body. He therefore hypothesized that the brain contains osmoreceptors that respond to the saltiness of the blood and thus trigger the release of the ADH that helps to regulate water balance.

It has long been known that an injection of solutions containing more than the normal 0.9 percent of salt (hypertonic saline) into the blood causes animals that have been satiated on water to drink. Andersson decided to test whether or not Verney's osmoreceptors in the brain could be responsible for thirst. While goats were under anesthesia, Andersson implanted tiny tubes leading down into the preoptic area of the brain, where the cells that secrete ADH are located, a likely place to look for the osmoreceptors. Some of these tubes also entered the nearby third ventricle, a chamber inside the brain that is filled with cerebrospinal fluid. He cemented the tubes to the skull and placed a small cap over them. When the goat recovered from the anesthesia and was behaving normally, he could inject fluid through these tubes. He found that a 0.9 percent solution of saline (matching the normal osmotic pressure in the body) had no effect, but a minute amount of a 2 percent solution caused the goats to drink eagerly. Thus, he showed that there are receptors in the brain that control drinking. Injections into other parts of the brain did not cause drinking.

Figure 7.3
The preoptic area.

Miller investigated whether Andersson's treatment merely elicited an automatic drinking reflex or produced the effect of normal thirst. Using cats that were moderately thirsty, he found that an injection of 2 percent saline would increase the amount drunk, but an injection of pure water would decrease the amount drunk. That these were not mere reflex effects was shown by the fact that the injection of saline would increase the rate of emission of a response reinforced by water, whereas the injection of water decreased the rate of responding. Injections of as little as 0.04 milliliter were effective.

In another series of experiments, Novin implanted, under anesthesia, special electrodes to measure the conductivity of the tissue, which in turn indicated how salty the fluids in it were. (Strictly speaking, this technique measured the amount of electrolytes, almost all of which were salt.) In this way, he found that, exactly as expected, depriving the animal of water caused the salt, as measured by conductivity, to increase and that drinking water caused it to decrease. An injection of water saltier than normal blood into the veins also increased the conductivity and caused the animal to drink.

Although each treatment produced the expected change, an exact comparison of the relative sizes of the changes showed an unexpected result. As Figure 7.4 shows, the amount of salt injected increased the conductivity more than did the period of water deprivation, but the deprivation caused the rat to drink more than did the injection of saline. If osmolarity were the only factor involved, the greater change in it produced by the injection of salt into the vein would have had to produce a greater amount of drinking. What caused the discrepancy?

It seemed plausible to Novin that the injection of saline slightly increased the blood volume whereas the period of water deprivation reduced it. Could this be the factor?

Some people who have lost or donated a significant amount of blood report that they are thirsty, but others do not. Animal experiments in which blood has been withdrawn from a vein had also yielded conflicting results. Perhaps the shock of losing whole blood is a confusing factor. In an ingenious series of experiments, Stricker injected rats with a solution that caused fluid of normal salinity (0.9 percent) to be removed from body circulation. This treatment caused rats to drink. Stricker also used chemical techniques to show that the osmolarity of the blood and body fluids had not been changed and that the volume of the blood, but not of the body fluids, had been reduced. In this way he showed that a reduction in blood volume can induce thirst. If these conclusions are correct, thirst must be regulated by volume receptors as well as by osmoreceptors. We do not yet know where these volume receptors are or exactly how they and the osmoreceptors respond so accurately.

In an extension of these experiments, Stricker and Wolf showed that when thirst is induced by injections of a salt solution that increases the osmolarity of the blood, drinking pure water, which is the best agent for reducing osmolarity, is most effective in satiating thirst. But when thirst is induced by a reduction in blood volume, drinking isotonic (0.9 percent) saline, which because of its osmotic effect is more effective in restoring blood volume, is more effective in satiating thirst.

Although drinking water restores the blood fairly rapidly, there is a time lag. Does the body have any mechanism for preventing drinking more than is needed? Experiments on dogs and on rats have shown that there is a quick-acting stop mechanism, activated in part by taking water into the mouth and swallowing it and in part by the volume of water in the stomach. Working together, these two mechanisms adjust the amount of water consumed to the amount that is needed, but their effects are not limited to the act of consumption—the animal will also stop working for water and will tolerate less bitterness in it. Thus, the whole cluster of effects that we find convenient to describe as thirst are stopped.

Figure 7.4

The effect of water deprivation and injection of salty water on drinking and on tissue conductivity.
(After Novin, 1962.)

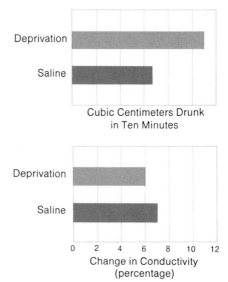

Hunger and the Regulation of Weight

It is important that the body have enough food for growth, for tissue repair, and for meeting its daily energy requirements. But it is also very important that an organism does not eat so much that it becomes overly fat. The body must therefore have a very finely tuned mechanism for regulating how much food is ingested. The critical importance of this mechanism can be illustrated by the following facts: if you overate by as little as two ounces a day, you would gain more than a hundred pounds in less than three years; undereating by two ounces a day would probably cause you to lose an equivalent amount over the same time span. The difficulty of resetting this control mechanism is shown by the problem that overweight people have in losing any weight at all and that underweight individuals have in gaining pounds. Apparently, once an individual's weight-control mechanism has been set, all but the most strenuous efforts to change it will fail.

As in the case of thirst, food deprivation produces a cluster of effects, which can conveniently be described as hunger. These effects usually go together, but, under unusual circumstances, they can be manipulated separately. Thus, within limits, the longer a dog has been deprived of food, the more it will eat, the easier it can be taught new tricks with food reinforcement, the more vigorously it will perform these tricks, the more likely it is to choose eating or looking for food to other activities, and the stronger the punishment that will be necessary to keep it away from food.

Brain Mechanisms in Hunger

We know quite a bit about certain areas of the brain that are involved in regulating eating. With lesions in a certain part of the hypothalamus, called the ventromedial nucleus (see Chapter 2), a rat will overeat until it becomes fat like

Figure 7.5
Lesions in the ventromedial nucleus have caused this rat to exceed the 1,000 gram capacity of the scale. A normal rat weighs between 300 and 500 grams.

the one in Figure 7.5, whose kilogram of weight is three to four times normal. Although such rats overeat on tasty food that is easy to get, paradoxically they do not show other symptoms of increased hunger. If we require these rats to press a lever to get food or put heavy weights on the lids of the food dishes, they will eat less than normal rats. This restraint in intake is not due to muscular weakness produced by the operation, as was shown by the fact that making the food bitter by adding quinine or requiring the rats to take a mild electric shock in order to get it also cuts down their eating more than it does that of normal rats. Finally, a short fast does not increase their eating as much as it does normal animals'. In sum, lesions in this area of the brain seem to make the rats less responsive to their internal needs for calories and more responsive to environmental factors that either facilitate or deter eating.

Tumors that damage the ventromedial nuclei on both sides of the human hypothalamus also cause overeating and obesity, but such damage is extremely rare. Nevertheless, it is interesting that many considerably overweight people seem to show the same pattern of effects as do the rats with ventromedial lesions. In an ingenious experiment, Schachter told fat and lean human subjects to rate the flavor of different large bowls of ice cream. He told them that they should feel free to take as much or as little of each bowl as they needed to get a good rating. In this way, he distracted their attention from the topic of food intake, something about which fat people often are sensitive. One kind of ice cream, called bitters, was mixed with quinine and tasted terrible. Another was the richest, tastiest, creamiest ice cream he could find. The lean subjects took the same amount, about a spoonful of each; the fat subjects barely sampled the bad-tasting ice cream but took huge amounts of the tasty kind.

In another experiment, Nisbett left each subject alone for lunch between parts of another experiment. Different amounts of sandwiches were placed on plates in front of different subjects and they were told that there were plenty more in the refrigerator, which they should feel free to get if the serving was not enough. The lean subjects tended to eat the same amount, irrespective of the conditions, leaving some on the plate if they were given too much or going to the refrigerator if they were given too little. The fat subjects ate what was set before them, cleaned their plates even if they were given a lot, but did not go to the refrigerator even if they were given only a little. These and other experiments show that at least some very fat people seem to respond to the sight and taste of food and that normally lean subjects seem to respond to their caloric needs. Although this behavior is like that of the fat rats, it does *not* mean that the fat people have tumors damaging the ventromedial nuclei of the hypothalamus.

Destroying the ventromedial nucleus causes rats, cats, monkeys, and men to overeat; stimulating it causes a hungry animal to stop eating. In a nearby area, the so-called lateral hypothalamic feeding-drinking area, destruction on both sides of the brain causes animals to stop eating and drinking, so that they die. That the interference with hunger is not a secondary result of extreme thirst is shown by the fact that they will not eat even if given plenty of water by tube feeding.

In this lateral area, electrical stimulation causes satiated animals to eat (and often also to drink). This is not a mere gnawing reflex, as has been proven by careful experiments that show that stimulation in this area has all the functional properties of the normal drive of hunger. For example, it will motivate rats to learn a new response, such as pressing the bar that delivers a pellet of food. The strength of the drive is shown by the fact that it will cause animals to continue

Ventromedial Nucleus in the Hypothalamus

Figure 7.6
The hypothalamus.

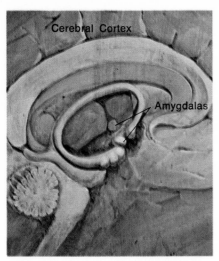

Figure 7.7
The amygdala.

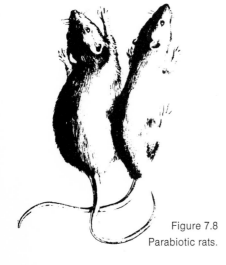

Figure 7.8
Parabiotic rats.

eating food that has been made so bitter by quinine that it is refused by animals that have been deprived of food for seventy-two hours. Furthermore, it can cause rats to overeat so much that they become very fat—gaining the amount of weight equivalent to a 150-pound man's going to over 200 pounds in nineteen days.

From these experiments, it is obvious that hunger is controlled by a balance between excitation from the lateral hypothalamus and inhibition from the ventromedial nucleus. This dual type of control is characteristic of many of the activities of the nervous system. Although the activity of the ventromedial and the lateral hypothalamic systems seems to play a very important role, it is known that eating is influenced also by the activities of other areas of the brain, such as the amygdala and the cerebral cortex. All the details of these interactions have not yet been worked out.

Because it takes quite a while for food to be digested and absorbed, there is an obvious need for some kind of short-term control to prevent the food-depleted animal from killing itself by eating too much at a single meal, as extremely hungry cattle sometimes do when they get into a cornfield. Experiments have shown that food injected directly into the stomach produces a prompt reduction in not only eating but also other measures of hunger, such as the rate of working for food. Mere distention of the stomach by a balloon does not produce as great an effect. Further evidence that there are some kinds of receptors in the stomach that can sense food is shown by the fact that hungry rats learn to go to the side of a T maze where food is injected directly into their stomach via a tube chronically implanted into the stomach in preference to the side in which an equal amount of isotonic saline is injected. But if an equal amount of stomach distention is produced by inflating a balloon when they choose one side and not when they choose the other, they learn to avoid the side where the balloon is inflated. It is clear that the stomach has some way of telling whether it is being filled by a balloon or by food.

Whereas food placed directly into the stomach produces a prompt reduction in hunger, food taken normally by mouth produces an even greater reduction in hunger, as measured by the rate at which the animal will work for food and the amount of bitter quinine required to stop it from eating. Thus, as in the case of thirst, it seems clear that there is a metering mechanism in the mouth and another one in the stomach, both of which help to put an end to a meal.

A rat can be forced to overeat and become fat in a number of different ways—by tube-feeding it large meals, by giving it injections of insulin, or by electrically stimulating it in the lateral hypothalamus. If, after it has been made fat by any one of these means, the treatment is stopped, it will virtually stop eating until it has lost most of its excess weight and will gradually resume eating the full normal amount only after it has come back to approximately its normal weight. How does the brain know that the body has too much food?

In one ingenious experiment, Hervey used *parabiotic rats*—the name given to Siamese twin rats that are created artificially by surgery. In such rats there is a certain amount of exchange in blood and body fluids, although the rate of exchange may be slow. Hervey found that when one member of the parabiotic pair had lesions in the ventromedial nucleus of the hypothalamus, it overate and became fat but its partner stopped eating and wasted away. His interpretation was that the tissues of the fat rat were sending out some sort of a signal into the bloodstream to tell the brain to stop eating but that this signal either was not received in the brain of that rat or was improperly translated because the ventromedial nucleus was destroyed. However, the rat with the normal brain received the signal all too well and stopped eating, actually wasting away until it died finally.

Other experimenters looked for a hunger signal by starving one member of a pair of parabiotic rats but have failed to notice any appreciable overeating by the other partner, who had access to food.

Many people have thought that Hervey's results may have been due to tissue incompatibility, much like that which causes transplanted hearts to be rejected, with the bigger rat being more likely to damage the smaller one than vice versa. This hypothesis is plausible because one member of a parabiotic pair often does die in this way without any ventromedial lesions in his partner. Recent work, however, has involved use of highly inbred mice who show no tissue incompatibility. A pair differed apparently in a single mutation: a type of diabetes characterized by obesity. When normal and potential diabetics were joined together as parabiotic twins, the fat one continued eating while the normal one stopped. This finding strongly suggests that there is some signal in the blood.

Mayer and other investigators have thought that this signal might be the amount of blood sugar, a plausible hypothesis because insulin reduces the amount of blood sugar and elicits eating. Thus far, injections of blood sugar have been singularly ineffective in satiating rats. We are therefore left with the important problem of discovering the signal, or signals.

Specific Hungers

When rats and many other animals are deficient in salt, they show an immediate strong preference for the taste of salt until they have restored their deficiency. This specific preference for salt has the properties of a drive in that animals will learn a new response to get salt.

In the case of the vitamin thiamine, rats do not seem to have a specific preference for the vitamin. But they develop an aversion for the foods eaten during the deficiency and therefore sample more novel foods. If one of the novel foods relieves the deficiency symptoms, they come to prefer it. Rats show other specific hungers related to specific deficiencies, such as having too little calcium, but these have not been studied in as much detail. The remarkable capacity for specific hungers is not perfect, however; for example, the rat's need for magnesium does not elicit any drive for it.

Hunger, Thirst, and Temperature

The way in which various physiological and behavioral mechanisms for homeostasis are interrelated is illustrated by studies of temperature regulation. The preoptic area is a moderately primitive, lower part of the brain. Electrical recordings from microelectrodes show that the preoptic area has some nerve cells that fire more rapidly when their temperature is slightly raised and others that fire

Figure 7.9
Warm or cool water or chemicals in solution may be delivered directly to this rat's brain.

more rapidly when their temperature is slightly lowered. Apparently, these cells function as, or are connected to, sense organs for temperature.

In order to study the functions of these cells, various scientists have implanted in the brains of animals fine tubes through which water can be circulated without discomfort after the animals have thoroughly recovered from the operation. Using warm water to slightly heat this area causes a variety of effects, all of which are useful to an overheated animal. The blood vessels in the skin expand so that more blood comes to the surface and the animal loses more heat. It also pants and salivates, thus cooling its tongue and mouth by evaporation. Other nerve cells in a nearby area function like tiny glands to secrete ADH, which is collected and released into the blood by the pituitary gland and permits the kidneys to reabsorb water so that a more concentrated urine is formed and the animal saves water that it will need for evaporative cooling. If the animal is hungry, it stops eating, which is adaptive because the processing of food would further raise its temperature. Finally, it becomes thirsty, so that it is motivated to seek and drink water, which has the function of anticipating the depletion by evaporative cooling.

Conversely, slightly cooling the preoptic area elicits constriction of the peripheral blood vessels; shivering; increased activity of the thyroid gland, which causes the body to create more heat by burning fuel faster; and hunger, which serves to motivate the animal to seek and eat food, which creates heat and restores the fuel deficits. All these activities would function to warm up a chilled animal to its normal temperature, but with the cooling limited to this minute area of the brain, they give the rest of the body a fever, thus illustrating the dominance of the brain in regulating temperature.

In this example, we see how the brain functions as a sense organ, as a gland, as a control center for various responses, and as a source of drives that motivate complex behavior. We see how all these functions work together in the regulation of temperature. Furthermore, abnormal temperatures can also serve as a drive for responses that are reinforced by restoring the normal level—a person or animal, for example, may learn to go out into the sun when he is cold or go into the shade when he is warm. If shaved rats are placed in a refrigerator, they learn to press a bar to turn on a heat lamp; placed in a hot environment, they learn bar pressing to give themselves a cooling shower.

Other Homeostatic Drives An excess of carbon dioxide is one of the main stimuli for deeper breathing. Try to hold your breath for ninety seconds. A terrific drive is created, so it is not surprising that animals learn a specific response, like pressing a bar, to regulate the amount of carbon dioxide in the air that they breathe. Experiments have shown that animals with an excess of water learn to avoid the side of a T maze where they get an injection of ADH that interferes with the formation of the urine that would get rid of the excess water. But if they have the problem of getting rid of excess salt because they have a deficiency of ADH, they learn to go to the side where they get an injection of ADH that allows them to form a more concentrated urine and thus get rid of the salt better.

Although not all cases have been investigated, it seems reasonable to suppose that a potential drive is involved in most, and perhaps all, cases in which homeostasis is mediated by the central nervous system. In some cases, indeed, the behavioral adjustment may evolve before the physiological one. Thus, if goldfish are given a chance to perform a response that regulates the temperature of the water in their tank, they will regulate it to approximately the temperature that produces the maximum rate of growth. If given the chance to swim about freely in a pond that has different temperatures in different places, they tend to swim to the places that have this optimal temperature.

Although sexual behavior is necessary for the survival of the species, it does not seem to be necessary for the survival of the individual or to have the same homeostatic functions as the drives that we have been considering. In lower animals, more of the details of sexual behavior seem to be innately determined and under the rigid control of sex hormones and of lower centers of the brain. In the higher mammals, the higher centers of the brain and learning seem to play a more important role. Interestingly enough, in any given species sexual behavior seems to be somewhat more under the control of hormones and the lower centers of the brain in the female than in the male.

Sexual Behavior—A Nonhomeostatic Drive

Different aspects of sexual behavior certainly have the attributes that characterize such drives as hunger and thirst. For example, an adult male rat will learn to run down an alley or to work at some other response in order to secure access to a receptive female. After sufficient access, he will act as though he were satiated. Although ejaculation is important if a sexual experience is to be maximally reinforcing, there is considerable evidence that other components of sexual activity also can serve as reinforcers. We have seen that even thirst is not a completely unitary drive and that there are specific hungers. It seems quite likely that sex is also complex and has a greater number of motivational components than, say, thirst or hunger.

The amount and type of sexual activity vary considerably with the testosterone that is secreted by the male testes and the estrogen and progesterone that are secreted by the female gonads. Testosterone also seems to be related to behavior that is loosely labeled as aggression. To date, most studies have concentrated on the effects of such hormones on the innate aspects of sexual behavior. Much less time has been devoted to a detailed analysis of the motivational components of sexual behavior.

There is interesting evidence that there is a certain critical period during which injections of male hormone into the female will produce so-called masculinization, eliminating female sexual behavior in the adult rat. Whether anything is involved beyond the fact that the estrous cycle is eliminated, so that the female never comes into heat, is not clear. Similarly, males castrated during a certain critical period of life show more female behavior, even when given hormone replacement therapy in adulthood, than do males that are castrated later in infancy or given similar replacement therapy early in childhood. For rats, the critical period is shortly after birth, and for guinea pigs it is before birth.

There is convincing evidence that sex hormones can act directly on the brain. If female cats are ovariectomized, they do not show receptivity. An implant of a small amount of an artificial form of female hormone in the preoptic area of the brain will elicit prolonged and excessive receptiveness, but a similar, or even considerably larger, implant under the skin or in other areas of the brain is ineffective. Injections of male hormone into the lateral preoptic area of either male or female rats will elicit male behavior consistently in some cases. If the standard tests for motivation were applied, these treatments probably would be found to have drive characteristics that increase the reward value of the sexual activity that they induce.

Fear is an important drive because it can be learned quite rapidly and can **Fear**

become very strong. Responses that allow the subject to escape fear are reinforced and hence learned. Thus, if a person escapes fear by behavior that is cowardly, he will learn to become more cowardly. But if a person learns to escape fear by bravely dealing adaptively with the danger, he will learn to become braver. The important thing is not how afraid you are but what you do when you are afraid, and especially what you are doing when the fear is suddenly reduced.

For example, students who are afraid of a crucial examination may be reminded of the examination and thus frightened when they open their book to study for it. One of the ways to reduce this fear is to close the book and seek a distraction that will crowd out all fear-inducing thoughts about the examination. The student may become engrossed in a bull session, a game of cards, or a movie. The temporary immediate escape from fear reinforces these responses. In this way, some students learn to avoid studying when they most need it.

The fact that the fear can be escaped by turning away from signs of danger and repressing thoughts about the danger is the source of a considerable amount of maladaptive behavior. It is also one of the weaknesses of trying to use fear as a way of influencing behavior (see Chapter 33).

Innate Elicitation and Reduction of Fear

Although most experimental studies have used pain elicited by electric shock as the basis for establishing fear, there is considerable evidence that fear can be aroused in other ways. If a dog raised in isolation is suddenly brought out into a complex normal environment, this abrupt exposure to a welter of novel stimulation is a traumatic experience, arousing strong fear from which the dog takes a long time to recover. Introducing the dog gradually into the novel situation avoids this trauma.

Loud sounds and sudden increases in stimulation often seem to induce fear, as do strange and unexpected situations. Thus, Hebb reports that chimpanzees may be terrified by a disembodied head or even by the appearance of a well-known caretaker wearing a strange mask. At certain ages, animals and children seem to develop a fear of strangers. Finally, the degree to which monkeys and chimpanzees fear snakes and snakelike objects suggests that certain patterns of stimulation may have an innate tendency to elicit fear.

Other stimulus situations seem to have an innate capacity to counteract fear. It is much harder, for example, to frighten an infant monkey when it is clinging to, rather than separated from, its mother. Exactly the same thing seems to be true of children.

Responses such as eating seem to be incompatible with fear. Thus, Pavlov found that if a very mildly painful stimulus was made the signal for giving food to an extremely hungry dog, as salivation and other feeding responses were conditioned to the stimulus, signs of emotional disturbance dropped out. Gradually, the strength of the pain could be increased without eliciting emotional disturbance. If the pain is too strong, however, the fear and other emotional responses can become dominant.

Other oral responses, such as thumb sucking, can reduce fear, and such reduction in fear may be one of the reinforcers for some thumb sucking. Complete muscular relaxation seems to be incompatible with fear and has been used as a therapeutic procedure to help to eliminate fear.

Extinction of Fear

Experiments have shown that responses originally reinforced by escape from fear extinguish readily when they are no longer effective in getting away from the fear-inducing cues. On the other hand, fear itself is often extremely persistent. For example, Figure 7.12 shows rats persisting for over 200 trials at pressing a bar to get out of a fear-inducing compartment, then gradually extinguishing. In other experiments, dogs have persisted for over 1,000 trials without showing any signs of experimental extinction.

This resistance to extinction has led psychotherapists to explore actively a variety of different techniques for helping patients to extinguish their fear. People who have snake phobias are helped to overcome the fear by first watching and then imitating models who have no fear of snakes. In an early experiment, counterconditioning was successful in removing a child's fear of furry animals that had resisted all other means of therapy. While the child was hungry and eating, a rabbit was very gradually brought nearer, until finally the child was eating with one hand and petting the rabbit with the other.

Learned Channeling

In experiments on the conditioning of fear, a previously neutral stimulus is made to elicit the drive of fear. Attempts to condition hunger and thirst in a similar way to date have led to singularly little clear success. When hunger is present,

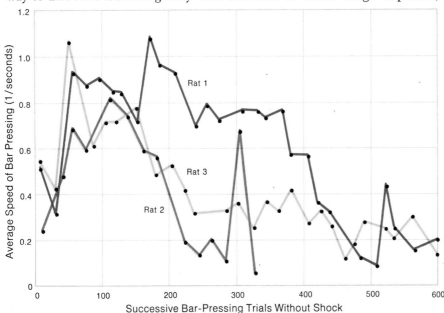

Figure 7.12
The gradual slowing of bar pressing to escape from a compartment once associated with shock.
(After Miller, 1951.)

however, food preferences can be learned. Thus, even though an animal is hungry, strange food may not serve as an effective reward but a familiar food does. Similarly, a person may not at first like olives or oysters but may acquire an appetite for them. In this case, one might say that their drive has been channeled, or perhaps that a new goal object for the drive has been learned.

Curiosity

Most mammals show curiosity. A series of experiments has shown that both rats and monkeys will learn new responses in order to get the chance to explore novel objects. In one such experiment, Butler showed that monkeys, confined in a monotonous cubicle, would press a bar that caused a shutter to be removed from a window so that they could look out and observe various types of activity outside. The monkeys would not only learn this new response but would continue to work hard to open the shutter.

The strength of curiosity is shown by the fact that if hungry rats are given a familiar food in a strange box they will take a nibble or two and then go off to explore the box, coming back from time to time to take a few more nibbles. It is only after they have thoroughly explored the box that they will settle down to steady eating.

Although we know something about curiosity, it needs much further study. We do not yet know either how to stifle or how to enhance the curiosity of a cat, and we have no scientific knowledge of the principles involved in developing or channeling the intellectual curiosity of a student. We know next to nothing about the neurophysiological mechanism of curiosity. Nor do we know whether the general type of activity that we loosely describe by this word really is a relatively unitary phenomenon or a hodgepodge of quite different phenomena mediated by different mechanisms.

Figure 7.13
The sight of an electric train will reinforce behavior in monkeys.

Much the same thing is true for what has been described as a drive for activity. We know that rats will learn to press a bar to secure access to a wheel in which they can run, but we do not know much more than that.

Aggression

If a certain part of the hypothalamus of the cat is stimulated via a chronically implanted electrode with a weak electric current, a spectacular burst of aggression is elicited. The hair bristles, the pupils of the eyes open wide, ears lie back, and the cat hisses and strikes out viciously and aggressively at either a gloved hand or a stick inserted into the cage. If there is a rat in the cage, it will be struck repeatedly with slashing swipes of the paw.

Stimulation in a slightly different area does not elicit the emotional components involving the hair, pupils, ears, or hiss but rather a silent, cold, stalking attack, in which the rat is seized by the neck with a bite that kills it by breaking its neck. This behavior has the true characteristic of a drive, for a cat stimulated in this way will learn to choose that arm of a Y maze that leads to a goalbox containing a rat to attack rather than the arm that leads to an empty goalbox.

The foregoing experiments demonstrate two rather different types of aggression elicited by stimulation in two somewhat different locations in the cat's brain. As Moyer has pointed out, it is quite possible that there are yet other types of aggression. In our ignorance, we do not yet know the extent to which these may have elements in common or may be quite distinct.

Figure 7.14
Aggression elicited by shocks may be displaced to a doll if another rat is not present.

We do know that aggressive responses can be elicited by frustration or by painful electric shocks. In the latter case, the tendency to fight can be increased if the fighting is rewarded by escape from shock. If rats are trained in this way to fight another partner, they will, as Figure 7.14 shows, attack the partner if he is

Figure 7.15
Aggression and threat elicited by brain stimulation. The apparatus strapped to the monkey's back receives the signal to deliver current to the brain.

present but generalize their attack to a doll if there is no partner there to attack. Clinical psychologists call this kind of generalization of an aggressive response displacement (see Chapter 27).

Animals also can be trained to be more likely to fight by being given a graded series of contests in which they first encounter an opponent they are certain to beat easily and then progressively more difficult ones. Similarly, they can be trained not to fight if they are matched with opponents superior to them.

When groups of social animals are in a natural situation, they usually organize themselves into a dominance hierarchy. After initial aggressive encounters, the more dominant animals control the less dominant ones by mere threats. If a monkey in the middle of a dominance hierarchy is stimulated to aggression by radio-controlled stimulation of the appropriate spot in its brain, it will always attack a less dominant monkey rather than a more dominant one.

In general, male animals seem to be more aggressive than female ones, but castration reduces their aggression. One should, however, remember the ferocity of some females in defending their young.

With aggression, as with so many of the other nonhomeostatic drives, we have enough successful research to show that it is possible to design experiments to study them in more detail at both the purely behavioral and the neurophysiological levels. The goal of understanding such motivations better is vital, and the means for achieving this understanding are at hand, but our present knowledge is tantalizingly incomplete.

HUMAN MOTIVATION

FOR THOUSANDS OF YEARS, philosophers, poets, and scientists have speculated about what kinds of motivation are innate to the human being and what are acquired in the course of life. Is the need to know the meaning of life, for example, an instinct, a drive, the action of a cognitive system, or simply a neurotic device for coping with more basic human functions? Perhaps all that exists in the human being as innate wishes is what experimental psychologists tell us exists in animals; perhaps a concern for the meaning of life is nothing but an instrumental act to come to terms with the fact that food was obtained on an irregular basis as a child. Most philosophical schools have made various assertions about what *really* constitutes human nature. Indeed, the history of modern psychology itself reveals a fierce ideological battlefield on this issue, in which the chief concern has been to cherish a single insight or research finding and strenuously draw up defensive lines against its corruption by another idea.

It is possible to see the sequence of ideas on human motivation in this century as falling into three stages. The first phase was that of the founders of modern psychology, men who saw new things about people and who consequently generated rich and seminal ideas. The second phase has been that of the essentially sterile defenders of the faith. There have been few really new ideas since 1940, and although there has been some useful nontheoretical research, it has not focused on resolving the theoretical disagreements. Fortunately, this period seems about to come to an end. The cumulative weight of several recent books indicates that psychology is about to return to theoretical issues and begin to explore the roots of human motivation and the way it develops in the course of human life.

Salvatore Maddi has introduced several new words that seem to hold promise in this exploration, if only by defusing some of the older unnecessary emotional issues that have collected around various positions. He suggests that psychology talk about the *core* elements of the individual (the organismic properties) and the *peripheral* elements (those characteristics acquired in the course of life). This approach is likely to be a bridge between the older theoretical positions and a half-century of empirical research and to open up a less fiercely ideological way of asking old but important questions.

As we turn our attention to the roots of human motivation, our concentration will be with the core elements and how research has been and can be carried out. This choice is made primarily because this is the least clear and most hotly contested area in motivational theory. In contrast, the logic of the explanation of the *acquisition* of motives is rather simple. It is essentially to show that key experiences occurred in childhood and are correlated with the presence of specific motives later on in life (for example, to show that a dependent child had been rewarded for showing dependent activity). The study of the core is more difficult, and therefore more interesting.

Instincts and the Human Core

Because the issue of the human core has been so controversial in modern psychology, it is important to take a serious look at how early ideas of instincts were developed, the kinds of phenomena first subsumed under them, and the methodological issues involved—spurious and real.

Within the early theorists' definitions of instinct, there were a number of criteria, most of which have survived the vicissitudes of the controversy over instincts in this century. These include the facts that: (1) a disposition is unlearned; (2) it is rooted in the physiology of the organism; (3) it produces behavior that accomplishes specific ends; (4) its produced behavior is accompanied by intrinsic pleasurable sensations; and (5) it determines the range of objects the individual perceives and becomes involved with. Among the many types of activities classified as instincts were flight, repulsion, pugnacity, self-abasement, self-assertion, parental behavior, sucking, spitting, smiling, playing, sociability, and acquisitiveness. Some were obviously absurd, like the instinct to sit on a chair or to be a Russian. Indeed, the list of instincts, by many hands, grew so rapidly that in 1924 Luther Bernard, a sociologist, set himself the task of compiling a master list. After surveying 500 books by social scientists, he arrived at a grand total of 5,759 separate instincts. With this achievement, the house of cards came tumbling down.

This well-deserved onslaught on the venture of instinct finding had been brought about by the careless approach used by social scientists. The difficulty was that every behavior that could in any way be distinguished from another was mindlessly given its own status as an instinct, regardless of whether or not it was a simple reflex, a general organismic reflex, an impulse to a specific end, an emotion, an organismic capability, a general behavior to no specific end, or an instrumental act. The hopeless confusion and the impossibility for scientific clarity that then prevailed served as one goad to what has been termed the behavioristic revolution in social science.

The Behavioristic Critique

The early behaviorists cut through this morass by arguing for a much simpler analysis of behavior. They refused to become involved with postulated internal forces and relied totally on what they could observe. They argued that personality is behavior, that behavior is learned, and that explanation consists of analysis in terms of environmental determinants. In other words, they wanted to explain behavior in terms of experience. The behaviorists felt that it is not valid

to posit perceptions and feelings in lower animals, and, because we can deal only with the activities of an organism, even when we come to deal with the human being we must define personality simply as the sum of all his activities. The behaviorists also argued that we can sufficiently account for the behavior of an organism by the environmental forces that impinge upon it without recourse to postulated instincts.

Social-Learning Theory

Because of the behaviorists' criticisms, psychologists began to shift their concern. An examination of the behaviorists' approach had made it clear that human behavior is not equivalent to those behaviors of lower organisms for which the concept of instinct did have some relevance. In the elaborately organized sequence of activities that occur in the mating dance of the stickleback fish, for example, a highly organized chaining of responses occurs first in one organism and then another. The first act by the male sets off another in the female, and the sequence repeats itself a number of times until the final consummation. The word "instinct" in this case inherently implies some notion of a fixed motor pattern. Human behavior, however, is characterized by great plasticity. In fact, it was this very plasticity that prevented psychologists from achieving their goal of listing a finite number of instincts.

Impressed with the extent of the plasticity, psychologists returned to a concept that has a long history—the concept of the empty organism. The idea here is that the behaviors, motives, and goals of the individual are implanted, by some means, through a process of social learning. In its simplest form, for example, the argument would be that aggressive behavior occurs because it has been rewarded in some way: a highly aggressive child results from parents who reward his various aggressive acts. This argument would hold similarly for virtually all human motivations. The psychological abstraction created to denote

Figure 8.3
Stickleback mating. The male's zigzag dance evokes the heads-up posture of the female, which stimulates the male to lead the way to the nest. His thrusts at the nest are the stimuli for her to enter it, and his subsequent prodding induces her to spawn.

this particular phenomenon is the *law of effect,* which maintains that if behavior is rewarded it will tend to repeat itself. A particular behavior that is not rewarded will drop out of the organism's repertoire.

Although almost all definitions of instinct imply that an instinct is unlearned, this is an exceedingly difficult proposition to prove conclusively. A number of instinctive motives in both lower organisms and man have been investigated recently—including aggression, maternal behavior, social behavior, and curiosity —and in all cases the logic of the research has involved a process of exclusion. Psychologists have sought, with sometimes ambiguous results, to establish, first, that the behavior is not in the service of another behavior. Second, they have tried to show that in the lifetime of the organism they are studying, it would have been impossible to learn that particular behavior. Unfortunately, it is virtually impossible to prove that nothing happened that might possibly teach the organism a particular behavior.

Criteria for Core Instincts

Psychology must nevertheless be extremely clear on the criteria used to arrive at decisions about motivation. A number of criteria have been proposed by Abraham Maslow, who sees motivation in terms of needs based in the organism. Maslow has attempted to build a systematic theory of motivation from the position of the human core by pulling together elements from empirical, theoretical, and clinical studies. His focus has been on human needs and potentialities within the framework of a concern for the development and growth of the human being. The basic general proposition is that the human being is not an empty organism to be filled by society. Needs indicate potentialities rather than final actualizations; we develop these impulses in the course of our lives. These impulses are weak and can be depressed or killed off by society and do not have a fixed behavioral sequence as their mechanism for finding gratification. Moreover, some parts of our inner nature are species-wide, for example, the need for love. Others are specific to the individual, such as musical talent. Finally, if this inner core is denied, sickness will result. On the basis of these internal forces, it is possible to build an absolute code of values: what is in us is healthy, and we should structure the world to provide a means of gratifying it.

Maslow has called these psychological forces *organismically based needs* and speaks of five levels of needs arranged in *hierarchical* order. The more basic level must be relatively well satisfied before the organism is able to function on a higher level. The most basic level of motivation, in Maslow's theory, is what he calls the *physiological needs,* including hunger, sex, and thirst (the homeostatic mechanisms maintaining optimal levels of salt, sugar, temperature, oxygen), as well as the need for sleep, relaxation, and bodily integrity. All of these must be satisfied before the organism can begin to function on a higher level.

When the physiological needs have been relatively well satisfied, the individual becomes concerned with a new set of needs, which are termed the *safety needs.* These are centered around the requirements of a predictable and orderly world. The world must not appear unjust, inconsistent, unsafe, or unreliable. If the safety needs have been deprived, the individual will feel mistrustful and insecure and will seek those areas of life that offer the most stability and protection. Further, he will attempt to organize the world to provide the greatest degree of safety and predictability possible.

After the physiological and the safety needs have been satisfied, there emerge the needs to possess affectionate relationships with other people and belong to a wider group. An individual functioning on this level desires warm and friendly

human relationships and is able to function well in interpersonal situations. These are called the *love* and the *belongingness needs*.

The fourth level in the hierarchy constitutes the *esteem needs*: the desire for achievement and competence, for independence and freedom, for reputation and prestige. When the satisfaction of all the lower needs has occurred, the level of *self-actualization* is reached by the full use and exploitation of talents, capacities and potentialities.

Throughout his development and the unfolding of these motivational patterns, the individual directs most of his activities toward frustrated needs rather than toward those that have already been satisfied. Activities based on needs not yet relevant are conspicuously absent in his activities.

This approach avoids the earlier method of simple *instinct listing*. Instead, using clear criteria, it has been possible to identify clusters of motives that seem to revolve hierarchically around general issues.

Measures of Human Motives

Theoretical interpretations of man's motives always ring truer if there is some empirical bulwark to shore them up. Although it may seem plausible that man is composed of hierarchically arranged needs that display themselves for satisfaction in regular orders according to regular rules, the basic conception of a need cries out for some objective statement and, if possible, measurement.

McClelland and his associates have developed to a high degree of excellence and practical usefulness a method of measuring human motives. Although their work started during World War II with a concern for measuring the hunger drive and its changes during prolonged starvation, the most important psychological impact has come from measurements of the *need for achievement* (nAch). It is intuitively clear that all of us share this need to some degree. The indolent fat types among us presumably have less of it than the active, striving, athletic executives, but each has at least enough need for achievement to turn a dollar or to open the refrigerator for the next meal. The problem is to find some way of determining the amount of need for achievement in a given individual so exactly that it can be assigned a number.

It is clear that simple questioning may not be effective. Many subgroups in our culture are not willing to display their full need for achievement in public on a questionnaire and some subgroups overreact and paint themselves as extremely desirous of success when in fact they are really quite lazy. Moreover, achievement may take many forms. For some, intellectual machinations represent the acme of achievement, but for others only sexual conquest, making money, or scoring touchdowns seems worth striving for. McClelland derived a system whereby any sort of achievement could contribute to an individual's score on need for achievement.

McClelland did not invent nAch but rather measured it. His measurement technique uses a unique combination of objective scoring and the productions of fantasy. An individual is shown several (usually four) ambiguous pictures, such as the set in Figure 8.8, and asked to write a story about what is happening in each one. The pictures each show a situation that can be interpreted in many ways. The assumption is that the individual will interpret the picture in terms of achievement to the degree that he has a need for achievement. The task of the objective scoring system is to tease out the relative degree to which the individual expresses achievement needs in his imaginary story.

Specifically, the individual is asked to write, for each picture, a story containing the following information. First, what is happening in the picture? Who is

Figure 8.8

An individual's need for achievement may be judged from the descriptions he gives of ambiguous situations like these.

doing what and why to whom? Thus, the subject is asked to identify the persons and to describe their current behavior. Second, what events, thoughts, and motives led up to the present situation? Third, what are the present thoughts, motives, hopes, and fears of the participants? And, fourth, what is going to happen to these people in the future? By answering these four questions in his story, the individual provides material for the objective evaluation system.

The scorer, who rates the story in terms of nAch, is a trained and experienced individual who has had long supervised practice with the scoring system under the tutelage of an expert. Experience has shown that it is possible to train scorers so that they almost exactly agree on the amount of need for achievement exemplified by a given story. The scoring system is gratifyingly reliable.

The system itself is based on an eleven-point scale. First, the scorer decides if the story has any evidence at all of need for achievement. If the task is ordinary and approached in an ordinary fashion, such as tying one's shoes in the morning, or if there is no task at all, the story is assigned a score of o or −1 and is not scored further. If the story contains an indication of an individual's striving to overcome a task or obstacle to reach a real goal, it is given one point, and the scoring continues.

Additional points are obtainable for each of ten categories. Remember that it is the *need* for achievement that is being scored, not necessarily its attainment. Additional points are given when the story contains reference to anticipated success or failure in reaching a goal, shows that there is an obstacle to the goal either in the person or in the environment, contains reference to personal forces aiding the individual in his striving for the goal, shows evidence of instrumental or mental activity related to obtaining the goal, indicates that the individual wants to reach the goal, shows positive or negative emotional attachment to the goal, and, finally, has the theme of achievement as the central one in the story.

The amount of need for achievement is expressed by the total score for the four stories written by the individual. The score may thus be as low as −4 (no task at all in any story) or as high as 44 (all 11 points earned in each story). A score between 25 and 30 indicates a substantial need for achievement.

The most comforting aspect of this sort of measurement of individual motives is that it seems to work in practice. We have indicated that the scorers are able to agree—that is, that the scoring is reliable. It also seems to be valid. Individuals low on need for achievement differ in a number of sensible ways from people who score high on need for achievement. Some of these differences are related to occupation, some to personality, some to cultural factors, and—one of the most

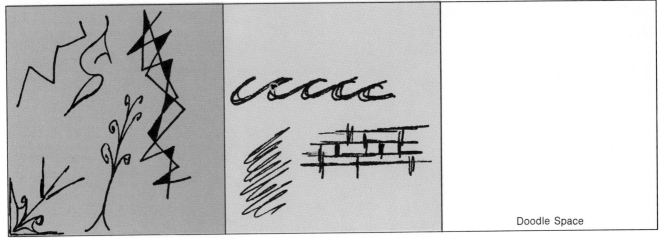

Doodle Space

interesting—some to the doodles people draw.

Aronson asked people with a variety of scores on need for achievement to participate in the following task. They were furnished with pencil and paper and asked to view briefly a page of doodles displayed on a screen in front of them. The exposure was long enough to let the person see the doodles and their placement on the paper, but not long enough to allow anywhere near an exact copy or even a fair memorization. Thus, this technique also relies on fantasy to some degree, because the individual must recall or confabulate the doodles he saw or generate his own.

The doodles were scored by an objective system, in its general principles similar to that used by McClelland for his stories. The outcome was a clear separation between the doodles produced by those high in nAch and those produced by individuals low in nAch, as measured by McClelland's system.

Before reading further, use the square in the margin to generate a few doodles of your own, then read the next paragraph to see what your score is on this kind of test.

Aronson's subjects showed that high values of need for achievement were associated with four characteristics of doodles: less unused space—if you filled the square, give yourself a plus nAch; more diagonal lines than vertical and horizontal—if you drew cubes, take a minus nAch; more S-shaped single figures—for many Ss, add a plus nAch; and finally, fewer regularly wavy lines containing more than one wave—take a plus or minus nAch accordingly.

Without scoring norms (see Chapter 23), it is of course impossible for you to arrive at an accurate numerical estimate of your own nAch, but by comparing your doodles to those shown in Figure 8.9, you should get some idea of where you stand on this particular motive.

Figure 8.9

Try doodling in the empty square, then compare your doodles to the others. Your need for achievement is high if your doodles are like the first set, lower if they are more like the second.

Applications of Basic Need Theory

To this point we have been talking about human motivation solely from the point of view of the individual. What most characterizes human beings, however, is the fact that they cannot be understood in isolation from others. They are continually involved in a social network. Thus, it is important to consider the role of motives in shaping the nature of social behavior.

The social sciences as a whole have long sought to link together the various processes each discipline has been studying separately, but no conceptual framework to date integrates these areas in a meaningful way. In the field of culture and personality, which has become the meeting ground for the various disciplines, the emphasis has been on the arrangements present in the culture to

produce human motives in order to maintain key aspects of the culture. The most generally accepted model of these processes has been offered by John Whiting, who argues that the primary elements in the social process are the economic structures. From these structures, the child-training practices of the culture are produced. These, in turn, create the specific personalities found in that culture.

Aronoff has hypothesized that both personality and sociocultural structures are the final products of three independent factors: environment, past sociocultural institutions, and organismically based psychological needs. He argues that neither the cultural nor the psychological phenomena the social scientist observes may be related to independent sets of determinants. Rather, they are the final product of the two in a particular setting. Aronoff suggests that specific environmental features create the possibilities and set the limits of cultural and personality development. The cultural institutions introduced to the setting adapt to its requirements to produce preliminary institutional forms. However, although this first arrangement will gratify the basic needs of the individual on some levels, it may deprive him on others. If the early social forms provide only limited degrees of gratification, they will leave deficiencies, particularly in other needs higher in the hierarchy. Because basic psychological needs must find some form of gratification, these deprived needs exert their influence on the general cultural system and restructure the initial institutional forms in such a fashion as to get as much gratification as is possible in that setting. This process of restructuring cultural forms should be seen as a period of changing the relationship among all factors until a resolution is reached.

Organizational Psychology

In the United States, the theory of motivation has attracted much attention in the area of industrial psychology. Managers, personnel directors, and industrial psychologists looking for a way to restructure their organizations to achieve both greater efficiency and higher morale have found useful direction by developing ways to provide gratification of lower levels of functioning—and thereby release higher levels. Perhaps the industrial psychologist who has had the greatest impact has been Douglas McGregor, who maintains that a theory of human nature, in the form of a set of assumptions, seems to underlie most industrial organizations. These assumptions, called *theory X*, are: (1) an individual dislikes work and will try in every way to avoid it; (2) therefore, the job of the industrialist is to find the means to coerce people to do their work; (3) the average person prefers to be directed, wishes to avoid responsibility, has little ambition, and wants security.

McGregor has called an alternative set of principles *theory Y*. Its assumptions about human nature are (1) the expenditure of energy is natural; (2) external control is not the only way to ensure the performance of a good job; (3) the commitment to objectives in work is related directly to the goals sought; (4) people like responsibility; (5) many people are creative; and (6) under present industrial conditions, only part of the human potential is reached.

A great many industrial psychologists and industrial managers have been interested in theory Y and have applied it to industry under the name of the *Scanlon Plan*. The methods of application can be seen in the experiences of one company that sought to mobilize the energy of the human being by providing an environment in which it was possible to express intrinsic forms of motivation. The action taken by the industrial manager was neither a training program nor a sermon; instead, he approached the problem with a concern for those dimensions

Figure 8.11
How the boss sees it: theory X.

Figure 8.12
An alternative view: theory Y.

of motivation inherent in the human being and attempted to develop social-psychological structures that might allow them to find expression.

A voltmeter factory that wanted to increase its production tried to do so at first by a variety of such standard inducements as paying their workers a good deal of extra money and giving them shorter work weeks. Their experience was that nothing they tried along the lines of what McGregor calls theory X had much effect. They then changed their approach to see if somehow they could institute organizational structures that would fit in with some of the principles stated in theory Y. This company originally had used a traditional assembly-line production in which each person did a small part of the job.

The solution this company reached was to reorganize the entire production system into small groups of approximately six to ten people, working in separate rooms. The intention was to give people a chance to get to know each other and to enjoy each other's company as they worked. The second innovation was to have the worker construct the product from the beginning to the end himself. The assumption was that if people are proud of their work, they will enjoy their work, take pains with their work, and do good work. The results of this innovation were startling. The company found that production skyrocketed; the quality of the work improved considerably; there was no sabotage of the work—as is so often found in the work done by alienated workers; absenteeism was down considerably; there was less job turnover; employees took fewer sick days; and, last, they enjoyed their work.

This experience has been repeated many times, and not only in industry. It is, for example, at the heart of a number of experiments in education. The principle is that students learn when they want to know something. Because optimal results do not ensue when students are forced to study, social structures were developed on the principle that it is essential to trust students to find out what activities are appropriate for them. Perhaps the most well-publicized experiment of this kind was carried out in England at the Summerhill school by A. S. Neill. Looking for appropriate ways to arrange social organizations in line with these principles, social scientists have been able to develop a range of institutions that can satisfy the basic needs of human beings, as well as lead to superior institutional functioning.

UNIT III

PSYCHOLOGICAL DEVELOPMENT

All organisms, including man, are born with certain genetically determined behavior patterns built into their bodily structure. These instinctual responses are sufficient to keep a human infant alive, but just as the infant must grow physically, so he must go through a period of psychological development if he is to become an adult. The stages of bodily maturation are determined genetically, for almost all children—given adequate nourishment and stimulation—grow at about the same rate and reach puberty and young adulthood at about the same time. But what of our personalities? Do all of us pass through the same psychological stages of development? The more complex the organism, in general, the longer this behavioral development takes; and the most complex form of behavior—that of language and thought—seems to take the longest of all.

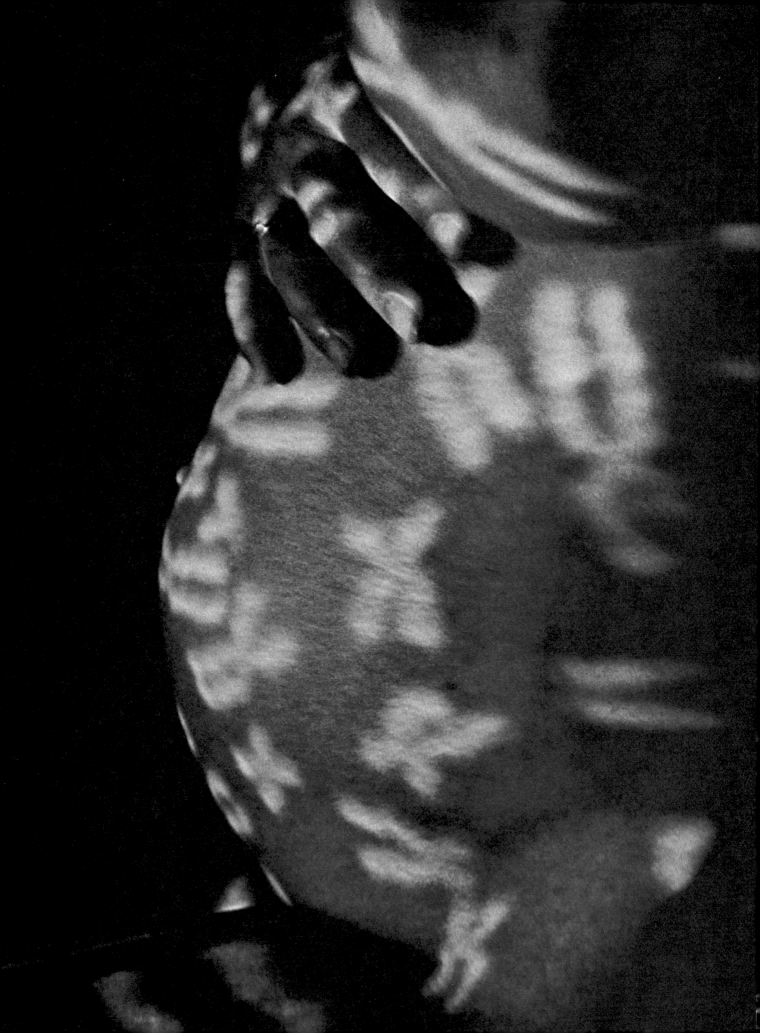

BEHAVIOR GENETICS

HEREDITY IS A SOURCE of both similarities and differences among individuals. The same hereditary mechanisms that lead to resemblance of parent and off-spring produce differences among members of a family. Similarly, there are some hereditary traits, such as instinctive behavior patterns, that are common to all members of a species; but, at the same time, there are many other hereditary traits that show tremendous variation both within and between species. In this chapter we are primarily concerned with the diversifying or differentiating role of heredity and its relevance to individual differences in animal and human behavior.

Heredity and Variation

In comparison to the inanimate materials studied in physics and chemistry, the behavior of living organisms shows an extremely high degree of variability, or individual differences. When laboratory rats are trained to run through a maze to obtain food, for example, it is invariably found that there are large differences in learning ability. Some rats learn very quickly, making few errors; others learn very slowly; and still others show various degrees of intermediate performance. The frequency distribution shown in Figure 9.1 indicates the extent of individual differences obtained by Tryon in the maze-learning behavior of laboratory rats. Each of Tryon's rats received 19 trials in a maze having 17 choice points. The learning score was the total number of errors, or incorrect turns at choice points, for 19 trials. The total number of errors for individual rats ranged from 7 to 224, compared to a maximum possible range of 0 to 323.

Other behavioral traits in animals and humans show a similar degree of variability. In human infants, for example, the amount of crying during the first week of life varies from 1 to 4 hours per day, and the age at which walking alone first occurs ranges from approximately 9 to 15 months; in later years, Stanford-Binet IQ scores range from 35 to 175, and the frequency of sexual behavior in males varies from 0 to 30 orgasms per week. The degree of variation revealed by these examples stands in sharp contrast to the situation existing in the physical sciences, where measurement of the electrical resistance of copper wires or the

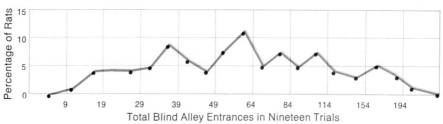

Figure 9.1

The variability of maze-learning
performance in laboratory rats.
(After Tryon, 1942.)

specific gravity of rocks of a certain type might show a range of only ±1 percent from the average value.

In addition to individual differences in behavioral traits, or stable response tendencies of organisms, it is often found that there are marked differences among members of a species in the effects on behavior of certain environmental or experimental conditions. A good illustration of this point is provided by the data in Figure 9.2, in which the rate of lever pressing by rats was studied as a function of the temporal conditions under which lever pressing was reinforced by food. For some rats, a decrease in the reinforcement ratio produced an increased rate of responding, whereas other rats showed decreased responding under the same conditions, and still other rats showed an increase in response rate followed by a decrease. In other words, different animals within a single species obeyed entirely different "laws" of behavior.

It is clear, then, that individual differences represent an undeniable fact of life in the study of behavior. In most areas of psychology, however, and particularly in experimental psychology, it is customary to pay attention only to the average or typical organism and to disregard individual differences completely. This is frequently accomplished by combining individual data into a performance curve based on group averages, which is then assumed to reflect a general principle or law of learning, motivation, perception, or some other process. The data in Figure 9.2 could be combined in this way, and although the resulting group curve might appear smooth and orderly, it would necessarily fail to de-

Figure 9.2

Rate of lever pressing as a function of the
proportion of time that reinforcement
is available. Data for individual rats are
presented at the left and the group
averages at the right.
(After Weissman, 1958.)

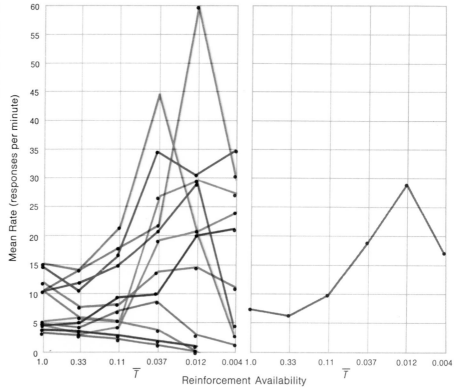

scribe the performance of a "typical" organism and could in no sense of the word be interpreted as a general law.

Experimental psychologists, then, treat individual differences as error, or random deviations from the norm; the field of differential psychology, which accepts variability as its basic subject matter, is concerned mainly with developing psychological tests that will accurately measure individual differences and with studying correlations among traits or test scores. Differential psychologists give relatively little attention to identifying the hereditary and environmental processes that actually produce individual differences. The field of *behavior genetics* treats individual differences as biologically inevitable facts of life and attempts to understand their genetic and environmental bases.

Behavior genetics combines the concepts and methods of genetics, based on knowledge or control of ancestry, with the concepts and methods of psychology and ethology, based on knowledge or control of experience. The concepts of genetics lead us to *expect* individual differences in behavior, because the mechanisms of hereditary transmission ensure that individuals are biologically unique prior to the onset of differentiating experiences.

Genetics can be described as a science of variability, in that its methods are designed to evaluate the manner and extent to which individual differences in observable traits are related to genetic differences among organisms. The question of whether individual differences in animal and human behavior are due to heredity or due to environment has been a source of heated controversy in the history of psychology. Modern genetics assumes that an organism's *phenotype,* or collection of observable traits, depends partly on the organism's *genotype,* or hereditary endowment of genes and chromosomes, and partly on the environmental conditions to which the organism is exposed. Similarly, individual differences are assumed to result from both genotypic and environmental differences among organisms. Before examining some of the evidence for genetic control of behavioral differences, we shall review some basic principles of genetics.

Genes and Gene Action

Every human begins life as a single cell weighing about one twenty-millionth of an ounce. This tiny bit of matter contains an individual's entire complement of genes and chromosomes. Encoded in the genes and chromosomes is a set of instructions that directs the development of a single cell into an adult organism consisting of trillions of cells, each containing an exact replica of the original genes and chromosomes. Each human cell contains 46 chromosomes and perhaps 100,000 genes. The chromosomes are threadlike bodies that occur in homologous (structurally similar) pairs in the cell nucleus. In man there are 23 such pairs. The genes, located at specific positions on the chromosomes, are the true functional units of heredity. Each gene has two or more alternative forms, called *alleles,* which represent differences in the chemical effects of the gene. Genes always work in pairs, in that two alleles of a particular gene (or two copies of the same allele) are located at corresponding positions on the two homologues of a chromosome pair. The combination of alleles present at a particular locus determines the effect of that locus on the functioning of the cell.

Chromosomes consist of three chemical substances: proteins, deoxyribonucleic acid (DNA), and ribonucleic acid (RNA). It is believed that DNA is the fundamental material of the genes. DNA is a highly stable substance but at the same time is capable of self-duplication; thus, it has the necessary properties to control the development of the organism and the transmission of hereditary instructions from parent to offspring. The DNA molecule is composed of deoxyribose (a simple sugar), phosphate, and four kinds of nucleotide bases (adenine, guanine, thymine, and cytosine), linked together in extended chains. According to Watson and Crick, the chemical components of DNA are arranged in two long strands twined about each other in the form of a double helix. Although it is not yet possible to translate individual genes into structural units of DNA, it is thought that the hereditary instructions carried by a gene are *coded* in the arrangement of adenine, guanine, thymine, and cytosine along the strands of the DNA molecule or molecules of which the gene is a part.

Genes exert their effects by regulating cellular processes that are involved in the growth and development of the organism and in the direct control of body functions. The most immediate effect of the genes is upon the synthesis of proteins in the ribosomes, which are tiny bodies in the cytoplasm, or outer portion of the cell. Chromosomal DNA never leaves the cell nucleus; it is thought that a special type of RNA, called *messenger* RNA, somehow takes on the code sequence of DNA and carries this information to the ribosomes, enabling them to fabricate a particular protein molecule. Depending on the types of proteins synthesized, an organism may develop into a rabbit or a human and may develop either a superior or an inferior nervous system.

The most thoroughly explored of the gene-controlled proteins are the *enzymes,* which regulate the rates of chemical reactions carried out by the cells. These reactions combine in a series of steps to carry out the complex metabolic and physiological processes of the body, including the functioning of the brain and central nervous system, which in turn regulate behavior. The manner in which genes and their primary products influence such behavioral traits as human intelligence and personality is not understood in detail, but it must be assumed that the pathways between genes and behavior are complex and indirect, involving a large number of interacting genes and a complicated network of physiological processes. Of course, environmental conditions can influence behavioral traits by producing effects on the same physiological pathways that are regulated by gene action. The same genotype that could otherwise produce a muscular athlete might produce a skinny weakling if the environment does not provide adequate nutrition. Probably the most important way in which environmental conditions produce their effects on behavioral traits is through the process of learning. One recent suggestion, made by Hydén, is that the composition of RNA in nerve cells or neurons provides the ultimate chemical basis of learning. In other words, an organism's learning experiences produce changes in the chemical structure of RNA, and thus in the synthesis of proteins and enzymes, without affecting the hereditary instructions encoded in DNA. This theory permits the genotypic individuality encoded in DNA to be propagated into the learning process (by the sequence of DNA producing RNA producing protein) and therefore has the advantage of reconciling the universal fact that learning occurs in all organisms with the equally obvious fact that there are vast individual differences in the rate of learning, or learning ability (see Chapter 4).

Gene Transmission

The mechanisms by which genes are transmitted from parent to offspring ensure substantial genotypic variability among members of sexually reproducing species. Thus, the principles of gene transmission provide our most fundamental basis for understanding individual differences in behavior.

We have described chromosomes as threadlike structures that occur in homologous pairs in cell nuclei, genes as specific chromosomal loci concerned with specific chemical activities, and alleles as the alternative ways in which the

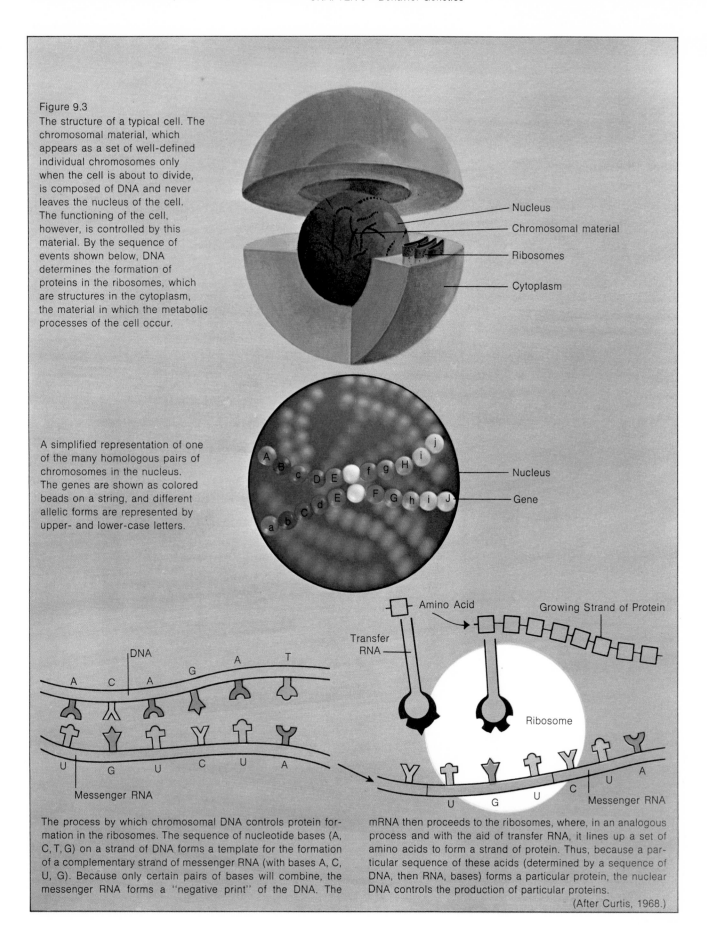

Figure 9.3
The structure of a typical cell. The chromosomal material, which appears as a set of well-defined individual chromosomes only when the cell is about to divide, is composed of DNA and never leaves the nucleus of the cell. The functioning of the cell, however, is controlled by this material. By the sequence of events shown below, DNA determines the formation of proteins in the ribosomes, which are structures in the cytoplasm, the material in which the metabolic processes of the cell occur.

Nucleus
Chromosomal material
Ribosomes
Cytoplasm

A simplified representation of one of the many homologous pairs of chromosomes in the nucleus. The genes are shown as colored beads on a string, and different allelic forms are represented by upper- and lower-case letters.

Nucleus
Gene

Amino Acid
Growing Strand of Protein
Transfer RNA
DNA
Ribosome
Messenger RNA
Messenger RNA

The process by which chromosomal DNA controls protein formation in the ribosomes. The sequence of nucleotide bases (A, C, T, G) on a strand of DNA forms a template for the formation of a complementary strand of messenger RNA (with bases A, C, U, G). Because only certain pairs of bases will combine, the messenger RNA forms a "negative print" of the DNA. The

mRNA then proceeds to the ribosomes, where, in an analogous process and with the aid of transfer RNA, it lines up a set of amino acids to form a strand of protein. Thus, because a particular sequence of these acids (determined by a sequence of DNA, then RNA, bases) forms a particular protein, the nuclear DNA controls the production of particular proteins.

(After Curtis, 1968.)

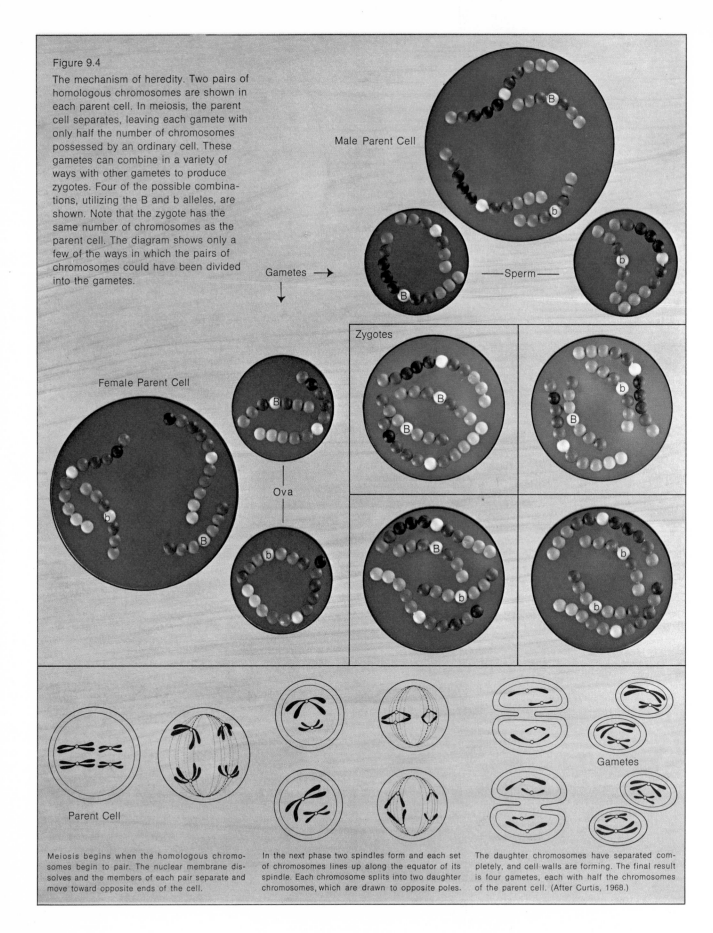

Figure 9.4

The mechanism of heredity. Two pairs of homologous chromosomes are shown in each parent cell. In meiosis, the parent cell separates, leaving each gamete with only half the number of chromosomes possessed by an ordinary cell. These gametes can combine in a variety of ways with other gametes to produce zygotes. Four of the possible combinations, utilizing the B and b alleles, are shown. Note that the zygote has the same number of chromosomes as the parent cell. The diagram shows only a few of the ways in which the pairs of chromosomes could have been divided into the gametes.

Male Parent Cell

Gametes →

—Sperm—

Female Parent Cell

Ova

Zygotes

Parent Cell

Gametes

Meiosis begins when the homologous chromosomes begin to pair. The nuclear membrane dissolves and the members of each pair separate and move toward opposite ends of the cell.

In the next phase two spindles form and each set of chromosomes lines up along the equator of its spindle. Each chromosome splits into two daughter chromosomes, which are drawn to opposite poles.

The daughter chromosomes have separated completely, and cell walls are forming. The final result is four gametes, each with half the chromosomes of the parent cell. (After Curtis, 1968.)

chemical activity may be carried out. Genes are transmitted from parent to offspring by way of *gametes,* or sex cells. Gametes are formed by the splitting of somatic cells, a process known as *meiosis.* The essential result of meiosis is that each pair of chromosomes in a cell separates, and one member of each pair is drawn into each gamete or daughter cell. Thus, human gametes contain twenty-three unpaired and nonhomologous chromosomes. Reproduction occurs when a female gamete (ovum) is fertilized by a male gamete (sperm) to form a single-celled *zygote.* In the zygote, two sets of unpaired chromosomes are combined to form one set of paired chromosomes, one member of each pair being of maternal origin and one of paternal origin. In this way each parent contributes 50 percent of his own genotype to each offspring.

Because the zygote receives a paired set of chromosomes—each parent contributing one member of each pair—it also receives a pair of alleles at each chromosomal locus. If homologues of a chromosome pair carry the same allele at a particular genic locus, the individual is said to be *homozygous* for that gene. If different alleles are received at a particular locus, the individual is said to be *heterozygous* for that gene. As an illustration we can consider a gene with two alleles, T and t, which in humans controls the ability to taste phenylthiocarbamide (PTC). To homozygotes carrying the alleles TT and to heterozygotes of genotype Tt, the compound has a bitter taste in solution, whereas to homozygotes of genotype tt, it is tasteless. The fact that heterozygotes are phenotypically indistinguishable from TT homozygotes indicates that the activity of the T allele masks that of t, preventing the latter from expressing itself in heterozygous combination. Masking alleles are said to be *dominant* over the alleles whose effects they cover, whereas masked alleles are said to be *recessive.* For some genes, neither of two alleles is dominant, so that the heterozygote shows a form of the trait that is approximately intermediate between the homozygous forms.

We have noted that the two homologues of a chromosome pair segregate to different gametes during meiosis. Thus, an individual who is heterozygous for the taster gene (Tt) can produce two types of gametes with respect to that gene, that is, gametes carrying the T allele and gametes carrying the t allele. A mating between two such heterozygotes ($Tt \times Tt$) can produce offspring of three different genotypes, namely, TT, Tt, and tt, in the expected ratio 1:2:1, as each parent will produce both types of gametes in equal numbers and these will combine randomly in the formation of zygotes. The expected ratio of tasters to nontasters among the offspring is 3:1. Notice that 3/4 of the offspring are expected to be phenotypically similar to their parents, whereas the remaining 1/4 (that is, the homozygous recessive nontasters) are expected to differ from both parents. The expected ratios of genotypes and phenotypes among the offspring of other types of matings can be calculated by entering the types of gametes produced by male and female parents along separate axes of a 2 × 2 matrix and representing genotypes of the offspring by cells of the matrix. The expected outcomes of several types of matings are shown in Figure 9.5. Observations of this sort on pea plants were the basis of Gregor Mendel's first law of inheritance, the *law of segregation.* Mendel postulated that each phenotypic trait of his pea plants was governed by a separate pair of "elements," which somehow divided and then recombined when a plant produced offspring. We now know that these elements are the allelic forms of genes and that meiotic cell division is the basis of their segregation.

Mendel's second law of inheritance, the *law of independent assortment,* describes the simultaneous inheritance of two or more traits. During meiosis, the

Parents	Gametes				Expected Progeny Ratio	
					Genotypes	Phenotypes
TT × TT ⟶			T	T	all TT	all tasters
	T	TT	TT			
	T	TT	TT			
TT × Tt ⟶			T	t	1/2 TT:1/2 Tt	all tasters
	T	TT	Tt			
	T	TT	Tt			
TT × tt ⟶			t	t	all Tt	all tasters
	T	Tt	Tt			
	T	Tt	Tt			
Tt × Tt ⟶			T	t	1/4 TT:1/2 Tt:1/4 tt	3/4 taster: 1/4 nontaster
	T	TT	Tt			
	t	Tt	tt			
Tt × tt ⟶			t	t	1/2 Tt:1/2 tt	1/2 taster: 1/2 nontaster
	T	Tt	Tt			
	t	tt	tt			
tt × tt ⟶			t	t	all tt	all nontasters
	t	tt	tt			
	t	tt	tt			

Figure 9.5
Expected progeny ratios for various matings involving the gene controlling taste sensitivity to PTC.
(After Murray and Hirsch, 1969.)

segregation of homologous chromosomes to gametes occurs independently for each pair of chromosomes, so that all combinations consisting of one homologue from each chromosome pair are equally likely in the gametes. Thus, alleles located on separate chromosome pairs also segregate independently to gametes, and traits related to them combine independently in the offspring. For example, an individual who is heterozygous for each of two genes located on different pairs of chromosomes (for example, $TtAa$) will produce four types of gametes with respect to the two genes, namely TA, Ta, tA, and ta. A mating between two double heterozygotes (represented by a 4×4 matrix) will produce offspring of nine different genotypes, as shown in Figure 9.6. If T and t are the alleles of the taster gene, and A and a are the alleles of the gene that produces albinism in man (AA and Aa individuals have normal pigmentation, and aas are albinos), the expected distribution of phenotypes is a 9:3:3:1 ratio of pigmented tasters, albino tasters, pigmented nontasters, and albino nontasters. Note that 7/16 or nearly half of the offspring are expected to be phenotypically different from both parents.

The phenomenon of independent assortment of chromosomes ensures genetic variability among members of a species, because it maximizes the number of genetically different gametes that can be produced by species members. A species with 2 pairs of chromosomes, Aa and Bb, will produce gametes containing 4 different combinations of homologues, namely, AB, Ab, aB, and ab, whereas only 2 different types of gametes would be possible if the assortment of one chromosome pair was dependent on the other. A species with 3 pairs of chromosomes (Aa, Bb, and Cc) will produce 8 types of gametes: ABC, ABc, AbC, Abc, aBC, aBc, abC, and abc, whereas 4 pairs of chromosomes will produce 16 types of gametes. In general, n pairs of chromosomes will produce 2^n kinds of gametes. Man, with 23 pairs of chromosomes, produces $2^{23} = 8,388,608$ types of gametes,

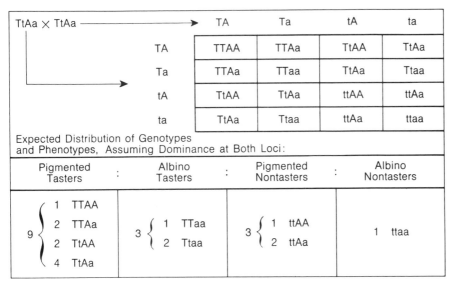

TtAa × TtAa		TA	Ta	tA	ta
	TA	TTAA	TTAa	TtAA	TtAa
	Ta	TTAa	TTaa	TtAa	Ttaa
	tA	TtAA	TtAa	ttAA	ttAa
	ta	TtAa	Ttaa	ttAa	ttaa

Expected Distribution of Genotypes and Phenotypes, Assuming Dominance at Both Loci:

Pigmented Tasters	:	Albino Tasters	:	Pigmented Nontasters	:	Albino Nontasters
9 { 1 TTAA, 2 TTAa, 2 TtAA, 4 TtAa		3 { 1 TTaa, 2 Ttaa		3 { 1 ttAA, 2 ttAa		1 ttaa

Figure 9.6

Expected outcome of a mating of double heterozygotes for two independent genes. (After Murray and Hirsch, 1969.)

each type carrying a different set of homologues. Thus, when a set of parents has two offspring (other than identical twins), the probability that the second will have the same genotype as the first is $(1/2^{23})^2$, or less than one chance in 70 trillion. The probability that unrelated individuals will have the same genotype is effectively zero.

Actually, the possibilities for genetic variation are even greater than is suggested by the above discussion. Instead of maintaining their integrity from generation to generation, as assumed above, chromosomes sometimes break, exchange parts, and then recombine during the course of meiosis—a process known as *crossing over*. This process permits the genes on a chromosome to segregate independently and thus increases immensely the potentialities for genotypic diversity. A second basis for increased variability is the fact that several alleles may exist for a given chromosomal locus rather than only two, as assumed in previous discussion.

It becomes clear, therefore, why individual differences are found in human populations. The hereditary mechanisms of segregation, independent assortment, and crossing over ensure that each human being is biologically unique from the moment of conception. We must remember, of course, that genes, not behaviors, are inherited. The task of behavior genetics is to discover what role inherited gene differences play in observed behavioral differences.

Polygenic Inheritance

Our discussion of heredity and variation has assumed that phenotypic traits are determined in an either/or fashion by single genes. Although the variation of some traits has been found to be governed by single genes (for example, in humans, ability to taste PTC, albinism, blood types), it is now thought that this mode of inheritance is the exception rather than the rule. Most behavioral traits, for example, have been found to depend on the combined effects of many genes acting together. Traits of this type are called *polygenic* traits, and the complex of genes involved is known as a polygenic system.

Generally, single gene traits are those that can be classified into a few sharply defined qualitative categories (for example, taster versus nontaster), whereas polygenic traits show continuous variation on quantitative dimensions. The genes in a polygenic system may be located on the same or on different chromosomes. Each gene in the system is assumed to behave as a discrete unit and to obey the usual rules of transmission (for example, segregation, independent assortment, and crossing over). However, the contribution of each gene to variation of the trait is small and cumulative rather than all-or-none. The action of a polygenic system is analogous to the simultaneous tossing of a large number of coins, where the alleles of each gene (assuming only two per gene) represent heads or tails, and the expression of the polygenic trait is determined by the number of heads. The result is continuous variation among members of a population. To complete this analogy, we could represent environmental conditions as the independent tossing of a second set of coins, such that heads and tails represent facilitative and inhibitory environmental effects; the total number of heads in both tosses determines trait expression. It is clear that the range of variation of the trait will be increased by environmental differences among members of a population.

Nature and Nurture

Psychologists have long debated the relative contributions of heredity and environment to the development of behavioral traits. At one time it was fashionable to take extreme positions in the nature-nurture controversy.

Although extreme statements are less common today, the nature-nurture issue still persists in psychology. In the light of concepts in modern genetics, however, the heredity-environment question proves to be a pseudoquestion to which there is no meaningful answer.

When applied to the individual organism, the question of whether a trait is due to heredity or due to environment is completely meaningless, because without heredity there is no organism, and without an appropriate environment the organism does not survive to display the trait. With respect to a population of individuals, however, it is meaningful to ask how much of the observed variation of a trait is due to genotypic differences among individuals and how much to environmental differences. In the language of genetics, this is equivalent to estimating the *heritability* of a trait—the percentage of trait variance that is attributable to genotypic differences among individuals. Even at this level, we must not expect absolute answers, because heritability is a measure of the relationship between a trait and the population in which it is studied, not a constant property of the trait per se. More specifically, a trait may have markedly different heritabilities in different populations as a function of the degree of genetic and environmental variability that exists in those populations.

Thus, a trait *must* have zero heritability in a population of genetically identical individuals (because none of the trait variance can be attributed to genotypic differences), but the same trait *might* have substantial heritability in a genetically heterogeneous population. The heritability of blindness, for example, has increased markedly since 1800 as a result of the elimination of smallpox and other communicable diseases as potential causes of blindness. Similarly, the equalization of educational opportunities should serve to increase the heritability of IQ scores by reducing environmental differences among individuals. Although this principle is fairly obvious, it is frequently ignored—for example, in statements asserting that a particular trait is 60 percent genetic and 40 percent environmental. One important implication of the heritability concept is that we can understand the genetic basis of individual differences only by understanding the genetics of populations.

Population Genetics

The term *Mendelian population* refers to a community of interbreeding individuals that is reproductively isolated from other individuals of the same species. Thus, rabbits inhabiting a forest in Norway, rabbits in Pennsylvania, Negroes in Rhodesia, and Caucasians in Rhodesia are four separate Mendelian populations, or isolated breeding units. Dobzhansky has emphasized that a Mendelian population possesses a corporate genotype, namely, its genetic structure, which, although clearly a function of the genetic composition of its individual members, nevertheless obeys its own laws of functioning, distinct from those that govern the genetics of individuals. These laws of genetic structure are the subject matter of *population genetics,* which studies relations between the distribution of genes and the distribution of individual differences in trait expression in Mendelian populations. Of particular importance are mechanisms responsible for change in gene distributions, as these underlie the process of Darwinian evolution in natural populations and provide a theoretical framework for analysis of the genetic correlates of individual differences in experimental populations.

The central concept of population genetics is that of the *gene pool,* which is defined as the totality of alleles carried by members of a breeding population, or briefly, the population genotype. If we assume that matings among members of a population occur on a purely random basis, then the formation of a zygote represents the random combination of two samples of alleles from the gene pool. Thus, if alleles A and a of a gene have relative frequencies p and q in the gene pool ($p + q = 1$), the proportions of AA, Aa, and aa genotypes in the population will be p^2, $2pq$, and q^2 respectively—the binomial expansion of $(p + q)^2$. As long as matings occur at random among these genotypes, the relative frequencies of both alleles and genotypes will remain constant in succeeding generations of the population. This principle, known as the *Hardy-Weinberg law,* is a fundamental concept of population genetics because it specifies a baseline against which the effects of change-producing mechanisms can be evaluated.

The mechanisms responsible for change in the genetic structure of a population include selection, mutation, inbreeding, and assortative mating. *Selection* refers to the existence of a correlation between genotype and reproductive capacity. If individuals of genotype aa tend to produce relatively few offspring, then the frequency of a alleles in the gene pool will decrease over successive generations of the population, and the distribution of AA, Aa, and aa genotypes and their correlated phenotypes will be correspondingly altered. *Mutation,* the inaccurate reproduction of a gene in cell division, may create new alleles in the gene pool or modify the relative frequencies of existing alleles (for example, if A mutates to a at a faster rate than a to A). *Inbreeding,* or the mating of blood relatives or genetically similar individuals, and *assortative mating,* where either similar or dissimilar phenotypes mate together, represent deviations from random mating in a population. The primary effect of inbreeding is to increase the probability that offspring will inherit the same genes from both parents. Thus, with respect to a particular locus, inbreeding will increase the frequency of homozygotes (AA and aa) and decrease the frequency of heterozygotes (Aa) in a population, without changing the relative frequencies of A and a alleles in the gene pool. However, if AA or aa genotypes are sexually infertile, inbreeding will facilitate natural selection and thereby produce indirect effects upon the gene pool. Assortative mating may facilitate selection in similar fashion by increasing or decreasing the frequency of the phenotype upon which mating is based. This result can occur, of course, only when the phenotypic trait is (1) to some extent heritable and (2) correlated with reproductive capacity.

Methods and Findings of Behavior Genetics

Much of our present knowledge in behavior genetics derives from laboratory studies of synthesized animal populations. While holding environmental conditions constant, it is possible to modify the gene pool of a laboratory population by such methods as artificial selection, inbreeding, and hybridization and to measure resulting changes in behavioral trait distributions. A significant phenotypic change under these conditions indicates that individual differences in behavior have, to some extent, genetic correlates. Man, of course, is not a laboratory animal and cannot be subjected to controlled breeding experiments. Nevertheless, useful information can be obtained in human behavior genetics by studying trait distributions in populations that have known breeding structures, by recording phenotypic similarities and differences among family members, and by microscopic study of the chromosomes in individuals of a particular phenotype. In this section we examine the research methods of behavior genetics and review some representative findings of both animal and human studies.

Selection   One of the most important research methods available in animal behavior genetics is *artificial selection*. In a selection experiment, the typical procedure is to measure a certain trait in all members of a laboratory population, then select and intermate only animals from the upper and lower extremes of the trait distribution (that is, high with high and low with low) to produce the next generation. Only the highest-scoring offspring of high parents and lowest-scoring offspring of low parents are selected in all subsequent generations. If individual differences in trait expression have genetic correlates, it is therefore expected that the mean trait scores for "high" and "low" groups will show increasing divergence in successive generations.

To illustrate, let us consider Tryon's use of selective breeding in studying the genetic basis of maze-learning performance in rats. Beginning with an unselected population in which maze-learning scores showed wide variation, Tryon mated fast-learning, or bright, rats with one another and similarly mated the dullest rats

Figure 9.7

Relative frequency distributions of maze brightness over several generations of inbreeding maze-dull rats and maze-bright rats.
(After Tryon, 1942.)

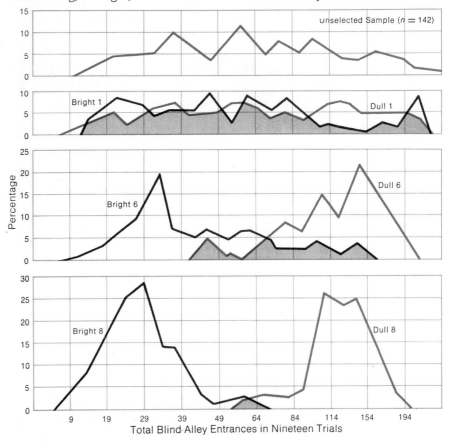

of each generation. As shown in Figure 9.7, the average maze-learning scores for the offspring of bright and dull parents gradually diverged over successive generations. After eight generations of selection, there was almost no overlap in the scores of the two lines. These results indicate that maze-learning ability is a heritable trait related to a large number of genes, or a polygenic system. We can designate the alleles that contribute to maze brightness as plus alleles and those leading to poor maze performance as minus alleles. The phenotypic divergence of the two lines can be assumed to result from the gradual accumulation of plus alleles in animals of the bright line and a similar accumulation of minus alleles in successive generations of the dull line.

When a phenotypic trait is controlled by a single gene, selection for the recessive expression of the trait can be completed within a single generation, as it is possible to intermate only the recessive homozygotes (*aa*) and to prevent reproduction in all individuals carrying the dominant allele (*AA* or *Aa*). Selection for the dominant form of a single-gene trait proceeds more slowly because some of the selected trait bearers—that is, the *Aa* heterozygotes—will transmit the recessive allele to the next generation. Selection for a quantitative, or polygenic, trait always takes place gradually, as in Tryon's study. The heritability of a polygenic trait in a particular population can be estimated from its response to artificial selection according to the adjacent formula, where "gain due to selection" is the average trait score of offspring of selected parents minus average trait score of original population, and "selection differential" is the average trait score of selected parents minus average trait score of original population.

$$\text{Heritability (\%)} = 100 \times \frac{\text{gain due to selection}}{\text{selection differential}}$$

This formula provides an estimate, ranging between 0 and 100 percent, of the proportion of trait variance that is due to genotypic differences among members of a population. Such an estimate is valid, however, only when the phenotypic effect of a certain environmental variable is the same for all genotypes, and the contribution of a particular allelic combination to trait variation is the same for all environments.

The selective-breeding method has been used for studying a wide range of behaviors in several species. Investigators working with populations of rats or mice have succeeded in developing lines selected for activity versus inactivity, as measured by the amount of motor activity in a revolving wheel; emotionality versus nonemotionality, measured by the amount of excretion in an open-field test; susceptibility versus resistance to audiogenic seizures, that is, convulsive behavior in response to auditory stimulation; as well as intelligence or maze brightness versus maze dullness. Other studies with *Drosophila* (fruit fly) populations have successfully selected for phototactic behavior—that is, approach versus nonapproach to a light source—and for either positive or negative geotaxis —that is, a preference for movement with or against the pull of gravity. Geotactic behavior was measured in the mass screening maze shown in Figure 9.8. At each of a series of choice points, the fly must move either upward (negative geotaxis) or downward (positive geotaxis). Flies that move upward at most choice points and reach the topmost collecting tubes are intermated to maintain a negative line, whereas flies terminating in the bottom tubes are intermated to maintain a positive line. Figure 9.9 shows the results of sixty-five generations of selection for positive and negative geotaxis.

Studies of natural selection in human populations are limited by the difficulties in obtaining data on thousands of individuals over several generations. There is evidence, however, that certain behavioral traits are correlated with reproductive fertility. Such a correlation provides the necessary condition for

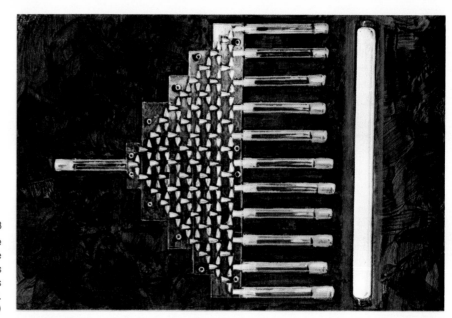

Figure 9.8
The geotaxic maze. Flies crawl through the maze, attracted by light and the odor of food, and are collected in the vials at the right. Small traplike funnels prevent backward movement.
(After Hirsch, 1959.)

Figure 9.9
Divergence of the response to gravity produced by selective breeding in successive generations of fruit flies.
(After Erlenmeyer-Kimling, *et al.,* 1962.)

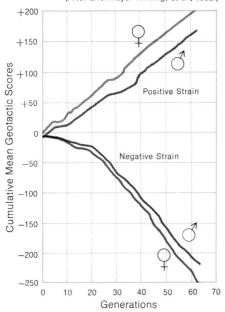

Strain and Race Comparisons

natural selection, provided, of course, that the trait in question has greater than zero heritability. Several investigators in different countries have found that persons suffering from the severe mental disorder schizophrenia tend to produce fewer offspring than nonschizophrenic individuals. This finding, along with other evidence that schizophrenia is partially heritable (see below), suggests that there should be a steady decline in the incidence of schizophrenics. Unfortunately, there is no evidence that such a decline is taking place. Several reasons can be suggested for the failure of schizophrenia to respond to negative selection. One possibility is that the effects of selection are being counterbalanced by the increased psychological stress associated with urbanization and industrialization. A second possible explanation is that the genes contributing to schizophrenia represent a balanced polygenic system. More specifically, it may be that schizophrenia depends on many genes in such a way that persons carrying more than a critical number of adverse alleles are afflicted, and selected against, whereas persons carrying less than the critical dosage (but more than nonschizophrenics) show such traits as inventiveness, imagination, and versatility and thus enjoy a selective advantage that serves to balance the negative selection operating above the critical level. The latter hypothesis is consistent with the general principle that individuals who are heterozygous for a given gene (for example, *Aa*) and thus carry a medium dosage of, say, the *a* allele, tend to be more viable and fertile than homozygous individuals (*AA* or *aa*), who carry either a zero or maximum dosage of the same allele.

Many of the data collected in behavior genetics come from comparison of naturally occurring strains of animals or of inbred laboratory strains. In general, a "strain" of animals refers to a reproductively isolated population within a given species. Wild rats and laboratory rats are separate strains, as are the various breeds of dogs. If two strains have been maintained in reproductive isolation, it is safe to assume that they will differ in the composition of their gene pools. Thus, if there are behavioral differences between two strains of mice or rats, and environmental circumstances are similar, it may be assumed that the behavioral differences are of genotypic origin.

An inbred strain is a reproductively isolated population, usually maintained under laboratory conditions, in which there has been a high degree of inbreeding. As previously noted, inbreeding is the mating of closely related individuals such as siblings and cousins. Because inbreeding increases the frequency of homozygotes (*AA* or *aa*) at many loci, it also tends to reduce genetic variability among members of a population. Thus, an inbred strain is both genetically uniform and genetically distinct from other strains. If intense (for example, brother-sister) inbreeding is continued over a large number of generations, an inbred strain will approach a completely isogenic state, that is, one in which all members of the strain are genetically identical. Under these conditions, all within-strain phenotypic variance is due to environmental sources.

Studies employing the strain-comparison technique have demonstrated the heritability of a large variety of behavioral traits. Strains of mice or rats have been shown to differ in aggressiveness, learning ability, hoarding activity, exploratory behavior, sex drive, alcohol preference, susceptibility to audiogenic seizures, and other traits. In addition to observing behavioral differences between strains, some investigators have undertaken more detailed genetic analyses of these differences by cross-breeding the strains and measuring trait distributions in one or more hybrid generations. Other studies have made comparisons of the response of two or more inbred strains to a range of environmental conditions, in order to determine the manner in which genetic and environmental factors combine in producing trait variation.

In many studies of this type, it is found that genetic and environmental effects are nonadditive; in other words, there is a *genotype by environment interaction* such that animals from strain A show one response to a particular environmental condition and animals from strain B show a different response to the same environmental condition. Wimer, *et al.,* for example, found that for one inbred strain of mice, massed practice (that is, intertrial intervals of five to forty seconds) produced better learning than distributed practice (intertrial intervals of twenty-four hours), whereas for a second inbred strain, distributed practice produced better learning than massed practice. Similarly, there is evidence that either handling or electric shock during infancy produces increased adult emotionality in one strain of mice but has no effect whatever upon the adult behavior of a second strain. The existence of these and other heredity-environment interactions shows that the generality of behavioral laws may be sharply limited by genetic boundaries. Different individuals may obey different "laws" of behavior because they are members of different Mendelian populations.

Human races are Mendelian populations that differ in the relative frequencies of various alleles in their gene pools. The fact that races are genetically different implies that we should expect to find behavioral differences between them, just as we find morphological and physiological differences and just as we find differences in the behavior of races and strains in nonhuman species. However, in any discussion of race differences it is important to remember that populations, not individuals, are being described. The principles of genetic transmission ensure wide diversity *within* races; thus, particular individuals in one race may be phenotypically more similar to members of another race than to members of their own group. Also, it is quite possible that racial groups could obtain exactly the same average score on a particular trait while still differing in the degree of trait variability or the shape of the frequency distribution of trait scores.

Racial differences are already well documented for at least two psychological traits, namely, color blindness and taste blindness for phenylthiocarbamide.

Approximately 30 percent of American whites are PTC nontasters, whereas 6–11 percent of Chinese and only 3–9 percent of African Negroes are nontasters. The frequency of various forms of mental illness has also been found to differ among races and other Mendelian populations. For example, in contrast to most other populations, manic-depressive psychosis is reported to be more frequent than schizophrenia in the mental hospitals of India and among the Hutterites, an isolated religious sect living in Canada and the northern United States. The latter findings must be interpreted with caution because the observed differences could have a cultural rather than genetic basis. A similar caution is necessary in interpreting the well-established fact that the average IQ score of American Negroes is approximately five to fifteen points below that of American whites. This difference may be due to environmental impoverishment of Negroes, to the middle-class bias in the content of intelligence tests, to gene-pool differences between the races, or to some combination of these factors (see Chapter 23).

Family and Twin Correlation Controlled breeding experiments are not possible in human behavior genetics, but useful information may be obtained through the study of phenotypic similarities and differences in families and twins. If genetic differences contribute to variation of a trait, it is expected that blood relatives will resemble one another in trait expression more than do randomly selected individuals and, furthermore, that the degree of phenotypic similarity between relatives of various categories (siblings, cousins) will depend on their degree of genetic similarity. Phenotypic similarity with respect to qualitative traits is usually expressed as a *concordance rate*—defined as the proportion of cases in which both members of a pair of relatives show the same expression of a trait (for example, color blindness, blood type). Phenotypic similarity with respect to quantitative traits can be expressed by a statistical index known as a *correlation coefficient* (see Chapter 3). The value of this measure for pairs of relatives can range from a minimum of .00, indicating a purely random degree of similarity, to a maximum of 1.00, indicating perfect agreement of trait scores. (The correlation of a trait between individuals of two groups—such as IQ scores of fathers and sons—should be distinguished from the correlation between two traits measured in the same group of individuals).

The left-hand column of Table 9.1 shows the degree of genetic similarity, expressed in terms of percentage of genes shared in common, for various categories of relatives. Although a parent and offspring share almost exactly 50 percent of their alleles (because a given offspring receives twenty-three chromosomes from each parent), the genetic similarity between two offspring (siblings) of the same parents will vary from 0 to 100 percent but will *average* 50 percent (because a second offspring will receive a new random sample of chromosomes from each parent, so that the two offspring will share, on the average, 25 percent of their maternal and 25 percent of their paternal alleles). Table 9.1 also shows correlations of intelligence-test scores between pairs of relatives and concordance rates for schizophrenia in relatives of hospitalized schizophrenics.

It is clear that family resemblance with respect to both IQ and schizophrenia depends on the number of genes shared in common. Although this result is consistent with the view that genetic factors are responsible for phenotypic differences, it does not preclude the alternative interpretation that trait correlations between relatives are due to varying degrees of environmental similarity. A basic difficulty in interpreting family correlation data is that relatives tend to have similar environments as well as similar genotypes, so that the causes of

Table 9.1—Correlation of Intelligence Scores and Schizophrenia

Relationship	Genetic Similarity	Correlation of Intelligence Test Scores*	Concordance Rate for Schizophrenia†
Unrelated	0.0%	.00	0.9%
First cousins	12.5	.29	—
Half-siblings	25.0	—	7.6
Grandparent-grandchild	25.0	.34	4.3
Uncle (aunt)-nephew (niece)	25.0	.35	3.9
Siblings	50.0	.53	11.5
Parent-offspring	50.0	.49	12.8

*From C. Burt and M. Howard, "The Multifactional Theory of Inheritance and Its Application to Intelligence," *British Journal of Statistical Psychology,* 9 (1956), 95–131.
†From F. J. Kallman, *The Genetics of Schizophrenia* (New York: Augustin, 1938).

phenotypic resemblance remain ambiguous. It should be noted, however, that Mendel's law of segregation of alleles provides a substantive and a priori basis for explaining the fact that *differences* as well as similarities are found among family members. Given only an unrefined notion of environmental similarity for members of a family, it is difficult to explain how a pair of brown-eyed parents can produce a blue-eyed offspring or why some family members develop schizophrenia and others do not.

Many investigators have turned to studies of phenotypic correlation in twins in order to avoid the confounding of genetic and environmental similarity that occurs in family studies. About one-third of American Caucasian twins are monozygotic (MZ) and two-thirds are dizygotic (DZ). Monozygotic twins derive from the splitting of a single fertilized ovum and therefore are genetically identical, sharing 100 percent of their alleles in common. Dizygotic twins result from the fertilization of two ova by two sperm and therefore are no more alike genetically than ordinary siblings; that is, they share, on the average, 50 percent of a common set of alleles. Like-sexed DZ twins can be distinguished from MZ twins on the basis of intrapair dissimilarities in physical traits such as hair or eye color, blood type, and fingerprint patterns, or, if these tests are inconclusive, by virtue of the fact that reciprocal skin transplants will "take" permanently only in MZ co-twins.

The general rationale of the twin-study method is that phenotypic differences between MZ co-twins should reflect environmental influences alone, whereas phenotypic differences between DZ co-twins should reflect the combined effects of hereditary and environmental factors. Thus, the extent to which intrapair similarity is greater in MZ than in DZ twins should provide an estimate of the heritability of a particular trait in the population studied. Table 9.2 summarizes the results of studies reporting MZ and DZ intrapair correlations and concordance rates for a variety of behavioral traits. It may be noted that, consistent with the family correlation findings, both schizophrenia and intelligence show a large MZ-DZ discrepancy, indicating substantial heritability. The other findings in Table 9.2 suggest that gene differences play a major role in such traits as manic-depressive psychosis, male homosexuality, and extraversion but a somewhat more minor role in the etiology of suicide and psychopathic personality.

The validity of the twin-study method is based on the assumption that MZ and DZ twins are essentially equal in the degree to which members of a pair experience similar environments. Some investigators have questioned this assumption. It is suggested, for example, that MZ twins are treated more alike by parents and peers and that they tend to model their behavior upon one another.

Table 9.2—Behavioral Traits of Monozygotic (MZ) and Dizygotic (DZ) Twins

Trait	Investigator	Intrapair Concordance Rate		Intrapair Correlation Coefficient	
		MZ	DZ	MZ	DZ
Schizophrenia	Kallman (1953)	86%	15%	—	—
Manic-depressive psychosis	Kallman (1953)	93	24	—	—
Psychopathic personality	Slater (1953)	25	14	—	—
Alcoholism	Kaij (1957)	65	30	—	—
Male homosexuality	Kallman (1953)	98	12	—	—
Hysteria	Stumpfl (1937)	33	0	—	—
Suicide	Kallman (1953)	6	0	—	—
Intelligence	Newman, et al. (1937)	—	—	.88	.63
Motor skill	McNemar (1933)	—	—	.79	.43
Vocational interests	Carter (1932)	—	—	.50	.28
Extraversion-introversion	Gottesman (1963)	—	—	.55	.08
Depression	Gottesman (1963)	—	—	.47	.07
Neuroticism	Eysenck & Prell (1951)	—	—	.85	.22

Each of these factors might serve to inflate MZ trait correlations, thus leading to overestimates of heritability. To counter this argument, other investigators have compared MZ twins reared apart from an early age with MZ and DZ twins reared together. One study of this type reported a correlation of .77 between the IQ scores of MZ twins reared apart, and in a second study the concordance rate for schizophrenia in adult MZ twins separated for an average of 11.8 years was 78 percent. The fact that identical genotypes subjected to different environments (MZ twins reared apart) are more similar with respect to intelligence and occurrence of schizophrenia than different genotypes subjected to similar environments (DZ twins reared together) suggests the importance of hereditary factors. The role of environment is indicated by the fact that MZ twins reared apart are less similar phenotypically than MZ twins reared together.

Human Cytogenetics

For many years the normal chromosome number in man was assumed to be forty-eight rather than forty-six. The earlier chromosome count was corrected in 1956 following the development of new and improved techniques in *cytogenetics*—the direct microscopic study of chromosomes. The improved methods of tissue culture that made this discovery possible have also been responsible for increased accuracy in the identification of individual chromosomes and for subsequent investigation of relations between chromosome anomalies and certain human behavioral pathologies.

Chromosomes for microscopic examination are obtained in cells cultured from bone marrow, from skin, or from the white blood cells of peripheral blood. Treatment of cell cultures with hypotonic salt solution produces swelling of the cells and spreading of the chromosomes, so the latter are more easily distinguished as separate bodies. Chromosomes prepared for examination in this way are seen in Figure 9.10; each body is a single chromosome in the process of dividing (during cell duplication). The left side of the figure shows the chromosomes arranged in pairs and numbered in order of decreasing size.

For human behavior genetics, the most important result of the new techniques in chromosome study has been the discovery of correlations between chromosome aberrations and several conditions associated with mental retardation. One such condition is *Down's syndrome,* also called mongolism, which accounts for up to 10 percent of individuals in institutions for the mentally

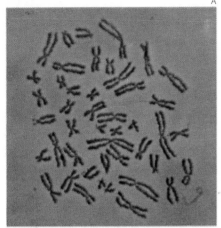

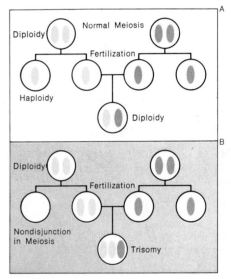

Figure 9.10

(A) Photomicrograph of human chromosomes. (B) Chromosomes arranged in homologous pairs, except for the example of trisomy in chromosome 21.

subnormal. In addition to extremely low mental ability (IQ between 20 and 60), Down's syndrome includes such morphological features as thickness and fissuring of the tongue, flattening of the face, and slanting of the eyes. (The latter features led to the unfortunate designation of the syndrome as mongolism or mongolian idiocy.)

It has been known since 1959 that all individuals with Down's syndrome have forty-seven rather than the usual forty-six chromosomes in their cells and, furthermore, that they carry chromosome number 21 in triplicate rather than in duplicate (right side of Figure 9.10). The chromosome trisomy is thought to be the result of *nondisjunction* occurring during meiosis. Nondisjunction refers to the failure of a pair of chromosome homologues to separate and be distributed to different gametes during meiosis, with the result that some gametes lack the chromosome entirely but others receive it in duplicate. At fertilization, union of a gamete containing two homologues with a normal gamete produces a zygote carrying the chromosome in triplicate (see Figure 9.11). Since the original reports of an abnormal chromosome number in Down's syndrome, further case studies have revealed that reciprocal translocation (exchange of parts during meiosis) between chromosome 21 and one of the other chromosomes represents another mechanism that may produce trisomy 21. It is also known that the chromosomal aberrations leading to Down's syndrome are more likely to occur in the offspring of mothers who are older than the average.

Several investigators have reported cases in which females showing Down's syndrome have produced offspring. Normal and affected individuals are observed in approximately a 1:1 ratio among the offspring of affected mothers. This result is explained by the fact that a mother with trisomy 21 should produce ova containing one homologue and ova containing two homologues in equal frequencies. Only the latter type of ovum will produce Down's syndrome.

Figure 9.11

(A) Gametes produced in the normal meiotic process unite to form diploid zygotes.
(B) Trisomy in the zygote may occur as a result of nondisjunction during meiosis.
(After Hirsch and Erlenmeyer-Kimling, 1967.)

181

10

THE DEVELOPMENT OF THE INDIVIDUAL

THE SHAPE OF YOUR BODY was fairly well decided at the moment you were conceived. The chromosomes you inherited from your mother and father determined not only whether you would be male or female, but also what color your eyes would be, the color and texture of your hair, and the slant of your nose. These same chromosomes also played a major part in determining how tall you would grow, whether your eyesight would be weak or strong, the limits of your intelligence, and, to some extent, how long you would live; but the last two attributes were determined jointly by genes and the environment in which you developed. The prenatal environment is fairly constant from one child to the next—so most prenatal development follows much the same course from one individual to another. A doctor can look at the unborn fetus and tell, almost to the day, how old it is. Fetuses develop much as a flower unfolds—unless the environment interferes, the petals open on schedule. Unlike flowers, however, humans develop socially and emotionally as well as physiologically. Personal development is a process of interaction between the psychological structures and adaptation of the person and the organization of his many environments. How would you go about testing such an idea scientifically?

Scientists have shown that human physiological development is gene-determined by demonstrating that anything other than radical changes in the environment has little or no effect on the way our bodies develop biologically. Psychologists point to the fact that most humans go through similar stages in the development of their personalities, no matter what culture they grow up in, and that most attempts to accelerate or retard these stages meet with little or no success. Both these factors suggest that the shape of our personalities is determined at conception much as is the shape of our body.

Stages of Development

The cycle of individual development begins with the newborn's initial actions. Immediately after birth, the neonate goes through a sensorimotor stage, during which the purely biological organization of his personality is gradually changed into a biopsychological organization through the infant's contacts with

183

the world into which he is born. During this period begins the child's construction of a cognition about himself and about his environment, but it is a highly idiosyncratic or individualistic construction.

Toward the end of this sensorimotor stage, the child begins to make symbolic representations about his world, a development that serves to transform the young child's predominantly biopsychological organization into a predominantly psychosocial organization. Toward the end of the child's symbolic operational stage, he begins to construct cognitions of the actual, concrete, conventional status of objects and events in his world, including himself. Then, during adolescence, the individual begins to be able to perform abstract, formal operations on his world, including the abstract-reflective operation of thinking about his own thinking. This new stage of development allows him to handle possibilities and potentialities as well as actual events in his environment. Then, the final and most mature form of his self-development comes with construction of a principled, logical hierarchy of values that guides his conduct. Such a construction requires that he be able to see social and interpersonal interactions from the perspective of others as well as from his own point of view. This hierarchy of values constitutes the individual's personal ideology and includes an integration of all his ethical, aesthetic, and logical principles. Now let us look at each of these developmental stages in greater detail.

Sensorimotor Stage   The first year and a half of life forms the transition period from biological, purely reflexive functioning to psychological evolution. During the first six weeks, the infant spends most of his time sleeping. When he is awake, however, he already engages in much active interaction with his environment that serves to stimulate his psychological and social development. The question of what the newborn experiences has puzzled students of human psychology for a long time. It was usually answered by something like William James' conclusion—a blooming, buzzing confusion. Today we know better. From some experiments by Bower, for example, we have learned that by the age of eight weeks, and possibly as early as the day of birth, the infant (1) is capable of discriminating between different depths and orientations of objects and (2) perceives objects as having constant size and shape even when they are receding and rotating so that the image they cast on the infant's retina is constantly changing.

Interaction With Environment   From birth there is continual feedback and influence among and between the neonate's acts and his physical and social environment. There exists, for example, interaction between his posture and sucking motions and the posture of the

Figure 10.1
Very young children can discriminate depth and fixate particular objects in their environment.

person holding him and the nipple being offered for him to suck on. At the same time, the child's cognition of his interactions may be characterized as an extreme inability to differentiate among himself, his acts, external objects, and their actions. This initial cognition is featured by a state of fusion or radical egocentrism and means that events are not yet psychologically real for him as differentiated but integrated aspects of his own interactions.

Such observable performances as the neonate's initial tendency to suck reflexively upon any object touching his mouth are of interest to the student of development. They suggest that the neonate constructs these interactions as if he judged all things he is actively sucking upon as suckables. He does not yet discriminate between essential and peripheral aspects of things. In effect, his construction of *objects* is "all such things are suckables." His construction of space is limited to what is immediately contiguous to his actions. It is as if *space* to him is "all things that touch my mouth are suckables." Time is limited to

transient, momentary glimpses—as if *time* were "all things are suckables as long as they touch my mouth." His sense of *causality* may be like "all things that touch my mouth that I suck upon are suckables."

First Reasoning This most primitive form of mentation contains the germ of two types of reasoning that become progressively differentiated and integrated in the course of growing up. One is a sense of *personal effectiveness.* This necessary condition for an individual's awareness of his developing competence allows him to be effective and to influence his own fate. It becomes the person's source of intentionality. It is the mode of causal reasoning that determines the person's subjective, internal reasons and feelings for the nature of events—the purpose he attributes to his experience. Another is a sense of *phenomenal connection* between things that are contiguous in space and time. This is the necessary, but not sufficient, condition for the attribution of the relation of physical causality between things. It becomes the mode of causal reasoning by which independent power or influence is attributed to aspects of the external environment.

In sum, the neonate's experience is initially that of a perceptually constant but conceptually nonpermanent here-and-now world. To obtain some intuition of his state—although it is impossible to capture the neonate's true state—imagine yourself dreaming or intensively involved in watching a movie. Now imagine that you are dreaming of or perceiving a magician making a pigeon disappear; imagine that you felt the pigeon really dissolved into nothingness so that you would not search for it. Then you may have some intuition for the neonate's state of awareness.

Perspectivism We know that such actions as sucking on any object serve, even at the beginning of the neonate's existence, as a postural-gestural sign of the object he is referring to—the nipple that he desires. Although it is one fused action, it nevertheless communicates his desire to get and to take to another, a mother figure. By sharing and giving the child what he wants, the mother is reading his action as a communicative sign, even though he will not understand her actions as communicative. For this reason, communication is a one-way avenue that is only truly available to the nonegocentric participant, the mother. True communication requires the ability to be *perspectivistic,* that is, to realize that there are multiple viewpoints and to be able to take the other's perspective.

The infant's need and desire is to take in, and the people taking care of him desire to give him what he needs. This is the first interactive step toward the child's developing perspectivism. Mutuality of taking and giving is the social and sexual foundation, according to psychoanalytic theory, of the person's incorporating an image of individuals (and their sexual roles) with whom he will identify or whom he will try to emulate. Eventually he himself will become the giver.

This primordial sharing situation has its basis, according to Freud, in the instincts that energize human mental functioning. The instinct to live, to preserve one's self, and to reproduce make up the sexual instinct *Eros;* its energy is called *libido.* In accordance with a maturational plan of epigenesis or unfolding, libidinal energy is focally invested, at birth, in the oral (mouth) zone of the child's body. The primary function of this zone is to interact with the environment in order to incorporate both physiological and experiential nourishment.

Developing Conceptual Awareness As we noted earlier, the neonate's initial experience is that of a somewhat perceptually constant but conceptually nonpermanent here-and-now world. By

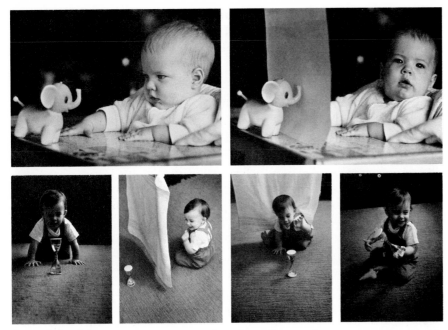

Figure 10.3
Hiding a toy ends its existence for the neonate *(top)*, but not for the older child.

the middle of the sensorimotor stage, when he is about eight to ten months old, his conceptual awareness has extended to the construction of a conceptually some-what permanent, as well as perceptually constant, world. For the first time, the infant will search for hidden objects even after a delay. Thus, objects are judged to maintain their permanence beyond the immediate present, that is, even if they are not-here and not-now. Nevertheless, the infant's progress is limited—is still idiosyncratic—because his attribution of permanence depends upon his own actions and not the action of the object. If a thing is hidden behind a screen on the infant's right, he will search and find it there. If it is then hidden behind a screen on his left while he is watching where it is being put, he does not immediately look for it where it was hidden. Rather, he first searches for it in the place of his original activity and success, that is, on his right.

He also begins to understand that the causal status of his own desires and intentions is different from the phenomenal character of other objects. In one of his many studies, Piaget presented a baby in a crib with some rattles to which a string was clearly attached so that when the baby grasped the string, the rattles shook. Delighted, the baby sought to reproduce the interesting spectacle by pulling on the string. It was almost as if the child understood that pulling the string was the cause of the rattling.

To test this interpretation, the baby was presented with a control condition. Now the rattles and string were both present but clearly not attached. Under eight months, the baby continued pulling upon the string and expecting the rattles to shake. For this reason Piaget interprets the baby's causal reasoning at this point as being magicophenomenalistic. It is only after eight months that the infant both realizes the purposefulness of his own actions and begins to under-stand the spatiotemporal aspects of causality, as was indicated by his understand-ing that the intermediary, the string, had to be attached to the rattles for the rattles to shake.

During this same period the baby begins to construct gestural signals that portray in a playful and imitative fashion the permanent world he is now referring to (see Figure 10.4). Signals are bodily gestures. Piaget observed that one of his

Gestural Signals

Figure 10.4
Facial expressions are early signals
used in social communication.

children would ordinarily suck her thumb before going to sleep at night. While playing with her pillow one day she began to suck on its fringe. This action seemed to remind her of going to sleep, because she lay down in her sleeping position while holding the fringe of the pillow and sucking her thumb for half a minute. Then she got up and went back to playing with the pillow.

Signals also include vocal gestures. Werner and Kaplan report the vocal productions of a baby who at nine months made sounds like *dididi* to represent either scolding or comfort, at ten months *nenene* to represent disapproval, and at twelve months *mjamjam* to represent food or tastes.

With the advent of gestural signaling, the child's environment must be social as well as physical. The relationship is no longer one that could, even in principle, be achieved by a flexibly programmed physical environment. Rather, the relationship has become one of communication, requiring the presence of another person who has the same symbolic function and can thereby communicate by symbols with the child. During this period, the child is particularly dependent upon others for social communication. He requires social communication that will foster the development of his symbolic function so that events can acquire representational meaning as well as immediate presentational significance. Consequently, this may be a critical period during which social deprivation of institutionalized orphans, for example, may lead to lasting psychological debilitation and pathology.

The importance of this period for later social interaction has been especially noted by psychoanalytic theorists. Psychoanalytic theory speculates that the baby's social dependency on others culminates in a crisis of trust. During this period the child is being weaned, leading to a fear of not being nourished. This, in turn, results in a universal crisis between the formation of a basic sense of trust, primal hope, and goodness versus a basic sense of mistrust, primal doom, anxiety, and evil. The resolution of this crisis is said to mark the course of the child's future personality development—whether he will be basically trustful or suspicious, independent or dependent, and competent or incompetent.

Representational Development Toward the end of the sensorimotor stage (twelve to twenty-one months), once

Figure 10.5
Experimenting with the physical world.
Long thin objects will pass through the bars
only in certain orientations.

he has begun to work out a communicative relationship with a conceptually permanent physical and social world, the child is ready to develop a representational, albeit highly idiosyncratic, view of the world. The child engages in much experimenting—for example, dropping an object in different ways and observing what happens to the path of falling. This experimenting becomes progressively representational. For example, Piaget describes one of his children at one year and twenty days who watched him remove and then put back the top of his tobacco jar. The child could have performed the same action because the jar was well within her reach. Instead, she gesturally symbolized the movement of his hand by raising and lowering her hand without touching the jar.

Even idiosyncratic symbolization, however, permits the child to make tremendous advances in his conceptions, such as his cognition of his own intentional efficacy and the phenomenal causal characteristics of his environment. For example, the same child, at a later age, was taken away from a game she was playing and was placed in a playpen. First she cried; then she indicated that she wanted to go "pottie." As soon as she was taken out of the playpen, she rushed over to her game. This indication of her anticipation of the effects of her action was only possible if she could represent to herself the effects of the cause.

Developing Autonomy This capacity for symbolic representation permits the child to extend his scope of communications with others. It also permits him to begin to communicate with himself: he can, for the first time, construct ideas that he can consider and remember. His knowledge, then, can begin to transcend immediate events. Meaning becomes the way in which he represents events to himself. He is, as a consequence of his developing symbolic function, becoming increasingly autonomous in relation to his physical and social environment at the same time that he is becoming progressively able to understand it and to enter into mutual or reciprocal relations with it.

It is in this sense that we may understand the psychoanalytic notion that the child, in Erikson's phrase, begins to feel "I am what I will." Developing autonomy is probably the reason why psychoanalysis has disproportionately focused upon anal activity and toilet training as central to this phase of development. Freud claimed that the child's libido shifts during this age period from his oral to his anal zone and energizes the anal zone's evacuative and retentive functions.

Erikson hypothesized that the child's primary concern is to exercise his anal-urethral musculature by flexion and extension. These modes of physical functioning provide the prototype for the conflicting psychosexual modes of deriving autoerotic pleasure from retention and elimination. They also provide the prototype for the conflicting or ambivalent psychosocial modes of functioning—holding on or withholding versus letting go or expelling. In the normal course of events, the child's anal activities are met, at least in part, by parental attempts to control, inhibit, and regulate, leading to a battle for autonomy. According to Erikson, this battle is between the child's natural tendencies to assert himself and the parent's just as natural inclinations to introduce him to the limits of physical reality and social propriety. The resolution of this crisis will determine whether the child develops a lasting sense of autonomy or one of shame and doubtfulness about himself and his actions—whether he will develop a personality allowing independent yet proper behavior.

We may recognize the importance of anal phenomena without accepting the significance for later development attributed to them by psychoanalytic theory. They hardly cast the long shadow over future development that is suggested in psychoanalytic speculations. After all, anal phenomena represent only one aspect of the child's rich interactions with his environment during only one step in the long process of the development of individuality. Consequently, the results of anal functioning are bound to be overshadowed by the many new forms of interaction that develop during the subsequent stages.

Symbolic Operational Stage The first major shift from predominantly biopsychological to predominantly psychosocial development begins between the ages of one and a half and two years. Its major mark is the shift from overt sensorimotor acts to covert mental acts. Its major instrument is the development of the symbolic function. Its major consequence is representational, as well as presentational, interactions. It is directed primarily toward the progressive construction of the physical and social that transcends the child's idiosyncratic cognitions constructed during the sensorimotor stage.

The major significance of symbolic representation for the developing understanding of actualities is that it permits the child to break up his presentational experience into psychologically meaningful units. Sensorimotor acts do not permit the child to detach aspects of an event from that event and give them independent status. To obtain some intuition of the sensorimotor state of awareness, consider what your own experience would be like if you could limit it to the pure perception of events as they present themselves to you. If you saw a red car moving down the street, you would have no basis for detaching the property "red" from the action "moving" from its location "down the street." You would be recording the presented event much as a television camera does; consequently you could not abstract the property of color or the action of movement as being independent psychological units for grouping into classes that transcend the particular presentation.

For example, it is impossible for a TV camera to group all red objects that you have perceived, such as a red car and a red apple, as belonging in the same class. Symbolic representation, on the other hand, enables you to break up the sequential flow of presentational experience and to categorize it according to conceptual units, such as *redness,* that transcend presentational experience. It literally represents presentational experience according to the different conceptual units that are meaningful to the child during this stage of development.

During the symbolic operational stage, the child's development progresses through three sequentially ordered substages that bring him from his state of idiosyncratic cognitions and feelings to a fuller understanding of the actualities of his life and his environment.

The child's first representations of reality during the naturalistic substage, which lasts from about one and a half to four years, are playful and imitative, that is, naturalistic rather than conventional symbols. Often the child uses human action as a metaphorical, as-if model for making sense out of events. Werner and Kaplan cite the symbolic constructions of a three-year-old who was watching her mother turn on a hot water faucet. The water spurted out in jets, leading the child to exclaim, "O, Mamma, the water is choked; see how it coughs!" The human-action model may also underlie the child's animistic reasoning. Indeed, children during this substage of their development attribute life to all sorts of inanimate things, even stones, if they are in motion.

Naturalistic Substage

■DIFFERENTIATION

A major consequence of being restricted to naturalistic forms of representation is that the child cannot adequately differentiate between what belongs to his inner mental state and what belongs to the external physical environment. That is, the child cannot yet differentiate his subjective state from objective states of affairs. For example, children do not distinguish their thoughts and dreams from external material events that they perceive. When a four-year-old girl described a dream, for example, the interviewer asked her if he too could have seen the dream. She responded that he could not have, but only because men were not

allowed into her room. Her mother, on the other hand, could have seen the dream, according to this little girl, because she was allowed to come into her room at night.

■ EGOCENTRIC SYMBOLIZATION

Children also begin actively to imitate the speech they hear around them. But they can only understand and produce speech in a fashion that is significant for them by transforming it, often playfully, to what they already know (see Chapter 12). Thus, their speech is still primarily in an egocentric form that is natural to them rather than conventional. Consequently, communication between the child and his community is still limited, and others have difficulty understanding him, particularly if they are not members of his family. For example, Werner and Kaplan cite the changes in the use of the word "mammam" by a little girl. At twelve months, she used it as a name for her sister, bread, and cooked dishes, as well as for her mother. When she was seventeen months old, "mammam" also represented milk. Between nineteen and twenty-one months, she stopped using the term for all these things and began to use separate names for each. At the same time, she began to use the derivative, more conventional form "mama" as a specific name to refer to her mother.

Another example of the usage observed toward the end of this substage is provided by Piaget, who tried to teach one of his children, aged three years and three months, that the city Lausanne, where her grandmother lived, was all the houses in that city and not just her grandmother's house, Le Cret, which she identified as the Lausanne house. What the child understood instead was that all houses in Lausanne were Le Cret. Granny's house continued to be Lausanne for the child. Such examples of egocentric symbolization show that the ability to represent is very limited. The child does not yet clearly understand that the elements of a group are independent units that can be classified as parts belonging to a class. A further symptom of this conceptual fusion is the child's tendency to use the terms "all" and "some" interchangeably.

Their symbolic egocentrism makes it difficult for children to detach the essential from the peripheral properties of objects during this substage. As a consequence, for example, although children know that a mountain remains permanent when they observe it, as they travel past it they believe that its shape changes. That is, they do not yet conceive that objects maintain their identity regardless of spatial position. Moreover, events that are clearly distinct and spatiotemporally segregated are understood to participate in each other. For example, a shadow thrown on a table by a screen in a closed room is explained as if it were the result of other shadows—such as those cast by trees in a garden. Necessity is purely subjective because children do not differentiate physical causality from social obligation and desire. They still reason in the kind of magicophenomenalistic fashion where desire influences events, which are obedient to the child's needs.

■ THE OEDIPAL SITUATION

Freud pointed to an interesting phenomenon that he hypothesized arises in all children toward the middle of this substage. He called it the *Oedipal situation* after the Greek tragic hero who killed his father and then married his mother without knowing that they were his parents. Freud claimed that the Oedipal situation was a universal developmental phenomenon that results from the maturational shift in the child's libidinal instincts to his phallic zone. This shift activates his psychosexual functions of intrusion and inclusion and concomitantly activates his psychosocial function of going after desired objects and including those he would like to be by playing their role. Inherent in the child's playing make-believe roles is the danger of competing with his parent of the same sex for the affection and attention of the other parent. Thus, in the Oedipal situation the child wishes to be like or identify with the parent of the same sex in order to usurp that parent's powers and sexual prerogatives. It inevitably leads to feelings of transgression and guilt and fear of punishment.

Consequently, psychoanalytic theory claims that the Oedipal situation and the way it is resolved have two major developmental consequences for the child's life. The first consequence is what kind of identity the child introjects or adopts. That is, it determines whether he primarily identifies with the parent of the same or opposite sex and therefore whether he will develop a normal or abnormal personality. The second consequence is the kind of conscience he develops. The resolution of the Oedipal conflict and its attendant guilt is the acquisition of a sense of moral responsibility. The child begins to introject or adopt the rules and regulations of his social milieu, which is required if he is to obtain pleasure from performing appropriate roles and functions. In sum, the combination of identifying with the parent of the same sex and adopting conventional social rules serves to repress the child's Oedipal desires and resolve his conflict.

As interesting as are Freud's hypothesis of the Oedipal situation and its consequences for identity formation, we know from anthropological research that the Oedipal situation is not a universal developmental phenomenon. The Oedipal conflict does not seem to arise, for example, in societies where the social family unit does not consist of the biological parents but only of the biological mother and an uncle who acts as a guardian. Nevertheless, there are no radical differences in sex-role development and personal-identity formation in such societies.

We therefore come back to the hypothesis that the child's capacities to make believe, to identify the essential nature of events, and to distinguish between his internal self and external reality are limited by his naturalistic symbolic capacities during this substage. As noted earlier, he engages in many magicophenomenalistic, playful, and participatory interactions. Some limited set of these naturalistic interactions may look like Oedipal interactions in certain social contexts, but they are constructions of the kinds of psychological competences he has developed during this particular substage of his development. These competences construct the roles he plays and the identity he forms during this substage. They do not predetermine the identity sex role or the conscience he will form at subsequent stages of development. They await the new forms of competence to construct interactions that he will develop at subsequent stages. From the developmental point of view, the child is not the father of the man.

Intuitive Substage

In his attempts to learn about the actualities of the physical and social environment, the child is still limited in this substage, from the ages of four to seven, to mental operations that are basically intuitive. He thinks and communicates in representational symbols that are still relatively imitative, imagistic, and playful. For example, the typical definitions for the word "bottle" given by five- and six-year-old children are "There's lemonade in it," "Where you put water," "When a little boy drinks milk out of it," and "Where you pour something out of."

■ INTUITIVE REPRESENTATION

Intuitive representation means that the child's interactions are still relatively egocentric because they are determined by his own present actions more than by the actualities of the events. His interactions are still phenomenalistic because they are still tied to immediate perceptual experiences, and he is unable mentally to transform events. The child is therefore limited to considerations of events in the irreversible temporal sequence in which he experiences them.

The child also classifies events in terms of his irreversible phenomenal experience. He begins to distinguish between "all" and "some" and to classify different aspects of events as belonging to certain classes. Yet when presented with a bunch of flowers in which only some are roses, he classifies the bouquet in terms of his phenomenal intuitions. When asked, for example, whether there are more flowers or more roses, he responds that there are more roses.

The child's phenomenal intuition permits him to begin to understand that, in actuality, things, including himself, maintain their identity notwithstanding changes in peripheral properties. For example, a child no longer maintains that the shape of a mountain changes when he views it from different positions. However, the limitations of intuitive reasoning for the formation of identity judgments were revealed by a study in which children were asked questions like, "This father studied and became a doctor. Is he still a father?" Some 58 percent of the five- and six-year-olds answered that he is not. In effect, their judgment was that the person would not maintain his identity but would change.

The child begins to have some genuine ideas of physical causality, as well as ideas of his own motivation, as the source of events. However, his causal understanding is still highly phenomenalistic, as may be revealed by his belief that clouds set themselves in motion by acts of internal force because they wish to move. His nascent concern for physical explanation is indicated by such additions as the notion that once the clouds are moving, they are driven along by winds that the clouds produced by their flight. Yet even the six- to eight-year-old accepts his immediate percepts as true. For example, because the sun and the moon appear to follow him around, he believes that they are following him.

■PSYCHOSOCIAL DEVELOPMENT

This is the period of the child's life when he begins to go to school, whether formally or informally, and when he begins to interact actively with the people in his neighborhood as well as with his family. For this reason, psychoanalytic theory maintains that he begins to sublimate, that is, reroute, his libidinal energy into social acts that require learning cultural skills. Erikson hypothesizes that during the period from five to ten years of age the child's psychosocial functioning is directed toward making and completing things by himself and with others. This activity is fostered by people in his neighborhood or school who seek to enculturate him to the technology of real life by teaching him and by working with him. The central question, then, is whether the child will become adequately industrious, in his own and others' eyes, or whether he will feel inferior and inadequate. If he feels unable to master the basic tools of his culture, he is likely to develop a lasting sense of inferiority, according to Erikson. Consequently, he will limit his interactions and goals to working by himself on things he is sure he can handle. There is the further danger that he may develop a lasting conformist identity and become subject to technological enslavement.

Concrete Substage   The child achieves relatively full understanding of the concrete, but not abstract, actualities of his physical environment and the concrete conventions of his social environment during the period of about seven to twelve years of age. His relatively rigid intuitive phenomenalism gives way to relatively flexible mental operations. His thought is no longer bound to the phenomenal irreversibility of events but begins to perform reversible transformations upon events. In a classic series of experiments, Piaget demonstrated that the child does not comprehend that transformations are reversible until this substage. In one experiment, the child was shown equal amounts of liquid in two identical glasses (see Figure 10.9). After the child had judged the amounts to be equal, the liquid from one glass was poured into a differently shaped glass. When the child is in the intuitive substage of his development, he is unable to reverse mentally the operations he has observed and he therefore judges the amount of liquid in the two glasses now to be unequal. At the concrete substage, he knows that the original amount is actually conserved.

■CLASSES AND BASES OF SYMBOLS

During this substage, children finally begin to categorize objects in terms of their belongingness to a class. They begin to take into account and differentiate the physical quality or intension and the physical quantity or extension of elements of a configuration when classifying them into parts and wholes. Now when presented with a bunch of flowers, only some of which are roses, children assert that there are more flowers. However, they still do not understand the logic underlying the actualities of class membership.

It appears that important features of the child's symbolic representation, particularly the semantic features of his speech, are based upon the child's

Figure 10.9

Children in the intuitive substage of development judge a volume of liquid to be increased when it is poured into a tall thin cylinder.

observations of actual events during this substage. Werner and Kaplan cite the example of a seven-year-old girl who thought that "vanity" meant "a person looking in the mirror." These authors performed an extensive investigation into the acquisition of word meaning. They presented children with a series of six sentences, each of which contained the same artificial word. For example, the artificial word in one series was "hudray," and its adequate translation was "grow," "increase," or "expand." One of the sentences in that series was "If you eat well and sleep well you will *hudray*." After each sentence, the children were asked what "hudray" meant, how it fit into the context, whether or not the meanings they gave fit the preceding sentences, and why. Among other semantic features, the children did not differentiate between the meaning of the word and the actual context. For example, one ten-year-old defined "hudray" as "feel good" in the sentence given above. She then ascribed this context-determined meaning to the term in the other sentences, though it did not fit. "Mrs. Smith wanted to *hudray* her family" became "Mrs. Smith wanted her family to *feel good*."

■ PHYSICAL AND SOCIAL DETERMINANTS

The child's overriding concern with the actual character of events during this stage influences his physical and psychosocial interactions. Consider first his construction of physical causality. For example, at nine to ten years of age, the child realizes that if the sun and moon move because of the desires or movements of people, then they must follow other people besides himself. Consequently, he begins to realize that the sun and moon cannot follow everyone at the same time. He therefore deduces that they follow no one, even though each person sees them as just overhead and following him. Consequently, he gives priority to the spatiotemporal or mechanical properties of events to account for behavior. To illustrate further, clouds are said to move because the winds push them. This notion reflects causal explanation by spatiotemporal contact and transference of movement or force, but it is still based upon the child's concrete perceptions of the actual state of affairs rather than principled reasoning that imposes logical necessity upon causal relations.

The child's focus upon determining the actual character of psychosocial interactions is most interestingly revealed in his attribution of moral values because it is based upon his assessment of the physical and not the psychological features of actions and needs during the concrete substage. Kohlberg has devised a moral-judgment interview that consists of nine hypothetical moral dilemmas and corresponding sets of probing questions. His results reveal a tendency in children at this stage to assess the physical state of affairs and who has actual social power and prestige as the basis for determining who should be obedient, who has the right to punish, and who deserves to be punished. The orientation, then, is conformity to physical and conventional determination of one's social role and conduct.

Formal Operations Stage When the child has fully established the actual spatial, temporal, and causal properties of his interactions, he begins to be ready to construct more formal logical and ideological theories of physical and social conduct. These theories come to be relatively independent of particular events or instances, and actual events come to be merely a subset of what are possible perspectives.

Ability to Reason The first substage of formal operations begins at about eleven to thirteen years of age. The development of the logical capacities that go beyond merely determining the empirical actualities has been studied most extensively by Inhelder and

Piaget. In one experiment on the logical comprehension of physical events, subjects were presented with a pendulum apparatus (see Figure 10.10). The relevant variables they could manipulate were the length of the string, the weight of the object fastened to the string, the height of the dropping point (that is, the amplitude of the oscillation), and the force of the push given by the subject. The subject's task was to determine if he could control the rate of oscillation. The purpose of the experiment was to study the logic of his analysis of this problem, which requires separating the relevant variable from the irrelevant variables. The approach of children at this substage indicates that they are beginning to separate factors but that they still have difficulty varying them in a systematic fashion. That is, they still have difficulty reasoning in a principled fashion that allows them to distinguish and exclude irrelevant variables, all other things being equal.

These same difficulties in reasoning and arriving at conclusions and forms of conduct underlie the child's psychosocial functioning. If we consider the progress in the child's moral reasoning, we find that he is unable to form a principle of

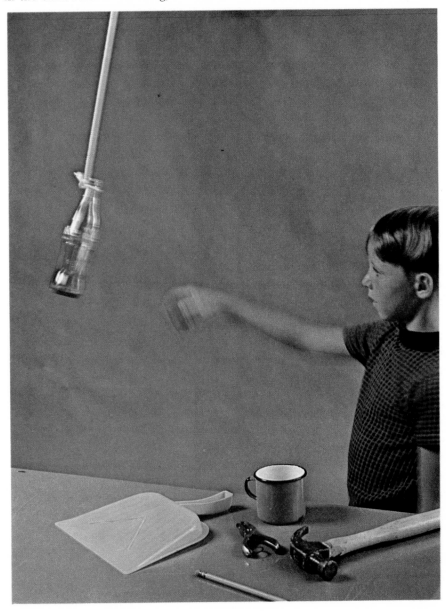

Figure 10.10
The logical capacities required to see how to control the rate of swing of a pendulum begin to appear at about eleven to thirteen years of age.

justice, all other things being equal. Rather, he resorts to conventional notions of law and order and loyalty.

Nevertheless, the competence that the adolescent begins to develop for the formation of possible perspectives begins to allow him to consider the perspectives of others as well as his own. This ability is the basis for his formation of a theoretical or ideological perspective about his own conduct and the conduct of other individuals with whom he is in direct contact. It may eventually lead him to form certain ideological or socioeconomic-political-moral views toward people, his society as a whole, and his place in the family of man.

Development of Identity

The problem of the adolescent is to find himself, to form and maintain a coherent sense of himself and his purpose. Psychoanalytic theory has focused upon the psychosexual manifestation of the problem. It notes that the adolescent's sexual impulses shift to a strange sexual object—a person of the opposite sex outside his family. Adolescence is a period of physiological upheaval, of tremendous bodily, especially sexual, maturation. It is also a period of intensified interpersonal interactions with peers, of the same and opposite sex, and with leader figures. Thus, it becomes imperative for the adolescent to construct his own personal, coherent view of life. The danger of all this for the adolescent's healthy mental development, according to Erikson, is that he may not further develop a sense of personal autonomy and integrity, which requires the formation of a personal identity with a principled hierarchy of values that makes certain aspects of life particularly meaningful to him. Therefore, he may feel lost—unmotivated and incompetent to invest himself in life. The result may be a disabling purposelessness and an inability to take hold, be one's self, and share being one's self.

The adult's social interactions center upon establishing reciprocal friendship and sexual, familial, and work relations. Erikson hypothesizes that the major problem facing the young adult is that of obtaining gratification from intimacy and solidarity with others rather than withdrawing from partnerships and becoming socially and personally isolated. Erikson claims that the resolution of this conflict has great significance in determining whether or not the adult's primary personal aim becomes that of establishing a family and creating a shared household with divided labor. It also has great significance for whether or not he will become an active member and molder of the social order to which he belongs. According to Erikson, the adult who has achieved gratification from reproducing, creating a family, and helping others to grow is equipped with the personal integrity necessary to face the final crisis of life—his own disintegration and death—which requires the wisdom to be through having been, to feel at one with mankind, and to face not being. This wisdom is also what the person may impart to his society.

Toward Principled Conduct

This full flowering of the person's potential for the formation of a mature identity and a coherent ideological perspective is dependent upon his progress to the final substage of formal operations, which involves developing the competence to systematically construct perspectivistic principles. The adult constructs physical concepts and principled moral judgments that appeal to logical universality, consistency, and necessity. He seeks to integrate shared laws with the dictates of personal conscience. Ultimately, he may form a coherent theory or ideology of social conduct and values.

The consequences of having developed to the formal level of moral judgment for moral action are revealed by two interesting studies. The first examines the implications of the person's level of moral reasoning for his conduct when asked to administer an electric shock to another person, who actually is a confederate of the experimenter. The subjects were asked to administer increasingly potent shocks to the confederate when he made mistakes on a learning task. In fact, the confederate made mistakes on purpose and only pretended to receive electric shocks. Although 87 percent of the subjects who were judged by earlier tests to be at conventional, law and order, and social-contract stages of moral development administered electric shock to the victim, by contrast, 75 percent of the subjects who were at the most mature principled stage of moral development refused.

The second study investigated the relationship of political activism to the individual's level of moral development. Among the groups studied were students at the University of California at Berkeley in 1964. One group consisted of students who had been involved in the free-speech movement and had been arrested for civil disobedience. This study revealed that more of these arrestees were at an advanced level of moral development than either University of California Peace Corps volunteers or a randomly selected group of fellow students.

As we have seen, the child's symbolic operations are directed toward the representation of the physical and conventional (social) actualities of his behavior and himself. The adolescent's and adult's formal operations, on the other hand, are more principled and flexible than the child's symbolic operations. They permit thinking about one's own thinking, whereas symbolic operations are more limited to the construction of direct thoughts or ideas about empirical events. Formal thought goes beyond empirical actualities to flexibly constructed theories of the operation of physical events and ideologies about social conduct and values. Thus, formal operations construct the possibilities of the person's interactions as well as the actualities. They construct the hypothetical or logical possibilities that are deductively necessary in order to understand events and integrate them with empirical, inductive means of verification. This integration is the mental basis for the highest forms of principled conduct and understanding that relate one's perspectives with those of others in a logical and moral way.

11

PERCEPTUAL DEVELOPMENT

PERCEPTION IS CONCERNED with how we see, hear, feel, smell—in short, how we obtain information about the world through the various senses. Whether the way we perceive the world depends upon learning or upon the way our sensory systems are constructed has long been of philosophical interest. The question has more recently become of practical interest. If we *learn* to perceive, then perhaps our perception can be modified by changing our early experiences. The implication that perception could not be modified if it somehow depended upon innate mechanisms may or may not be true. It certainly is not a logical necessity. Nevertheless, it is of considerable interest to know what a perceptually naïve organism, such as an infant, perceives if he finds himself in a normal world. Furthermore, the puzzle of how to infer the perceptual world of an infant is a fascinating exercise in its own right. Therefore, we shall begin with a discussion of how that puzzle can at least be tentatively solved. Subsequently, certain aspects of shape perception and the relationship of perception to intelligence in older children will be considered. Finally, the effects of experience on perception will be examined.

When we try to obtain knowledge about the infant's perceptual world, the main problem is one of communication. The infant could be perceiving the same world as we do but simply be unable to inform us of that fact. In addition, because of his relatively poor motor coordination, he seems to be unable to respond appropriately in many cases even if he perceives well. For example, he might perceive a ball approaching his face but be unable to catch it or even avert his head because of slow motor development.

    The difficulty in inferring the perceptual world of the infant is compounded if we expect to learn too much. We might like to know whether or not the

Communicating With Infants

infant's total perceptual experience is the same as ours, but this is a difficult question even if we are communicating with another adult. Success in understanding the infant's perception has thus come from asking simpler questions. What objects can an infant detect or register? What objects can an infant tell apart? Two major techniques have been used to answer such questions. One depends upon unlearned responses, in some cases reflexes. The other depends upon learned responses, or at least responses that do not initially occur when the object is first presented to the infant.

Unlearned Responses

The use of unlearned responses to determine infant activity can be illustrated by a series of examples. First, infants and animals show a reflexive eye movement consisting of pursuit or tracking of a moving object. If a series of objects moves slowly laterally across the field of view, the eye will track in the direction of movement, then jump back in the opposite direction and begin slow tracking again. This movement, called *optokinetic nystagmus,* has been used to measure the visual acuity of very young infants. The moving objects are vertical black and white stripes on a belt moving across the visual field of an infant lying in a cradle. The width of the stripes is varied from fine to coarse. The investigator has to note the minimum width of stripes at which the nystagmatic movements occur. Two assumptions (true for adults) are made: (1) when the stripes are too fine to be resolved by the infant's eye, a uniform motionless gray is seen; and (2) when the infant's visual system can resolve the stripes, eye movements will occur. By this method, the acuity of the one-month-old infant has been placed at better than 20/400 in the familiar Snellen notation. It gradually increases to 20/20 or 20/15 by the age of ten.

A second example of such an unlearned response occurs when a static object is shown to an infant. He will look at it—that is, fixate it—for a period of time that varies reliably for different objects. If infants fixate different objects for different lengths of time, it is reasonable to infer that in some sense they see these objects differently. One determiner of the duration of fixation apparently is complexity. There appear to be different optimum degrees of complexity for infants of different ages. In general, older infants spend longer times fixating objects of greater complexity. A variation of this technique is one in which a pair of objects is presented to an infant. It is possible to observe how long the infant looks at each. Again, reliably different durations of fixation are obtained for different objects, and again, complexity seems to be one important determiner of relative duration of fixation. This method has also been used to measure visual acuity in infants. In such a case, one of the pair of objects is a uniform gray field; the other, a field of black and white stripes. On successive presentations of the pair of objects to the infant, the stripes are varied in width. When the stripes are wide enough to be resolved by the visual system, the infant will tend to fixate that object rather than the uniform gray field. Acuity can be estimated by noting the minimum width of stripes that the infant reliably fixates for a longer dura-

Figure 11.1
Increasingly finer stripes are moved slowly across the infant's visual field until optokinetic nystagmus is no longer observed. The smaller the visual angle subtended by the stripes at this point, the higher the child's visual acuity is assumed to be.

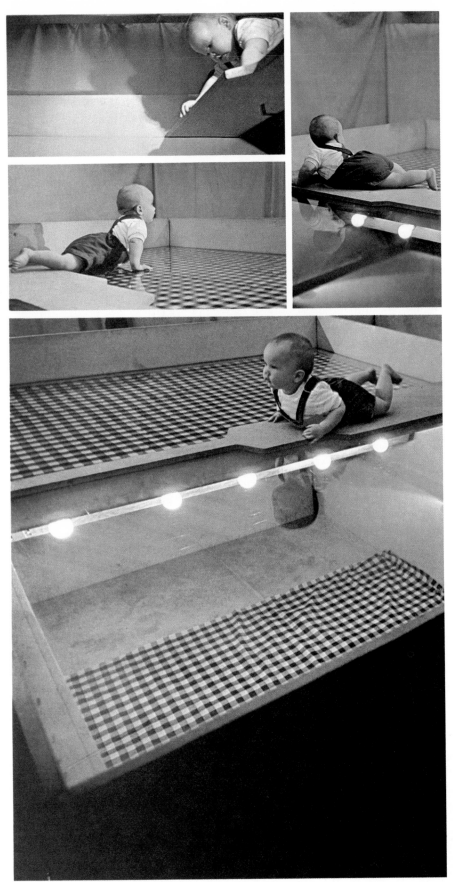

Figure 11.2
The visual cliff.

tion than the gray. Results obtained by this method agree very well with those obtained by the optokinetic method described previously.

A third example of the unlearned-response technique implies the perception of distance or depth by infants. This technique, devised by Walk and Gibson, employs a visual cliff. Infants are placed on a centerboard resting on a large glass table. On one side of the centerboard a textured surface is visible directly beneath the glass. On the other side of the centerboard, the same surface is visible some distance below the glass. Infants as young as six months, when they begin to crawl, tend to crawl off the centerboard onto the shallow rather than the deep side. It is possible to obtain some idea of the sensitivity of infants to differences in depth by gradually increasing the distance of the surface on the deep side and noting at what depth infants will begin to avoid crawling onto that side. Walk found that if the surface on the deep side was as much as 20 inches below the centerboard, 68 percent of the infants under 300 days of age would not crawl to that side.

Learned Responses

The second technique used to infer the perception of infants, learned responses, can also be illustrated by a number of examples. Perhaps the simplest form of learning is learning not to do something. For example, an infant will probably look in the direction of a strange sound in his surroundings, such as when an adult says peek-a-boo. However, if this sound is repeated a great many times, the infant will soon cease to respond; but if a new sound occurs, the infant will look once again toward the source of the sound. Thus, it is possible to infer by the recurrence of the looking behavior that the infant has distinguished between the two sounds. Although this technique has actually been used, the response of looking is not as sensitive as had been hoped. The infant might not look for a variety of reasons.

In addition to the response of looking, investigators have measured changes in heart rate. They noted that upon presentation of a novel stimulus, an infant's heartbeat changes briefly. After repeated presentations, this change ceases to occur, but it recurs if a new object is presented. Thus, the recurrence of the heart-rate change can be taken as evidence that the infant has distinguished between, say, sounds of different loudness. However, the most dramatic use was to show that infants at twenty-four weeks of age could distinguish between the syllables "ba" and "ga." Infants were exposed to a series of repetitions of the syllable "ba." Gradually, the initial change in heart rate disappeared, but it recovered completely when the syllable was changed to "ga." This is the first evidence that infants so young are able to distinguish phonetic differences important for speech.

Another type of learning has been used to show the presence in infants of a rather complex form of perception. Infants forty to sixty days old were trained to turn their heads slightly to the side when a twelve-inch cube was shown to them at a distance of three feet. In order to train the infants, an adult popped up in front of the children and said peek-a-boo as a reward for turning their heads. Once they had learned to turn their heads, in place of the twelve-inch cube at three feet they were shown a twelve-inch cube at nine feet, a thirty-six-inch cube at three feet, or a thirty-six-inch cube at nine feet. When the twelve-inch cube at nine feet was presented, they responded with the head turnabout as consistently as they did in the original learning. However, when the thirty-six-inch cube at nine feet was shown, they responded very little. The significance of this result arises from the fact that the thirty-six-inch cube at nine feet projects an image in

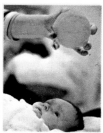

Figure 11.3
Infants will turn to look at a strange object but will not look repeatedly at similar objects.

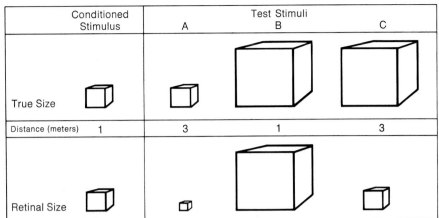

Conditioned Stimulus	Test Stimuli		
	A	B	C
True Size			
Distance (meters) 1	3	1	3
Retinal Size			

Figure 11.4

If the child turns his head to test stimulus A, even though its retinal image is small, he is showing size constancy. If he were to respond only to retinal size, he would turn his head when presented with a larger cube at the same distance (stimulus C). (After Bower, 1966.)

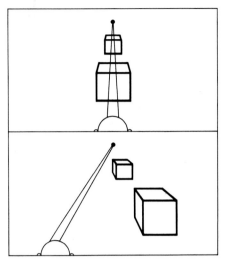

Figure 11.5

Because of motion parallax, our two eyes receive slightly different retinal images of the same object. This discrepancy increases for closer objects and thus provides one of the many cues we use to perceive depth.

Depth Perception

the eye of exactly the same size as in the original training. The low response to this stimulus suggests that they are taking into account the distance of the object and its size at a given distance. The possibility that the difference in distance from the original training caused the decrease in responding was ruled out by their reaction to the thirty-six-inch cube at a distance of three feet. This situation also elicited very little of the original responding. Thus, here is evidence that infants even younger than the age at which they can be tested on the visual cliff are sensitive to differences in depth and perhaps even make use of depth information in their perception of the size of objects.

This discussion of the perception of infants has stressed method of investigation because most of the work is very recent, and the infant's perceptual world has not been mapped out very systematically. We now know how to measure the infant's perceptual world and we have clues that it is much richer than was originally thought, but we still do not know its details.

The indication that infants are sensitive to distance is related to the problem of how we see depth, a question that has long fascinated philosophers and was of primary concern to the early psychologists in the middle of the nineteenth century. The perception of depth is paradoxical in that from a two-dimensional array of light distributed on the retina of the eye, we somehow perceive the world as being three-dimensional. It seems necessary to reason that somehow the two-dimensional information is processed and enriched to yield a three-dimensional world. One group of philosophers and psychologists argued that we learned on the basis of experience to interpret certain cues in terms of a third dimension. For example, it was noticed that in order to view objects that are close, the eyes have to converge greatly, but for distant objects, the eyes can be relaxed and point straight ahead. Thus, it was argued that sensations of strain in the eyes become associated with reaching or walking various distances to obtain objects. The result was that visual information was combined with proprioceptive or kinesthetic information of eye-muscle strain and associations of past experience to produce finally a perception of distance or depth.

Another group of philosophers and psychologists challenged this view by arguing that the brain and visual system are constructed so as to categorize our experience spatially without any necessary prior experience. Obviously, this is a question of the development of perception, and we have just seen that rather young infants are able to utilize depth information—a potentially damaging result for those who believed in the importance of past experience. However, it is possible that rudimentary depth perception is present early in life but that our ability to perceive depth improves markedly with age. Actually, most existent data suggest that children are quite good at estimating distances under normal conditions.

In analyzing how people perceive depth, psychologists have identified a number of cues or clues that can be sufficient. Degree of convergence of the eyes was mentioned previously, but there are a host of others. Some, such as linear perspective, interposition (one object cutting off a view of another), and aerial perspective (gradual blurring of more distant objects), have long been known to artists. Others, such as binocular parallax (the incongruent views the two eyes receive because of their different positions in space), motion parallax (the different relative motions that objects at different distances appear to have as a person moves his head), and accommodation (the change of shape of the eye's lens required to focus objects at different distances on the retina), have been identified and studied by scientists interested in vision.

Much systematic work has been done on the function of such cues in the perception of adults. But because of the tedious nature of the research, which typically requires hundreds or thousands of judgments by an observer, very little systematic work has been done with children. However, there have been demonstrations that children do get depth information from some of the cues. What is lacking is precise information about how much information they get and how accurate the children are in relation to adults. In the normal viewing situation, many of these cues function simultaneously. There is some evidence to suggest that if the number of cues is reduced artificially in a psychological laboratory, the accuracy of a child's perception is affected more than that of an adult. An inference from this result is that children are more dependent on the greater redundancy of real-life viewing.

Perception of Shape

The study of the perception of shape by children has considerable practical significance because it must be involved in the reading process at some level. Moreover, different objects in the world are identifiable mainly on the basis of shape. However, there is one difficulty in investigating shape perception that does not arise in the case of depth perception. In the study of depth perception, it is easy to determine how well a person performs because there is a clear physical metric. A person's performance can be compared to that of other individuals or it can be evaluated under various conditions, and there is a valid standard—physical distance. As was seen above, this possibility permits us to understand what cues are being used. The fact that shape does not have a clear metric has been a stumbling block for psychologists. Nevertheless, there have been four aspects of shape perception that have been examined in children: the influence of orientation, preferences for complexity, discrimination of letterlike forms, and susceptibility to illusions.

Orientation

Preschool children often look at and are seemingly able to name without trouble pictures that are upside down or rotated right or left. It is easy to believe that such children are indifferent to the orientation of objects, a view that is reinforced by the observation that many children confuse such letters as "b" and "d," or "p" and "q." One might wonder how a child can identify objects in peculiar orientations so well when it is sometimes difficult for an adult to do this. Children may be focusing their attention on features of the object that are unaffected by orientation. For example, any object with four protuberances and a few other characteristics might be a horse for a child; it may not make any difference what

orientation the object is in. An adult, on the other hand, may be trained to focus his attention on such things as facial expression—if the lips are curved up in a smile, it is quite different from when they are curved down in a frown. Rotating such objects disrupts the ordinary directional cues.

In an effort to verify experimentally whether it is indeed the case that children are indifferent to the orientation of objects, Ghent conducted a series of studies. In one, she showed children, ranging in age from four to eight, pairs of drawings of nonsense figures. Each member of the pair was a mirror-image inversion of the other. Examples are shown in Figure 11.7. The children were asked in each case to indicate which of the two figures they thought was upside down. Surprisingly, with many pairs the children would overwhelmingly choose a particular member as being upside down. In the case of the examples in Figure 11.7, the left-hand member was the one chosen as upside down by a majority of four-year-old children. In another study, Ghent showed that the speed with which children identified pictures of objects depended on their orientation. Objects that were right side up could be identified faster than upside down objects. Thus, these results do not support the generalization that children are indifferent to orientation.

Ghent has suggested an ingenious scanning hypothesis to account for her results. She suggested that young children typically scan objects from top to bottom. Their attention is also attracted to obvious "focal" points of objects. When the focal point is at the top, its attraction for attention is congruent with the beginning of the natural scanning tendency from top to bottom. When the focal point is at the bottom, there is an incongruency and the child judges the object as upside down. This explanation fits a large portion of the data: for example, the pairs of objects in Figure 11.7. However, some objects with rather definite focal points do not seem to obey these rules, and there are objects that are judged overwhelmingly as upside down by children although they do not seem to have anything that could be called a focal point. It would appear that there is more than one determiner of judgments of orientation. What the other factors are is still unknown.

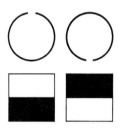

Figure 11.7
Children readily judge the left figures to be upside down.
(After Ghent, 1961.)

Infants seem to be responsive to the complexity of objects. Complexity is one **Complexity**

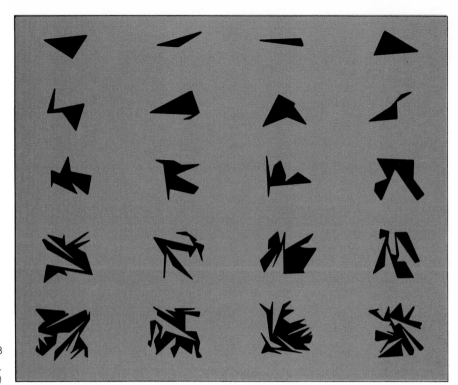

Figure 11.8
Random shapes of increasing complexity.
(After Thomas, 1966.)

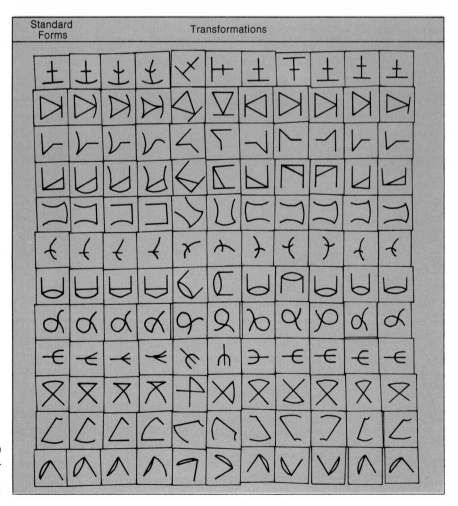

Figure 11.9
Gibson's standard forms and their
transformations.
(After Gibson, *et al.*, 1962.)

aspect of shape that can be measured, at least in a crude and arbitrary way, and a number of investigators have examined how differences in complexity affect the shape preference of children of different ages. In these experiments, nonsense shapes are typically used, and they are generated in a rather unusual way. A square grid forms the basis of the shape. Several cells of the grid are chosen at random, and a point is placed in the center of each cell. The points are then connected to form an outline shape, which serves as a stimulus for the experiment. The number of cells determines the number of corners, and the number of corners is arbitrarily used to define complexity. Examples are shown in Figure 11.8. In any experiment, shapes of different complexity are presented to a child and he is asked to express his preference. Results indicate that for the young children, preference is an increasing function of complexity—the more complex the shape, the greater the child's preference. For older children and adults, there appears to be an optimal level of complexity for such shapes; preference increases up to that level of complexity, but with further increases in complexity, preference decreases. In this respect, adults resemble infants, not young children.

The third aspect of shape perception to be considered here is more directly relevant to reading: the discrimination of letterlike forms. E. J. Gibson and her co-workers investigated the ability of children to make the kinds of discriminations necessary to differentiate among the letters of the alphabet. An artificial set of nonsense forms was constructed in order to study this problem without possible bias by the children's experience with real letters of the alphabet. For each member of the initial set of forms (called standards), four types of transformation were generated: (1) rotations and reversals, (2) changes of straight lines to curves and vice versa, (3) topological transformations (adding to or subtracting from the standard), and (4) perspective transformations (tilting the standard and reproducing the projected view). The set of standard forms and transformations is shown in Figure 11.9.

The first three types of transformation are variations that sometimes differentiate between such letters of the alphabet as "b" and "d," or "O" and "Q." The perspective transformations are never a critical kind of difference for distinguishing between letters. For example, A and ᴀ are still the same letter. The ability of children from three to seven to distinguish between the standard form and the various transformations was assessed. Individual children were shown a standard form over a row of transformations of the standard. The children were asked to pick out all the figures in the row that were the same as the standard. Errors in which children incorrectly picked a transformation to be the same as the standard indicated a failure of discrimination. The pattern of such errors for different transformations as a function of age is shown in Figure 11.10. Aside from the normally expected decrease in number of errors as the children get older, the pattern of errors is interesting.

The perspective transformations are difficult for the children at all ages. The ability to discriminate the line-to-curve changes and the rotations and reversals is poor for the younger children but improves rapidly at about the age when children are beginning to learn to read. Gibson and her colleagues have suggested that the younger children apply to this task the same kinds of distinctions they make in the world of real objects. Thus, topological differences between objects signify different objects in the world, and even the youngest children have learned to utilize these important differences. However, objects seen from different points of view, such as in the perspective transformations or rotations,

Letter Forms

Figure 11.10

Children's errors in matching variously transformed letters to standard letters. (After Gibson, et al., 1962.)

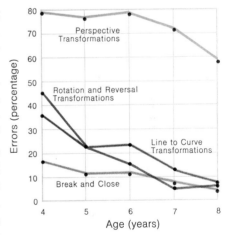

209

are still the same objects, and the young children have not found it necessary to pay attention to these differences. The same is true for line-to-curve changes that, for example, might characterize the same person in different bodily positions but still the same person. In the case of line-to-curve changes and rotations and reversals, children must learn to pay attention to such differences when they learn to read. They do not find it necessary to distinguish perspective differences. The interesting implication of the results, depicted in Figure 11.10, is that children come to pay attention to differences between objects and not necessarily to the objects themselves. There is also some *direct* evidence that at least initially children do just that; that is, they learn the characteristics that distinguish between objects rather than learning such properties as overall shape of individual objects.

So far, we have discussed a method of study that evaluates the performance of children in relation to variations of the stimulus objects shown to them and hence allows us to infer the underlying process. An alternative method of study is to observe directly the behavior of the child while he is perceiving in order to try to understand how he is perceiving. We could, for example, look at eye movements in the case of visual perception or at hand movements in the case of tactual perception. Eye-movement observation has not been extensively used for this purpose with children because it is technically quite difficult to accomplish in any precise way; it is known that people can be observing one thing while their eyes are fixated on another and, at least for adults, it is possible to perceive rather complex objects without eye movements at all. Nevertheless, Soviet psychologists have been interested in such overt behavior of children while they are performing perceptual tasks. Their results suggest that both for eye movements in visual perception and for hand movements in tactual perception, young children (three to four years) tend to have movements that appear random and chaotic in relation to the stimulus objects. Slightly older children (five to six years) show movements that conform more closely to the contour of objects they are exploring. Still older children (seven years) show much-abbreviated movements that begin to resemble those of adults in similar tasks.

In another study of children's eye movements, Vurpillot investigated how children performed a visual search task. Children were shown outline drawings of two houses. Each house had six windows, and the child's task was to state whether or not the objects in the windows of the two houses were exactly the same. One of the results of this investigation indicated how the memory capacity of the children affects their perceptual behavior. The older children (nine years) tend more often to scan several windows of one house before looking at the other house, whereas the younger children tend more often to look back and forth at the corresponding windows of the two houses. In some cases, it is possible to infer strategies from the search behavior of the children.

Perception and Intelligence

The existence of strategies in the activity of the child during perception raises the general question of the relationship between perception and intelligence. This is a question with a rather long history; early intelligence tests were rather heavily weighted with sensory and sensorimotor items. Unfortunately, such items were largely unrelated to behavior that we would intuitively think of as intellectual. Very recently, a number of educational, diagnostic, and remedial programs have assumed that a large number of problem children in the schools are suffering from perceptual or perceptual-motor deficits, although there is not a great deal of evidence for such claims. More careful and systematic research has

Figure 11.11
Perceptual constancy *(top to bottom):* size constancy—when the houses are seen at different distances they appear to be of the same size; shape constancy—a change in perspective distorts the retinal image but not the appearance of the rectangle; brightness constancy—a white cat is still white at dusk; position constancy—although the retinal image changes as we move past, we do not see the man by the road moving.

been conducted on the relationship between intelligence and perception in the context of two classical problems of perception: constancy and illusions.

Constancy

Constancy refers to the fact that an object perceived from different points of view still looks like the same object. The paradox that has intrigued psychologists is that the immediate stimulus at the eye can be very different from different points of view. For example, the size of a retinal image of a person standing ten feet from you is three times as large as the size of the retinal image of the same person when he is thirty feet away, yet you see him as approximately the same size. This phenomenon is an illustration of *size constancy*. Similarly, the retinal image of a plate on the table, when viewed from directly above, has the shape of a circle, but when viewed from a normal eating position, its retinal image takes on elliptical form. Yet in both cases, the plate is perceived as round—an illustration of *shape constancy*. Constancy, then, like depth perception, is one of those perceptual phenomena in which our perception seems to be better than it ought to be on the basis of an analysis of the retinal image. Also, like depth perception, one resolution of the paradox is the possibility that the nonveridical (incorrect) retinal information has to be corrected by the perceiver on the basis of his past experience or additional current information. It would therefore seem reasonable to expect the degree of constancy to increase through childhood as children gain more experience. Simply put, when young children view people on the ground from the top of a large building, they might perceive them to be the size of ants, whereas older children would perceive them to be their actual size.

In systematic studies of size constancy, the expected increase in constancy as a function of age was found. Perhaps even more impressive was the finding that the greatest discrepancy in degree of size constancy between younger and older children was at the longer distances. Apparently, at short distances—at which presumably even young children have had much experience—size constancy is no problem. It is only when the younger children are faced with size judgments of objects far away, where their experience is presumably less, that they show any deficiency.

It would also seem reasonable to expect that the degree of size constancy would be greater with greater intelligence. If size constancy does actually involve some kind of correction of an incorrect retinal image, more intelligent people might be expected to make this correction better than less intelligent. Here the results have not generally supported the hypothesis. The question of the relationship between intelligence and size constancy was investigated by trying to rule out the effects of age; at least with children, intelligence typically varies with age and experience. The age effect was ruled out by comparing retarded and normal subjects of the same chronological age. No difference in size constancy was found. When retarded and normal subjects of approximately the same mental age but different chronological ages were tested, the older subjects showed higher constancy. The greater size constancy of older children was again found, but there was no support for the hypothesis of an intellectual or cognitive relationship with constancy. The results still do not resolve in any final way the question of if and how prior experience might be involved in the development of constancy in children. There could be some maturational process going on through childhood that could account for the changes in constancy, or they might be accounted for by experience that affected something other than the traditional intellectual processes.

Illusions   The phenomenon of constancy illustrates a process in which perception is more accurate than one would expect. Illusions are a phenomenon in which perception seems to be worse than one would expect. Perhaps the most familiar illusion is that of motion pictures, in which a series of still pictures are perceived as a continuous scene (see Chapter 18). Less familiar but equally striking are the geometric illusions that psychologists have carefully studied. Typical of these are the Müller-Lyer and Ponzo illusions shown in Figure 11.12. Because the perception of such figures does not correspond to the information at the eye (or, in

Figure 11.12

Illusions. In (A) the Müller-Lyer and
(B) the Ponzo illusions, the subtended lines
appear to be of unequal length. The sides
of a square within concentric circles
(C) appear to bend inward. In (D) the
Poggendorf illusion, the two halves of the
diagonal line do not appear to be aligned.
(After Carraher and Thurston, 1966.)

this case, to physical reality), some psychologists have reasoned that the retinal image stimulation must be modified on the basis of other information, such as that from prior experience. In the case of the illusions in Figure 11.12, one hypothesis as to why they occur is that people interpret the line drawings as perspective representations of three-dimensional stimuli. For example, in the Müller-Lyer illusion, the *A* member represents a sawhorselike object with the top close to the observer and the legs extending away, whereas the *B* member represents a sawhorse with the top away from the observer and the legs extending toward him. In such an illusion, the observer registers as equal the images of the two really equal segments *A* and *B* on his retina. Then, in producing his ultimate percept, he resolves the question of how two segments at different distances could give rise to equal retinal images: the one farther away must actually be larger. This "answer" appears in the resultant perception. The whole process must be unconscious, because no observer ever reports that he is actually consciously working through such an inference. One hypothesis is that such an inference should increase as a function of experience in interpreting line drawings as representations of three-dimensional objects. Such an inference should also increase as a function of experience in viewing the right angles of objects like sawhorses and the corners of rooms and buildings when they are projected to the retina as oblique angles.

The Ponzo illusion portrayed in Figure 11.12 is thought by some to occur because both segments are embedded in the series of lines projecting toward a vanishing point on the left, giving rise to an impression of distance from linear perspective. Again, segments *B* and *A* project to the eye equal line segments, but *B* is inferred as farther away because it is closer to the vanishing point. As in the Müller-Lyer illusion, if two stimuli project equal images to the eye and one is farther away, it must be larger. The same age trend then might be predicted for the Ponzo illusion as for the Müller-Lyer illusion. As a person gains more experience in interpreting linear perspective cues in line drawings or registering real distance, the illusion should become more compelling.

The results of developmental studies, however, go in opposite directions. The magnitude of the Ponzo illusion does increase in children as a function of age, but the magnitude of the Müller-Lyer decreases. A rather striking confirmation of the age trend in susceptibility to the Ponzo illusion was reported by experimenters who examined the magnitude of the Ponzo illusion in adults who were hypnotically age-regressed to nine years and five years of age. The results obtained from the hypnotized subjects showed the same age trend as that obtained from subjects of truly different ages, that is, an increase in magnitude of illusion as a function of age. This study notwithstanding, the different direction of age trends for the Müller-Lyer and Ponzo illusions makes untenable the general hypothesis of the effects of prior experience in producing these illusions. An analogous phenomenon is analyzed in Figure 11.13.

Another contemporary view of the relation of intelligence to susceptibility to illusions is that held by Pollack. Following Piaget, Pollack grouped illusions according to whether they increased or decreased in magnitude with age. He noted that many of the illusions that showed an increase with age involved a successive comparison of parts of a figure by an observer rather than a simultaneous comparison. An example of such an illusion is the Uznadze illusion: if two concentric circles are presented successively, the inner circle after the outer circle, the inner circle appears to be smaller than it really is. (In an impressive demonstration of the generality of the observation about successive versus simul-

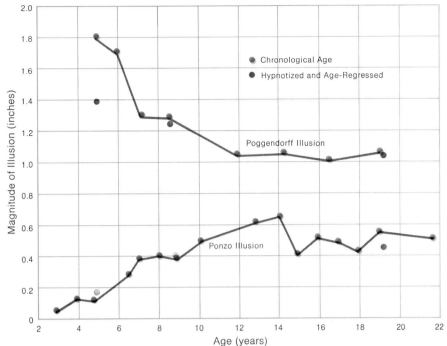

Figure 11.13
Susceptibility to the Ponzo and Poggendorf illusions as a function of chronological age and hypnotically induced age regression. The Poggendorf illusion shows the same age trend as the Müller-Lyer, opposite to the trend for the Ponzo. The inconsistency of age trends in illusion susceptibility is not well understood.
(After Parish, *et al.*, 1968.)

taneous comparisons, Pollack devised a successive form of the Müller-Lyer illusion. When this form of the illusion was presented to children of different ages, the magnitude of the illusion increased with age, reversing the usual trend.) Pollack suggests that such phenomena, which seem to show similar age trends and involve integrating information across time, are related to intellectual ability. He has found remarkably high correlations between susceptibility to such illusions and intelligence-test scores. On the other hand, a number of illusions that decrease with age and do not involve temporal integration show very little relation to intelligence. It is not surprising to find that intellectual ability is related to ability to make perceptual comparisons successively or across time. However, why this temporal integration is accompanied by a greater magnitude of illusion is not clear. It gives rise to the deduction that the intelligent people are less stimulus-bound, more illusory.

Thus far, we have focused on normative aspects of children's perception; that is, perception of children of different ages has been described. Suggestions have been made about the effects of prior experience on perception, but few data have been described in which the effects of early experience on perception have been directly assessed experimentally. Obviously, drastic manipulations of the environment in order to assess effects on perception cannot be carried out on humans. Indeed, even mild manipulations of environment should not be carried out on humans unless there is good evidence that they are beneficial or at least not harmful. It is possible to modify the environments of animals and study the effects of such manipulation on their later perception. Although one must be very cautious in extrapolating the results of such experiments to humans, they at least provide clues for possible effects at the human level.

The first experiments manipulating early perceptual environments were done in the hope of answering such ultimate questions as whether perception was learned or innate. However, the question has turned out to be too complicated to be answered by a few simple experiments and, in fact, will not yield a yes or no answer in the end anyway. In the first place, there are so many components of

Perceptual Modification

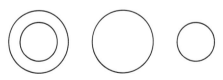

Figure 11.14
The Uznadze illusion. Is the smaller of the two circles to the right the same size as the inner circle in the figure to the left?

perception that the task of proving a general statement that perception is learned would be monumental. More important, however, is evidence that heredity and environment interact in so many complex ways that it is meaningless to talk about heredity in the absence of environment or environment in the absence of organismic structure (see Chapter 9). Research focusing on smaller, more manageable questions is beginning to show how heredity and environment interact in perceptual development. Generally speaking, there are three ways that the perceptual environment can be modified: by impoverishment, enrichment, or rearrangement.

Impoverishment The most obvious perceptual impoverishment is total deprivation, which is relatively easy to accomplish with vision: animals can be raised in complete darkness. In one set of studies, rats were raised in the dark for ninety days and were then tested on the visual cliff described earlier. They showed the same positive preference for the shallow side and avoidance of the deep side of the cliff as normally reared rats. These rats, however, did show a deficit in their response to texture as a cue for depth. Kittens who were raised in the dark for twenty-six days, on the other hand, seemed to be functionally blind, stumbling off the centerboard indiscriminately; that is, they showed no particular preference or apparent discrimination of depth when first exposed to the light. However, they did develop the normal preference after living in light for several days. The perception of a chimpanzee raised in the dark for the first year of life was clearly deficient, but it turned out that such drastic deprivation had resulted in damage to the visual system. A second experiment was carried out in which a chimpanzee was raised without patterned visual experience but did receive daily ninety-minute periods of exposure to diffuse light. Such treatment prevented obvious damage to the visual system. Nevertheless, the chimp's size and shape perception were deficient, though its color perception was normal. Thus, complete visual deprivation seems to lead to deficits in perception, at least for the animals higher on the phylogenetic scale.

It is not clear whether total absence of patterned visual stimulation is necessary to produce these effects or whether there are specific components of necessary visual experience. A number of experimenters have addressed themselves to this question. Riesen and Aarons raised different groups of kittens in four different environments for the first fourteen weeks of life: one group was given an hour per day of diffuse unpatterned visual stimulation; a second was given one hour per day of patterned stimulation, but with their heads held immobile during that period of time; a third group was given one hour per day of patterned stimulation with freedom of movement; and a fourth group was raised normally in the laboratory with much patterned stimulation and freedom of movement in their cages. Between fourteen and eighteen weeks of age, the kittens were trained to discriminate between a stationary and moving object and to discriminate between the relative brightness of two objects. There was no difference in the four groups in the brightness discrimination. However, the third and fourth groups were better in the discrimination between a stationary and moving form. Apparently at least some freedom of movement in the presence of patterned stimulation (third group) is necessary for the normal development of the ability to distinguish stationary and moving visual forms.

An experiment by Held and Hein suggests that such experience is also necessary for the normal development of depth discrimination. These investigators raised kittens in the dark until approximately ten weeks of age. At that age, the kittens were divided into two groups: actives and passives. For three hours a day an active kitten and a passive kitten were linked together at opposite ends of a pivoted bar. The bar was set inside a vertically striped cylinder, and the kittens were harnessed in such a way that every action of the active kitten moved the passive kitten through an equal distance. The passive kittens were raised off the floor and so could not move themselves. The experimental situation is shown in Figure 11.15. Because of the uniformly striped cylinder, the visual stimulation for the active and passive kittens was approximately identical. The difference was that in the case of the active animals, the changes in patterning of stimulation were correlated with their own movements. In the case of the passive kittens, any movements were essentially uncorrelated with changes in visual stimulation because these depended on the movement of the active kitten. Results of visual-cliff testing of these kittens as well as other tests of depth perception showed that the passive kittens, in contrast to the active ones, show no discrimination of depth. Held and Hein interpret their results to mean that visual feedback from self-produced movement is necessary for normal perceptual development.

The enrichment technique is typified by an experiment conducted by Gibson and Walk. Rats were raised in cages on the sides of which were hung metal triangles and circles. The performance of these rats in learning to discriminate between triangles and circles when they had reached ninety days of age was clearly better than rats raised without such objects. The triangles and circles used in the discrimination test were actually stimuli painted on a background rather than the cutouts that were hung on the cages during the rearing or exposure period. A series of subsequent experiments by the same investigators sug-

Enrichment

Figure 11.15
Through the arm and chair arrangement shown, movements of the active kitten in every plane produce similar movements for the passive kitten.
(After Held and Hein, 1963.)

217

Figure 11.16

A playroom for monkeys. Exposure to such an environment may be necessary for normal perceptual development.

gested that the exposure stimuli had to be distinct objects; that is, they could not be painted figures like the ones used in the discrimination test. In interpreting their results, the investigators point out that the characteristics that the relatively flat cutout objects have in contrast to painted figures are edges at a depth from the background. As the animals move in relation to these edges, they provide motion parallax. Again, feedback from self-produced movement seems to be a significant factor.

Rearrangement

The technique of rearrangement is typified by experiments that employ systematic visual distortion. One frequently used distortion is that produced by wedge prisms, which, when worn as spectacles, optically displace all objects in the visual field toward the apex of the prism. Thus, if the wedge prisms are oriented with the base or thick portion toward the left and the apex toward the right, all objects will appear farther toward the right than they really are. In trying to reach or to obtain objects, the subjects, at least initially, will be off target. After some exposure, organisms may adapt or adjust to the distortion. If an animal is raised with such a distorting device and does not adjust, it might be inferred that the spatial-directional system involved is innate. If he does adjust, then the system is experientially determinable. Actually, the inferences probably cannot be that strong, except possibly in the case of nonmodifiability. In only one study has anyone actually raised animals under conditions of rearrangement. In his study, Hess raised chickens for several days after hatching with prisms that displaced objects about seven degrees to the side. The chicks, of course, initially missed the grains at which they pecked. More importantly, they never adjusted to the displacement, suggesting that their perception was determined by an inherent, unmodifiable mechanism.

Although only one early experiment has been done using a rearrangement procedure, a large number of studies of adult humans have been conducted with distorting devices. Of course, studies of adults must be applied with caution to developmental questions. However, the work of Held and his colleagues is particularly relevant here. Held has found that human adults adapt to the optical displacement of prisms to a greater degree (and possibly only) if they actively move about and experience the changing pattern of visual stimulation that is contingent upon their self-produced movement. The fact that feedback from self-produced movement has proved important in normal perceptual development in deprivation, enrichment, and now rearrangement experiments with human adults suggests that it is a very important specific component of visual experience.

Although most early-experience studies are conducted for obvious reasons with animals, it is possible to take advantage of natural situations of deprivation to try to assess the effects of various kinds of early experiences on adult human behavior. There also have been a few studies in which the perceptual experience of children has been systematically and purposefully altered and the effects on perceptual development studied. The most dramatic of the natural situations examined is the study of congenitally blind cataract patients whose sight has been restored. Senden reviewed a large number of such cases, obtained from sources ranging from medical reports to newspaper articles. His review, which suggested that such patients have great difficulty in learning to perceive visual shape, must be interpreted cautiously because the cases were obtained from nonscientific sources. However, one careful scientific examination of such a patient has been carried out by Gregory and Wallace. Their results indicated that the patient could visually identify shapes with which he was tactually familiar, for example, upper-case letters. He could not identify complex visual stimuli such as the expressions on people's faces. He also could see objects in depth, although his distance scale was somewhat distorted.

Knowledge of the effects of early perceptual experience on the perceptual development of humans could be of immense practical importance. A good many of the early-experience programs such as Head Start have as part of their goals enriched stimulation of children. There is some evidence that increased stimulation—for example, of institutionalized children—will increase their intellectual performance. However, the only evidence of such effects on perceptual development comes from the work of White. He enriched the environment of institutionalized infants by simply increasing the amount of stimulation: they were handled an increase of twenty minutes per day in one case, and specific attention-attracting objects were introduced into their cribs in another case. The increased fondling of the infants had the effect of increasing the amount of their visual attention or looking behavior. By introducing into and removing the specific objects from their cribs at various times, White was able to accelerate or retard the normal course of the perceptual-motor development of their reaching behavior.

The typical enrichment programs being carried out in this country are very general in nature. Neither the intervention nor the analysis of effects can be very specific. However, if such massive enrichment yields substantial effects on perception, it will be theoretically important to undertake analytical investigations to help us understand specifically what is producing the effects.

Effects of Early Experience on Humans

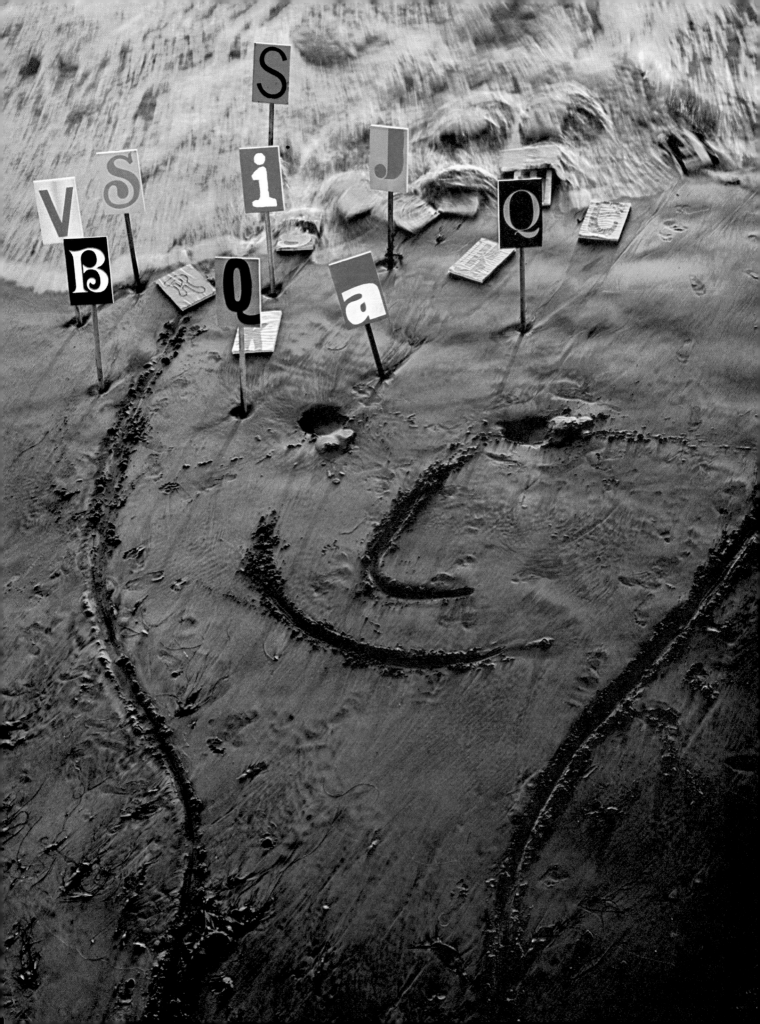

12

LINGUISTIC AND COGNITIVE DEVELOPMENT

HUMAN CULTURE, with its vast systems of social organization, technology, and ways of thinking, rests in deeply fundamental ways upon the existence and use of language. Because we can tell ourselves what we want and can interpret the world in words, we are not slaves to immediate biological impulses at all times. Man can work ceaselessly for verbally formulated goals, can fight and die for symbols, can torture himself with fears, and can formulate the loftiest intellectual and aesthetic creations. In this chapter, we shall attempt to explore these ideas and follow up some of them in greater detail. To what extent are man's thought and action actually molded by language? How does the ability to speak affect the course of mental development in the child? And do people who speak different languages necessarily think differently?

The ancient question of whether or not thought and speech are inseparable still has not received a definitive answer in the annals of philosophy or psychology. The most extreme affirmative answer to the question was formulated by John B. Watson, the father of American behaviorist psychology, who stated that thought processes are really motor habits in the larynx. The assertion that thought is no more than covert speaking stemmed from the early reluctance of American behaviorism to postulate any intervening variables between stimulus and response.

A middle position has a rich history in Russian psychology. One of the earliest scientific hypotheses regarding this problem was put forward in 1863 by Ivan M. Sechenov, the innovative Russian physiologist and mentor of Pavlov, who held that language and thought are closely linked in childhood but that in the course of development, adult thinking becomes free of language in some ways—at least free of overt or covert speech responses.

Completely opposed to the behaviorist tradition is the work of Jean Piaget and his colleagues in Geneva, Switzerland, discussed in greater detail in Chapter

10. It is the position of Piaget's school that cognition follows its own laws of development in the child and that, more often than not, the development of language follows the development of thought, perhaps amplifying and extending processes of intellect but not forming those processes or their underlying structure to any significant degree.

Thought, Speech, and Language

Before we deal with questions of human development, let us ask whether or not any sort of intelligent, higher-order cognitive processes can occur in the absence of language. First, however, we must be careful to distinguish between *language* and *speech.* Language is an abstract system of word meanings and syntactic structures, whereas speech is the actual physical process of uttering sounds. Watson's position actually equates *speech* and *thought,* but the more cognitive approach of Piaget relates inner structures of *language* to *thought,* without necessarily implying that these inner structures need be reflected in the articulatory movements of the speech apparatus.

There are many arguments against the strong Watsonian hypothesis, the most obvious of which seems to come from the implication that a man who had no use of his speech musculature would lose the ability to think. Striking counterevidence has been presented in experiments in which subjects have retained their ability to think even when totally paralyzed by the drug curare.

Although the naïve equation of speech and thought can be dismissed, the question persists of whether or not it is possible to think without inner speech—that is, without some internal mediation of language, even if not articulated. A number of thought processes seem to be prelinguistic or nonlinguistic. Everyone is certainly familiar with the unpleasant phenomenon of groping for a word or trying to find the best way to express himself. Why would we ever have to grope for words if thought were simply a matter of inner speech? The Soviet psychologist Vygotsky expressed this matter well when he stated that thought is not merely expressed by means of words—thought comes into existence through them. Clearly, one cannot *equate* thought with either speech or language, but language nevertheless must play an important role in some cognitive processes. One of the clearest areas in which such a role can be seen is in studies of memory, which have often been conceptualized in terms of verbal mediation.

Language and Memory

There are three problems with memory—acquisition, storage, and retrieval. Assuming that material is acquired and somehow stored, how do you get back to it when you need it? In this regard a very puzzling aspect of retrieval is the problem of remembering early childhood experiences. Most people cannot remember much, if anything, of their personal lives before the age of two or three. Why should it be that autobiographical memory is so poor for very early experiences?

Freud believed that early memories are repressed because of the shame and guilt associated with infantile sexuality. The question to be raised here is whether we simply repress childhood memories or whether they are inaccessible to retrieval because of other, more "cognitive" reasons. This problem has been discussed at length by the psychologist Ernest Schachtel, whose analysis is well worth reviewing in the light of the role played by language in memory.

Schachtel has two principal objections to the Freudian interpretation. First, he asks why the repression of sexuality should lead to the repression of *all* memories of very early childhood. Second, he points out that it is generally impossible to resurrect such memories, either through psychoanalysis or by other means. The child's way of perceiving the world is so different from the adult's that the two are almost mutually incomprehensible. Note how difficult it is for us to imagine what a child, much less an infant, is really thinking and feeling. As we shall see in Chapter 18, adults tend to code and remember their experiences in linguistic and symbolic terms. Because we cannot very well remember an entire event, we seem to store a short description or label of the event and try to reconstruct it later in memory from this label.

In this sense it is probably true that *memory* is more governed by conventional patterns than is perception or direct experience. Adult memory of life experiences tends to follow certain cultural forms—what Schachtel calls signposts. In recounting their lives, people mention standard facts—college, marriage, jobs, trips, and so on. It is very hard to capture the nature of specific experiences in retelling—this is the special art of the good writer—and it is impossible for us to tell and to live at the same time. (This point is frequently made in reports of drug experiences but is also an aspect of everyday experience of which we are generally not aware.) It is as if there were two "modes" of living or remembering—the experiential and the symbolic, or "told." Regarding childhood amnesia, Schachtel makes two strong points: (1) there are no schemata available to the child for the preservation of his very earliest memories, and (2) those schemata he learns later in childhood are not appropriate to his early experience. The memory of early experiences may be not so much willfully repressed as simply inaccessible, though not forgotten.

It should be clear by now that language is not the sole instrument of cognition, but we have yet to explore more fully the degree and nature of its significance. The point has been made that we have various means for representing experience to ourselves, and the question here—quite literally—is how people *re*-present experience to themselves. How can one call something forth at a later time? Jerome Bruner has spoken of three main modes of representation, and his scheme provides a useful beginning point.

Language and Cognitive Development

One way we can represent things to ourselves is through action—what Bruner calls *enactive* representation. If you were asked what "shrug your shoulders" means or what a square knot is, for example, you might very likely demonstrate by doing. Many of our activities, and many things we know about, are in the status of being represented by actions or by some sort of muscular imagery. For

Representations of Reality

adults, the enactive mode is probably used primarily for representing motor skills; for children, however, it may be an important initial means for representing objects.

Another means of representation uses imagery as its mode. There is no good English adjective for "imagistic," so we shall use here the term proposed by Bruner, *ikonic*. Ikonic representation—or visual-spatial imagery—achieves one of the critical things missing in the enactive mode of representation: simultaneity. If you have a map (or a "cognitive map") to guide you about a city, you can look at the whole scheme at once, then figure out where you are and where you are going; you do not have to go back to the beginning of your route and feel your way along.

Visual imagery—or the ikonic mode—is one important means of action-free representation. The most important, however, is obviously linguistic representation, or, to use Bruner's more general term, *symbolic* representation. The symbolic system is the last to arise ontogenetically (that is, in the course of child development). The advantages of linguistic representation over ikonic representation are obvious: we can make up symbols for anything, and we can reshuffle them and recombine them to deal with all manner of *possibilities,* going far beyond things and events we have experienced directly.

Bruner's categorization is useful in giving us three major techniques for representing reality: action, imagery, and symbolism. As adults, we use all three techniques, depending on the task at hand, and we use them in interrelation. No one technique serves all human purposes; we must learn motor skills, spatial arrays, rituals, rules of behavior, and so on. In addition, there must be inarticulate forms of thought that precede the formation of acts, images, and symbols.

Development of Imagery With age, visual imagery seems to become more and more important to the child. Experiments on change in imagery with age point to three interesting conclusions about the differences between children and adults: (1) children use *more imagery* in carrying out intellectual tasks; (2) their imagery is more *particularistic,* rather than generic and schematic; and (3) children's images seem to have *greater vividness and detail.*

In *Studies in Cognitive Growth,* Bruner and his co-workers report a number of studies carried out at the Harvard Center for Cognitive Studies documenting the use of imagery by children in intellectual tasks and the shift with age from ikonic to symbolic modes of representation. For example, if children are given a collection of pictures to be sorted into categories, the younger children sort on the basis of such perceptual features as color, size, and pattern, but older children sort on the basis of some broader functional concept. A six-year-old may group together *boat, ruler, doll, bicycle, scissors, saw, shoe, gloves, barn, candle, pie, nails,* and *taxi* because "Some are red, some are gold, and some are yellow. One is white, some are brown, and some are blue." Or he may group together *screw, ruler, nails, candle, hammer, taxi, coat, scissors, sword,* and *bicycle* because "They have a part that you get dressed with, or they have holes in them, or you use them for tools, taxi goes with bicycle."

Bruner reports that increasingly with development children isolate one or more attributes that are common to all the items in the group: "They are all tools," or "You can eat with them," or "They can all move." Response to the vividness of the way things look may prevent superordinate grouping for young children because what is most vivid perceptually may vary greatly from one moment of comparison to the next. Perhaps the increasing ability to code and

Figure 12.4
Grouping by appearance *(top)* and grouping by function *(bottom)*.

compare attributes of objects linguistically acts to free the child from the immediate perceptual impact of one attribute or another.

Bruner suggests that the important determiner of the use of language in cognitive growth is the school. In school, children must learn to read and write; but also, within the broader range of linguistic tasks, a child must learn to perform in a school setting. Bruner's studies suggest that the sort of intellectual training a child receives is more important than the particular language he speaks—as far as the general course of his cognitive growth is concerned.

An important consequence of use of language is that the child can pursue new knowledge by means other than direct test. In solving a problem, he can eliminate possibilities by ruling out whole classes of events and follow up on leads that before meant little to him. The idea of *possible information* emerges—something that *may* be so upon further inquiry rather than simply being so or not so.

We still are not in a position to unravel, however, the extent to which the emergence of such abilities requires language. Perhaps human beings develop complex cognitive competence with or without language, and with or without schooling. Much of Piaget's work has suggested that language reflects rather than determines cognitive development. He and his followers made careful attempts to train children in problem solving by teaching them new ways of talking about the problem at hand. The general finding has been that special linguistic training will be of no avail to children whose level of cognitive development has not yet reached the point at which it can embrace the relevant concepts represented by the words.

Hans Furth and his co-workers, in their extensive studies of deaf children and adults, offer important evidence in regard to the role of language in cognitive development. The deaf provide a significant control group of children deprived

The Role of Language

Figure 12.5
Modes of the categorization of pictures as a function of age.
(After Olver and Hornsby, 1966.)

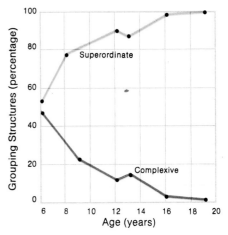

225

of verbal language and of much formal schooling. If their cognitive development does not differ markedly from that of normal children, we will have important evidence that Bruner has overemphasized the role of language and that Piaget's emphasis on cognitive maturation guided by various sorts of experience is more appropriate. The central question here is whether the possession of language itself makes for the stages of cognitive development observed by Piaget and others or whether language merely provides experiences that help make this development possible. If the latter is more nearly true, then perhaps equivalent amounts of experience in the absence of language will also move a child forward in cognitive development.

Furth reports that deaf children in America do not learn any sort of formal language—reading, writing, speaking, or sign language—until rather late in life (unless their parents happen also to be deaf, in which case gestural sign language develops normally, and early, in the deaf child). As a matter of fact, most American deaf never learn English adequately. Furth claims that it remains almost a foreign language for most deaf people and criticizes the policy of most American schools for the deaf for withholding the sign language from deaf children in the hope that they will learn English instead. This unfortunate situation, then, has provided us with a very valuable "natural experiment" in which we can observe the cognitive development of children who are grossly deficient in language. The striking finding is that *in a vast number of studies* deaf children are not very different from children who can hear. They go through the same sequence of stages of cognitive development, sometimes at the same rate, sometimes a little slower. The slowness may well be due to the fact that their environment is generally experientially impoverished rather than specifically impoverished in regard to linguistic input. By adulthood, according to Furth, the cognitive abilities of the deaf are the same as those of hearing people, though most of them can barely read and write or speak English.

Furth concludes, on the basis of his many studies, that language has an indirect, rather than a direct or decisive, effect on cognitive development. That is, language can accelerate development by acting as a channel for additional experience and information, by allowing for efficient and frequent communication, and by providing ready-made symbols for important ideas. But such a

Figure 12.6
Gestural sign language in deaf children.

conclusion means that people who are in some way "language deficient" are not necessarily permanently impaired in cognitive facility. Rather, they may be temporarily slowed down because of lack of relevant experience, and this retardation may be especially marked on specific tasks that are greatly facilitated by linguistic means of formulation or solution. Language clearly plays some role in some aspects of cognition and cognitive development. The task remaining is to characterize the varying roles played by language in cognitive functioning.

Linguistic Relativity and Determinism

The notion that different languages have different effects upon thought is associated with Benjamin Lee Whorf, the linguist whose name is familiar in the form of the *Whorf hypothesis*—the hypothesis of linguistic relativity and determinism. In an early statement of the problem by Edward Sapir, who was Whorf's teacher, language (it is not specified what aspects of language) is held to influence *all* experience—seeing, hearing, and experiencing generally. It is not clear in Sapir's discussion how strong he believes this influence to be; early in his statements he says that we are at the mercy of language, but he later simply says that the language habits predispose certain choices of interpretation. The earlier statement is a strong one; the later is a weaker one (and more in consonance with the arguments developed earlier in this chapter). Finally, he says that the language habits of a given community are operative—that is, different languages have different effects. Here we have a kernel statement of both linguistic relativity (differences between languages) and linguistic determinism (effects of language), proposed in both a strong and a weak version. Let us examine these proposals in more detail.

Lexical Differences Between Languages

To begin with, why should we expect different languages to have different effects on cognitive processes? What sorts of facts have led people to talk about linguistic relativity? For one thing, we know that language deals with *categories* of experience. Categories are represented in various ways in a language: (1) by individual words (for example, *house, green*); (2) by parts of words that perform grammatical functions (for example, *horse, horses, horse's; color, to color, colorful, colored; green, greener*); and (3) by a variety of grammatical processes (such as word order used to distinguish subject and object in English: *The man bit the dog* versus *The dog bit the man*). Linguistic relativity becomes relevant when languages are compared and the diversity of categories of experience embodied in various languages is uncovered.

The differences that attract investigators go deeper than the well-known fact that there are no really perfect translation equivalents for individual words. In order to grasp this matter of relativity, it is useful to think of two general sorts of ways in which categories are expressed in language. One way is in terms of individual words—this is a matter of relativity from a *lexical* point of view; the other is in terms of *grammatical* processes.

■ LEXICAL 1: TERM LACKING

To begin with, when you compare two languages, you may find that one of them has a term for which there is no single-term equivalent at all in the other language. For example, there is no clear English equivalent for the German *Gemütlichkeit*. Nevertheless, we are able to learn what the German term means and borrow it for use in English, as we have borrowed words from other languages whenever necessary. It could be argued, in this regard, that Germans may be more sensitive to the attribute of *Gemütlichkeit* than we are, but this would be a very different sort of nonlinguistic behavior to measure. Moreover, when

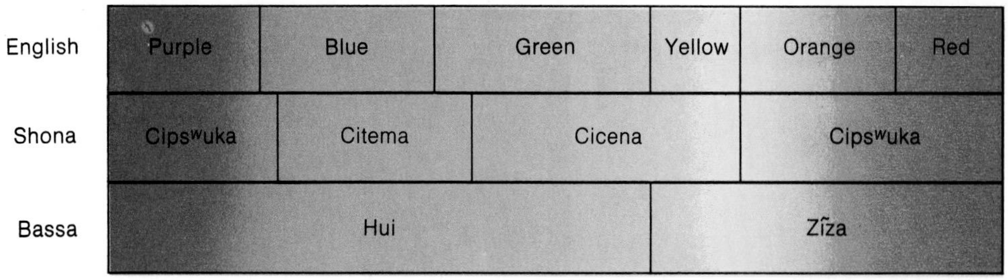

English	Purple	Blue	Green	Yellow	Orange	Red
Shona	Cipsʷuka	Citema	Cicena		Cipsʷuka	
Bassa	Hui			Zĩza		

Figure 12.7

In some languages, the principal color words break down the spectrum quite differently from the English color vocabulary. (After Gleason, 1961.)

new concepts arise, we invent new words to refer to them: *hippie, de-escalation,* and so on.

■ LEXICAL 2: SUPERORDINATE MISSING

Languages differ in providing superordinate terms for various classes. For example, we have the superordinates *animal, bird, insect,* and *creature,* which some languages lack; on the other hand, we do not have a superordinate term for "fruit and nuts," but the Chinese do.

■ LEXICAL 3: DIFFERENT SPLITS IN REALMS

One of the most popular areas of investigation on this level is the color continuum, because it is so objectively definable. Some languages make more cuts on this continuum, some fewer, and some simply different sorts of cuts. A comparison of divisions of the spectrum by speakers of English, Shona (spoken in Rhodesia), and Bassa (spoken in Liberia), as shown in Figure 12.7, elicits some significant points. Consider, for example, a color that we call yellowish green. This color lies on the boundary between two English color categories and must be named by a compound rather than a single word. If a yellowish-green chip is presented to an English speaker to be labeled, his response time will tend to be longer than if a "pure" yellow or green chip is offered (that is, a chip from the center of the named category). On the other hand, the same chip may be a good example of *cicena* to a speaker of Shona and may be quickly and easily labeled by him. Each semantic system carries with it the implication that a given stimulus will be the best exemplar of a named category and that naming difficulties occur at the boundaries between named categories.

Likewise, research has shown that color labels influence memory for color, along lines suggested by the discussion of language and memory earlier in the chapter. For example, a slightly off-green may be remembered as green because there is no easy way of coding "slightly off-green." Another familiar example of different splits in a realm can be observed in the language of the Eskimos, who have more words for snow than we do. Note, however, that in all these cases it is the presence or absence of a *single* word that is offered as evidence for linguistic relativity and determinism. As is obvious, of course, every language allows for productive *combinations* of words. We are able to refer to different kinds of snow, for example, by the use of phrases; indeed, Whorf could not have explained the Eskimo distinctions without being able to do so. In all these cases, we are dealing with what Roger Brown calls the problem of *codability*. This is another way of stating the weak form of the hypothesis: In some languages it may be *easier* to think about or talk about certain phenomena because there are handy linguistic expressions with which to do so.

These three aspects—missing terms, missing superordinates, and different splits in realm—characterize the lexical differences between languages that attract the attention of investigators. Here the question seems to be one of the relative codability of concepts. Although it is a debatable point, many theorists tend to believe that any concept can somehow be coded in any language—the question is one of how easily it can be done—and thus, in regard to the lexical level, favor the so-called weak form of the hypothesis. The important distinction here is between *potential* and *habitual* behavior. For example, most men can discriminate many colors, but, in everyday practice, a few habitual categories are used by most ordinary people. Although it may be true that anything can be said in any language, usually the conventionally coded and codable things are said, and experience is frequently assimilated to the categories for the code. Thus, if you look at the words that are frequently used in a culture, you will have some indication of the concepts that are frequently communicated and are probably especially important to members of that group. Other concepts can be conveyed by circumlocutions, but this is not economical for important discriminations.

Grammatical Level

When *grammatical* level is examined, the question of determinism becomes quite intriguing, because there are a variety of mandatory classifications embodied in grammar to which we do not usually attend and that do not even become obvious until a comparison of languages is made. A most graphic example of such classifications is revealed by the use of pronouns of address in various languages. In German, for example, one must choose between the "familiar" *du* and the "polite" *Sie,* and in French between the corresponding *tu* and *vous,* using, at the same time, the appropriate verb conjugational forms. These are obligatory grammatical distinctions when speaking.

Another sort of argument advanced on the grammatical front of the Whorf hypothesis is the semantic implication of the part of speech of a word. For example, *heat,* in Indo-European languages, may be a noun. The noun class is made up, to a large extent, of concrete things. Perhaps this is why so many

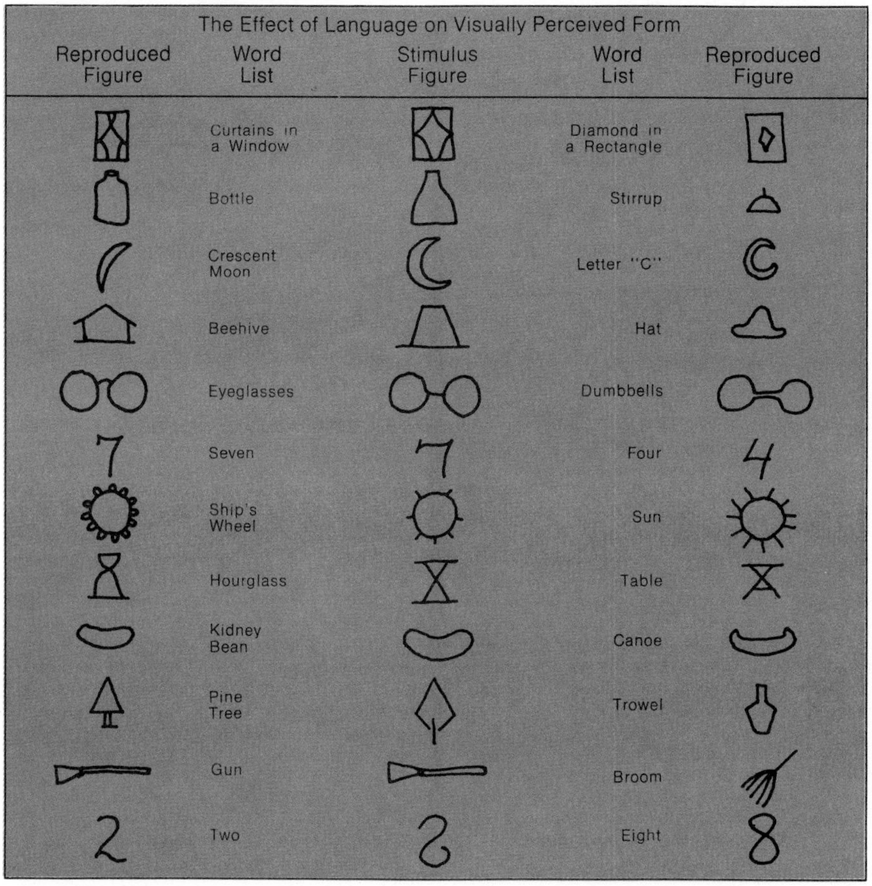

The Effect of Language on Visually Perceived Form				
Reproduced Figure	Word List	Stimulus Figure	Word List	Reproduced Figure
	Curtains in a Window		Diamond in a Rectangle	
	Bottle		Stirrup	
	Crescent Moon		Letter "C"	
	Beehive		Hat	
	Eyeglasses		Dumbbells	
	Seven		Four	
	Ship's Wheel		Sun	
	Hourglass		Table	
	Kidney Bean		Canoe	
	Pine Tree		Trowel	
	Gun		Broom	
	Two		Eight	

Figure 12.8

The reproduction of ambiguous figures is influenced by the names associated with them. After being shown the series of stimulus figures, subjects were given one of two different word lists and produced the two different series of figures. (After Carmichael, *et al.,* 1932.)

Figure 12.9
In the rumor effect, stereotypes and expectations affect the verbal coding of events—especially ambiguous events open to several interpretations.

fruitless decades were spent in the history of Western science looking for a heat substance, like "phlogiston" or "caloric." Perhaps if our scientists had spoken a language like Hopi, where *heat* is a verb, they would have started out with the more appropriate kinetic theory of heat, which they finally arrived at. (But note that in spite of the language—if it were a determiner—Western scientists did eventually free themselves from the notion of a heat substance when this notion proved itself inadequate.)

These examples should give a good idea of why so many people have been so struck with linguistic relativity as to propose some sort of cognitive differences between the speakers of different languages. There are many other differences like these, but the main point is simply that languages do seem quite different, one from the other, in both the lexical and the grammatical categories they embody. If you look at all these linguistic differences carefully, though, you will have to conclude that languages differ not as much in *what* they are able to express as in what they regularly must and do express. The same basic functions are performed by all languages—making and negating assertions, asking questions, giving commands, and so on.

The fate of the Sapir-Whorf hypothesis today is interesting: our concern now is more with linguistic universals and cultural universals than it is with linguistic and cultural relativity. Chomsky has proposed that Whorf was too much concerned with surface structures of languages and that, on their deeper levels, all languages are of the same universally human character. Cultural anthropologists are looking to cross-cultural studies for the underlying structures of culture in an attempt to understand general laws of human behavior and development. Perhaps in an age when our world has become so small and the most diverse cultures are so intimately interrelated in matters of war and peace, it is best that we come to an understanding of what all men have in common. But at the same time, it would be dangerous to forget that different languages and cultures may indeed have important effects on what men believe and what they do.

Psycholinguistics

As we pointed out above, there is little doubt that language influences the way we perceive the world and the way we respond to our environment. For the most part, the environment or culture into which we are born decides for us which language we will use. That is, we acquire whatever language is dominant in the society into which we are thrust. But how does a child go about the confusing task of learning to speak?

Psycholinguistics brings together the theoretical tools of linguistics and the empirical tools of psychology to study the mental processes underlying the acquisition and use of language. Linguists are engaged in the formal description of an important segment of human knowledge: the structure of speech sounds and meanings and the important and complex system of grammar, which helps to relate sounds and meanings. Psychologists are concerned with the ways by which children acquire such systems and with the ways in which such systems function when people are actually speaking and understanding sentences.

In brief, then, psycholinguists are interested in the underlying knowledge and abilities that people must have in order to use language as adults and to learn its use in childhood. The expression *"underlying knowledge and abilities"* must be used because language, like all systems of human knowledge, can only be inferred or guessed from the careful study of overt behavior—in this case, speech and reactions to speech. Thus, the problem of the psycholinguist is that of all social scientists who venture beyond description of behavior: namely, postulating underlying bases of apparent orderliness in observed behavior.

The question of how a child learns to speak has intrigued and puzzled adults since antiquity. The cognitive abilities of a young child seem to be generally rather limited, yet he masters the exceedingly complex structure of his native language in the course of only three or four years. Moreover, each child, exposed to a different sample of the language and generally to little or no conscious teaching on the part of his parents, arrives at essentially the same level of grammar in this brief span of time. That is, each child becomes a full-fledged member of his language community, able to produce and comprehend an endless variety of novel sentences in the language he has mastered.

At the very beginning, of course, the child's attempts to communicate are quite different from adult language. They consist of gross responses like crying and gesturing. Then there is a babbling period, out of which parents try to recognize the "first word." This normally appears before the first birthday, but still the sounds are not what we would call language because the child cannot build more complex messages. Each word probably functions as a total utterance, its meaning dependent on the situation. *Mama* can mean *Mama come here* or *I see Mama,* and so on. During this period the child cannot be said to have an active grammatical system or grammatical rules for forming sentences, because words are not combined into sentences. All his utterances are one-word sentences. At this stage, however, the very young child may have a passive grammatical system—he may have rules for decoding or understanding many grammatical patterns—but we do not yet have adequate experimental techniques for studying the comprehension of language in children so young.

■TWO-WORD UTTERANCES

At the age when the child starts putting words together, one can begin investigating his grammar. It is possible to demonstrate that children's language is *structured* from the two-word stage on, that it soon takes on a *hierarchical structure,* that it tends to be *regular,* that the structures change with age, and that they do not always correspond to adult structures.

One cannot speak about grammar until the child starts putting two words together to make primitive sentences, typically somewhere around eighteen months of age. The growth of such two-word utterances is slow at first, but it rapidly accelerates. For example, the cumulative number of one child's *different* two-word combinations recorded in successive months was 14, 24, 54, 89, 350, 1,400, and over 2,500. Clearly, we are dealing with very large numbers of new combinations, produced in a short time span.

Distribution analysis reveals that these utterances are not random or unstructured juxtapositions of two words; rather, two classes of words can be discerned. There is a small class of what have been called pivot words, or operators, as well

The Child's Development of Grammar

Figure 12.10

The increasing number of a child's two-word utterances as he approaches two years of age.
(After Braine, 1963.)

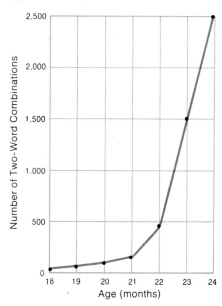

Table 12.1— Fragment of Pivot of One Child	
Pivot	Open Class
allgone	car
more	dog
my	door
see	girl
there	glass
this	house
	man
	milk
	toy

as a large, open class of words, many of which were previously one-word utterances. For example, a child may say things like *bandage on, blanket on, fix on,* and *take on.* The word *on* is a sort of pivot here—it is always in second position, and a large collection of words can be attached to it. The child may also say things like *allgone shoe, allgone vitamins, allgone outside,* and *allgone pacifier.* In this case, there is a pivot in the first position—*allgone*—which is followed by a large class of words in the child's speech. These words can be called pivotal because other words can be attached to them. A pivot word may be the first or second member of a two-word sentence, but whichever it is, its position is fixed. The membership of the pivot class expands slowly; that is, only a few new pivots enter each month.

The other class is large, is open, and contains all the words not in the pivot class. All the words in this open class also occur as single-word utterances, but some of the pivots never do. Table 12.1 presents a sample of part of the pivot grammar of one child. On the left is the total list of first-position pivots; on the right is a partial list of the open class (which may contain hundreds of words). Generally, any of the words on the left can be combined with any of the words on the right to form a sentence in this child's language.

An important thing to note is that from the point of view of the child's system, he has but two classes of words, though these words belong to a number of different classes in adult language (adjectives, nouns, and so on). Thus, although the child has a system of his own, it is not a direct copy of the adult system. At this stage—and certainly at later stages—many of the child's utterances, although consistent with *his* system, do not directly correspond to adult utterances and do not appear to be reduced or delayed imitations of adult utterances. As Braine has pointed out, the pivot stage is rich with charming examples of such childish utterances: *allgone sticky* (after washing hands), *allgone outside* (said when door was shut, apparently meaning "The outside is all gone"), *more page* (meaning "Don't stop reading"), *more wet, more car* (meaning "Drive around some more"), *more high* (meaning "There's more up there"), *there high* (meaning "It's up there"), *other fix* (meaning "Fix the other one"), *this do* (meaning "Do this"). It is quite unlikely that the child has ever heard utterances quite like these. Rather, it seems that, using the limited tools he has, the child is already trying to express himself in his own way, producing novel utterances within his system. He seems to have a grammatical system of his own, which is *based* on what he has heard but is not a direct reflection of sentences he could have imitated from adult speech.

■HIERARCHICAL CONSTRUCTIONS

By the beginning of the three-word stage, it is possible to analyze sentences in terms of immediate constituents, or structural subunits. Thus, the basic organizing principles of language mentioned above emerge very early. Hierarchical constructions enter the child's linguistic system when a pivot construction comes to replace one of the open-class words in an open-open sentence, as shown in Figures 12.11 and 12.12.

These figures, called tree diagrams, are used by linguists to indicate the parts of a sentence that go together as constituents. The branches from a node in the tree indicate a constituent. In this case, *pivot-open* is a constituent in the sentence on the right-hand sides of both figures because it functions as a single unit, playing the same role as an open-class word.

In Figure 12.11, the pivot construction *other man* can serve as a phrase in place of *man* in the open-open sentence *man car*, giving the sentence *other man*

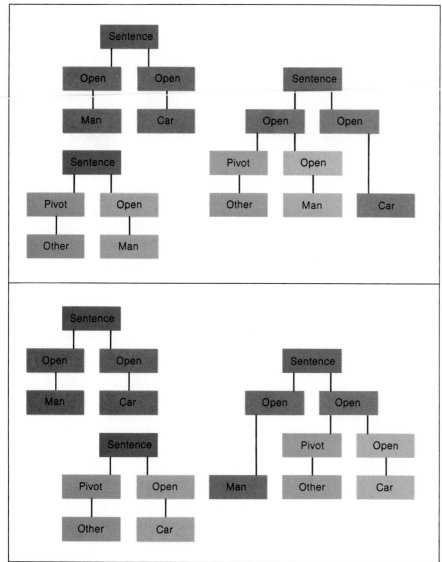

Figure 12.11
Tree diagrams showing how a three-word utterance may emerge when a pivot construction replaces the first member of an open-open sentence.
(After Slobin, 1969.)

Figure 12.12
A different sentence is produced if the pivot construction replaces the second of the open-class words.
(After Slobin, 1969.)

car, meaning, perhaps, "The other man is in the car." In Figure 12.12, conversely, the pivot construction *other car* can replace *car* in the same open-open sentence, giving the sentence *man other car,* perhaps meaning "The man is in the other car." That these sentences are hierarchical is clearly shown in the fact that the tree diagrams have some depth.

■REGULARIZATIONS

An important point noted above is that children's speech deviates from adults' speech in systematic fashions—thus implying that the deviations are creatively constructed by the child on the basis of a partial analysis of the language and on the basis of inherent cognitive tendencies of the child's mind. An area in which consistently deviant utterances appear is the overregularization of inflections. It is common knowledge, for example, that children say things like *comed, breaked, goed,* and *doed.* That is, the irregular (or "strong") verbs are inflected for past tense in the same manner as the regular (or "weak") verbs. Other familiar types of regularizations include such plurals as *foots* and *mouses.* This tendency to regularize continues well into elementary school for some children.

The crucial point here is that the strong verbs, though they are frequent, are each unique: they do not follow a pattern, and *evidently it is a pattern that children are sensitive to.* As soon as they find one, they try to apply it as broadly as possible, producing words that are regular but that they have never heard spoken. One is left very impressed with the child's great propensity to generalize, to analogize, to look for regularities—in short, to seek and create order in his language. One is fascinated by the child's *autogenic behavior*—the behavior that follows from his own attempts to organize the world.

■ RULES AND THEIR ORIGINS

The discussion so far has made reference repeatedly to the individual's knowledge of the rules of his language and to the child's development of various sorts of rules. The great productivity of human language—the ability to produce and understand an endless number of novel sentences—impels us to speak of the formation of grammatical rules rather than the learning of large numbers of specific word combinations. But this notion of rule is rather tricky and can be easily misunderstood. The use of the word "rule" may imply that psycholinguists believe that explicit rules of grammar can be stated and that children learn such rules. On the contrary, no psycholinguist can state all the rules of English grammar. (If they could, linguists would have nothing to do.) Perhaps this important notion of "rule" can be clarified by asking about the sort of behavioral evidence that would enable one to speak of a person's possession of a rule.

There are various levels of evidence for rules, from less stringent to more stringent. The simplest sort of evidence comes from analysis of the spontaneous speech of the child. Take, for example, the elementary case of two-word utterances, discussed above. Already regularities can be detected, for not all possible combinations of units occur. This is the earliest sort of evidence for rules—*regularities of behavior.*

A more stringent test for the existence of rules is the extension of regularities to new instances. We have such evidence in the spontaneous speech of the child when he says things like *it breaked* and *two mouses,* as discussed above.

On the next level, one can ask if the child can detect deviations from regularity, if he can judge if a given construction is right or wrong. This *normative* sense of rules is a later development in ontogenesis and corresponds to what linguists refer to as a sense of grammaticality. Actually, there are several levels of evidence here.

The first comes, again, from spontaneous speech. If a child stops and corrects himself, this is evidence that he is comparing his speech with some standard of correctness. He is monitoring it in regard to his rules. Three-year-olds are frequently heard to stop and correct themselves while speaking. Consider, for example, the following bit of spontaneous talk by a three-year-old girl: *She had a silly putty like me had . . . like I . . . like I did.* Clearly this child is applying a sense of grammaticality to her speech. But note that she can only be comparing what she says to her *own* rules, not to adult rules; although her sense of rules is already normative, the norms are of her own form, for at another point she stops and corrects herself in the following fashion: *Why . . . Why . . . Why ducks have not . . . Why ducks have no hands?*

A more difficult test of this sense of grammaticality is to see if the child can detect ungrammaticalness in speech of others. At some point, children usually begin to correct each other (and their parents).

The most difficult test of grammatical judgment is the direct question. The child can be asked if it is, for example, "better" or "more correct" to say *two mouses* or *two mice.* These are extremely important data for the linguist working with adult informants. It is, however, an ability that develops late in childhood

and, unfortunately, is thus of little use in dealing with very young children. Developmental psychologists in the United States have collected much evidence indicating that children develop, discard, and refine systems of grammatical rules, ultimately arriving at adult linguistic competence.

Furthermore, individual children go through strikingly similar stages of development. What little information we have on children who acquire native languages other than English suggests a universality of stages and processes of acquisition. The thrust of theory and research in this field has been to emphasize universality and the existence of innate, biological determinants of such universality. The arguments over the issue of innate factors in language acquisition are complex and heated. In addition to the universality of stages of language development, theoreticians are struck by the complexity of the task facing the child—especially the problem of discovering underlying structures and meanings of sentences. This complexity has made it plausible to postulate that the child's mind is somehow set in a predetermined way to process the sorts of structures that characterize human language. Indirect evidence for this approach also comes from the fact that there seems to be a biologically determined critical stage for language acquisition in humans. There may even be special structures in the human brain for performing linguistic functions. But these issues are far from being settled unequivocally.

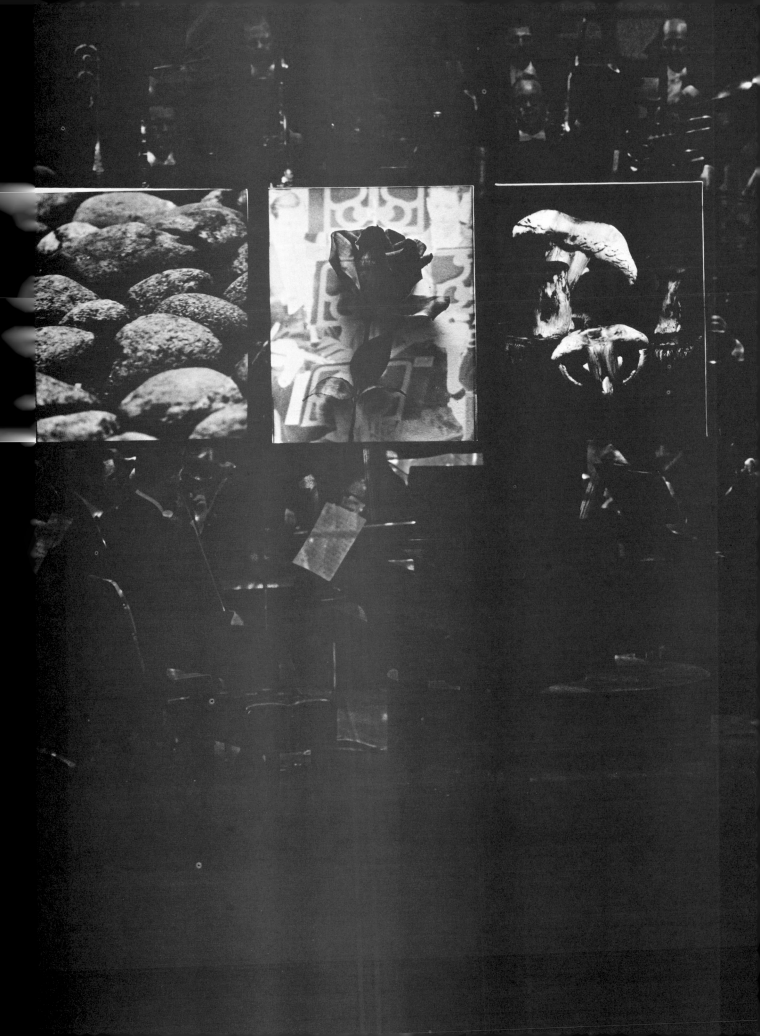

UNIT IV

THE SENSORY WORLD

You are strongly influenced by the physical world around you and are dependent on that world for stimulation to keep you awake, alive, and alert. But oddly enough, you never have direct contact with your environment. Everything that you know about your body, about other people, and about objects and events outside you comes to you through your sense organs. Even your best friend exists to you only as a shifting, complex pattern of stimuli. You generate your knowledge of the world around you from the information available from your sense receptors. We cannot hope to understand very much at all about the way we function in the world unless we know the way these receptors—the eye, the ear, the nose, the tongue, and that conglomeration of receptor processes we call touch—function to bring the world to us.

13

CONSCIOUSNESS AND AWARENESS

PLEASE LOOK AT YOUR FEET, then answer the following questions. Your feet are a part of your body; your mind is also a part of your body, but does it exist in your feet? As you look at your feet, do you feel that there is a *you* of some kind that has a separate existence from the rest of your body? Where is this *you* located? In your head?

Now, wiggle your toes. You are aware of your toes both from seeing them wiggle and from feeling them as they move. But where does this awareness come from? What causes consciousness? Does it exist in your toes, or just in your brain? When you concentrate on reading a book, why are you no longer aware of your feet? When you go to sleep, why can't you feel your toes wiggle?

Now, stop for a moment and look at the world around you. If you are reading this book in your room, pick out a table a few feet away and concentrate on it. The table will appear of a certain size, of a certain shape and color; it will probably seem quite substantial, perhaps with several objects resting on it. If you pounded on it, you would hear a solid *thunk;* if you smelled it, it might have a woody odor of some kind. If someone asked you, "Is this table real—does it really exist?" chances are you would insist that it does exist. Yet you would be hard-pressed to prove philosophically that the table was anything other than a figment of your imagination.

The Nature of Awareness

We commonly assume that our conscious experience is an awareness of objects and events in the external world, such as tables, trees, cars, sounds, smells, and our bodily responses to them. We react to these objects and events by manipulating them, thinking about them, solving problems related to them, and developing feelings and attitudes about them. Most of us assume that our senses mirror the external world exactly and that our sensory neural pathways somehow transmit copies of it to the brain. Many of us have grown up with the Walt Disney metaphor of consciousness that portrays our sensory systems as sending copies—

images or pictures—of the external world to some sort of central switchboard where they are displayed on a screen of consciousness that reflects the ebb and flow of our experience and awareness of the world. In general, when we think about the nature of our experience we tend to conceive of it along these lines. But if we think about it a little more deeply, we realize that this is not a sufficient explanation of how we perceive and experience the world and that there are many exceptions that are unaccountable for in terms of this seemingly simple, direct, and parsimonious view.

If, indeed, the world is rerepresented in such a fashion on a screen of consciousness, very much as a projector displays action on a movie screen, who sees it? Who, or what process, abstracts the properties, the theme, and the story and classifies and stores the information as a record or memory of past experience? Let us start by examining some of the possible difficulties of rerepresenting the world via the senses and some of the exceptions to such a direct and simplistic view.

First of all, we can be made to see without our eyes' receiving light. If you close your eyes and press on them (take off your contact lenses!), you will see a

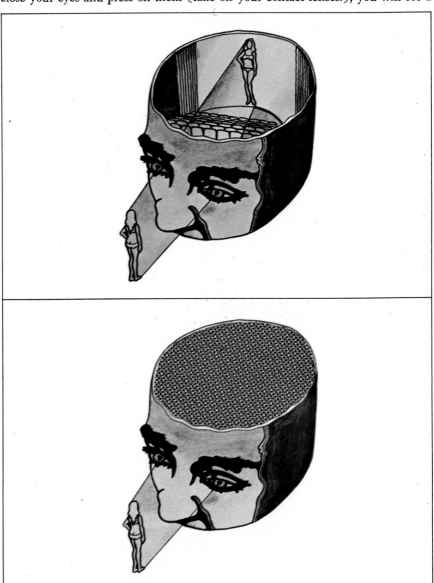

Figure 13.1

Our sensory systems do not transmit copies of the external world to an audience in the brain but rather perform complex encodings of information that are somehow interpreted in higher centers.

240

purplish light flash. Where does this flash come from? No real light flash occurred, yet you experienced light. Your visual system and your brain have been tricked, in a sense, for a visual experience has been created without actual light stimulation. Usually the receptors (the rods and cones) in the retina of the eye respond to light energy from the external world and generate neural impulses that are transmitted across two synapses (neuron junctions) in the retina and fire impulses along optic nerve fibers toward the brain. But the retina can be made to fire impulses by such other means as pressure on the eyeball or electrical stimulation applied to the cornea of the eye. Luminous impressions produced in this way are called phosphenes, but they are nevertheless visual experiences originating in the eye without light stimulation.

As a matter of fact, even the eye and the retina are not required to produce visual experiences. If electrodes are applied to the visual receiving area of the brain and electrical impulses sent through them into the tissue of the visual cortex, experiences resembling ordinary light flashes occur. Thus, the brain of a person may be made to see something without light flashes, and even without the eye or the visual pathways to the brain. This kind of demonstration is very important to our understanding of the nature of awareness.

We do *not* always see with our eyes. We can sometimes have visual experiences without using them, auditory experiences without using our ears, and so on. If our eyes could somehow be connected to the auditory area of the brain, we could presumably hear light. Our conscious experience, then, is a brain process determined by which cells in the brain are activated. Usually in ordinary experience, this process is activated when the senses respond to some external occurrence in the world, but such external stimuli are not necessary to activate the process. Perhaps our most common, rich, and complex experiences of this sort are dreaming, for which there is no sensory input. Sometimes, too, we hallucinate—we see things that are not there. In general, our consciousness is constructed from direct sensory input, assisted by memory (see Chapter 18).

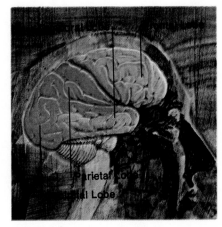

Figure 13.2
The visual cortex is in the occipital lobe.

It becomes clear, then, that we do not see with our eyes; we see with the help of our eyes. The common comparison of our eyes to a camera is consequently incorrect. Although we may speak of an image "formed" on the retina, an analysis of the retina shows that it does not really work like the film in a camera. Instead of the formation of an image, a set of receptors is excited and sends impulses to the brain. Moreover, this mosaic of receptors does not merely mirror the world. We have probably evolved a visual system that transmits enough information to our brain for us to manipulate objects in the world, to avoid accidents, and to survive, but our senses do not respond to *all* the external world. Instead of mirroring the world, our sensory systems seem to have the primary function of selecting out of the enormous stimulus array only a few relevant dimensions of stimulation and transmitting these to the brain. In short, it seems that one of the major functions of our senses is to *throw away* some of the information about the world and to select out only a few things.

The way in which such selectivity works can be seen by studying a lower organism whose visual system throws away much more information than ours does. The frog's eyes perform a calculation and analysis of the visual world and transmit only a limited amount of information to its brain. Neurophysiologists have inserted microelectrodes into the optic nerve of the frog, the connection between the frog's eye and the brain. By recording from this microelectrode in different portions of the optic nerve while they displayed different stimuli in front of the frog, they found that the frog's eyes responded to only four different

Figure 13.3 *(opposite)*
Our sensory systems filter the information pouring in, selecting some of it, rejecting the rest.

Figure 13.4
The frog's visual world.

Figure 13.5
Before you continue reading, turn the page and quickly count up the aces of spades in the display of cards in Figure 13.6.

kinds of stimulation. One optic nerve fiber transmitted a picture of sustained brightness contrasts, perhaps a sketchy outline of the world of the frog. A second nerve fiber responded to a moving edge of light or a shadow; a third nerve fiber, to a sudden reduction of illumination. Perhaps this fiber could be thought of as part of a bird-of-prey response system. The fourth type of nerve fiber responded only when a small black object in constant motion appeared in the frog's field of vision: a bug-perceiving system. The frog's total visual experience does not include color or form as we know it, or brightness, or many of the other dimensions that we can experience. Although its senses function to discard more information than ours, nevertheless we basically have the same kind of visual apparatus, a sensory system that abstracts a limited amount of information from that available and transmits it to the brain.

If we understand, then, that our awareness is not a direct registration of some sort of copy of the world but a pattern of electrical events in the brain, we are free of many of the questions that have concerned us about consciousness. For example, those who have taken the idea of the retinal image literally have been bothered by the fact that an image formed by a lens is upside down. This phenomenon has led to the question of how we experience the world right side up if the image on our retina is upside down. It would indeed be a problem if a copy of the world was sent to the brain upside down, but if we understand that what is transmitted to the brain is merely a *pattern of excitation* of certain receptors in a given system, then it does not really matter how this pattern is coded—upside down, sequentially in time—as long as it is consistent. What determines our experience ultimately is the *brain process*, not an image registered in a sensory system.

Some psychologists have demonstrated that our experience of the world depends on much more than what is "really" there. Jerome Bruner, for example, in a long series of experiments showed that our motivations and needs often determine our experience. We all have often noticed that when we are hungry, we tend to notice restaurants or to smell food we might usually ignore. To do this, we must be able to "tune" our sensory systems to receive different kinds of information, depending on our intention. This ability can be easily demonstrated

Figure 13.6
Playing cards.

Figure 13.7 *(opposite)*
All the shapes could be retinal projections of a circle.

Figure 13.8 *(opposite)*

The trapezoid on the right might be the square on the left tipped backward.

Figure 13.9 *(opposite)*

The left view suggests that the second shape really is a trapezoid. When seen from another angle *(right),* the circle and ellipses above all appear as ellipses with differently oriented long axes. From the information available, there is no way to determine what these shapes really represent.

at a party. First, pick out one person's voice and listen to him, then tune him out and listen to someone else. You can tune in or out at will. Moreover, Bruner showed that we often tune ourselves to see what we expect to see. He took a deck of playing cards and turned them over one by one, asking people to name them. As a part of our experience of the world, we have learned that clubs and spades are black and that hearts and diamonds are red; presumably we have tuned ourselves to receive these combinations. In Bruner's deck, however, there were such anomalous cards as a red ace of spades. When these cards were turned over, they were miscalled; the red spade, for instance, was often called an ace of hearts. Bruner called this phenomenon *perceptual readiness,* indicating that we are aware of what we are ready to perceive.

Our awareness consists of an *interaction* between ourselves and the environment. We often are not given all the information we need for "correct" perception, so we supply the rest. A circle, for example, may be registered many different ways on the retina (see Figure 13.7). Thus, not only does our sensory system respond rather selectively to stimulation, but any pattern of stimulation is in itself usually ambiguous. The pattern shown in Figure 13.8 may be a trapezoid standing upright or a rectangle whose top is farther away than its bottom, or any of a number of other shapes. Given such ambiguity in sensory input, we usually make a calculated guess as to the nature of the object in the world, and we develop our own theory of the world this way. Over a lifetime of learning, our

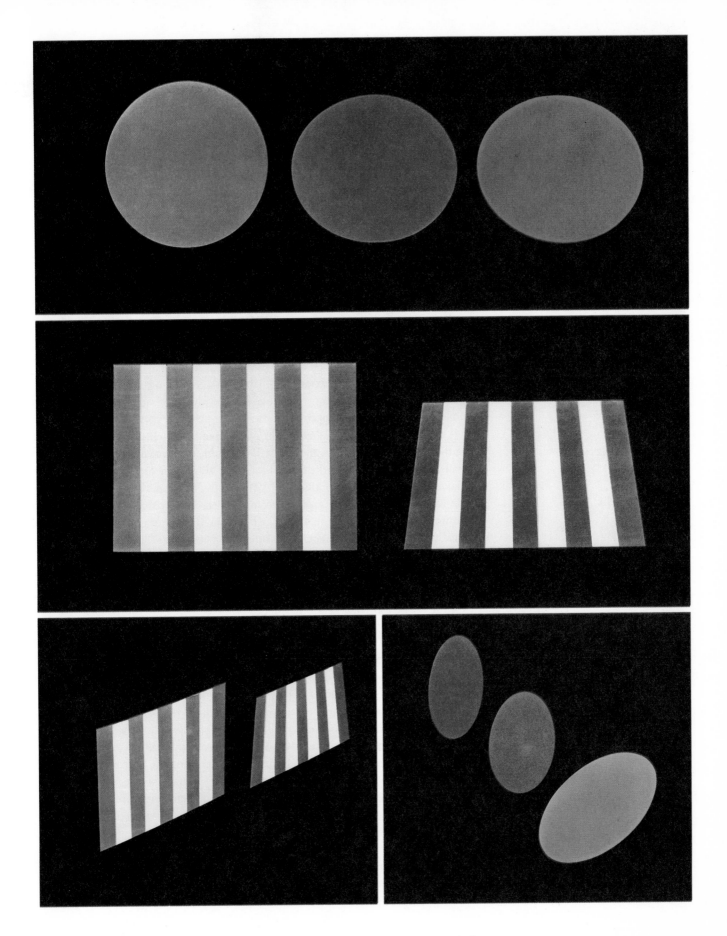

Figure 13.10
An Ames room.

assumptive world becomes rather reliable. We would not last too long if we theorized that a wall was transparent and soft or that a car approaching would do no harm or that objects appear larger the farther away they are.

The scientists who emphasize the assumptive aspect of awareness are known as the *transactionalists,* a name that reflects their idea that awareness consists of transaction between us and the world. One of their demonstrations uncovered a major aspect of our assumptive world. Normally, all rooms are rectangular, and we can safely bet that any given room will be. But no matter how good our assumptive world is, we can be tricked. Just as the pattern in Figure 13.8 can "really" be a trapezoid, rectangle, square, or just four lines unconnected, a "room" could look like almost anything (see Figure 13.10). Our assumption is that the room is rectangular—but in this case our assumption is wrong. If the room is a rectangle, then the men must be very different sizes, for this is the way we experienced it. If we assume that the room is trapezoidal in shape, then the men look equal in size, but this is almost an impossible assumption to make if you are brought up in a rectangular-room, linear-perspective culture.

The nature of the interaction that determines our awareness is not limited only to selection of input. If, for example, you push your eye sideways with your finger, the visual world seems to jump. Why? One reason is that when your eye was moved, the visual input changed because the eye was in another position. But if you had moved your eye with *your eye muscles* (the way you normally do) over the same path, the world would not have jumped. This means that we monitor our own movements and correlate them with the sensory signals that come in so that we can cancel out the effects of natural eye movements on perception. If we do not know how we move, our perception becomes distorted and disturbed.

We have already considered that the senses select information and that we can tune in to various stimulus dimensions. Pribram and Spinelli have further demonstrated, on a physiological level, how the brain can *control* its input. By recording from the visual system, they mapped the response of a single cell in the visual system to stimuli. When they stimulated the frontal cortex of the brain

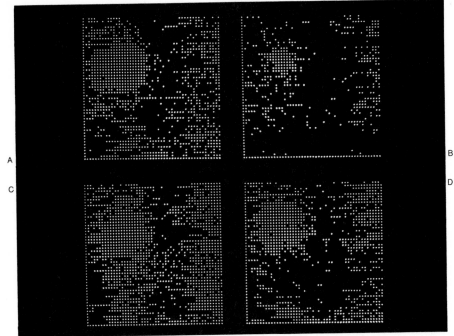

Figure 13.11
Map of points on the retina at which a light spot produces responding in a particular lateral geniculate cell in the brain of a monkey. A and D show receptive-field maps obtained under ordinary conditions. Stimulation in the inferior temporal cortex reduces the field (B), and stimulation in the frontal cortex expands it (C).

(thought to control input), the cell's response to stimuli was dramatically altered (see Figure 13.11). Such experiments thus demonstrate that we are much more flexible than the frog. Even though our senses select a limited range of stimuli from the world, we have some control over that selection. Our awareness of the world comes from input that is selected, modified, controlled, and then correlated with past experience. It is a process of construction rather than one of bringing a copy of the world onto a consciousness screen. With this fact in mind, we can now explore some of the different "states" or "levels" of our awareness.

Sleep

One of the best physiological indicators of the state of awareness is the brain's electrical activity, called the *electroencephalogram* or EEG. Electrodes are placed on the scalp of an individual and the electrical activity generated in the brain is amplified and recorded by a complex machine called an electroencephalograph, which traces the waxing and waning of electrical potentials in the brain. EEGs have been recorded during sleep, relaxed wakefulness, varying degrees of attentiveness, and other normal as well as pathological states of awareness. During relaxed wakefulness, in the absence of special stimulation and with the subject's eyes closed, rhythmic *alpha waves* of about ten per second are the most prominent feature of the EEG record. The most striking physiological changes are observed as the subject goes to sleep, changes that are related to the variations in the level or degree of consciousness.

One of the states of awareness that most of us have wondered about is that of dreaming. Do all people dream? What are the functions of dreaming? Do different people dream different things? Why are we aware of our dreams when we are not aware of the external world? The use of an objective indicator of a subjective state of awareness such as the electroencephalogram has allowed us an opening into the study of our experience during sleep. In 1953, Aserinsky and Kleitman noticed the appearance in sleepers' EEGs of regular periods of eye movement and a brain wave resembling those of an awake person. They awakened subjects sleeping in the laboratory when this *rapid eye movement* (REM) period was occurring and found that it was highly associated with dreaming. When people were awakened immediately following an REM period and asked to describe their dreams, their dreams corresponded well to eye movements made during the REM period. In one case, walking down five steps was accompanied by five downward deflections of the subject's eyes during the REM period.

Although many people believe that they do not dream, laboratory tests have shown that almost everyone has rapid eye movement periods totaling one hour in duration out of every four hours of sleep. Perhaps people who feel that they never dream merely do not remember their dreams when they are awake. Furthermore, such subjects awakened immediately following an REM period usually report that they were dreaming.

Although the main distinction in sleep has been made between the REM and the non-REM periods, four distinct stages have been identified, indexed by the EEG. The patterns are shown in Figure 13.12.

The REM state is unusual in many ways. During REM periods, there are accelerations and irregularities in heart rate and in respiration, elevations of blood pressure, tumescence of the penis in men, and perhaps a characteristic change in every type of bodily function. All these physiological changes are associated with arousal; how then does most of our body appear to remain in the placid, relatively immobile state we associate with sleep? The answer seems to be that the brain somehow paralyzes most of the major body muscles during REM periods; that is, most of the bodily reflexes that can readily be elicited during ordinary sleep are suppressed. Apparently, part of the great increase in brain activity during REM periods is channeled into suppressing most muscular function. A few muscles are spared—those of the eye, the middle ear, and the respiratory system. It is also true that one can occasionally observe brief, miniscule twitches of the muscles in the extremities, all of which seem to be associated with the content of the dream the sleeper is experiencing. The noted French scientist Michel Jouvet succeeded in removing the small part of the brain responsible for this muscular inhibition in cats. REM periods continued to occur in these cats, but after the operation, the sleeping cats jumped up and ran about the room spitting

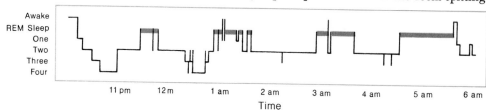

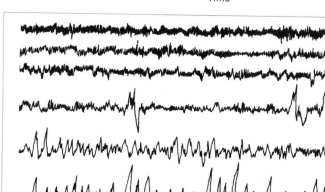

Figure 13.12

Record of a night's sleep *(top)*.
(After Naitoh and Johnson, in press.)
EEG patterns used to identify
stages of sleep shown above *(bottom)*.
(After Rechtschaffen and Kales, 1968.)

248

and hissing. Their eyes remained functionally closed, however, and they appeared to be oblivious to the world around them. Apparently, during REM periods, we attempt to act out whatever the dream is about, but one small part of the brain acts as an inhibitory center to prevent us from impulsively acting out the dream.

It is difficult to say why we dream or what the functions of dreams are, but we do know that if we are awakened each time the REM state appears, thus depriving us of dreams, we tend to make up these lost periods whenever given the chance. This "rebound" phenomenon is found both in humans and in lower animals. A cat deprived of REM sleep for any length of time becomes hypermotivated in many ways when awake. Sexual behavior is greatly enhanced or increased, as are aggressive tendencies and food-seeking behavior. Most other kinds of behaviors do not seem to be affected at all by REM deprivation. Apparently the body has a strong need to undergo REM periods at regular intervals, but the function of these periods is still unclear. We might expect that a person deprived of REM sleep for long periods of time might eventually start dreaming or hallucinating while still awake, but this seems not to be the case.

The connection between REM sleep and hallucinations is unclear, but tantalizing fragments of evidence suggest that such a connection does exist. For example, actively ill schizophrenic patients do not show the usual rebound effect when deprived of REM sleep, although all normal humans and all lower organisms tested do. Perhaps these patients, who hallucinate frequently, are discharging during their waking hours the types of brain activities that normal people discharge only during the REM period of sleep. Whatever the case, REM periods do seem to be connected with motivational states in both humans and infrahumans. When we learn the exact connections, we may well be close to finding an explanation for some of the more common types of mental disturbance.

Habituation

Our normal awareness is an interlayering of numerous experiences, but any processes that repeat over and over seem to disappear from awareness. When, for example, we enter a room and a clock is ticking, we normally hear it for a little while, then tune it out even though it is still there. When we are learning something new, such as driving a car, little complexities like the proper way to let out the clutch soon become automatic—we do them almost without awareness. This *habituation* to the repetition of various stimuli in the world and the automatic response state we often fall into because of habituation are quite common in our everyday lives. They show that we are normally more aware of changes in the world than of steady states.

We can *monitor* many things in the world without necessarily being aware of them. We can, for example, detect when a ticking clock stops. Awareness is multiple—many things, many dimensions, many levels, all at once.

Meditation

The practice of meditation produces alterations in awareness similar to those induced by drugs. In viewing many forms of meditation and prayer, one is struck by a great overall similarity in technique across cultures and across times. Most forms of meditation involve a repetitious process, a focusing or concentrating on one thing or one world, with the result that brain input is restricted. In a form of Yoga, for example, a mantra is used, a sonorous word repeated over and over, like the prayers of the Jewish and Greek Orthodox religions.

Another form of meditation involves concentrating upon an object—a sacred picture, a wall, a mandala. Here, again, an attempt is made to focus on one

thing, to expose the nervous system continually to the same input. The mandala, for instance, is designed so that one's gaze returns to the center. Both Zen meditation and Yoga have similar exercises in which concentration is on breath, and in Zen a single question, or koan, may be the focus of concentration for years. The similarities between these meditation exercises and prayers all over the world, as well as similarities in the descriptions of the state they induce, are striking examples of the communalities of our nervous system.

A single item, kept in consciousness for a long time, leads to a certain kind of state, which is meditation. We can conceive of this state as a shutting down of awareness, of awareness focused on one object. Practitioners claim that they experience something the thousandth time in the same way that they did the first. They see everything freshly. This tuning out, then, leads to a dehabituation process—a diminution of the normal selections of awareness. Meditation is in this way similar to the alterations of awareness produced by psychedelic drugs: both alter the selection process and open channels usually closed.

In meditation, the alpha rhythm, associated with closed eyes, relaxation, and the cessation of activity, becomes prominent. Moreover, when an attempt is made to control input by the use of a stabilized image (one that always stimulates the same part of the eye) or a completely homogeneous visual field (a Ganzfeld) as well as during meditation, one obtains similar subjective experiences. While viewing a stabilized image, people report a loss of the sense of vision completely. In the Ganzfeld, subjects report a visual "white-out" and contact with the world disappears, an experience similar to that of meditation. In these situations, constant input leads to a turning off of perception and the appearance of the alpha rhythm in the EEG.

A new technique has evolved using the EEG to train people to alter awareness. Joseph Kamiya and others have developed a system that informs a person of the state of his EEG. Given this information—usually not available in consciousness—a person can learn to control his own EEG, or at least to increase the amount of alpha activity. A number of studies have found that when a person is producing a large amount of this wave form, he is relaxed, passive, alert—a state much like that of meditation. This method has sparked a new line of research, the study of which aspects of awareness can be controlled by feeding back information to the subject. The possibility that we may all learn to control our blood pressure, heart rate, and consciousness as well as do experienced meditators has significant implications for medicine, as well as for psychology.

Time The continuing experience of time is part of our daily life and intertwines always with our experience of vision and hearing. In contrast to the clarity of these experiences, however, it is not very clear how our time experience occurs. With vision, for example, we can observe that some sort of established sensory-input brain-process relationship finally becomes our experience. But what of time? How do we experience it?

One long-held idea about time is that each organism has its own internal clock—some kind of interior organ that controls the perception of temporal durations. But it is not at all clear how such a special organ—which no one has ever found—could give rise to our experience. Instead, we should look again to the idea that our time experience is constructed somewhere in the brain, perhaps from the content of memory.

We continually experience the brief instant of the present, the forever-changing and fleeting *now*. What we call *now* is probably a series of actions that

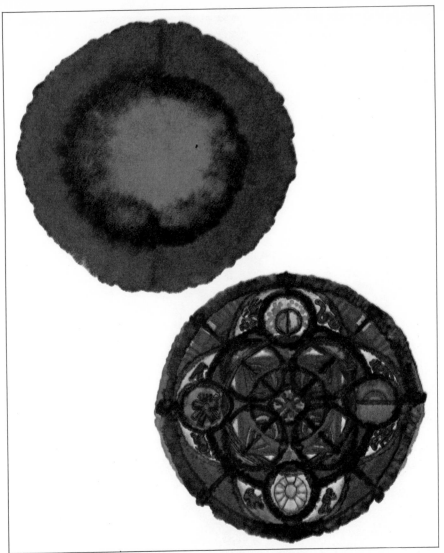

Figure 13.14
Observation of a simple figure does not extend our sense of time.

Figure 13.15
Observation of increasingly complex figures prolongs our experience of time.

are as yet uncompleted. When they become completed they are no longer *now* but part of the past.

Another level of our time experience is that of duration. Duration can most easily be understood as a function of the amount remembered of a given interval. When we are aware of and remember many things, an interval seems quite long. In a related sense, a drug that increases our awareness—such as LSD or marijuana—lengthens our duration experience (see Chapter 22). Moreover, when we look at a complicated figure, we experience time as longer than when we look at a simple figure (see Figure 13.14). This observation suggests that the amount of information we process determines at least in part our time experience.

Sensory Isolation

We are very effective at manipulating symbols, at using language, at doing calculations, and in general at handling information-processing situations. However, although we can deal efficiently with a moderate information-processing load, this specialization makes it difficult for us to cope with situations that do not have much input. The structure of the brain is such that one of the systems, the reticular activating system (RAS), maintains alertness by sending signals to the cortex to plan the next course of action. When input continues to come in, the cortex remains alert, but when the input begins to slow down or become

Figure 13.16
Human subjects find prolonged
confinement in an environment in which
there is very little stimulation intolerable.

Figure 13.17
Rats sometimes follow longer routes
for variety.

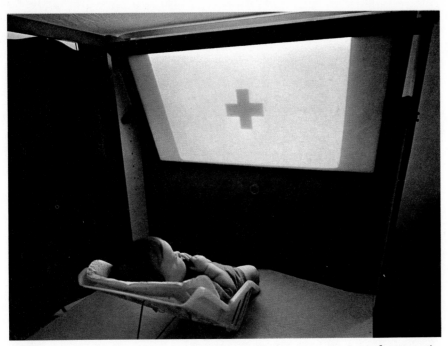

Figure 13.18
The amount of looking an infant does can be measured for each of several stimuli of varying complexity presented to him.

monotonous, the cortex seems to shut down. When an attempt is made to restrict input completely—by covering the eyes, ears, and all sense organs of the subject and putting him in an environment where he receives as little stimulation as is possible—his consciousness is altered: his judgment is impaired, he sometimes has hallucinations, and he loses track of his thoughts. Thus, it seems that we have to maintain a certain level of external stimulation to function effectively. When this stimulation is not present, our awareness is drastically altered—it seems that if we do not receive a certain amount of stimulation, we seek it. Consequently, hallucinations in sensory-deprivation situations may act as a sort of substitute for external stimulation.

Many organisms besides man also seem to need variation and stimulation. For example, a rat who is given two routes to food sometimes takes the longer one, perhaps just to get some variety. In our everyday life, we do not like to have nothing to do. We find that we get very bored and begin to fill up the time with some form of stimulation. We hum or tap our fingers just so that something is happening. Even newborn babies often choose to look at complex rather than simple figures.

Many of these different levels of awareness can be understood as altered functions of our normal awareness. We normally *select* information from the world, modify it, correlate it with our own movements, and finally *construct* our normal awareness out of a combination of this input and memory. Altered levels of awareness are produced by changes in this process.

STIMULATION AND SENSATION

SOME EXISTENTIALISTS HAVE HELD that man is ultimately isolated from his fellow man because all his contact with other humans is indirect and mediated by the senses. No information from the environment ever reaches the brain without first getting by the sensory receptors and the neural pathways; man never has *immediate* knowledge of the world's objects, other people, or anything. Psychology has thus come to consider the physical world as *stimulus,* its effects on a person as *sensation,* and his interpretation of the effects as *perception.*

With respect to man's two major senses, seeing and hearing, the physical stimuli are well defined. For hundreds of years physicists have worked in optics and acoustics, and much is known about the stimuli for seeing and hearing. The development of two distinct branches of physics, one dealing with light and one with sound, is the result of the overriding importance of seeing and hearing in the life of man. Had his sense of smell been as important to modern man as to the dog, physics would probably have a branch called "osmics." As it is, much less is known of the physical stimuli in smell, as well as in touch and taste.

"Sensation" and "stimulus" are the two terms used to separate the perceptual and subjective from the physical and objective. Knowledge of the physical dimensions of the stimulus is the first and perhaps the least interesting step for psychologists. Ultimately, it is the effect of the stimulus on the individual—the sensation—that is the particular domain of psychology. The difference between our sensations and the physical stimuli that give rise to them is shown in the discrepancies between certain aspects of our sensations and certain aspects of the stimuli, which are revealed by measuring both the sensation and the stimulus.

The Physical Stimulus We consider the measurement of the physical objective stimulus first because in large part it determines our subjective perception. Normally, a sensation arises when some minimal quantity of physical energy activates a receptor organ such as the eye or ear.

Light and sound, different as they are, have certain important similarities. Both may be described as a wave motion of energy that is propagated from a distance to the eye and ear. Both are subject to absorption, reflection, and diffraction by objects in their path. Despite these similarities, their differences are fundamental. Light is electromagnetic radiation that consists of the emission of packets of energy called *photons*. Light differs from radio waves and X rays only in the frequency of its wave motion. As we shall see, its effect on the visual system is photochemical. Sound, on the other hand, is a mechanical movement, usually of air particles. The movement of the air particles sets up vibrations in the auditory system. Sound thus affects the auditory system mechanically.

Light Physical studies have indicated that light can be characterized by its wavelength and by its intensity. Of these, the wavelength is the most important to vision because it determines not only whether the light will be seen but also the *color* of the light. The *intensity* determines (along with wavelength) whether the light is seen and how *bright* it looks.

The amount of light may be specified in a number of ways. The two most common ways are *luminance* and *illuminance*. Luminance refers to the amount of light emitted by a source such as a neon tube or incandescent bulb. Illuminance refers to the amount of light falling on a surface or object. Both measures take account of the total amount of light energy per second that is emitted from or falls upon a defined area. In vision, the measured physical energy is weighted according to the characteristics of the human eye, whose sensitivity to light depends on its wavelength. Energy at wavelengths to which the eye is more sensitive is counted more heavily than energy at wavelengths to which the eye is less sensitive. Energy at wavelengths to which the eye is completely insensitive, as in the ultraviolet region, are not counted at all—the weight assigned is 0. Luminance is expressed in a number of different units of measurement whose values depend on the size of the area—whether cm^2, m^2, or ft^2—over which the energy is measured. The most popular unit is probably the *millilambert*. Illuminance also is measured in many different units, of which the *foot-candle* is the most popular. The recommended illuminance for various working conditions is given in Table 14.1.

Measurements of luminance and illuminance are usually made by having an observer match the unknown light or object to a standard light. The standard light's luminance is calculated from a physical analysis of its spectrum, which gives the amount of energy at each wavelength, and by the appropriate weighting of the spectrum according to the properties of the human eye.

Sound Sound is motion. The source of the motion is usually a solid body set in motion—a vibrating string or vocal cord, the impact of shoes on a floor, the turning of a fan. The vibrating body impresses a regular motion on the surround-

Table 14.1—
Recommended Illuminance

Working Conditions	Foot-Candles
Hospital operating table	300
Shop windows, main street	100
Very fine work (watchmaking)	100
Fine work (weaving)	30–50
Office work	20
Workshop, general lighting	10–20
Rough work, warehousing	7
Corridors and stairways	3

Source: Y. Le Grand, *Light, Colour and Vision* (London: Chapman & Hall, 1957), p. 83.

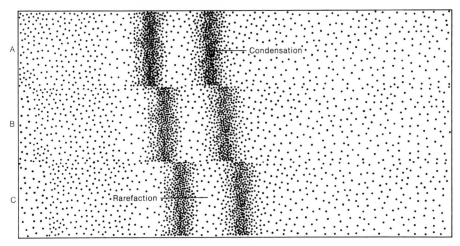

Figure 14.1
The propagation of a sound.

ing air particles. The vibrating body expands and contracts, first pressing out against the particles to create an area of *compression* and then releasing the pressure to leave an area of *rarefaction*. Figure 14.1 shows the relative density of air particles as a sound wave moves through them. Part B shows the density a moment later than part A. As the sound moves from left to right, the particles are set vibrating back and forth in the same direction as the sound moves. Because the particles move back and forth around their average resting place and do not advance with the wave, a sound wave requires a medium such as air that contains particles that can be set in motion. In a vacuum, there are no sounds.

In its simplest form as a pure tone, the motion of a sound wave is *sinusoidal,* as shown in Figure 14.2. The change in the *pressure* of the wave at a given point in space is plotted as a function of time. Pressure is maximum at the onset of the sound and then gradually decreases through zero until it becomes again maximum but in the opposite direction.

The physical characteristics of a sound wave are its *frequency* and its *amplitude*. Frequency is usually measured in cycles per second or hertz (Hz), while amplitude is typically measured in terms of *sound pressure,* that is, the effective amount of mechanical pressure that a given sound actually exerts. In general, the higher the frequency, the higher the tone sounds to us; and in general, the greater the sound pressure of the tone, the louder it sounds to us. But *loudness* is a psychological dimension, not a physical dimension, and the relationship between sound pressure and loudness is a complex one.

The range of sound pressures to which the ear is sensitive is so enormous that auditory intensity is usually measured in a logarithmic unit known as the *decibel*

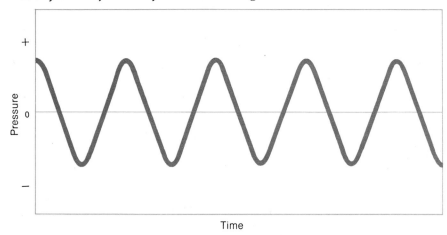

Figure 14.2
The wave form of a pure tone.

(dB). The *sound pressure level* (SPL) is measured in decibels according to the following formula: number of dB $= 20 \log P/.0002$ dynes per cm², where $P =$ sound pressure. The value of .0002 dynes per cm² was chosen as the reference because it is close to the smallest pressure detectable by the human ear. Thus, because log 1 equals 0, 0 dB is close to the faintest sound we can hear. The range of sounds we typically hear in the world around us varies up to about 140 dB (a sound many times louder than an acid rock group performing through a large power amplifier). Ordinary conversation typically comes in at about 70 dB. Figure 14.3 gives the dB levels of many common sounds.

A pure sinusoidal tone is largely a product of the laboratory. In nature most sounds are not so regular, not even the warble of a bird, but any periodic sound no matter how complex can be broken down into a number of sinusoidal components. Sounds composed of more than a single tone are called *complex* sounds. In comparing two or more waves, a third variable, *phase,* becomes important. Phase indicates at which part of a cycle a sinusoidal motion falls at a given instant relative to some arbitrary reference point in time. When there is only one tone, phase is unimportant, but the phase relation between two or more tones does become meaningful and is important because it helps us to localize sounds of low frequency. If information about phase is not important, then the stimulus can be represented in a simpler fashion on a *spectrum* in which amplitude is plotted as a function of frequency. Figure 14.4 gives the spectra for several musical sounds; each comprises many frequencies.

A common and useful laboratory stimulus is *white noise,* so called by analogy to white light because the noise contains all audible frequencies at randomly varying amplitudes. White noise sounds like an unvoiced long *sh,* as in the word

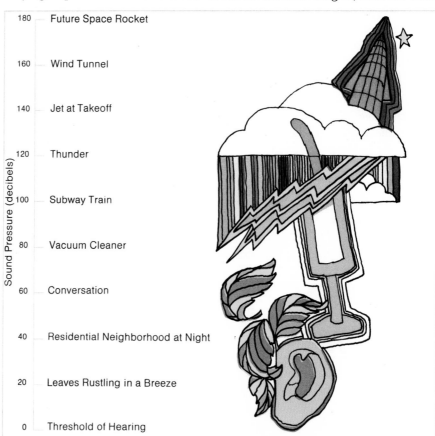

dB	Sound
180	Future Space Rocket
160	Wind Tunnel
140	Jet at Takeoff
120	Thunder
100	Subway Train
80	Vacuum Cleaner
60	Conversation
40	Residential Neighborhood at Night
20	Leaves Rustling in a Breeze
0	Threshold of Hearing

Sound Pressure (decibels)

Figure 14.3

The position of some familiar sounds on a decibel scale of sound pressure level.

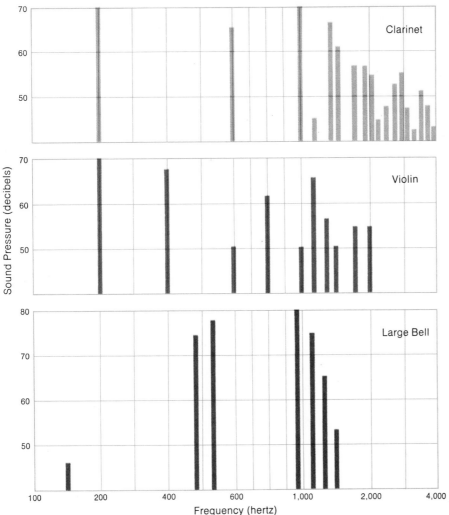

Figure 14.4
The sound spectra of a clarinet,
a violin, and a large bell.
(After Fletcher, 1946.)

"*sh*oe," and is approximated by the sound of falling water, as in a shower or waterfall. White noise is particularly useful in the study of masking, discussed later in this chapter.

Attributes of Sensation

In measuring sensations, we ask the subject to tell us about their *attributes*. An attribute is defined as a quality of a sensation that can be held constant while in all other respects the sensation is varied. It turns out that a simple sound has four attributes: the familiar pitch and loudness, and also volume (how large it appears to be) and density (how compact it appears to be). Consider, for example, the musical notes produced by the piccolo and the tuba. The piccolo produces notes that are high in pitch and usually relatively low in loudness. In addition, reflection and a little imagination reveal that the piccolo's notes appear to be dense and to occupy little space. The tuba's notes, on the other hand, are of lower pitch and probably of considerable loudness. In addition, they seem to fill the entire concert hall with their volume. But they have very low density; they do not seem compact. Loudness, pitch, volume, and density are the attributes of auditory sensations because an observer can, by adjusting the frequency and intensity of the physical stimulus, hold constant any one of these attributes despite variations in all the others. For example, the loudness of a tone is an attribute because it can be held constant while the tone's pitch, volume, and density are changed. To do this, the listener must be free to vary both the

259

intensity and the frequency of the tone. If the frequency is increased, for example, the loudness may be held constant by decreasing the sound pressure level. At the same time, the tone rises in pitch and becomes denser but less voluminous.

Psychologists and physiologists investigate by a variety of techniques the ways in which attributes are related to the physical stimulus and how the attributes are coded in the nervous system. The goal of this research is to show how a physical stimulus gives rise to nervous activity that in turn leads to predictable human responses. Apart from its role in providing an understanding of man, such information can help in the development of techniques for the prevention and treatment of malfunctions in the sensory systems and the development of therapeutic devices such as hearing aids. It may also facilitate the building of machines, mainly computers, to duplicate certain human functions.

Measurement of Sensation

It was not always clear how sensation—an internal, untouchable, unpublishable event—could be measured. Most of the earliest measurements were concerned with the smallest detectable changes in stimulus and sensation.

Weber's Law

Weber's law, established in 1834, states that the just-noticeable difference or change in a stimulus is a constant proportion of the stimulus, $\Delta S = kS$, where S = stimulus, ΔS = just-noticeable difference, and k is a constant whose value depends on the type of stimulus and the sense modality. The larger or stronger the stimulus, the larger the change required for an observer to notice that anything has happened to it. An inch added to a ten-inch line is obvious. Added to a ten-foot line, it is not even detectable.

Fechner's Law

Fechner so extended Weber's measurements that he is considered the father of the measurement of sensation, which he called *psychophysics,* the study of the relation between the sensation and the stimulus. Using Weber's law and making some seemingly reasonable assumptions, he claimed to be able to state the precise relation between the magnitude of any sensation and the magnitude of its appropriate stimulus. Fechner's law is $\psi = a \log S$; ψ stands for the magnitude of the sensation, S for the magnitude of the physical stimulus, and a is a constant whose value depends on the sensation investigated and the units of measurement.

Figure 14.5

An illustration of Weber's law. It is much easier to see that the short lines are different in length than to see that the long lines are, even though there is a physically greater difference between the long lines.

Fechner's law was extremely important because it said that almost any sensation stands in the same mathematical relation to its stimulus, whether the relation be between brightness and light intensity, loudness and sound pressure, felt weight and physical weight, and so on. Fechner's and Weber's laws were the first general, quantitative laws in psychology, the first laws about behavior. Unfortunately, Fechner's law turns out to have been incorrect; nevertheless it implanted the notion that behavior can be studied scientifically and that psychology can strive toward the goal of all science, the uncovering of invariant, unambiguous relations, stated as precisely as possible, preferably in mathematical equations.

Fechner's major error was in assuming that a just-noticeable physical change in a stimulus always occasions a change in sensation that is *constant*. Such an assumption implies that while the magnitude of a just-noticeable stimulus change increases with stimulus magnitude, the amount of change perceived in the sensation is always the same. Intuitively it may seem plausible that the sensation corresponding to a stimulus change that is only just barely noticeable would always be the same regardless of the size of the change. Fechner and his followers thought that sensation magnitude could not be measured directly but must be inferred from measurements of just-noticeable changes. Thus, he did not attempt an experimental test. Rather, using Weber's proportionality law and his own assumption about the subjective equality of just-noticeable differences, Fechner arrived at his logarithmic law.

Stevens' Power Law

In the twentieth century, techniques for the direct measurement of sensation have been invented. In one technique, *ratio production*, listeners are given control of the intensity of one sound and asked to make it twice as loud as another, or five times or one-half as loud. From data like these, changes in loudness are measured as a function of intensity, and the psychophysical law is directly obtained. These direct procedures are sometimes called the *new psychophysics*. Their validity rests on (1) their repeatability—different groups of subjects and different techniques give essentially the same results (in another type of direct procedure, *magnitude estimation*, subjects assign numbers to sounds proportional to their loudness; if the first tone in a series is called 2 and the second tone sounds 3 times as loud, the subject calls it 6, and so on); and (2) their predictive power—the obtained sensation functions can be used to predict responses in other experiments.

The recent burgeoning of these direct measurements has resulted in a new general law of psychophysics—*Stevens' power law*. These measurements have shown clearly and convincingly that the subjective magnitude, ψ, is proportional to the physical magnitude, S, raised to a power, n. That is, $\psi = kS^n$, where the value of n depends upon the particular sensation and attribute measured and k is an arbitrary constant of proportionality that depends on the unit of measurement.

Figure 14.6 gives examples of three power functions—electric shock applied to the finger, length of line, and loudness. The functions are straight lines plotted on double logarithmic coordinates because, in logarithmic notation, the power law is $\log \psi = \log k + n \log S$, which is the equation for a straight line with a slope equal to the exponent, n. Electric shock grows more rapidly than any other stimulus tested thus far (exponent = 3.5)—doubling the stimulus intensity makes the sensation grow tenfold. Length of line has an exponent of 1, which means that doubling the physical length of the line causes it to *appear* twice as long—estimates of length are relatively, at least, very accurate. Loudness has a slope of 0.3 when the sound energy is measured—doubling the sound energy increases the loudness only about 25 percent, and a tenfold increase in energy is needed to double the loudness.

Plotted on ordinary linear coordinates, the lines of Figure 14.6 look like those in Figure 14.7. Most attributes of sensation that have been measured are a power

Figure 14.6
Psychological magnitude as a function of physical magnitude. Magnitudes increase logarithmically on both axes.
(After Stevens, 1962.)

Figure 14.7
The same functions with psychological and physical magnitudes plotted linearly.
(After Stevens, 1962.)

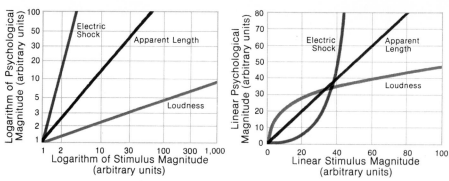

function of some physical measure of the stimulus. Table 14.2 lists a number of representative exponents of the power functions relating psychological magnitude to stimulus magnitude. The pervasiveness of the power law suggests that the nervous system imposes this relation on our sensations. A power relation, regardless of the value of the exponent, means that equal ratios of one variable correspond to equal ratios of the other variable. Perhaps perception is facilitated when most of the attributes of sensation are related to their physical counterparts in such a way that equal ratios in the stimulus domain correspond to equal ratios in the sensation domain.

Limits of Sensory Sensitivity   Our eyes and ears can detect extremely small amounts of energy. Although reference is often made to receptor events, threshold, by definition, refers to the

Table 14.2—Representative Exponents

Continuum	Exponent	Stimulus Condition
Loudness	0.60	binaural
Loudness	0.54	monaural
Brightness	0.33	5° target—dark-adapted eye
Brightness	0.50	point source—dark-adapted eye
Lightness	1.20	reflectance of gray papers
Smell	0.55	coffee odor
Smell	0.60	heptane
Taste	0.80	saccharine
Taste	1.30	sucrose
Taste	1.30	salt
Temperature	1.00	cold—on arm
Temperature	1.50	warmth—on arm
Vibration	0.95	60 cps—on finger
Vibration	0.60	250 cps—on finger
Duration	1.10	white-noise stimulus
Repetition rate	1.00	light, sound, touch, and shocks
Finger span	1.30	thickness of wood blocks
Pressure on palm	1.10	static force on skin
Heaviness	1.45	lifted weights
Force of handgrip	1.70	precision hand dynamometer
Vocal effort	1.10	sound pressure of vocalization
Electric shock	3.50	60 cps—through fingers
Tactual roughness	1.50	felt diameter of emery grits
Tactual hardness	0.80	rubber squeezed between fingers
Visual velocity	1.20	moving spot of light
Visual length	1.00	projected line of light
Visual area	0.70	projected square of light

Source: S. S. Stevens, *In Pursuit of Sensory Law;* second public Klopsteg lecture (Evanston, Ill.: Technological Institute, Northwestern University, November 7, 1962), p. 7.

behavior of intact organisms. *Threshold* is often defined as the stimulus intensity at which the observer reports detecting a signal on 50 percent of the trials. The limits of human sensitivity have been measured under optimal conditions with respect to both stimulus and subject variables. Threshold is determined by stimulus variables such as intensity, frequency (or wavelength), duration, size, and rate of presentation, as well as by subject variables such as adaptational state, training, age, motivation, and health; experimental procedures also affect thresholds. One of the most difficult problems is motivation and the subject's criterion for stating that he saw or heard something.

Certain procedures allow the experimenter to classify the observer's response as right or wrong. For example, in one version of the procedure called *forced choice,* a trial consists of two portions. In hearing, the two portions or intervals are temporarily separated, and in vision they are usually spatially separated. On each trial, the observer reports which interval of time contained the signal. The signal is set at a fixed level and presented in one of the two intervals on each of as many as a hundred consecutive trials. Blocks of trials are run with the signal set at different levels. The observer's responses provide an objective measure of the proportion of correct judgments at each intensity level. Threshold is taken as the stimulus level that elicits an arbitrary proportion of correct responses—often 75 percent correct is used. Forced-choice procedures tend to be long and tedious because so many trials are required at each level.

A quicker, more commonly used but less precise procedure is the *method of limits.* The experimenter alternately increases and decreases the intensity level in discrete steps, and after each change the observer reports whether or not he detected the signal. Figure 14.8 gives a set of results in which the frequency of a tone was varied in order to determine the lowest detectable frequency. When the observer changes his response, the experimenter skips several steps on the frequency scale and then starts changing frequency in the opposite direction. Threshold is taken as the average of the frequencies at which shifts in judgment occurred. Many variations of the method of limits are used. One variation especially popular in hearing is the *tracking* method devised by Békésy. The observer controls the stimulus intensity. Pressing a switch causes the sound intensity to increase; releasing the switch causes it to decrease. The observer is instructed to increase intensity until he just hears the sound and decrease it until he just stops hearing it. A pen records the change in intensity. Besides giving a continuous

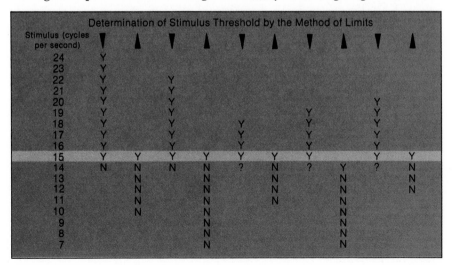

Figure 14.8
The method of limits. Alternatively, the experimenter presents decreasing frequencies until the observer says he cannot hear the sound; then, starting quite low, the experimenter increases the frequency until the observer says he can hear the sound.
(After Woodworth and Schlosberg, 1954.)

Figure 14.9

The intensity of the dimmest light that can be seen varies as a function of wavelength and depends on the area of the retina stimulated. (After Hecht and Hsia, 1945.)

Figure 14.10

The smallest amount of intensity change necessary to produce a detectable difference in brightness as a function of the intensity of the stimulus for four stimulus sizes. (After Steinhardt, 1936.)

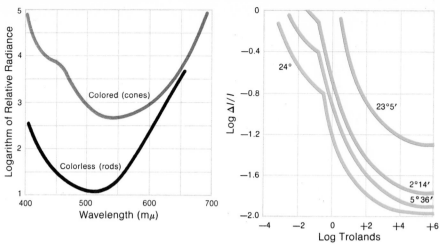

Figure 14.11

The smallest change in wavelength that will produce a detectable difference in hue as a function of wavelength. (After Judd, 1932.)

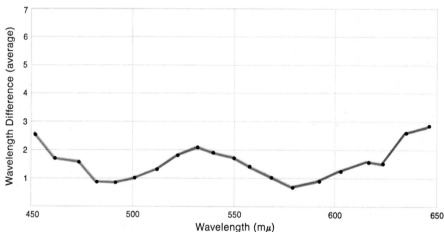

record of the observer's responses, this procedure has the advantage of permitting the experimenter to vary frequency while the observer varies intensity. Usually the frequency is increased slowly as the observer tracks his threshold so that a whole *audiogram* is obtained in fifteen or twenty minutes, showing how an individual's threshold depends on frequency.

Visual Sensitivity

Figure 14.9 shows how the intensity of a light that can just be seen (threshold) varies as a function of wavelength. Two curves are presented: one curve is obtained by directing light to the center of the eye, the fovea; the other, by stimulating an area in the periphery about 20 degrees from the center. The fovea is most sensitive at about 560 millimicrons ($m\mu$), the periphery at about 500 $m\mu$. Maximum sensitivity shifts from the longer to the shorter wavelengths. This also happens as light dims, and is called the *Purkinje shift* after the nineteenth-century Austrian physiologist who pointed out in a book on the phenomenology of vision that blues and violets (short wavelengths) become relatively brighter and oranges and reds relatively dimmer at twilight.

So far we have considered only *absolute* thresholds—the minimum amount of detectable light intensity. *Differential thresholds* concern the minimum detectable *change* in a stimulus or the minimum detectable difference between two successive or adjacent stimuli. Figure 14.10 shows how intensity discrimination varies as a function of light intensity for stimuli of various sizes. A break occurs for the larger stimuli that extend out beyond the fovea, but not for the stimuli under 2 degrees that cover the fovea only. Figure 14.11 shows the

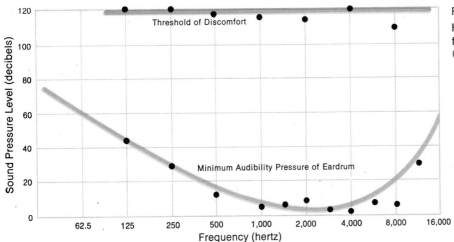

Figure 14.12

Hearing threshold as a function of frequency.
(After Davis, 1960.)

smallest wavelength difference required for observers to report a difference between two lights that are equal in brightness and all other respects. A difference of only one or two millimicrons is needed.

Auditory Sensitivity

Figure 14.12 gives, as a function of frequency, the minimum audible sound pressure that young adults can hear. The tones were presented via a loudspeaker in a specially constructed *anechoic room*, in which there are almost no echoes. Figure 14.12 also shows the upper pressure limits beyond which sounds become uncomfortable. People disagree about when a sound begins to cause pain or discomfort, but the boundary is somewhere between 100 and 140 dB. Sounds more intense than 140 dB are likely to cause permanent damage to the ear.

Several other factors affect the auditory threshold. As the bandwidth (the separation between the lowest and highest frequency components) of a complex signal is increased beyond a certain value that depends on frequency, the threshold goes down. Mode of presentation also counts; a sound presented binaurally, to both ears simultaneously, is easier to hear than the same sound presented monaurally (to only one ear).

Also influencing threshold is preceding auditory stimulation. Adaptation or fatigue is prominent in hearing as well as in seeing, although it plays a much less important role. After exposure to a loud sound, the absolute threshold is temporarily raised. The longer and more intense the exposure, the larger the threshold shift and the longer before hearing returns to normal. Much work has been done on the problem of temporal threshold shift in the hope of gaining

Figure 14.13

An anechoic chamber. Sound waves are absorbed rather than reflected by the floor, walls, and ceiling. The observer is supported on a wire grid, which disrupts sound waves negligibly.

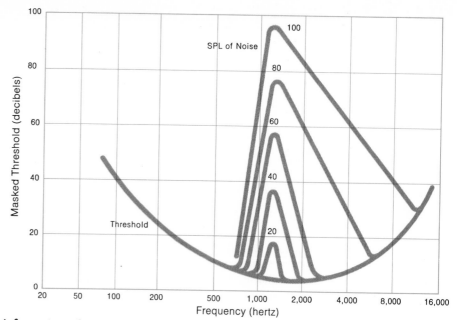

information about permanent threshold shifts—auditory damage—that come from long-term exposure to intense noise in factories, airports, and so on.

Masking

Usually, we hear more than one sound at a time, and it is generally harder to hear one sound in the presence of another than alone. The effect of one sound upon the threshold of another sound is called *masking*. The amount of masking in decibels is the increase in the threshold for the second sound caused by the masking sound or *masker*. Perhaps the most striking fact about masking is that low frequencies mask high frequencies much better than the other way around. Figure 14.14 shows how the threshold varies as a function of frequency when a tone is masked by a narrow-band masker centered on 1,200 Hz and set to various sound pressure levels. The more intense the noise band, the more it masks tones within its frequency limits (1,100 to 1,300 Hz) and *above*. Frequencies below the noise band are hardly affected. Within the frequency limits of the noise band, for every increase of 10 dB in the noise level, threshold rises 10 dB. These results are true for a narrow band of noise located anywhere in the audible frequency spectrum.

Often the masking sound covers a wide band of frequencies. *White noise* is a common laboratory example. Such a sound raises the thresholds for all frequencies. Careful investigations have shown, however, that only a small part of the noise, those frequency components in the immediate vicinity of the masked tone, contributes to the masking. Figure 14.15 illustrates how, as a white noise is narrowed, the threshold for a tone at first is unaffected but then, when the noise is very narrow, the tone becomes clearly audible. At low frequencies, only a narrow band of the noise contributes to the masking, but at higher frequencies, a much larger part of the noise contributes. This contributing band is called the *critical band,* and its width is plotted as a function of the frequency of the masked tone in Figure 14.16. The critical band plays a role in many other kinds of auditory phenomena, including loudness, as indicated above, and probably represents a basic property of the auditory system.

An interesting and still unexplained phenomenon in masking occurs when a listener adjusts the intensity of a low-frequency tone so that he just barely hears it against an intense background noise. Both tone and noise are presented

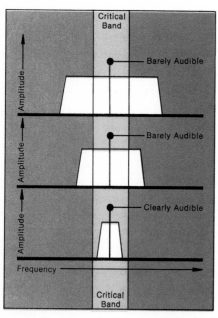

monaurally to the same ear. Now the noise is added to the other ear so the listener is bombarded with twice as much noise. One would expect the tone, barely audible in monaural noise, to disappear altogether in binaural noise. Instead, the tone is clearly audible. To set the tone back to threshold, the tone's intensity must be reduced. It seems that the monaural tone is easier to hear in binaural noise because the tone and noise are localized in different places—the tone is heard at the earphone and the binaural noise in the middle of the head. Adding a tone to the other ear moves it to the middle of the head, where the binaural noise is, and the tone is therefore harder to hear. These results may be related to our ability to attend to one of many voices in a roomful of people. The one voice can stand out partly because it comes from a different place from all the others. This so-called cocktail-party effect also depends on other differences (temporal, intensive, frequency) between the attended voice and other voices.

Measurements of the differential threshold in hearing reveal a baffling sensitivity to frequency differences. Within the audible frequency range (20 to 20,000 Hz), we can detect changes as small as 3 Hz in frequencies under 1,000 Hz and changes as small as 0.2 to 0.3 percent in frequencies above 1,000 Hz. These values apply only at levels higher than 30 dB above absolute threshold. Below about 30 dB, the just-noticeable difference at all frequencies rises as threshold is neared. In other words, soft tones are more difficult to tell apart than loud tones.

Weber's law holds fairly well for intensity discrimination. From a point about 40 dB above threshold upward, an intensity change of 0.5 dB is detectable at most frequencies.

The threshold is a statistical concept. It is the energy level at which a stimulus is detected a certain percentage of the time. In a yes-no experiment where the observer responds on each trial whether he detects the signal or not, threshold is usually taken at 50 percent. At energy levels below threshold, the observer detects the signal on less than 50 percent. Classical theory ascribes this variation to fluctuation in the observer's sensitivity, with the nonsensory variables supposedly canceling out.

Two major difficulties with this approach have been that observers appear more or less sensitive depending on their *criterion* for deciding whether a signal was presented, and often they say a signal was presented when there was none. A cautious observer uses a high criterion; he does not say he detected a signal unless he is quite sure. A daring observer chooses a low criterion and reports signals about which he may be very unsure. Criterion selection is determined not only by personality variables (daring versus cautious) but also by the experimental situation, the importance and value of the decisions to the observer, the observer's attitudes, and so on. Classical procedures have attempted to estimate the criterion by inserting so-called catch trials in which no signal is presented. The observer with a low criterion gets caught more often, gives more *false alarms,* than the observer with a high criterion. But why should there be false alarms if there is a threshold, below which every no-signal trial must fall? Signal-detection theory tackles this question and provides separate measures of the contributions of motivation and sensitivity to performance on threshold tasks.

Signal-detection theory ascribes false alarms mainly to real sensory events that occur even when no signal is present. We have already seen that spontaneous neural activity is inherent in the auditory and visual nervous systems. Confronted with a series of trials on which very weak signals are sometimes

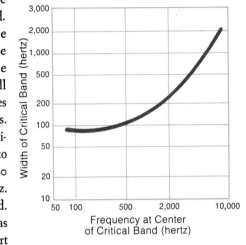

Figure 14.16

The width of the critical band as a function of the frequency of the masked tone. (After Zwicker, *et al.,* 1957.)

Signal-Detection Theory

presented, the observer may easily mistake spontaneous activity for activity evoked by a signal. Signal-detection theory assumes that the spontaneous activity fluctuates so that it sometimes reaches levels as high as or higher than the level of signal-evoked neural activity. Thus, we can think of the observer as having to make his decision on the basis of the two overlapping distributions shown in Figure 14.17.

One distribution presents the probability of neural activity's reaching various levels when only spontaneous activity (internal noise) is present, the other distribution when a signal is presented whose evoked activity is added to that of the spontaneous activity or noise. (Often in auditory tests of signal-detection theory, white noise is presented on every trial and on some trials a tone is added; the fluctuations in white noise can be specified, which simplifies analysis because the much lower and unspecifiable "internal noise" or spontaneous neural activity can be ignored.) The two distributions overlap so that the observer is bound to make mistakes. Or is he? After all, the observer does not have these distributions before him. On each trial, he has a sensory experience on the basis of which he decides whether it is more likely that his experience came from the noise-alone distribution or the noise-plus-signal distribution. It is assumed that early in a series of trials the subject chooses some *criterion* or level of sensation that serves to divide his responses into the two required categories, yes and no. This is criterion (C) in Figure 14.17. If, on a given trial, his experience exceeds C, he says he detected a signal. If his criterion is high, far to the right of the line, then he will almost never give a false alarm because almost no noise-alone event will exceed his criterion. However, he will miss many signals, too, because many noise-plus-signal events will also fall below his criterion. A subject with a low criterion, far to the left, will detect most of the signals but at the price of a large number of false alarms. With the criterion as shown on the curves, the subject would detect about 50 percent of the signals and give false alarms on 16 percent of the no-signal trials. These percentages are taken from the proportion of the normal curves to the right of C.

As the criterion shifts, so does the ratio of hits (correct signal detections) to false alarms. These shifts are usually graphed as a *receiver-operating characteristic* (ROC) curve. The percentage of hits is plotted as a function of the percentage of false alarms. Figure 14.18 shows the results of one experiment in which the criterion was artificially shifted by the experimenter (by changing the a priori probability of a signal's occurring). An increase in the percentage of hits is always accompanied by an increase in the percentage of false alarms if only the criterion is changed. If the signal strength is increased, then for a given criterion, the percentage of hits will increase without changing the percentage of false alarms because increasing the signal shifts the whole noise-plus-signal distribution to the right, away from the noise-only distribution. A more sensitive observer for whom the effective signal strength is higher will also do better, as shown in the second part of Figure 14.18.

Signal-detection theory is a derivative of statistical decision theory. The observer in a threshold experiment is treated like a statistician who has to make a decision about a hypothesis. The hypothesis is that a signal was presented. The alternate hypothesis is that no signal was presented. Because only two hypotheses or responses are allowed and on each trial a signal either was or was not presented, it is possible to set up a 2-by-2 *pay-off matrix*, shown in Figure 14.19. Variations in the value of each cell can alter performance considerably by affecting the choice of a criterion. If hits are highly rewarded and false alarms lightly

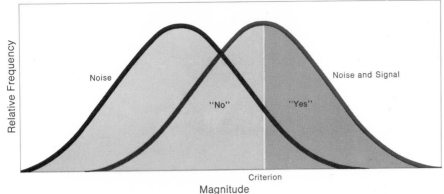

Figure 14.17
A diagram of the kind of statistical decision made by observers according to signal-detection theory.

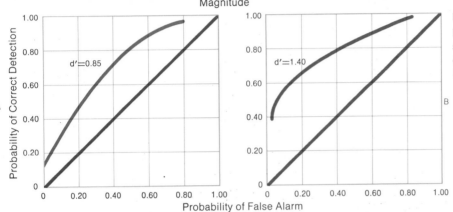

Figure 14.18
ROC curves generated by artificially shifting the observer's criterion. In B the effective signal strength is higher than in A.
(After Swets, 1961.)

punished or ignored, an observer will usually pick a low criterion, and so on.

The important contribution of signal-detection theory to sensory psychology is the provision of sophisticated mathematical procedures for the design and analysis of detection experiments. These procedures separate the response criterion from sensitivity. This separation was shown in Figure 14.18, where we saw that a change in criterion shifted both the hit and false-alarm rates whereas a shift in sensitivity shifted only the hit rate. The curves shown in Figure 14.18 are theoretical and are determined by the observer's responses and information about the stimulus. Given only one point on an ROC plot, the appropriate curve can be drawn with its associated sensitivity and criterion values. Another advantage of signal-detection theory is that it provides a measure of how an "ideal observer" would do, given certain noise and signal values. Actual human observers do not do as well as the ideal observer, but their performance can be compared to a meaningful standard.

Simply separating sensitivity and criterion is extremely valuable, and it also helps determine the effects on detection of higher-level, cognitive processes such as attention and response dependencies. The results so far seem to have yielded much new information about sensory processes; they form a crest of the psychophysical wave of the future.

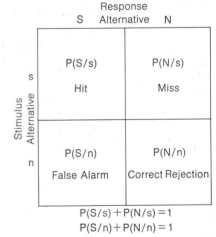

Figure 14.19
Payoff matrix in an experiment in which two stimulus alternatives and two possible responses combine to produce four possible trial outcomes.
(After Green and Swets, 1966.)

15

AUDITORY, CHEMICAL, AND OTHER SENSES

As far as our sensory world is concerned, the eyes have it. The number of neurons connected with vision is much greater than with any of the other senses, and it is estimated that as much as 25 percent of the total energy expended by the brain goes toward the upkeep of our visual apparatus. Our eyes are so acute, our environment so colorful, that we often tend to denigrate hearing and the other senses such as taste, smell, and touch. Taste, smell, and touch, for example, are typically referred to in textbooks as being "the lower senses," although no one ever bothers to mention in what sense they are lower.

Psychology tends to follow the trends set in the world around us. Thus, most work on sensation has been devoted to vision, so we know enough about seeing to devote a separate chapter to that subject, whereas hearing and the other senses are combined. There is no doubt that vision is important to us, and the world would be a much less exciting, interesting place were we blind. But we should avoid rank-ordering the various senses in terms of how much information scientists have gathered about them lest we end up giving vision more than its due. The other senses have their own exquisite contributions to make to all our lives.

Sense of Hearing

For man, hearing is the social sense, just as for many animals smell is the sense facilitating their social interaction. Of the myriad sounds heard each day, those that make up the speech of others and of ourselves are the most important. Some people for whom social intercourse is paramount view the loss of hearing as imposing a greater burden than the loss of sight—they can dispense with the accompanying looks and gestures as long as they can hear the sounds of speech, with its linguistic content and its intonations that reveal the emotions of the speaker as well as or better than visible signs.

Language and thought are not irrevocably dependent on hearing, but speech perception and the development of speech are. Mammalian hearing evolved to

271

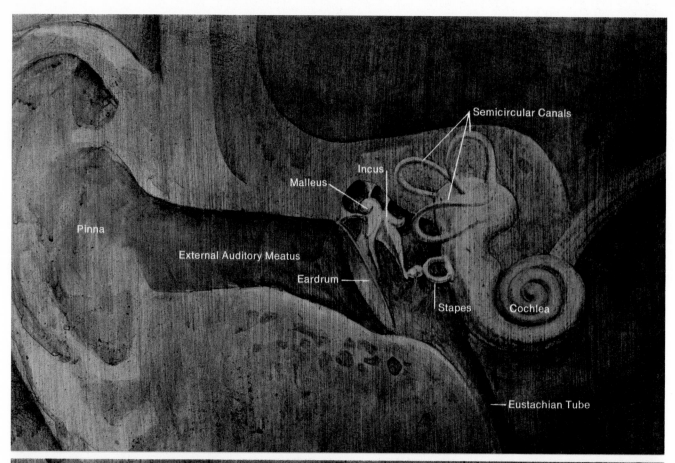

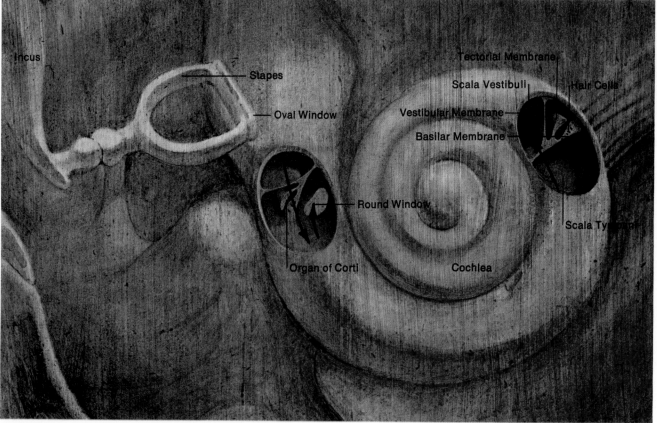

serve nonspeaking animals; speech and man's vocal apparatus probably evolved, in part, to accommodate the already established auditory mechanism.

We shall treat the auditory system as a *sensory-transducing device,* that is, a device for changing sound waves into neural impulses that eventually give rise to the sensation of hearing.

The Ear

The ear changes stimulus energy into neural energy. Figure 15.1 shows the middle ear with the outer ear (pinna and auditory canal) and the cochlea. (The three rings are part of the vestibular apparatus that provides cues to body position and movement.)

Sound reaching the eardrum sets it and the ossicles vibrating to and fro, transmitting the movement of the air particles to the cochlea buried deep in the body's hardest bone. The cochlea has the extremely sensitive *basilar membrane* coiled up inside. The basilar membrane and the rest of the interior of the cochlea are shown in cross section in Figure 15.2. Sound energy entering the cochlea via the oval window sets up a pressure wave that travels from the oval window to the apex of the cochlea, causing a progressive displacement along the basilar membrane. Pressure against the oval window is relieved by the flexibility of the *round window,* which lies on the other side of the basilar membrane.

When the basilar membrane is wobbled by the traveling wave, the *organ of Corti* lying on it also moves up and down. In the organ of Corti are the hair cells with their extensions or hairs embedded in the *tectorial membrane.* This membrane and the basilar membrane move somewhat differently, so that the hairs are bent by the tectorial membrane in a kind of rubbing or shearing action. The bending of the hairs causes, in an undetermined manner, the hair cells to send neural impulses to the auditory nerve. At the threshold of hearing, the basilar

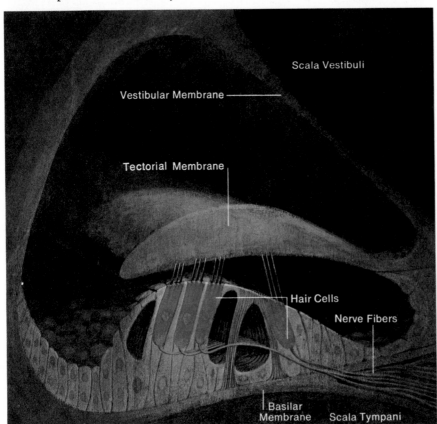

Scala Vestibuli

Vestibular Membrane

Tectorial Membrane

Hair Cells

Nerve Fibers

Basilar Membrane   Scala Tympani

Figure 15.1 *(opposite)*
The organs of hearing.

Figure 15.2 *(opposite)*
The cochlea. The arrows show the path of pressure waves set up at the oval window and absorbed at the round window.

Figure 15.3
Cross section of the cochlear duct.

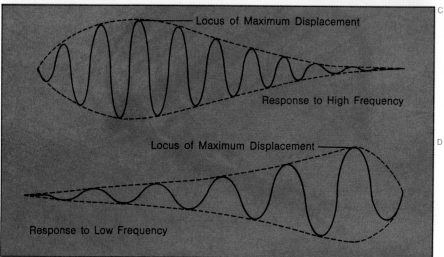

Figure 15.4
(A) The basilar membrane showing the locus of maximal excitation corresponding to various frequencies. (B) The cochlea may be represented as a straight (rather than coiled) tapering cylinder so that the motion of the basilar membrane in response to (C) high-frequency and (D) low-frequency stimulation may be illustrated. (After Stuhlman, 1943.)

membrane vibrates over a distance 100 times smaller than the diameter of a hydrogen atom. Somehow, this infinitesimally small movement leads to hearing.

Using ingenious techniques, Békésy has observed the displacements of the basilar membrane under high-powered microscopes when an intense pure tone is introduced into the ear. Békésy found that different parts of the basilar membrane were maximally excited by different frequencies. High-frequency tones affect the region near the oval window the most. As the tone decreases in frequency, the locus of excitation moves down the membrane toward the apex of the cochlea. Thus, frequency is encoded by the *place* of maximum displacement on the basilar membrane.

Neural Coding in the Auditory System

The basilar membrane transduces stimulus energy into neural energy. Transduction is mechanical in the ear.

In the basilar membrane the hair cells make synaptic connection with the fibers of the auditory nerve, which pass out to the cochlear nucleus in the medulla. Figure 15.5 shows the pathways followed from both ears to the auditory cortex. Note the four relay stations—cochlear nucleus, superior olive, inferior colliculus, and medial geniculate—and the large amount of crossing over from one side of the brain stem to the other.

Despite its great complexity, the auditory system retains its tonotopic organization—that is, the correlation between place and frequency noted on the basilar membrane—in the auditory nerve, the cochlear nucleus, and the auditory cortex. For example, in the auditory cortex the place of maximum electrical response to stimulation by pure tones shifts as a function of frequency. Other studies have

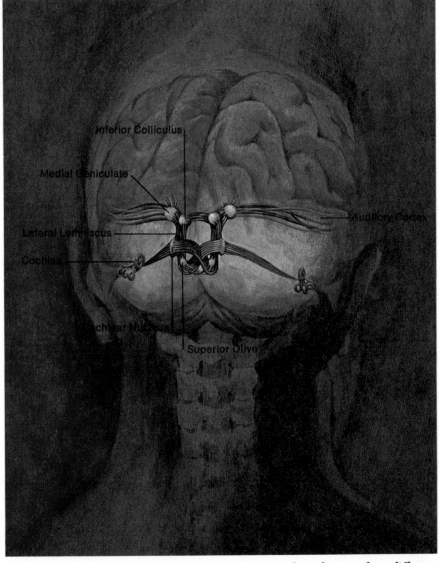

Figure 15.5
Auditory pathways in the brain.

shown that the basilar membrane may be represented in three or four different places on the cortex. The correlations support a projection theory of pitch perception. However, pitch perception is so much more accurate than would be predicted from the flatness of the traveling wave pattern that it is not clear how a simple projection of mechanical events on the basilar membrane can be the basis for our fine frequency discrimination.

The fibers of the auditory nerve seem to be excited only when one of the ossicles, the stapes, pushes in against the oval window. An outward motion, corresponding to rarefaction at the eardrum, inhibits the auditory nerve response and decreases neural firing below the spontaneous rate.

Although frequency discrimination has been the major theoretical problem in hearing, the coding of sound intensity also poses problems. It is thought that loudness depends upon the number of active fibers and the degree of their activity, as reflected primarily in their rate of firing. As in most neural fibers, the discharge rate increases with stimulus intensity. In the auditory nerve, it increases over a stimulus range of 40 to 50 dB. But loudness increases steadily over a range of about 140 dB. Frequency of firing cannot by itself, then, encode all the intensity information. The number of active fibers also increases with intensity because the spread of displacement over the basilar membrane increases with intensity, thereby activating more and more fiber. But even this effect is not sufficient to explain how we hear loudness. A full explanation of loudness simply is not yet available to us.

Another important aspect of auditory perception is localization. Sounds usually can be localized in space. This ability depends primarily on tiny physical and temporal differences between the sounds arriving at the two ears. For example, a sound from the left arrives at the left ear about 7/10,000ths of a second sooner than at the right ear. This small time difference causes the listener to hear the sound as being on the left. Localization, like frequency discrimination, may depend on which fibers are most active.

Basic Phenomena of Hearing

A consideration of the basic phenomena of hearing—loudness, pitch, binaural interaction—provides a basis for understanding the main functions of the auditory system: the identification and localization of sound sources. Pitch is the basic variable in identification; loudness, in detection and in determining the distance and size of the sound source; and binaural interaction, in determining the direction of the source.

■LOUDNESS

Loudness is the subjective magnitude of strength of a sound as distinct from its physical intensity. The match between loudness and physical magnitude, such as sound pressure, is poor, but loudness does have a predictable relation to sound pressure. For a given change in the sound pressure, the loudness changes a given amount; generally, when the sound pressure level (SPL) is increased threefold, corresponding to about a ten-decibel increase (see Chapter 14), the loudness doubles.

How, the reader must wonder, do we find out how loudness changes? What is the measuring instrument? The listener is. The experimenter presents a stimulus at a variety of known sound pressures to the listener, who is asked, in one commonly used procedure called *magnitude estimation,* to assign the number 10 to one sound of intermediate loudness and to assign a number to each other sound that corresponds to its loudness relative to the sound of loudness 10. Observers agree remarkably well in the relative numerical values they assign.

What effects do such factors as frequency, complexity, and duration have on loudness? The loudness function shown in Figure 15.6 is for a pure tone with a frequency of 1,000 Hz, but the same function, or very nearly so, holds for pure tones at frequencies between about 500 and 4,000 Hz. This statement is based not on measurements at all those frequencies or even on magnitude estimations at more than a few of them. Long before psychoacousticians believed one could learn about loudness by asking subjects to judge loudness directly by assigning numbers, they were busy finding out how intense tones at different frequencies must be in order to sound equally loud.

In this type of measurement, the listener is asked to adjust the sound pressure of one tone to make it as loud as a standard tone. The two tones alternate, and the listener is given control of one of them by means of an intensity-control knob similar to that on a radio or TV set. The standard tone is set at a given frequency and sound pressure, while the other tone, at a different frequency, is adjusted in sound pressure by the listener. This procedure reveals how much sound pressure is required for a tone at one frequency to sound as loud as a tone at another frequency. As would be expected from the hearing-threshold curve (Chapter 14), low and high frequencies must be more intense to sound as loud as the

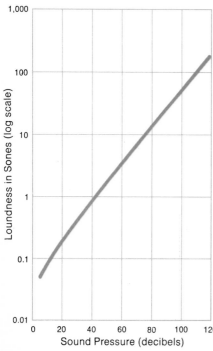

Figure 15.6

The relation of loudness to sound pressure. (After Stevens and Davis, 1938.)

middle frequencies. However, as the sound pressure of the standard tone is increased, differences among frequencies become smaller (Figure 15.7).

■ PITCH

Pitch is closely related to frequency, but the two should not be confused: *pitch* refers to the subjective attribute and frequency to the physical variable. Figure 15.8 gives the measured relation between pitch and frequency. The unit for pitch is the *mel*. Although Figure 15.8 is for pure tones, complex sounds also usually have a characteristic pitch. Sound sources are most often identified by their pitch quality; the sounds of speech, on the basis of pitch.

Pitch has been the center of attention in auditory theory, but every theory of pitch perception faces two difficult problems. First, there is the problem of the

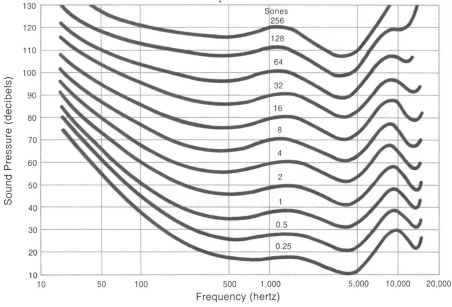

Figure 15.7

Equal loudness contours for pure tones: the curves show the physical intensities at which tones of varying frequency sound equally loud.
(After International Standards Organization, 1961.)

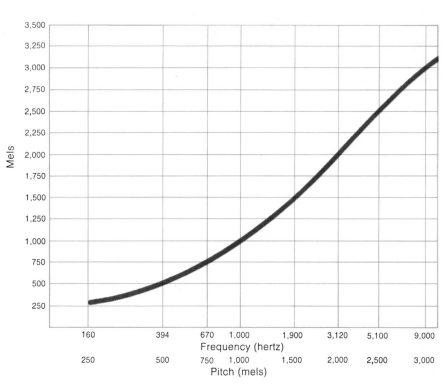

Figure 15.8

Pitch in mels as a function of frequency.
(After Stevens and Davis, 1938.)

large number of different pitches distinguishable at most sound pressure levels—something like 1,000 under optimal testing conditions. Second, a listener can distinguish more than one pitch at a time. Indeed, *Ohm's law* states that we can hear the individual components of any complex sound. Although this statement is not strictly true—if the components are too close or too many, they become confused—we nevertheless can distinguish the violin from the drum and from many other instruments in an orchestra. How then is frequency represented or coded in the auditory nervous system so as to enable us to detect small pitch differences and to hear different pitches simultaneously?

Two types of explanation are offered. One theory says that frequency is translated into a locus of excitation on the basilar membrane and is recognized according to the principles we discussed earlier. An alternative theory says that frequency is directly represented in the nervous system by some repetitive event with the same frequency as the sound's. The first theory relies on the observed ordering of frequency on the basilar membrane. The second theory relies in part on the observations that the cochlea duplicates some aspects of the stimulus waveform and frequency and that the firing of the auditory nerve follows, within limitations, the stimulus frequency. In its modern guise, the second theory, known as the *volley theory,* includes the first.

Having observed the traveling wave on the basilar membrane, Békésy assumed that pitch is related to the place of maximum displacement, whose location along the basilar membrane depends on the frequency of the stimulus—high frequencies produce a maximum displacement near the oval window, low frequencies near the apex of the cochlea. In essence, Békésy claimed that pitch is determined by the most active neural fibers.

To study how this localization might be produced, Békésy used a model of the cochlea. He filled a plastic tube with fluid. A vibrating piston set the fluid in motion, producing traveling waves like those in the cochlea. Békésy tested the possibility that the skin's and the basilar membrane's nerve supplies are similar in the way they process deformations produced by traveling waves. His reason for expecting a similarity between the skin and basilar membrane was that they have a similar evolutionary and embryological development and both have receptors extended over a large surface. The plastic tube was made large enough to support the forearm. Figure 15.9 shows the subject's arm placed on the model. Although

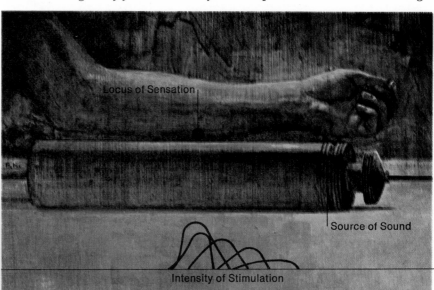

Figure 15.9

Békésy apparatus for studying the similarities between the localization of maximum amplitude of vibration on the skin and the localization of frequency response on the basilar membrane.
(After *Sound and Hearing* ©1965 Time Inc.)

simple-looking, the model was constructed according to dimensional analysis so as to have those properties of the cochlea that produce traveling waves when the stapes is set vibrating sinusoidally. The piston substitutes for the stapes. The subject with his arm laid out along the tube was aware of being stimulated over only a small part of the arm; for some subjects at some frequencies the area was as small as a quarter of an inch, even though the traveling wave caused a displacement with a flat maximum along much of the tube. Subjects were stimulated with frequencies from 40 to 160 Hz. Under careful controls for temperature change in the fluid for muscular tension in the arms, trained subjects could locate the place of maximum sensation quite easily. As the frequency was increased from 40 to 160 Hz, the place of maximum stimulation moved from the elbow toward the hand, where the vibrating piston was located.

These measurements on the skin are extremely important because they show how a stimulus pattern spread over a large surface area and with a flat maximum gives rise to a concentrated, easily localized sensation and how the locus of the sensation varies monotonically with frequency. In listening, we do not hear tones at different places on the basilar membrane; rather, we hear different pitches—but the analogy is clear.

■ LOCALIZATION

The auditory system bases its localization of sound sources on the detection of extremely small time and intensity differences between the two ears. The size of these *binaural differences* depends upon the direction and usually the frequency of the sound.

Figure 15.10 shows how the intensity difference between the ears varies at some sample frequencies as a function of the azimuth of the sound. Azimuth is the angle between the sound source and a line passing forward through the center of the head, perpendicular to an imaginary line connecting the ears. At frequencies below about 1,800 Hz, the change with azimuth is small. Because identical intensity differences occur for sounds behind and ahead of the listener,

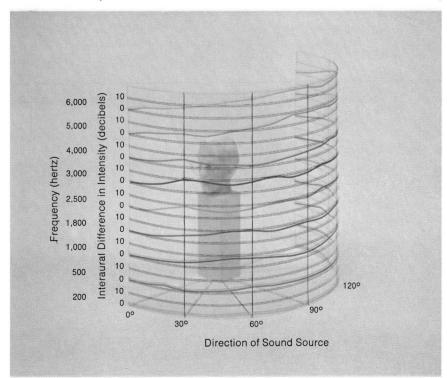

Figure 15.10
Intensity difference in decibels between the ears as a function of the azimuth of the sound source. The curves for nine different frequencies are shown one on top of another.
(After Feddersen, *et al.*, 1957.)

279

it is difficult for an observer with his head in a fixed position to distinguish front and back. Figure 15.10 also shows that the same intensity difference arises for a very different azimuth at one frequency as at another frequency so that confusion would arise unless the auditory nervous system also took into account the frequency of the tone.

Given these binaural intensity differences, how good is the human listener at judging the direction of sound sources? To answer this question, Stevens and Newman took turns sitting in a high chair on the roof of a building and, blindfolded, judged the location of a loudspeaker emitting pure tones, which was at various azimuths. They sat on a roof to minimize sound reflections from surrounding objects, for most surfaces reflect a substantial portion of the sounds hitting them, and consequently the stimulus at the subject's ear would be complicated by echoes. Out in the open, the problem is much less severe. Figure 15.11 shows that the listeners seldom made an error of localization exceeding 20 degrees; the error was smallest below 1,000 Hz and above about 6,000 Hz.

How do we discriminate direction at the lower frequencies, where, owing to the long wavelength of the tones relative to the size of the head, intensity differences between the ears are almost nil? For brief sounds and sounds chang-

Figure 15.11

Error in judging the direction of a sound source as a function of the frequency of the sound.
(After Stevens and Davis, 1938.)

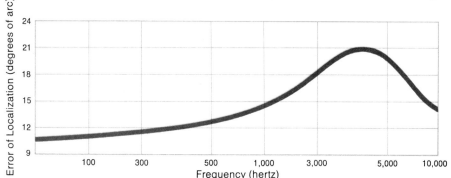

ing in frequency content, the important cue to localization is a difference in the time of arrival at the ears of the onset of the sound or of a change in the sound. Sound travels about 1,100 feet per second—fast, but still slow enough to produce a clear time difference between the two ears, separated as they are in the average adult male by about 7 inches or 0.60 foot. A sound at 90 degrees azimuth, directly opposite one ear, arrives about 0.7 millisecond sooner at the nearer ear than at the farther ear. As the sound source moves toward a position directly in front (or back) of the listener, the time difference decreases until for a sound at 0 degrees azimuth, the sound reaches both ears simultaneously. The time difference at 1 degree azimuth is about 0.01 millisecond. These small differences are heard as differences in the location of the sound. To check that the time differences are the relevant cues, tones can be presented in earphones and the time difference electronically controlled. Time differences of the order of 0.01 millisecond are detectable, but as differences in the location of the tone in the head rather than in space.

In general, only binaural differences in the time of arrival can tell a listener about direction independently of the frequency of the stimulus. Because most sounds we hear are either brief or fluctuating, time differences are probably the most important cues in everyday life for localization. In our daily experience, we also have the advantage of being able to turn our heads, thereby affecting both time and intensity differences in ways that depend upon the direction of the sound source. Another cue to direction is afforded by the external ear flaps, or pinnae, which block high-frequency sounds from the back more than those from the front. The whorls of the pinna may also provide cues to direction by transforming high-frequency sounds in ways that depend on the direction and distance of the sound source.

One final point about the psychophysics of localization. Although time and intensity differences between the two ears are largest when a sound is directly opposite one ear, detection of a *change* in azimuth is best when the sound is directly in front or in back. This seeming paradox occurs because the interaural differences change fastest around the median plane and slowest around 90 degrees.

Outside the laboratory, the everyday sounds that we most frequently encounter contain both low frequencies and high frequencies and mostly fluctuate so that both time and intensity differences contribute to localization. Under normal conditions, sounds are most likely to be heard in areas where objects and surfaces abound. These surfaces reflect the sounds in different ways depending on their distance from the sound source. Although the echoes or reverberations reach the ear later than the original sound, they are not heard as separate from the original sound but are suppressed. This suppression is called the *precedence effect*. Nevertheless, the reverberations markedly affect the quality of the sound, as any acoustical architect will testify as he struggles to make optimal the reverberation time—the delay between the arrival of the original sound at the ear and the arrival of the first reverberations. We hear echoes only when the reverberation time exceeds about 50 milliseconds.

Auditory Pathology

The causes of deafness may be classified in two categories. *Conductive impairment* involves pathology of the conductive mechanisms of the external or middle ear: auditory meatus, eardrum, or ossicles. *Sensorineural impairment* involves pathology of the cochlea or the auditory nervous system, including the auditory cortex. Within each category, the pathology may take many forms.

A common conductive-impairment problem affecting about 1 percent of the general population is *otosclerosis*, in which new bone forms around the stapes, impeding its movement. Infection in the middle ear may reduce the movements of the whole ossicular chain. Perforation of the eardrum may make it less responsive to sound. An example of sensorineural impairment is damage to the organ of Corti by exposure to intense sounds or to large doses of certain drugs like neomycin and dihydrostreptomycin. Tumors of the auditory nerve damage the

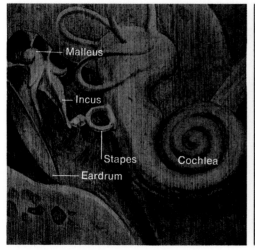

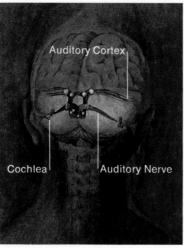

Figure 15.12
Location of conductive impairment.

Figure 15.13
Location of sensorineural impairment.

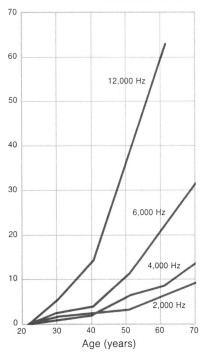

Figure 15.14

Amount of sensitivity loss at several frequencies as a function of age. (After Hinchcliffe, 1959.)

fibers and interfere with the transmission of nerve impulses to the brain. Circulatory trauma such as hemorrhage or thrombosis in those parts of the brain concerned with hearing, primarily the temporal lobe, may reduce hearing and speech perception. Often, a hearing deficiency present from an early age is inherited or results from faulty embryological development, as may occur, for example, if the mother contracts rubella (German measles) during the first few months of pregnancy.

Of all the causes of hearing impairment, aging is certainly the most common. For most people, the average sensitivity to pure tones declines markedly beyond the age of thirty. An example of a set of pure-tone thresholds measured on a large, randomly selected group of subjects is shown in Figure 15.14. Note that the thresholds increase much more with age at the higher than at the middle and low frequencies. Why? One clear factor is that as a population grows older it is more likely to include people who have developed some type of hearing impairment not related to the aging process itself. Hearing impairment caused by long-term exposure to intense noise is a good example, and such exposure affects the high frequencies much more than the middle and low frequencies. At the same time, deterioration of brain cells is part of the normal aging process, and the loss in sensitivity may reflect central neural deterioration.

The diagnosis of hearing loss is primarily an attempt to ascertain the site of the pathology, for the site is critical in determining how to treat the patient. As in other types of ailments, diagnosis is based mostly on the patient's history and the symptoms felt by the patient and uncovered when he responds to sounds in a test situation. The basic test is the measurement of pure-tone thresholds. The amount of hearing loss and the frequency range involved reflect in large part the severity of the ailment and help in the diagnosis. For example, a person who has normal thresholds up to about 3,000 Hz but unusually high thresholds around 4,000 Hz very likely is suffering from exposure to noise, which can be verified by his history. On the other hand, a person with about the same moderate degree (30 to 40 dB) of threshold elevation at most frequencies may be suffering from otosclerosis. However, loss of sensitivity per se usually helps to define only the seriousness of the disturbance.

Although threshold measurements are the mainstay of diagnostic tests, loudness measurements are also very helpful. Loudness functions are usually much steeper for patients with a cochlear impairment than for normal listeners and for patients with a conductive or more central sensorineural impairment. Despite his high thresholds, a person with a cochlear impairment may hear intense sounds just as loud as a person with normal hearing. It would seem advantageous that loudness becomes normal at higher levels; actually, it is a distinct disadvantage because the sounds are not clear and speech perception is poor. Moreover, patients with this disability usually find intense sounds unpleasant and consequently are difficult to fit with a hearing aid that intensifies all the sounds reaching the listener.

Another even more annoying symptom often present in cochlear impairment is *tinnitus,* or ringing in the ear. Impaired hair cells apparently send strong signals to the brain although no sound is reaching the ear. Usually, medication can relieve the symptoms.

What can be done about deafness? Infections can be treated with antibiotics and diseased tissue can be removed by surgery and the middle ear reconstructed. Tumors can be removed, although their removal usually does not relieve the hearing difficulties and may not prevent further deterioration. Cochlear impairment cannot generally be reversed, either. Conductive impairment is subject to the most extensive direct treatment. For example, otosclerosis may be treated by removing the stapes and replacing it with a prosthetic device such as a plastic tube. This operation is extremely delicate but otherwise requires only two or three days in the hospital and is usually performed under local anesthesia. Because conductive impairment does call for an operation in most cases and sensorineural impairment does not (or it requires a very different type of operation, such as removal of a tumor), it is essential that a correct diagnosis be made of the site of impairment. Psychoacoustics, with its threshold and loudness measurements, has contributed substantially to diagnosis.

Man's third major distance receptor, besides seeing and hearing, is smell, or olfaction, the sensitivity to odors emanating from distant sources. Man's sense of smell is not nearly as sensitive as that of many animals and insects. Male moths, for example, can smell female moths several miles away.

Smell requires that appropriate molecules enter the nasal passages, where the olfactory epithelium is located. Figure 15.15 shows the lateral wall of the right nasal cavity. The epithelium is about 2.5 cm² and contains millions of *hair cells*, each with up to 1,000 hairs per cell. An electromicrograph of a human hair cell with its fingerlike projections is shown in Figure 15.16. These cells are thought to respond to chemical properties of the stimulus and are therefore classified as chemical receptors.

The hair cells both transduce the stimulus and transmit nerve impulses through their axons, which constitute the olfactory nerve and which lead directly to the olfactory bulb of the brain. Because the olfactory receptors are accessible only to gases, to be odorous, substances must be volatile—that is, readily vaporized from a liquid or solid to a gas. Most odors to which man is sensitive are organic compounds, but little else is known about why some substances are odorous and others are not or why certain groups of odors smell alike. A search

Sense of Smell

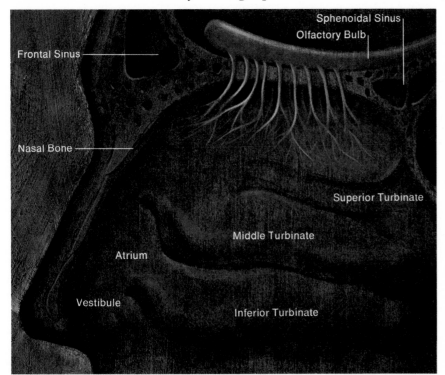

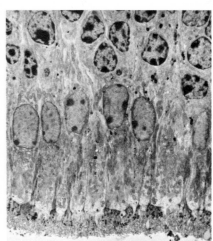

Figure 15.15
The organs of smell.

Figure 15.16
Electron micrograph of the surface layer of the olfactory epithelium. Hairs end at the border of the nasal cavity, at the bottom of this picture.

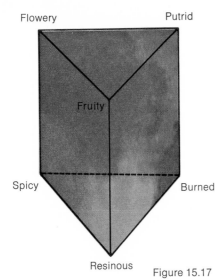

Flowery

Putrid

Fruity

Spicy

Burned

Resinous

Figure 15.17
Henning's smell prism.

for the stimulus key to the classification of odors has so far been unsuccessful. A subjective classification scheme based on judgments by humans is also not entirely certain, but the most popular one seems to be Henning's smell prism (Figure 15.17). Six supposedly pure qualities form the corners of the prism, and the intermediate qualities lie along the surface.

The search for the basis of odor differences and similarities is a search for common chemical properties among the members of each class of odors that distinguish it from all the other classes. The recently proposed *stereochemical theory* of odor, for example, suggests that classification depends on molecular shape: certain shapes fit certain receptor cells, like keys in locks. On the basis of similarities in molecular shape, odors are classified into seven primary categories not too different from Henning's scheme. Nevertheless, the theory seems unable to account for many odors. Moreover, there is no evidence for seven different types of receptor cells.

Lack of knowledge about what stimulus properties are important in smell makes stimulus control more difficult. In vision and hearing, the important properties are known, easily measured, and easily controlled. In smell, the one known property is the concentration of the odorous substance in air, but specifying the concentration at the receptors is extremely difficult because of the inaccessibility of the olfactory cells in the recesses of the nasal passages. Despite these difficulties, it has been calculated from threshold measurements that a human olfactory cell is excited by at most eight molecules and very likely by only one molecule of the appropriate odorous substance. At least forty molecules are necessary to produce a sensation.

The subjective intensity of smell increases as a power function of the concentration of the odorous substance. For coffee odor, subjective magnitude grows more slowly than physical magnitude. The slow growth occurs even though the effective stimulus range is usually of the order of only hundreds to one. Perhaps the subjective magnitude grows slowly because of very rapid adaptation. We are all aware of the efficiency of adaptation to odors. Odors disappear within a few minutes of exposure, and generally the more concentrated the odor, the more rapid the adaptation.

Smell plays a small role in modern civilization, but enough to encourage large perfume and deodorant industries. Nevertheless, its major role is probably in connection with taste.

Sense of Taste

Taste, or gustation, may be considered in two ways: as the global sensation or perception that accompanies ingestion or as the specific sensation that accompanies stimulation of specialized organs in the mouth. The global taste perception includes a very strong olfactory component (as shown by the cold sufferer's insensitivity to taste owing to a "stuffed nose"); temperature and touch (which includes size, texture, consistency) from tissues in the skin, lips, and mouth; and kinesthetic cues from muscles of the tongue and joints of the jaw. We shall consider here only the gustatory organs that respond to chemical properties of the stimulus.

The dorsal surface of the tongue (Figure 15.18A) is dotted with *taste buds* grouped in large numbers (on the average, 200) as *papillae*. A few papillae are also found in the pharynx and larynx and on the palate, tonsils, and epiglottis. Figure 15.18C is a diagram of a single taste bud, which consists of several receptor cells with small hairlike processes that project beyond the surrounding epithelium into a sharp depression or pit in the tongue surface. Nerve fibers

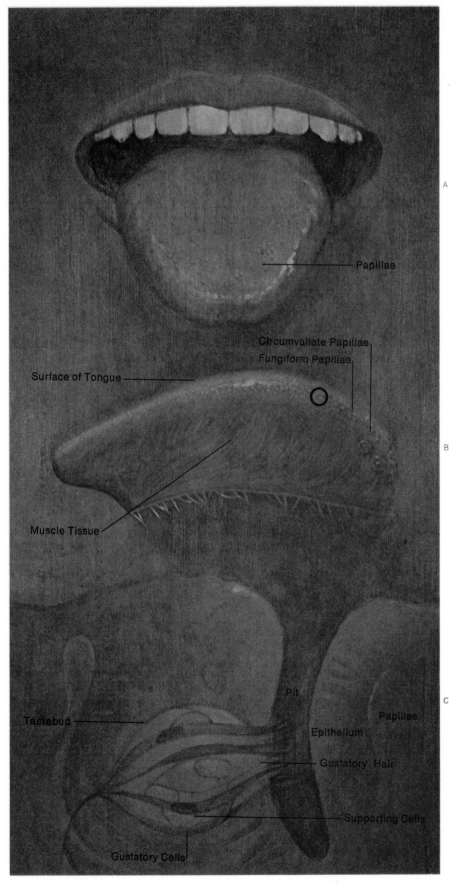

A

Papillae

Circumvallate Papillae
Fungiform Papillae

Surface of Tongue

B

Muscle Tissue

C

Pit

Papillae

Tastebud

Epithelium

Gustatory Hair

Supporting Cells

Gustatory Cells

Figure 15.18
The organs of taste.

supplying these buds wind about and terminate on the surfaces of the taste cells. Taste buds are constantly dying and being replaced, but not quite fast enough; the number of sensitive buds decreases with age, starting in childhood. It is assumed that chemical changes initiated in the neighborhood of the buds trigger neural activity in the receptor cells and thence in the nerve fibers.

Man has four primary taste qualities: *sour, salty, bitter,* and *sweet.* These qualities can be elicited in more or less pure form by stimulation of the taste buds with concentrated solutions and by stimulation of individual papillae with electrical DC pulses. The fact that electrical stimulation affects only these four taste qualities suggests that four kinds of papillae, differing somewhat in shape, are responsible for the four primary taste qualities.

But how do the stimuli that elicit the four qualities differ? That question can be answered only slightly better for gustatory than for olfactory stimuli. All taste stimuli must be at least partially soluble because they must be dissolved in the saliva of the mouth in order to reach the taste buds in their cavities. The salty and sour tastes seem to depend on ionic action; thus, molecular dissociation must take place: NaCl (common salt), for example, becomes the anion Cl^- and the cation Na^+; HCl (hydrochloric acid, which is very sour) ionizes to H^+ and Cl^-, the hydrogen ion being the critical ion. No common property such as ionization applies to sweet or bitter. Consequently, it is not possible to state a single chemical or physical property that characterizes taste quality.

Most of our taste sensations are mixtures among the four primaries. In one study, subjects were asked to match standard foods to the four basic taste qualities represented by sucrose, quinine sulfate (bitter), tartaric acid (sour), and sodium chloride. The relative matches to each of the qualities are shown in Table 15.1, where the maximum possible value is 100 for any given cell.

Because the function of taste is to keep an animal or man from eating poisonous and nonnutritive material and to steer him toward nutritive food, it is not surprising that it has a strong affective or emotional component. Affect—that is, our liking or disliking a given stimulus—depends on both the nature of the stimulus and the physiological condition of the eater. A case history illustrates this relation. A three-year-old boy, admitted for examination in a hospital because

Table 15.1—Taste Mixtures of Selected Food Products

Food Product	Sweet	Bitter	Sour	Salty
Cola drink	11.2	2.2	5.0	1.3
Ale	2.5	28.2	10.0	1.3
Unsweetened grapefruit juice	3.2	2.0	35.5	2.0
Consommé	1.4	1.3	4.5	7.9
Tokay wine	10.0	4.2	4.2	1.8
Riesling wine	1.0	7.5	6.7	1.3
"Root" tonic	4.2	1.3	3.2	1.3
Coffee, unsweetened	1.0	42.3	3.2	1.0
Coffee, 5% sucrose	3.2	23.8	3.2	1.3
Anchovy fillet	1.3	23.8	5.6	10.0
Sweet pickles	3.2	3.2	13.4	3.2
Sour pickles	1.0	1.8	18.0	3.2
Raspberry jam	23.8	1.8	10.0	1.3
Honey	56.4	2.4	1.8	1.3
Means	8.8	10.4	8.9	2.7

Source: G. A. Geldard, *The Human Senses* (New York: Wiley, 1953), p. 315. Data from J. G. Beebe-Center, "Standards for the Use of the Gust Scale," *Journal of Psychology,* 28 (1949), 411-419.

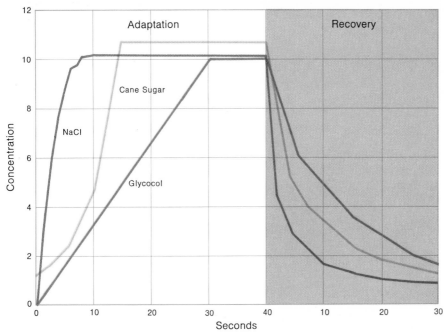

Figure 15.19
Smallest detectable concentrations of chemical stimuli as a function of time after the presentation of the stimulus (adaptation) and after removal (recovery). (After Pfaffman, 1951; from Hahn and Taeger, 1938.)

of irregular physical development, died after a week. Autopsy showed that his adrenal glands had been allowing salt to pass out with urine faster than he could accumulate it on the regular hospital diet. It turned out that the boy had had a craving for salt and had previously survived because he received large extra amounts of salt at home. He would gulp down a tablespoon of salt or eat directly from a salt shaker. Tests on rats whose adrenal glands are removed show the same preference for salt.

Adaptation to chemical stimulation is rapid. Figure 15.19 shows, for three different stimuli, that threshold increases to an asymptote in from ten to twenty-five seconds, and then is back to normal about thirty seconds after removal of the stimuli. The greater the concentration of the adapting stimuli, the more the threshold increases. What is the effect of one chemical on the threshold for another? It has been shown that adaptation to any one of twenty-four different kinds of salt does not affect the threshold for the other twenty-three. On the other hand, adaptation to any one acid raises the threshold for all other acids. Such cross-adaptation is shown also for some, but not all, sweet and bitter stimuli. The failures of cross-adaptation complicate theories that assume separate taste receptors.

Vestibular Sense

The vestibular sense—the sense of balance—unlike the senses of hearing, seeing, and smell, is a sense we are never directly aware of; we have no vestibular sensation that we can ascribe to a particular body organ. Nevertheless, we are very much aware of our posture, movements, and orientation in space. Nor does seasickness pass easily unnoticed. This awareness depends upon neural input from the kinesthetic, visual, and vestibular senses.

Figure 15.20A shows the vestibular organ and the cochlea, which together form the labyrinth, or inner ear. In man, only the cochlea is concerned with hearing. (In certain fish, limited hearing is ascribed to the saccule, from which the cochlea probably evolved.) The vestibular organ lies buried in temporal bone above and to the rear of the cochlea. Its prominent section is the three semicircular canals, which lie at right angles to each other. At both ends of each canal is an enlarged section called the *ampulla*, which contains the receptor cells that signal rotational acceleration and deceleration. When the head starts turning in the plane of a given canal, the inertia of the endolymph causes it to move relative to the wall of the canal. The endolymph then presses against the *cupula,* a gelatinous mass inside the ampulla, which sits on the *crista.* The movement of the cupula bends the endings of the receptor *hair cells,* which are lined up in the crista. These hair cells and the cupula are analogous to the hair cells and tectorial membrane of the cochlea. A schematic diagram of the observed change caused by rotational acceleration of a live cod is given in Figure 15.20B. When the acceleration stops, the cupula slowly swings back to its normal position. The hair cells have synapses with the endings of the bipolar cells of the *vestibular nerve,* which joins the auditory nerve to form the VIIIth cranial nerve.

Our discriminations of up and down, of body position, and of linear acceleration seem to be based in the utricle and saccule, which also contain hair cells along their inner surfaces. These hair cells with their supporting cells form the *macula.* Above the macula is a gelatinous mass that contains many heavy, stone-like particles called *otoliths.* When the head is erect, the macula of the utricle lies directly under its otoliths, but the maculae of the saccule form an angle of about 30 degrees with the vertical plane. The endings of the hair cells are embedded in the gelatinous mass. Linear acceleration or change in head position would bend the hairs. A change in gravitational force would, presumably, change the pressure exerted by the heavy otoliths on the macula of the utricle, and a change in centrifugal force would change the pressure on the almost vertical maculae of the saccule.

As in the cochlea, little is known about how the bending of the hairs is transduced to neural impulses. Studies of the neural response itself have shown that rotational acceleration in one direction increases the firing rate in some vestibular fibers and acceleration in the other direction decreases it below the resting rate in other fibers. Generally, the more rapid the acceleration, the greater the increase in firing rate in the excited fibers.

The stimuli for vestibular responses are rotational or linear acceleration, falling, and tilting of the body or head. A common test of the vestibular function in humans uses a rotating chair. The observer feels the rotation and shows *nystagmus* (back-and-forth movement of the eyes) as long as the chair's rotation increases every second by at least 1 degree per second. If the chair continues to rotate at a constant speed, the observer stops feeling any movement (provided visual, auditory, and tactual cues are excluded), and the nystagmus disappears. Interesting effects occur when a rotating chair is suddenly stopped. The observer feels as if he is turning in the opposite direction, and nystagmus returns. These effects last no longer than twenty or thirty seconds. They may be similar to the ocean traveler's feeling that the land is moving when he steps off the boat.

Bodily movement is not always necessary to stimulate the vestibular organs. Irrigating the ear canal with warm water (above body temperature) sets up convection currents that apparently cause the endolymph in the semicircular canals to move, thus producing the symptoms that are associated with rotational acceleration. This procedure is used frequently in the clinic to test the adequacy of the vestibular organs and nerves.

The vestibular apparatus is phylogenetically ancient and has undergone little evolutionary development (aside from the probable development of the cochlea from the saccule). Its neural connections and interrelations with other body-control mechanisms have evolved so that man can get along quite well without his two vestibular organs, provided his visual and kinesthetic senses are unimpaired. In fact, a person with one vestibular organ intact and one removed is

Figure 15.20 *(opposite)*
The organs of motion and orientation.
(A) The vestibular organ. (B) The movement of the endolymph and the crista in a semicircular canal; a drop of oil was injected into the canal to make visible the movement of the endolymph under rotational acceleration.
(After Geldard, 1953.)
(C) The utricle and saccule.
(After CIBA, 1962.)

A

Superior Canal

Posterior Canal

Lateral Canal

Utricle

Cochlea

Saccule

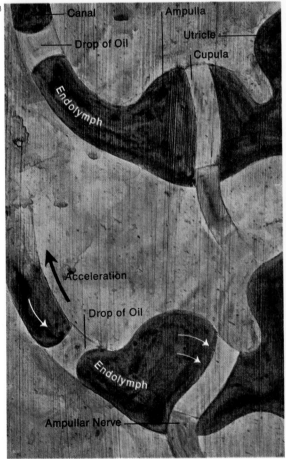

B

Canal

Drop of Oil

Ampulla

Utricle

Cupula

Endolymph

Acceleration

Drop of Oil

Endolymph

Ampular Nerve

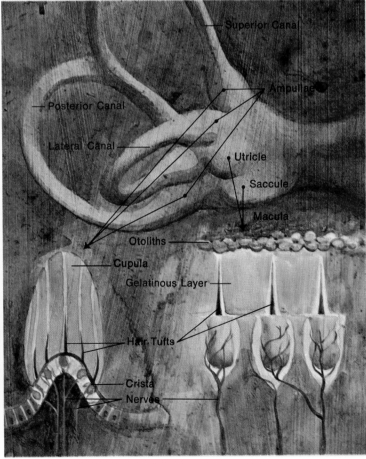

C

Superior Canal

Posterior Canal

Lateral Canal

Ampullae

Utricle

Saccule

Macula

Otoliths

Cupula

Gelatinous Layer

Hair Tufts

Crista

Nerves

worse off, for one or two months, than a person who loses both organs. The unilateral loss results in severe dizziness, nausea, and nystagmus. After these symptoms clear, the unilateral loss goes unnoticed. The bilateral loss results in permanent damage to equilibrium, which, however, is noticeable only when vision is absent. It is also a problem in water, because the afflicted person is as likely to swim downward as upward in trying to reach the surface. Interest in the vestibular organs has revived as astronauts and cosmonauts travel in spaceships where a long absence of gravity might disturb vestibular functions.

Kinesthesis

Kinesthesis refers to the sense of movement and position of the body. It cooperates with the vestibular and visual senses to maintain posture and equilibrium. The sensation of kinesthesis comes from nerve endings located in the neighborhood of the more than 100 body joints. Receptor endings are located in the tissue in and about the joints, in the ligaments, and in the joint capsules. The endings in the capsules respond to movement of the joint by an initial rapid burst of firing, after which the discharge rate is a function of the speed and extent of the movement. Which receptors respond depends on the direction and angle of movement. Other nerve endings in the muscles and tendons signal overloads and provide the feedback necessary for regulation of active body movement. Some of the receptors in the muscles respond only to passive, others to both active and passive, stretch. *Passive stretch* has to do with stretching muscles not in use for lifting weights; active stretch, with moving a limb. The detection of movement of various parts of the body is keenest at the hip, big toe, and shoulder joints. Slow displacements of from 0.2 to 0.7 degrees are detectable.

Skin Senses

Touch comes to our awareness in three distinct forms: as pressure changes, as warmth and cold, and as pain. As commonly used, the term "touch" refers both to active exploring touch by the hand and fingers and to passive touch as when the top of a pencil is pressed against the palm of the hand. Active touch involves kinesthetic as well as tactual cues. This section deals with passive touch and the resulting pressure, thermal, and pain sensations.

Figure 15.21 shows the two layers of the skin, the relatively thin *epidermis* and the inner *dermis*. The outer surface of the epidermis is a layer of dead cells containing neither blood vessels nor nerve fibers. Many free nerve endings innervate the rest of the epidermis but no blood vessels go there. The dermis is

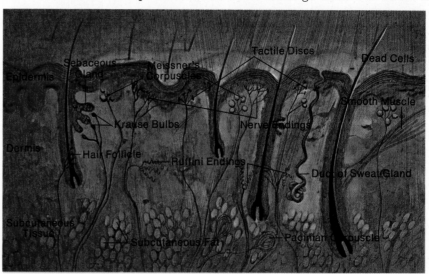

Figure 15.21
Diagram of the skin in cross section.

richly supplied with a variety of nerve endings, blood vessels, and cutaneous receptor organs. The major types of nerve endings are gathered together in the composite diagram of Figure 15.21. The function of the free nerve endings is probably related to pain, and the function of the Pacinian corpuscle is probably related to vibratory pressure. The specific functions of the Krause bulbs, Ruffini endings, Meissner's corpuscles, and tactile discs are not known, and the typology of the nerve endings is not clear-cut in any case.

The anatomical structure of the nerve supply to the skin areas is well known. Figure 15.22 shows the areas or *dermatomes* of the body surface served by thirty of the thirty-one pairs of spinal nerves (only the first cervical pair has no sensory roots) and four of the cranial nerves. Each area is served by a posterior root of the spinal cord. The dermatomes served by the spinal cord are represented in sequence on the central gyrus of the cortex (Figure 15.23), giving a faithful projection of the body surface. The size of the cortical region representing a given body area is related to the density of neural innervations at the body surface, not the dimensions of the surface. Thus, such areas as the hand, foot, and mouth have the largest cortical representation.

Exploration of the skin surface with various probing devices such as calibrated hairs and tiny hammers has revealed a pattern of pressure-sensitive spots, as shown in Figure 15.24. These spots represent areas of high sensitivity, and it is assumed that they lie closer to the receptor endings than their surrounding areas. Whatever the endings may be, they are sensitive only to a pressure gradient. Once the skin is displaced, the sensation disappears, more or less rapidly depending on the force exerted. In other words, we are more sensitive to changes in

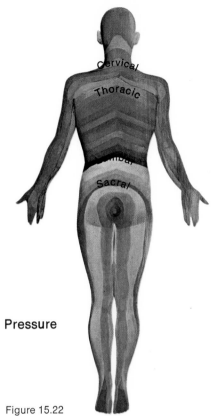

Pressure

Figure 15.22

Dermatomes: each colored area is innervated by a different spinal nerve. In most individuals considerably more overlap of innervation is found than is shown here. Areas of similar color are innervated by the groups of spinal nerves indicated. (After CIBA, 1962.)

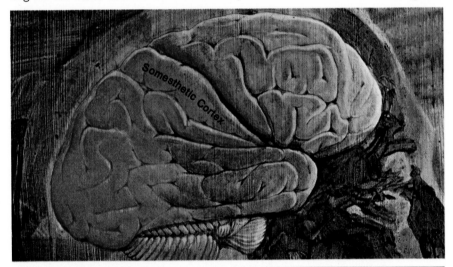

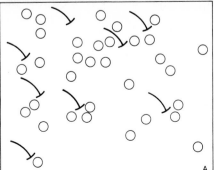

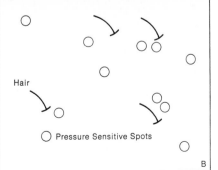

Figure 15.23
Location of the central gyrus.

Figure 15.24
The distribution of pressure-sensitive areas (A) on the face and (B) on the back. (After Woodworth, 1938.)

Figure 15.25
Von Frey hair used to stimulate the skin with constant pressure. Hairs of varying stiffness pressed down until they just begin to bend.

energy than to steady states. Otherwise, we would probably be constantly aware of our clothes pressing lightly upon us.

The sensitivity of the skin to pressure varies with locus. The energy needed to make tiny impacts to the skin just detectable is perhaps smallest on the ball of the thumb, the tips and balls of other fingers, the underside of the forearm, the lips, and the tip of the tongue. These thresholds are among the lowest for man's skin, yet the energy values are from 100 million to 10 billion times greater than those required by the eye and ear at threshold.

Warmth and Cold

We are generally aware of two kinds of temperature—air temperature and the temperature of isolated parts of the skin, which is the immediate topic. Touching the skin with stimulators at skin temperature, usually 32 degrees Centigrade, yields no thermal sensation and so is referred to as physiological zero. Generally, warmth is associated with temperatures greater than physiological zero and cold with lower temperatures. Because the stimulus in both cases is a change in temperature and only the direction varies, one might expect that a single receptor serves for both warmth and cold. However, exploration of the skin with small points of warm and cold materials shows that warmth and cold are not felt at every point on the skin, only at specific spots. Generally, in a square centimeter there are about six cold spots but only one or two warm spots. Table 15.2 gives the distribution of warm and cold spots per square centimeter over the body. As noted above, it is not known what are the receptors for warmth and cold. However, their separate identity is generally accepted, especially because sometimes stimulating a previously identified cold spot with a very warm stimulus (45 to 50 degrees Centigrade) yields a cold sensation—hence, the name *paradoxical cold* for this phenomenon.

Warm and cold spots if stimulated simultaneously may give a clear sensation of heat, even dangerous heat. This fact can be demonstrated with rows of tubes filled alternately with cold water (12 to 15 degrees Centigrade) and warm water (42 to 44 degrees). No single tube feels hot, but if the forearm is placed over several rows, the first impression is of intense heat. Apparently, warmth and cold fuse to yield the sensation of heat, but the mechanism of such fusion is not understood.

Thermal sensitivity undergoes rapid and complete adaptation when individual warm or cold spots are stimulated, even if the stimulus is very cold or very warm. In contrast, adaptation under a real stimulation is complete only if the stimulus is no colder than 16 degrees and no warmer than 42 degrees, and then complete disappearance of thermal sensation may take several minutes, as shown in Figure 15.26. Of course, once a subject has adapted to a warmer or colder stimulus, physiological zero changes; and thus, if you have become used to a warm bath, tap water only a little less warm feels cold.

Table 15.2—Distribution of Warm and Cold Spots in Human Skin

Location	Number per cm²	
	Cold Spots*	Warm Spots†
Forehead	5.5– 8.0	—
Nose	8.0–13.0	1.0
Lips	16.0–19.0	—
Other parts of face	8.5– 9.0	1.7
Chest	9.0–10.2	0.3
Abdomen	8.0–12.5	—
Back	7.8	—
Upper arm	5.0– 6.5	—
Forearm	6.0– 7.5	0.3–0.4
Back of hand	7.4	0.5
Palm of hand	1.0– 5.0	0.4
Finger dorsal	7.0– 9.0	1.7
Finger volar	2.0– 4.0	1.6
Thigh	4.5– 5.2	0.4
Calf	4.3– 5.7	—
Back of foot	5.6	—
Sole of foot	3.4	—

*After H. Strughold and R. Porz, *Zeitschrift Biologie*, 91 (1931), 563.

†After H. Rein, *Zeitschrift Biologie*, 82 (1925), 189.

Source: Y. Zotterman, "Thermal Sensations," in J. Field (ed.), *Handbook of Physiology—Section 1: Neurophysiology* (Washington, D.C.: American Physiological Society, 1959), I, 432.

Pain

Pain is associated with more than just the skin. However, little is known about pain from the interior of the body except that it seems to be deep, dull, and much more unpleasant than the bright, sharply localized pain from the skin. Many kinds of stimuli—scratch, puncture, pressure, heat, cold, twist—may produce pain. Their common property is real or potential injury to bodily tissue. It is also true that, in general, overstimulation of any sensory modality—loud sounds, bright lights, intense pressure—is painful.

The evidence points to the free nerve endings distributed throughout the epidermis and dermis as the receptor organs for cutaneous pain. Apparently,

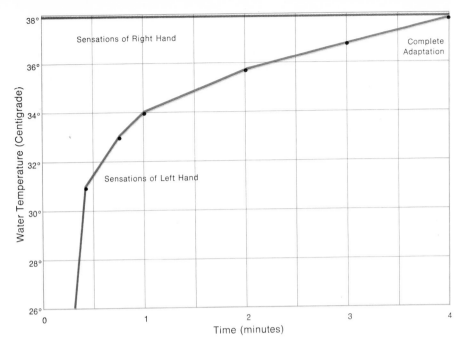

Figure 15.26

Thermal adaptation. On the ordinate is plotted the water temperature that feels the same to the right hand (which is completely adapted to 38-degree Centigrade water) as 26-degree water feels to the left hand after the varying periods of exposure time plotted on the abscissa. After four minutes in 26-degree water, the left hand feels the same as the right hand does in 38-degree water.
(After Hahn, 1929.)

injury to the tissue involves injury of the nerve fibers themselves, because at some spots on the skin, puncture by a fine needle is not painful; these few spots are probably not served by the free nerve endings. Pain from such places as the cornea and gum pulp, which have a rich supply of free nerve endings and no other types of receptors, is easily aroused. What part of the brain mediates pain is not clearly known.

Measurement of pain in man is not easy, owing largely to problems of stimulus control as well as subject resistance. Nevertheless, Hardy and his associates have developed a radiant-heat technique for producing pain that allows accurate measurement of the heat transfer to the skin. They found that thresholds for pain vary little from observer to observer and from time to time. Adaptation to pain is not striking. In the laboratory, however, mild cutaneous pain can be shown to disappear with prolonged stimulation.

Sensitivity to pain is sometimes absent—induced genetically, by neurotic reactions, or by hypnosis. The genetic absence of pain graphically illustrates the importance of pain in helping us to guard against noxious stimuli and to treat injury and illness appropriately. In a particular type of neurotic reaction called hysteria, a person may be insensitive to any stimulation, painful or otherwise, of a particular part of his body. Similarly, a hypnotized person may report no pain if he is told that he is insensitive. However, nonhypnotized observers may do equally well in submitting to painful stimulation if they are highly motivated.

16

VISUAL SENSATIONS

OUR ABILITY TO SEE is perhaps our most important sensory capacity. The loss of any sensory system represents a serious handicap to the individual, but vision plays a major role as we move around in our environment, as we communicate with others, as we learn in the classroom.

Light, as you recall from Chapter 14, is a form of radiant energy, and we are able to see only when we have some source of radiant energy available. We see either the radiant source itself or surfaces that reflect the radiations of such a source. During the day, the primary source outdoors is the sun, but secondary sources do exist, such as the particles in the atmosphere that provide the lightness of the sky. Most of the objects we see are made visible by the light they reflect from such sources. With the technological advances made by man came a large variety of so-called artificial light sources, including the incandescent and fluorescent bulbs with which we are all familiar.

If we ask the physicist what light is, he will say that it is a narrow band of the electromagnetic spectrum, which itself is extremely broad and includes such radiations as cosmic rays, gamma rays, X rays, ultraviolet rays, infrared rays, and radio waves. These labels refer to various portions of this broad spectrum, with radiations having wavelengths ranging from .0000000000001 to 1,000,000 meters. Thus, the longest wavelength in the radio portion of the spectrum is about 100 million million million times longer than the wavelength of the cosmic-ray portion of the spectrum. The visual system, however, operates by using only one small section of this very broad spectrum. The longest wavelengths to which our eyes are sensitive are only about twice as long as the shortest wavelengths to which we are sensitive. The visible spectrum is situated between the infrared rays and the ultraviolet rays; we see the long wavelengths in the visible spectrum as red and the short wavelengths as blue or violet. A representation of the electromagnetic spectrum is shown in Figure 16.1.

The band of electromagnetic radiations we call *light waves* are given this name because we can see them. We separate off this band because our eyes are sensitive to radiations in this region. We must avoid a logical circularity. We do

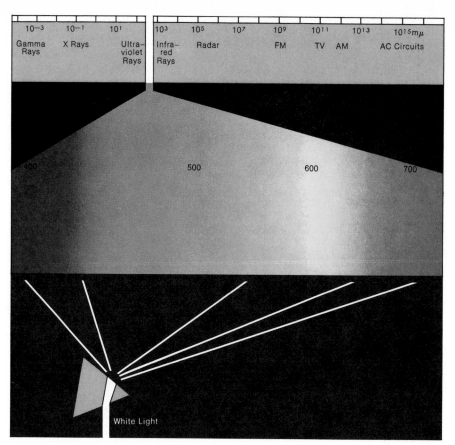

Figure 16.1
The composition of white light and the position of this visible radiation on the total electromagnetic spectrum. Wavelength is expressed in millimicrons (10^9 millimicrons = 1 meter).

not make such progress if we say that the eye is sensitive to light and then define light as the radiant energy to which the eye is sensitive.

The Eye Light reaching the eye is focused on the retina, where it elicits complex neural responses. The light first passes through the cornea, then the aqueous humor, then the pupil, then the lens, and finally the vitreous humor before reaching the retina. Figure 16.2 outlines the structure of the human eye. The lens, by changing its shape—*accommodation*—focuses the light on the retina. The lens thickens in order to focus near objects and returns to its flatter shape to focus far objects (twenty feet or farther away). Near-sightedness (myopia), the inability to distinguish far objects clearly, results when the lens is not flat enough to focus the light rays on the retina. An example of a near-sighted eye with rays coming in parallel from a distant object is shown in Figure 16.3A. Near-sightedness usually is not the fault of the lens; the retina is too far from the lens, so that the far object is focused on a plane in front of the retina and the retinal image is blurred. This figure also shows how a normal eye focuses a near and a far object.

The pupil regulates the amount of light reaching the retina by changing its size. Vision is sharpest when the pupil is smallest because light then passes through only the center of the lens and cornea, where spherical and chromatic aberrations are less than toward the periphery.

Our diagrams always picture the eye as stationary. In fact, the human eye is highly mobile. Some six muscles control its movement so it can focus over a wide area. Even when we hold our eyes stationary, they are constantly vibrating, just as our finger does if we try to hold it steady with our arm outstretched. It turns out that this *nystagmus*, or eye tremor, is essential to vision. Under special

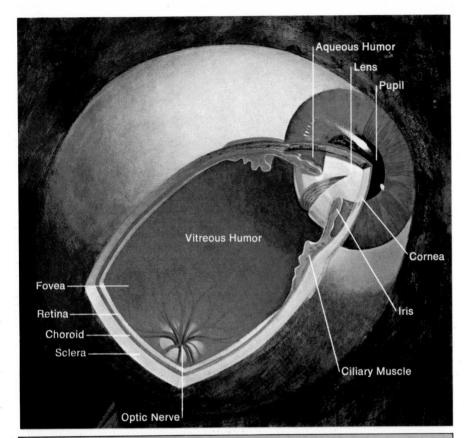

Figure 16.2
The eye.

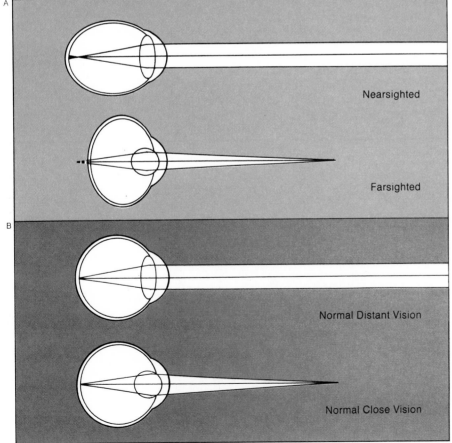

Figure 16.3
(A) The nearsighted and the farsighted eye
(B) Accommodation to near and distant
objects in the normal eye.

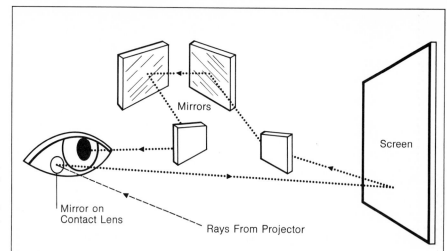

Figure 16.4

By first reflecting the stimulus image off a mirror mounted on the eye, the movements of the eye may be compensated for precisely, so that the image is stationary on the retina.
(After Riggs, et al., 1953.)

optical arrangements, an image can be fixated on one section of the retina (see Figure 16.4). The image disappears within a few seconds as the receptor cells adapt to the unchanging pattern. Rather than interfere with vision as originally thought, nystagmus is essential to it.

At the retina, the light does not immediately affect the receptor cells. First it must pass through the nerve fibers and blood vessels. At almost the last layer of the retina lie the *rods* and *cones,* the highly specialized cells containing pigments that, upon the absorption of light, undergo chemical changes that result in electrical neural impulses. A picture, based on Polyak's, of the complex structure of the retina is shown in Figure 16.5. The bottom of the picture faces the front of the eye. The rods are the thin cells at the top alternating with the thicker cones. The human eye contains 6 or 7 million cones, which are concentrated largely in the *fovea,* where vision is sharpest. The rest of the retina, the *periphery,* contains between 75 and 150 million rods, with the highest concentration of rods about 20 degrees from the fovea. Distance on the retina is measured in degrees because the retina covers the inner surface of a sphere. Similarly, the

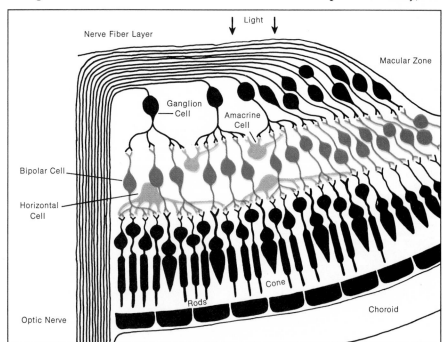

Figure 16.5

Schematic representation of the retina in cross section. Note that the receptor cells are not the first structures exposed to incoming light. Note also the decreasing specificity of innervation of the receptor cells away from the macular zone, around the fovea.
(After Graham, 1966.)

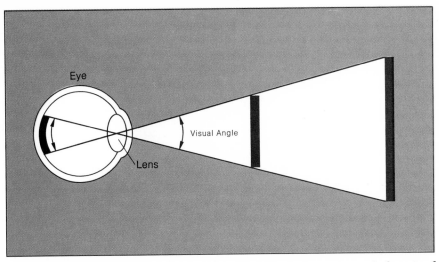

Figure 16.6
The visual angle subtended by an object decreases as the object moves away from the eye.

size of images formed on the retina may be expressed in terms of the *visual angle,* as illustrated in Figure 16.6.

The distinction between rods and cones lies not only in their shape but more importantly in their behavioral correlations and in their pigmentation. Rods are more sensitive to light than cones, are essentially color blind, and are less suited for sharp spatial discrimination partly because groups of them share the same neural connections. Cones require more light before they begin to respond, are sensitive to color, and are usually served by a single unshared neural fiber. The rods are most useful in night vision, when maximum sensitivity is required; the cones in daylight, when color distinctions can also be made.

A difference between rods and cones is noted in the electrical response of the eye to light. The response has the waveform shown at the top of Figure 16.7 when a deep violet light is used to stimulate primarily the rods; it has a more complex waveform (bottom of Figure 16.7) when an orange light is used to stimulate both cones and rods. The latter waveform includes both the rod and the cone responses. These waveforms, called *electroretinograms* (ERGS), are recorded from humans by placing an electrode embedded in a plastic contact lens on the cornea and a second, indifferent electrode on the forehead. The ERG is probably generated in the retina, primarily between the receptor cells and the bipolar cells. The ERG may be useful in the clinic for testing for early signs of eye disease and for testing infants and young children.

The chemical basis for rod action has been very carefully worked out, largely by George Wald and his collaborators. Rods contain the chemical compound *rhodopsin,* which is bleached by light. When light strikes it, the rhodopsin

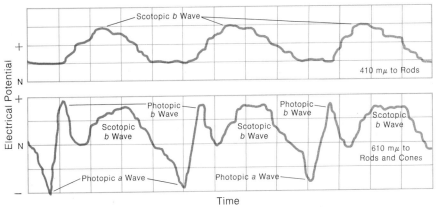

Figure 16.7
Electroretinograms: waveforms of the electrical changes occurring in the eye in response to light stimulation.
(After Riggs, 1966.)

absorbs photons that initiate a rapid formation of retinene and other chemical substances. Because vitamin A is essential in this process, vitamin-A deficiency may lead to "night blindness."

When the eye is dark-adapted, threshold is determined entirely by the rods. Measurement of the weakest luminance detectable over the whole range of visible wavelengths gives the *scotopic* threshold curve shown in Figure 16.8. The crosses were obtained by measuring the absorption of light of different wavelengths by rhodopsin, outside the living eye. The close correspondence with the threshold curve suggests that the form of the latter is determined primarily by rhodopsin. Figure 16.8 also gives the *photopic* curve for the light-adapted eye stimulated by a small spot of light on the fovea, where cones abound.

Neural Coding by the Eye

The eye, like the ear, transduces energy. Light energy is turned into neural, electrical energy. A major difficulty is that the final transduction, from light energy in the eye and from sound energy in the ear, is not known precisely. Moreover, lateral connections among the receptors and efferent fibers (fibers that send impulses from the brain out *to* the retina and basilar membrane) enormously complicate the picture.

The retina is embryologically a part of the brain, and so the highly complex neural organization revealed in Figure 16.5 is not unexpected. Three levels of neural cell bodies are shown. At the top are the rods and cones, whose tips are embedded in the cells of the choroid layer. The cones, which are thicker than the rods, generally connect directly with a single *bipolar* cell located in the next neural layer. Several rods share a single bipolar cell, which may send branches to cones as well. A second synapse in the retina occurs between the bipolar cells and the *ganglion* cells, whose axons are the fibers of the optic nerve. These fibers all collect at the *blind spot,* where they exit as a bundle. We are unable to see in this spot because it contains all nerves and no transducers.

The optic nerve from each eye bifurcates, as shown in Figure 16.9, before synapsing in the thalamus and finally arriving at the occipital lobe in the back of the brain. Note the interconnections among the ganglion cells. Similar lateral connections exist among the bipolar cells and perhaps even among the receptor

Figure 16.8

The decrease in the intensity of a light that can just be seen as the eye dark-adapts.
(After Hecht, *et al.*, 1935.)

Figure 16.9 *(opposite)*

(A) Visual pathways from the eyes to the occipital cortex, showing how the right side of each retina sends information to the right occipital lobe and how the left side of each retina sends it to the left occipital lobe. (B) Bifurcation and crossover in the optic nerve.
(After Graham, 1966.)

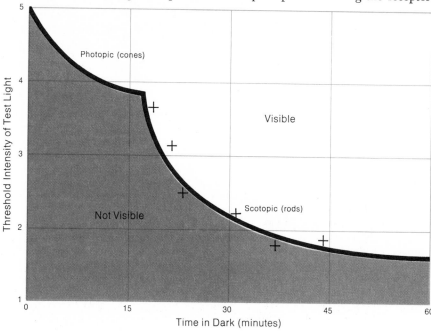

A

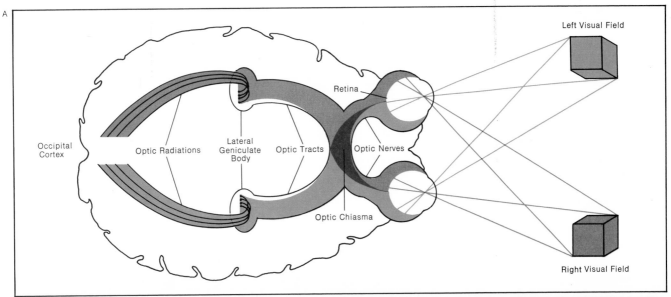

Left Visual Field

Retina

Occipital
Cortex

Optic Radiations   Lateral
Geniculate
Body   Optic Tracts   Optic Nerves

Optic Chiasma

Right Visual Field

B

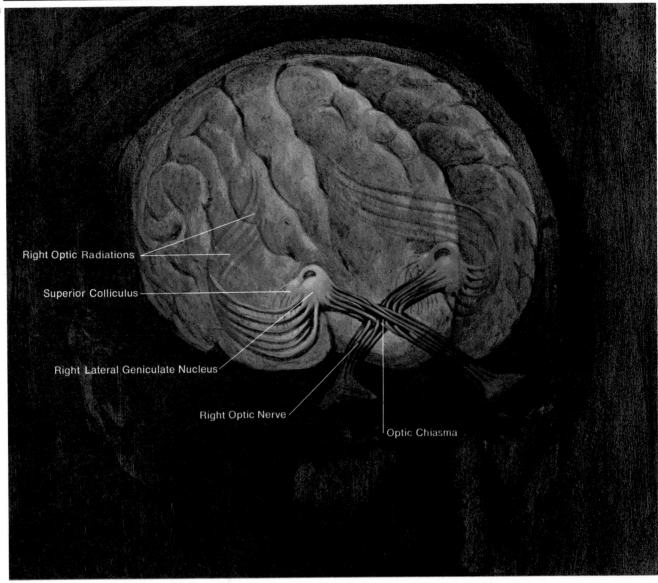

Right Optic Radiations

Superior Colliculus

Right Lateral Geniculate Nucleus

Right Optic Nerve

Optic Chiasma

Figure 16.10

The firing of a fiber in the brain of a monkey when the monkey's eye is stimulated for a second at a time with lights of varying wavelength. (After De Valois, 1966.)

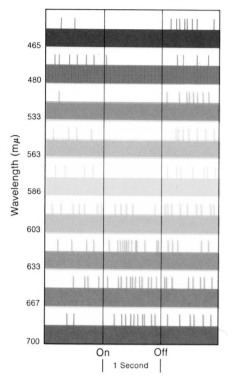

465
480
533
563
586
603
633
667
700

Wavelength (mμ)

On   Off

| 1 Second |

cells themselves. The neural complexity of the retina suggests that much of the coding takes place there.

Even in the absence of external stimuli, the retina is constantly discharging impulses to the brain. This *spontaneous activity* may either increase or decrease upon the onset of stimulation. Excitation and inhibition together provide the basic means by which information is processed in the nervous system. The interplay of inhibition and excitation may determine the code for some of the basic attributes of the visual stimulus.

The presence of cones with three distinct pigments provides the basis for color vision. The three different cones apparently have complex inputs to the higher levels that give rise to "opponent" cells. Located in the lateral geniculate nucleus of the thalamus, the opponent cells are excited when the eye is stimulated by light at certain wavelengths and inhibited at other wavelengths. An example of a fiber (from the thalamus of a Macaque monkey) that is excited by wavelengths in the red region and inhibited by wavelengths in the green region is shown in Figure 16.10. This cell presumably has excitatory inputs from cones that are most sensitive in the red region and inhibitory inputs from cones most sensitive in the green region. Another type of opponent cell is excited by blue (excitatory inputs from blue-sensitive cones) and inhibited by yellow (inhibition from either red or both red and green cones). Opponent cells with the opposite relation of excitation and inhibition are also found—for example, cells inhibited by red light and excited by green light.

When you realize the enormous number of interconnections that exist among adjacent and nearby receptor cells, you may consider it something of a miracle that we can perceive sharp visual contours at all. In their search for an explanation of how the parts of the eye interact to yield clear perceptions of complex objects, scientists have made use of a "living fossil," the horseshoe crab (*limulus*). Not really a crab at all, but more closely related to the spider, this marine animal existed hundreds of millions of years ago in much the same form as it does today.

The eye of the horseshoe crab has provided scientists with a simple model for the complex visual system of man and other mammals. The compound eye of the limulus is composed of about 1,000 tiny, separate eyes (ommatidia), shown in Figure 16.11. Neighboring ommatidia cover partially overlapping sections of the visual field. The ommatidia feed into *eccentric cells* whose axons form the optic nerve with no intervening synapses. The eccentric cells always interact when the

Figure 16.11

(A) Photomicrograph of the compound eye of a limulus in cross section. The cornea has been removed; the dark bodies are the sensory parts of the ommatidia. (B) The surface of the limulus eye.

A

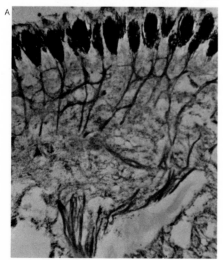

B

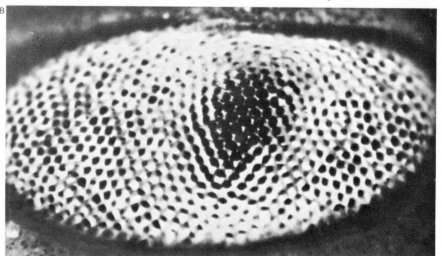

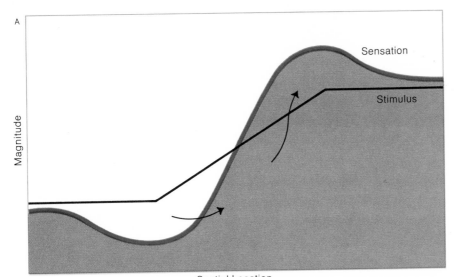

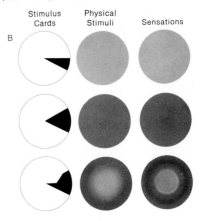

Figure 16.12
(A) Mach's law: the psychological gradient (brightness) is steeper than the physical gradient (intensity) over the edge of the stimulus border. (B) Rotation of stimulus cards produces the stimuli and sensations shown.
(After Békésy, 1958.)

ommatidia are stimulated by light, and the interaction is always inhibitory. The amount of inhibition increases with the activity rate of the inhibiting neuron and decreases with its distance. Thus, lighting up the whole compound eye produces little activity because all the cells inhibit each other. However, at a border where light intensity changes, some very interesting effects occur. The lighted cells nearest the border are inhibited only by excited cells on one side because the other side is dark and contributes no inhibition. Cells farther away from the border are inhibited more because they are surrounded on all sides by excited cells. Thus, the greatest rate of firing would be just over the bright side of the contour. On the dark side, the greatest inhibition is at the border from the excited cells just on the other side, so that those darkened border cells have depressed firing rates. The expected pattern of firing has a dip on the dark side of the border and a hump on the bright side (Figure 16.12).

The line shown in Figure 16.12 is not from limulus but from man. It traces the subjective brightness reported by human observers when stimulated with a light distribution given by the black line. For the human observer, the contour is sharpened by a brighter area on one side of the border and a darker area on the other side. These lines are called *Mach bands* after the physicist Ernst Mach, who first investigated them at the end of the nineteenth century. In the limulus eye, it has been conclusively shown that the contour enhancement results from inhibition via lateral neural connections among the eccentric cells. Quite possibly, a similar mechanism of *lateral inhibition* causes the Mach bands in the human eye.

Another way to explore the spatial organization of the visual system is by moving a small point of light across the eye while recording the responses in a single fiber or cell in the nervous system. In the limulus eye, the responses of a single cell reveal a spatial pattern on the retina called the *receptive field*. Figure 16.13 shows the pattern that follows from the interaction of excitation and inhibition in limulus, as described above. When the spot of light falls on an ommatidium, the cell's rate of firing increases; when it falls on neighboring ommatidia, the rate decreases. The distance over which some inhibition is effective is about the same in all directions so that the receptive field for a single ommatidium is somewhat circular.

Kuffler uncovered a similar pattern when recording from ganglion cells in the cat's eye. A typical result is shown in Figure 16.14. The increased size of the

Figure 16.13
Receptive fields in the limulus eye. The minuses (—) indicate points at which light stimulation reduced cell firing; the pluses (+) indicate points at which stimulation increased firing.
(After De Valois, 1966.)

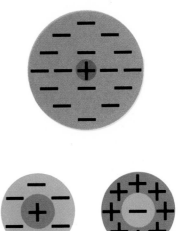

Figure 16.14
Receptive fields for two ganglion cells in the cat.
(After De Valois, 1966.)

central excitatory area indicates that the receptive field for the ganglion cell covers a number of receptor cells, not just one, as in limulus. Moreover, Kuffler found about as many ganglion cells with an inhibitory center and an excitatory surrounding. The ganglion cells can then serve the same function in contour sharpening as the eccentric cells. Cells at the next level in the cat's visual system, in the thalamus, have similar receptive fields. They and the ganglion cells could then be the site of, for example, the neural activity behind Mach bands.

Basic Phenomena of Vision

In this discussion of how the eyes play their important role in providing information about the environment, we shall emphasize three properties: (1) the ability of the eye to detect differences in intensity and to adjust to a large range of intensities, (2) the ability of the eye to detect differences in spatial position of a stimulus and to respond differentially to a large variety of spatial configurations of light, and (3) the ability of the eye to detect differences in the wavelength composition of energy coming from a source or reflected from an object and to see these differences as differences in color or saturation. The eyes can perform many other diverse functions, but these three properties will sample some of the characteristics of our visual system and give us some indication of how the process of seeing is studied.

Adjustment to Intensity

The visual system is remarkably adaptable. The range of intensities to which we can adjust is exceedingly large, covering a range of somewhere between a millionfold and a billionfold. It is important to note that we have used the word "adjust" rather than "respond." There is no doubt that we can also respond to an extremely large range of intensities, but it is important to distinguish between the adjustment of the eye to intensities and our ability to respond to different intensities.

The study of this adjustment leads us to the topic of light and dark adaptation. Suppose that a normal subject is placed in a completely darkened room for about an hour and then that we measure the smallest amount of light that is barely visible to him. Now imagine that we briefly present a light that is a thousand times the intensity of this just-visible stimulus. Such a light will undoubtedly be judged as being very bright. Momentarily, perhaps, it will be somewhat uncomfortable. Now let us take the same subject and let him adjust for an hour to a high light intensity—for example, of the magnitude that is found on a clear, sunny day at a beach. If, after he has adjusted to this high intensity, we immediately place him in a completely darkened room and flash this previously very bright light, he probably will not see it. In fact, it may not become visible until he has remained in the dark for a period of one or two minutes. If the subject stays in the dark for an hour, this light that is a thousand times as intense as his absolute threshold in the dark will again appear to be very bright.

The important thing to remember from this imaginary procedure is the fact that at any given moment the eye may or may not be able to respond to the full range of intensities to which we know it can respond. In other words, what the eye can do depends, in an extremely important way, on the state it is in at the time that we test its functioning. If we are adjusted or adapted to very bright lights, then lights that are much weaker or lower in intensity than the adapting lights will not be immediately visible. They become visible only after dark adaptation. Moreover, this experiment indicates that what is judged as dim, bright, or very bright is not uniquely linked to the intensity of the visual stimulus. The label depends upon the state of adaptation of the viewing system;

a light of fixed intensity can be made invisible, dim, or bright by appropriately adapting the eye.

One technique that has been used to study these processes is to light-adapt the eye to a fixed high intensity and then follow the time course of the amount of light that can be barely detected. The intensity that is required for a light to be barely seen is called the *threshold*. Figure 16.15 shows clearly that when a subject adapted to a high-intensity light is placed in complete darkness, the absolute threshold is very high at first. It then falls in two stages: it drops rapidly at first, then begins to level off after a couple of minutes; then it falls rapidly again, leveling off after about an hour. This is one of many phenomena observed in the study of vision suggesting that we have two different visual systems, a question we shall comment on in more detail later.

If, as we have said, the curve in Figure 16.15 is a plot of the intensity of light just required to make the light visible, then all intensities above this curve should be visible to the observer (the unshaded area in the figure). It is important to realize, however, that although we are most sensitive to light after being adapted to the dark for a long period of time, this fact should not be interpreted as meaning that the eye will function best in all capacities when it is dark-adapted. When the eye is dark-adapted, it is most sensitive to the detection of weak lights. What other tasks can be performed and how well they are performed remain to be examined. We can nevertheless anticipate some of these results by making one general statement: our ability to see fine detail, to see small differences in intensity, to detect a light as alternating in brightness, and to perform many other visual activities is usually best when we are adapted to an intensity level near but slightly below the intensity level at which we are going to test the visual function. It seems that the visual system responds efficiently over a range that is much narrower than the total range of its sensitivity and that the process of adaptation or adjustment is one of setting the eye for responding appropriately over a given range of intensity. If we want to see small details efficiently or to detect small differences in intensity at the levels that are found on a sunny beach, then we must allow time for the eye to adjust to levels approximately equal to those involved in the test stimuli.

The kind of results obtained in such experiments as the one represented in Figure 16.15 depends on a very large number of detailed features of the testing procedure. Mentioning a few of these will indicate the complexity of the system that we are dealing with. For example, we obtain the lowest thresholds for seeing when we present the test stimulus slightly to the side of our direct line of sight. In other words, we have a better chance of seeing a very dim light not by looking directly at where it should be but by looking slightly off to the side. If we can control the placement of the test stimulus so accurately that it falls directly in the center of our optical line of sight of the eye, then the dark-adaptation curve we get will not go any lower than the first limb of the curve that is shown in Figure 16.15.

We mentioned earlier that there was overwhelming evidence for the fact that we really have two visual systems in each eye. Histological evidence has shown that we have two major kinds of sense cells in the eye: the *rods* and the *cones*. It is believed that the first part of the dark-adaptation curve is due largely to the functioning of the cones and the second part to the functioning of the rods. We also know that we have only cones in the very center of the eye, the fovea. Consequently, if the stimulation is limited to the center of the eye, we do not obtain the second portion of the dark-adaptation curve. There are many other

Figure 16.15
Threshold changes during dark adaptation.
(After Hecht, *et al.*, 1935.)

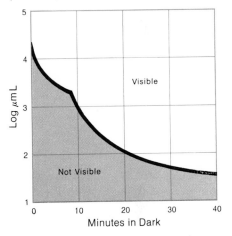

factors that influence the shape of the dark-adaptation curve, for example, the color and size of the test stimulus.

Our discussion so far has been concerned with the measurement of adaptation by a simple detection procedure. We simply ask what amount of light is needed for the subject to see the light. There are many other procedures for measuring the ability of the eye to adjust to different levels of intensity. As we have noted, saying that the eye is most sensitive does not guarantee that it is most efficient in operating at different levels. The ability of the eye to adjust in order to just detect the existence of light is not the same as the ability of the eye to adjust in order to perform some different task. Let us study, for example, the ability of the eye to adjust to light and ask if the eye can see some simple pattern—perhaps a series of dark and light lines, the so-called grating pattern.

In this case, the eye adjusts quickly to test stimuli that require very fine acuity, but the intensity levels that are required remain quite high. If we use acuity objects—in this case a grating figure that requires relatively poor acuity—the eye shows a rapid adaptation, as the first segment of the adaptation curve in Figure 16.16 shows, then continues to adapt more slowly to lower levels of intensity. Once again, the data shown in Figure 16.16 suggest that we are dealing with two visual systems. Thus, although acuity improves as we adapt to the dark, we must recognize that the measurement of our ability to see depends upon the performance required.

Unfortunately, there are limits to what might be called the dynamic range of any physical detector. For example, photographic film can respond over a very large range of intensities. If we simply ask if the photographic film is responsive, then intensities that completely darken the film but do not allow for any resolutions of differences in intensities could be considered to be effective stimuli. At high light intensities, the film would not be responsive to differences in intensity. If we ask a more subtle question—for example, over what range is there discriminability in the intensity of light stimuli—then we find that most physical detection systems are quite limited in the range over which they are responsive.

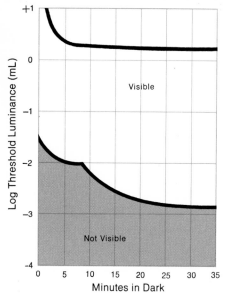

Figure 16.16

Threshold for discrimination of a grating during dark adaptation.
(After Hecht, et al., 1935.)

Adjustment to Spatial Detail

When we discussed the question of dark adaptation and visual acuity, we introduced the problem of resolving lines. Another example of acuity is the average person's ability to detect a dark line against a light background, even a one-fourth-inch-wide line approximately one-half mile away. This kind of acuity is frequently labeled *minimum visible acuity*.

A second kind of acuity involves a *repeating pattern*, such as that found in a grating or that of horizontal and vertical lines forming a checkerboard design. A third type, *vernier acuity*, concerns our ability to detect the offset of a line. In this case, the subject is required to respond by saying whether a line is broken or not. Other types of clinical tests of visual acuity include the *Landolt ring*—a black ring with a broken segment that the subject is required to detect. Another task, the *Snellen chart*, involves a kind of form discrimination by requiring the recognition and naming of printed letters of the English alphabet. Examples of these various acuity figures are shown in Figure 16.17.

Although these measures are loosely related, the kind of measurement used depends on the aspect of the visual system being considered. Measurements of the minimum visual acuity and minimum separable acuity, as represented by a grating or checkerboard figure, provide perhaps the most basic information on the resolving power of the visual system. However, if information on the ability to detect complex forms is sought, then the Snellen chart is of considerable use.

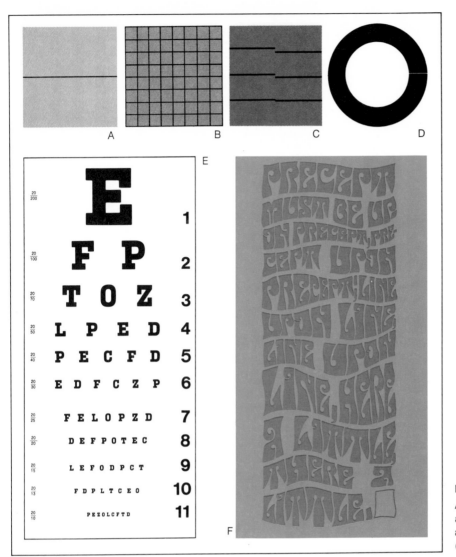

Figure 16.17
Acuity discrimination stimuli: (A) visual acuity, (B) grating pattern, (C) test of vernier acuity, (D) Landolt ring, (E) Snellen chart, (F) design lettering.

If we employ such a test, many variables enter that are very difficult to evaluate. These variables include the amount of training we have had in seeing printed letters and words and the naming of such letters, as well as how they are printed—for example, in bold outline or artistically varied. At this point, distinction between visual acuity and form discrimination is very hard to specify.

The kinds of stimulus figures commonly used in studying visual acuity represent only one of the many sets of analyses of spatial relations that can be performed by the eyes. Even when only black lines on a white background are used, the analytic power of the visual system is impressive. The length, width, and direction of simple straight lines can be discriminated. We can tell whether or not two lines are parallel and whether a line is straight or curved, horizontal or vertical. We can see lines as having different shapes or enclosing different areas. We can see two lines as meeting and forming different angles. The list of such visual cues is extensive. In spite of this vast array of visual information, lines are only a special case of the many spatial arrangements of light that we can discriminate. Even drawings in black and white, for example, have variations in the degrees of shading. The number of possible variations increases sharply when we turn to the somewhat more realistic light distributions represented by photographs and becomes almost infinite when we consider real-life looking at the objects in our environment. Moreover, add to all the variations in patterning those that take place in the dimension of time, which involve us with perception of the moving patterns that form so much of the visual world in which we must operate.

It is not possible to consider the many forms of perception that are encountered with complex configurations of light stimuli. Many data are available indicating the ability of the human observer to judge such things as the lengths of lines, the distances between points or between lines, the direction of lines, and whether or not two lines are parallel. We have data on our ability to discriminate size and area and to recognize or identify such special shapes as circles, triangles, and squares.

Nevertheless, there are also many things we do not know about these complexities of vision. A major problem is that we do not have an adequate language for describing the stimuli. We have been able to make the greatest progress in studies that deal with the elementary figures of geometry and trigonometry, such as points, lines, angles, and enclosed figures. Unfortunately, the visual system is not always guided by such simple geometric forms, and any analysis of our response to spatial patterns must cope with some of these interesting variations. We can illustrate this by examining Figure 16.18. Column A presents three simple geometric figures—a triangle, a square, and a circle. Most observers will also label the figures in columns B and C by the same names as their counterparts in column A. That is, all the figures in row 1 will be labeled triangles, those in row 2 will be labeled squares, and those in row 3 will be labeled circles. There is no suggestion that the observer cannot tell the difference between the various columns; he certainly can. The question of how the visual system can integrate these discontinuous figures—sequences of dots or dashes or combinations of them—and read them as straight lines is intriguing. The phenomena of such figure perception will be discussed more fully in Chapter 17.

Detection of Color   There are three rather interesting observations about the detection of color. Two of these seem to lead to one kind of conclusion; the third raises a question about, but not an insurmountable barrier to, this conclusion. The first observation is that subjects apply relatively few names to the various portions of the spectrum. Among the wavelengths that a subject calls red, he may be able to detect differences in stimuli but he does not possess appropriate labels to describe reliably the differences in information contained in the stimuli. The second observation, derived from basic research on color mixtures, is that it is possible to select three appropriate primary monochromatic stimuli and with these match every other color of the spectrum. This basic experimental finding has led to the

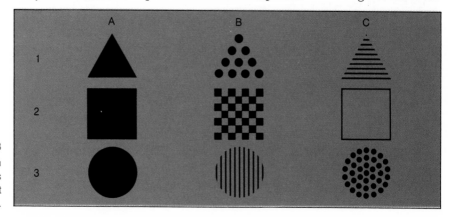

Figure 16.18
The way in which the visual system responds to figures like those in columns B and C was of interest to Gestalt psychologists.

trichromatic theory of color vision: that color vision depends on a relatively small number of color receptors. These first two observations are consistent with this conclusion.

A difficulty arises from the third observation: within the visible spectrum from wavelengths of 400 mμ (millimicrons) to 700 mμ, the normal observer can distinguish more than 125 different steps.

We have already mentioned the fact that different wavelengths of the visible spectrum are typically perceived as having different colors or hues. For example, if we present a normal subject with a visual stimulus that has a wavelength of 450 mμ, the subject will typically say that it appears blue to him. Likewise, a stimulus of 70 mμ will be perceived by most subjects as being red. However, we should make one point rather clear. The visual stimulus itself has no color; color is a psychological experience, a response to the stimulus. The color is, quite literally, in the eye of the beholder, not in the stimulus itself. Thus, we should always say that a visual stimulus (such as a traffic light) *appears* red to us, not that the traffic light *is* red. A great many organisms, including humans that have defective color vision, will not see the light as being red at all. The question is how it is possible to make so many fine discriminations over a range of approximately 300 mμ with a very small number of different receptor processes.

Before we discuss the possible mechanisms for color vision, let us first describe briefly several of the color phenomena that have played important roles in influencing color theory. One of the major sources of data is experiments on

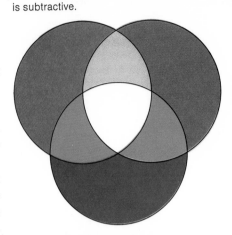

Figure 16.19
Color mixture. Superposition of projected lights adds the energy at each wavelength. Colored filters remove energy, and therefore the mixture with filters is subtractive.

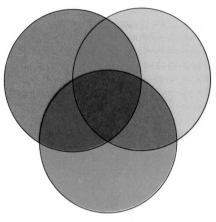

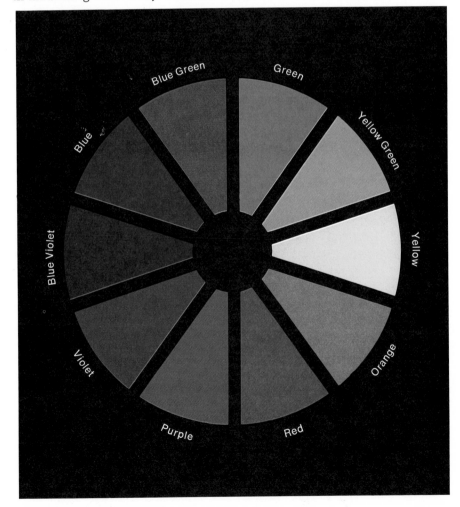

Figure 16.20
Color wheel. Colors opposite one another are complementaries.

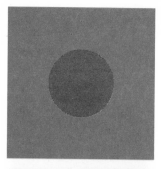

Figure 16.21
The centers of these two figures are
physically identical.

color mixture. Within very broad limits, it is possible to select a set of three monochromatic stimuli and by adjusting their relative intensities match any color in the spectrum. There are a few restrictions in the selection of these three so-called primary colors. For example, no two of them can be complementary colors, that is, pairs that when mixed together in correct proportions yield an achromatic or colorless stimulus. The existence of complementary colors is simply one example of a variety of color phenomena involving some kind of two-by-two linkage in color vision. We also encounter this kind of duality in the study of color contrast, which can be illustrated in an analogous way. If a gray disk is surrounded by a bright green stimulus, the disk will appear to have a red tint; conversely, if the surrounding colored field is red, then the gray center will appear to be green. These induced colors do not always correspond exactly to the complementaries of the inducing field, but the match is close enough to be interesting.

Similarly, this pair-wise linkage can be observed in the study of color afterimages. If a brief flash of an intense yellow light is presented, a subject is likely to report that shortly after the flash he sees blue light. Alternatively, if a brief intense flash of a green light is presented, the subject reports seeing a red patch after the cessation of the flash. The afterimages do not correspond exactly to the complementaries, but they are close to both the complementary color and the induced color in simultaneous color contrast.

We have noted that there is a substantial amount of data to support the notion that we possess a relatively small number of color receptors or color processes. The exact number is not easy to determine on the basis of psycho-physical experiments. We can deal with most of the color vision data by assuming that there are just three different types of color receptors, but we can also explain the same data by assuming that there are four or five. It is important to recognize, as was pointed out by Selig Hecht, one of the leading early investigators in the field of vision, that this is not a mathematical matter but a biological problem. Important recent physiological results suggest quite strongly that there are three different types of color receptors in the human, and more generally, the primate eye.

From the point of view of color theory, there remains the question of how the activity of these three types of cells is organized and analyzed by the nervous system. One of the notions that is widely discussed at the present time is that these three types of cells are linked together in such a way that they form three different opponent systems. One of these is a red-green system, in which a red and a green system act in opposition to each other. The second system is a yellow-blue system, and these two also act in opposition to each other. The third system is a broadly sensitive achromatic or brightness system that can be either excitatory or inhibitory in nature. This system would adequately explain such phenomena as complementary colors, afterimages, and color contrast. However, these phenomena can also be explained by a trichromatic theory, and at this point the physiological data suggest that both theories are to some extent correct. If by trichromatic theory we mean that the assumption is made that we have three different color receptors, then the physiological data strongly suggest that this assumption is correct. If we interpret the opponent-processes theory as assuming that we have red and green color mechanisms operating in opposition to one another, then the physiological data also support this assumption. Such observations and conclusions are not contradictory if we note that in one case we are talking about *receptors* and in the other case we are talking about *mechanisms* or *processes.* In fact, modern opponent-process theories do assume that there are three different types of color receptors.

What color is the grass in springtime? What color is an American Beauty rose? Are they the same color? Some 90 percent of the people in the world see grass as being bright green, and a rose would seem red to them. If your color vision is normal, there is an almost indescribable difference between red and green. To someone who is partially or completely color blind, however, there may be no perceptible difference at all between the color of grass and the color of a rose—both may seem vaguely yellowish, brownish, or even dark gray.

About 10 percent of the population has difficulty of some kind seeing colors, but it is a mistake to call most of them color blind, because they are neither blind nor insensitive to all the colors of the visual spectrum. The easiest way to describe color blindness is in terms of the number of colors that a person needs to mix together in order to match all the hues of the rainbow.

As we pointed out above, the normal individual needs just three well-chosen hues in order to reproduce all the colors of the spectrum. Such a person is therefore called a *trichromat.* People who are partially color blind need but two hues to reproduce all the colors they can see; we call them *dichromats.* If the dichromat is red-green blind, he can match all the hues he can see with just two colors—yellow and blue. The way he sees the world is reproduced in Figure 16.24. Red-green dichromatism is by far the most widespread form of partial color blindness. A few dichromats are yellow-blue blind; that is, they can reproduce all the hues they perceive by mixing red and green. The way this type of dichromat sees the world is shown in Figure 16.25. A very few individuals are totally color blind; they see no color at all, and to them the world is nothing but blacks and whites and shades of gray. Such a person is called a *monochromat* because he needs but one color (any color at all—they are all the same to him) to reproduce all that he can see.

Most forms of partial color blindness are sex-linked genetic anomalies that are passed from father to daughter to grandson. Men are rather unlucky in this respect, for they will be color blind if their mother carried the gene whether or not she was herself color blind. For a woman to be color blind, both her parents must carry the defective gene. If a woman has a color-blind father but her mother's color vision is normal, the woman will have normal vision herself, as will her daughters, but all her sons will be color blind. This complicated form of inheritance is outlined in Figure 16.27 and described more fully in Chapter 9.

In point of fact, even partial color blindness is not usually an all-or-nothing thing. There are many trichromats who actually can see all the colors and who need three hues to match the spectrum but who need abnormal amounts of one of the hues. Such a condition is called a *tritanomaly.* A tritanomalous individual who was green weak would see the leaves on trees as being a grayish green, but at least he would be able to perceive green as a separate and distinct color. The red-green *blind* individual is unable to see green at all, no matter how intense the stimulus is.

Although we are not entirely sure what the neural correlates of color blindness are, it seems a good bet that the proper cones are either missing or malfunctioning. Confirmation of this theory comes from careful studies of how the totally color blind person, the monochromat, sees the world. The fovea, which is at the center of the retina, contains nothing but cones. A monochromat should see only with his rods, and studies show this to be the case. The totally color-

Color Blindness

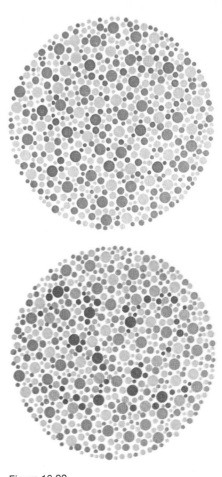

Figure 16.22

Test for color blindness. The discrimination of the numbers in these figures depends entirely on the ability to see colors, because the dots are equated for brightness. (The Dvorine Pseudo-Isochromatic Plates.)

Figure 16.23
The visual experience of the trichromat.

Figure 16.24
The visual experience of the
red-green–blind dichromat.

Figure 16.25
The visual experience of the
blue-yellow–blind dichromat.

Figure 16.26
The visual experience of the monochromat.

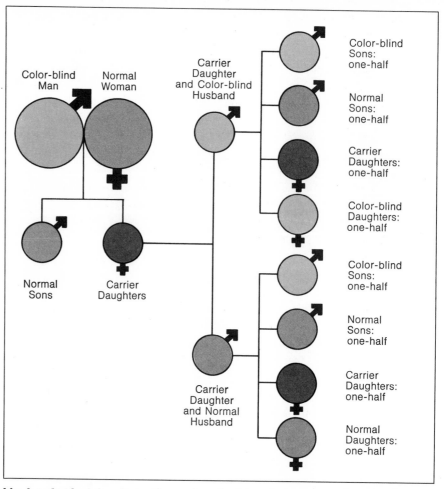

Figure 16.27
The sex-linked inheritance of color blindness.

blind individual has little if any foveal vision—he sees peripherally. But the center of his visual field—that part that contains the most detail for the rest of us—is lacking. To compensate for this handicap, he moves his eyes back and forth rapidly to scan the world with that peripheral part of his visual apparatus that still works. Monochromats see better in dim light than in bright light because some of the neural mechanisms that help normal eyes to adapt to the light are missing in their visual apparatus. As you might expect, too, their dark-adaptation curves are rather simply shaped because only the rods are adapting.

For the most part, those of us who have normal color vision fail to take into account the fact that color blindness exists. Most dichromats and tritanomalous individuals have difficulty with reds and greens but see yellows and blues quite well. Why then are stoplights red and green (which are easily confused) instead of being blue and yellow? A large number of automobile accidents could have been avoided if traffic engineers had taken the facts of color vision, and color deficiency, into account when stoplights were first designed.

The Role of Vision

The problems encountered in studying vision are similar to many of the problems found in other areas of psychology. We observe many forms of behavior in response to visual stimuli, ranging from something as simple as stopping at a traffic light when it is red and starting when it is green to the complex reactions that may result from seeing a beautiful painting or the judgments we may make about another person by observing the way he dresses or his facial expressions. In all cases, one of our most serious problems is attempting to describe accurately the critical dimensions of the stimuli that control these responses. In some areas of vision, our understanding of the stimuli has reached an advanced level; in others, we have far to go before we can be confident that we are on the correct path in our analysis. If we can learn one thing from the history of psychophysics in general and the study of vision in particular, it is that we cannot, without careful investigation, be satisfied that our intuitive notions and our subjective impressions can provide the proper guide for this analysis. There is no better place to start the analysis; at no time should we stop this analysis until we can give an accurate account of the relation between the changes in the environment described in the language of the physical sciences and the behavior of the living organism as we understand and can describe it at any given time.

We have attempted to provide a number of examples of terms that are quite acceptable in our everyday language but that on one occasion may seem to imply that we are talking about a stimulus and on another occasion clearly indicate that we are talking about the response of the observer. In everyday language, we encounter this confusion with such a phrase as "the brightness of a light." Under controlled circumstances, there are lawful relations between the intensity of a light stimulus and the brightness as judged by the observer. We have attempted to show that this relationship is complex. With the freedom of the experimenter to adjust the test circumstances, we can obtain judgments of equal brightness to stimuli that in physical terms may differ by a factor of a million or more. Although perhaps less striking numerically, we certainly encounter equally important influences in our perception of the spatial arrangements of light. This state of affairs contributes to the difficulties of studying sensory activity; it is also what makes the study both important and interesting.

The visual system responds differentially to the environment by enhancing certain features of the physical changes taking place and by deemphasizing others. It has no alternative. The total amount of information contained in all the physical changes taking place in our environment is far beyond the capacity of any living organism to register, much less analyze. The problems that confront the scientist working on the visual system are how this selection and analysis take place and what factors control it.

No small part of the problem that confronts the psychologist is attempting to account for how the human handles all the visual cues. Why he handles them in the way he does may be attributed to the fact that we live in an extremely visually oriented culture. The acceptance and rejection of geometrical representations of such figures as squares, circles, and cubes are but simple examples of many perceptions that may be influenced by the tremendous amount of visual display material that occurs in printed media, movies, and television. Representations designed to enhance certain features of objects or materials can hardly fail to have their effect on the criteria we use for acceptability, realism, and accuracy.

17

PROBLEMS OF PERCEPTION

THERE IS MORE TO SEEING THAN MEETS THE EYE. The physical aspects of stimuli, as they are delivered to the sense organs, determine many aspects of the subjective sensation. Thus, as we have seen, the luminance of an object rather tightly determines its apparent brightness and its dominant wavelength, its color. But it is relatively easy to demonstrate that our *perception* of the world depends on factors other than those we immediately see. If we can understand how this happens, we will understand seeing.

To the psychologist concerned with understanding behavior and brain function, the study of perception is attractive because even very simple experiments can give repeatable and suggestive results. There are many clearcut perceptual phenomena to investigate, and they cut across many areas—psychology, physiology, photochemistry, optics, and art. Also involved are the deep philosophical problems of the nature of knowledge, of how we come to understand things. If it were true that all our knowledge comes through the senses, it would be as foolish of the philosopher to ignore the phenomena, the limitations, and the embroidery of perception as it would be for the astronomer to disregard the distortions and limitations of his telescopes.

317

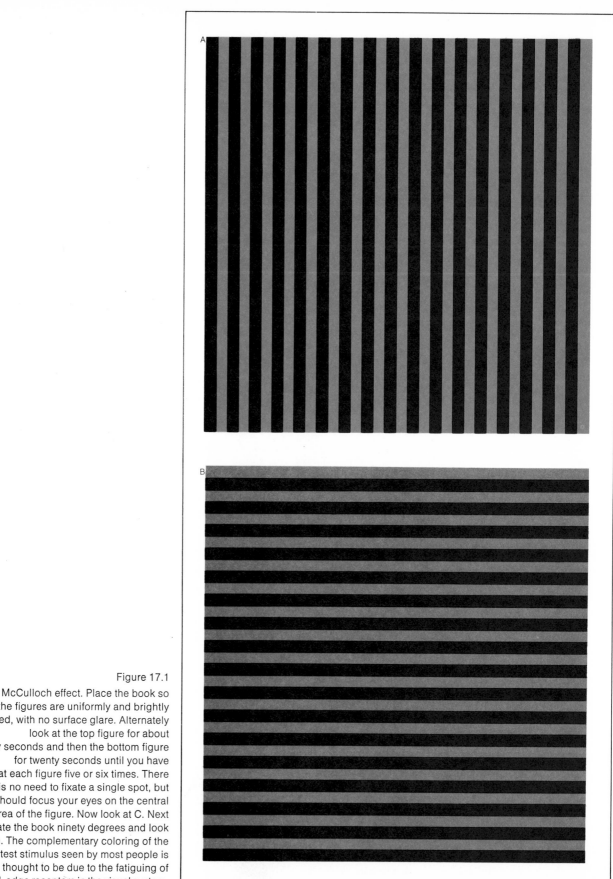

Figure 17.1
The McCulloch effect. Place the book so that the figures are uniformly and brightly lighted, with no surface glare. Alternately look at the top figure for about twenty seconds and then the bottom figure for twenty seconds until you have looked at each figure five or six times. There is no need to fixate a single spot, but you should focus your eyes on the central area of the figure. Now look at C. Next rotate the book ninety degrees and look again. The complementary coloring of the test stimulus seen by most people is thought to be due to the fatiguing of colored-edge receptors in the visual system.

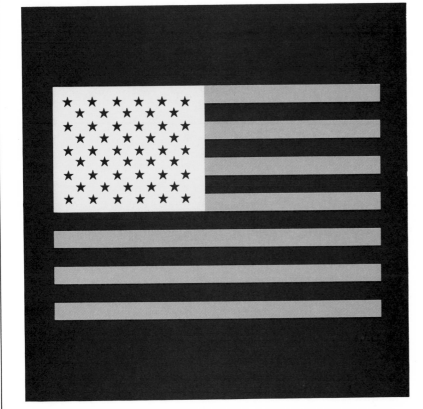

Figure 17.2
Simultaneous contrast. In the first pair of figures, the same gray square is made darker by surrounding it with white, then lighter by surrounding it with black. In the second pair, the tendency of a colored surrounding to produce a complementary hue in the central square is used to modify the apparent color of a blue.

Figure 17.3
Afterimages. Stare intently at the star in lower right-hand corner of the cluster for forty-five seconds. Then look at a white area, where you should see the flag in its correct colors.

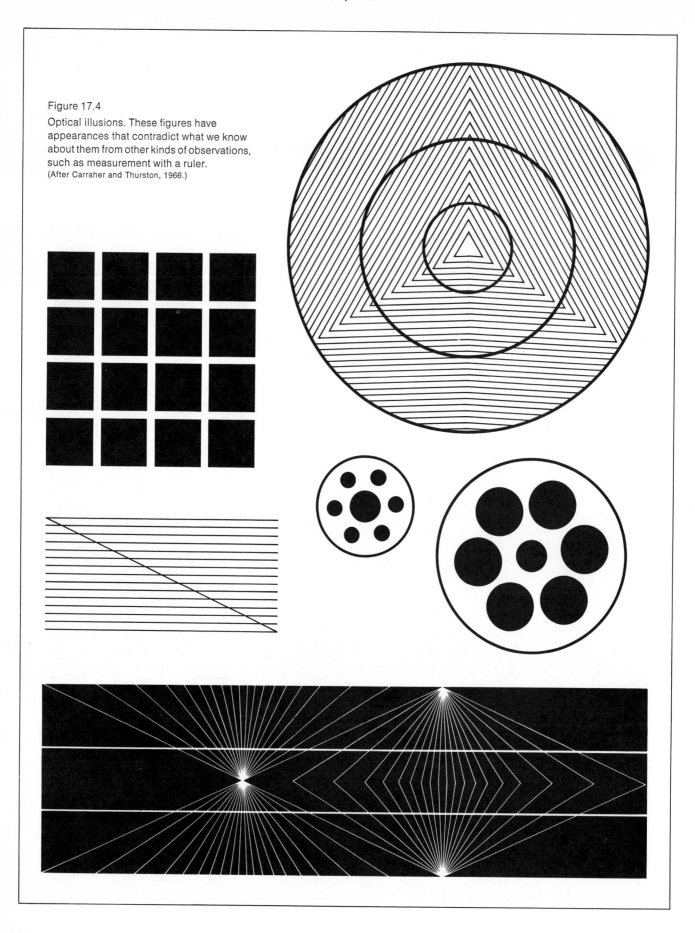

Figure 17.4
Optical illusions. These figures have
appearances that contradict what we know
about them from other kinds of observations,
such as measurement with a ruler.
(After Carraher and Thurston, 1966.)

Figure 17.5
Ambiguous figures that our nervous system
can interpret in more than one way.
(C after Bugelski and Alampay, 1961;
others after Carraher and Thurston, 1966.)

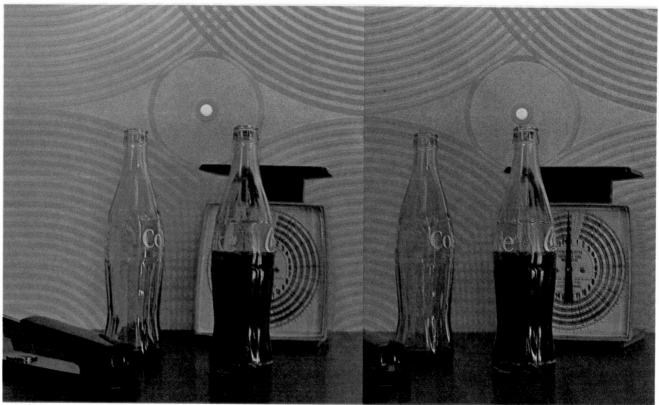

Figure 17.6
If the two slightly different pictures above are viewed in the way shown to the left, so that each eye sees a single picture, the two images may be fused into one and thus give an appearance of depth. Binocular fusion of the disparate images received by the two eyes is said to yield stereoscopic depth.

Figure 17.7
The moon illusion. The moon appears larger near the horizon—an effect that is even stronger when one is actually looking at the moon.

Figure 17.8
When photographed from a certain point, a distorted picture of a house painted on the floor looks like a normal three-dimensional building. The interpretation of the unusual combinations of size, distance, and orientation that can be obtained in this situation produce some baffling effects.

Perhaps the distinction between what we mean by patterns and objects is a philosophical question, but it must be faced to understand the nature of perception. By a *pattern* we mean a more-or-less orderly sequence of events in space or time. Stimulus patterns are sequences of events at the eye or the ear or in contact with the skin, signaled to the brain by trains of nerve impulses through fibers— sometimes through just a few or, as in the eye, through up to a million. Stimulus patterns represented in this way to the brain are interpreted in terms of events and *objects of the external world*. This is the remarkable miracle of perception: so little information from the senses conveys so much to the mind. Fleeting patterns of light and shade and color on the retina allow us to infer the existence of and behave appropriately to a wide variety of objects that are not at that moment and may never have been fully represented in retinal images. Real objects are different from and far more complex than any sensory patterns of stimulation. An object has a past and a future; it may be heavy, brittle, hot—and it has a form that is never entirely represented in the retinal image at any one time. In perceiving objects, we classify retinal images as plates, cups, tables, or books and behave according to this classification, whatever the available information may be that allows us to recognize it for what it is.

Behavior is geared to objects and object properties, not directly to stimulus patterns. Probably most of what we perceive is not signaled directly but is inferred from present and past stimulus patterns. Perceptual inference is common in everyday experience. When we put a book on a table, we do not check that the table is hard or solid. We do not generally check that a chair will bear our weight before we sit down; we assume that it has four sound legs, though they may be hidden. We assume that the ground is solid before us as we walk and that a smile means friendship but a frown, danger.

Perception is also forward-looking, predictive. It is not difficult to see why this is so: the nervous system takes some time to transmit and to translate input signals into appropriate behavior. The response delay (reaction time) for an unexpected signal is at least 0.2 second, but behavior is not generally delayed with respect to external events. If it were, fast games would be impossible; indeed, we would not survive for long. It has been found experimentally that when a subject is presented with a familiar or predictable wavy line on a moving paper strip and asked to follow it as accurately as possible with a stylus, he often follows the track with *no* temporal delay. But an unpredictable change of course will be followed only after a delay of around 0.2 second. It is thus clear that tracking is not controlled directly by visual input but rather by a continuous series of predictions of what is about to happen. When prediction is impossible, appropriate behavior is delayed.

Prediction is vital for any strategic or planned action, and planned behavior is a vital characteristic of higher animals. Events are anticipated, and behavior is geared to the anticipation. For example, if a rat maze is modified by shortening a run, rats familiar with the maze will rush headlong and bang into the new, unexpected wall. It follows that they are not running the maze simply as sensed but are running the expected maze, as based on their past experiences.

Such considerations show that although we study perception with stimulus displays of various kinds, perception is not generally geared directly to current sensory inputs. It is geared to a belief in the—mainly non-sensed—properties of external objects. Moreover, behavior is directed not so much to objects as they *are* but rather to how they *probably will be* by the time action is carried out.

Patterns and Objects

Perception and Prediction

Figure 17.9 A

Despite the continuity of our retinal images, we perceive objects as separate from each other and from the background.

Objects and Space When we look at objects against the sky or another unstructured background (Figure 17.9A), it is not difficult to imagine how we decide, from the pattern of the retinal image, which regions represent *objects* and which represent *spaces* between objects. If spaces always lacked structure, then we would merely interpret structured regions as objects and unstructured regions as space. Very often, however, objects are seen against a structured background yet are perceptually distinct from the background (Figure 17.9B). Moreover, although objects may be touching each other, we still see them as separate; they are seen as separate *objects*, though the retinal *patterns* are continuous (Figure 17.9C).

There are often, however, direct indications that objects are separate from their background and from each other. Movement of the observer generates parallax shifts between objects lying at different distances, and stereoscopic depth perception, produced when both eyes function, is important for separating nearby objects. But the fact that we can isolate and recognize objects as represented in photographs and pictures shows at once that distinct objects can be recognized even if only a static pattern is given to the eye. Pictures are very useful for perceptual research, because it is easy to control the stimulus pattern and to reduce in stages every helpful kind of information in order to discover the irreducible minimum the eye requires. Motion parallax and stereoscopic information are lost in pictures, and we can go on to remove color, contrast, and sharpness. We can also reduce the viewing time by using a tachistoscope, which illuminates pictures for controlled durations, and we can introduce conflicting, disturbing, or masking features.

It is most important to realize that pictures are essentially artificial in presenting objects *as though* they were lying in three dimensions (indicated by perspective and shadows and so on) although the object—the picture itself—is but a flat sheet with a pattern on it. The picture surface is generally visible as a flat texture, so the perspective and other depth-suggesting features tend to be seen as artificial. This conflict never occurs when objects are viewed directly. There is considerable evidence from anthropological studies that seeing pictures is something of a special skill, for even excellent photographs may at first make little sense to people unfamiliar with pictures. Although pictures are useful for perceptual research, it is vital to treat them as artificial visual inputs that may give misleading results when we are interested in how objects are perceived.

Gestalt Psychology

The Gestalt psychologists of the 1920s and 1930s made much use of dot patterns to reveal what they called the *organizing principles of perception*. They presented dot patterns like that of Figure 17.10A and pointed out that although the dots physically are equally spaced, we tend to see them in groups forming squares or rows. The subtle aspect is not that the dots are not at the same time seen as dots or that they appear to shift in space—it is that they seem to *belong* to each other in groups forming patterns. When the spacings are changed, quite stable groupings are formed. In Figure 17.10B, for example, the dots are seen in pairs. If the dots are still closer, the effect is even more apparent, as in Figure 17.10C. Evidently, then, dots close together tend to be seen as belonging to each other. But this is not all there is to the matter. Look carefully at Figure 17.10D. The lowest dot of the inclined line is nearer to a dot on the vertical line than to any other, and yet it does not belong to the vertically arranged dots. It belongs to the inclined row even though the gap is greater. Thus, mere proximity does not appear to explain belongingness completely. Continuity is also important and can be more important than proximity in organizing dot patterns.

Another important factor is similarity. Figure 17.11A, for example, is seen as rows of As and rows of Bs. We get much the same effect for individual elements less meaningful than letters, as can be seen in Figures 17.11B and 17.11C. On the

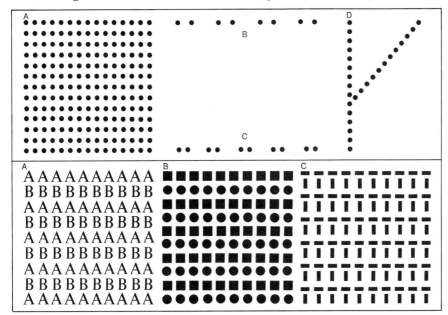

Figure 17.10

Gestalt principles describe the perceptual organization of dot patterns.

Figure 17.11

Our perceptions of patterns are influenced by the similarity of their components.

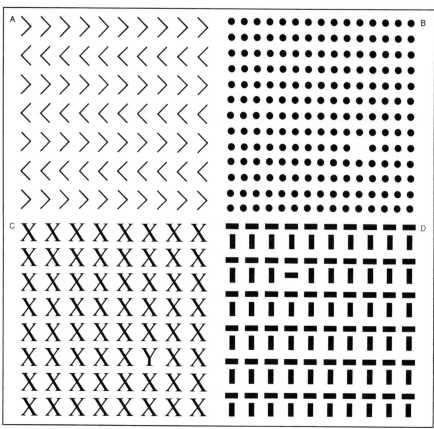

Figure 17.12
Figures demonstrating our varying
perception of irregularities.

other hand, some individual shapes do not cohere when arranged in equally spaced blocks in this way; see Figure 17.12A.

A slight deviation from a repeated arrangement may be readily seen, as in Figure 17.12B—but not always (see Figure 17.12C). A break in a sequence is detected most readily (see Figure 17.12D).

The demonstration-experiments that are presented in Figures 17.10–17.12 are typical of the Gestalt approach to perception. Gestalt psychologists presented figures that were closed or open in form, and they performed some interesting experiments with simple moving displays or with lights switched on and off in sequence to generate apparent movement; generally, they simply asked people what they saw. They summarized the results of the dot pattern experiments in a series of *laws of organization*, including such factors as *proximity, continuity, closure,* and the *common fate* of dots moving together against a background of stationary or differently moving dots. They thought that the ways dots belong to each other reveal basic, underlying units of perception. These principles, or laws of organization, and the associated units, or gestalts, were supposed to be inherited, to be given innately and not derived from experience with the world of objects. The Gestalt psychologists did acknowledge some perceptual learning, but it was played down. They also proposed a rather curious physiological theory based on the notion of isomorphism—that seen shapes are represented by similarly shaped electrical brain fields that have innate tendencies to form simpler, more closed shapes. They extended the notion of gestalts and isomorphism to music, holding that sequences of notes forming melodic units are similar to visual perceptual groupings of dots.

There are serious physiological objections to the Gestalt psychologists' isomorphic brain field—for example, placing conducting wires in the visual region of chimpanzees' brains does not seem to produce perceptual distortion. Moreover, there are logical objections. If two-dimensional patterns are represented as flat pictures on the cortex, are three-dimensional objects represented as three-dimensional brain fields? The Gestalt psychologists were never very clear about this question, partly because they most often considered flat patterns and tended to ignore perception of objects in three-dimensional space. If we consider other properties of objects, such questions arise as whether or not movement is represented by corresponding movement of the similarly shaped brain fields. Furthermore, if the object is green or blue, is its corresponding region of the brain supposed to turn green or blue? Is a hard object supposed to be represented by a hardening of the brain and a soft object by brain softening? Such extensions of the theory become so implausible that we must reject the notion for nonshape properties of objects. And if it does not hold for them, why should it be accepted for shape?

The Gestalt writers started from a metaphysical position that emphasized a priori truth, so a theory of innate perceptual knowledge of the world was attractive to them. It is less appealing to empiricists, who put far more emphasis on learning and experiences in order to account for perceptual organization. It is possible to accept the validity of the Gestalt writers' organizing principles and hold that they are not given innately but are inductively derived from experience of objects that generally *are* closed in form, have visual features in close proximity, and have parts that display "common fate."

The great nineteenth-century scientist Hermann von Helmholtz took a view of perception very different from the Gestalt view. An eminent physicist and physiologist, he tended to distrust phenomenalism. In modern terms, he would argue that observed phenomena are unlikely to reveal the truth directly. Rather, observation must be used for suggesting and testing conceptual models of underlying processes, which may appear very different from the observed phenomena. (The Gestalt grouping phenomena might be generated by a digital computer. This would not mean that the computer worked with isomorphic fields or anything like them, for the logical structure of the digital program could give such properties without in any simple way resembling them.)

Helmholtz suggested that perception of objects from the stimulus patterns is given by a process of *unconscious inference*. He argued that an individual's unconscious generalizations based on his previous experience produce the principles by which patterns are grouped and interpreted as objects.

The notion of unconscious inference has traditionally been unpopular with psychologists, but with the development of and familiarity with computers, any philosophical objection there may have been is disproved. We no longer require that there be consciousness for inference. We can suppose that the visual brain infers objects from images without supposing that there is any sort of conscious little man inside making the inferences. We can go on to ask what kinds of inference and what data and what assumptions are used for perception.

Perceptual Inferences
Figure-Ground Decisions

The first decision involved in perception is distinguishing between figures and the spaces between figures. The classic work in this area is that of the Danish psychologist Edgar Rubin. He presented such line drawings as that in Figure 17.13, which spontaneously changes, the white region sometimes appearing as a face and sometimes as mere background. The most famous example is the pair of faces looking at each other (Figure 17.14); sometimes the picture appears as two faces, but at other times the background between them becomes a figure—a

329

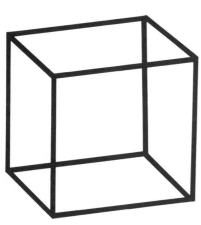

Figure 17.13
The interpretation of this drawing depends on what is seen as the ground.
(After Rubin, 1915.)

Figure 17.14
The goblet figure, which may also be seen as two faces.
(After Rubin, 1915.)

vase—and the faces fade perceptually to become background in their turn. These are examples where there is no adequate information to decide which is object and which background. The reversals can be entirely spontaneous and do not depend on any changes of stimulation at the eye. Perceptual set and individual interest may, however, affect which alternative tends to be dominant.

Depth-Reversing Figures

The best-known reversing figure is the Necker cube (Figure 17.15), a drawing, with no perspective, of a skeleton cube. Because the back and front are drawn equal in size (they would not be by perspective), there is no information on which face is nearer. The brain evidently entertains alternative hypotheses—and never makes up its mind. Normally, only one kind of object has a high probability of being perceived (which is indeed most surprising when we think of the vast numbers of kinds of objects that exist), but the Necker cube is a case where two acceptable possibilities exist. This effect is very far from trivial. In the first place, it is interesting that we have only two alternative perceptions. Why, indeed, should it be accepted as a cube object at all? This same drawing could be the flat projection, the retinal image, of an infinity of different objects—truncated pyramids and so on—and yet only two possibilities (both based on the cube assumption) are entertained. This phenomenon at once suggests that perception is a matter of selecting from available data the most likely kind of object. In this case, it is a cube, but it *could* be any of an infinite number of very different three-dimensional shapes.

The phenomena of reversible depth suggest several characteristics of perception. First, perception is not inevitably determined by stimulus patterns, as is demonstrated by the fact that the same pattern can give alternative perceptions. Second, perception involves selection from a finite number of object hypotheses, or available answers to the question "What object is producing the pattern at the eye?" Moreover, it is likely that some kind of probability hierarchy exists, the Necker cube being a rare case where the probabilities of two object hypotheses are equal but mutually exclusive, so that they cannot be selected at the same time. Finally, although the Necker cube *as drawn on paper* (it also exists as a wire model) does not change its shape when it reverses, if it is presented with *no*

Figure 17.15
The Necker cube.

visible background, the face that is apparently farther away always appears larger than the nearer, though in fact they are the same size. This phenomenon shows that *constancy size scaling* (discussed below) can be set purely by the prevailing internal object hypothesis and not necessarily by the stimulus pattern.

The effect of size change with change in apparent distance of the faces of the figure when it reverses in depth is best seen with flat luminous wire models. Viewed glowing in a dark room, they appear as luminous line figures with no background. When light is added to reveal a background, the differences are striking. When there is no visible background, the flat wire figure changes in form so that the apparently farther face always looks larger than the nearer, whichever that may be. When the background is clearly revealed with light, though the figure reverses (as in Figure 17.16), there is no change in the relative size of the faces with reversal. Depth in all drawn or photographed figures with backgrounds is *paradoxical,* for we see the figure both in depth and also lying on the flat background. Necker cubes drawn on paper have this paradoxical depth. The size and shape changes associated with seen distance do not occur when depth in pictures is, in this sense, paradoxical. Removing the background removes the paradox—we see the figure in the depth of normal objects, even though it is illusory.

When an object recedes, its image shrinks to half its size with each doubling of the distance of the object from the eye. This effect is the same as the shrinking of camera images with increasing object distance. In normal perception, however, we do not see this decrease but rather see objects as almost the same size over a wide range of distance. We compensate for the geometrical shrinking of images with distance, to give *size constancy,* which can easily be demonstrated with no apparatus except our own hands (Figure 17.17). Put one hand at arm's length and the other at half that distance (judged by the elbow of the extended arm), and note the relative sizes of your hands. They will look very much the same size although the farther will give but half the image size to the eye. Now move the nearer hand so that it partly overlaps—partly hides from view—the farther. Immediately, they will look quite different sizes. Although you know intellectually that your hands are the same size, the farther hand will appear to be that of a midget. Evidently, the partial overlapping has prevented perceptual size scaling, normally giving constancy, from working, so that we see our hands as they are presented at the eye.

Size constancy can be easily demonstrated with afterimages. An afterimage is given by fixating a bright light, preferably a photographic flash. Extreme stimulation produces a relatively long-lasting image on the retina. At first, we see a positive picture of the stimulating light, which changes after a few seconds to a longer-lasting negative afterimage. The afterimage appears to be in external space. In darkness, it generally appears to be ten to twenty feet distant. When we look at a surface, such as the wall of a room, the afterimage appears to lie on the surface. The more distant the wall, the larger it looks. With each doubling of distance, it looks (almost) twice as large. This linear increase in size with distance is known as Emmert's law and is said to demonstrate the active principle giving size constancy. The effect is much the same as the size-distance effect with the Necker cubes with no background. There is, however, a difference, which is often missed. In the Emmert's law situation, the total retinal image does change when we look at the nearer or farther wall because the screen is part of the total retinal image. Consider the afterimage on a distant wall and a nearer one. In

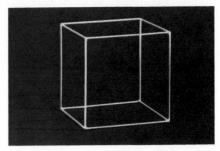

Figure 17.16
A Necker cube shown with a background reverses, but the relative sizes of its surfaces do not change.

Size Constancy

Figure 17.17
You can demonstrate size constancy and its breakdown by looking at your hands at different distances and then moving them so that their images overlap.

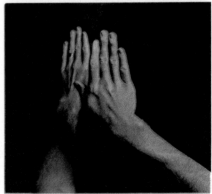

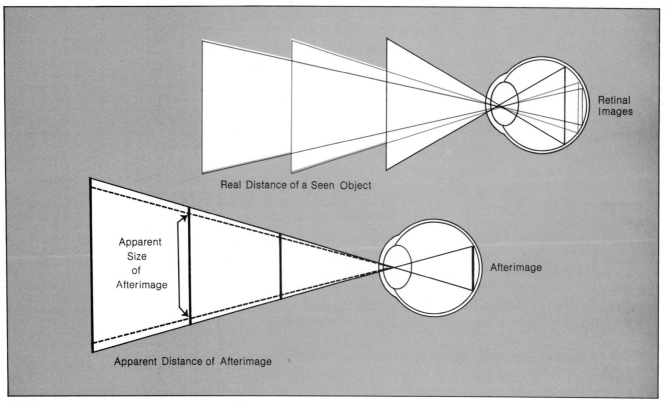

Retinal Images

Real Distance of a Seen Object

Apparent Size of Afterimage

Afterimage

Apparent Distance of Afterimage

Figure 17.18

(Top) Size constancy. Although the retinal image of a receding object grows smaller, we do not see a shrinking object. *(Bottom)* Emmert's law. When the retinal image size is constant, the image appears larger the more distant it appears to be.

relation to any pattern or texture on the wall, the afterimage will be relatively larger on the distant and smaller on the nearer wall in *physical* terms. So although Emmert's law is usually given as a clear demonstration of a brain process called constancy scaling, the law can be criticized.

The size changes with the depth-reversible figures are not open to this complication, for there is no change in the retinal image. They do indeed show that there is a central process, size scaling, associated with apparent distance. It remains, however, an open question whether or not size constancy is set *purely,* and throughout its range, by this central scaling mechanism. The relative-size effect shown in Figure 17.18 may well play a part—as it does when we judge the size of objects in pictures. There is also reason to believe that apparent size is determined in part by another kind of perceptual scaling system that also affects the well-known distortion illusions.

Distortion Illusions

Distortion illusions such as the Müller-Lyer arrow figures (Figure 17.19) and the Ponzo converging-lines figure (Figure 17.20), discussed in Chapter 11, have been investigated for a century, but no fully accepted theory to explain them has emerged, even though they are predictable and highly repeatable phenomena occurring in almost all observers.

The earliest theory of distortion illusions was given by the father of experimental psychology, Wilhelm Wundt, who suggested that the pictures produce abnormal eye movement, which in turn affects the apparent position as well as the apparent size of the lines. This suggestion cannot be correct, because the illusions persist in afterimages or when the image is optically fixed (stabilized) in the retina. Also, the distortions can occur in several directions at the same time (for example, in a pair of Müller-Lyer arrows).

There is evidence that the distortions have their origin in the brain from experiments in which part of a distortion figure is presented to one eye and the rest to the other eye. This has been done in two ways: by breaking the figure up into very small regions so that neither eye sees any recognizable picture and by presenting the distort*ing* parts to one eye and the distort*ed* parts to the other. Given certain precautions, in both methods the distortions remain unimpaired by splitting the figure between the eyes. Thus, the origin of the distortion must be in the brain, which has access to the information from both eyes.

Other theories have suggested that these patterns upset visual shape analyzers. It has been noted that acute angles tend to be overestimated and obtuse angles underestimated, but no one has suggested why this should happen or why errors of angle should produce distortions of length or position. Thiéry, in 1896, made a different kind of suggestion: that the distortions arise through the brain's handling them not as *patterns* but as *objects*. He suggested that the illusion figures have perspectivelike features that typically indicate distance. This effect is seen most clearly in the Ponzo illusion (Figure 17.20): the converging lines certainly can be regarded as perspective lines, in which case the upper of the two horizontals would be more distant than the lower. The Müller-Lyer arrows (Figure 17.19) can be regarded as skeleton drawings of corners, the outward-going fins being the lines, say, of the floor and ceiling of the *inside* corner of a room, and the inward-going fins an *outside* corner. We see the same arrowlike shapes generated by perspective in photographs of corners (Figure 17.22). What Thiéry pointed out is that when the figures are regarded in this way, features indicated as distant are expanded. This effect is just what occurs when size scaling is set by apparent distance, so it is very tempting to believe that the illusions are the result of *constancy size scaling* being set *inappropriately* by perspective depth features in pictures. The scaling is inappropriate because the illusion figures are actually flat, so that there is no compensating shrinking of the

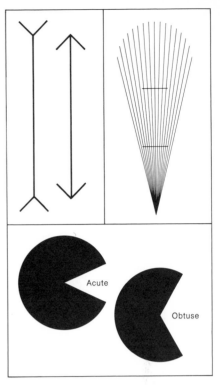

Figure 17.19
The Müller-Lyer illusion. The vertical lines are identical in length.

Figure 17.20
The Ponzo illusion. The subtended lines appear to be of unequal length.

Figure 17.21
Acute angles seem smaller and obtuse angles seem larger than they really are.

Figure 17.22
The reason that the upright in A appears longer than the same upright in B may be that it is seen as more distant—a striking example of the Müller-Lyer illusion.

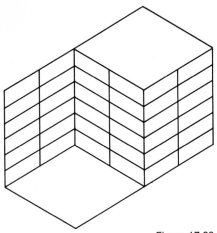

Figure 17.23
In this reversible figure, the square in the horizontal plane that is seen as more distant appears larger.
(After Carraher and Thurston, 1966.)

image. What is normally an appropriate and useful compensation would produce errors in this situation, where depth features are presented without depth.

It is important to note that there is something odd here, because the reversing cube figures do *not* show size-distance changes when their background is visible. Why, then, should constancy scaling operate in the quasidepth of the illusion figures whose background is visible? In other words, why should it work when we see the figures as flat? At this point, we must either drop the idea that the distortions are given by inappropriate constancy size scaling or suggest that the scaling mechanism is somewhat more complicated than has been assumed. This is a classic situation in science. The simplest hypothesis that covers the facts should be adopted, but when it is inadequate, we are free either to reject it or to add to it until the facts are covered.

In the present case, we can cover the facts by adding one extra idea: *size scaling is set directly by typical (perspective) depth features.* Normally, perspective shrinking and convergence of the retinal image are determined by the distances of objects in the external world, and the consequent direct setting of scaling by these perspective features should be appropriate. It seems that we can explain the distortion illusions if we suppose that they are the result of constancy size scaling being set inappropriately when indicators of depth are presented without any (or with different) true depth. To cover all the facts, however, we must suppose that size scaling can be set in two ways: (1) directly by apparent depth—by the prevailing internal hypothesis of the distance of the object; or (2) directly by typical (perspective) depth features of retinal images, even when depth is not seen because it is countermanded by other information, such as the texture of a picture's background. Normally, these sets will agree with each other and also with reality, but if either is set inappropriately, there will be a corresponding size error—a distortion illusion.

The Ames Demonstrations

Adelbert Ames, a painter, produced some very striking visual demonstrations. He made several models (some were full scale) designed to give the same retinal image as familiar objects although the models were a very different shape. This effect is possible because an infinity of three-dimensional shapes can give the same plane projection—the same retinal image—from a chosen viewpoint. The best-known demonstration is the Ames room, which gives the same image to a viewer placed at a critical position as does a normal rectangular room although it is far from rectangular. The far wall recedes to one side (Figure 17.24) and is correspondingly larger to maintain the retinal image of a rectangular wall. Why do we accept this retinal image as indicating a rectangular room when, demonstrably, it could represent an infinity of oddly shaped rooms? We must suppose that we select the *most probable* interpretation of the image—a rectangular room. Piquancy is added to the situation when familiar objects, such as people, are placed inside the room (Figure 17.26). *The room appears rectangular but the people appear to be of impossible sizes.* One person seems twice the height of another. What is needed here, surely, is a control situation for the experiment. What we want is an Ames room without the room. Consider Figure 17.27, which shows two people actually at relatively great distances, as in the Ames room. Now, do they look different in *distance* or in *size*? Does the smaller look twice as distant or shrunk to half the size? Most people say that she looks more shrunk than distant—so, is the assumption of rectangularity all that strong?

It is most important to realize that the Ames room is not a distortion illusion like the distorting figures discussed above, for there is no perceptual modification

Perceived Rectilinear Room

Actual Distorted Room

Peephole

Figure 17.24
Floor plan of the Ames room, showing the rectangular interpretation observers make of what they see.
(After *The Mind* ©1964 Time Inc.)

Figure 17.25
The construction of the Ames room.
(Courtesy of Dr. William H. Ittelson.)

of the size of the retinal image. What this figure does bring out are the assumptions that we make to decide between size and distance. The assumption that a room is rectangular is quite strong, but evidently not as dominating as is usually suggested.

It is interesting that visual perception of the Ames room is modified by active exploration with a long stick. Gradually, the room comes to look its true odd shape. On the other hand, intellectual knowledge of its shape does not give correct perception. Although perception involves a kind of problem solving, evidently perception is largely autonomous, as is strikingly demonstrated by a wire Necker cube model. If you hold it in your hand while it is glowing in a dark room, it will reverse visually—in spite of the touch information—and the visual and touch worlds separate. If you now slowly rotate the cube in your hand, it will *visually* rotate *backward,* for motion parallax is wrongly referred to

Figure 17.26
The Ames room illusion.

Figure 17.27
The Ames illusion without the room.

back and front—a most weird experience. Evidently, vision is largely autonomous, though it can be affected by touch or other information.

Perception of Movement

Figure 17.28
The illusion of movement may be produced by a stationary figure.

Perception of movement is of primary biological importance, for moving objects are likely to be potential danger or food. Some primitive eyes respond *only* to movement, as does the extreme periphery of the human retina. Try watching a television set with your eyes directed about 90 degrees away and you will see movement but no form.

Movement is signaled to the brain in two distinct ways: (1) by the image running along retinal receptors and (2) by the eyes following the moving object. When we look from object to object, the world does not swing around in the opposite direction, as it does when you pan with a motion-picture camera. It seems that the velocity signals from shift of the retinal image are canceled by the brain's signals to move the eyes. These signals are equal and opposite, so the world remains stable in spite of eye movements. If you push your eye with a finger, however, the world does swing around, for in this case there is no eye-movement signal to cancel out the retinal velocity signal produced by the passive eye movement.

The Gestalt writers made a great deal of apparent movement, the *phi phenomenon*. This phenomenon is common in illuminated displays where lights are switched sequentially; we see movement though nothing is moving. Of course, there *is* sequential firing of the retinal receptors, much as for true movement, so we may suppose that is why we see the phenomenon as movement. It has been suggested, however, that perception of movement in the two cases is essentially different.

It is well known that immediately after viewing movement, such as a running river or a rotating wheel or spiral, an illusory afterimage of movement in the opposite direction is observed for up to twenty seconds. This aftereffect does not result from experience of movement per se, for it occurs only when the original movement was signaled by sequential stimulation of the retinal receptors. If moving objects are followed with the eyes, no aftereffect is produced. The aftereffect of movement is interesting—actually, it is paradoxical—for although we see movement, we do not see change in size or position.

An effect of movement that is more closely related to the perception of objects is Michotte's work on the perception of causality. This is essentially like causality in cartoon films (see the flip series in Chapter 18). Michotte worked with various velocities and time relations and described many interesting effects. He regarded the perception of causality as innate because there was strong agreement between observers.

Readjustment of Perception

One of the most famous experiments in the field of perception was performed by Stratton, who wore spectacles that invert the retinal image to find out whether or not the brain would compensate perceptually. After about a week, he found that he could walk around fairly normally. He was not aware that things were upside down, though at the same time they did not look quite normal. Certainly, some kind of adaptation had taken place. Ivo Kohler, at Innsbruck, found that it was perfectly possible to ride a bicycle, or to fence, after a few weeks of continuous inverted vision. Both these writers, however, are hesitant to say that the world ever comes to look quite normal.

Held and his colleagues have carried out a series of experiments on the relative importance of active and passive touching on visual adaptation to retinal images displaced by deviating prisms. They conclude that active touching is far more effective, and perhaps vital, for producing motor behavior corrected to displaced images. To the question of which adapts—vision or motor output—they give no definite answer. It has generally been assumed, since the time of Berkeley in the eighteenth century, that touch is primary to vision because it gives unambiguous information of spatial form, whereas retinal images are always ambiguous. A few recent writers have challenged this hypothesis, suggesting that prism-adaptation results are best explained by supposing that it is not so much the visual as the touch and position senses that adapt.

At the present time, we are beginning to conceive computerlike machines that will see the world in the same way as higher animals and people do. With this technical possibility, the study of how the brain interprets images in terms of objects has suddenly taken on a new significance and excitement, for once we reach a fundamental understanding of perception, we should be able to translate brain processes into intelligent seeing machines. Apart from its possible technological implications, research on perception is important for understanding and helping people who are brain-damaged or partially blind and for such things as improving the layout of road intersections and airport runways in order to reduce accidents resulting from visual errors and illusions of various kinds. This application extends to assessing the visual hazards of space travel—how much human perception can be trusted in conditions far removed from earthly experience, such as a moon landing, where the eye may be misled by a strange visual environment.

What sort of a system, then, is the perceptual system? It is clearly *not*, in engineering terms, a straightforward input-output control system. In biological terms, it is *not* a stimulus-response system (except in certain atypical conditions), as is shown from the simple fact that responses to unexpected events (for example, flashes of light) are delayed by the reaction time of at least 0.2 second whereas in normal continuous behavior the reaction time is not evident. Behavior and perception seem to be geared not to the current retinal image but to what is predicted in the immediate future both from prevailing sensory information and from generalizations about the world of objects induced from past experience. We read the present with generalizations and assumptions derived from the past in order to deal with the future. But when the present situation differs from the past and is read with yesterday's assumptions, perception breaks down and the future may come as an unpleasant surprise.

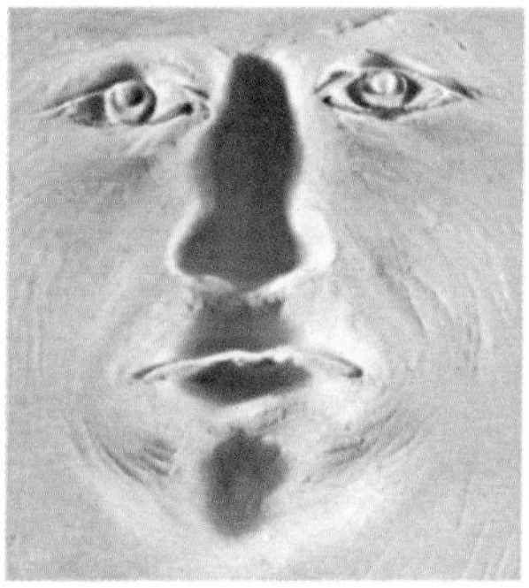

Applications of Perception Studies

Figure 17.30

This is the face shown at the beginning of the chapter, but now the physical properties of the object are apparent. The face is not in relief but rather set into the surface.

UNIT V

HUMAN FUNCTION

Most of us look at people from the outside in—that is, we observe their behavior today not because we are interested in what goes on deep inside them but because we are interested in what they are likely to do tomorrow. Psychologists have learned that they must often take the opposite tack, that is, look at people from the inside out. They must determine what basic processes exist inside all of us in order to understand, and predict, our future behavior. All of us receive information from the world around us, process it, store it away in memory, and use it in trying to solve the problems that confront us in the real world. Sometimes our solutions are not as good as they could be and lead to the expression of emotionality on our part. Some of us may even escape into the nether world of drugs in an attempt to control this occasionally overwhelming emotionality. The study of man from the inside out is the psychological study of human functioning.

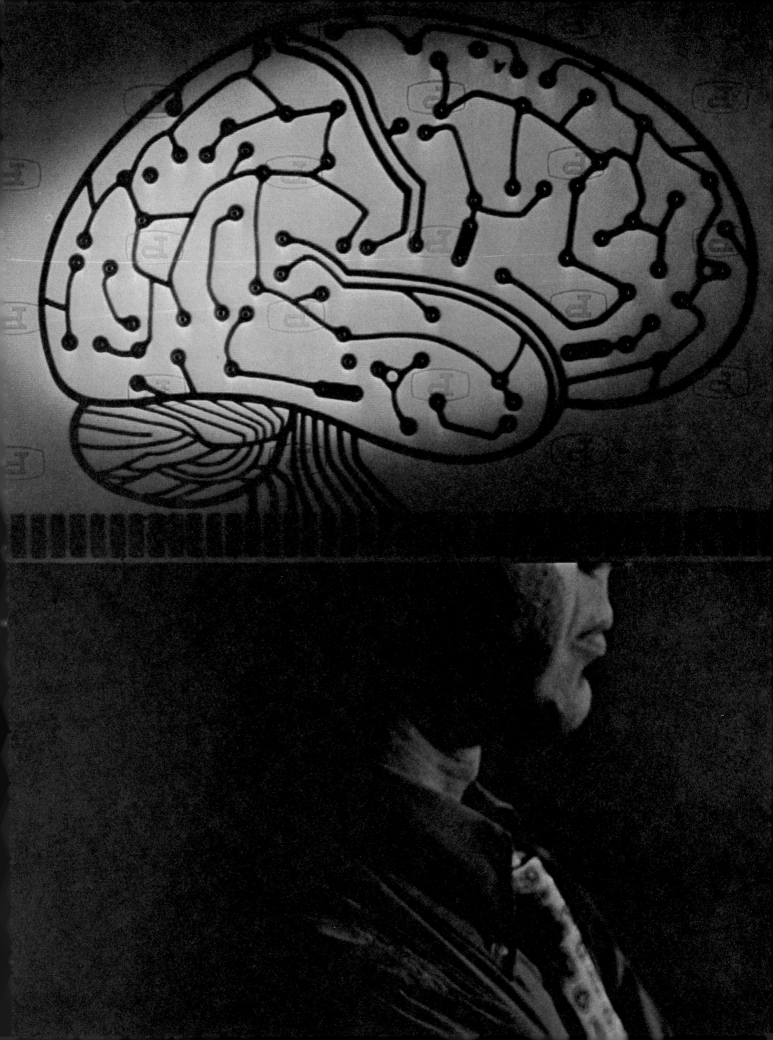

18

HUMAN INFORMATION PROCESSING

IF YOU ARE A FAN of professional sports, you may have seen televised sportscasts in which the play-by-play announcer stands in front of a bank of small television screens, each of which displays a different program. A number of cameras picking up different views of the action send pictures to this central location. The director of the telecast must sit in front of this electronic display and choose which of the cameras will be "live" at any given moment—that is, the director selects from many different inputs the one that will be sent out for the television audience to watch. As the action of the game progresses, he switches back and forth from one camera to another, and while one camera is live, he tells the other cameramen what they should focus on next. He also has available to him an instant-replay feature, a video tape recording of what has happened on the field during the past minute or so, as well as video material made days or even months earlier that can be interjected whenever he wishes to let the audience compare the day's action with previous events.

Running such a television show is a very challenging job, for the director must keep up to nine different inputs in mind all the time, remember what material is available for instant replay and what is on permanent film, and scan the various displays continuously and pick the critical one to show to the audience at any given moment. He must also be able to anticipate how the action on the field is likely to go so that he can direct the cameras ahead of time to focus on what he expects to happen next.

Although the analogy is far from perfect, the conscious part of the brain can be likened to such a television program. Information comes streaming into the central nervous system continuously from many different sensory channels (the eyes, ears, nose, tongue, skin, and various receptors in the internal organs of the body). The "director" of your own television show must somehow select which of these channels you will pay attention to at any given instant in time, must pull out of what is called short-term memory certain information about what you have just seen or heard, match this information with what you have stored away in permanent, or long-term, memory, and then direct the body to prepare for what changes might be expected next in the external world.

Information Processes

In any more exact and detailed examination of human attention and memory, we must begin by picking up information as it arrives at the sense receptor. Then we must trace it as it is converted, or transduced, into physiological patterns by the receptors and channeled to the central nervous system, then processed by the brain, then stored away, then finally retrieved at a later time. This type of analysis not only emphasizes the information-processing capability of humans but also gives us a helpful theoretical structure for explaining various experimental observations about attention and memory. Because most of the work on information processing has involved language, we shall for the most part restrict our discussion to an analysis of *verbal* material—that is, words and other meaningful items presented both visually (in printed form) and auditorially (spoken).

For convenience, we shall divide the organization of information processes into five stages and summarize each briefly, for the detailed workings of any one stage cannot be appreciated fully without an understanding of the whole system. Note, however, that this explicit division of the initial information processing is made primarily for purposes of explication; the actual divisions in the human are not nearly as neat and well established as the discussion in this chapter might indicate.

Briefly, the five stages are these:

1. *Sensory transduction.* Incoming information arrives first at our sense organs, but the physical energy of sound and light must be transformed, or *transduced,* into some physiological representation before the nervous system can start its analysis. The ear must not be thought of as a mere microphone, nor the eye as a simple television camera, for these analogies imply that the ears and eyes simply pass a complete, accurate picture of the sensory events to the brain. On the contrary, as was noted in Chapter 14, many important transformations of the sensory information are performed at the level of the receptor organ itself. Thus, the pattern of excitation that the receptor organ sends to the central nervous system has already gone through an initial processing that makes the job of extracting the information content of the arriving signal much simpler for the brain.

2. *Attention.* Once the incoming stimuli have been transduced into physiological energy patterns and sent to the brain, they are put through the second stage of information processing. The signals may be stored briefly in short-term memory (instant replay), or they may trigger a search of the long-term memory banks to determine if the stimuli have been experienced previously. Depending on the state of the organism and the read-out from the memory banks, the

incoming stimuli may be *attended* to, that is, may reach the stage of conscious awareness.

3. *Short-term memory* (STM). The brain appears to have a mechanism of some kind, separate from permanent storage of information, for holding recently experienced material for brief periods of time. The capacity of this holding mechanism is quite limited—somewhere between five and nine items. Retrieval of an item stored in STM is simple and direct, requiring very little conscious effort (see Chapter 19).

The process of attention appears to have its final influence at this stage. Thus, although information about all sensory events does seem to be stored temporarily, these data will be lost completely unless they are selected for further processing by the mechanism of attention.

4. *Long-term memory* (LTM). After an item has been held in STM for a limited period of time, it is either forgotten or somehow transferred to more permanent storage. The capacity of LTM is difficult to measure, but it is generally accepted that it is immense and, for all practical purposes, unlimited. Some scientists contend that if material enters LTM it is never forgotten, but no one has yet devised a method by which this contention could be proved true or false. One important aspect of LTM is that retrieval is often very difficult and is directly related to the way information is organized within LTM (see Chapter 19).

5. *Retrieval.* The last stage is the key process in the use of any large memory system, and the problems of retrieving the one correct item from the millions or billions that are stored seem to have dictated much of the overall structure of the other four stages.

In a detailed discussion of each of these stages, it is important to keep in mind that these somewhat arbitrary divisions serve primarily as a convenient outline of the process. The division of memory into two types, short- and long-term, is particularly arbitrary. Although this division is now widely accepted, there may actually be much finer gradations in the memory system, with many stages of intermediate-term memories intervening between the short- and long-term stages. However, our division of memory into two systems is supported by data from numerous laboratory experiments that suggest that there are at least two basic physiological processes involved in memory formation and storage: one process for temporary storage and a quite different one for permanent storage.

Sensory Analysis

Verbal material is processed chiefly in terms of its *meaning*, a fact that poses something of a problem in our attempts to explain the workings of the brain, for the verbal signals (stimuli) that arrive at the eyes and ears can have no innately determined biological significance. The printed symbols that make up letters and words, for example, are arbitrary; many types of symbols and alphabets have been invented. The particular combinations of sounds that make up our speech are also arbitrary, a fact that the wide variety of spoken languages illustrates nicely. Moreover, the correspondence between the spoken and the written word is even more arbitrary—the best example perhaps being the Chinese language. People from different regions of China can read the written symbols of this language with ease yet cannot understand each other's speech.

Before the operations of the memory system can be analyzed, then, we must consider how arbitrary visual and auditory inputs are translated into the meanings they represent. This process of translation is extremely difficult, and no machine can yet do it satisfactorily. Moreover, the analysis of the meaning of one symbol can never be performed without taking into account the meaning of the whole message in which it is embedded.

Feature Extraction

In order to analyze the sensory inputs, we must first extract the important features of the physical signals, which is not an easy task. We are able to read and understand material that is very much distorted: words may be mispronounced, and written text may be sloppily printed, with the letters ambiguous, distorted, or defaced; different people speak differently—they have colds, they speak in low voices and high voices, rapidly and slowly. Yet these major physical variations cause only minor difficulties in our ability to understand verbal material. Apparently we do not recognize material by matching it up with a single stored representation (a template), for if we did, every sound or letter would have to have an exact form or would fail to match the template properly. Evidently we extract the important *features* of incoming information and identify items by trying to match the features we have learned. Note again, however, that it would be impossible for us to interpret material properly if we analyzed it sound by sound or letter by letter.

In order to interpret stimuli properly we have to use *contextual* information; we have to combine our expectations of what we think should be occurring with what actually does occur. This fact means, of course, that the message we get from a physical signal may depend as much on what we expected the stimulus to be as on what it actually was. In fact, we often see what we expect to see rather than what actually occurred.

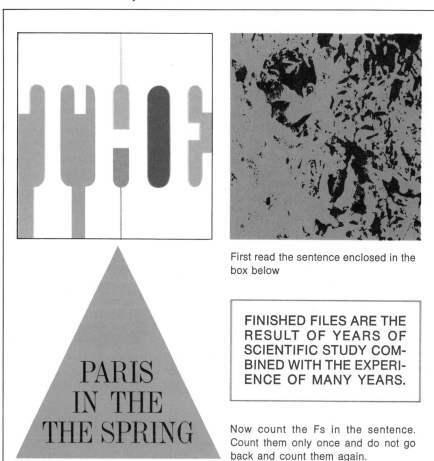

First read the sentence enclosed in the box below

FINISHED FILES ARE THE RESULT OF YEARS OF SCIENTIFIC STUDY COMBINED WITH THE EXPERIENCE OF MANY YEARS.

PARIS
IN THE
THE SPRING

Now count the Fs in the sentence. Count them only once and do not go back and count them again.

Figure 18.1
The top figures show how difficult feature abstraction may be under some conditions. In the bottom figures, some results of our expectations in reading are shown.

There is an easy way of proving that we do not simply recognize letters and words by matching up the perceived image with a stored template: read aloud some printed material that is upside down. Note how difficult reading becomes. The important demonstration comes after you have been doing this for several seconds. First, with practice, your ability improves, but usually it remains a relatively hard task, one that is performed rather slowly.

As you read, try to introspect about what you are doing. You will discover a number of interesting things about the way you interpret the material. For one thing, you do not recognize words by first recognizing each letter. You may puzzle out the first few letters of a word, then tend to say the entire word directly, without having gone through all the letters. Moreover, you find that words in the middle of a phrase are somehow easier to read than words at the beginning of a sentence. Finally, as you begin to speed up, you will find yourself making errors of a particular sort: the words you say probably start correctly (that is, you get the first few letters correctly) and probably have the correct number of syllables (you notice how long the word is), but the word you actually say is likely to be dictated by the rest of the sentence you have just read rather than by what word is printed on the page. In fact, you will find that you tend to read by looking at each word only long enough to confirm that it is what you *expected* rather than to discover what it is.

This important aspect of human functioning appears to operate by a process of internal synthesis, in which an image of the world is created and matched against the sensory input. By taking into account all our past experiences and the rules of behavior and language, we can predict with reasonable accuracy at any point the set of events that can be expected to occur next. Using this technique of synthesizing and confirming, we are able to operate much more efficiently than we could have done otherwise, and we are able to extract information in the face of much confusion. This method of interpreting sensory inputs does lead to error, however—the kinds of errors you made when you read material upside down. To illustrate the point further, try reading the adjacent nonsense material—ungrammatical material that is not in sentences—and see how poorly you perform when rules of grammar are not relevant.

A special type of memory system is involved in the initial stages of information processing. This memory, called a *sensory-information store* (SIS), has been studied primarily in the visual system, but there is some evidence that it may exist in other sensory systems. The SIS operates primarily at the level of the sensory receptors themselves.

Consider the rather thorny problem posed to visual theorists by the motion picture. A movie camera records action by taking about twenty-four still pictures a second. When we watch a film, what actually happens is this: the projector throws a still photograph on the screen for about one-fiftieth of a second, then the shutter in the projector closes and the screen is black for about one-fiftieth of a second, then the shutter opens again and another still picture is projected, followed by yet another blackout. How does the brain generate the perception of motion from a series of still pictures presented in sequence? The answer seems to lie in the manner in which the eye processes information.

Suppose we have a human subject sitting in absolute darkness and we present to him a slide taken at a football game. Let us further assume that the slide is an action shot, taken in color, and that we flash it on a screen for exactly one-fiftieth of a second. How long does the subject actually see the scene in the photograph? If he has sat in the dark for several minutes prior to this experi-

Expectations in Reading

In Figure 18.1, did you notice an extra "the" in the triangle? The boxed sentence contains six Fs, but because the "f" in "of" sounds like a "v," the Fs are often overlooked.

the man walked by my house is green and shiny smiling face is pleasant to see a flower and a flower bloomed in spring the grass is green

Sensory-Information Storage

Figure 18.2

If you use your right thumb to rapidly flip the next thirty-six pages, you will see movement as it is produced by the successive frames of a movie.

345

ment, he might well see the photograph floating in front of him for several minutes afterward. When a very brief stimulus impinges on a dark-adapted retina, the photochemicals in the rods and cones are excited by the physical energy that makes up the stimulus. The complex chemical reactions that are thus triggered by this very brief period of stimulation can continue for many minutes, during which time the eye continues to send detailed information to the brain about the stimulus that has vanished.

We usually detect this odd property of the eye only under experimental conditions, for normally the next stimulus comes along and alters the process by changing the chemical reactions taking place. If the next stimulus is darkness, the original photograph is not erased at all but is maintained, and minutes later the subject can describe in detail what the scene was all about. When we present a series of such stop-action pictures, one after another, with brief periods of darkness in between, the eye maintains each picture during the intervening periods of darkness until a subsequent picture erases the previous one. This momentary storage of sensory information allows the brain to generate the perception of motion from a series of static inputs.

The SIS system provides several good examples of how man processes information. Not only does this system seem to retain a detailed image of prior sensory events, but also there is more information stored in the image than the brain can extract during the very brief duration of the image. This discrepancy between the amount of information held in the SIS and the amount that can be used during later stages of analysis is very important, for it implies some sort of limit to the capacity of the later stages, a limit that seems not to be shared by the sensory processes of the body. The limitation appears to be on our ability to encode or make sense out of the material presented.

Much of the tremendous amount of information carried in a sensory image is of no importance in trying to interpret its meanings. In fact, for many purposes, too many details make the job harder. Computer devices that attempt to read printed text, decode speech waveforms, or even read printed music are easily thrown off by trivial details in the input that are never noticed by a human doing the same task. Tiny dirt spots or breaks in printed letters confuse computers, but humans often overlook even gross misspellings.

Attention When a visual stimulus reaches the retina and excites the rods and cones, the eye

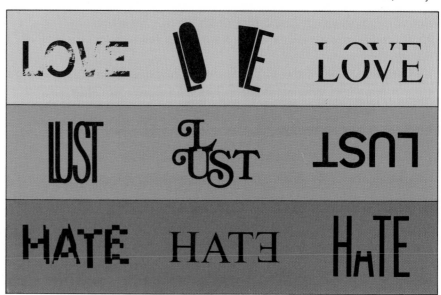

Figure 18.3
We are able to abstract familiar patterns in spite of considerable distortions and disruptions.

transduces the physical energy of the stimulus into physiological energy and sends it streaming toward the brain. The main pathway of nerves over which this material moves is called the *straight-line sensory system*. In the case of vision, this system runs from the eye straight through to the primary visual projection area in the occipital region of the brain, shown in Figure 18.4 (see also Chapter 2). But the eye also sends information about the stimulus to the brain via a secondary pathway, the *reticular activating system* (Figure 18.5). The straight-line sensory system is the information-carrying channel; if it is destroyed, the person is permanently blinded. The reticular activating system carries little information as such; rather, it is the means by which the eye alerts the brain that information is coming through on the straight-line system. If the reticular system is destroyed, the organism lapses into a deep coma from which it usually cannot be aroused.

Our brains are dependent upon external stimulation for proper functioning. If we were to isolate you in a completely changeless environment, the chances are that you would very soon drop off into a deep sleep. If, when you awoke hours later, you were still in this changeless environment, you would very soon notice long lapses or breaks in your stream of consciousness. You would find it very difficult to think at all. If we gave you a simple arithmetic problem to solve, you might fluff it; if we asked you to recall something important that had happened to you in the past, you might not be able to remember it very well.

The brain is alerted to changes in the world around it by messages arriving over the reticular system. The straight-line sensory system carries the actual stimulus information, but important data *about* the stimulus appear to be sent to the brain via the reticular activating system.

Sensory Gating

As you might guess, the more novel, radical, or unexpected a stimulus is, the more important it is that the organism pay attention to it. It is likely, then, that the mechanism of attention is influenced chiefly by data arriving in the brain via the reticular system. There also seems to be a feedback system of some kind that goes from the brain to the sense receptors themselves and acts as a kind of damper or gating mechanism on sensory activity. When we are attending to a visual stimulus, the brain sends messages to the ears and to other senses, cutting down the volume, as it were, of the information coming through on these channels so that they do not distract our attention unless something unusual

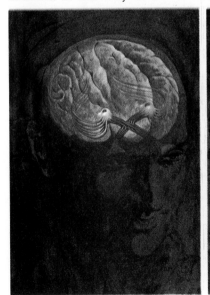
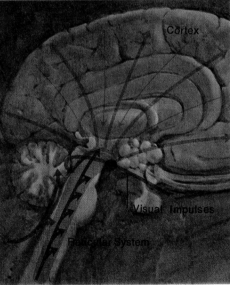

Figure 18.4
Visual pathways in the brain.

Figure 18.5
The reticular activating system.
(After CIBA, 1957.)

happens. This type of stimulus attenuation is called *sensory gating*. But if our ears detect a strange or unusual sound—or even an unexpected silence—the reticular activating system alerts the brain at once that something novel has occurred, and our attention shifts, at least briefly, away from visual input to scan the message the ears are trying to get through to us.

An illustration of a more complex type of selective attention is our performance at a party. We can attend to one conversation out of the babble of voices that arrives at our ears while completely ignoring the content of other conversations—including, perhaps, the one in which we are supposedly taking part. Moreover, if we do try to take part in (or even just listen to) two different conversations simultaneously, we typically fail. It is quite possible to keep up with one conversation while maintaining a rough check on who is saying hello or good-bye to whom throughout the room, but it is quite difficult to keep track of two complicated conversations simultaneously.

Sometimes, however, we find it of benefit to use the presence of one type of stimulation to allow us to maintain our attention on another. For instance, if you

are reading this book in rather noisy surroundings, you will surely find yourself distracted fairly often. If you turn on a phonograph or a radio to provide you with background music while you study, the chances are that you will be able to concentrate much better, for the music will mask out most of the other noises, thus reducing the number of inputs the brain must pay occasional attention to. "Music to Study By" typically is bland and familiar, just the sort of stimulation the brain can quite easily block out.

Shadowing

Much of the modern experimental work on the limits of attentional capacity has involved the use of a technique called *shadowing*, in which the experimental subject listens to a series of words or numbers spoken at a regular rate. His job is to recite the words as soon as he hears them (to shadow the sequence of words like a detective) and to make as few errors as possible. It turns out that shadowing with accuracy is difficult for most people.

In a typical experimental situation, material to be shadowed is presented to the subjects through one phone of a pair of earphones. At the same time, other material is presented over the other earphone. The usual finding is that subjects remember little or nothing of this other information. If, for example, a variety of other spoken material is presented to subjects who are shadowing, they later remember neither the words (even if they have been repeated numerous times) nor the language. But the subjects do notice whether a man's or a woman's voice spoke and often recall if the voice changed during the experiment. They also notice nonverbal material, such as musical tones.

Finally, a subject often notices his own name when it is included in the material; and if the items that are not to be shadowed happen to fit the context of the material that he is shadowing, the subject often makes mistakes and shadows the wrong material. That is, if the nonsense sentence to be shadowed is "The boy hit the on the other side of the book . . ." while the words not to be shadowed are "The diagram is ball soundly and with great skill . . .," the subject is likely to shadow the phrase "The boy hit the ball soundly and with great skill" before stopping and apologizing for becoming confused.

Short-Term Memory

Short-term memory is an important concept because we can use it to explain a number of different phenomena. It explains, for example, the "What did you say?" phenomenon. Often when we are asked a question, we sit up and say, "Uh, what did you say?" Yet before the question is repeated, we can re-create it from STM. It also accounts for our ability to make sensible-sounding responses to a conversation in which we have no interest ("Um—um, yes, that's right") although later we are completely unable to recall what the other person said.

STM differs from SIS in that SIS stores raw, relatively unprocessed sensory information at the level of the sense receptor whereas STM stores processed information—items rather than stimuli—and is a mechanism of the central (rather than the peripheral) nervous system.

The short-term memory system has a very limited capacity; no more than five to nine items can be stored at once. Obviously this limited size does not allow a human to retain much information about events that have just happened. Moreover, that material stored in STM is severely affected by interference. For example, if we are undistracted, we can look up a number in a telephone directory and retain it long enough to dial the number correctly. If, however, we are interrupted in the process, whether by a question from someone else or by making a mistake in dialing, we are very apt to have to look it up again.

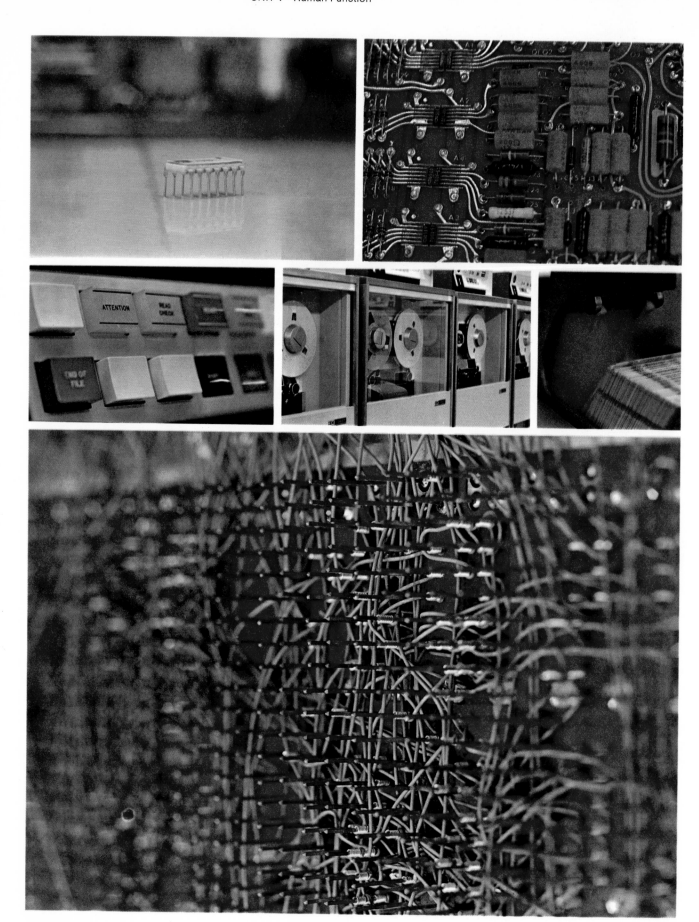

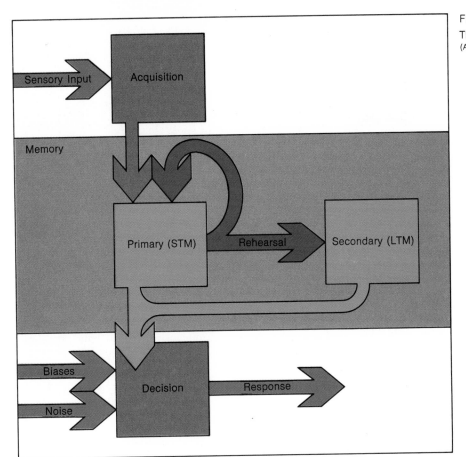

Figure 18.8
The flow of information in human memory.
(After Norman, 1969.)

Rehearsal

One important feature of short-term memory is rehearsal. No one knows exactly what occurs during the rehearsal of material stored in STM, but the phenomenon is well known. You can often retain a telephone number for a long period of time by rehearsing it over and over—by saying it to yourself. Rehearsal need not always be so directly observable or so tied to the speech mechanism, but it does appear to have many of the properties of the silent speech you can "hear" yourself going through when you attempt to retain material or to learn it permanently.

Rehearsal appears to have two functions: (1) it prolongs the retention of material in STM, and (2) it helps transfer the material into long-term memory. In fact, it has been suggested that the reason new material interferes with the retention of old is that it interrupts the rehearsal process (see Figure 18.8).

Coding

Material that is stored in STM appears to be encoded auditorially by most people. Thus, even when we retain information we have seen—such as a printed name or number—most of us seem to store it in STM by its sounds. It is as if we recode everything in STM by saying it to ourselves rather than by trying to maintain a visual image of it. Thus, if we are presented with the printed letter "Q" but later make an error in recalling it, we are much more likely to recall that the letter was a "U" (which shares some sounds with "Q") than an "O" (which shares some visual characteristics with "Q"). This peculiar result should be interpreted with caution.

The fact that most people remember the sounds of words rather than their shape may not necessarily reflect any basic property of the human brain. It might simply be an accidental result of the fact that we learn to produce and under-

stand spoken language much earlier than we learn to read and write. In fact, learning to read consists in large part of learning to associate the correct sound with the visual image of a word. It is really not too surprising that the storage in STM reflects this early training. Thus, we make confusions among sounds, not among meanings. If we are given a list of words to remember, including the word "hare," we are much more likely to erroneously retrieve "hair" than "rabbit." In fact, the latter confusion almost never comes about in STM.

We have now put together a picture of the initial processing of information. Spoken and written material is transformed into a physiological pattern by the appropriate sense organs. The receptors hold the stimulus briefly in sensory-information storage but send two types of messages to the brain during this holding process. One message, which contains the actual detailed information about the stimulus, passes along the straight-line sensory system of the central nervous system; the other message, which contains information about the importance or novelty of the stimulus, is channeled to the brain via the reticular activating system. If the stimulus is important enough, it is attended to; if not, it vanishes almost immediately from SIS.

By the time the material gets into short-term memory, it has been recognized. This is an extremely important point. During sensory processing, the material is represented primarily in terms of its physical characteristics. Noise, clarity, and the temporal duration of the material all affect the sensory processing. In STM, however, all three factors appear to be stripped away. All that remains is the psychological content. Thus, it does not matter whether a word was perceived clearly or with difficulty, whether it was long or short. Clarity and length do affect the likelihood that the word will be perceived correctly in the first place, but once the word has been perceived (correctly or incorrectly), it is stored in STM no matter how difficult or easy the original perceiving was. Thus, we say that the span of immediate memory is limited primarily by the number of items that have been presented to it. The span is not affected by making the items hard to see or hear or by changing their information content.

Long-Term Memory We understand very little about the nature of long-term memory. The acquisition of new information into LTM appears to be a difficult process, often requiring active participation on our parts. Some types of information are relatively easy to acquire, whereas other types are quite difficult. In general, a unique item to which we can easily attach verbal labels and associations is easy to retain, but homogeneous items or material that is difficult to organize can pose problems. Thus, although we remember visual images of the world around us, we find it hard to retain the exact words of conversation that we have heard. Yet, presumably, we attend as much to spoken words as to details of visual scenes.

We do know that associations play an important role in the organization of material within LTM (see Chapter 19), and most of the research on the properties of memory has actually been on the nature of associations within LTM. We know, for example, that the more highly structured or organized the material, the better it can be remembered, but we do not know if this readiness of recall is due to ease of storage or ease of retrieval. We also know that it is better to space learning trials out in time rather than massing them all together in a "cram" session if we want to retain the items for any length of time.

Our inability to maintain more than a limited number of items at any one time in STM suggests that organization of LTM is by meaningful categories. If only five items can be held in STM, organization in LTM logically ought to be in units of five, and recent experimental results indicate that this is a very plausible working hypothesis. Our total capacity of memory is not limited, however, for even if we can remember only five items within one category, we are able to recall more than five items because we can treat categories as items and organize five categories into a metacategory. This metacategory can contain about five categories, each of which contains about five items. The process is recursive, so if in any one category we can hold five items (or other categories), then the number of items within a category at each level increases exponentially: 5 items at the first level, 25 at the second level, 125 at the third level, and so on. This chunking together of more elementary material is a very important aspect of human memory.

The process of organizing material into categories for insertion into LTM can be difficult. We retain information better if it has been presented to us already organized into categories. Thus, if we were given a list of a hundred words, we would have trouble learning them all at one sitting. If, however, the same words were presented to us organized in terms of categories, we might find the task very easy. We would need at least three levels of categories. In the

Figure 18.10

Categories and metacategories that might be used in the organization of animal names in memory.

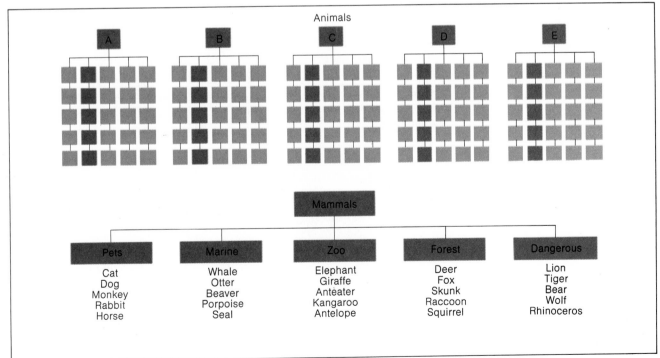

highest level there would be four categories—call them A, B, C, and D. Each of these four categories themselves would be organized into five subcategories, so that A might be organized into A^i, A^{ii}, A^{iii}, A^{iv}, and A^v. Then, in turn, each of these twenty, second-order categories would contain five of the words in the list, as is shown in Figure 18.10.

Retrieval The nature of retrieval from human memory is too poorly understood to allow a precise description. Some of the problems encountered in the study of retrieval, however, are indicative of the general nature of the process. We know that some types of searches through memory are more successful than others. The most difficult method of questioning memory is to require recall of previously presented material with minimal cues or prompts. It is much easier to recognize material than to recall it. Thus, although we may be unable to recall the name of the book we seek, we are often able to recognize it from a set of names. A forced-choice procedure, in which we are shown several items but told that only one is relevant, is an even more successful means of searching memory.

The usual explanation for the differences among test methods is that in recall we are required to search our entire store of LTM for the one, unique memory trace relevant to the test question. We must somehow find that one particular item even though we have few cues or prompts to tell us exactly what we are looking for. The more we know about the nature of the item we are looking for, the easier the search becomes. Recognition is easier than recall because the target item is given to us. Our task is merely to decide whether we can place the target item in the proper context, whether it is relevant to the question we have been asked about it. Usually, given the cues that exist in the item itself, it is not too difficult to reconstruct the contexts in which we have experienced it previously. Forced-choice is easiest of all because we know that one of the items given to us must be correct. We need merely decide which of a limited set of items seems most relevant without having to search our long-term memory in detail.

Errors So far we have been talking as if information is either stored or not. The process of memory appears to be a continuous one, however, and in the continuum between perfect retrieval and complete lack of retrieval, there is a stage in which errors are made. As we have said, in STM errors are usually acoustical confusions, even when information is presented visually. In LTM, errors appear to have some semantic relation to the item we are trying to locate in storage. Similar sounds seem not to be confused with one another in LTM, but items with similar meanings are often confused.

One of the most common LTM errors is that of transposing the order in which items are stored. Most of the mistakes we make in trying to recall telephone numbers, for instance, are transpositional errors. A number such as 755-3166 comes out 755-1366 when we attempt to dial it. Our memory for the digits themselves is usually better than for the order in which they were originally presented. The scientific study of errors can sometimes tell us a great deal about the factors that underlie the memory process; many personality theorists believe that the types of errors we make in trying to recall past events may be influenced by the emotional content associated with the events themselves.

In summary, let us return to our original analogy. The process of attention can be likened crudely to the actions of the director of a televised sports event such as a football game. Several cameras (sense organs) follow the activity on

354

Figure 18.11
The problem of retrieval is the problem of finding in a huge mass of information the one piece that is desired now. In a library, indexing makes it possible to do this quickly, but it is not known exactly how the job is done in the brain.

the field (our external environment), transducing the physical energy of light and sound waves into electrical energy that is sent along wires (the straight-line sensory system) to a central location (the brain). The director chooses among the various inputs, for under most circumstances only one channel can be broadcast at a time (selective attention). When one camera is on the air, the director informs the others to stand by (sensory gating) and also tells them what should happen next (expectation). At the director's request, some of the incoming information can be recorded for instant replay (short-term memory) but is erased if not used almost immediately. Those parts of the game that the director decides are the most exciting are recorded permanently for later use (long-term memory). The director also has available to him a large stock of permanent recordings of past games that he can switch on the screen at will, provided his technician can find them in time (retrieval). And, as anyone who has ever watched a televised game knows, occasionally the equipment malfunctions or the technicians pull out the wrong films (errors).

This analogy should not be taken too seriously, for the human body is not a television station, nor are the processes of attention and memory more than rough analogues to a television program. But perhaps this way of organizing the material will help you store it away rapidly in long-term memory and retrieve it easily in the future.

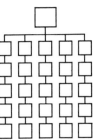

19

HUMAN LEARNING AND MEMORY

IN THE FILM 2001: *A Space Odyssey,* a group of American astronauts takes what is supposed to be man's first trip to the planet Jupiter. The spaceship on which they travel is run, for the most part, by a very complex computer called HAL. Somewhere this side of Jupiter, HAL goes mad and manages to kill most of the astronauts before he is put out of operation. In order to regain control of the spaceship from HAL, the surviving spaceman goes to a large room at the center of the computer and begins removing HAL's memory storage units. One by one, the spaceman pulls the metallic boxes from the storage bank. As each unit is pulled out, HAL regresses further and further into a kind of computer childhood and is finally rendered helpless when almost all his memory has been removed.

There are a number of points about men and computers that the authors of this screenplay (Arthur C. Clarke and Stanley Kubrick) make, perhaps unwittingly. Leaving aside their obvious deep-seated fears that man's mechanical marvels may someday prove his undoing, these very talented writers clearly point out the difference between man's memory and the computer's. HAL is supposed to be the most complex machine ever built. HAL is almost as bright as the astronauts he serves—perhaps brighter in some ways—but his memory storage units take up an incredible amount of room. Man's memory storage units are jammed into a few pounds of brain a fraction the size, or weight, of HAL's.

Computers are very impressive machines, but the brain is infinitely more impressive. HAL's memories were pigeonholed neatly in hundreds of containers, each bit of data in its proper file. Man's memories are stored away somewhere in the brain, but not in neat, labeled boxes. The surviving astronaut could open HAL's memory center and remove whatever items he desired taken out—just those particular items, nothing else. No one can open your brain and remove a box of related memories, much less a single, particular item.

We know how HAL's memory worked; after all, computers are a product of human hands and human ingenuity. No one knows how man's memory works, which is perhaps why psychology is at once a more primitive and yet more fascinating field of study to many people than is computer science.

Normally, our memory works so rapidly and smoothly that we take it for granted. We notice it primarily when it fails and usually think of our own memory ability in terms of its weaknesses. After all, who has not wished for a perfect memory—such as the one HAL supposedly had—for the ability to recall whole pages of text after one brief glance and to remember which names go with which faces? With all its faults, however, human memory in general is the most perfect of all the memory devices that now exist, whether constructed by man or by nature. Moreover, it seems unlikely that mechanical memory systems will soon equal either the capacity or the retrieval capabilities of human memories, even with the expenditure of vast sums of monies, with equipment that fills an entire room, and with basic speeds of operation measured in thousandths of millionths of seconds (nanoseconds). (It would be dangerous, of course, to make the prediction that computer memory capacity will *never* surpass that of a human.)

Thus far, no limit has been established to the size of human memory, that is, to how much information it can hold. Obviously there must be some limit, for the brain is of finite size. Regardless of anecdotes to the contrary, there is no evidence of serious difficulty in fitting new information into memory no matter how much has previously been learned. That is, under the proper circumstances, you *can* teach an old dog new tricks. The retrieval of previously learned material is amazingly rapid in light of this large capacity, but even more impressive is the ability to know when you do not remember something. Do you recognize the word "tralidity"? Hopefully not. The knowledge that "tralidity" is a new word comes very rapidly—too rapidly, in fact, for you to have made an exhaustive search of your memory. If our recognition of words, scenes, and previously encountered experiences were not so rapid, the speed at which we read and speak would be substantially slower.

Remembering   Before we discuss these phenomena and try to piece together some of the properties of the human memory system, let us divide the process of remembering into three basic parts: acquisition, storage, and retrieval.

Acquisition   The process of *acquisition,* or inserting new information into long-term memory (LTM), is the learning stage. A distinction must be made between the acquisition of new information into LTM—which may be the most difficult process of all—and insertion into short-term memory (STM)—which is direct and automatic. For example, if we tell someone our telephone number and he dutifully recites it back to us, we should not be surprised if he has forgotten it by the next day. The correct recitation proved only that the number reached STM; but unless it got into LTM as well, future retention is not possible. The only way to check LTM storage is to ask for the telephone number thirty or sixty minutes after it was first stated. Only if it can be retrieved with a reasonable delay after it was "learned" do we stand a chance of getting it back in the future.

Storage   *Storage* is the actual, physical retention of information in LTM. Usually when we say that something is remembered, we are referring to the fact that it is stored. Not much is yet known about how information is put in permanent file in the brain. We do not know whether the storage comes about from the growth of new connections at the synapses of neurons, whether there is some chemical or

358

molecular change, or even whether a particular memory is stored at one specific location in the brain, stored scattered about in a unique pattern, or stored many times in many different places. In some sense, all we know about storage is that it does take place. Our studies of acquisition and retrieval, however, tell us something about the informational and organizational properties of human storage.

Retrieval

Retrieval, the way we finally get access to stored information, in some ways is the key property of memory, although obviously it depends upon successful acquisition and storage. Two basic methods of retrieving information can be identified: recognition and recall—although there are variations on each.

The easiest way to get to something is by *recognition.* You need only decide whether the object, word, sound, or experience before you is the one you are seeking. You used recognition to decide whether or not you knew the word "tralidity"; the lack of recognition indicated that you did not know it. We do make errors in recognition—if we fail to recognize an item that is actually in storage, we have a *miss;* if we claim to recognize an item that we have never seen before, we have a *false recognition* or *false alarm.* In general, however, we are extremely accurate in recognition. Moreover, we usually know exactly how accurate we are being; we not only can say whether or not we recognize something but also can state our confidence in the accuracy of our response.

The second major type of retrieval is *recall.* In this method you name or recover information after being given only the barest of cues: What was that word we asked if you recognized? Recall is typically very difficult. We stumble in speaking, trying to recall the exact word we want, or fail to recall a name, yet know that we should be able to do so. When recall occurs, it is usually accurate. Thus, the most common error in recall is failure to get anything, a *miss. False recalls* (called intrusions) are rare, and when they do occur it is usually possible to give plausible reasons—such as strong, familiar associations—for why they might have happened. As with recognition, it is possible to state our confidence in the accuracy of the recollection.

Recognition differs from recall in a very basic way. In recognition, we are given an item and asked if it is the appropriate one. We do this task, presumably, by finding the item in storage and asking whether or not it has the appropriate

Figure 19.3
In recognition, the question is simply whether or not this is a bear. The answer is obtained by comparing the stimulus with information about "bear" in the memory. In recall, the question is what the words describe. A search through memory for possible answers might on occasion yield a wrong one, as shown, but more often yields a correct answer or nothing at all.

cues associated with it. In recall, we are given the appropriate cues but are asked to generate the item corresponding to them.

We thus see that to speak of remembering something really means to speak of successful acquisition, storage, and retrieval. When we claim to have forgotten something, however, any one of these processes may be at fault. The implication of the word "forgotten" is that material we once knew (like our first-grade teacher's name) is no longer in storage. The fact that we once knew it proves that the acquisition process worked. But the failure to recall the item at a later date does not indicate whether the material is truly forgotten—gone from storage physically and never to be retrieved any time in the future—or whether we simply are unable to retrieve it at the moment. Moreover, there does not appear to be any sure way we can tell if material in storage ever actually disappears and is truly forgotten. The only evidence we have to the contrary is that successful retrieval of information can take place quite unexpectedly. The success of psychiatrists and psychoanalysts (and professional hypnotists, for that matter) at recovering what are thought to be long-lost memories points out the remarkable storage capacity of memory and the extreme difficulties faced by the retrieval mechanisms.

■ CONFABULATION

Motivation affects recall, as it does most human activities. A person offered a thousand dollars to remember the name of his first-grade teacher is more likely to come up with the correct answer than is the person who is merely offered ten cents. But under conditions of high motivation, we often commit a memory error called *confabulation*. That is, when we are unable to reproduce a certain item from memory, we simply manufacture something else that seems appropriate. For some time, psychologists were impressed by the apparent ability of people in deep states of hypnosis to report in considerable detail events that had occurred during childhood. The hypnotist, using a technique called hypnotic age regres-

sion, would tell the person being hypnotized, "Go back, back, back to when you were very, very young," and then ask the subject to describe, for instance, his sixth birthday. Typically the hypnotee, if in a deep trance, would thereupon give a lengthy and quite impressive account of a birthday party, complete with cake, candles, presents, and guests. The hypnotee would seem absolutely convinced that his report was accurate, but objective evidence usually contradicted him. Almost always it could be shown that the person had confabulated—that is, he had mixed in details of several other birthday parties and, even under further questioning, could not tell which part of his story was real and which was imaginary.

Hypnosis induces a state of high motivation in most people, as well as making them much more suggestible than usual. The hypnotized person strives to please the hypnotist and responds to even the most subtle vocal and facial cues given by the hypnotist. If the hypnotist suggests that his subject ought to be able to remember something, the subject complies eagerly, even if he must resort to confabulation to satisfy the request. Newspaper and magazine accounts of "memory magic" under hypnosis should therefore be viewed with skepticism.

Confabulation also occurs as a symptom in some types of physical and mental disabilities. Korsakoff's syndrome is a condition associated with the type of vitamin deficiency commonly found in alcoholics; people suffering from this condition lose much of their recent memory. If you ask a person with this type of disability to describe what happened to him yesterday, he is unable to respond correctly but invents a series of fictitious events that often have little or no plausibility. Loss of recent memory is also a common symptom of general paresis (the condition associated with syphilitic damage to the central nervous system) and of advanced senility. In all these cases, memories of events that occurred many years ago may remain relatively intact.

■ THE DECISION PROCESS

We have spoken as if acquisition, storage, and retrieval were fixed operations that ran their course smoothly and without hesitation, but storage may be the only part of the human memory process that is rather automatic and not under direct control. One of the interesting distinctions between the human memory system and that of computers is this automation of storage. Specifically, once something is present in human storage, it does not appear possible for the human to erase it or otherwise forget it deliberately. Most computer memories, on the other hand, are constructed to allow for information to be added or deleted at will. Whenever this erasure is not possible in a computer, the memory is called a read-only or a nonerasable memory system.

Human memory appears to be nonerasable, a fact that suggests that we must be careful to take at face value someone's statement that he has deliberately forgotten something. What the person means by such a statement (whether he will admit it or not) is that he has repressed this information—that is, he has set up the retrieval mechanism so that it by-passes this information whenever it is encountered. Indications that the information actually has not been erased from storage can be observed in such aspects of the person's behavior as hesitations in his speech when he talks about the critical items, increased sweating (as well as change in the galvanic skin resistance), and changes in heart rate or surface blood vessels (blushing), as well as by the ability of a skilled psychiatrist to extract the supposedly forgotten material.

A decision mechanism thus plays an important role in retrieval, both in protecting ourselves from material we do not wish to remember and in allowing

us to adjust our performance to the demands of the situation. One such adjustment concerns the criterion that will be used to accept or reject information provided by the storage system. In fact, the retrieval of information from memory has many features in common with the standard communications problems of detecting a weak signal embedded in noise and with problems in making decisions based on incomplete and unreliable information—that is, what do you do when the memory image retrieved is unreliable, incomplete, and ambiguous?

Consider what happens when you are trying to recall a name that is on the tip of your tongue. If you are merely talking with a friend, you can set a low criterion on the accuracy you demand of the output before being willing to say it. This way, the two of you might together stumble across the correct name. Thus, you can say, "It's Fishmonger . . . no, Fishman . . ." In this situation, false recalls incur no penalty, but if you are face to face with the person, it would be best to use a high criterion and say nothing unless there is an extremely high chance of your being correct. The cost of a false recall—that is, of incorrectly addressing him as Mr. Fishmonger—would be extraordinarily high, whereas the cost of the other type of error (avoiding mentioning his name entirely), a miss, is nominal.

This type of adjustment of criterion for the retrieval system implies certain things. First, there must be some way of assessing how accurate the response is going to be. Second, there must be some trade-off between the rate of emitting false recalls and misses; in particular, as one error rate increases, the other should decrease (see the discussion of operating characteristics in Chapter 14). Finally, it should be possible to determine the relative virtues and costs of correct recalls, false recalls, and misses. All three conditions are usually satisfied in practice.

Organization of Memory The most critical aspect of storage is the filing system used to organize material. The problem is perhaps best illustrated by considering a large library. The most important aspect of a library is its organization. The user must be provided with sufficient guides and reference sources so that when he specifies some aspect of the item he seeks, he can find the exact location of the book. To help with this job, librarians provide various organizational schemes, including classification codes and indices organized by topic and authors' names, as well as published indices and abstract services. Organization of all the records, files, and cross references that must be established before a book can be placed on the shelves with some hope that users will be able to find it is so complicated that libraries have difficulty in storing new books. It would be a simple matter for the librarian to insert a new book anywhere on the shelves of the library, but this simple act of storage would be pointless, for no one would be able to find that book again except by accident. It does the user no good whatsoever to be assured that the book he seeks is somewhere within the library if he does not know how to get to it, for an exhaustive search of the contents of the library—or of any large storage system for that matter—is completely impractical.

The most important point in the analogy to the library is that the key role in large memory systems is played by the organizational structure. If we apply the library analogy to human memory, a few concepts start falling into place. We can see, for example, why it is so difficult to acquire new material and why it is easiest to fit material into a previously learned structure. Unfortunately, however, if we wish to probe the organization of memory we find that most of the crucial studies have not been done. Although a few psychologists have been examining organizational factors in human memory for the past decade, their experiments have primarily illustrated the important role that organizational factors play in the memory process.

Almost nothing is known about the exact organizational structure of human memory, but some interesting correspondences between the limitations of short-term memory and the organization are evident. If we postulate that to form a new organization within the structure of memory all the material to be organized together must be worked on simultaneously, then we would expect the limit on the amount of material that can be organized to be determined by STM, and this, indeed, is what we find. The most common grouping of information appears to be in clusters of fives, as has been pointed out in Chapter 18.

The most interesting material about organization appears to come from the study of memory systems, aids, and mnemonics. Yet mnemonics used to be a dirty word in psychology. It was considered a trick or gimmick, merely the collection of techniques used primarily by night-club entertainers—and therefore not worthy of study. Recently, however, the picture has changed, and the study of mnemonic systems is becoming popular, primarily because—be they magic or gimmick—they really do work.

Mnemonics

The simplest mnemonic scheme is organization into rhymes of material to be learned: " 'I' before 'E' except after 'C' "; "Thirty days hath September . . ." These systems work by letting us take advantage of the fact that we have no difficulty in remembering the individual items (the names of the months or the letters) but that our difficulty is learning the proper ordering. The rhyme helps because it imposes an external constraint on our memory; if we remember incorrectly, the rhyme fails to scan properly. The use of a rhythmic mnemonics illustrates one other property of mnemonic systems in general: once we learn an instance, we must recall everything to get back anything. Can you recall how many days hath June without going through the rhyme?

The oldest mnemonic scheme appears to be the method of places (*loci*), credited to the Greek poet Simonides by Cicero, and the act of creation is honored by an anecdote. It seems that Simonides was invited to a banquet by a nobleman named Scopas. In the midst of the banquet two unknown visitors asked to see Simonides. He left the banquet hall but was unable to find anyone outside. In his absence the building collapsed, killing everyone inside and leaving them beyond recognition. But Simonides was able to identify the bodies by picturing the banquet in his mind and remembering where each person had been sitting.

Thus the mnemonic system of loci: Form pictorial images of things you would remember, then mentally walk through a well-known building (such as your house), placing the things to be remembered in corners, on chairs, or in other easily visible places. To recall the objects, mentally walk through the house again, looking in the corners and on the chairs. This system was popular for several centuries among orators, who, by tradition, spoke eloquently for hours without any visible aids or notes. In fact, the system was so popular that specific buildings were designed solely for the purpose of placing mental objects in the corners and against the pillars.

Historical interests aside, what kind of memory system do humans have that can profit from such peculiar tricks? Suppose I tell you to remember a rhinoceros. Do so by putting it (mentally, of course) under the sheets of your bed. Will you remember that? How can you help it? You are now stuck with a rather clumsy bed partner. Your protests of "Of course, I remember it—it is unique,

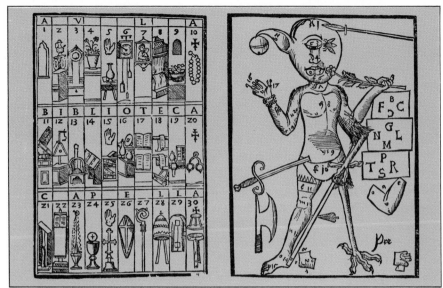

Figure 19.5
Two medieval examples of mnemonic
devices.
(The Bettmann Archive.)

original, special" do not explain how the method works; they simply emphasize the beauty of the system. Put peculiar objects in unusual locations and you will remember them.

Remember:

One is a bun.
Two is a shoe.
Three is a tree.
Four is a door.
Five is a hive.
Six is sticks.
Seven is heaven.
Eight is a gate.
Nine is a line.
Ten is a hen.

Another popular mnemonic scheme is the *key-word* or "peg" *system,* illustrated by the adjacent list. First note that this list itself is easy to learn; the words associated with the numbers are concrete, easily visualizable, rhyming nouns. Suppose you wish to learn the number 4391. Say, "4-3-9-1, door-tree-line-bun; I see a little door in a big tree and when I open the door there is a line leading to a bun." Silly? Perhaps, but it works.

There are many other systems of mnemonics, but they all use one of the basic principles illustrated in the preceding examples: rhymes, loci, or key words made into images. One final system should be noted because it is extremely basic and is used in most courses on memory improvement.

The *number-consonant alphabet,* first used in its modern form in the early 1600s, provides a way of translating numbers into letters (consonants) of the alphabet. Numbers can be extremely difficult to remember because they do not have the richness of meaning attached to them that words or pictures do. That is, they are difficult to organize. The number-consonant system solves this problem. The method is always to associate the sounds (note: learn the sounds, not the letters) to the numbers, as shown in Table 19.1.

Given some arbitrary number to learn—say, the telephone number 447-8132—simply replace each number with the corresponding consonant, getting "rrngftmn." Then, with some thought, it is possible to redo the letters as "r-r-ng f-t m-n," then as the phrase "roaring fat man," which turns out to be very easy to learn. Simple? No, not really, but it does work. With practice, it is possible to construct these images very rapidly—rapidly enough to amaze your friends with your memory ability. (Now, without looking back, what was the phrase? The telephone number? The bed partner? The four-digit number?)

Mnemonics illustrates almost all the principles of organized storage. For example, the ability to remember events learned by mnemonic techniques does not come easily. Also, the primary aid is the organization imposed on the material and the resulting simplification of the retrieval task. The penalty one pays is the effort required to do the organization during the acquisition process. It takes practice to learn these organizational rules—sometimes years of practice—then

Table 19.1—The Number-Consonant Alphabet

Number	Letters and Diphthongs	Sounds	Rule for Remembering
0	s, c, a	ess, zzz	"Zero" starts with "z."
1	t, d, th	t	The vertical bar of "t" looks like a one.
2	n	en	A written "n" has two strokes.
3	m	em	A written "m" has three strokes.
4	r	r	The number 4 ends in "r."
5	l	el	"L" is 50 in Roman numerals.
6	sh, j, ch, g	sh, j, or soft g	No rule; just remember it.
7	k, q, g, ng	hard k or g	A printed "7" looks somewhat like a printed "k."
8	f	ef	A written "f" looks like an "8."
9	b, p	b, p	The letters "b" and "p" are turned-around 9s.

concentrated effort applied to the items that are to be learned to put the rules into play.

Human memory, then, is not subject to any magical principles denied other forms of storage systems. It works effectively only if there is proper organization. To be able to use memory more efficiently, one has to work at it, concentrating on the material and trying to establish some organizational structure.

Learning

The act of learning new material can be identified with the successful organization, acquisition, storage, and retrieval of information in the long-term memory system. The most important of these various steps appears to be the proper organization of new material going into LTM. Without this step, retrieval may fail; but if this stage is successful, the other steps probably will be automatically satisfied.

As we noted in Chapter 18, successful acquisition of new information depends upon our paying full attention to that information at the time that it is presented. Although nonattended material may reside temporarily in short-term memory and although we do have some ability to divide our attention among several tasks at the same time, it is quite evident that successful organization and storage of new, complex material requires the undivided attention of the learner. In fact, because many signals from the environment are subjected to analysis even when we supposedly are not attending to them, the most efficient learning would require that we isolate ourselves from all possible distracting influences when attempting to learn new material or that we use masking sounds such as background music if isolation is not practical.

Preparation

To acquire new information, it is easiest to decide upon the proper organization first, then to begin to learn the material. This, of course, is a recursive process, for the proper way of organizing new material cannot be determined until something about the nature of the material itself is known. Therefore, the material should be examined closely enough to permit organizing it so that it can be added to already familiar material. Then, new concepts and ideas within this previously determined framework can be learned. In other words, proper preparation is as important to learning as is rote recitation of the material.

Proper organization of new material can be accomplished only if several limitations of the memory system are kept in mind. First, it is not possible to retain more than five to nine items at any one time in STM. Thus, the STM system is the main bottleneck through which the information must pass, and the organizational structure should be designed so that no new concept requires learning more than five unrelated items at any one time. Second, the organizational scheme itself should be learned before it is used to acquire new information. If the framework must be learned simultaneously with the material it is supposedly organizing, overall memory performance will suffer.

Review   It is wise to check on new material after about thirty minutes, for successful retrieval at this stage not only guarantees that the learning attempt has been satisfactory but also constitutes another opportunity for reorganizing and learning the material. If we wait too short a period of time before attempting this first recall, we may delude ourselves into thinking that we have learned the material when, in fact, we have not; for we can almost always remember material for brief periods of time whether or not we have actually stored it away in LTM. It is too easy to decide erroneously that something has been learned simply because it can be recalled from STM or from other partial cues.

Thus, the process of acquiring new material requires adequate preparation, adequate study time, and adequate review and testing. Often these three steps are effortless, but occasionally this process requires hard work. It is noteworthy that many commercial speed-reading courses emphasize these techniques. In fact, try following these steps before reading a new book: skim the book for its structure and examine the table of contents, jacket notes, and section headings so that you can organize the material *before* you start reading. Then test yourself at the end of the book. You will probably find that your reading speed has increased, even without any instructions or practice in the act of reading itself.

Rote Learning   Traditionally, the experimental psychologist has been concerned with the way that the memory image is formed, stored, and retrieved. He has wanted to know the best method for presenting material to ensure successful formation of the memory image and has wanted to know how retrieval and memory performance are affected by the nature of the material that he uses and by the prior and later experiences of his subjects. To help him perform these studies, the psychologist has created a very careful, special technology: *rote learning*, which is substantially different from the information-processing approach. Rote learning consists of the acquisition of new material by repeating it until it "sticks." Rote learning is an important aspect of acquisition, for if the acquisition process consisted only of the organizational scheme described in the preceding paragraphs, nothing completely new could ever be learned. Rote learning by adults seldom takes place in pure form, however, for stories, images, mnemonics—in short, elements of organization—are unconsciously applied in almost all situations.

Traditional Studies of Memory   The classical study of the memory process by Ebbinghaus was first published in 1885. In his experiments, carried out with extreme care and patience on himself, he sought precise, numerical estimations of memory performance. For this purpose he invented two useful experimental devices: the nonsense syllable and the measure of memory performance called savings.

As we have seen elsewhere in this chapter, when subjects are asked to learn material, they try to do this by imposing some sort of order on the items presented. They confabulate or make up stories, use mnemonics, invent peculiar relationships among the items—anything to help them organize the items in

366

their memory system. Traditionally, however, psychologists have avoided studying this type of behavior for several reasons. Basically, psychologists have been primarily interested in how unorganized, novel material is stamped into memory by rote processes. Moreover, each subject has his own unique way of learning material, and even one subject changes his methods.

Nonsense Syllables

To avoid the contaminating effects of the subjects' own particular methods of learning, it is necessary to devise material for which these strategies are useless. A most useful experimental technique is the *nonsense syllable* devised by Ebbinghaus, who discovered that he could put together meaningless words by combining a consonant (c) with a vowel (v) and ending with a consonant (c). This cvc syllable, or trigram, can be pronounced but when properly selected means little or nothing to the subject. QUK, KIZ, ZAL—no immediate associations come to mind. Although Ebbinghaus did his work in German, the principles do not change from language to language.

Savings

The second major innovation in experimental technique devised by Ebbinghaus was a method of measuring retention called *saving,* in which he measured the difference in the number of trials required for relearning material compared with the number of trials needed for its original acquisition. Thus, if he wished to know how much could be retained after a lapse of thirty-one days, Ebbinghaus would methodically teach himself a list of nonsense syllables until he had reached some reasonable criterion of knowledge, satisfying himself that he had learned them. He recorded the number of trials required to reach this state, then waited thirty-one days, presumably without thinking about the items during this time period. At the end of the waiting period, Ebbinghaus relearned the syllables, counting the number of trials needed to reach the same level of performance achieved the first time. Typical savings results are shown in Figure 19.6. Note that forgetting appears to occur rapidly at first but then slows.

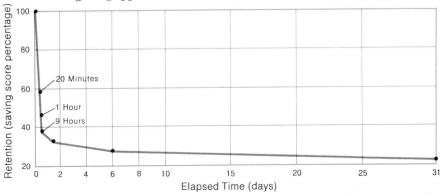

Figure 19.6
Retention. The savings score plotted as a function of time since learning.
(After Ebbinghaus, 1885.)

Ebbinghaus' savings score is a particularly sensitive way of assessing exactly how much has been retained by subjects, even when they retain so little information that they can neither recall any of the items nor recognize them. For this reason, the method of savings was an important addition to the psychological study of learning and memory.

Association Value

Recent experimental work has pointed out a number of difficulties with the Ebbinghaus nonsense syllables. Essentially, most of the trouble arises because there really is no such thing as a true nonsense item. Because subjects manage to make some sense out of any combination of letters, it is important to divide nonsense syllables into classes. Even when a cvc (consonant-vowel-consonant)

combination fails to make up a legitimate word, some are closer to words than others. By using various tests, we can measure the associability or association factor of each nonsense syllable. Words like LUV and MUN are much more meaningful, have higher association value, and are easier to learn than VEQ and QAX, which in turn are easier than CCCs (three consonants), such as CPQ and KXL.

Association value changes the ease with which syllables are learned, and many theorists have attempted to discover why. Usually, syllables with high associative value seem to be similar to well-learned items already in memory, and this previously formed knowledge apparently helps us to remember the new items that we are trying to learn.

Paired-Associate Learning

Although items to be learned are frequently presented in simple lists, this is not the only method psychologists use. A favorite technique for studying the learning of new associations among items is *paired-associate learning,* in which a subject is asked to learn the relationship between a pair of items, such as XOP-TAZ. Later his knowledge is tested by presenting one item to him—XOP—and asking him to recall the other. The lefthand member of the pair of items is usually considered the *stimulus* item, because it usually is presented to the subject when he is asked to recall the other. The righthand item serves as the *response* item. The ability of subjects to learn stimulus-response pairs depends upon the nature of the material used for the two items and whether the subject knows the stimulus items before he starts the experiment or is exposed to them for the first time during the experiment. Moreover, similarity and association values between the stimulus and response items obviously are important variables that must be considered in this type of experiment. The learning of paired-associate lists is very similar to the acquisition of the vocabulary of a foreign language. For example, in trying to learn that the English word "cow" is "vaca" in Spanish, "cow" is the stimulus item (in this case, a well-learned stimulus item), and "vaca" is the response item (in many ways simply a nonsense syllable—a CVCV quadragram—because the letters do not form an English word).

Forgetting

One of the major questions psychologists are interested in answering is why something well learned should ever be forgotten. Two different explanations of forgetting are popular. One assumes that forgetting takes place through the passage of time—that when two items are learned, some sort of memory trace is formed in the brain; the better the items are learned, the stronger the trace. With time, however, the strength of this memory trace decays and eventually disappears: it then cannot be recalled.

The alternative explanation is that forgetting results from the interference of other material. Thus, when we must learn a great deal of similar material, it becomes difficult for us to distinguish the present associations from the many other similar associations we have learned in the past.

Interference

The notion of forgetting as a result of interference from similar traces has much support. For example, a subject forgets substantially less when he is asleep than during an equal period when he is awake (see Figure 19.7). Such a phenomenon would hardly occur if memory were to decay only as a result of the passage of time.

Extraneous material learned by a subject can interfere both with placing new items in LTM (learning) and with recalling them once they have been stored (retrieval). If a subject is required to learn two lists of words, A and B, and if the learning of A makes it more difficult than usual for the subject to learn list B, then *negative transfer* has occurred.

If some time much later we ask the subject to recall the items in list B and we find that he remembers fewer than we would have expected, then apparently something about having learned list A first has affected his ability to recall the items on list B—a condition psychologists refer to as *proactive interference*. If the items on list B disrupt the subject's ability to recall the items on list A, we speak of *retroactive interference*.

An important variable that affects the severity of proactive or retroactive interference is the degree of similarity of the interfering material to the material to be retained (see Figure 19.8). Thus, if you spend an hour studying Spanish, it would be better to spend the next hour learning a dissimilar language such as

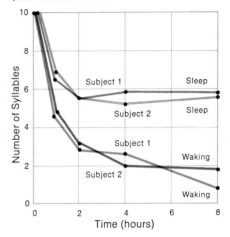

Figure 19.7
Amount of recall as a function of time since learning when the subjects slept between learning and recall and when the subjects stayed awake.
(After Dallenbach, 1963.)

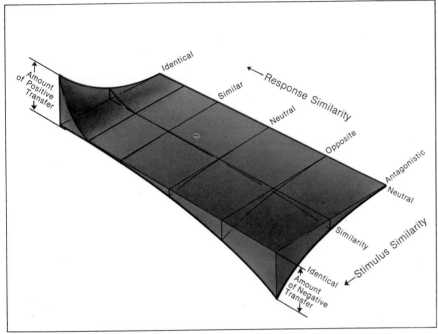

Figure 19.8
Osgood's transfer surface for paired-associate learning. The subject first learns a series of paired items. Later, when presented with a stimulus item, he must give back the other member of the pair, the response item. The extent to which learning a previous list helps in the learning of a new list (amount of positive transfer) is plotted as a function of the similarity of the stimulus items in each list and as a function of the similarity of the response items in each list.
(After Osgood, 1949.)

Chinese than in learning another Romance language such as Portuguese. (Better yet, spend the second hour learning to play tennis, for the more dissimilar the next task, the less it will disrupt your memory of Spanish.)

An important experimental result has shown that the combination of proactive and retroactive interference produces a *serial-position effect*: in general, we remember best the first and last items on a list, whereas things in the middle are remembered poorly if at all. Thus, when subjects are asked to learn lists of words, they invariably learn the words at both ends better than those in the middle. The superiority of the first part of the list is called a *primacy effect*; the superiority at the last part of the list is called a *recency effect*. This bow-shaped serial-position curve, shown in Figure 19.9, occurs in learning new tasks, in perceiving a briefly exposed word, in motor skills, and in verbal habits.

In the context of an experiment on memory, the serial-position curve appears to express the interactions between attention and short-term memory. During the presentation of the first few words of a list, there is little for the subject to do except learn the words. He is aided in this by two things: first, he can "label" the first word by the fact that it is first. Second, he had only one word to learn (and then two, three, and so on). By the time a number of words

Figure 19.9
The serial-position curve.

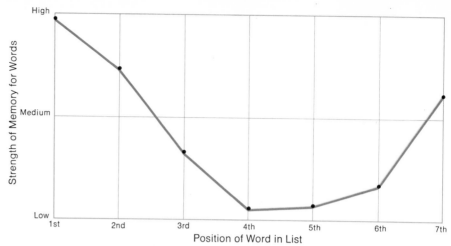

have been presented, however, the subject is bogged down. He is trying to learn many items simultaneously, some of the earlier words have already been lost from STM, and there are no obvious position clues that he can use. At the end of the list, although all the factors that caused problems in the middle of the list are still present, the subject has some extra time. That is, after the presentation of the last item, he can concentrate on the last few items presented (because they still reside in STM) and try to organize and rehearse them until they finally fade away. Thus, the first and last parts of the list receive an advantage in the organizing process over items in the middle.

Short-Term Memory and Rehearsal

Recently, psychologists have shown increased interest in short-term memory, that is, the memory of material presented once and tested very shortly afterward. One of the first experiments in this area was performed at Indiana University in 1959. Subjects were asked to learn a three-letter CCC trigram—say, CPQ—then immediately afterward they had to start counting backward by threes from a randomly selected point—say, 497, 494, 491 . . . They were not allowed to spend much time thinking about the trigram before being asked to do this irrelevant counting task. Some time after the subjects had been counting, they were stopped and asked if they could remember the trigram. Usually all the memory for the trigram had disappeared after about eighteen seconds of counting (see Figure 19.10).

Figure 19.10

Recall as a function of time when an irrelevant task is used to prevent rehearsal.
(After Peterson and Peterson, 1959.)

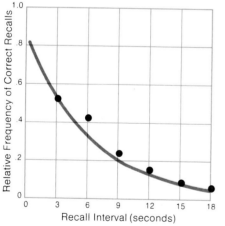

This result does not mean that items in short-term memory disappear after eighteen seconds, for the subjects were performing a task that may have produced certain retroactive interference. Unfortunately, it is not possible to measure the time in which short-term memory "decays" without using some sort of interfering task, for subjects asked to do nothing during the time between presentation of the letters and the test would probably spend that time rehearsing the items. This type of silent repetition of items has the same effect as repeating a telephone number after looking it up in a directory. Active rehearsal by the subjects makes it impossible to determine exactly how the memory decay would take place if rehearsal were not present. Moreover, instructions to subjects not to rehearse seem to be unavailing.

Rehearsal is thought to be such an important part of the memory process that some psychologists believe it a crucial step that makes possible the transition of material from a short-term storage system (much as the one that was illustrated in Figure 18.8) to a more permanent, long-term storage.

The Structure of Storage

The problem of getting access to stored material can be illustrated by another example of a nonsensical word, say, "mafterling." It could be an English word—the sequence of letters follows the proper rules. But you can immediately determine that the word is not in your memory. Obviously you looked it up in memory and found that it was not there. But how did you do it so quickly? It sometimes takes quite a long time to find an item you know is in memory, so why should it take less time to discover the absence of something?

The answer appears to be that the very ordering of the letters (or perhaps the sound of a word) tells us where to look in storage, and when we do, that spot is empty. Thus, the structure of memory appears to be based on the features of the input. This hypothesis does not exclude the existence of other methods of storage, but it would explain why recognition of words in a sentence is so rapid and easy and why recognition is so much easier than recall. Furthermore, it would seem to make sense from a consideration of the neurological organization of the brain (see Chapter 2). Such a system, in which the features of the items themselves determine where they are stored, is called a *content-addressable storage system*. Many people believe that efficient computer memories will not come into being until such content-addressable systems are available at reasonable prices, for the major problem with the use of computers with large-capacity memories is figuring out where information is stored. The human memory does this job well, perhaps because of its heavy emphasis on organizational variables coupled with its apparent use of content-addressable storage.

Pigeonhole Memories

There are many possible ways by which a memory system might be organized. In a digital computer (such as HAL, the machine in *2001*), material is stored in a system very much like post office pigeonholes. The boxes are arranged in some logical order and each has a unique number, called its address. Each box is of a fixed size and can hold anything that fits within it. If there is too much material for one box, the overflow has to be put in a separate location, and a note telling the user the overflow address is inserted. It is easy to store and retrieve information if the box number is known. If the number is not known, however, storage and retrieval are less efficient, and unless the proper indexes to the box exist, retrieval can become impossible.

This pigeonhole system has many disadvantages, the primary one being that the way of getting to a box—its numerical address—is unrelated to the material stored in it. In the use of digital computers, clever programmers have devised

techniques that allow us to circumvent some of the difficulties of the computer's memory system. Efficient index systems are provided that make it possible to determine the proper address of stored information. Organizational aids and outlines to the memory system are provided by making up interconnected lists of the stored items and their relationships with one another. Moreover, special programming languages have been designed that allow the user to manipulate these lists in an easy and direct manner. The problem with these systems is that they are tacked on to the existing pigeonhole-type memories of computers. As a result, they are inefficient and slow. Thus, in large-scale information-retrieval systems, much time is spent simply in keeping track of the empty memory locations—especially locations that were used temporarily and then became free again. This job is so common and necessary, yet so distasteful and time consuming, that it has been given a name: garbage collection. The lesson we learn from studying computer information-retrieval systems is that proper organization of information is essential in a large memory and that it would be best if the memory itself were designed with this purpose in mind.

Human Memory There is good reason to believe that human memory is structured quite differently than are the memory systems used in computers. That is, the brain does not

seem to contain the physiological equivalent of empty pigeonholes, waiting to be filled up with information. Rather, the storage location of information seems to be given by the information content itself. Moreover, once a memory has been laid down permanently, it does not become erased—"garbage collection" is therefore unnecessary in the brain. Finally, the relationships among stored material in the brain seem to be an essential part of the storage of that information. Indeed, these relationships may be more important than the material itself.

It should not be thought that when we retrieve something we are necessarily re-creating an accurate image of the original event. On the contrary, we tend to acquire rules, schemes, and abstractions of the events that actually occurred, so that later, when we try to recover our memories, we actually synthesize a new version of the previous occurrences. Thus, many of our memories tend to be re-creations rather than actual recoveries. We do not so much remember what has happened as we make up a logical picture based on our experiences in general and what we do remember in specific about an event.

Examples of this phenomenon are numerous; it is one reason for the notorious unreliability of eyewitnesses. It comes about primarily from too much reliance on organizational factors—in some sense, we make the events we are experiencing fit into our preconceived organizational framework even if they do not belong there. Then, when later asked to recall something, we actually fabricate our version of what should have happened. This fabrication is neither deliberate nor even conscious. It is quite normal that we remember things by reconstructing them from the cues we have remembered. Usually, this turns out to be an extremely efficient method of operating, for we can take full advantage of the redundancies in events, of our expectations, and of the organizational scheme we have developed in memory. Only when we lose all new input into LTM, or when some physiological condition of the brain causes us to lose our organizational schemes as well as losing LTM, does this kind of confabulation become pathological.

Perhaps the single most important point to remember about human memory is that we do not actually remember—rather, we remember how to remember.

Images or Ideas?

20

PROBLEM SOLVING

ONE OF THE largest corporations in the world has as its motto the trenchant command *THINK!* In an apocryphal anecdote about this corporate giant, the president, a hard-working, no-nonsense sort of fellow, arrived at his office a little earlier than usual one morning and found the company's chief scientist sitting in the president's chair, his feet on the desk, a faraway look in his eyes as he blew smoke rings at the legend *THINK!* emblazoned on the wall behind him. The president thought about the situation briefly, then decided not to make too much of an issue of this transgression because the scientist's many creative inventions had helped put the company in its present position of dominance. So the president merely asked, "Might I ask what you're doing?" "Just following your directions, Sir—I'm thinking." "And what are you thinking about?" responded the president, hoping for news of a great new laboratory breakthrough that would earn the corporation even greater fame and fortune. The scientist smiled. "I'm thinking that if I had been really creative, I would have invested a few thousand dollars in this company when it was founded and I'd be boss around here now."

The verb "to think" has many dictionary meanings, two of the major ones being to think *of* and to think *about*. When the president asked the scientist what the man had been thinking about, the corporate leader was using the term as a synonym for problem solving. When the scientist replied, however, it became clear that he was using the term to mean that he had been daydreaming—that is, thinking of better times. Although psychologists have studied both types of mental activity extensively, in this chapter we shall limit ourselves chiefly to a discussion of thinking about, or problem solving.

Mental activity is very difficult to study scientifically, for much the same reasons that the structure of the atom is difficult to study—in both cases, scientists cannot see what they are studying with their own eyes. The best the physicist can do is to postulate what the inside of an atom is like, then perform experiments that he thinks should somehow affect or change that structure in a particular way. If he gets the results that modern atomic theory says he ought to get, this fact gives him additional evidence that the theory is correct.

The physicist, however, never can test his scientific hypotheses about the atom directly in the same way that you, for instance, can test the hypothesis that if you set off a firecracker behind a friend when he is not expecting it, he will act startled. You can witness the startle reaction with your own eyes, and you can demonstrate it to anyone who is skeptical. But can you demonstrate to anyone that you *think*? Thinking is a private affair; it goes on inside you. Science must deal with public affairs, events that can be witnessed by anyone who cares to watch. No one can see your thoughts, although you are probably quite convinced that they exist. The best the psychologist can do in studying thinking is to set up experiments in which his subjects must think in order to solve certain problems and, by studying the solutions the subjects come up with (as well as their comments on how the solutions occurred to them), make inferences or guesses about the invisible psychological processes that underlie the activity of thinking.

Many people believe that thinking distinguishes human organisms from other forms of animal life. This controversial proposition is not easily resolved, but let us examine a few of the questions involved. Suppose that a laboratory rat is trained to make the following responses: Run from point A to point C for water reward, and run from point B to point D for food reward. If the rat is then made hungry and placed at point A, he shows evidence of combining these previously unrelated experiences; rats trained in this way run to point B (and then on to point D) more often than to point C. When a comparable task is given to children, older children do better at it than younger. Moreover, monkeys, after being given extensive practice with various discrimination problems, learn to solve problems with remarkable ease (see Chapter 4).

In contrast to these findings, which suggest a continuum of thinking ability, it is clear that thinking is most characteristic of humans and that adult human organisms are capable of thinking in a variety of ways and at levels of complexity

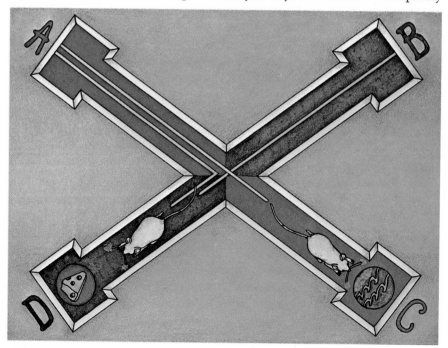

not seen in other species. Actually, distinctions must be made among humans; an infant is perhaps more like a monkey than an adult in terms of his performance. A critical characteristic in distinguishing among children is their facility with language, for language is the common medium for representing the environment symbolically in thought. However, language is not the only means of representing the environment; people also use visual images rather than words under certain circumstances. Furthermore, despite the availability of efficient symbolic systems, human thinking is far from perfect. Solving a problem may involve an extended sequence of operations or the consideration of many things simultaneously. Because there are limits to the amount of information that people can deal with at any time, a person's system can be overloaded. He will forget where he is in the process of attaining a solution or produce an inferior solution because of his inability to utilize all the relevant information. Thinking can also be impaired by certain biases or weaknesses in the symbolic system employed.

Logic and Thinking

Psychologists are interested in determining the degree to which people reason logically and what affects the likelihood of their reaching a correct conclusion. Such analyses are well undertaken within the field of logic, a branch of mathematics that provides a system for determining if a conclusion follows validly from the stated premises. The process of evaluating conclusions for logical validity is often called *syllogistic reasoning*. One important feature of logic is the symbolic system used to present the premises and conclusion in a syllogism. Consider the adjacent syllogism. Does the conclusion follow from the premises? Many people say yes, but the answer is no. More people will reject the conclusion if the content of the syllogism is altered as is next shown.

All A is B.
All C is B.
Therefore, all A is C.

All humans are animals.
All dogs are animals.
Therefore, all humans are dogs.

All sparrows have wings.
All birds have wings.
Therefore, all sparrows are birds.

Although people usually perform better when syllogisms are stated in concrete rather then abstract terms, other biases can occur when familiar terms are used. Consider the adjacent syllogism. In this case the conclusion is factually correct and people are likely to accept it as a logical conclusion, but it is not (substitute "airplanes" for "sparrows"). Although they are initially more difficult, syllogisms stated in abstract terms have the advantage of being free of biases due to the factual truth or falsity of the statements involved. Logical thinking is further aided by the use of a different representational system, called *Euler's circles* or *Venn diagrams* (see Figure 20.2). The use of these diagrams seems to make the meaning of the premises clearer and enables a person to determine if he can construct a situation in which the premises are true but the conclusion is not true.

The propositions described thus far have been universal statements, referring to all members of a class. Syllogisms involving particular statements appear to be more difficult (for example, "Some animals are cats"), as are those including negative statements. At least part of this difficulty can be attributed to the

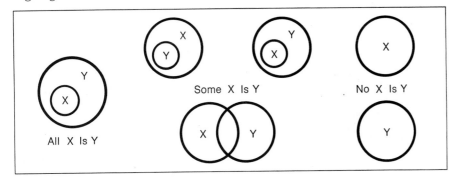

All X Is Y
Some X Is Y
No X Is Y

Figure 20.2

In a Venn diagram, the statement "All X is Y," for example, would be diagrammed by showing all of an area labeled X inside an area labeled Y. The validity of a syllogism may be tested by seeing whether or not the conclusion is correctly represented in a diagram to fit the premises.

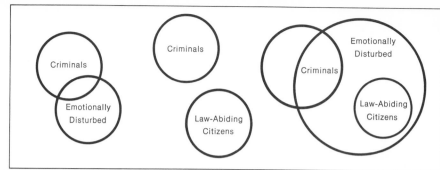

Figure 20.3
A Venn diagram for the premises of the criminal syllogism does not represent the conclusion reached.

Some criminals
 are emotionally disturbed.

No criminal
 is a law-abiding citizen.

Therefore,
 some law-abiding citizens
 are not emotionally disturbed.

different meanings of "some" in logic and ordinary language. Logically, "some" means "at least some, and perhaps all," but in ordinary usage, "some" means "at least some but not all." Taking the logical meaning of "some" into consideration, try the adjacent syllogism. It is difficult to reject the conclusion, but it does not follow. As you can see in Figure 20.3, we can construct a situation in which the premises are true but the conclusion is not.

Syllogistic reasoning is also affected by other factors. The atmosphere of the premises is an important factor in erroneous reasoning. The *atmosphere effect* refers to the tendency to accept an affirmative conclusion if the premises are affirmative, a particular (some) conclusion if at least one premise is particular, and so on. Also, syllogisms involving emotional material are more subject to erroneous evaluation. The most elementary forms of reasoning, then, are affected, usually adversely, by biases. Similar influences occur in other problem-solving situations.

Characteristics of Problem Solving

In most studies of syllogistic reasoning, people are given the task of evaluating the adequacy of the conclusion. In other types of problems, however, different aspects of thinking are emphasized. Four distinguishable activities occur during problem solving: *knowing* a problem exists, *preparing* to find a solution, *attempting* to produce a solution, and *evaluating* the adequacy of a solution attempt.

Very little is known about the variables affecting awareness of a problem because in almost all studies of problem solving people are told that they will be given a problem or the situation is so constructed that it will be immediately obvious that a problem exists (a goal is indicated and the obvious response fails). Similarly, preparation is seldom studied; this phase refers to figuring out what are the requirements of the situation and of an adequate solution. Typically, the experimenter tells the problem solver what criteria his solution must meet and the limitations under which he must try to find the solution before work on the problem is begun. That is, most psychologists prepare the person to solve a problem rather than observing the person preparing himself. In the few studies of preparation that have been conducted, it has been found that preparation time increases with the number of requirements imposed on the solution, as you might expect.

In most cases, studies of problem solving involve only production and evaluation. Many researchers, however, have used problems for which evaluation is assumed to be simple, and consequently they have devoted their attention to production. It is assumed that a person takes a long time to solve a problem or fails to solve it because of his inability to produce the solution rather than his inability to evaluate potential solutions. Although this assumption is probably correct in many situations, it is clearly wrong in others. Occasionally, when a person who has failed to solve a problem is told the answer, he says something like "I thought of that but decided it was wrong." Evidently, some of the difficulty attributed to production has in fact involved evaluation.

The assumption that difficulty in solving a problem reflects primarily production is most appropriate when the problem is fairly simple and each potential solution can be easily judged as right or wrong. Psychologists attempting to program computers to solve problems have employed more complex problems and have pointed to the importance of evaluation in producing a solution. Consider a person (or computer) choosing his first move in a game of chess or checkers. He has a number of alternatives to select from, and, for each of his alternative moves, his opponent has a number of replies, to each of which there are a number of rejoinders, and so on. The selection of a move thus leads to a geometrically expanding "tree of possibilities," each branch of which eventually leads to either a win, lose, or draw outcome. The problem lies in evaluating all these possible sequences of play in order to select the best move.

Algorithms

A method that leads its user to consider systematically all possibilities with respect to their eventual outcomes is called an *algorithm*. In principle, algorithms could be specified for many problems, but it is doubtful that they could ever be used for any but the simplest problems because they take far too much time to apply. For example, it has been estimated that there are 10^{40} alternative sequences of play in a checkers game; if three alternatives were evaluated every millimicrosecond (one-millionth of one-thousandth of a second), evaluating all the alternatives would require 10^{21} centuries. It is clear that neither human nor computer would be an efficient problem solver using such methods. The alternative is to limit search and evaluation in some way.

Heuristics

Techniques for limiting search, called *heuristics,* are rules of thumb that enable the problem solver to select some potentially fruitful alternative in a reasonable amount of time. The quality of the solution depends on the adequacy of the heuristic; a person who employs the heuristic, considering only moves that do not place a piece in jeopardy of capture, would play a very limited game of chess. To program computers to solve problems efficiently, psychologists have attempted to identify the better heuristics used by humans to solve the same problems and have had noticeable success for chess, checkers, logic problems, and mathematics.

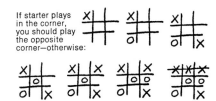

Solution Discovery

With the exceptions noted above, psychologists have been most interested in how people discover the solution to a problem. Solution discovery has been studied most extensively in the following two types of situations. In one case, the subject is provided with a number of alternatives and his task is to locate the alternative that satisfies the requirements of the situation. A good example of such *search* or *selection problems* is a trouble-shooting task: a piece of equipment does not function because one of its ten components is not in working order; the subject must locate the faulty component. The other type of problem is one that can be solved only if the person himself thinks of the solution. For example, choosing the right move in a chess game, solving a mathematics problem, and designing a proper scientific experiment have solutions that are by no means certain to occur. In each case there are too many alternatives to search algorithmically or the alternatives may not be clearly indicated.

An extensively studied laboratory situation with these characteristics is the two-string problem. A person is either actually brought into or told to imagine himself in a large room in which two strings are hanging from the ceiling. His task is to tie the strings together, but they are too far apart for him to take one in hand and walk to the other. There are a number of objects in the room, and he is told that he may use any of them to solve the problem. In most cases, the situation is structured so that only the pendulum solution is acceptable; the subject must tie an object of sufficient weight to the end of one string, set it swinging, then walk to the other string and wait for the weighted string to swing over to him. Of the objects available, usually only one can be used as a pendulum weight, and it is an object not typically used in this way (for example, a pair of pliers). This problem is fairly difficult for college students, a small percentage of whom are usually unable to solve it even after fifteen minutes of trying.

In a number of similar problems, the solution requires an unusual use of an ordinary object (building a hatrack from boards and a C clamp, using a screwdriver blade in place of an electrical wire, rolling a piece of paper to use as a funnel, and so on). In general, the subject is given very little idea about how to approach the problem and must think of the right approach himself.

Problem Difficulty   When a person has to find the correct item among a set of alternatives, the difficulty of solving the problem increases with the number of alternatives. One reason that chess is harder than checkers, or bridge than pinochle, is that there are more alternative plays to consider in chess and bridge.

Amount of Information   The amount of information in a problem is related to the best way to search through a set of alternatives. If each successive choice or check eliminates half of the alternatives remaining, the desired alternative will be located with certainty in the least number of choices. For example, suppose that you have to find the faulty component among a set of 64 and that you can test one or more components against a standard at one time. One approach is simply to try them one at a time; sometimes you will be lucky and find the faulty one with a few checks, but you also will sometimes take a very large number of checks—on the average, this strategy would require 32 checks to locate the one sought. The *split-half technique* is faster. Divide the components in half, then check 32 of them at once. If the test indicates that the faulty one is among those 32, divide them in half, checking one of the subsets of 16. Continue by dividing one of the sets of 16 into

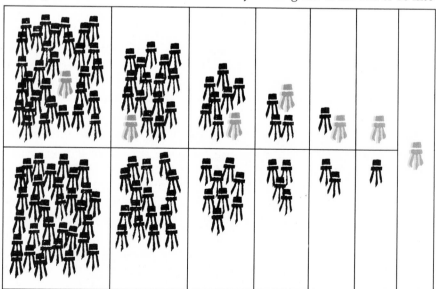

Figure 20.5
The minimum number of yes-no questions that will yield the solution is a measure of the amount of information or uncertainty in a problem.

8s, one of the 8s into 4s, one of the 4s into 2s, reaching the last step in which you check one of the 2 remaining possibilities. If it is all right, then the one remaining is faulty. People do not often think of using this technique on their own, but it can be taught to them, and their trouble-shooting performance improves.

Strength of the Correct Response

The order in which people think of possible solutions to a problem is partly determined by their experience with various alternatives. In general, people tend to produce responses in order of their frequency of experience. When asked to name as many uses for an object as they can, they first give frequently occurring, common answers and mention less frequent uses only after some time. If similar behavior occurs in solving problems, a problem whose solution is a high-frequency response should be easy (solved rapidly), but a problem requiring a low-frequency response should be more difficult. Testing this notion requires that something be known about the relative frequencies of the possible responses. For this reason, problems based on language have often been used.

One such extensively studied problem is the anagram, a set of letters that can be rearranged to make an English word (for example, ALBKC—BLACK). It has been repeatedly found that anagrams whose solutions are high-frequency words are easier to solve than those with low-frequency solutions. Moreover, if subjects are shown a number of words including the solutions before they see the anagrams, their performance improves.

These findings indicate that the difficulty of solving a problem is inversely related to the strength of the required response. One important limitation on thinking of possible solutions is that subjects often do not think of all the possible alternatives. In other words, although a person tries high-frequency responses first, there is no guarantee that he will think of the correct alternative even if it is of high strength.

Response Complexity

Solving a problem can involve a varying number of steps, and difficulty increases with complexity. If each part of the solution can be solved separately, then difficulty is linearly related to the number of steps. However, if the steps are related to each other (if the difficulty of a later step depends on what you have done previously), then difficulty increases faster than the number of steps. An example of this relationship is provided by the "spy problem." Subjects are told to imagine themselves as running a spy ring. For security reasons, not all spies can communicate with each other. After learning which other spies each spy can talk with, a subject is required to get a message from one spy to another, doing the problem in his head. Solution times increased much more rapidly than the number of steps involved in the communication.

Thus, three characteristics establish the basic difficulty of a large number of problems. The difficulty increases when the number of alternatives from which the solution must be selected becomes greater, when the correct response is less frequent, and when the solution is more complex. Problem solving, however, is impaired by other factors.

Factors Impairing Problem Solving
Functional Fixedness

A problem is more difficult if its presentation stresses an ordinary function of the critical object and the solution requires using the object in an unusual manner. This inability to see familiar objects in a new light is termed *functional fixedness*. Functional fixedness can be observed in the difficulty most people have in breaking a given object up into its component parts—they see the object as a whole, not as a collection of smaller items. If people are asked to describe a mirror hanging on a wall, they tend to describe it in just those terms rather than saying that it is a piece of silvered glass supported by a piece of wire hanging from a nail on the wall. A further illustration of functional fixedness comes from a study of the candle problem.

In this problem, a person is given a candle, a book of matches, some tacks, and a small box, and he is told to attach the candle to a cardboard wall in such a way that the candle burns freely and does not drip wax on the table or floor. The situation is constructed so that solving the problem requires tacking the box to the wall and using it as a platform for the candle. This problem is much more difficult when the box is presented filled with the tacks than when the tacks are on the table along with an empty box. One interpretation is that when the box is filled, people tend to see it as a container, thus making it more difficult for them to think of the box as a platform. However, when describing the situation, people who failed to solve the problem within fifteen minutes tended not to mention the box at all or to describe it in an undifferentiated fashion ("a box of tacks"). But if each object, especially the box, is separately labeled when the problem is presented, people will notice the box as a separate object even when it is filled with tacks. Labeling the objects apparently makes the problem easier. These findings indicate that functional fixedness sometimes occurs because people tend not to differentiate the critical object at the time that they perceive the problem situation.

Attitudes and Motivation

Researchers have consistently found that men perform better than women on arithmetic and similar problems. This sex difference may be partly due to the fact that men may have more of the knowledge necessary to solve such problems, but another possibility concerns attitudinal factors. In our culture, the ability to solve these types of problems is predominantly a part of the masculine role; the attitude that men take toward such challenges is therefore likely to favor their finding the solution. Consistent with this analysis are the findings that women profit from discussions of problem solving, in which their attitudes toward the subject apparently are improved.

A related issue is the manner in which motivation affects problem solving. You might expect exceptionally high or low levels of motivation to impair problem solving, but this seems too simple a statement of the facts. Performance does appear to be impaired by very high motivational levels when problems are difficult; for example, students who tend to become anxious on examinations perform poorly on problem-solving tasks. Similarly, experiencing failure on a number of problems impairs subsequent performance, perhaps because of increased anxiety produced by frustration. The difficulty of reaching a simple conclusion is indicated by the fact that increasing stress (through time pressure, by telling people that intelligence is being measured, and so on) has ambiguous effects on problem solving. Furthermore, students characterized as either low-anxious or high-anxious suffer greater impairment due to functional fixedness than those with medium anxiety. The effects of changing motivation seem to depend on the difficulty of the task, the actual level of motivation, and the relationship between motivation and problem solving.

Factors Aiding Problem Solving

One way in which problem solving can be facilitated is by familiarizing subjects with typical solutions before testing them. The more specific the hint is, the better it works; less direct procedures are usually less successful. For example, although psychologists at first expected that practice at giving many uses for an object would subsequently aid subjects in using that object to solve a problem (like the two-string problem), it appears that such facilitation typically does not occur. Watching demonstrations of problem solving or working on simpler versions of problems has been found to aid problem solving, but each technique has also been observed to hinder solution. A similar state of affairs holds for a technique with considerable intuitive appeal, giving hints.

The best answer to the question of whether or not hints help is probably "Don't bet on it." The idea of giving a hint is quite clear—a hint is designed to lead a person in the direction of solving the problem, to suggest a crucial idea to the problem solver. Some success has been reported with giving hints, but most evidence indicates that hints have no effect. Perhaps the problem with hints is that if you know the answer, the relationship of the hint to the solution is obvious, but the person receiving the hint unfortunately does not know the answer—he's trying to discover it. A hint can actually mislead a problem solver, and it is also possible that hints will not work because people ignore them.

Experience and Problem Solving

We have already examined a number of effects of prior experience on problem solving. Now we turn to what happens to problem solving as a person gains experience. The degree and kind of change to be expected depend on the relationships between the problems the person has experienced. Both helpful and interfering changes are much more pronounced when rather obvious relationships exist between successive problems.

Learning to Solve

If a person improves his performance as he gains experience in solving problems of a certain type, we would say that he had learned to solve. It is clear that improvement over a wide range of problems is unlikely to occur because there is no very general problem-solving skill. On any given problem, there will be sizable individual differences in performance, but a person who is good at solving one kind of problem cannot necessarily be expected to be good at solving any other kind of problem. The generality of problem-solving skills is quite limited.

Experimental studies of learning to solve have not been conducted with great frequency, but there is an apparent pattern to the results. For problems involving sequences of choices or information-gathering moves, people tend to improve with practice. Learning to solve has been observed with simple search problems, the game of twenty questions, and concept-identification tasks. For each of these problems, the person's goal is to find a solution in the least number of choices or moves. Each successive choice provides him with additional information about the problem and its solution. Improvement with practice generally reflects increased use of strategies that maximize the amount of information gained with each choice.

In contrast, for problems requiring a person to think of the correct answer on the basis of information received at the beginning of the problem, the typical finding is that people do not improve with practice. This lack of improvement has been found with anagrams, word-guessing problems, and problems that, like the two-string problem, require an unusual use of an object for solution. One possible reason for this is that success on these problems is essentially a function of the familiarity of the individual solution to the problem solver and that strategy differences are relatively unimportant.

Problem-Solving Sets

With respect to solving problems, a *set* can be defined as a tendency to try a particular method of solution or to seek a certain kind of solution. Some sets are

383

Figure 20.6
Sets in everyday experience.

very specific. For example, a letter-order set in anagram solving may be a tendency to employ a particular rearrangement of the anagram letters to make a word (for example, the third letter of the anagram is the first letter of the word). When such a set is established, it may be detected in the eye movements of the problem solver, who will fixate the letters of the anagram in the order in which they occur in the word. Some sets are more general. For example, a category set may be a tendency to look for words in a particular class (such as animal names).

Sets are established primarily by having a person solve a series of problems with related solutions. The strength of a set is an increasing function of the number of set-inducing problems that are given. As a person solves successive problems in the set-inducing series, his performance improves. Thus, through training, a set develops gradually and increases in strength. Very strong sets can be established with immediate effects through instructions, as by simply telling people to look for flower names as anagram solutions. Thus, the development of a set facilitates performance on problems requiring the set solution.

But after set training, if a problem is presented that requires a new solution, the set interferes with solving to a degree dependent on the strength of the set. Recent studies suggest that a single problem requiring a new solution breaks the power of the set; that is to say, solving a problem with a new solution decreases the strength of the set to the same low level regardless of how much previous training with the set the person has had.

Factors Affecting Set

If, during set training, problems requiring the set solution are intermixed with problems requiring different solutions, the amount of set produced is lowered. The strength of a set is also reduced as the time increases between successive set-inducing problems. An interesting feature of sets is that once they are established, little forgetting is observed over periods up to several days. In this respect, set is quite different from induced functional fixedness, which is rapidly forgotten. Finally, it has been demonstrated that people can develop a set to adopt a set. In a recent study, people who were first given set training with anagrams were more likely later to develop a set with modified arithmetic problems than those not given anagram-set training.

Originality and Creativity

To the extent that a person develops sets as he becomes experienced at solving problems, he will presumably be less likely to produce an original or creative solution to such problems. By its very definition, an original solution is unusual or infrequent, and because a set results in a common solution's becoming quite dominant, the existence of this very strong response is expected to interfere with the production of unusual responses. There is evidence that repeating the same response a number of times lowers subsequent originality and that practice on problems having multiple solutions results in the production of more solutions to test problems than practice on problems having only one solution. These findings are consistent with the opinion that a newcomer to a field of knowledge, if he has the requisite information, is more likely to produce creative solutions to its problems than a long-time worker in the field.

There is fairly high agreement among researchers as to the meaning and measurement of original responses, but there is considerable disagreement regarding creative behavior. An original response is simply one that is infrequent. Maximum originality is exemplified by the unique response, given by only one person. Creative behavior may be roughly defined as that which is original, relevant, or practical to the solution of a problem. Many tests of creativity have been proposed, based on rather different assumptions that reflect the diversity of opinion regarding this subject. Part of the difficulty comes from the fact that, in many situations, the identification of behavior as creative depends on someone's judgment.

That such judgments are unreliable can be seen by the pitfalls into which psychologists have fallen when they have attempted to develop tests to identify creative workers in various fields. To demonstrate that a test works, one must show that it differentiates the more creative from the less creative workers in the profession. One solution to this problem that has been widely adopted (and is thus not itself creative) is to rely on the judgments of superiors or experts, but the problem is accentuated when judges do not agree. A topic of great interest to psychologists is the possibility of increasing originality or creativity through training, and our discussion of this research will emphasize the differences between these two kinds of behavior.

Increasing Originality

In this discussion, the word "originality" refers to responses that are infrequent, whereas "creativity" refers to responses that are both original and either relevant to the solution of a problem or judged practical. Earlier it was pointed out that people given a task tend first to give frequent or common responses, only later producing infrequent or original responses. Thus, as people continue to respond in a given situation, the originality of their responses increases. With this fact in mind, consider a training technique in which people are asked to free-associate to stimulus words, giving a different association each time a stimulus word is repeated. The basic idea is that requiring repeated responding will produce more original responses and that this tendency might generalize to other tasks. This technique has been found to increase originality on subsequent free-association tasks, as well as to increase originality in giving uses for objects. It is important that people respond repeatedly to each stimulus. Thus, giving 1 association to each of 125 words produces less transfer of originality than giving 5 associations to each of 25 words. There are some limitations to the general technique, however, because practice at giving uses for objects does not lead to greater originality on subsequent free-association or uses tests. A simple and direct way to increase originality is through instructions. Although people instructed to be original tend to give a smaller number of responses, they do produce more original responses.

The Criterion of Relevance

Although it is relatively easy to increase the originality of responses, it is noticeably difficult to increase creativity. One possible explanation for this difficulty is suggested by the effects of instructions. Direct instructions to be original, to be practical, or to use wild imagination affect both the originality and the practicality of the responses but not the number of creative (original *and* practical) responses. Most original responses generated under such conditions are impractical. In a similar vein, although it is relatively easy to increase the originality of responses, there are but remote chances of raising the probability that the subject will come up with the one original response relevant to the solution of a problem.

What then can be done to promote creative behavior? The requirement of sufficient knowledge cannot be underestimated; a person must have the elements of a creative solution at least potentially available to have a chance for success. Because a creative response must be original, extended effort is called for; the suggestion has been made that in many studies of creativity people have not been

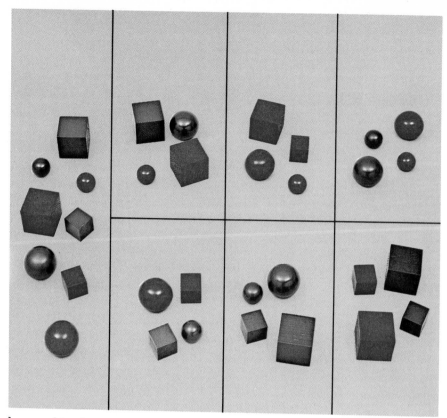

Figure 20.7
A set of eight objects may be generated by varying combinations of two colors, two sizes, and two shapes. Three simple ways of defining a concept by subdividing the set are shown. Can you see a mistake in one of the subdivisions?
(After Bourne, 1966.)

kept working long enough on a problem. Finally, the context in which work on a problem takes place seems important.

Identification of Concepts

Many of the points previously considered are exemplified by research on the problem of identification of concepts. A *concept* may be defined as a system for classifying stimuli. As the problem is usually presented, subjects are shown a series of stimuli and the groupings to which they belong, and then they are asked to determine the system used to form the groups. For example, geometric forms varying in a number of ways (color, size, shape) are shown, and the category is indicated for each form (a large red square is in group A, a large blue triangle is in group B, and so on). The subject must figure out the system being used, such as all red forms in group A, all others in group B.

The number of ways in which stimuli can be grouped is enormous, so the problem solver is faced with a task of considerable complexity. As he learns the category membership of more and more stimuli, the number of possible solutions decreases until, at some point, only one remains. The efficiency with which a subject can discover the solution depends on how information about the solution is provided and on his ability to use this information. There are two basic ways in which such information can be presented. In one method, the subject is shown an arbitrarily chosen sequence of stimuli; in the other, he is allowed to select the stimuli about which he receives category information. College students have been found to solve problems more efficiently when they are allowed to select stimuli. In this case, the student can adopt a strategy for obtaining information and choose stimuli so that the information they provide will fit with the strategy. When he is not allowed to select stimuli, he must adapt his strategy to the sequence of stimuli he is given. When subjects are allowed to select stimuli, their performance improves as they gain experience in solving concept-identifica-

386

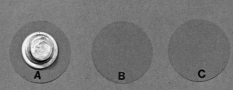

In this cross of pebbles, if you count from A to B or from C to B or from D to B, you will count 9 pebbles. How can you take 2 pebbles away from the cross and rearrange the pebbles so that you get the same answer by counting to and from the same points as before?

Use a water glass to draw three circles on a sheet of paper, then label the circles A, B, and C. On circle A, stack a dime, a penny, a nickel, a quarter, and a half-dollar in order of size, with the half-dollar on the bottom. The problem is to move them all to circle B—in the smallest number of moves possible—so that they are stacked in the same way. Note, however, that only one coin at a time may be moved, and a coin may be moved only to another circle. Moreover, you may not place a coin on top of a smaller coin (for example, you may not place a penny on top of a dime). The minimum number of moves required to move the coins from A to B is 31.

If the puzzle you solved before you solved this one was harder than the puzzle you solved after you solved the puzzle you solved before you solved this one, was the puzzle you solved before you solved this one harder than this one?

Arrange 16 toothpicks, as indicated, so that they form 5 squares of equal size. The problem is to move 3—only 3—toothpicks in such a way that the 16 toothpicks now form 4 squares of equal size. Can you think of a "rule" that would help in the solution?

Take any 4 red-suit and any 4 black-suit cards from an ordinary deck. Arrange them into a small deck so that if you alternately place a card on the table and a card on the bottom of the deck—first card on the table, second card on the bottom of the deck, third card on the table, and so on—when you have finally laid all cards on the table, they will alternate red and black.

A prisoner who was attempting to escape from a tower found in his cell a rope that was only half long enough to permit him to reach the ground safely. He therefore divided the rope in half, tied the two parts together, and escaped. How did he do this?

See page 389 for solutions.

387

tion problems. This increase in problem-solving efficiency is correlated with the increased use of strategies that maximize the amount of information received from each stimulus choice.

Variation in Stimulus Attributes

When stimuli are sorted into categories, only some of their attributes are relevant to the categorization. The problem solver must discover which of the many ways stimuli differ are relevant to the solution. For example, a person trying to figure out the basis on which animals are sorted into "dogs" and "cats" must discover that the color of the animal, the speed with which it runs, the sex of its owner, and the side of street on which it lives are irrelevant to the categorization. In other words, the problem solver must search through all the attributes of the stimuli for those relevant to the solution. With simple search tasks, the difficulty of search increases with the amount of information contained in the set of alternatives, and the same holds true for concept identification.

It was pointed out above that people bring to problems differential experience with various possible solutions. This factor also affects stimulus dimensions, because people exhibit preferences for certain dimensions over others. If the concept to be discovered is based on preferred or high-strength dimensions, the problem is easier to solve.

Forgetting of Previous Information

In a concept-identification situation, information about the concept is received from a succession of stimuli separated in time. To solve the problem, information from a number of stimuli must be used. If previous stimuli are no longer present, however, a problem solver tends to forget some of the information provided by them, and his performance is impaired. The degree of forgetting of stimulus information is directly related to the number of subsequent stimuli presented. For example, if a person is asked what he thinks the concept might be after he is shown the tenth stimulus in a series (earlier stimuli having been removed), his statement is likely to be consistent with the information contained in the stimulus he is looking at but may contradict the information contained in previously shown stimuli. Because people tend to forget previous information, it follows that decreasing the memory load should aid solution of the problem. The efficiency with which subjects identify a concept is directly related to the number of stimuli allowed to remain in view, and the advantage of having more stimuli available increases with the amount of irrelevant information in the problem.

Another way in which memory is involved in identifying concepts concerns the degree of separation of stimuli belonging to the same category. A person usually obtains the best information about a concept when he can compare two stimuli from the same category because any and all ways in which these stimuli *differ* must be irrelevant to the concept. For example, if you find that a small, open, green triangle belongs to category A and that a large, solid, red triangle also belongs to category A, it must be true that the category contains triangles. When subjects are allowed to choose the stimuli about which they will get information, their optimal strategy is one that allows comparisons of this sort. Experiments show that those people who use such a strategy identify concepts with greater efficiency, and as they gain experience in solving conceptual problems, they adopt this strategy.

Clearly an informative comparison of stimuli from the same category is much easier if the stimuli are seen in succession. If their occurrence is separated by the presentation of stimuli from other categories, then the subject will have to remember longer what the earlier stimulus was like. More generally, any reduc-

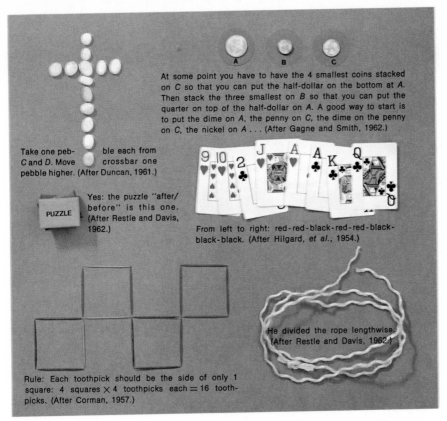

At some point you have to have the 4 smallest coins stacked on C so that you can put the half-dollar on the bottom at A. Then stack the three smallest on B so that you can put the quarter on top of the half-dollar on A. A good way to start is to put the dime on A, the penny on C, the dime on the penny on C, the nickel on A . . . (After Gagne and Smith, 1962.)

Take one peb- ble each from C and D. Move crossbar one pebble higher. (After Duncan, 1961.)

Yes: the puzzle "after/before" is this one. (After Restle and Davis, 1962.)

From left to right: red-red-black-red-red-black-black-black. (After Hilgard, et al., 1954.)

He divided the rope lengthwise. (After Restle and Davis, 1962.)

Rule: Each toothpick should be the side of only 1 square: 4 squares × 4 toothpicks each = 16 toothpicks. (After Corman, 1957.)

tion in reliance on memory facilitates concept identification, and this is one important function served by efficient strategies.

The study of problem solving is directed toward the development of an accurate description of the process and the identification of factors that affect this behavior. Three important factors in problem solving are the amount of information the person has to deal with, his familiarity with the solution, and the complexity of the solution. Much more is known about solving problems whose solutions are definite than about the production of creative solutions. When a person must discover the solution on the basis of information received when the problem is presented, success appears to be primarily a function of the familiarity of the solution and the probability of its being included in the set of alternatives a person thinks of. With other problems, the solution involves obtaining and using information from a sequence of choices or presentations. People adopt information-gathering strategies of varying degrees of efficiency in attempting to solve such problems and tend to improve their performance as they gain experience. Moreover, strategies can be taught, thus facilitating problem solving, but the limitations on problem-solving transfer have not yet been well defined.

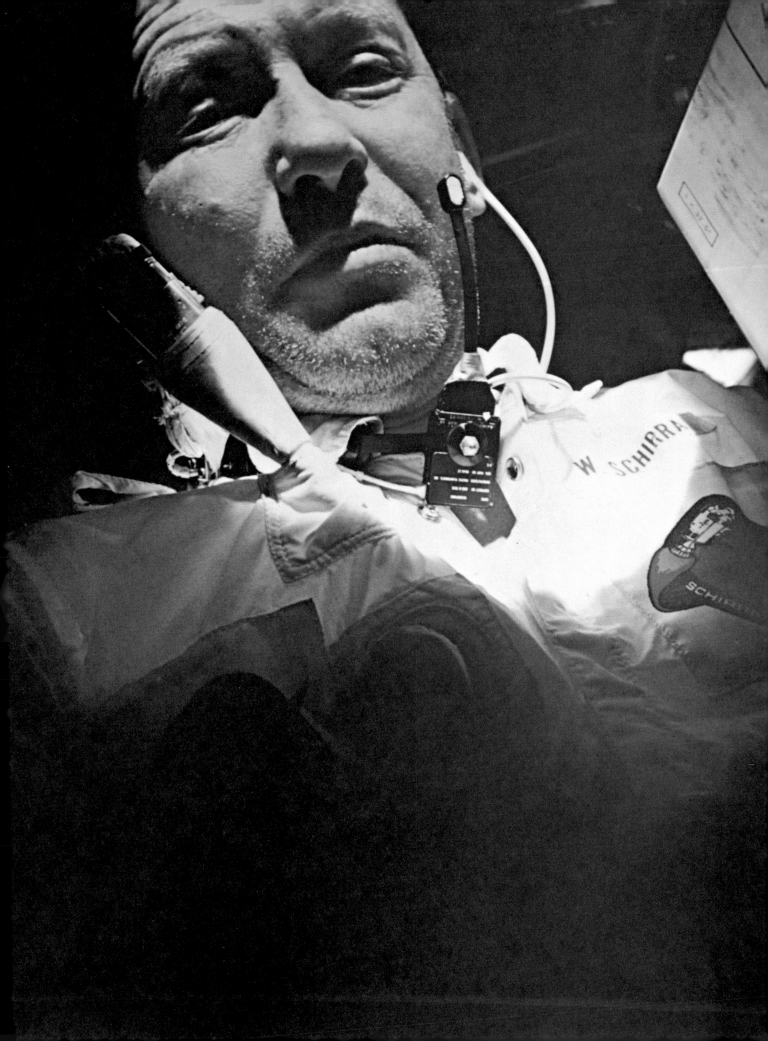

21

EMOTION AND FEELING

IT WAS NOT A NEW CAR, but it was new to him, and very special. He had painted it the green color used by many British racers, he had selected the oversize tires himself and carefully mounted them on the car, and he had fiddled with the engine until it put out considerably more power than its conservative Detroit makers would ever have admitted publicly it could.

When he had finished fixing the car up, he was so proud of it that he took time off from school to drive it out to a nearby track to put it through its paces under the best of conditions. Around the track he went, slowly at first to gain confidence, then faster and faster until he reached speeds well over 150 miles per hour. Then, as he slowed down slightly to enter the tightest curve on the track, it happened. Making a sound like a small cannon, the right rear tire exploded. The car began to vibrate dangerously and spin out of control. Almost immediately he knew what had happened and, frightened almost out of his wits, he felt a strong urge to dive for cover under the dashboard. His heart pounded so loudly he could hear it above the roar of the car's huge engine and his hands began trembling so violently that he could barely clutch the steering wheel. Immediately he caught himself, told himself that this panic wouldn't help, grasped the wheel firmly, and began to fight for his life.

No matter how often the human being is compared to an information-processing machine and his kinship to increasingly complex electronic computers is pointed out, we know we are different. For one thing, we have feelings and emotions. We love, we hate, we fear, we laugh, we experience joy and sadness. We experience a wide variety of feelings and emotions throughout our daily lives, and these experiences have a profound effect on everything we do.

Some psychologists prefer to reserve the term "emotion" for a few dramatic states such as fear, anger, and ecstasy. Yet there are quieter emotions—the feeling a mother has when she is holding her child, the mild irritation of boredom, the uneasiness of living in the nuclear age. There is an emotional quality of some sort to all the interactions we have with our surrounding environment. It has been suggested that we use the term "feeling" to refer to the milder states and "emotion" to the stronger ones.

Feelings and emotions can be described in terms of a felt attraction or repulsion. A tendency for action is involved—for example, when we have an urge to attack when angry or run away when afraid. These tendencies are associated with a number of bodily changes such as muscle tension, increased breathing rate, and changes in heart rate.

The physiological changes associated with emotion, particularly such strong emotions as fear and anger, are so striking that they have often been the focus of research efforts. In fact, at one time, emotional experience was thought to be dependent entirely upon the perception of internal bodily changes. We shall return to this belief later, but we know now that the internal changes occur too slowly to account for the entire emotional experience. Nevertheless, it is obvious that sensations from internal bodily changes play an important role in emotion.

In a theoretical analysis of emotion, Magda Arnold has taken the position that internal bodily changes provide a secondary source of sensations. The primary source of emotional arousal is stimulation from the external environment as it is perceived and evaluated by the person in light of his past experiences. The person then perceives and evaluates his own bodily reactions in a phase Arnold calls *secondary appraisal*. In general, Arnold believes that psychologists have overemphasized the second half of the emotional sequence—experienced emotion, bodily reaction, and behavioral activity—rather than the first half—perception, appraisal, emotion. She suggests a sequence something like this:

1. Perception—The young man in the car hears the sound of an explosion and feels an immediate change in the car's handling.

2. Appraisal—He realizes that the right rear tire has blown and the car is going out of control.

3. Emotion—He feels an almost overpowering urge to escape by throwing himself under the dashboard.

4. Bodily change—His heart begins to pound wildly, his hands shake, and he can barely keep them on the steering wheel.

5. Secondary appraisal—He notices these bodily changes and decides that he is experiencing an incapacitating panic that may cost him his life.

6. Action—The driver forces himself to take control of the car and to try to bring it safely to a stop.

In this chapter, we shall attempt to cover the facts about emotion using, as a framework, Arnold's description of the sequence of events in emotion.

Perception and Appraisal

The relative importance of perception and appraisal in the arousal of emotion depends on the nature of the stimulus, the species and state of the organism, and the amount of learning involved.

Fear

Some years ago John Watson found that human infants become emotionally aroused, presumably fearful, in reaction to three types of stimuli: (1) painful stimuli, (2) loud noises, and (3) sudden loss of support. However, the stimuli that arouse the most intense fear change as the child grows older. For example, from ages two to twelve, the fear of noises and strange objects decreases, but fear of animals and social threats increases.

The critical factors in the arousal of fear in children seem to be not only the intensity of the stimulus but its strangeness and suddenness. As the child de-

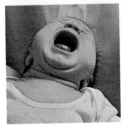

velops, he becomes familiar with noises and less fearful of them, but he comes into more frequent contact with strange animals that arouse fear. The matter of degree is important here. A mildly novel stimulus arouses curiosity, but a really strange stimulus may arouse fear.

The fear aroused by a specific stimulus may spread to other stimuli by means of *conditioning* (see Chapter 4). In a famous experiment, an eleven-month-old boy was shown a white rat. He showed no signs of fear of the rat and even tried to play with it. The experimenters then sounded a loud noise as the rat was presented several times. The child reacted with fear to the loud noise and, after several pairings, reacted with an anticipatory fear to the white rat. Furthermore, the fear generalized to other white and furry objects such as a rabbit, a fur piece, and a man with a beard. (Fortunately, what can be learned can be unlearned; at the end of the experiment, the child's fear of furry objects was removed by again presenting the rat but this time pairing it with food and affection.)

More complex learning is also involved in the arousal of fear. For example, a good deal of perceptual learning is required before the child can respond to strangeness—a factor that may explain why fear of strangers peaks at about eight to ten months in the infant.

■APPRAISAL

The appraisal part of the emotional sequence refers, essentially, to evaluating an environmental event in the light of one's thoughts or cognitions based on previous learning experiences. The evaluation may be slow and deliberate but more often is a rather rapid, intuitive judgment that the individual may find difficulty in reporting verbally. Arnold uses the analogy of the outfielder who "senses" *where* a fly ball is going and automatically adjusts his speed and direction. The player who stops to reflect, Arnold says, is soon out of the game.

■ EFFECTS OF COGNITION

The way in which cognitions can alter the appraisal of an environmental stimulus and thus one's emotional reaction was demonstrated in an experiment in which the stimulus was a motion picture made by an anthropologist of the puberty rites of the Arunta, a primitive tribe of Australian aborigines. When several tribal elders hold down a boy and perform a subincision operation—an opening is made on the underside of the penis with a crude stone knife—most viewers react not only to the boy's obvious pain but to the castrative implications of surgery on the genitalia. The film is an exceedingly successful emotion-arousing stimulus: viewers report strong feelings, and physiological measures such as heart rate show a strong response.

The cognitive appraisal of the Arunta movie was manipulated by adding different sound-track commentaries to the original silent film. The emotional response, in terms of both reported feelings and internal physiological response, was increased by a commentary in which the painful and disturbing aspects of the boy's experience were emphasized. The emotional response to the movie was *decreased* by either of two *defensive* commentaries. One relied on *intellectualization,* a cool, detached analysis of the procedure as social custom. The other defensive commentary used *denial,* in which the painful aspects were minimized and the joyful aspects of the ceremony emphasized. Some subjects—in particular, college students—were helped more by intellectualization, whereas others—businessmen, for example—responded better to denial.

Differences in cognitive appraisal explain why some people react to a stimulus with little feeling and others with great fear. For example, one person approaches a public-speaking engagement calmly, but another may be so fearful as to be unable to go on. The first person sees the situation as a simple task to be accomplished, but the second person may construe the occasion as an evaluative one in which he may fail. Some people see almost every life situation as threatening and may become incapacitated as a result. We usually consider such individuals to be psychopathological (see Chapter 27).

Anger The term "anger" is frequently used in conjunction with, and sometimes interchangeably with, two other terms—"frustration" and "aggression." For the sake of clarity, however, we shall use *anger* to refer to the emotional experience or feelings; *aggression,* to overt behavioral acts of an attacking nature; and *frustration,* to the blocking of an ongoing, goal-directed sequence of behavior.

The idea that anger and aggression are aroused by environmental frustrations was first proposed by Sigmund Freud but was elaborated later as a formal hypothesis by John Dollard and his associates. The *frustration-aggression hypothesis* states that frustration produces a tendency toward aggression and that aggression, particularly the angry sort of aggression, is traceable to frustration. Thus, for example, a child who wants a toy is frustrated when the parent refuses to buy it, and the child may become angry and aggressive toward the parent.

The effects of frustration depend on a number of factors, including the strength of the original motivation toward the goal. Thus, the child would be more emotionally aroused if the refusal came after the toy had been heavily

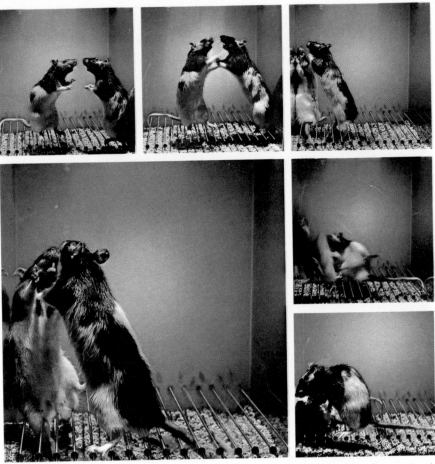

Figure 21.2
Inescapable shock causes rats to fight.

advertised on children's television programs for a week. So, too, the frustration is greater the closer the person is to the goal. The child's reaction would be considerably greater if the parent actually took him to the store but refused to buy the toy after seeing the price tag.

The way in which cognitive appraisal can alter the reaction to frustration was shown in a study in which about half of a group of third-grade children were subjected to a frustration procedure in the course of a block-building task. The frustration procedure involved a sixth-grade confederate of the experimenter, who made sarcastic remarks, interfered with the block building, and caused the third-graders to lose a quarter in prize money. On a questionnaire, the frustrated children indicated a rather strong dislike for the confederate.

The third-grade children were then divided into groups for special treatment. Some groups were allowed to shoot guns at a target, and others were allowed to talk in a social way with the adult experimenter. The important group was one that was not only allowed to talk to the experimenter but also given a new interpretation of the previous behavior of the confederate. These children were told that the confederate had been sleepy and upset and that he might have cooperated if offered some of the prize money. This intervention clearly suggests a reappraisal of the frustration.

The results of the study showed that the new interpretation significantly reduced the negative feelings of the third-graders. This result was shown both in questionnaire ratings and behaviorally in a situation in which the children believed they were shocking the confederate. The results support the idea that the reaction to frustration can be modified by a reappraisal of the threat.

There is relatively little known about love and other positive emotions. Psychologists have tended to emphasize the negative emotions in both research and theory. Nevertheless, for the sake of completeness, we will at least touch upon some relevant findings.

The infant shows a reaction, shortly after birth, that has been called *delight,* which is manifested by relaxation and smiling. This positive reaction is aroused by stroking, feeding, and warmth. As the infant develops throughout the first year of life, he begins to react in a positive way to the fondling, kissing, and other affectionate behavior of specific persons.

A complex emotional and behavioral reaction to a maternal figure can be seen in many species, but it has been studied extensively in the monkey. The infant monkey becomes attached to the mother or to an artificial mother surrogate during the first few months of life. Clinging to even a crude mother surrogate made of cloth-covered wire brings a reaction called *contact comfort* in the infant monkey. The contact comfort can be seen most dramatically when the monkey is frightened, runs to the mother, and shows a visible emotional change. Contact comfort appears to be reciprocally related to fear. Similar phenomena can be seen on the human level.

Following the perception and appraisal of an environmental stimulus, we may experience an attraction or aversion depending on our intuitive evaluation of the stimulus. This felt *action tendency* is what we experience as emotion. The action tendency may lead to bodily changes and to overt behavior, but the action tendency itself is a psychological experience presumably dependent on brain functions alone.

Although Arnold emphasized the two basic action tendencies of approach and avoidance in emotional experience, it is clear that people report a much larger number of emotional experiences. Because we cannot observe emotional experiences directly, we must rely on verbal reports. The seemingly limitless vocabulary of feeling and emotion may suggest that there are thousands of different emotions. However, many of the words we use are synonyms or near synonyms. Many other words refer to varying degrees of the same emotion. Therefore, psychologists have been interested in finding out whether verbal reports of emotional experience can be described on the basis of a few simple dimensions. In the last century, the great German psychologist Wilhelm Wundt proposed a three-dimensional theory of feeling and emotion. The three dimensions he suggested were pleasantness-unpleasantness, excitement-quiet, and tension-relaxation. A number of research studies have been carried out since the time of Wundt, and two basic dimensions consistently turn up: an evaluative dimension corresponding to Wundt's *pleasantness-unpleasantness* dimension and an intensity dimension that cuts across Wundt's last two dimensions and is today usually called *level of activation.* A third factor related to introversion-extraversion sometimes appears, but not consistently.

The way in which these basic dimensions are used to describe emotion is illustrated by a study in which subjects were asked to rate words describing emotion on several seven-point scales. One scale, good-bad, represented the evaluative dimension; another, active-passive, represented the intensity dimension. Each word could be located on both dimensions at the same time, as is shown in Figure 21.4. "Joy" is rated high on both the evaluative and intensity

Love

Emotional Reaction

Dimensions of Emotional Experience

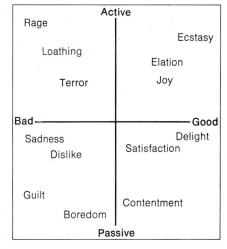

Figure 21.4

Some words describing emotions located in a two-dimensional space of goodness-badness and activity-passivity.

dimensions; "rage" is high in intensity but toward the "bad" end of the evaluative scale; "sadness" is low on both dimensions, and so on.

The evaluative aspect of the pleasantness-unpleasantness dimension is reminiscent of tendencies to approach or avoid. Pleasant emotional experiences include contentment, joy, and ecstasy. Unpleasant emotions might include guilt, disgust, and terror. As we shall see later in this chapter, the pleasant-unpleasant quality of emotional experience is extremely important in understanding many aspects of behavior.

The dimension of level of activation is related to the distinction made earlier between mild feelings and stronger emotions. Emotional experiences are described in such a way as to suggest an intensity dimension. Thus, contentment or boredom represent a more quiescent state than anger or joy. The level of activation is independent of the pleasantness-unpleasantness dimension. Contentment is a mild but pleasant feeling, whereas dislike is mild and unpleasant. Pleasant emotions of an intense sort include joy and ecstasy, but terror and loathing are intense unpleasant emotions.

Overt Bodily Expression

Often we judge the emotions of others not entirely on the basis of what they say but also on clearly observable behavioral changes. A person's voice may be relaxed, tense, or angry. He may laugh or cry. His fists may be clenched or his hand may tremble. His whole posture may change. Above all, we rely on changes in facial expression for clues to a person's emotional experience.

According to Charles Darwin, many of the features of emotional expression are inherited patterns with survival value. The startle pattern to a sudden stimulus, for example, may help the organism jump away from danger. Many aspects of emotional expression in man have prototypes on the animal level. For instance, the growling and baring of teeth in the dog may be the forerunner of the sneer of the human being.

The emotional reactions of children show an increasing complexity and differentiation over the first two years of development. At birth, the infant displays only a generalized excitement or quiescence. By the end of the first year, one can distinguish between such reactions as fear, anger, delight, and elation.

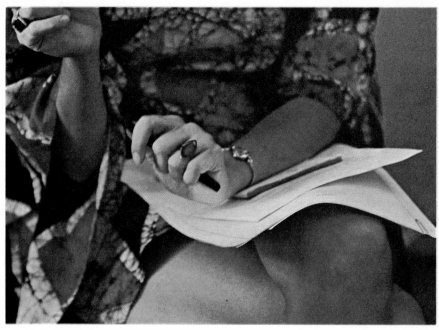

Figure 21.6
Emotional expressions in the dog.
Aggressiveness increases to the right, and
the expressions in the bottom row are those
of a more fearful animal than are
those in the top row.
(After Lorenz, 1966.)

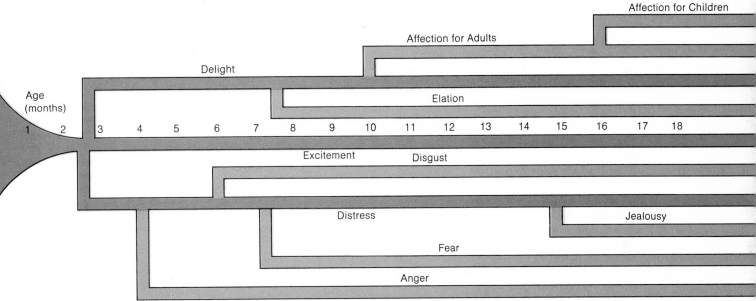

Figure 21.7
Observations of growing children suggest
that the emotions are gradually differentiated
from very general states.
(After Murray, 1964.)

By the end of the second year, more complex emotions such as affection and jealousy can be observed. Some of the changes consist of shifting old reactions to new stimuli, but the emotional reaction itself also shows a change through development. For example, at about three months of age, anger or a reaction to frustration becomes differentiated from general distress. At this age, anger is shown by a change in the tone of crying, increased breath holding, and vigorous leg thrusts. Near the end of the first year, the child's face becomes flushed and he screams when thwarted. A little later, true temper tantrums appear. Finally, at about eighteen months, anger is shown toward other children by hitting them and toward adults by obstinate behavior.

Are the various forms of overt bodily expression innate or learned? Many of the patterns, such as laughing, crying, and frowning, appear to be universal and require little learning. Some of the emotional patterns are the same in children born deaf and blind as they are in normal children. On the other hand, most of

399

the patterns can be modified by social learning. Some actors can cry on command. Some people learn to maintain a fixed smile no matter what their internal feelings. Moreover, there are cultural differences. Many Occidentals find the Oriental inscrutable, but Orientals have little difficulty in reading one another's facial expressions.

Internal Bodily Changes

Let us consider what happens when a person is in two distinctly different emotional states. In the first state, a man is sitting in his own chair, feeling calm and relaxed after a good day's work and an excellent dinner. He is happy and content as he chuckles at a cartoon in the newspaper. The man's brain is functioning at a moderate level of arousal, perhaps even showing brain waves suggesting drowsiness from time to time. The man breathes easily, his hands are warm and dry, and his heart is beating regularly and slowly. The most active system in the body is probably the digestive tract. Blood has been shunted from the brain and muscles to the digestive system. Many of the activities of these visceral organs are controlled by the parasympathetic branch of the autonomic nervous system. The housekeeping functions of the body are in ascendance.

The man then turns to the front page of his newspaper and begins to read about violence at home and abroad. His pulse quickens, he fidgets, the mood is spoiled. Then he turns to the local news and reads that the city council is going to allow a supermarket to be built half a block from his heavily mortgaged house. He sits upright with tensed muscles and a highly aroused brain. His digestive system comes to a halt as blood is shifted to the muscles and the brain. Heart rate and blood pressure go up. Hands sweat. The pupils of the eyes open. Breathing deepens. Sugar is released from the liver and white blood corpuscles from the spleen. The man is emotionally aroused, with fear, perhaps, or rage.

The Harvard physiologist Walter Cannon described this changed state of the internal organs as an *emergency reaction*. The changes can be viewed as preparation for concerted action, either *flight* or *fight*. In general, the aroused visceral changes are associated with the influence of the sympathetic branch of the autonomic nervous system.

There are two important systems in the brain that appear to be related to the visceral changes controlled by the autonomic nervous system as well as many of the overt bodily patterns of emotional expression mentioned earlier. These two systems are the *reticular activating system* and the *limbic system* (see Chapter 2). The physiological alerting function of the reticular activating system appears to bear some correspondence to the level-of-activation dimension of verbally reported emotional experience. The other important dimension of emotional experience, pleasantness-unpleasantness, may be related to the limbic system— that part of the brain most closely related to the activities of the visceral organs and to a number of emotional patterns. Electrical stimulation of certain parts of the limbic system in laboratory animals produces recognizable fear, rage, and other emotional reactions. Of most interest is the fact that there appear to be areas for pleasure and pain in the limbic system. Thus, for example, a laboratory animal will press a bar at a high rate to get an electrical stimulus to the pleasure area through an implanted electrode. Quite possibly the limbic system is involved in the intuitive appraisal of incoming stimuli as positive or negative as well as in the felt tendency to approach or avoid.

Figure 21.8
(A) The reticular activating system.
(B) The limbic system.
(After CIBA, 1957.)

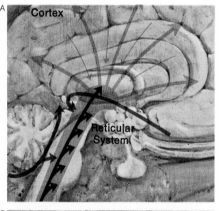

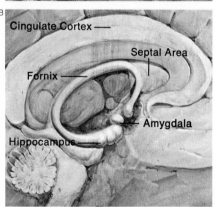

Prolonged Stress and Psychosomatic Disease

Up to this point we have been discussing the bodily reactions to acute stress. The various circulatory and autonomic changes of the emergency reaction constitute the immediate reaction to a stressful stimulus. But what happens when the organism cannot eliminate the stress or move away from it? What happens when the organism is subject to chronic stress?

In studies of the long-term reaction to stress the phrase *general adaptation syndrome* has been used to describe the generalized reaction of the body to a large number of specific stimuli. Laboratory animals have shown this generalized reaction, similar to the emergency reaction, to such stresses as near-freezing temperatures, confinement in a small cage, forced muscular work, drugs of various types, and infectious agents. This general reaction, called the *stage of alarm,* is particularly characterized by the swelling of the adrenal glands and the release of hormones that control inflammation.

If the stress persists long enough, the animals' reactions change, and they enter the so-called *stage of resistance,* in which the adrenals return to normal size, the visceral reactions return to normal, and the animals seem to be adapting beautifully. However, this outwardly excellent adaptation is somewhat deceptive, because the stage of resistance seems to consume all the adaptive resources of the organism. Thus, if the external stress continues unabated long enough, the signs of the first stage reappear: the adrenals enlarge again, and the organism may die. This final period is called the *stage of exhaustion.*

A second type of observation suggests that the adaptational resources of the organism are being strained during the stage of resistance. If, during this period, a second stress is applied—one that the organism could ordinarily handle—the adaptation breaks down and the stage of exhaustion may appear. This additive process can be seen in everyday life when we seem to come down with colds and other ailments more frequently during periods of emotional stress.

Prolonged stress and additive stress are probably involved in many *diseases of adaptation* such as ulceration in various parts of the digestive track, high blood pressure and heart disease, kidney disease, and rheumatism. We shall examine one disease, gastrointestinal ulcers, as an example. A few days after a severe stress such as extensive burns on the skin or intense aerial bombardment during war, many patients exhibit bleeding ulcers in the stomach or duodenum. The temporal sequence here is consistent with the fact that although acute fear

Figure 21.9
After several weeks, daily sessions of shock avoidance produced ulcers in these monkeys.

reduces the flow of stomach acid, chronic fear or tension increases it. Prolonged frustration and inhibited anger are also effective in producing ulcers. What happens is that the stomach juices start, literally, digesting part of the stomach or duodenal wall.

Gastrointestinal ulcers have been produced experimentally in laboratory animals. In one study, for example, monkeys were required to press a lever every few seconds over a period of six hours to avoid getting an electric shock. This procedure, six hours on and six hours of rest, was continued over a period of weeks, and the monkeys eventually developed massive ulcers in their digestive tracks. Interestingly enough, the upsurge in stomach acid and thus the tissue damage occurred during the rest periods rather than the periods of acute stress.

Secondary Appraisal

Common sense suggests that we have an emotional experience and that bodily expression follows. Thus, we see something frightening, feel afraid, and run away. Nevertheless, the most persistent controversy in the area of emotion concerns the *James-Lange theory,* in which the common-sense sequence is reversed.

According to William James, one of the originators of the theory, the perception of a feared stimulus produces a bodily reaction that is followed by the subjective experience we call emotion. Thus, we feel sorrow because we cry, anger because we hit, and fear because we tremble. James based his conclusion on introspective evidence that if one eliminates all bodily symptoms from an emotional experience nothing is left. For example, he suggests that we try to imagine a funny experience unrelated to a feeling of laughter. The James-Lange theory puts particular emphasis on changes in the circulatory system and other internal organs.

This theory has been criticized on many grounds. It has been pointed out that the visceral organs react too slowly to the autonomic nervous system and to various hormones to account for what are often very rapid emotional reactions. Furthermore, the visceral reactions are too diffuse and indiscriminate to correspond to the myriad emotional experiences reported by human subjects. Finally, injections of fear-related hormones do not produce the same experience as a regularly induced emotional state; the subject may report that he feels "as if" he were afraid but that the feeling is not the same as fear.

Perhaps one reason why the James-Lange theory continues to attract attention is that we all know, introspectively, that it contains an element of truth. The visceral reactions may not precede the emotional experience, but they play some role in it. Level of arousal may be similar in different emotions but it is still a noticeable aspect of many emotions. How are bodily reactions and emotions related?

A new approach to the role of visceral feelings in emotional experience has been taken recently by several psychologists. In one study, for example, it was shown that the internal physiological state has an effect on the cognitive processes involved in the appreciation of humor. Subjects were given injections of epinephrine, which typically produces a palpitation of the heart and a slight tremor; a tranquilizer; or a control solution of salt water. The subjects were then asked to watch a movie and rate it on funniness. The group given the epinephrine showed the most amusement and rated the movie high on funniness. The tranquilizer group showed the least amusement, and the control group was intermediate.

The results of this study do not mean that the internal sensations preceded or determined the amusement reaction. What is suggested is that ordinarily when we react with amusement to an external situation, the amusement is followed by some signs of internal arousal that provide a secondary source of stimulation. This secondary, internal stimulation adds to a spiraling emotional increase. Good comedians know how to create this effect by warming up an audience and building up to big laughs. The epinephrine used in the experiment apparently added to the secondary internal stimulation, whereas the tranquilizer reduced such stimulation.

In another study, the other half of the relationship between cognition and bodily sensation was examined, that is, the effects of cognition on the appraisal of internal sensations. In this study, subjects were told that they were getting a vitamin injection but were actually given either epinephrine or a placebo. The subjects injected with epinephrine were also given one of two sets of instructions. One set of instructions *informed* the subjects exactly what to expect in the way of physical symptoms. The other group was *uninformed* about these symptoms and led to believe that there would be no side effects.

The subjects were then exposed to one of two situations designed to manipulate the subjects' cognitive appraisal of the situation. In the *euphoria* condition, the subjects were put one by one in a room with a stooge posing as a fellow subject. The stooge began acting in a wild, euphoric manner. He kept up a manic conversation and invited the subject to join in. The second condition was *anger*. The subject was required to answer a long and infuriating questionnaire. The stooge, working alongside him, finally tore up the questionnaire, declared he would not waste any more time, and marched out of the room noisily.

The results showed that there was a marked difference in the reactions of the control and informed groups, on the one hand, and the uninformed groups on the other hand. Subjects in the control and informed groups tended to stare incredulously at the antics of the stooge in the euphoria condition and to remain calm in the face of the stooge's behavior in the anger condition. In the control condition, the subjects did not have internal physical symptoms and in the informed group they could account for their symptoms.

The most interesting results were those with the uninformed subjects. These subjects were influenced by the stooge. In the euphoria condition these subjects caught the mood of the stooge, joined in his activities, and added new activities of their own. So, too, subjects in the anger condition became angry with the stooge. In the case of uninformed subjects, there were unexplained and unexpected internal sensations from the epinephrine. However, this undifferentiated internal arousal became either euphoria or anger, depending upon the external influence of the stooge. A complete emotional experience, then, consists of a cognitive integration of external stimuli and internal bodily sensations.

Emotion and Action

Feelings and emotions are aroused through perception and appraisal. Changes in personal experience, expressive behavior, and physiological functioning follow. What then? What effects do feelings and emotions have on behavior? We shall consider the effects of two emotions, fear (or anxiety) and anger, on behavior.

Fear and Anxiety

As we have seen, an external stimulus may be appraised as negative or harmful in some way and thus lead to a felt tendency to avoid that stimulus. An avoidance tendency of this sort can be established on the basis of classical conditioning—a neutral stimulus can be paired with a negative stimulus so that eventually the previously neutral stimulus evokes a fear reaction. Behavior that

Figure 21.10
In the shuttlebox, the animal comes to exhibit fear of a neutral stimulus that signals shock.

in fact leads to an escape from or avoidance of the feared stimulus will be reinforced by a reduction of fear.

This process was demonstrated in a classic experiment in which laboratory rats were placed in an apparatus containing a white and black compartment with a sliding door between them. The floor of the white compartment was a metal grid by which the animals could be shocked. The animals were placed in the white compartment and given mild electric shocks. They were allowed to run through the open door into the black compartment, which had no grid floor and no shocks. The animals learned to escape from the shocks quite readily.

Next, the animals were tested for acquired fear by placing them in the white compartment without shock. They showed a fear reaction to the cues of the white compartment. Fear had been conditioned to these cues. Finally, it was shown that the fear could motivate the learning of new responses. The door between the compartments was shut and could only be opened by the rats' turning a small wheel. The animals learned to do this task and run into the black box. They also learned a different response, bar pressing, when this was necessary to open the door. Thus, the acquired fear motivated the learning of new responses and fear reduction served as a reward.

"Anxiety" is a term often used to describe more general fears of a social nature in human subjects. In humans, anxiety is usually measured by a questionnaire. In relatively simple tasks, anxiety facilitates learning and performance, but in complex tasks, anxiety interferes with learning and performance. So, too, when anxiety is aroused experimentally by failure, the findings suggest that moderate anxiety facilitates performance but severe anxiety is disruptive.

Anxiety relating to tests may have an effect on students' performance. Many students become very tense, with pronounced physiological symptoms, before and during an examination. This test anxiety does not seem to make too much difference with extremely high- and low-aptitude students, but for the majority of students, the level of anxiety is clearly related to grade-point average. Students with high anxiety do much more poorly than those of comparable scholastic aptitude with low anxiety. Furthermore, the grade-point averages of highly anxious students have been raised by therapy in a college counseling center.

Anger and Aggression

Although anger and aggression are often closely related, they may occur separately. Anger is an emotional reaction, and aggression is an overt behavioral response. Anger may be aroused by frustration or personal attack, but aggression is only one of a number of responses that may be motivated by anger. So, too, an aggressive response may be learned in a given situation without the intervening emotion of anger, as can be seen in professional sports, where a highly aggressive response may be learned as an instrumental skill.

The emotional arousal produced by frustration may motivate new learning or increase performance. For example, if a laboratory animal is frustrated by the experimenter's omitting an expected reward, the animal may increase the vigor of his response on subsequent trials.

Frustration and the subsequent emotional arousal may lead to responses other than aggression. These other responses may include *regression,* or immature behavior; *fixation,* or a stereotyped, repetitive sequence; *withdrawal,* or a retreat; or even *problem solving* of a positive sort. To a large extent, the response to frustration depends on the person's previous learning. In one study, for example, children were taught by direct reward to show either aggression or constructive behavior. Later, they were frustrated. Those children taught to be

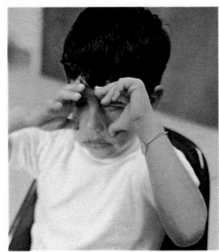
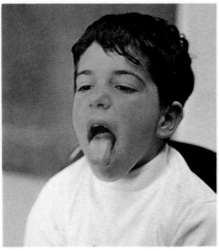

Figure 21.11
These responses to frustration may be strengthened if they are rewarded.

aggressive showed aggression, but those children taught constructiveness showed constructive behavior.

Emotion and Motivation

Some theorists distinguish between emotions and motives on the grounds that emotions are disruptive of behavior but motivation has an organizing and adaptive influence. However, we have seen that emotions such as fear and anger may have an organizing or facilitative effect on behavior at moderate levels. At intense levels, emotions may have a disorganizing effect.

Motives also have both organizing and disorganizing effects, depending on the level of intensity. For example, problem solving by chimpanzees is facilitated by increasing hunger up to twenty-four hours of food deprivation, but increasing hunger beyond twenty-four hours of deprivation interferes with problem solving. The chimps reach out for the food reward instead of trying to solve the problems and throw temper tantrums when they fail to get the food.

A number of theorists have suggested that motives and emotions are essentially alike in that both involve levels of arousal. Level of arousal in turn has widespread effects on many aspects of behavior, depending on the prior history of the person, and may be considered a fundamental dimension of behavior.

The pleasant-unpleasant dimension of emotional experience is also related to the motivation of behavior. Thus, for example, in the *hedonic theory of motivation,* all behavior is assumed to be directed toward either *approaching* stimuli associated with the arousal of pleasant emotion or *avoiding* stimuli associated with the arousal of unpleasant emotion. According to this theory, emotion is the key to understanding human motivation.

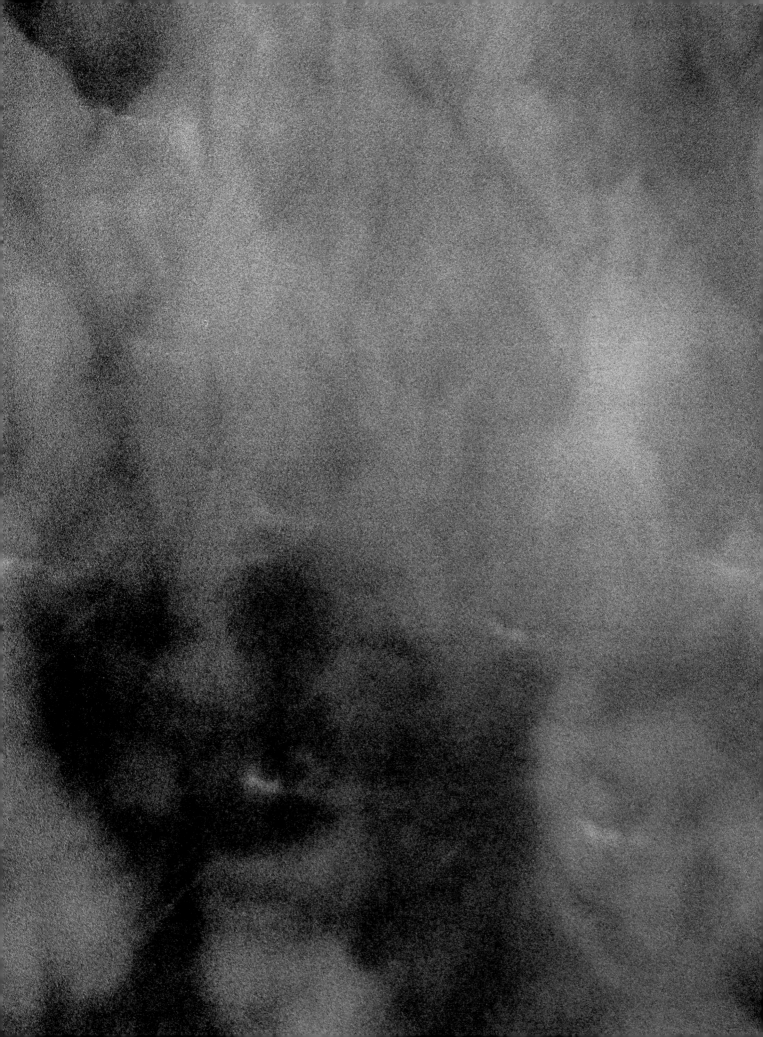

22

DRUGS AND BEHAVIOR

In the Middle Ages, a scourge of horror and death descended on Europe in the form of the physically and psychologically crippling disease ergotism. Caused by eating ergot—a fungus that grows on rye—the disease at first causes psychological disorientation, peculiarities of organization, and malaise but progresses rapidly to physical afflictions, extensive and pernicious gangrene, and finally death. All Europe was in the grips of the cold panic that envelops nations under scourge.

Today, many people feel that we too are visited by a scourge, introduced by a close chemical relative of an ergot: the synthetic diethylamide of lysergic acid. Its chemical name is d-lysergic acid diethylamide, but in the telegraphic patois of both commerce and fear, it is LSD. This so-called scourge of the 1960s, however, well may prove to be something of a blessing, albeit in a darkly puzzling and deeply challenging disguise, for pharmacologists are finding in the LSD reactions a road toward understanding the complex chemical structure of the brain itself. Moreover, studies involving all the so-called psychiatric drugs, as well as alcohol, have extensive social implications in addition to their medical and behavioral applications.

The major psychiatric drugs are catalogued and characterized in Table 22.1. There are some multiple listings, reflecting the complexity of the psychological effects of certain of the drugs.

Psychotherapeutic drugs are typically used in the treatment of many psychological and psychiatric disorders. *Antipsychotic* drugs, for example, are used

Psychiatric Drugs

primarily to treat such major illnesses as schizophrenia, manic-depressive states, and senile psychoses. *Antianxiety* drugs are used to combat insomnia, induce muscle relaxation, treat neurotic conditions, and reduce psychological stress. *Antidepressant* drugs are effective in the treatment of psychiatric depression and phobic-anxiety states. Stimulants, which some consider within the psycho-therapeutic group, are considered below.

Psychotogenic drugs produce changes in mood, thinking, and behavior. The resultant drug state may resemble a psychotic state, with delusions, hallucinations, and distorted perceptions. These drugs have little therapeutic value.

Stimulants are drugs that elevate mood, increase confidence and alertness, and prevent fatigue. *Analeptics* stimulate the central nervous system and can reverse the depressant effects of an anesthetic drug. Caffeine and nicotine are mild stimulants.

Most *sedative* and *hypnotic* drugs produce general depression (sedation) in low doses and sleep (hypnosis) in large doses. They are used to treat mental stress, insomnia, and anxiety.

Anesthetics, analgesics, and *paralytics* are drugs widely used in the field of medicine. *General anesthetics* act centrally to cause a loss of consciousness; *local anesthetics* act only at or near the site of application. Analgesic drugs, many of which are addicting, typically produce euphoria and stupor and are effective pain relievers. Paralytic drugs act primarily at the neuromuscular junction to produce motor (muscular) paralysis and are commonly used by anesthesiologists.

Neurohumors (or *neurotransmitters*) include compounds known to be synaptic transmitters in the nervous system. Other naturally occurring compounds may also be neurotransmitters.

Tranquilizers

Tranquilizing drugs such as chlorpromazine have been used quite successfully to reduce tension, destructiveness, and the severity of hallucinatory experiences. With the aid of tranquilizing drugs, many patients are able to live in the community again and may be more receptive to psychotherapy. Mild tranquilizers are also used with individuals with less severe problems and with relatively well-adjusted people going through a period of stress.

Tranquilizing drugs may produce *depression* in some patients if given in large doses. Reserpine, for example, which is used in lowering high blood pressure in hypertensive patients, can produce a deep depression indistinguishable from depression produced by psychological factors. In fact, correlational evidence suggests that the mood swings of manic-depressive patients are related to the metabolism of amines.

Energizers

Several types of drugs seem to facilitate the activity of amines and thus produce an elevation in mood. *Amphetamines,* or pep pills, have a psychologically stimulating effect by releasing norepinephrine in the brain. Unfortunately, amphetamine has a rebound effect, and prolonged use consequently produces depression and fatigue.

More effective antidepressant drugs are the psychic energizers, such as iproniazid and imipramine, which increase the available level of amines. These drugs may reverse a depressive mood and produce a mild euphoria.

LSD

Psychedelic drugs seem to be related to amine activity. LSD, psilocybin, and other psychedelic drugs are very similar in chemical structure to the important brain amine *serotonin,* which is thought to be important in emotional, perceptual, and cognitive brain functions. The psychedelic drugs sometimes seem to act like serotonin in producing excitement, agitation, pleasurable sensations, and hallucinations. At other times, the psychedelic drugs act to block the action of serotonin and produce deep depression. The effects of the psychedelic drugs are, then, quite complex and may be dangerous, and some people may have a long-term psychotic reaction to them.

Any evaluation of LSD requires knowledge of its effects, unbiased as much as possible by the special languages of either cult philosophy or science. A large number of both clinical and experimental studies on individuals of many different types, as well as the personal observations of trained and trustworthy scientists and medical men, have made clear the major phases of an LSD "trip."

A Trip

The typical sequence of effects in man begins with an acute *intoxication state* lasting some three to four hours. This phase is characterized by a heightened— and often illusory—sense of perception, by enhanced sensitivity to the surroundings, and by a somewhat diminished control over the subject's own thoughts, sensations, and memory. Thoughts tend to shift rapidly and become more plastic and vivid, somewhat as in a dream. Characteristically there is a sense of the self seeing the self—a sort of internal TV show—and an enhanced self-observation of the self experiencing an altered and vivid world. Thus, there is a split of the self into two parts, one of which perceives vivid experiences while the other is a relatively passive monitor rather than an active, focusing, and initiating force. Some people seem to reexperience this effect long after taking the drug.

The loss of control over sensory input and cognitive functioning poses a lurking and often overt threat to the individual. Events both within and without the individual take on a trajectory of their own, and the concept of importance in the external world shifts to allow most mental activity to be absorbed either in monitoring the novelty of experience or in maintaining the very integrity of the self. Moreover, a compelling sense of immediacy diminishes the normal evaluation of past and future. "Nowness" is overevaluated; the fickle pursuit of the novel prevails. Goal-directed, efficient behavior is impaired, along with integrative and synthetic functions and abilities.

The mergings of sensory objects, the plastic rearrangements of sensations and thoughts, the intense focusing on hitherto unseen or disregarded fine details cannot be compared to any organized arrangement in which boundaries between the self and between others are essential. Originality may indeed be induced, because this experience requires the facility for seeing new meanings; but there is *nothing* about the drug effect that specifically enhances the synthetic and organizing facilities. Indeed, it would be more accurate to say that the *need* for synthesis—not the *ability* to synthesize—is what is enhanced in the drug state.

Important features of the drug state are an enhanced dependence upon the environment for structure and support and a heightened vulnerability to these essential forces. In the LSD experience, other persons or a group usually are used for control, for help in knowing what is inside and what is outside, for comfort, and for finding and balancing the fragmenting world. Absorption in holding the personality together renders major changes in the external world of minor importance or makes slight changes seem of critical and overwhelming significance.

Persons or objects in the environment are seen as objects—not to be related to or evaluated in their own right, but either to be clung to as an anchor or to be contemplated as a threat. This change in one's relationship to others can lead to

409

socially valued outcomes such as wisdom, humor, and perspective, but it can also lead to disaster. This leaning on others for structure and control to an overwhelmingly abnormal degree may damage irreparably the subtly predisposed but apparently normal personality.

After the first few hours of an LSD reaction, perception and thinking are no longer grossly distorted, but mental functions are still subtly altered by the drug. Until the drug wears off, in approximately eight to twelve hours with moderate doses, the distorted ideas of reference remain, though to a lesser degree than the induced changes in mood and manner seen in the first stage. Depression, increased suspiciousness and a heightened self-centeredness are characteristic. At twelve to forty-eight hours after drug ingestion there may or may not be some letdown and slight fatigue. There is no craving for a drug to relieve this state if it occurs, nor are there true physiological withdrawal symptoms, as is the case with opiates, alcohol, sedatives, and certain tranquilizers. One such trip may lead to another, but one trip also may be the only one desired by the normal personality for weeks, months, or even years.

The effects of the drug on a given individual depend upon his own personality and the situation in which he finds himself, both in internal organization and with respect to the psychologically relevant milieu. It is rare to find extraverted, successfully well-integrated, traditionally value-conscious personalities in the LSD fringe of our society. Moreover, it seems to be more rare to find disintegration, inability to function, or self-destructive impulses emerging in any subject after and as a result of taking LSD when such impulses were not present before. The instances of LSD causing abnormalities are far fewer than the cases where abnormalities cause the taking of LSD.

Chemical Effects

Scientific study of LSD has focused not only on its great pharmacological potency but also on the structural similarity of LSD to the chemical *serotonin,* which is produced by the brain. Serotonin is a potent vasoconstrictor as well as a stimulator of smooth muscle contraction, and it has a potent effect on the metabolism of the brain. An excess of serotonin brings about stimulation of cerebral activity, but a deficiency causes a depression. Serotonin is itself metabolized or broken down with the help of an enzyme, a monoaminoxydase, and destruction can be slowed by an inhibitor of this enzyme to produce a surplus of serotonin and a consequent stimulation of brain activity. Thus, interference by LSD with serotonin at critical sites in the brain might lead to the chain of events characteristic of the drug.

In a study of the effects of drugs on the synthesis and destruction of serotonin, LSD was found to cause a quite small (20 percent) but reproducible increase in the amount of serotonin in the brain. Moreover, there is considerable evidence that LSD results in a shift of the dynamic equilibrium and location of serotonin in the brain to produce an excess or deficiency at certain critical sites. Some notion such as this seems absolutely necessary to account for the orderly effects of LSD on behavior, because these effects do not seem to be simply a matter of generalized excitation or of generalized depression.

Overall, studies of the relationship between LSD and serotonin lead to the theoretical speculation that when a dose of LSD sufficient to produce grossly observable behavioral effects is administered, the drug first acts at certain sites in the brain closely related to the production, metabolism, or nervous effects of serotonin. The LSD then leaves the brain, but concurrently there is a binding of serotonin at certain critical sites in the brain in response to the effects initiated by

LSD. The change in the level of serotonin at the critical site is thus in large measure a by-product of an LSD-induced change in the distribution of serotonin throughout the brain. Regardless of whether these speculations are correct, it has been shown that only with the clearance of the drug from the brain does the serotonin increase begin to be observed. However, the acute effects on behavior can be observed prior to the rise in serotonin.

Although studies have built a web of circumstantial evidence indicating a link between LSD and the brain's own systems for regulating serotonin, it is clear that a number of precise correlations of a more refined nature—on both the behavioral and the biochemical sides—remain to be established and investigated. But it is also clear that we are approaching an era in which it will be possible to conceive of, and perhaps to understand, not only the biochemical structure and function of the brain but also the controls that the brain itself exerts over its functioning and that LSD seems to distort. The ultimate goal of the pharmacologist is to explain the chemistry of the brain and the mind. We have to begin, however, with what we can learn about how behavior is organized and with what nature can teach us about the ways in which the chemical organization of the brain is related to the dimensions of mind. In this quest, LSD may prove a useful laboratory tool.

Although painstaking pharmacological and biochemical research would seem to hold the ultimate key to unraveling the mystery of LSD, psychiatrists and psychotherapists have found uses for the drug in the treatment and study of certain types of mental illness.

The effects of LSD on parts of the body other than the brain are not well understood. Relatively large doses of LSD injected into pregnant rats and mice can cause spontaneous abortion and fetal damage, but there is no reliable evidence that humans are affected in the same way (there are many drugs that affect rats and other lower animals but do not affect humans, and vice versa). Early reports suggested that LSD could cause chromosomal damage in humans, but later studies have questioned the validity of the earlier work, so the issue remains in doubt. If chronic LSD use did cause chromosomal aberrations, one might expect a marked increase in birth defects among children born to mothers who have taken LSD. Studies made of "hippy" mothers (almost all of whom admitted to taking LSD before and during their pregnancies) show that the incidence of birth defects among the offspring was no greater than average. Long-term studies of chronic LSD users need to be made before the issue can be settled one way or the other.

LSD Therapy

Psychotherapists have attempted to use the loosening of associations and the intensity of experiences produced by LSD in order to influence behavior change. Coincident with the use of LSD by society at large, LSD therapy has a history of both use and abuse. In the late 1950s many physicians not only were struck by the drug-induced phenomena but were apparently addled by them. Because these physicians insisted on taking the drug themselves during the therapy sessions, their lack of intellectual control over the events that they were presumably monitoring resulted in a type of therapy that was nothing more than a healing cult. There is no evidence that any progress was made by those therapists who insisted on drugging themselves.

Within responsible psychotherapy, two major modes of treatment prevail. The treatment employed by many Europeans is a method by which certain defenses are breached. The patient has a strong drug-enhanced tie to the

therapist, and feelings and memories are allowed to emerge vividly and unforgettably while the therapist helps his patient discharge their strength. During later therapy sessions, the drug-produced confidences are examined carefully. The dosage of the drug is carefully regulated with a view to the patient's capacity to steer a course between being utterly lost, on the one hand, and overly constrained by his habitual defenses, on the other. A kind of active participation is sought through the drug's loosening effects. Preserved throughout is a certain autonomy and directiveness, the inner capacity to integrate and pull together the personality and experience, something that is lacking in the unskilled or overdosed user. The integration of the personality that follows is a collaborative venture requiring the active participation of the therapist and the patient. The danger, of course, is that the entire therapy will come to depend upon the patient's being drugged, because any lasting therapeutic effects of the treatment must somehow prevail in the behavior of the undrugged patient.

There are also the so-called psychedelic therapies, which employ an immense amount of preparation—of salesmanship with an evangelical tone in which the patient is confronted with hope and positive displays of it—before he has his one great experience with a very high dose of drug. The experience is structured by music and by confident good feelings. With the support of the positive therapist throughout this experience, the patient is encouraged to see his life in a new light and to think of his future accordingly. In this method, there tend to be rather long periods of follow-up and support of the patient. Formerly, this mode of therapy attempted to avoid the intricate problems of the relationship of therapist and patient, with the single dose of the drug used as a therapy almost unto itself. The current approach is more explicitly ritualized and rational. For example, ego dissolution under the drug and subsequent ego building with the help of the therapist may turn out to be of particular benefit in dealing with the egocentric problems of the alcoholic. The efficacy and selectivity of current therapies is far from settled, and research is still in progress. Obviously careful follow-up is essential, for the immediate glow that occurs with drug-induced personality change can be deceptive for therapist, for patient, and for society.

Some researchers believe that the effects induced by LSD might be similar to "model" psychosis. This does not mean the effects *are* a psychosis but that certain processes are present to some extent in both the drug state and the psychosis. There are obvious differences between the two, just as there are obvious differences between psychosis and our nightly dreams. The similarities between the drug state and a psychosis such as schizophrenia include the enhanced value and intense attention placed on the self, the rush of vivid memories from the past to compete with current reality, the heightened tension, and the diminished control—all of which lead the trained psychologist to hope that through a careful and controlled examination of the LSD-induced model he can arrive at some understanding of the processes that have gone awry in schizophrenia. Moreover, because the drug-induced state is reversible for the stable personality, the psychiatrist can study the observations of a selected and specially trained individual who has recently been in a state akin to schizophrenia as a result of the ingestion of LSD. Formerly, such observations were limited to those few individuals who were purportedly cured of schizophrenia and who were articulate enough to enunciate publicly their descriptions and impressions of their ordeal. The immense challenge that LSD offers to psychiatry and psychology is thus being met at the level of therapy as well as at the level of the brain's chemistry. Its use in other than clinical or laboratory settings is open to question, however.

Marijuana

One of the most interesting social phenomena of the 1960s was the dramatic increase in the use of marijuana in the United States. Prior to 1960, its use was restricted almost entirely to such minority groups as Latin American farm laborers, ghetto Negroes, and that segment of the culture associated with jazz musicians and arty enclaves in big cities. By 1960, however, the college population had discovered marijuana, and since that time the number of users of the drug in the United States has increased by a factor of perhaps ten thousand. Accurate statistics are difficult to come by, because possession of the drug carries stiff legal penalties, but some social scientists have estimated that at least 10 percent of the American public smokes, or has at least tried smoking, marijuana. The physician in charge of student health services at one major American university has stated that as much as 50 percent of the student population of urban colleges has had experience with the drug. One national magazine insisted that at least 100 million Americans have used the drug; a more likely estimate is that 20 million people have tried marijuana at one time or another and that 5 million to 10 million people use it regularly.

Source

The active ingredient in marijuana is a complex molecule called tetrahydrocannabinol (THC), which only recently has been synthesized from inorganic materials. THC is found naturally in resin exuded from the flowers, leaves, seeds, and stems of the female plants of a common weed, *Cannabis sativa,* or Indian hemp. Male plants, which are used chiefly as a source of hemp fiber, contain little or no THC. It has been estimated that up to 10 percent of the weeds growing wild in many parts of the United States are *Cannabis sativa,* but the amount of THC present in most such plants is fairly low. Marijuana is technically any part of the top of the female plant that is harvested and dried; *hashish* is a gummy powder made just from the exuded resin. Typically both marijuana and hashish are smoked, although they may be ingested in cookies or candy. In its prepared state, marijuana consists chiefly of short, dried green fibers (hence the nickname "grass"). In some cultures it is steeped in hot water in a teapot and then drunk (which may explain why it is sometimes called tea or pot).

Introspective Reports

Marijuana has been used as an intoxicant among Eastern cultures for many centuries; in some societies, marijuana (hashish) is legally and morally acceptable, but alcohol is not. Although the effects of the drug seem to vary somewhat from one person to another and are dependent upon the setting in which it is taken, there is considerable consensus among regular users as to how it affects them. When marijuana containing at least 0.5 gram THC is smoked and inhaled, the user undergoes a condition known as "getting high." Sensory inputs are greatly enhanced or augmented—music sounds fuller and larger, colors are brighter and livelier, smells are richer, and foods taste better than when the person is not "high." The user becomes elated, the world seems somehow more meaningful to him, and even the most ordinary events take on a kind of extraordinary profundity. The user's time sense is greatly distorted; a short piece of music may seem to last for hours, perhaps because the normally smooth-flowing stream of consciousness is somehow fragmented into separate vignettes only loosely tied together. He may become so entranced with a painting that he sits and stares at it without moving for many minutes. He may report that a music

413

phrase of no more than a few seconds' duration has stretched out in time until it becomes entirely isolated from the rest of the composition, allowing him to perceive it in such rich detail that he insists he has never really heard it before. The physiological mechanism responsible for this temporal distortion is unknown.

As many users of marijuana have discovered, the drug tends to enhance unpleasant as well as pleasant experiences. If the user is in a frightened, unhappy, or paranoid mood when he takes the drug, he stands an excellent chance of having these negative experiences blown up out of proportion so that his world, temporarily at least, becomes terrifying.

Unlike alcohol, marijuana has few if any known physiological side effects, and it appears difficult if not impossible to inhale a fatal dose. The long-term debilitating effects of marijuana have not been studied scientifically but appear (from clinical evidence) to be considerably less deleterious than those of alcohol.

Experimental Report

Although it was clear to many people more than a decade ago that the growing use of marijuana constituted a grave social and legal problem, social pressures were apparently such that the first well-controlled scientific study on its effects in humans was not undertaken until 1968. The subjects of the research were seventeen college students in the Boston area who ranged in age from twenty-one to twenty-six years. Nine of the subjects had never smoked marijuana before; the other eight were "experienced users." All subjects were given psychiatric screening beforehand, and all were volunteers. The marijuana smoked in the experiment was supplied by the Federal Bureau of Narcotics.

The naïve or inexperienced subjects were put through four experimental sessions, each a week apart. During the first session they were taught the proper technique of smoking and inhaling the drug. At each subsequent session, they smoked one of three types of cigarettes: the first contained a high dose of marijuana (2.0 grams THC), the second contained a low dose (0.5 gram THC), and the third was a placebo cigarette that contained no THC at all. The naïve subjects were not told which type of cigarette they were smoking. The experienced users were tested only on the high-dose cigarettes. Before the sessions and for a period of three hours after they had inhaled the marijuana, all the subjects were given various psychological and physiological tests. The results of these tests are of considerable interest.

Marijuana increased the heart rate moderately in all subjects, seemed to cause little or no change in respiratory rate, and had no effect on blood sugar level. Unlike many other drugs, marijuana did not affect the size of the subjects' pupils, but it did cause the eyes to become bloodshot (an effect noticed more in experienced than in naïve subjects).

No adverse reactions occurred in any of the subjects; indeed, the reactions several subjects showed to the tobacco used during the training sessions were far more spectacular than any of the effects produced by marijuana.

Only one of the inexperienced users actually became high (that is, reported the euphoria typically associated with marijuana smoking); the subjective experiences they reported were considerably different from those reported by experienced users. The naïve subjects demonstrated significantly impaired performance both on intellectual and on psychomotor tests after smoking marijuana. In many cases, the heavier the dose, the greater was the impairment. Surprisingly, however, regular users of marijuana (all of whom got high on the dose given them) showed no impairment either of intellectual function or of motor

skill; to the contrary, in some cases their performance appeared to improve slightly after smoking marijuana. The effects appear to reach maximum intensity within thirty minutes, to be diminished after an hour, and to be almost completely gone at the end of three hours.

There is no evidence in the scientific literature to suggest that marijuana is physiologically addictive—that is, the body does not become dependent upon the chemical effects of marijuana as it does with heroin. The question of psychological dependence is more difficult to discuss because the phrase has little real meaning. Usually it refers to a condition in which the person has a strong craving for a given substance presumably because it gives him some kind of intense pleasure. If offered a choice of pleasures, he tends to pick this same one over and over again. The difficulty with the phrase becomes obvious when one realizes that, by this definition, most American children are addicted to peanut butter, hot dogs, and soda pop, and most adults are addicted to steaks, sex, and the *Reader's Digest*.

Dependence

There is no evidence in the literature to suggest that smoking marijuana is but the first step in a chain of events that inevitably leads to taking heroin or some other narcotic. Although it is true that many addicts smoked marijuana before trying heroin, the causal connection between these two correlated events has not been established experimentally (see Chapter 3 for a discussion of causality and correlation). Indeed, the correlations between heroin addiction and smoking tobacco or drinking alcohol are higher than between heroin and marijuana. Police estimate that fewer than 100,000 Americans are heroin addicts at the present time and that addiction is growing little faster than is the overall population. These statistics suggest that fewer than 1 percent of marijuana smokers become narcotics addicts.

Hard-narcotic trade has long been illegal in the United States, but it is so profitable that it is hard to eliminate. Moreover, the heroin addict, for example, achieves such a sense of euphoria and relief from pain and anxiety from the drug that the demand is kept ahead of the supply.

Hard Drugs

Heroin is addicting in that a series of physiological symptoms appear when access to the drug is cut off. Within six hours after the last dose a craving for the drug occurs, and within twelve hours the addict may begin to vomit, sneeze, and sweat and have hot and cold spells, cramps, pains, and perhaps hallucinations or delusions. Most of these symptoms are gone within five to seven days. Despite these painful experiences at withdrawal from the drug, long-term usage (as much as twenty years) is not thought to produce any more physical damage than does excessive use of alcohol. The social problem posed by drugs is to be found in the drug taker's obsession with the drug experience, the costs of illegal acquisition of the drug, and the social setting in which drug taking often occurs.

Attempts at treatment of drug addicts have been less than successful. Withdrawal of drugs has proved to be only a temporary measure: an estimated 90 percent of addicted patients return to the habit when they are released from custodial care. Substitution of a less addictive drug such as Methadone is a controversial practice, and such rehabilitation centers as Synanon remain limited enterprises that are primarily effective with those whose personality matches the method.

It is evident that the solution to drug addiction cannot be found in remedy of the affliction after the fact. The social and psychological conditions that induce drug use must be alleviated as a preventative measure to reduce the number of persons newly recruited to chemical forms of problem solving.

Alcohol and Alcoholism It is estimated that 5 million Americans have a severe drinking problem, and the cost of this national hangover is impossible to estimate. Alcohol, administered slowly in small doses, is a kind of social wonder drug that loosens inhibitions and makes people gregarious. Beyond that magic point, it causes disorders of sensation and perception and stimulates behavior that violates common social codes.

Because these effects are characteristic of many drugs besides alcohol, the many who have fallen prey to alcohol in one generation might well have taken to other drugs had they been born at a different time or in another culture.

Many people think of alcohol as a stimulant because drinking is so predictably followed by loudness and hilarity, but alcohol is really a chemical depressant that affects those parts of the brain that suppress, control, and inhibit our thoughts, feelings, and actions. As the depressant is administered in larger doses and accumulates in the body, there is a steady deterioration in all functions. How rapidly this initial stimulation and consequent decline will occur depends on how much and how rapidly alcohol enters the bloodstream.

Three stages of alcoholism were described by E. M. Jellinek. In the *prealcoholic* stage, the drinker discovers that alcohol reduces his tensions, gives him self-confidence and a sense of courage, and eases psychological and social pressure. In the *prodromal* stage, a beverage is turned into a drug. The drinker drinks heavily and furtively; he may begin to suffer memory blackouts and be unable to recall events during his drinking bouts. In the final, *crucial* stage, he drinks compulsively, beginning in the morning; he becomes inefficient in his work and may go on benders that last for days or weeks. He feels a powerful need for alcohol when he is deprived of it.

By this point, the problem drinker imbibes continuously, eats infrequently, and is unable to alter his compulsive self-drugging despite the anguish he causes others or the obvious destruction of his social life. As Jellinek pointed out, however, each alcoholic has a unique personality and temperament, and the drinking pattern differs accordingly. The so-called periodic alcoholic, for example, may not abide by general social rules of when, where, or how much to drink, yet he is able to stop drinking completely for brief periods of time when it is crucial that he do so. He may never progress to the most extreme form of alcoholism even though he bounces in and out of an alcoholic haze most of his life. In the most severe type of alcoholism, the victim's body builds up a tolerance for the drug. He may develop such a psychological dependence on alcohol that he feels normal only when he has been drinking and experiences severe and painful physical symptoms if he stops.

It is estimated that five or six men are alcoholic for every woman with this problem. Such statistics are not very trustworthy, however, for many fewer women have the visibility the male has in his work and contact with the outside world. No one knows, for example, how many suburban housewives secretly drink at home attempting to drown their problems, boredom, and anxieties.

There are many theories as to why some people can handle alcohol but others cannot. Some theorists suggest that this destructive dependence is part of an inherited malfunction or biochemical disorder of the body. Perhaps, they speculate, alcoholics are those whose bodies fail to manufacture some essential (but unknown) products necessary to proper nutrition or metabolism. Thus, the alcoholic drinks as others do but his body cannot manage alcohol chemically.

There is, unfortunately, very little scientific backing for biological theories of the cause of alcoholism—there is only hope that future research will yield more information.

Other theorists look to the differences in the rate of alcoholism in various cultures and suggest that this problem is a national characteristic related to the family pattern; that is, the family structure in wine-drinking cultures may differ from that of whiskey-drinking cultures. This broad cultural theory of alcoholism fits comfortably with the views of dynamic theorists such as Freud and the neo-Freudians, who look to the nature of the individual's psychological experience in growing up.

A great many attempts have been made to pin down precisely the dynamics of the alcoholic, but only a quite broad and general description of how problem drinking comes about has been evolved. The dynamic theorists suggest three general characteristics of alcoholics: egocentricity, dependency, and hostility.

Egocentricity. The alcoholic is immature and more concerned with himself than others. Like a jealous child, he feels that people pick on him and favor others. He easily feels sorry for himself and justifies his drinking accordingly. As he developed from childhood, he failed to become mature and takes the alcoholic escape route from his problems.

Dependency. The alcoholic is a passive person who needs to be cared for by others and cannot manage enough independence to face problems alone. When the necessary protection is not available, he becomes anxious, feels others are more capable, secure, and able, and retreats to the bottle to ease his discomfort.

Hostility. He is angry and resentful at being thrust into the world unready to face life's problems; he is angry that others do not support him but keep making demands on him. Consciously he feels he loves those close to him, but his hostility lies just below the surface.

Being egocentric, dependent, and hostile, he does not manage his tensions well and avoids (as much as he can) being caught in situations in which there might be conflict between people.

A usual first step in treating the alcoholic is to sober him up by cutting off his supply. Food, vitamins, and medical care are then administered to restore the body to some reasonable shape. This is easily done, as far as the doctors are concerned, but may be excruciatingly unpleasant for the alcoholic. Deprived of alcohol, his pulse, blood pressure, and body temperature may rise, and he experiences racking pain and feels depressed, frightened, restless, and shaky. Such symptoms may last for months.

Once restored to a reasonable state of health, the alcoholic may be exposed to electroshock, tranquilizers, antidepressants, or traditional psychotherapy. These efforts have all had less than the hoped-for success. The alcoholic may also seek relief in such lay groups as Alcoholics Anonymous. A variety of techniques have been used in attempts to help the alcoholic, but only a microscopic part of the social resources needed have been devoted to this pursuit. It is as if our culture has, over the years, developed a tolerance for the alcoholic.

Drug Addiction The mechanics of drug addiction are not well understood at either a psychological or a physiological level. There are some hints, however, that addiction is in part a function of the addict's personality. Of the Americans who are exposed to alcohol, about 5 percent become alcoholics. Of the hospital patients who are given morphine as a painkiller, about 5 percent become addicts. Although there are no comparable figures for heroin addiction (because heroin is seldom given

MARTY GUNSAULLUS

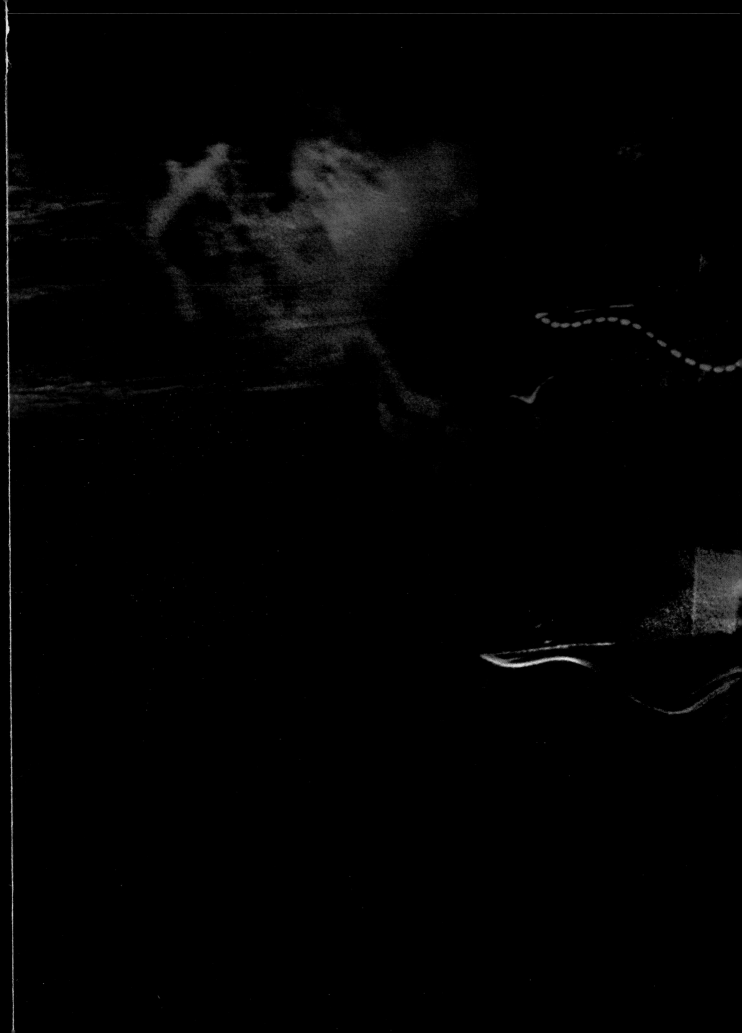

Table 22.1—Major Drugs

Drug Group	Example	Trade or Common Name	Natural or Synthetic	Usage	How Taken	First Used	Evidence of Addiction?
PSYCHOTHERAPEUTICS							
Antipsychotic							
Rauwolfia alkaloids	reserpine	Serpasil	natural	greatly diminished	injected, ingested	1949	no
Phenothiazines	chlorpromazine	Thorazine	synthetic	widespread	injected, ingested	1950	no
Antianxiety							
Propanediols	meprobamate	Miltown	synthetic	widespread	ingested	1954	yes
Benzodiazepines	chlordiazepoxide	Librium	synthetic	widespread	ingested	1933	yes
Barbiturates	phenobarbital	see SEDATIVES					
Antidepressant							
Monoamine oxidase inhibitors	tranylcypromine	Parnate	synthetic	diminished	ingested	1958	no
Dibenzazepines	imipramine	Tofranil	synthetic	widespread	ingested, injected	1948	no
Stimulant	amphetamine	see STIMULANTS					
PSYCHOTOGENICS							
Ergot derivative	lysergic acid diethylamide	LSD, Lysergide	synthetic	widespread?	ingested	1943	no
Cannabis sativa	marijuana	hemp, hashish	natural	widespread	smoked	?	no
Lophophora williamsii	mescaline	peyote button	natural	localized	ingested	?	no
Psilocybe mexicana	psilocybin		natural	rare	ingested	?	no
STIMULANTS							
Sympathomimetics	amphetamine	Benzedrine	synthetic	widespread	ingested, injected	1935	yes
Analeptics	pentylenetetrazol	Metrazol	synthetic	rare	ingested, injected	1935	no
Psychotogenics	lysergic acid diethylamide	see PSYCHOTOGENICS					
Nicotinics	nicotine		natural	widespread	smoked, ingested	?	yes
Xanthines	caffeine		natural	widespread	ingested	?	yes
SEDATIVES AND HYPNOTICS							
Bromides	potassium bromide		synthetic	widespread	ingested	1857	no
Barbiturates	phenobarbital	Luminal	synthetic	widespread	ingested, injected	1912	yes
Chloral derivatives	chloral hydrate		synthetic	rare	ingested	1875	yes
General	alcohol		natural	widespread	ingested	?	yes
ANESTHETICS, ANALGESICS, AND PARALYTICS							
General anesthetics	nitrous oxide	laughing gas	synthetic	rare	inhaled	1799	no
	diethyl ether		synthetic	greatly diminished	inhaled	1846	no
	chloroform		synthetic	rare	inhaled	1831	no
Local anesthetics	cocaine	coca	natural	widespread	applied, ingested	?	yes
Analgesics	procaine	Novocaine	synthetic	widespread	injected	1905	no
	opium derivatives	morphine, heroin	natural	widespread	injected, smoked	?	yes
Paralytics	d-tubocurarine	curare	natural	widespread	injected	?	no
NEUROHUMORS (NEUROTRANSMITTERS)							
Cholinergic	acetylcholine		natural synthetic	laboratory	injected	1926	no
Adrenergic	norepinephrine		natural synthetic	laboratory	injected	1946	no
Others (?)	5-hydroxytryptamine	5-HT, serotonin	natural synthetic	laboratory	injected	1948	no

under legal conditions in the United States), it is known that large numbers of people try heroin but do not become addicted to it. Therefore, it seems possible that a certain small percentage of people who try any given drug will like it so much that they become "psychologically addicted" to it and that this psychological addiction leads the person to use the drug long enough to become physiologically addicted to it if the drug is a true narcotic (marijuana is not a true narcotic in this sense of the word).

Whatever the case as far as addiction is concerned, it remains true that all drugs constitute a kind of psychological crutch and that any form of real dependence upon such drugs can lead to severe personality problems.

Societal Implications

We know that many serious persons have reported some transient or long-term value in the use of certain drugs, especially the psychedelics. They say that their aesthetic appreciation has been enhanced, and there is some hard evidence for a slight shift of this sort for part of a group of normal subjects. If, however, we search for major productions of art, letters, music, or visionary insight, exceedingly few clear-cut and lasting monuments to drugs are available. Effects of drugs simply do not seem to have compelled creativity. Aldous Huxley's greatest output, for example, preceded his experimentation with drugs; thereafter, he tended to write *about* drugs, not to *create with* them.

Numerous cultures through the ages have used drugs that induced the sort of experience garnered through LSD, but none of these cultures eradicated mental disorders and disease. In fact, the use of such drugs is often associated with some form of psychosocial deprivation on the part of the user or on occasion with marked privilege (as in Brahmins in India and college students in the United States and Canada). That private satisfactions might have been achieved by the individuals and that groups may have achieved some spiritual equilibrium seem apparent, but whether such drugs have been an overall palliative in the general titre of human misery is another question.

At the present time, when the legal penalties for possessing drugs such as marijuana are so great, the social consequences of its use can also be disastrous. If the present explosion in the number of young Americans using the drug continues, however, as these young people grow older and become the cultural leaders of tomorrow, one might predict considerable change to occur in society's attitude toward the use of these drugs.

In general, we have been more awed than aided by our experience with many drugs. Here undoubtedly are agents that reveal previously hidden consciousness and modes of thought, but revelation, although perhaps instructive, is not tantamount to understanding. For that we must employ our mental faculties in the undrugged state. This is the lesson of civilization.

UNIT VI

PERSONALITY

Science is a systematic way of handling data, of putting facts together so that they make sense. But science has difficulty handling unique events. A physicist can tell you how many radioactive particles a pound of uranium will emit in a second's time, but not when a given atom will yield up a particle. The electric company cannot predict just when you will turn on your reading lamp, but it does know approximately how many such lamps will be lit at any given time in the evening. If each person in the world were totally different from everyone else, there could be no science of psychology; for science deals with communalities, with the ways in which large numbers of objects or organisms are similar. Psychologists measure those aspects of personality that each of us shares—intelligence, ability, adjustment to the world—in order to handle the much more difficult problem of understanding how we are different.

423

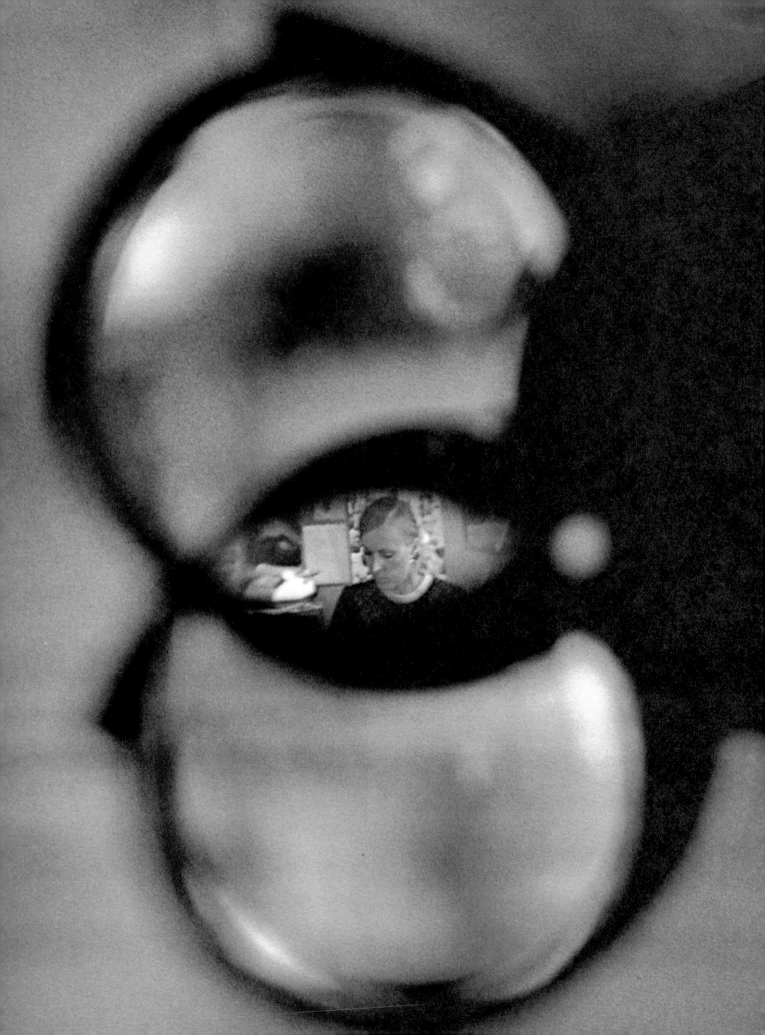

23

INDIVIDUAL DIFFERENCES AND THEIR MEASUREMENT

IT IS A FACT that, on the average, black Americans score lower on standard intelligence tests than do whites. Does this fact mean that Negroes are innately inferior to whites?

It is a fact that, on the average, urban populations (black or white) score higher on intelligence tests than do rural populations. Does this fact mean that the brighter farmers tend to migrate to the city, leaving their duller neighbors behind to raise the nation's food?

It is a fact that many large corporations have designed personality and aptitude tests that, on the average, allow them to determine which job applicants are likely to do well and which are not. Some of the tests include rather detailed questions about the applicant's sex life. Even if the answers to these personal questions are of considerable help in screening applicants, is it ethical for the corporation to make use of such data?

Psychologists have, over the years, devised a whole range of instruments that, when used properly, can measure skills, aptitudes, intelligence, interests, and even basic personality patterns. The fact is that, in today's complex world, these tests are being used more and more widely. The ethical and moral issues raised by this usage all stem from one additional fact: Each person is unique. Among the billions of people who have walked this earth, are now inhabiting it, or will be born in the future, no two individuals are exactly alike. The fact of individual differences has been a challenge to human institutions and social relationships in all periods of history, and schools and shops, courts and congresses, and manufacturing plants and military establishments must be designed to take these differences into account.

Mankind has met this challenge in a variety of ways. Out of the attempts to reveal individuality have come great works of art—novels, plays, portraits. Although in the past individuals have been sorted out into types or classes to be dealt with in different ways for many purposes, what is new in the efforts modern man has been making to deal with differences is his attempt to measure them scientifically.

Early Studies

This undertaking can be said to have begun in 1816, when the German astronomer F. W. Bessel was struck by an account of an incident that occurred in 1796 at the Greenwich Observatory and became curious about what it meant. A young assistant had been dismissed for systematic errors in the time recorded for an event he was routinely required to observe. He was always a little late. Bessel started wondering whether or not it might actually take some persons longer than others to make visual observations. When Bessel tested his idea on several of his fellow astronomers, he found that he was right. For each person, there was a certain minimum time required for him to react to something he was observing. Bessel called this phenomenon the *personal equation*. Later psychologists were to refer to it as *reaction time*.

The next major effort to measure individual differences occurred in Sir Francis Galton's laboratory in London. Galton's book *Inquiries Into Human Faculty and Its Development,* published in 1883, still makes interesting reading. Along with discussions of physical characteristics in which individuals differ, he gives an account of ingenious techniques for measuring differences in sensitivity to various kinds of stimuli, imagery, associations, and sentiments.

During the last quarter of the nineteenth century, laboratories were set up at several German universities for research in the newly defined field of experimental psychology. Most of the psychologists involved in the new movement were attempting to understand general processes and formulate general laws of learning, perception, and thinking—as indeed most experimental psychologists are doing at the present time. But a few of them—notably James McKeen Cattell, an American who took his degree at Leipzig—focused their attention on the differences in the performance of individual subjects who participated in these experiments. It was in this way that the mental-testing movement was born. In 1890 Cattell became the first person to use the term "mental test." He and a number of other investigators who were working in various places at about the turn of the century set out to explore the possibilities of this new concept by developing ways of measuring many aspects of such characteristics as attention, discrimination, and speed of reaction, then finding out how the differences they identified were related to success in real-life situations.

Intelligence Studies

The overall characteristic in which all the early researchers were most interested was intelligence. The first real breakthrough in measuring it came when the French psychologist Alfred Binet, with the collaboration of a colleague named Simon, published in 1905 a graded series of standardized tasks to be administered to children. The level of the last test the child could handle successfully indicated how far his intellectual development had proceeded. In later editions of the intelligence scale, Binet grouped the tasks by year levels and invented the term "mental age" to serve as a summary evaluation of an individual child's attainment. Regardless of his actual chronological age, a child who passed tests typically failed by persons under twelve but who failed tests passed by those above twelve, for example, could be said to have a mental age of twelve.

Binet was able to show that the ability to answer questions and solve problems of the kinds included in his intelligence scale did indeed increase with age throughout the childhood years and that it corresponded fairly closely with the quality that teachers evaluated as brightness or dullness in their pupils. Binet's most important contribution to the science of individual differences was his demonstration that *complex* human abilities, as well as the simpler processes experimental psychologists had been exploring, could be measured.

Much of the history of scientific research on individual differences since Binet's time has involved the elaboration of a tremendous number of intelligence tests for many different special purposes and situations. There are tests of scholastic aptitude for all levels of education from preschool to graduate school. There are infant tests and adult tests, tests for draftees, for job applicants, for mental hospital patients. They range from highly verbal instruments based entirely on vocabulary to completely nonverbal instruments in which even the instructions are given in pantomime. Although there is a tendency for high-scoring individuals to do well and low-scoring individuals to do poorly on all of them, each test makes specific demands on the respondent, so that the judgment as to how intelligent an individual is depends to a certain extent on which test he takes. *No person has a certain fixed, unchangeable intelligence score that shows up no matter how he is tested.*

Intergroup Differences

One of the things early psychologists hoped to do with intelligence tests was to obtain definite answers to age-old questions about whether or not there were intellectual differences between groups. Some set out to compare men and women or boys and girls. Others were interested in comparing Negroes and whites or in ranking nationalities as a basis for decisions about American immigration policy. Unfortunately, it has become increasingly clear with the progress of research that intelligence tests are not suitable instruments for such investigations. Because a person's score reflects what he has learned from his experience as well as his genetic potential for intellectual development, persons whose childhood environment has been quite different from that of the majority of American and European children tend to have lower scores on tests developed in this country. This difference, even when statistically significant, cannot be accepted as evidence that various groups differ in *innate* potential.

The fact that researchers in earlier periods were not as clear on this point as today's social scientists has led to considerable controversy in this area. Social scientists have largely given up efforts to discover whether any race or either sex is inherently inferior and are concentrating their energies instead on analyses of the aspects of the environment that help to shape intellectual development and the meaning of the larger individual differences that are found *within* each racial or sex group.

Varieties of Tests

In the years since the mental-testing movement began, methods for measuring many kinds of human characteristics besides intelligence have been devised. At the present time, their number runs into the thousands. There are tests of school achievement at all levels and in all subject-matter areas. There are tests of vocational aptitudes of many sorts. There are tests of interests, aptitudes, values, and many aspects of personality adjustment. Tests are used in every corner of American society—by schools, clinics, industries, businesses, governmental agencies, and many other organizations.

The magnitude and pervasiveness of the mental-testing enterprise has recently led to some concern on the part of thoughtful observers of social trends. Is testing retarding social mobility, assigning some persons at an early age to an inferior position in society? Could the existence of personality-test scores in biographies, given an awe-inspiring permanence through modern computer technology, work to the disadvantage of individuals years after the tests were taken? How about privacy? Does one citizen have the right to ask another one personal questions about his sexual or religious life? All these ethical and social questions are being seriously considered today.

Characteristics of a Test Although writing a test, publishing it, and selling it to the public may seem similar to the processes the author of a book goes through, they are very different in several ways. Unless certain kinds of research have been done and certain kinds of information collected before the test is made available for general use, a test is not simply worthless but potentially harmful. Because people use tests in making important decisions affecting the course of their own and other people's lives, it is essential that certain standards be understood and followed. Consequently, guidelines to the nature of the essential information that test publishers and test users must obtain has been summarized in the American Psychological Association's *Standards for Educational and Psychological Tests and Manuals.*

Validity The most important considerations for the nature of tests are classified under the general heading of *validity.* The term points to the fact that in order to use test results intelligently we must know *what the test measures.* The title an author gives a test does not tell us this, and the history of the mental-testing movement presents numerous illustrations of tests that were designed for one purpose but turned out to measure something quite different, such as social-intelligence tests that really measured verbal ability and introversion tests that really measured neuroticism.

The kind of evidence that must be assembled to demonstrate validity varies with the nature and purpose of the test. For example, in a school achievement test designed to find out how much individual students know about geometry or American history, the questions asked in the test must constitute an adequate sample of all the things there are to know in that particular field. In judging such a test, one looks for information about how its items are selected. How many experts had a hand in this selection, and how expert were they? Any one course in American history may be biased in the direction of the instructor's interests, but such biases offset one another when a committee of fifteen equally competent people make the decisions.

In the case of an intelligence or aptitude test, the information necessary to establish its validity is some evidence that the behavior of individuals in situations outside the testing room corresponds with their test behavior. This correspondence need not be perfect in order for the test to be useful, but at least a moderate correlation must be demonstrated. If all children who score low on a so-called intelligence test do as well in school as the children who receive moderate or high scores, the test cannot be considered a valid measure of intelligence, or at least the kind of intelligence that schoolwork requires. The indicator of per-

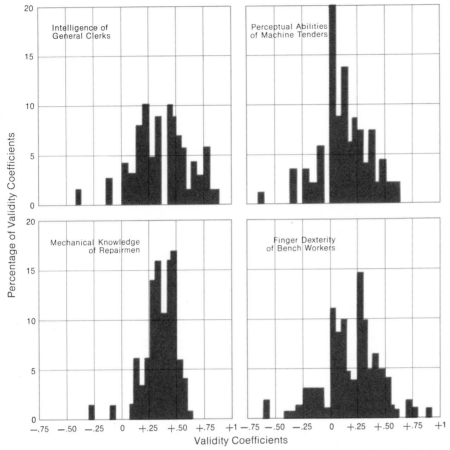

Figure 23.1

Relative frequency distributions of validity coefficients showing examples of the correlations of job proficiency with scores on tests of abilities related to those jobs. Good repairmen tend to have a high level of mechanical knowledge *(bottom left)*, but perceptual abilities are not strongly related to machine-tending performance *(top right)*. (After Ghiselli, 1966.)

formance in real life against which a psychological test is evaluated is called the *criterion*.

It has become clear that test validity is a very complex matter. To ensure that tests do more good than harm, society must make certain that those who offer tests to the public as measures of abilities and personality traits collect the information that is needed to establish what the tests are measuring and that those who use the tests—teachers, personnel managers, and psychotherapists, for example—know and make use of this whole body of research data as a basis for their interpretations of what scores mean.

Reliability

The validity question is by far the most important that must be asked in judging how good any psychological test is, but there are other questions as well. A test's reliability, or accuracy, must always be considered. To what extent do the scores individuals make depend upon the trait the test is designed to measure and to what extent are they a matter of chance? This too has turned out to be a more complicated question than the early mental testers thought it was. There are all sorts of chance factors that can influence scores. Some reflect variations in the way any one individual reacts to the test situation at different times, variations in how hard he tries, how anxious he is, how much he is distracted by what he was thinking about when he came to take the test. Others arise out of variations in how different items in the test are related to particular experiences of the individuals who answer the questions. For example, if the word "philately" is an item in the vocabulary section of an intelligence test, the testees who happen to have watched a television program on stamp collecting the night before will probably give the right answer whether they are highly intelligent or not. All test scores contain chance components. What the person who constructs a test must do is try to keep them to a minimum and to provide the users of the test with the kind of research evidence that will enable them to make proper allowances for such components.

Norms Still another kind of information that must be provided if a test is to be useful comes under the general heading of *norms*. A score in itself tells an individual very little unless he knows what kinds of scores other people have made. It is customary for mental testers to take the arithmetic average as a reference point and indicate how far above or below average any given score is. There are many ways of doing this. On the IQ scale with which the public is most familiar (see below), 100 is the average figure; and scores, at least for young children, can range all the way from 0 to about 200. But because there are many more scores near the average than in the most extreme categories, about 67 percent of the population when tested on a commonly used test of intelligence obtain IQ scores between 85 and 115. Figure 23.2 shows norms for several well-known tests.

The most common systems for translating the actual "raw" scores individuals make into figures that relate them to the whole distribution of scores for a group of persons are the *percentile* system and the *standard-score* system. Each has many variations. The essential thing a percentile shows is the proportion of the individuals in the group who scored below a designated point in the distribution. The essential thing a standard score shows is the distance of the individual score

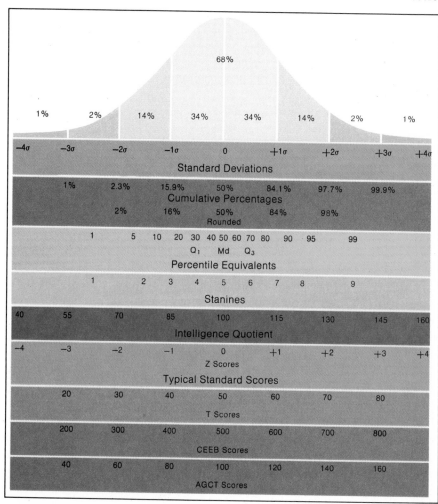

Figure 23.2
The relationships among several types of derived scores and the scores from several well-known tests.
(After Seashore, 1955.)

from the point designating the average. To generate norm tables of either sort is not difficult after a group of people has been tested. What is more difficult for the producer of a test is to make sure that the group on which norms are based is really representative of the population in which the test will be used. The users of tests must consider carefully the information about the composition of the group on which norms are based if they are to interpret obtained scores correctly.

Many other characteristics of good tests might be mentioned, but none are so important as the three we have discussed. If a test is a valid measure of a characteristic in which we are interested, if it is fairly reliable or accurate, and if the norms facilitate clear interpretations of where individuals stand in the groups with which they may be reasonably compared, then we may consider the test's length, its attractiveness, the clarity of the instructions, the ease of scoring, and many other things. Any one of these factors may determine which of several tests available will be chosen for a particular purpose. But no advantage in convenience or attractiveness can compensate for negative or nonexistent evidence with regard to what the test measures, how accurate the scores are, or how the norm group was chosen. For a standardized test designed to be used in many situations, these three requirements are essential.

Although there have been many arguments about the definition of intelligence and many sophisticated discussions of what intelligence tests measure, the fact of gross intellectual differences between individuals and the need to adapt social institutions to such differences are as obvious today as they were in the late 1800s, when psychologists initiated serious attempts to construct intelligence tests. Most of us have encountered a mentally retarded child who, though he may look quite normal, has extreme difficulty even in following simple directions, to say nothing of mastering the reading, writing, and arithmetic that schools require children to learn. Many of us have also met or at least heard of some extremely bright child who at six was studying calculus and astronomy and at ten had moved on to Einstein's theories of relativity. All the evidence we have on the subject suggests that these differences are to some extent hereditary.

When the average man uses the term "IQ," it is usually these innate differences to which he refers. Psychologists are much more cautious. They have learned from nearly a century of research how complex the problem of separating heredity from environment really is. Although they would agree that differences in what we measure with intelligence tests are to some extent genetically determined—research on identical twins has produced the clearest evidence of this—they know that an individual's score also reflects his upbringing, especially his education, as well as his genes. It is not really necessary to establish that a test measures innate differences in order to draw limited conclusions from it. We should confine our judgments of people to such limited conclusions. For example, test scores alert a seventh-grade history teacher to the fact that one student is equipped at the outset of the course to do excellent work and should be held to a high standard, whereas another may have much more difficulty in grasping the main ideas and should be given special help. The teacher need not concern herself with whether the differences reflect heredity or environment.

One more misconception about IQ should be mentioned before specific tests are discussed. The term "IQ" was designed to be used for tests scaled by age levels, as Binet's original test was. A child's *mental age* indicated the age of the children in the norm group whose performance his performance just matched. If he could pass the test for ten-year-olds but not for eleven-year-olds, his mental

Intelligence Tests

Figure 23.3

The distribution of IQ scores on the revised Stanford-Binet Intelligence Scale. (After Terman and Miller, 1937.)

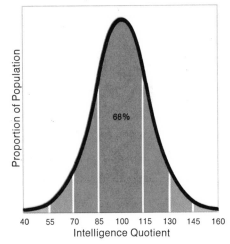

age was ten. It was an easy step from this concept to an index of the rate of mental growth. One simply divided the child's mental age by his chronological age to obtain an *intelligence quotient* (multiplying by 100 to get rid of the decimals).

The IQ turned out to have serious defects, and it is now seldom used as a general index of intellectual quality. The term, however, had been taken up by the public and made a part of common speech. Thus, it is still used as a label for derived scores involving no *quotient* of any sort. It would be less ambiguous to employ some other label, but people in general seem to prefer this one. We need to understand that a person's IQ is not immutable and does not indicate *how much* of any hypothetical capacity he possesses. It simply tells us how much above or below average his present performance is for the group with which he has been compared. The average, of course, is 100.

Intelligence tests can be classified in many ways, but the two most comprehensive categorizations are *individual versus group* and *verbal versus performance*. We shall look at a few examples from these categories.

Individual Tests

The individual test that has had the longest continuous use, the Stanford-Binet scale, follows the pattern Binet set up of grouping tests by age levels. In order to stimulate and maintain interest, the group of tests for each age consists of a variety of tasks, both verbal and performance. The examiner is trained to carry out the standardized instructions exactly but at the same time to put the child at ease, to make friends with him, and to get him to pay attention and try as hard as he can. The best way we can be sure that differences in scores do not reflect

---

WAIS RECORD FORM
Wechsler Adult Intelligence Scale

Name _____
Birth Date _____ (MO DAY YR.) Age _____ Sex _____ Marital: S M D W (CIRCLE ONE)
Nat. _____ Color _____ Tested by _____
Place of Examination _____ Date _____
Occupation _____ Education _____

TABLE OF SCALED SCORE EQUIVALENTS*

Scaled Score	Information	Comprehension	Arithmetic	Similarities	Digit Span	Vocabulary	Digit Symbol	Picture Completion	Block Design	Picture Arrangement	Object Assembly	Scaled Score
19	29	27-28		26	17	78-80	87-90					19
18	28	26		25		76-77	83-86	21		36	44	18
17	27	25	18	24		74-75	79-82		48	35	43	17
16	26	24	17	23	16	71-73	76-78	20	47	34	42	16
15	25	23	16	22	15	67-70	72-75		46	33	41	15
14	23-24	22	15	21	14	63-66	69-71	19	44-45	32	40	14
13	21-22	21	14	19-20		59-62	66-68	18	42-43	30-31	38-39	13
12	19-20	20	13	17-18	13	54-58	62-65	17	39-41	28-29	36-37	12
11	17-18	19	12	15-16	12	47-53	58-61	15-16	35-38	26-27	34-35	11
10	15-16	17-18	11	13-14	11	40-46	52-57	14	31-34	23-25	31-33	10
9	13-14	15-16	10	11-12	10	32-39	47-51	12-13	28-30	20-22	28-30	9
8	11-12	14	9	9-10		26-31	41-46	10-11	25-27	18-19	25-27	8
7	9-10	12-13	7-8	7-8	9	22-25	35-40	8-9	21-24	15-17	22-24	7
6	7-8	10-11	6	5-6	8	18-21	29-34	6-7	17-20	12-14	19-21	6
5	5-6	8-9	5	4		14-17	23-28	5	13-16	9-11	15-18	5
4	4	6-7	4	3	7	11-13	18-22	4	10-12	8	11-14	4
3	3	5	3	2		10	15-17	3	6-9	7	8-10	3
2	2	4	2	1	6	9	13-14	2	3-5	6	5-7	2
1	1	3	1		4-5	8	12	1	2	5	3-4	1
0	0	0-2	0	0	0-3	0-7	0-11	0	0-1	0-4	0-2	0

SUMMARY

TEST	Raw Score	Scaled Score
Information		
Comprehension		
Arithmetic		
Similarities		
Digit Span		
Vocabulary		
Verbal Score		
Digit Symbol		
Picture Completion		
Block Design		
Picture Arrangement		
Object Assembly		
Performance Score		
Total Score		

VERBAL SCORE _____ IQ _____
PERFORMANCE SCORE _____ IQ _____
FULL SCALE SCORE _____ IQ _____

*Clinicians who wish to draw a "psychograph" on the above table may do so by connecting the subject's raw scores. The interpretation of any such profile, however, should take into account the reliabilities of the subtests and the lower reliabilities of differences between subtest scores.

motivation rather than ability is to try to ensure maximum motivation in all subjects tested.

In administering the scale, the examiner tries the child out on some questions, often from the vocabulary test, to locate the proper level at which to start. If it appears that he is at least as bright as the average nine-year-old, he is given the test for year nine. If he misses some of them, the examiner drops back to year eight. After locating the *basal age,* he proceeds with the more difficult tests at later year levels, and the child is given extra credit for the ones he can pass. When a child reaches the difficulty level at which no tests can be passed, the testing session ends. In the final scoring, the mental age indicates how high a level of development the testee has reached, and the IQ indicates how his rate of growth up to this point compares with that of his age mates. At the same time, the examiner has picked up a good deal of qualitative information about how the child's mind works, information often very useful to teachers or psychotherapists who deal with him. The original Binet tests were designed for school-age children, but the successive revisions of the Stanford-Binet tests have extended the scale downward into the preschool levels and upward into the adult levels.

The other individual scales that have been most frequently used are those developed by Wechsler: the WAIS (Wechsler Adult Intelligence Scale) and the WISC (Wechsler Intelligence Scale for Children). These tests, like the Stanford-Binet, are made up of both verbal and performance tests, but they are arranged

Figure 23.7
Wechsler test.

differently, with verbal tests and performance tests in a ratio of about 6 to 5. Within each half, tests of the same kind are grouped together and arranged in order of difficulty. The examiner administers these sets of tests, one by one, starting at the beginning with a very easy item and continuing until the end or until the person has missed three items in succession.

Mental-age scores are not obtained on the Wechsler tests, but one does come out with separate scale scores for each kind of subtest—vocabulary, information, arithmetic, picture arrangement, block design, and so on—and separate verbal and performance IQs. (These scale scores are primarily indications of how much above or below average for his norm group the testee is.) Here too the examiner is able to sketch a qualitative picture of how the individual reacts to different kinds of challenges, and this finding can be a valuable supplement to the scores themselves.

Group Tests

Group intelligence tests, whose ancestors are the famous Army Alpha and Army Beta, developed during World War I for classifying soldiers, also come in verbal and performance varieties and in many combinations of the two. The convenience and economy of group testing have led to their use in preference to individual tests in schools, employment offices, and many other mass testing situations, whereas individual tests still dominate the clinic.

One of the most important differences between group and individual tests is that group tests tend to be more specialized in content and range of applicability. Unfortunately, however, it is not possible to pick out one or two tests that are as representative of group tests as the Stanford-Binet and Wechsler instruments are of individual tests. Rather, it has turned out to be more feasible to build special tests for particular purposes in particular situations than to construct all-purpose group testing instruments. Whatever their particular titles, tests of scholastic aptitude are specialized intelligence tests, made up of the kinds of items that correlate most closely with school success. There are scholastic aptitude tests for kindergartners, grade school children, high school students, college students, and graduate students. None of them works very well if used at the wrong level.

Tests like the AGCT (Army General Classification Test) and the measure of general intelligence used in state employment offices as part of the GATB (Gen-

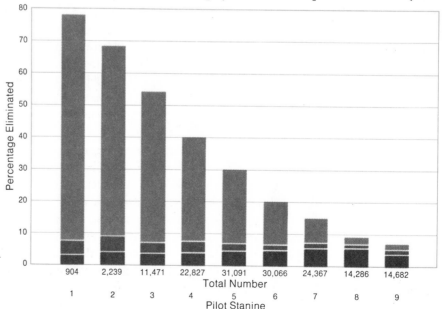

Figure 23.8
The predictive validity of a test used to select men for pilot training. The percentage of men eliminated from training is shown as a function of their performance on the test prior to training.
(After Tyler, 1965.)

eral Aptitude Test Battery) include other kinds of content that have been shown to be related to occupational criteria.

When the same group of people is given several of these tests, all intended as intelligence measures, the correlation between the sets of scores is positive but of only moderate magnitude. Typically, high scorers on one show up better on all the others than low scorers do. But there is such variation in the scores any individual obtains on different tests that it is unsound practice to label him on the basis of any single one he happened to take.

Besides their important applications in facilitating decisions by or about individuals, intelligence tests have served as tools in the investigation of several research questions, including that of the development of mental ability. It is clear that children grow mentally as well as physically, but the important questions are whether or not the individual grows at a constant rate, at what age growth ceases, and whether an individual's ultimate level is maintained or lowered as he ages. As research evidence has accumulated, the answers to all these questions have become somewhat equivocal.

Research Applications

As far as the constancy of the IQ is concerned, it is apparent that individual children differ in their growth patterns. Some show steady acceleration from year to year, so that children with average IQs of about 100 blossom out into distinguished adults with IQs of 130 or higher. Some children show the opposite pattern, their IQ decreasing steadily from early childhood through adolescence. Still others manifest great irregularity from year to year.

In spite of these individual differences, however, there is a general tendency for the initial level of intelligence to be approximately maintained, at least throughout the school years. Bright children tend to remain bright; dull children usually remain dull. Furthermore, some things are known about the factors underlying accelerating and decelerating growth curves. For one thing, children become similar to their parents as they approach maturity. Thus, average children of well-educated parents tend to go up in intelligence, and average children of illiterate parents tend to go down. Moreover, boys are more likely to gain IQ points during their growing years than girls are, perhaps because personality traits of independence, initiative, and aggressiveness are related to IQ gains. Children from remote or backward areas who receive little schooling manifest IQ losses from age to age. What all these studies show is that experience plays a large part in mental development. The total pattern is not laid down at birth.

The studies set up to find out when mental growth stops indicate that this growth pattern seems to depend primarily on education. Children who leave school early show no further increases in intelligence-test scores after fifteen or sixteen on the average, but those who continue through high school and college continue their intellectual growth into the early twenties.

Attempts to find out what happens to intelligence during the years from twenty to eighty have produced even more equivocal results. Those studies that have compared different age groups with one another at a given point in time have usually pointed to a steady decline from age thirty on, but when the same adults have been tested at age thirty and then retested years later, slight increases have generally been obtained, at least up to the sixties. Again, experience, especially early experience, seems to be involved. Persons now in their sixties and seventies grew up in a simpler world than today's and received less formal education. The fact that they score lower now than adults presently in their thirties or forties may indicate that the older group never actually attained as

435

high an average level rather than that they have declined since middle age. However, some evidence indicates that there probably is a genuine falling off with greatly advanced age, varying in its magnitude from one individual to another.

"Intelligence," as the word is used in common speech, is a broad term with many meanings. What psychologists have been measuring by means of intelligence tests is a much more limited quality. This discrepancy, poorly understood by the test-using public, has led to confusion and at times to unwise decisions about individuals. Intelligence tests *do not* measure all-around adaptability. They do not measure common sense. In spite of the fact that scores are clearly related to measures of school success, they do not measure general learning ability either—in fact, evidence indicates that there is no such thing as general learning ability. Those who manifest the most rapid improvement in learning to play the piano, for example, may be slow to develop skill in golf or tennis, and rapid language learners are not necessarily the best learners of mathematics.

Each variety of motor or mental skill draws upon unique learning abilities not measured by intelligence tests. Thus, industrialists who select the highest-scoring applicants in order to get men who can learn factory skills quickly and educators who channel the highest-scoring children into rapid-reading sections are basing their decisions on a misconception, one that may have unfortunate consequences, both for those chosen and for those rejected.

Let us not, however, minimize the contribution that intelligence tests do make to decisions by and about individuals. They do show how well individuals are equipped to handle the acquisition of certain kinds of knowledge—through reading, paying attention, thinking, grasping concepts, and organizing what is read and heard and thought about in coherent patterns. In our kind of civilization, this kind of mental ability is of crucial importance. Tests can help to discover how far along each person is in his development, so that he can be stimulated to greater development. This is one of their central purposes.

Achievement and Aptitude Tests

The construction of achievement tests designed to assess accurately how much individuals know about subjects taught in school and the construction of aptitude tests designed to find out how much talent or capacity individuals have for particular lines of work began as separate enterprises carried on by different psychologists with completely different objectives. As time passed, however, the distinction between achievement and aptitude tests became more and more blurred. As has already been noted for intelligence, evidence accumulated that what at first had been thought to be measures of aptitude—defined as *innate* ability or talent—were partly reflections of different kinds of experience, so that they must be considered in some sense achievement tests. On the other hand, achievement tests often turned out to be the best predictors of many kinds of occupational criteria, so that they were in some sense aptitude tests. Thus, the distinction has come to rest more on purpose than on composition. A test *used* to evaluate what a person knows is an achievement test. The same test *used* to predict how successful he will be is an aptitude test.

Validity Criteria

Different bodies of validity information must, however, be examined for the two purposes. If one is interested in achievement, the important consideration is *content validity,* or how satisfactorily the test samples the concepts and intellectual skills involved in a subject-matter area. If one wishes to assess aptitude, one seeks evidence about the test's *predictive validity,* or how high the correlations be-

Figure 23.9
Mechanical-aptitude test.

tween scores on the test and later criterion measurements in occupational situations are.

Test Construction

In building an achievement test for wide general use, a test-construction agency first secures the cooperation of a committee of experts in the field under consideration. This committee—consisting often of college, high school, or elementary school teachers (depending upon the level at which the new test is to be pitched)—formulates the objectives and lays out the general blueprint for the examination. The items are usually written by professionals employed by the test-construction agency but may be modified by the subject-matter experts.

Trial forms are then administered to groups of several hundred students similar to those for which the final forms are to be used. Careful statistical analysis follows to determine how difficult each item is and whether or not it contributes its fair share to the total score. The reliability and the comparability of parallel forms is also determined. On the basis of this preliminary analysis, sets of test items having the desired characteristics can be put together. Before the new tests are offered for sale, they must be given to carefully selected norm groups so that meaningful scores showing where each respondent stands as compared with other people can be derived. It is important that much of the background information, statistical and otherwise, be put into a user's manual.

In building a test designed to measure aptitude for some kind of work, the criterion is (or should be) the first consideration. The psychologist tries to find a situation in which the performance of a sizable group of workers can be evaluated, then devise some quantitative system (test) for making such evaluations. It need not be precise or highly differentiated to be useful. Just separating the successes from the failures or dividing the whole set of workers into upper, middle, and lower thirds may be sufficient. Good criteria are hard to obtain. Ideally, the next step is to test a new group of applicants and then hire them without reference to their test scores. After a suitable period of time, the psychologist obtains criterion ratings and computes correlations to show how good a prediction of job success can be made from the test scores.

Application

Unlike school achievement tests, which can be used in any school or college with a more or less standard curriculum, aptitude tests must be put through a trial run in each new situation where they are to be used to select workers. Because a test has predicted with reasonable success in one factory does not guarantee that the results will be equally good in another. Consequently, one must be very cautious about inferences from aptitude tests.

The most impressive work in aptitude measurement has been done by the United States Employment Service, which produced a two-and-a-half-hour set of tests, the General Aptitude Test Battery (GATB), that makes it possible for a client to find out whether or not he meets minimum standards for each of a considerable number of occupations. This kind of aptitude information is of considerable value to prospective workers and their counselors.

There was a period when it was hoped that achievement testing would lead to signal improvements in education and that aptitude testing would enable each person to find a niche in life that suited him. Several decades of work have not accomplished these purposes, and it now seems unlikely that further efforts along the same lines will. But useful techniques and instruments have resulted from these efforts. In the hands of people who understand their advantages and their shortcomings, available tests can aid the development of many individuals.

Tests of Interests and Personality Traits

No.	Occupation	L	I	D
1	Actor	Ⓛ	I	D
2	Advertising Man	Ⓛ	I	D
3	Architect	Ⓛ	I	D
4	Military Officer	L	I	Ⓓ
5	Artist	Ⓛ	I	D
6	Astronomer	L	Ⓘ	D
7	Athletic Director	L	Ⓘ	D
8	Auctioneer	L	Ⓘ	D
9	Author of novel	Ⓛ	I	D
10	Author of technical book	L	I	Ⓓ
11	Auto Salesman	L	I	Ⓓ
12	Auto Racer	Ⓛ	I	D
13	Auto Mechanic	L	Ⓘ	D
14	Airplane Pilot	Ⓛ	I	D
15	Bank Teller	L	Ⓘ	D
16	Designer, Electronic Equipment	L	Ⓘ	D
17	Building Contractor	L	Ⓘ	D
18	Buyer of merchandise	L	Ⓘ	D
19	Carpenter	L	Ⓘ	D
20	Cartoonist	Ⓘ	I	D
21	Cashier in bank	L	Ⓘ	D
22	Electronics Technician	L	Ⓘ	D
23	Chemist	L	Ⓘ	D
24	Civil Engineer	L	Ⓘ	D
25	City or State Employee	L	Ⓘ	D
26	Minister, Priest, or Rabbi	Ⓛ	I	D
27	College Professor	L	Ⓘ	D
28	Foreign Service Man	L	Ⓘ	D
29	Dentist	L	Ⓘ	D
30	Draftsman	L	I	Ⓓ
31	Editor	L	Ⓘ	D
32	Electrical Engineer	L	Ⓘ	D
33	Employment Manager	L	Ⓘ	D
34	Geologist	Ⓛ	Ⓘ	D
35	Factory Manager	L	Ⓘ	D
36	Income Tax Accountant	L	Ⓘ	D
37	Farmer	L	Ⓘ	D
38	Labor Union Official	L	I	Ⓓ
39	Art Museum Director	Ⓛ	I	D
40	Foreign Correspondent	Ⓛ	I	D
41	Governor of a State	L	Ⓘ	D
42	Hotel Manager	L	Ⓘ	D
43	Interior Decorator	Ⓛ	Ⓘ	D
44	Interpreter	L	Ⓘ	D
45	Inventor	L	Ⓘ	D

Figure 23.10
Strong Vocational Interest Blank.

The gap that separates the instruments for measuring personality characteristics from those measuring abilities is wider than the gaps that separate the various kinds of ability tests from one another. The big difference is that in attempting to quantify things like interests, values, attitudes, and adjustment, psychologists have proceeded by asking subjects to report on their own behavior directly, as an intelligence test or an achievement test does. Correct answers to questions on an intelligence test indicate that the testee can, in fact, do certain kinds of thinking and solve certain kinds of problems. Correct answers (those receiving credit according to the scoring key) on a social-adjustment inventory indicate only that the person *says* that his relationships with other people are of a satisfactory sort. Anyone familiar with the complexities of personality organization knows that a person may have a variety of reasons for saying what he does about himself.

One way of reducing the ambiguity about what scores on inventories of personal characteristics mean is to develop scoring keys without regard to the apparent significance of the questions and answers. One does this by collecting information about how persons in clearly defined groups actually respond to individual items. This method has worked particularly well in the measurement of vocational interests. The Strong Vocational Interest Blank was constructed by tabulating the responses to each item of a group of men successfully employed in a particular occupation with the responses of a group of "men in general." (A similar instrument for women was developed later.) Only the responses for which there was evidence of clear-cut differences were included in the scoring key for the occupation. The procedure was repeated again and again for the different occupations. The most recent edition of the Strong Vocational Interest Blank for Men can be scored for fifty-nine occupations, and the form for women can be scored for twenty-nine occupations.

What does a person find out about himself by answering these questions about his likes, dislikes, and preferences and receiving a report back from the scoring agency? He should understand first what it does *not* tell him. Because the answers he has given to the questions in no way indicate how competent he would be in the work an occupation requires, the score cannot possibly demonstrate that he has a special ability or talent. A high school dropout can get an A on the engineer scale, for example, and an illiterate can score an A for writer.

438

Statements such as "The test says I should be a lawyer," made after an interest test, indicate an unsound inference. What the scores are related to is the *direction* in life the individual finds most natural or satisfying. There is much evidence that scores on the Strong blank are related to choices individuals make later about entering and remaining in occupations. Years before they even enter medical school, for example, premedical students in college tend to get high physician scores. Many years later, they are likely to be practicing medicine, but those who initially had low scores but went to medical school anyway are likely to have shifted to some other occupation.

The other principal strategy used in developing instruments for personality measurement has been *factor analysis*. Especially since the advent of computers, it has become feasible to correlate the responses individuals in a representative group give to each item with their responses to every other item on the test. What factor analysis serves to do is to reveal the pattern of these correlations. Separate scoring keys can then be constructed for sets of answers that tend to cluster together. If all the items turning up in one of these correlated sets have to do with preferences for thinking, reading, and other kinds of attention to one's inner experience rather than social activity, it is natural to call the set thinking introversion. The Cattell 16 PF (16 personality factor) inventory is probably the most widely known product of this approach to personality measurement, but the GATB also uses factor analysis to clarify what different tests have in common.

Whatever the approach, the problem of *validation* is crucial, as it is in the case of ability measures. We must not jump to conclusions about what a test measures. Evidence must be obtained and its import communicated to test users.

The Significance of Individual Differences

The foregoing discussions have made it clear that there are many deficiencies and unsolved problems related to the measurement of individual differences. Tests for assessing important aspects of human ability and motivation are only partially valid. The inferences we make from these must be tentative and must be checked by evidence from nontest sources.

However, the attempt to take individual differences into consideration is so important an undertaking that we should never lose sight of it when we criticize particular measurement techniques. Ways must be found to provide enough flexibility in our educational system at all levels so that each individual student can learn in his own way, at his own pace, the things it is essential for him to know. Society must provide the organizations and services to enable each person to work at things he can do well and obtain satisfaction from doing, for the diverse contributions of a variety of individuals make any kind of complex social order possible.

24

MEASUREMENT OF PERSONALITY

OF THE FOUR SETS OF ALTERNATIVES listed below, which one of each pair would you prefer doing?

1. Reading the latest novel by one of your favorite authors, or reading the latest scientific textbook in a field of your major interest?

2. Seeing the latest Broadway play, or watching a television documentary on the latest monetary crisis in Europe?

3. Talking to someone you know quite well and trust about current world problems, or talking about your own personal problems?

4. Talking to someone you know quite well about your own personal problems, or talking about his or hers?

Most people are more interested in people than in things or in ideas and concepts; and the person most of us are chiefly interested in is ourself. Socrates' admonition to know thyself is a command most of us are quite ready to heed. And if we are honest with ourselves, most of us will admit that we learn something new about ourselves almost every day. Have you ever heard two of your friends (or worse, two of your enemies) discussing you when they thought you could not hear them? If you have, you know there are facets of your personality that others see but are often hidden from you. What are you really like, from a psychological point of view?

Few areas in psychology stimulate as much interest and curiosity as personality assessment. The layman finds this area interesting because it may offer a key to self-understanding. For the psychologist, this field provides an opportunity for studying one of the richest and most complex phenomena in existence: the human personality. The psychologist is particularly challenged by personality assessment because the personality being studied rarely wholeheartedly enters into the task of revealing himself but rather shows the very human tendency to reveal himself in a favorable light, to describe himself as a sympathetic friend might rather than as a critic would. Consequently, a great deal of research effort has gone into the problem of accurately measuring personality, and a great deal of ingenuity has been directed at overcoming the biases that inevitably creep into measurement. These efforts have produced a remarkable variety of techniques, ranging from personality questionnaires to tasks involving perception of the vertical and perception of inkblots. An equally broad range of characteristics, traits, dispositions, attitudes, and modes of thinking and behaving have been uncovered.

The scope of personality assessment is almost as large as the number of situations in which an individual can reveal his personality. For example, personality can be revealed in attitudes, in vocational interests, and in the functioning of intellectual abilities, and there are corresponding tests and assessment devices to tap these facets of personality. Usually, however, when we think of personality measurement, we think of characteristics that help us understand the quality of a person's relationships with other people; his characteristic orientation to work, to play, and to duty; his reaction to authority; and his characteristic way of evaluating his own self-worth. We also tend to think in terms of those characteristics that, although found in some degree in normal people, take on an extreme form in psychopathological conditions. Similarly, the clinical psychologist interested in assessing psychopathology may use a variety of techniques to uncover various types of perceptual distortion, of limited self-control, of overriding hostility, or of excessive dependence upon repression and denial as defensive mechanisms or upon tendencies to exaggerate physical symptoms, as might be found in a hypochondriac. Thus, although personality is defined very broadly and the number of situations that might be used to reveal something about the nature of the person is very large indeed, the focus of this chapter is upon those techniques that seek to assess characteristic variables at the core of personality.

Personality Variables

Attempts to conceptualize and categorize types of people extend almost to the beginning of written history. About twenty-three centuries ago, Hippocrates adapted the early Greek conception of the four basic elements of air, water, fire, and earth to the basic four substances postulated to exist in the living body, namely, blood, phlegm, yellow bile, and black bile. Claudius Galen, anticipating modern developments in endocrinology and psychopharmacology, sought to link the four substances in the human body to types of temperament. An abundance of phlegm was thought to produce a phlegmatic person; yellow bile and black bile produced the choleric and melancholic person, respectively. Although Galen's conception has persisted for almost 1,800 years and has made its way into the vocabulary and the lay conception of personality, its major failure, above and beyond the discredited physiological theory upon which it rests, is that its scope is too limited. More recent historical efforts to systematize and classify personality have had perhaps equally profound effects upon our ways of thinking about personality but have similarly not been entirely satisfying in their completeness.

In this century, attempts to characterize the kinds and natures of men have been as frequent as personality theories and theorists. Each of the theories of personality discussed in Chapter 25 has, in fact, its own list of the essential attributes of individuals that characterize them and make them unique among their fellows.

Personality Inventories

All theories of personality and all thinking about man, his nature, and his difficulties share in common certain concerns, and it is these that have attracted the most persistent attempts at measurement. People range from normally well adjusted to pathologically out of touch with reality. They have a variety of specific problems that can be characterized rather accurately. They are interested in a variety of different things. They are suited for different kinds of work and play. They hold different values, and their opinions about issues differ. Working with these differences, a personality inventory attempts, from the answers to direct or indirect questions, to characterize the personality of an individual.

The three personality inventories discussed below span a variety of different kinds of measurable human characteristics, from psychopathology to values to psychological needs, and also illustrate different approaches to the problems of measuring personality. Two of these personality inventories—the Minnesota Multiphasic Personality Inventory and the Allport-Vernon Study of Values—are old and widely used. The third—the Personality Research Form—is relatively new and embodies the latest developments in theory and computer technology as it is applied to personality assessment.

The Minnesota Multiphasic Personality Inventory (MMPI)

About thirty years ago Hathaway and McKinley undertook a series of studies that had important implications for personality assessment and resulted in the most widely used personality inventory, the MMPI. The MMPI was developed by contrasting the answers of normal persons with those of psychiatric patients in order to identify items where the pattern of response was different. These items were then combined into groups called *scales,* which were used originally to aid in the evaluation and diagnosis of mental illness but have been used more recently in a much wider variety of situations.

The authors began with a set of approximately 560 statements. Many of these items dealt directly with psychiatric symptoms—including delusions, hallucinations, ideas of reference, obsessive and compulsive states, and sadistic and masochistic trends—but most of the other items ranged very widely over a variety of questions dealing with physical health, general habits, family and marital status, occupational and educational problems, and attitudes relevant to religion, sex, politics, and social problems. It is fortunate that the MMPI items were so diverse, because many of the items apparently irrelevant for the initial purposes of the inventory have been found to be useful not only in studying psychopathology but also in developing a variety of other scales, many measuring characteristics of normal people.

The authors next identified over a period of three or four years 800 carefully studied clinical cases at the Neuropsychiatric Division of the University of Minnesota Hospitals. Each one of these cases had been carefully diagnosed according to one of a number of categories used for psychiatric diagnosis at that time. In addition to the patients, the authors administered the basic MMPI items to 724 people considered normal who happened to be visiting relatives or friends in the university hospital and indicated that they were not at the time under the care of a physician. Other normal groups used in the development of MMPI scales included young persons of college age seeking guidance at the University of Minnesota Testing Bureau, WPA project workers, and individuals on medical wards of the University of Minnesota Hospitals.

■ SCALE CONSTRUCTION

The scale construction can be illustrated by a single scale based on the differing responses of a clinical group showing relatively uncomplicated depressive patterns and normal individuals. The entire set of 560 items was administered to depressive patients and normal subjects. From this large set, about 53 items were found to differentiate the two groups significantly. Not surprisingly, the majority

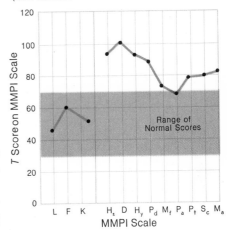

Figure 24.2
An MMPI profile.
(After Dahlstrom and Welsh, 1960.)

443

of these items dealt with pessimism of outlook, mood state, energy level, control of impulses, feelings of hopelessness and worthlessness, a lack of quickness in thought and action, and thoughts concerning death and suicide. These are, of course, predominant symptoms of clinical depression. Later, a few additional items were added to sharpen the discrimination between other types of psychiatric patients. Although the original criterion group involved the differentiation of patients who carried mainly a psychotic diagnosis, the MMPI D (for Depression) scale has subsequently been found to be a highly sensitive indicator of less severe forms of depression—and indeed of varying mood states—and of reaction to various forms of psychological treatment.

In a similar way, eight additional clinical scales were developed for the original MMPI, as well as a scale of masculinity-femininity based on the different responses of males and females to that set of items. This scale, though not a clinical scale in the same sense as the others, has been found useful in understanding not only clinical patients but people within the normal range. In addition, four validity scales were constructed. These scales described not so much the individual's personality directly but rather the manner in which he took the test. Their primary value, therefore, is in revealing the degree of confidence we can place in the results of psychological testing. Four validity scales are used in the MMPI: (1) a scale indicating the number of omissions or "cannot say" responses; (2) a lie scale, revealing the individual's tendency to respond in an implausibly desirable direction; (3) the F scale, revealing a pattern of deviation in responding that is sometimes suggestive that the individual might not have understood the questions; and (4) the K scale, reflecting the tendency to be defensive and to deny certain types of symptoms.

In addition to the thirteen scales already described, over 200 special scales have been devised for the MMPI by a great variety of investigators. These scales vary from such specific types of psychopathology as "bizarre sensory experiences" to such normal and even desirable qualities as the extent to which an individual possesses a "counselor personality," as well as a scale to predict college achievement and a scale for ego strength.

■ INTERPRETATION

The number of research studies using the MMPI is very large, covering extensively the range of possible investigations in personality. A decade ago, when Dahlstrom and Welsh compiled their MMPI handbook, they cited over a thousand titles dealing with MMPI research. Since that time, this figure has probably tripled. Many of these investigations have been clinical in nature, but others have focused upon the psychology of responding to a questionnaire, and still others have used the MMPI primarily as a device for understanding different facets of personality.

Clinically, the usual interpretation of an MMPI protocol is based upon the patterning of the scale scores rather than upon the absolute elevation of the scores. A great deal of information has been gathered about thousands of people who have been classified by the MMPI profile and the pattern of symptoms revealed by the individual. Since the mid-1950s, the electronic computer has come into its own, and with its availability there has emerged a development of computer programs to write clinical reports based largely on MMPI data. Many clinical psychologists believe that the results from either computer-based characterizations of personality or the use of statistical tables to generate descriptions of personality will yield more accurate portrayals than will the use of trained judges, and there is increasing evidence to support this contention. This objective approach, starting in the personality-assessment area, has become more general in other disciplines. It has uncovered the advantages of an actuarial or statistical over a clinical approach in areas where there is a degree of uncertainty, such as in medical diagnosis and in weather forecasting.

■APPLICATION

The MMPI has found its greatest utility in the psychiatric clinic and hospital. Nevertheless, it has been used for a variety of other purposes, including employment screening, college student counseling, and personality research. Its major advantage, and the major reason why it will probably be around for quite some time, is the tremendous storehouse of knowledge gained about its utility in different situations. Although it has not proved to be as accurate a diagnostic tool for the differential diagnosis of psychiatric disorders as its authors had hoped, it undoubtedly has exceeded their aspirations in regard to the wide range of applications that it has been found to have. Its major disadvantages are the extent to which its accuracy can be upset by response biases, such as the tendency always to choose desirable or undesirable alternatives, and its predominantly psychopathological content.

The Study of Values, developed by Allport and Vernon, is very different from the MMPI in that it does not focus at all upon pathological aspects of personality but rather upon the view that personality is best revealed through a study of an individual's values or his evaluative attitudes. Unlike the MMPI, the Study of Values is most appropriate for college students or adults with higher than average educational backgrounds. The authors recommend that the Study of Values be used primarily in contexts where the full cooperation of the subjects is obtained, such as might be expected in vocational counseling, classroom demonstration, and research. Although it has been shown to have important implications for vocational choice and vocational satisfaction—it was found, for example, to be quite highly predictive of occupational career choice of Wellesley students during the period up to fifteen years after graduation from college—it is not recommended as a device to be used for personnel selection unless specific research is undertaken to demonstrate its applicability in a particular setting.

The Study of Values

■UNDERLYING TYPOLOGY

The Study of Values is based on a typology first advanced by Eduard Spranger, who maintained that a person is best understood by his interests and intentions rather than by his achievements. Thus, it is extremely important to investigate the nature of the values that distinguish different people. For Spranger, values could be summarized in terms of six major types, each of which was considered to be a kind of idealized individual, very much the same as the Jungian extravert

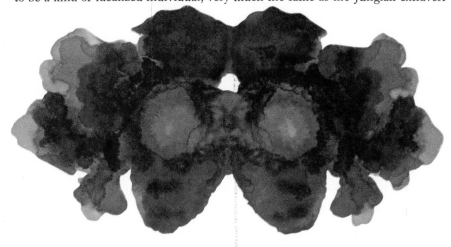

445

and introvert types. The six ideal types, according to Spranger, were the theoretical, the economic, the aesthetic, the social, the political, and the religious. Although Spranger believed that an individual could be characterized primarily in terms of a single value type, he also allowed for combinations, an approach consistent with that used by the authors of the Study of Values in developing a profile of values.

■ INTERPRETATION

A great wealth of data has accumulated about the interpretation of the value scores. One source of information is based on the scores obtained by people in different occupations. Figure 24.4 is a relative representation that contrasts the average scores obtained by three different male occupational or student groups: undergraduate students at a college of engineering, personnel and guidance workers, and clergymen. Figure 24.5 similarly describes three contrasting female occupational groups: freshman medical students at a number of medical schools, students at a school of design, and social workers at Veterans Administration

Figure 24.4
The Study of Values. Relative scores of three male populations.

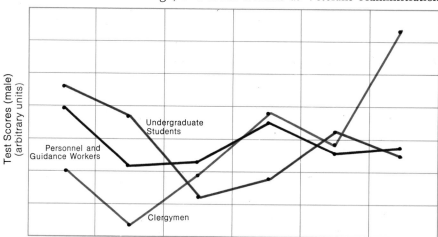

Figure 24.5
The Study of Values. Relative scores of three female populations.

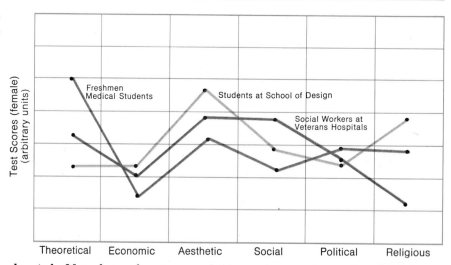

hospitals. Note that with quite remarkable consistency, the profiles of the groups conform quite well to what one would expect. Individuals within each group might be expected to vary within a considerable range, but it is reasonable to expect that individuals most satisfied with a particular occupation would be those whose value profiles were consistent with and typical of those individuals already in the occupation.

■ APPLICATION

The role of different values has been shown to affect a variety of different kinds of performances and to be influential in the choice of friends and mates. In general, profiles of married couples and of friends tend to be similar. Values have also been found to be important determinants of perception. In one study of selective perception, words were flashed on a screen for very brief intervals. Each word appeared for such a short fraction of a second that the subjects had difficulty in recognizing them. Each of the words was related to one of the value areas. For instance, there were words like "profit" and "money" that were linked to the economic value, and words like "beauty" and "poetry" that were linked to the aesthetic value. The experimenters presumed that each individual's recognition threshold would be lowest for words most closely related to whatever value area he scored highest on, a presumption that the results of the experiment tended to confirm.

In a similar study, recorded words were presented to subjects at such a low volume that the subjects could barely hear them. Again, the subjects recognized most accurately those words most closely related to their own values. These findings indicate that values may represent a very central and fundamental aspect of personality, determining not only such things as what an individual believes but even what he is likely to see when confronted with an ambiguous or barely perceptible situation. Indeed, values have caused some to begin wars but have caused others to undergo privation to avoid war; a value may serve as the motivating force to erect a thing of beauty or may serve to justify such institutions as child labor and slavery. Very little of history, and even less of personality, would be understandable without some appreciation of the diversity of human values. The fact that they can be manifested in measurable form renders them more susceptible to scientific study.

The Personality Research Form

The Personality Research Form (PRF), recently developed by Jackson, is one of the first personality-assessment devices to make use of the upsurge in knowledge in personality assessment and theory over the last decade and, at the same time, the flexibility and capacity of the modern digital computer in scale development. Prior to the development of the PRF, most personality questionnaires were based on a single strategy of scale construction such as the method of empirical item selection with an outside criterion, used for the MMPI. The PRF, however, utilizes a sequential strategy of scale development with a number of steps, ranging first from a very careful definition of the variables to be employed to a series of statistical procedures designed to maximize homogeneity of content, freedom from response bias toward desirable answers, and the distinctiveness between scales. It is available in both a long form, containing twenty-two scales, and a standard form, consisting of fifteen scales.

■ASSESSMENT ITEMS

The initial definitions of the characteristics to be measured by the PRF were the variables of personality described by Murray and his associates (Chapter 25). In the three decades following publication of Murray's personality variables, however, a great deal has been learned about these variables and personality more generally than could be incorporated into the system.

Table 24.1 provides an illustration of the method of item selection used in the PRF for the aggression scale. Note that in Table 24.1 three items are listed that are each highly correlated with the total aggression scale, indicating high representation of the content they are supposed to be reflecting (aggression). Note also that for the first three items, all the correlations with irrelevant scales are substantially lower than they are for the relevant aggression score. Furthermore, the correlations between each item and a scale reflecting desirability bias are also

447

lower than for the relevant aggression scale. Finally, the proportion of people endorsing the first three items ranges between .30 and .52. Had these been too extreme, below .05 and above .95, the item would not have been incorporated into the PRF. Examples of items that did not meet criteria for inclusion in the final form are represented by items 4 and 5 in Table 24.1. Note that the first of these items correlated more highly with the order scale than they did with the aggression scale. Such an item would be a better measure of the relevant scale than it would be of aggression, but because it does correlate moderately with both aggression and order, it was considered preferable to eliminate such items entirely in the PRF construction than to rekey them. The fifth item is an illustra-

Table 24.1—PRF Item Selection Method: Aggression Scale*

Item	Correlation with Total Scales				
	Endorsement Proportion	Aggres- sion	Desir- ability	Achieve- ment	Order
1. When I am irritated, I let it be known.	.52	.76	−.32	−.30	−.14
2. I swear a lot.	.44	.70	−.41	−.23	−.29
3. Life is a matter of "push or be shoved."	.30	.57	−.31	−.28	−.10
4. I think that it is a help to other people when I point out their faults to them.	.73	.17	.19	.03	.20
5. I am often jealous of others.	.46	.41	−.43	−.40	−.13

*There were a total of 140 items and 142 subjects in the original test.
Source: Items from the Personality Research Form published by Research Psychologists Press, Inc., © by Douglas N. Jackson. Reproduced by permission.

tion of a statement that is too heavily representative of a bias to choose the desirable response. It proved to correlate more highly with a scale reflecting tendencies to respond desirably and undesirably than it did with aggression. In this particular instance, the item is primarily eliciting tendencies to respond undesirably.

In general, a scale made up primarily of such items would not be as useful as one made up of items heavily representative of the content that they were designed to measure because scores on such a scale would primarily reflect the façade of a particular respondent who consciously or unconsciously reveals himself more desirably than does the average person. In the construction of the entire set of 22 PRF scales, over 3,000 items were written; and after such obviously unsuitable items as 4 and 5 in Table 24.1 were eliminated, the items on each scale were ranked in terms of a statistical index that sought to maximize relevance to content while minimizing bias. The final sets of scales proved to be relatively free of bias and have been shown to possess a property of *convergent and discriminant validity*. Thus, these scales show a substantially higher correlation with distinct criterion measures, such as might be represented by behavior ratings of traits like aggression by persons who know the respondent well, than with irrelevant traits.

■ PRF PROFILES

The PRF scores are usually summarized in the form of a profile. Figure 24.8 gives an illustration of the PRF profile of a twenty-one-year-old female college student who during her senior year of college became president of the student association while also serving on the university debating team and achieving a level of scholastic performance that consistently placed her on the dean's list. Note that the salient features of the profile are consistent with this pattern of performance. There are elevations for exhibition and dominance, both of which have been

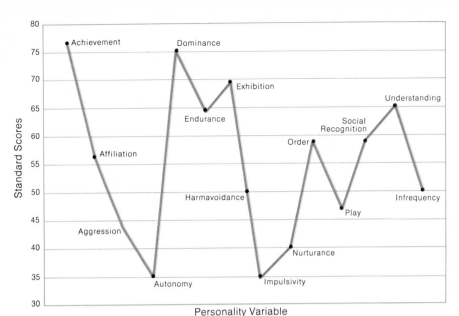

Figure 24.8
Personality Research Form profile of an outstanding college girl.
(After Jackson, 1967.)

shown to be associated with the tendency to be ascendent and talkative in small groups. There are also elevations for achievement and understanding. Because achievement involves the seeking of standards of excellence and understanding primarily involves a kind of intellectual curiosity, we might conclude that these characteristics are consistent with her outstanding level of performance in academic work. Note that the score for autonomy is relatively low, implying that she prefers to work with people rather than independently and that her interaction with others is more affiliative than aggressive.

■ INTERPRETATION

In the interpretation of personality-inventory profiles, a great deal of attention is often directed at interpreting *patterns* of total scores rather than the scores directly. There is a tendency to seek to capture a total life style as revealed by the relative importance of various traits in the individual's personality. Predominant dimensions of personality have been shown to be associated with vocational interests, indicating that one's orientation to other people, to work, and to characteristic activities may be revealing of a life style that also reveals itself in the choice of an occupation and the tendency to be satisfied in one line of work rather than another.

In a study linking PRF scores to scores derived from the Strong Vocational Interest Blank, seven dimensions common to both vocational interests and personality were identified. One of these was particularly interesting in that it contrasted different modes of either controlling or expressing impulses. At one extreme, PRF scales for order and cognitive structure, which together imply a certain planfulness and care with details, were associated with scales reflecting interest patterns of accountants and office workers. At the other extreme of this same dimension were the PRF scales for impulsivity, change, exhibition, and autonomy. Associated with these were the vocations of author-journalist, lawyer, clinical psychologist, and advertiser. Each of these occupations would seem to have in common the possibility of some freedom of expression and escape from routine. This dimension is presented in Figure 24.9, together with a second dimension labeled human-relations management.

Projective tests get at personality characteristics by asking persons to interpret or tell stories about ambiguous or meaningless material. The idea is that because there is no certain meaning specified by the testing material, any meaning that

Projective Tests

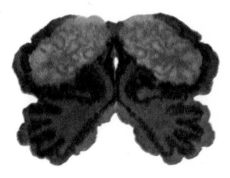

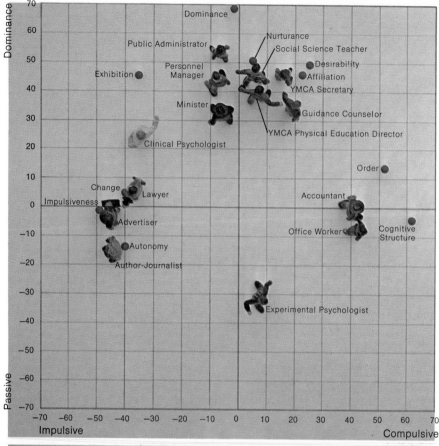

Figure 24.9

The positions of members of several occupations and the positions of several PRF characteristics (red points) on the dimensions of impulsivity-compulsivity and dominance-passivity. Note that occupations that are very close on one dimension may be widely separated on the other, suggesting that these are independent dimensions of personality. (After Jackson, 1967.)

the person puts into his story about it must come from himself and may thus be revealing of his personality.

The projective tests are based on a different set of principles than are personality questionnaires. Instead of focusing upon specific traits and seeking to measure these with high precision, projective tests place an individual in an ambiguous situation and provide him with an opportunity to reveal both his strengths and his weaknesses by the idiosyncratic manner in which he may perceive or interpret a particular situation. Some involve highly ambiguous materials, like inkblots. Others involve the individual's tendency to interpret a social situation as represented in a picture. Others involve doing drawings, modeling with clay, or even acting out roles, as in psychodrama.

The Rorschach Technique

Perhaps the best-known projective technique is the set of inkblots developed by Hermann Rorschach, the Swiss psychiatrist, who with remarkable insight and considerable preliminary exploration developed a set of ten inkblots. Rorschach developed a scoring system that has been modified but is still in wide use today.

■ADMINISTRATION

Typically, the Rorschach, as well as other projective techniques, is administered in a situation in which the examiner and the subject are seated facing each other. The subject is instructed to report his interpretation of materials, and cards are handed to him one by one. With the Rorschach technique, administration is divided into a free-association period and an inquiry period. During the free association, the individual simply identifies what he sees. For example, a certain area of a blot might resemble an airplane or a rocket. During the inquiry, the examiner asks certain general questions in order to establish the manner in which each percept may be scored.

■INTERPRETATION

In general, scoring involves the use of three major categories. The first indicates the extent of the inkblot used, ranging from small or even minute detail to the whole blot. The second category relates to the determinants of the response—whether form, color, shading, or the activity level were primarily responsible for the individual's seeing the inkblot the way he did. Combinations of determinants are possible, and provision is made for scoring in terms of quality. The third major category of scoring the Rorschach test is in terms of content.

In most scoring systems content is the least important aspect of the individual's performance, although to the layman this would seem to be the primary function of giving the test. Certain types of responses to inkblots, however, are considered *pathognomic,* that is, indicative of the possibility of serious psychopathology, because they occur with substantial frequency in certain types of mental patients and more rarely in normal individuals. These responses include *contaminations,* the tendency to mix indiscriminately parts belonging to different animals and humans, and *confabulations,* referring to the tendency to go far beyond the material at hand in responding, often with somewhat bizarre overtones (see Chapter 19).

It would be a mistake to place too much emphasis upon the scoring techniques used by Rorschach examiners. More than a psychometric device, the Rorschach method is impressionistic, based to a large extent upon the individual clinician's insight, his capacity for careful observation, and his awareness of the manner in which psychopathology is revealed not only by the formal qualities of a person's reported perceptions but also by the nuances involved in the interpersonal situation. An individual's reaction to the test situation itself may be used as part of the assessment procedure. Some subjects, for example, are extremely defensive and wary in the test situation, but others define it in authoritarian terms, seeking to be extremely submissive to the examiner's every wish. Still others view it as a competitive task, with the expectation that their performance will be evaluated against some standard and judged in terms of its quality. Each one of these interpersonal styles within the situation may be judged by the examiner as revealing of the individual's personality structure. The fact that the individual has great latitude in how he acts in the situation, while detracting from the possible reliability of the results, at the same time provides an opportunity for him to reveal himself.

The lack of structure involved in the Rorschach technique, as in many projective techniques, is both a strength and a weakness. It is a strength in the sense that it broadly samples behavior and permits at least the possibility for certain patterns to emerge that might not emerge otherwise. For example, the possibility that an individual might reveal sadistic trends in a more structured test is less likely. Such behavioral tendencies are not commonly revealed in the general population, but like many other kinds of behavior that have low probabilities of occurrence in any given situation, Rorschach's variety of stimulus materials and the relatively unstructured situation permit such trends to appear. The disadvantage of such an approach is that although the possibility exists that a great variety of behavioral tendencies could appear, the test situation itself does not focus clearly on any single set of these.

In a sense, one pays a price for the broad view, and the price is low resolution. Because the stimulus materials are not focused on any one content area, there is no assurance that behavior relevant to this area will be assessed, and if this is the case, many judgments about a particular trait, such as an individual's competitiveness, will not be based on substantial and reliable information. It should also be recognized that the Rorschach technique focuses on aspects and qualities of the individual's receiving and thinking, not necessarily upon the total personality. Better techniques are available for establishing the quality of an individual's interpersonal relationships and of such traits as his integrity, loyalty to friends, and devotion to certain principles.

The Holtzman Inkblot Technique

One of the disadvantages of the Rorschach test is that the scoring categories are often interdependent, illogical, and difficult to interpret. For this reason much of the interpretation of the Rorschach has been on an impressionistic basis. Holtzman recognized the value of a projective device like the Rorschach but, having been trained in psychological measurement, believed it possible to combine the advantages of the projective technique with sound measurement principles. The result was the *Holtzman inkblot technique,* which, although derived from the Rorschach, involves completely new materials and a different scoring system; it is modeled after the Rorschach but has many novel features, all designed to be improvements. Basically, the Holtzman technique involves parallel sets of forty-five cards. Ordinarily, only one response is permitted to each card. This limitation avoids one of the most serious difficulties in Rorschach scoring, namely, that all scores tend to be highly related to the total number of responses that the individual has given. The primary advantage of the Holtzman inkblot technique is that it combines careful standardization with highly reliable scoring. Each card was selected by virtue of its ability to distinguish between groups of college students and of schizophrenic hospitalized patients. The assumption was that cards that did not distinguish between these diverse groups might not be very useful for other purposes. Two forms of the Holtzman technique were developed, designed to be parallel and to yield essentially the same information. The major advantages of the Holtzman technique over the earlier Rorschach are that the scoring procedures, and hence the reliability of the scores, were more rationally conceived and more reliable. Another major advantage is the excellent normative data that have been gathered on groups ranging from five-year-old children to various types of psychologically disturbed adults.

A number of studies have indicated that the Holtzman technique is quite useful for distinguishing between individuals showing different diagnostic symptom patterns and for revealing the distortions in perception and cognition that often accompany psychopathology. The great variety of scores that are possible with this technique, ranging from movement energy level to hostility and sex, provide a continuing basis for research investigations into the relationship between perception and personality. Holtzman has thus provided a technique that while preserving many of the features of the original Rorschach also permits a high degree of reliability in scoring.

Although also a projective device, the Thematic Apperception Test requires a different kind of response than those required by the Rorschach and Holtzman inkblot techniques.

■ADMINISTRATION

The TAT, developed by Murray, consists of a series of twenty cards containing vague pictures of a variety of situations, some of which may seem quite unusual. The examinee is asked to present a coherent story about the picture, including what led up to the situation, what the characters are thinking and feeling, and how it will end. The original suggestion of the authors was to present the pictures in two one-hour sessions, the first involving the more unusual and even bizarre scenes; but most clinical psychologists employing the test select their own series from cards originally developed for children, for males, and for females.

■INTERPRETATION

Analysis of the stories is usually very much a task for the individual clinician. A number of scoring procedures have been devised, but these are rarely used, even by their authors. Originally, Murray suggested that the TAT be interpreted in terms of the need and press system described in Chapter 25, but a variety of other theoretical positions, including psychoanalytic theory, are also employed, depending upon the situation and the taste of the person doing the interpretation.

Figure 24.12
The kinds of pictures used in the TAT.

This procedure would appear to rely heavily upon the skill of the clinician making the interpretations, and in fact research indicates that clinicians agree only moderately well regarding interpretations and predictions. Indeed, their accuracy does not exceed that of psychology students who have not received specific training in TAT interpretation.

All interpretative systems depend on certain underlying assumptions regarding the use of the sort of fantasy tapped by the TAT—for example, that the hero of the story is the one with whom the storyteller identifies, that his fantasies will be revealing of his motives, and that uncommon responses are more likely to be personally significant than more common ones.

A number of very interesting studies have employed the TAT, including studies involving changes arising from unusual states induced by sensory deprivation and the use of drugs. Equally important, the TAT has led to the development of a variety of techniques useful for measuring particular traits like the need for affiliation and McClelland's extensive studies of the need for achievement as judged from the TAT in our own as well as in less achievement-oriented cultures.

Other Projective Tests of Personality

The number of projective personality tests is very large. Some of these tests involve very elaborate scoring systems; others resemble the typical interview in that they merely allow observation of another person in a single situation.

■THE WORD-ASSOCIATION TECHNIQUE

One of the earliest techniques for personality assessment was the word-association technique, described by Sir Francis Galton almost a hundred years ago. In this simple technique, the subject is merely instructed to say the first word that comes into his consciousness after hearing a stimulus word. A large number of words are ordinarily read by the examiner, and the subject responds to each of these. Jung systematized the procedure as it applies to assessment. He carefully selected his words so that they might be revealing of psychiatric problems and analyzed responses primarily in terms of reaction time, content, and the nonvocal responses that often accompany a response. For example, if a subject cannot think of any response to the concept "Mother" but flushes and wrings his hands, this reaction might be duly noted and interpreted.

Further adaptations of this technique at the Menninger Foundation not only focused on areas of psychological disturbance but also used the procedure as a method to study formal thought processes. The approach involved techniques for analyzing the possibility of peculiar or disturbed association processes and the possible impairments in thought that might be revealed, for example, by a loss of memory for the associates when the list is repeated a second time. The Menninger approach is one manifestation of a trend in psychoanalytic thought that pays increasing attention to the formal properties of the organization of thought rather than merely seeking to uncover an individual's unconscious motives and fantasies.

There are trends at present to formalize the use of the word-association technique by developing norms for common or popular responses and uncommon or deviant ones, together with techniques for classifying the content of responses and providing a higher degree of control over the conditions under which the test is administered. All of these will serve to place the use of word-association techniques on a more scientific footing and will allow a more critical evaluation of their worth.

■ LIE-DETECTOR TESTS

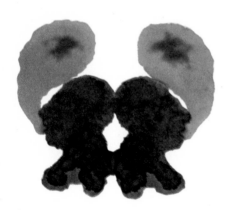

Another trend, which has been embraced wholeheartedly by personnel officers, is the use of the word-association technique in relation to the galvanic skin response and other measures of complex emotional reaction. These have been incorporated into many lie-detector tests. The theory underlying the use of these procedures is that a person will reveal an emotional response not to the truth or falsity of his response but to the word that arouses the emotional response. It should be recognized, however, that individuals vary widely in their susceptibility to this sort of procedure. There are both "false positives" and "false negatives." That is, some individuals will show a heightened reactivity to a variety of words, even where there is little cause for concern, whereas others will show almost no reaction, even when it is known from independent evidence that they have been implicated in a crime of some kind.

A number of different word-association lists have been prepared. They are usually interpreted impressionistically in relation to other information available about the person. The items are ordinarily chosen to identify sources of likely psychological difficulty, although as with structured techniques, it is not always possible to hit upon the areas that are precisely the most relevant to the individual's functioning.

■ THE SENTENCE-COMPLETION TECHNIQUE

Another widely used projective technique for personality assessment is the sentence-completion technique. In this procedure, only the first few words of a sentence are presented to a subject, and he is asked to complete the sentence without being given any clearly formulated guidelines. For example, he might be asked to complete the following sentences: "The thing that upsets me the most is . . . ," "My parents . . . ," "I felt like quitting when they . . ."

A number of variations of this procedure have been developed. Notable is the Rotter Incomplete Sentences Blank, which employs a rating for maladjustment of each response given to forty statements. Rotter developed a set of criteria for judging the adjustment and maladjustment implicit in the various responses. Although the scoring of the responses to this technique is fairly objective and reliable, it should be recognized that the scores obtained will be very much a function of the individual's willingness to reveal sources of maladjustment. His willingness to describe himself in desirable or undesirable terms will have an important effect on the scores.

Because a projective test typically leaves it up to the examinee to reveal that portion of his personality that is salient at the time of testing, there is no assurance that particular needs of interest to the examiner will emerge. Thus, the assessment of specified dimensions of personality will ordinarily proceed more efficiently and more validly with structured techniques.

A number of expressive tests of personality have been developed, including the *Draw-a-Person test* popularized by Machover and the *House-Tree-Person projective technique* devised by Buck, as well as techniques involving construction of miniature situations out of toys or out of various pictures of figures. Although a sensitive clinician can use these tests as a means for observing the individual and the way he thinks, taken singly they have not yet demonstrated a sufficient degree of validity to be classified as scientifically acceptable assessment devices for measuring particular traits.

The one exception to this general trend is the use of the Draw-a-Person test, which involves the instruction simply to draw a person and then afterward to draw a second person of the opposite sex. This test has been found to be revealing of a dimension of psychological differentiation, a trait that is as much intellectual and cognitive as it is a personality dimension, revealing itself in the individual's tendency to be analytical and to seek to structure a situation carefully and accurately. It is revealed in human figure drawings by a tendency to incorporate many details, to maintain sex differentiation, and to avoid simplification of drawings and in a variety of other ways. The high validity found for figure drawings using this technique is to be contrasted with the generally negligible validities or nonexistent data pertaining to some impressionistic statements made about figure drawing, such as the belief once held that unruly hair was associated with a low level of morality.

Expressive and stylistic behavior is potentially a valuable source of information about an individual's personality, quite apart from particular traits. Many years ago, Allport and Vernon did a remarkable series of studies investigating stylistic consistencies in behavior. An individual's gait, his tempo of talking, his characteristic facial expression, and his posture all proved to be measurable and consistent. Allport distinguishes this kind of behavior from that of traits per se, suggesting that although stylistic behavior is only surface behavior, ultimately it may be possible to show that it is revealing of personality characteristics of more central concern.

The major difficulty with most projective techniques, and particularly with the Rorschach, is that their reliability is open to considerable question. The basic principle—that each person tends to structure an ambiguous situation according to his own personality—seems tenable enough. Thus, the responses that someone gives to the Rorschach inkblots may very well indicate a great deal about that person's basic character, but the responses themselves usually constitute an ambiguous stimulus to the person who attempts to score or interpret the responses. Thus, a purely clinical interpretation of a person based on his Rorschach protocol may tell us more about the person who did the interpretation than about the person who actually produced the responses in the first place. When the Rorschach and the MMPI are compared experimentally, the MMPI almost always proves to be a better predictor of future behavior than does the inkblot test. It is one of the unfortunate facts of life that while the more structured tests may not

Expressive Techniques

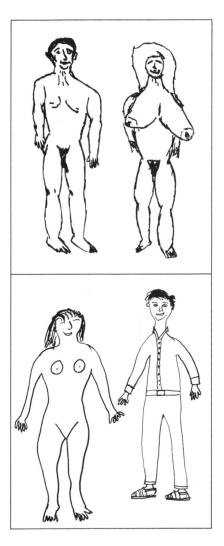

455

tap as deeply into the personality structure as do the projective, one can usually place a great deal more faith in information yielded by properly constructed structured techniques.

Other Bases for Judging Personality
Formal Interview

Probably the most widely used technique for personality appraisal is the interview. Few employers would wish to make a hiring decision prior to the opportunity to have a face-to-face talk with the prospective employee. The interview is also used in counseling, in clinical assessment, and in educational decision making.

■TECHNIQUES

Interviewing techniques vary widely, ranging from those that leave the interviewee free to discuss whatever he wishes to those that involve such highly formal question-and-answer procedures as to be very close to questionnaires. Many books have been written on the interview, particularly the clinical interview, discussing a wide variety of techniques regarding how to elicit information, as well as how to bring about counseling or therapeutic change. Attorneys have given a great deal of attention to a certain type of formal interview, namely, that conducted in a court of law. Although the latter usually involves fact finding, there is one classic book in the area concerning the art of cross-examination that makes particular reference to the importance of sizing up the witness's personality and conducting one's interview accordingly.

■APPLICATION

Many studies have investigated the validity of the interview in a variety of situations. The validities are usually higher when a single trait is at issue and when the interviewer knows what to look for prior to the interview. On the other hand, where a great deal of information is sought and the interviewer has not had an opportunity to decide beforehand what is most important, lower validities usually obtain. Even in the face of this sort of evidence, interviews continue to be used for a number of important reasons.

First, an interview can provide a great deal of information, for example, about the individual's manner of dress, his poise, his sensitivity to certain topics, his fluency and style of speech, and his level of anxiety. It would be difficult to appraise all these qualities as effectively in the same amount of time using another technique. Of course, to appraise these characteristics individually, more reliable and more valid procedures might be obtained, but the interview has the peculiar property of allowing for diverse assessment of improbable consequences.

Another important function of the interview is that it affords an opportunity to obtain personal history and background data more readily than other techniques. Although personal-history forms have been devised for a variety of purposes, individuals for one reason or another may be motivated to distort the information they prepare. In an interview, however, they have less opportunity to prepare prevarications. In addition, it is sometimes more appropriate to ask personal questions in an individual interview than it is in a standardized questionnaire. Indeed, psychologists have found that the use of highly personal questions in a standardized questionnaire is a potent device for arousing aggression.

One of the problems with the interview is that interviewers vary widely in their skill at eliciting information. They also vary widely in the accuracy with which they can judge traits emerging from an interview. A skilled interviewer will show high sensitivity both to cues meriting further investigation and to those relevant to particular personality traits.

A number of ingenious procedures have been developed to assess personality. Some of these involve various types of business games, in which certain essential materials must be obtained from competitors, thus offering an opportunity for a person to demonstrate his skill as a negotiator. Others involve frustration or stress. Some of the most ingenious procedures were those devised by the staff of "Station S" of the Office of Strategic Services (oss) during World War II. These staff members had the task of selecting and training espionage agents and other individuals preparing to work behind enemy lines. Some of the particular problems in this kind of situation were that the assessment specialists employed on the project had relatively little direct experience with the criterion performance, no scientific literature on which to base their knowledge of the criterion, and little faith that typical performance tasks such as might be involved in a standard clinical interview or personality test might apply in a situation that required maximum performance.

One procedure used was a construction task in which a candidate was shown a plan and a set of building materials. The staff member suggested to the candidate that he build a certain type of building, offering him a plan and the assistance of two individuals, who were actually other staff members. The staff members were instructed to behave in a very frustrating manner, although not to disobey orders. The candidate, of course, did not know of these secret instruc-

Situational Measures of Personality

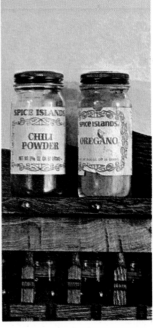

Figure 24.16
Such common phenomena as preferred use of herbs and spices can be used in certain situational measurements.

457

tions to the two assistants. One acted extremely sluggishly, took no initiative, engaged in projects of his own, and offered no advice.

The other assistant was extremely aggressive, criticizing any weakness he observed in the candidate, offering irrelevant suggestions, expressing dissatisfaction. For example, if the candidate did not immediately introduce himself and ask for the workers' names, this assistant would suggest that a boss interested in getting along well with his men would at least find out their names. He constantly looked for weaknesses in the candidate's performance, often complained of inadequate instructions, suggested that the candidate was inexperienced, wondered aloud what he was doing as a candidate on the project, suggested alternative methods for construction, kicked inadequate portions of the structure, distracted the candidate from the job, and accused him of being the poorest leader they had ever seen.

The particular direction the needling took often involved a high degree of imagination and almost invariably resulted in some degree of frustration on the part of the candidate. The emotional reactions elicited by this task provided a rather good gauge of tolerance for frustration. At times, it even surpassed some candidates' level of control. Some men were so shaken up by this experience that afterward they asked to be released from the assessment program and from their assignment. The situation was also used as a measure of leadership and of emotional stability, but it proved best as an assessment of the individual's tolerance for interpersonal frustration.

Another ingenious procedure developed by the oss staff was the stress interview. It assessed what an individual might do when placed in the role of a person who had been caught looking at the secret files of an enemy power. Circumstances necessitated that he develop a cover story and resist interrogation. The interrogation techniques used by the staff were highly effective for arousing stress and for uncovering weaknesses in the candidates, providing them with insight into their own weaknesses, and even causing some individuals to resign from the program.

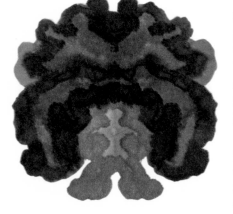

These procedures have in common the view that assessment ought to be realistic and relevant to the situation in which it will occur. Assessment in the oss program was not an appraisal of static traits that might emerge in any situation but of those that emerged under circumstances where the individual was put to test, a procedure consistent with the highly unusual assignments many of the candidates were given.

Use and Abuses of Personality Measurement

Personality measurement involves potentially valuable information that may be used appropriately and fruitfully for the betterment of individuals in institutions. Such information may also be misused with potentially serious effects. It is hardly necessary here to outline the many potentially helpful applications of personality assessment. Techniques such as those outlined in this chapter have been applied with increasing success in vocational counseling, in clinics, in hospitals, in educational institutions, and in industry. The widespread acceptance of personality assessment has not been without its critics. Many of the critics seek constructive alternatives to present practices. Others see little value in any sort of assessment. Such criticism, whether well founded technically or not, often serves a positive function in that it orients the users of assessment devices to the broader questions relating to the appropriateness of their use.

Many questions concerning the appropriateness of assessment are essentially technical questions. For example, one can ask, "Is the personality test valid for the purposes for which it is being used?" or "Can the questions asked be legitimately answered in terms of the data collected with the personality-assessment techniques employed?" Most qualified psychologists could answer such questions without a great deal of difficulty. If such a question were difficult to answer, it would be a fairly simple matter to review the information available about the test in the technical manual accompanying its publication or in handbooks of reviews written specifically for this purpose.

There are, however, broader questions concerning the use of personality-assessment devices, ones with which the public at large has some interest. Although a company or organization might quite legitimately inquire into a person's interpersonal relationships as these might affect his job performance, is it appropriate for the organization to inquire into his fundamental beliefs or his fantasies? Is it appropriate for colleges to use attitude questionnaires as an aid in selecting students because they claim that they wish to ensure a certain homogeneity in the student body? Is it appropriate for business organizations to give tests originally intended for psychiatric patients, such as the Rorschach, in order to assess the potential of executives? To what extent should personality tests be used in government employment decisions, under circumstances where these have proven to be valid—for example, in predicting adjustment to living overseas? Should personality tests be used in college admission decisions, even where they have been shown to be valid?

Undoubtedly, you have opinions concerning these questions, but these issues are often far more complicated than they appear at first, and they usually involve not a clear, unequivocal value but a resolution of competing values or issues. For example, in the case of the question about using personality tests to select individuals for overseas government service, one is balancing the value of privacy of the individual with the very legitimate interest on the part of the government to send the best-qualified people overseas, those who might best serve the country they are visiting and also best serve their own country. Under such circumstances, one might wish to give a qualified answer, possibly suggesting ways in which the individual's right of privacy might be preserved. For example, reduce personality-test data to numerical values and identify each applicant with a numbered code placed in the computer, but keep this information from the individual's supervisor or associates.

As is the case with many tools in a modern technological society, personality tests may be used for desirable ends or to create mischief. The most important safeguard is that the individual using such a tool, whether it is a surgeon's knife or a personality test, knows what he is doing and knows the potential and limitations of his instruments. But such a person must be more than a mere technician. He must be aware of and sensitive to the ethical problems involved, the rights of individuals, and the legitimate interests of institutions and of the scientific community.

25

THEORIES OF PERSONALITY

WE ALL WEAR MASKS. Only an as-yet-unsocialized infant shows himself to the world as he really is; the rest of us have learned to hide our feelings, disguise our moods. We are like the ancient Greek actors who held stylized masks up to their faces to denote what character they were playing, what emotion they were trying to convey. We change our personalities (at least, that part the rest of the world sees) in a twinkling of an eye; and even when we wear the mask of comedy, can the world really say that we are happy deep down inside?

The term "personality" has an interesting derivation. It comes from the Latin *per sonare*, "to speak through," and refers to the masks that actors put before their real faces and "spoke through" on stage. Sometimes when we use the word, we mean the characteristic behavior patterns that a given individual displays in public. More often, when a psychologist uses the term, he has reference to the actor himself rather than just to the public roles he plays. Personality theories, then, are attempts to explain in scientific terms what the actor is really like and why he wears the masks that he does.

Conceptions of man prior to the twentieth century were largely the work of philosophers, theologians, poets, and novelists. With the rise of scientific psychology and psychiatry at the end of the nineteenth century, theories of the nature of man based upon empirical observations and research began to appear. The number of rival theories that have evolved since 1900 is so great that we can present only some of the more prominent ones here.

Theories of personality may be classified in a number of ways. Many of them have been developed within the context of the therapy situation, where the behavior of the whole person is under observation. Others have been developed in the laboratory under controlled experimental conditions. Some personality theories were evolved by psychiatrists, others by psychologists. Some personality theories emphasize the importance of unconscious determinants, others the importance of conscious determinants.

Personality theories may also be differentiated on such dimensions as heredity versus environment, the importance of childhood experiences, the role of the past versus the role of the future, a single sovereign motive versus a pluralism of motives, holism, uniqueness of the individual, and the centrality of the self-concept. Some theories have generated a great deal of research, others have generated little.

What, then, is a theory of personality? Ideally, it is a formulation or system of interrelated statements that describe and explain all aspects of man's nature. The fact that there are so many different and often contradictory views of man, each supported by a body of clinical or experimental data, suggests that no one theory is completely adequate to account for man's complex nature. The broadest one is Freud's, but even his sophisticated conception of man is incomplete. Each theory, therefore, despite its shortcomings, should be looked at objectively.

Freud's Psychoanalytic Theory

Freud's theory of personality was the first and is the most detailed one that has been formulated. It is based upon Freud's fifty years of experience as a psychoanalyst working intensively with a fairly large number of individuals in the intimacy of the therapeutic situation.

Freud, known as the *premier* explorer of the unconscious mind, was born in Freiberg, Moravia (now Czechoslovakia), in 1856 and died in London in 1939, but for most of his life he lived in Vienna. He received his medical degree from the University of Vienna and soon afterward began to practice psychiatry. Dissatisfied with current methods of treating patients, he developed new ones in collaboration with Joseph Breuer. In 1900, his *Interpretation of Dreams* was published and the new technique of psychoanalysis was introduced to the world. People came to Vienna to learn Freud's methods, and soon there were psychoanalysts practicing in a number of countries.

Freud's theory of personality consists of three major provinces: structure, dynamics, and development.

Structure

Personality, according to Freud, comprises three separate but interacting systems: the *id,* the *ego,* and the *superego.* Freud used these terms as analogies, as ways of explaining what he saw in his patients' behavior. He did not know if someday neurophysiologists would find structures or systems within the central nervous system that would be congruent to the psychological systems that he described. Somewhere in the development of psychoanalytic theory, however, these descriptive terms took on a life of their own, and much of the analytic literature is written as if each person had within him a cast of characters with an existence almost independent of the person within whom they lived and acted out their parts (personae). We must keep in mind, when discussing Freud, that he spoke

Figure 25.2
Sigmund Freud.

in analogies. And as Freud himself said, analogies prove nothing, but they do make us feel at home.

■ THE ID

The id is the original system of the personality; it is the material out of which the ego and the superego become differentiated. It is the reservoir of psychic energy, which it obtains from the instincts, and it is completely unconscious. You can never know your own id directly but only through its manifestations in your behavior.

The id cannot tolerate tension, so it tries to discharge immediately any tension that arises in it. The id is said to obey the *pleasure principle,* that is, to reduce painful tensions to the lowest level possible.

■ THE EGO

Because the id does not have any direct contact with the external environment, the ego is formed to handle transactions with the outside world. It operates according to the reality principle. The distinction between the pleasure principle and the *reality principle* may be illustrated by the following example. If a person becomes hungry and imagines that he is getting food and eating it, the pleasure principle is operating. Obviously these fantasies of food do not satisfy his hunger. He must find food in the environment and eat it if the tension caused by the hunger is to be removed. When he does this, the reality principle is functioning.

The ego is said to be the executive of the personality because it controls the gateways to action, selects the features of the environment to which it will respond, and decides what needs will be satisfied and in what manner. Its principal role is to mediate between the needs of the organism and the objects and conditions in the surrounding environment. Unlike the id, much of the ego is conscious or readily becomes conscious.

■ THE SUPEREGO

The superego is the internal representative of the traditional values and ideals of society as interpreted to the child by his parents and enforced by means of a system of rewards and punishments imposed upon the child. The superego is the moral arm of personality. It represents the ideal rather than the real, and it strives for perfection rather than for pleasure. Its main concern is to decide whether something is right or wrong so that it can act in accordance with the moral standards authorized by the parental agents of society.

The main functions of the superego are (1) to inhibit the impulses of the id, particularly those of a sexual or aggressive nature, because these are the impulses whose expression is most condemned by society; (2) to persuade the ego to substitute moralistic goals for realistic ones; and (3) to strive for perfection.

Dynamics Because work is performed by the personality, it must have sources of energy that it can tap. These sources are the *instincts* and *external stimulation.* The instincts, the more important of these two sources, fall into two large classes, which Freud named the *life* and the *death instincts.*

■ INSTINCTS

The life instincts serve the goals of individual survival and propagation of the race. Hunger, thirst, and sex are in this category. The form of psychic energy by which the life instincts perform their work is called *libido.*

The life instinct to which Freud paid the greatest attention is sex, and in the early years of psychoanalysis almost everything a person did was attributed to this ubiquitous drive. Actually, the sex instinct is not one instinct but many; that is, a number of separate bodily needs give rise to erotic wishes. Each of these wishes has its source in a different bodily region, or *erogenous zone*. An erogenous zone is a part of the skin or mucous membrane that is extremely sensitive to irritation and when manipulated in a certain way produces pleasurable feelings. The lips and mouth constitute one such erogenous zone, the anal region another, and the sex organs a third. Sucking produces oral pleasure; and massaging or rubbing, genital pleasure. In childhood, the sexual instincts are relatively independent of one another, but during adolescence they tend to fuse together and come to serve the aim of sexual union and reproduction.

The death instincts perform their work much less conspicuously than the life instincts, and for this reason little is known about them other than that they inevitably accomplish their aim. Freud postulated that organic matter evolved out of inorganic matter and that the death instinct is a manifestation of the unconscious wish to return to the inorganic. "The goal of all life is death" is one of Freud's most famous assertions.

An important derivative of the death instincts is the aggressive drive. Aggressiveness is self-destruction turned outward against external objects and persons.

An instinct has four characteristic features: a *source*, an *aim*, an *object*, and an *impetus*. The source is a bodily condition or need—for example, hunger. The aim is the removal of the bodily excitation. All the activity that intervenes between the appearance of the instinct and its satisfaction is subsumed under the heading "object." The impetus of an instinct is its force or strength, which is determined by the intensity of the underlying need.

Let us briefly consider some of the implications inherent in this way of conceptualizing an instinct. In the first place, the model that Freud provides is a tension-reduction one. The behavior of a person is activated by internal irritation. In this sense, an instinct is *regressive* because it returns the person to a prior state, one that existed before the instinct appeared. An instinct is also said to be *conservative* because its aim is to conserve the equilibrium of the organism by abolishing disturbing excitations.

The source and aim of an instinct remain constant throughout life, but the object or means by which the person attempts to satisfy the need can and does vary considerably. This variation in object choice is possible because psychic energy is *displaceable*: it can be expended in various forms of behavior. When

the energy of an instinct is more or less permanently invested in (or directed toward) a substitute object—that is, one that is not the original and innately determined object—the resulting behavior is said to be an *instinct derivative*. Thus, if the first sexual object of the child is the manipulation of his own sexual organs and he is forced to give up this pleasure in favor of more innocuous forms of bodily stimulation such as sucking his thumb and playing with his toes, the substitute activities are derivatives of the sexual instinct. Freud's theory is often called a *reductionistic* one because it reduces all behavior to the biological instincts.

This displacement of energy from one object to another is the most important feature of personality dynamics. It accounts for the apparent plasticity of human nature and the remarkable versatility of man's behavior. Practically all the adult person's interests, preferences, tastes, habits, and attitudes represent the displacement of energy from original instinctual object choices. They are all derivatives. Freud's theory of motivation is based solely on the assumption that the instincts are *the* sole energy source for man's behavior, for even external stimulation must arouse an instinct in order to have any effective influence.

■ ANXIETY

Transactions with the external environment not only reduce tension but may also increase tension by threatening or harming the person. This kind of tension is experienced as *anxiety*. In addition to anxiety caused by environmental threats (Freud called it *reality anxiety*), two other types of anxiety were described by Freud: *neurotic anxiety* and *moral anxiety*, or feelings of guilt. Neurotic anxiety is fear that the instincts will get out of control and cause the person to do something for which he will be punished. Moral anxiety is having a guilty conscience; one does something or thinks of doing something that is contrary to the moral code he learned from his parents. Both neurotic anxiety and moral anxiety are based upon reality anxiety.

■ DEFENSE MECHANISMS

The function of anxiety is to warn the person of impending danger so that he may do something to avoid the danger. Under the pressure of excessive anxiety that cannot be relieved by realistic methods, the ego is forced to use unrealistic methods. These measures are called *defense mechanisms*. All defense mechanisms have two characteristics in common: (1) they deny, falsify, or distort reality; and (2) they operate unconsciously so that the person is not aware of what is taking place. The principal defense mechanisms are *repression, projection, reaction formation, fixation,* and *regression*.

Repression was one of the earliest and most important discoveries of Freud. He observed that his patients were unable to recall traumatic events in childhood without considerable probing and analysis using free-association techniques. Traumatic memories, Freud concluded, had been repressed into the unconscious and were held there by strong counterforces.

If anxiety that arises from the individual's own instinctual impulses or from threats of conscience can be projected onto the external world, it is easier to deal with. In employing the defense mechanism of *projection*, one says, in effect, "My father hates me," instead of the unbearable truth, "I hate him."

Reaction formation involves the replacement in consciousness of an anxiety-producing impulse or feeling by its opposite. Hate is replaced by love.

In the course of development, a person passes through a number of stages. Each new step that is taken entails a certain amount of anxiety. If the anxiety is too intense the person may withdraw from taking the next step. He remains fixated. The child who remains overly dependent upon his parents and later in his life on other persons exemplifies defense by *fixation*.

By *regression* is meant that a person returns to an earlier stage of development when threatened. A young married woman who has difficulties with her husband may return to the security of her parents' home, or a man who has lost his job or his wife may seek solace in drink because alcohol reduces his responsibilities to those of a child.

Development

Freud was the first psychological theorist to emphasize the developmental aspects of personality, and in particular to stress the decisive role of the early years of infancy and childhood in laying down the basic character structure of the person. Indeed, Freud felt that personality was rather well formed by the time the child entered school and that subsequent growth consisted of elaborating upon this basic structure. The two principal mechanisms by which development takes place are *identification* and *displacement*.

■ IDENTIFICATION

Identification is the process by which a person takes over the features of another person and incorporates them into his own personality. The two persons with whom the child is most likely to identify are his mother and father. Typically, the boy identifies with his father, the girl with her mother. This is called *narcissistic* identification because the boy sees in the father the embodiment of his own male gender and the girl sees in the mother her female gender. One may also identify with another person out of fear. For example, the child identifies with the prohibitions of his parents in order to avoid their wrath. This kind of identification is the basis for the formation of the superego. Identification is also a method by which one may regain an object or person that has been lost through death, separation, or rejection. By identifying with a lost loved person, the lost person becomes reincarnated as an incorporated feature of one's personality.

■ DISPLACEMENT

When an original object choice of an instinct is rendered inaccessible, displacement to a new object takes place. The development of personality consists in large measure of a series of displacements from the original object. Because a substitute object is rarely if ever as satisfying as the original object, a pool of undischarged tension accumulates that then acts as a permanent motivating force for behavior.

Freud pointed out in *Civilization and Its Discontents* (1930) that the development of civilization was made possible by the inhibition of primitive object choices and the diversion of instinctual energy into social organization and the development of culture. A displacement that produces a higher cultural achievement is called a *sublimation*. Freud observed, for example, that Leonardo da Vinci's interest in painting Madonnas was a sublimated expression of a longing for reunion with his mother, from whom he had been separated at a tender age. Because sublimation does not result in complete satisfaction, any more than any displacement does, there is always some residual tension. This may discharge itself in the form of nervousness or restlessness—conditions, Freud pointed out, that were the price man paid for his civilized state and the reason he must periodically blow off steam in war and other primitive behaviors.

■ STAGES OF DEVELOPMENT

Freud believed that the child passes through a series of dynamically different stages during the first five years of life, following which for a period of five or six years, during the period called *latency,* the dynamics become more or less stabilized. With the advent of adolescence, the dynamics erupt again and then gradually settle down as the adolescent moves into adulthood. The three early stages, collectively called the *pregenital stage,* are the *oral,* the *anal,* and the *phallic.* Each is organized around a zone of the body.

The first source of pleasure derived from the mouth is that of eating, or more specifically, sucking. Later, when the teeth erupt, the mouth is used for biting and chewing. These two modes of oral activity, ingestion of food and biting, are the prototypes for many character traits that develop later. Gullibility is derived from the oral incorporative mode: a gullible person will swallow almost anything. Biting or oral aggression may be displaced in the form of sarcasm, biting wit, and argumentativeness. Further, because the oral stage occurs at a time when the baby is almost completely dependent upon his mother for sustenance, feelings of dependency arise during this period that tend to persist throughout life and come to the fore whenever the person feels anxious and insecure.

When toilet training is initiated, usually during the second year of life, the child has his first decisive experience with the external regulation of an instinctual impulse. Depending upon the particular method of toilet training used by the mother and her feelings concerning elimination of waste products, this training may have far-reaching effects upon the formation of specific traits and values. If the mother is very strict and repressive in her methods, the child may hold back his feces in defiance of her and become constipated. If this mode generalizes to other forms of behavior, the child will develop a retentive character: he will become obstinate and stingy. Or under the duress of repressive measures in the bathroom, the child may vent his rage by expelling his feces at the most inappropriate times. This is the prototype for all kinds of expulsive traits such as cruelty, wanton destructiveness, temper tantrums, and disorderliness, to mention only a few. Many other character traits have been traced to the anal stage.

During the phallic stage of development, which lasts from about the age of three to six, sexual and aggressive feelings associated with the functioning of the genital organs come into focus. The pleasures of masturbation and the fantasy life of the child that accompanies autoerotic activity set the stage for the appearance of the *Oedipus complex.* Freud considered the identification of the Oedipus complex, which takes its name from the Greek king who killed his father and married his mother, to be one of his greatest discoveries. Briefly defined, the Oedipus complex consists of sexual attraction to the parent of the opposite sex and hostility for the parent of the same sex. The boy wants to possess his mother and remove his father; the girl wants to possess her father and displace her mother.

The *castration complex* also appears during the phallic stage. In the boy, this complex takes the form of fear of being castrated. Specifically, he is afraid his father will castrate him because he (the boy) is a rival for the mother's love. In the girl, the complex takes the form of *penis envy.* The girl is envious of the more visible sexual organs of the boy. Her envy can express itself by her trying symbolically to castrate the male. However, her envy is somewhat reduced by getting possession of a man's penis by marriage and by having children.

The impulses of the pregenital period are narcissistic in character; that is, the individual obtains gratification from the stimulation and manipulation of his own body plus the fantasies that accompany these activities. Other people are valued only because they feed the narcissistic pleasures of the child. After the latency period, that is, during adolescence, some of this self-love becomes channeled into genuine object choices. During this period, called the *genital stage*, sexual attraction, socialization, group activities, vocational planning, and preparations for marrying and raising a family begin to manifest themselves. By the end of adolescence, the person has become transformed from a pleasure-seeking, narcissistic individual into a reality-oriented socialized adult—not everyone, of course, nor without many regressions. The principal biological function of the genital stage is that of reproduction; the psychological aspects help to achieve this end by providing a certain measure of stability and security.

In spite of the fact that Freud differentiated these four stages of personality growth, he did not assume that there were any sharp breaks or abrupt transitions in passing out of one stage and into another. The final organization of personality represents contributions from all four stages.

Jung's Analytical Theory

One of the earliest followers of Freud was Carl Jung, born in Switzerland in 1875. Jung received a medical education and became a psychiatrist; his acquaintance with Freud began in 1906, and he joined the psychoanalytic movement soon thereafter. In 1913, he broke away from Freud and started his own school of psychoanalysis, which became known as *analytical psychology*. Jung died in 1961 at the age of eighty-five.

Structure

Like Freud, Jung recognized the great importance of unconscious factors in determining behavior, but he distinguished two levels in the unconscious. One level, the *personal unconscious*, contains experiences the individual has had that were once conscious but have been repressed or forgotten; the contents of the personal unconscious are capable of returning to consciousness. The other level, the *collective unconscious*, is the storehouse of memories and behavior patterns inherited from man's ancestral past. It is almost entirely detached from anything personal in the life of the individual, and all human beings have more or less the

Figure 25.8

Jung believed that the mandala, a figure common to the art of many cultures, expresses the archetype of the self.

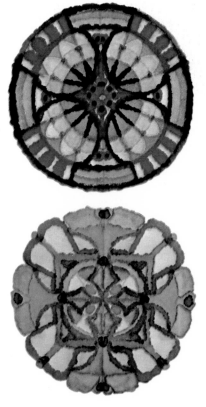

same collective unconscious. Jung attributes the universality of the collective unconscious to the similarity of structure of the brain in all races of men, and this similarity is due to a common evolution. Jung felt that the collective unconscious is the most unique feature of his theory of personality.

■ARCHETYPES

The contents of the personal unconscious are organized into complexes, or universal thought forms that contain a large element of feeling. The nucleus of a complex in the personal unconscious is archetypal. For example, everyone inherits a *mother archetype* because human beings have always had mothers. This archetype of the mother causes the child to perceive and react to his actual mother in predetermined ways. Out of these actual experiences, a mother complex is formed. An archetype can never become conscious. It can only be inferred from outward manifestations.

■ CHARACTER TYPES

Jung also developed a system of character types. The components of this system consist of two *attitudes* and four *functions*. The two attitudes are *introversion* and *extraversion*. The extraverted attitude orients the person toward the external, objective world; the introverted attitude orients the person toward his inner, subjective world.

The four functions are *thinking, feeling, sensing,* and *intuiting*. The thinking function is concerned with ideas. By thinking, man tries to comprehend the nature of the world and of himself. Feeling is the valuing function; it gives value to things with reference to the individual. It is responsible for man's experiences of pleasure and pain, anger, fear, sorrow, joy, and love. Sensing is the perceptual or reality function. It yields concrete facts and information about the world. Intuiting refers to knowledge that is gained from unconscious sources. The intuitive man tries to get at the essential nature of the world by means of mystical experiences.

Jung believed that the principle of compensation operates between the conscious and unconscious. Too little development in one means overdevelopment in the other. Ideally, the attitudes and functions should all be equally developed in order to achieve unity.

Development   Jung, unlike Freud, believed that there is a forward-going character to personality development. Man is trying continuously to realize himself. His goal is to achieve complete unity within his personality. This end is accomplished, first, by developing all parts of the personality, a process that Jung called *individuation*. After individuation has been achieved, then the *transcendent function*, as it is called, unites the disparate systems of personality into a fully realized self. Of course, Jung realized that this is an unrealizable goal but held that it nevertheless is the great driving force of all of man's behavior.

Social Psychological Theories   Freud and Jung have often been criticized for being too biological in their orientation, and as a reaction against this orientation new theories have been formulated that place more stress upon the social determinants of personality.

Alfred Adler   Adler, like Jung, was an early associate of Freud's who broke with him to start his own version of psychoanalysis. Adler, like Freud a Viennese, was born in 1870; he died in the United States in 1937.

In sharp contrast to Freud's major assumption that man's behavior is motivated by inborn instincts and Jung's principal axiom that man's conduct is governed by inborn archetypes, Adler assumed that man is motivated primarily by social urges. Man, for Adler, is inherently a social being—a concept of major importance for personality theory. He relates to other people, engages in cooperative social welfare above selfish interest, and acquires a style of life that is predominantly social in outlook.

Adler's second major contribution to personality theory is his concept of the *creative self*. Unlike Freud's ego, which consists of a group of psychological processes serving the ends of inborn instincts, Adler's self is a highly personalized subjective system that interprets and makes meaningful the experiences of the organism. Moreover, it searches for experiences that will aid in fulfilling the person's unique style of life; if these experiences are not to be found in the world, the self tries to create them.

A third feature of Adler's psychology that sets it apart from classical psychoanalysis is its emphasis upon the uniqueness of the individual personality. Adler considered each person a unique configuration of motives, traits, interests, and values; every act performed by the person bears the stamp of his own distinctive style of life.

Finally, Adler made consciousness the center of personality. Man is ordinarily aware of the reasons for his behavior. He is conscious of his inferiorities (Adler's famed *inferiority complex*), and he is conscious of the goals for which he strives. Moreover, he is a self-conscious individual who can plan and guide his actions with full awareness of their meaning for his own self-realization.

Erich Fromm

The essential theme that runs through Erich Fromm's writings is that man feels lonely and isolated because he has become separated from nature and from other men. In his book *Escape From Freedom* (1941), Fromm develops the thesis that as man gains freedom he feels increasingly alone. Freedom then becomes a negative condition from which he tries to escape. In so doing he often engages in self-destructive acts like war and totalitarianism.

What is the answer to this dilemma? Man can either unite himself with other people in the spirit of love and shared work or he can find security by submitting to authority and conforming to society.

There are five specific needs that arise from the conditions of man's existence, according to Fromm. First, there is the *need for relatedness,* which stems from the stark fact that man in becoming man was torn from the animal's primary union with nature. Man has a *need for transcendence*—an urge to overcome animal nature, to become a creative person instead of remaining a creature. Third, there is a *need for rootedness;* man wants to be an integral part of the world, to feel a sense of belonging in it and of brotherliness. But man also wants a sense of *personal identity*—he wants to be distinctive and unique. Finally, there is a *need for a frame of reference* that will give stability and consistency to his behavior.

Fromm believes that the ways in which these needs express themselves are determined by the social arrangements under which he lives. His personality develops in accordance with the opportunities that a particular society offers him. In a capitalistic society, for example, he may gain a sense of personal identity by becoming rich or develop a feeling of rootedness by becoming a dependable and trusted employee in a large company.

From the standpoint of the proper functioning of a particular society, it is absolutely essential, Fromm points out, that the child's character be shaped to fit the needs of society. The task of the parents and of education is to make the child *want to act as he has to act* if a given economic, political, and social system is to be maintained. Thus, in a capitalistic system the desire to save must be implanted in people in order that capital is available for an expanding economy. A society that has evolved a credit system must see to it that people feel an inner compulsion to pay their bills promptly.

By making demands upon man that are contrary to his nature, society warps and frustrates him. It alienates him from the fulfillment of the basic conditions of his existence. Fromm also points out that when a society changes in any important respect, as occurred when the factory system displaced the individual artisan, such a change is likely to produce dislocations in the social character of people. The old character structure does not fit the new society and thus adds to man's sense of alienation and despair.

Harry Stack Sullivan

Adler and Fromm were identified with psychoanalysis and are sometimes referred to as neo-Freudians. We consider now a man who developed a new theory of personality, which he specifically called an *interpersonal theory*. This man was Harry Stack Sullivan (1892–1949), an American psychiatrist. Personality, Sullivan asserted, is a purely hypothetical entity that cannot be isolated from interpersonal situations, and interpersonal behavior is all that can be observed as personality. Consequently, it is vacuous, Sullivan believed, to speak of the individual as the object of study because the individual does not and cannot exist apart from his relations with other people. From the first day of life, the baby is a part of an interpersonal situation.

Nursing provides the baby with his first interpersonal experience. The baby develops various conceptions of the nipple, depending upon the kinds of experiences he has with it. There is the good nipple, which is the signal for nursing and a sign that satisfaction is forthcoming. There is the good but unsatisfactory nipple when the baby is not hungry, and the wrong nipple, which does not give milk. There is the bad nipple of the anxious mother, which is a signal for avoidance.

During *childhood,* the child begins to develop a conception of gender, and he plays at being grown up. One dramatic event of childhood is what Sullivan calls the *malevolent transformation*—the feeling that one lives among enemies. It makes it impossible for the child to respond positively to the affectionate advances of people and causes him to withdraw into himself.

The *juvenile period,* which extends through the grade school years, is the period of becoming social, of acquiring experiences of social subordination to authority figures outside of the family, of becoming competitive and cooperative, and of learning the meaning of ostracism, disparagement, and group feeling.

The relatively brief period of *preadolescence* is extremely important because it marks the beginning of genuine human relationships. In earlier periods, the interpersonal situation is characterized by dependence of the child upon an older person. During preadolescence, the child begins to form peer relationships. He has a strong need for an intimate relationship with a peer of the same sex, a chum in whom he can confide and with whom he can collaborate in meeting the tasks and problems of life.

Early adolescence is highlighted by the development of heterosexual activity, and *late adolescence* by initiation into the privileges, duties, satisfactions, and responsibilities of social living and citizenship.

When the person has ascended all these steps and reached the final stage of *adulthood,* he has been transformed, largely by means of his interpersonal relations, from an animal organism into a human. Sullivan did not believe that personality is set at an early age. It may change at any time as new interpersonal situations arise; the human being is extremely plastic and malleable.

The most important educative influence is that of anxiety, which forces the young organism to discriminate between increasing and decreasing tension. The second educational force is that of trial and success. Success stamps in the activity that has led to gratification.

Henry Murray, formerly director of Harvard's famed Psychological Clinic, was one of the first American psychologists to be deeply influenced by psychoanalysis and to make it part of the academic scene. The research carried on by him and his students has helped to give a strong empirical base to many of Freud's concepts and theories. Murray was medically trained and earned a Ph.D. in biochemistry, but soon thereafter his interests turned toward psychology. He attributes this conversion to his personal contact with Jung. Unlike most medically trained individuals, Murray is a research worker rather than a psychotherapist. He has worked primarily with normal people rather than with neurotics or psychotics.

Murray's most distinctive and respected contribution to an understanding of personality is his *theory of motivation*. Murray has insisted that an adequate understanding of human motivation must rest upon a system that employs a sufficiently large number of variables to reflect the tremendous complexity of human motives. He has also made serious efforts to provide empirical definitions

Murray's Personology

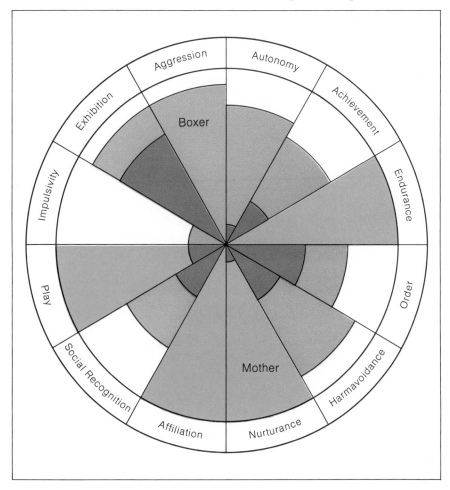

Figure 25.11

A representation of the personalities of a boxer and a new mother in terms of their needs.

Table 25.1—Murray's Needs

Need	Description
Abasement	To submit passively to external force. To accept injury, blame, criticism, punishment. To become resigned to fate. To admit inferiority, error, wrongdoing, or defeat. To confess and atone. To blame, belittle, or mutilate the self. To seek and enjoy pain, punishment, illness, and misfortune.
Achievement	To accomplish something difficult. To master, manipulate, or organize physical objects, human beings, or ideas. To do this as rapidly and as independently as possible. To overcome obstacles and attain a high standard. To excel oneself. To rival and surpass others. To increase self-regard by the successful exercise of talent.
Affiliation	To draw near and enjoyably cooperate or reciprocate with an allied other (an other who resembles the subject or who likes the subject). To please and win affection of a cathected object. To adhere and remain loyal to a friend.
Aggression	To overcome opposition forcefully. To fight. To revenge an injury. To attack, injure, or kill another. To oppose forcefully or punish another.
Autonomy	To get free, shake off restraint, break out of confinement. To resist coercion and restriction. To avoid or quit activities prescribed by domineering authorities. To be independent and free to act according to impulse. To be unattached, irresponsible. To defy convention.
Counteraction	To master or make up for a failure by restriving. To obliterate a humiliation by resumed action. To overcome weaknesses, to repress fear. To efface a dishonor by action. To search for obstacles and difficulties to overcome. To maintain self-respect and pride on a high level.
Defendance	To defend the self against assault, criticism, and blame. To conceal or justify a misdeed, failure, or humiliation. To vindicate the ego.
Deference	To admire and support a superior. To praise, honor, or eulogize. To yield eagerly to the influence of an allied other. To emulate an exemplar. To conform to custom.
Dominance	To control one's human environment. To influence or direct the behavior of others by suggestion, seduction, persuasion, or command. To dissuade, restrain, or prohibit.
Exhibition	To make an impression. To be seen and heard. To excite, amaze, fascinate, entertain, shock, intrigue, amuse, or entice others.
Harmavoidance	To avoid pain, physical injury, illness, and death. To escape from a dangerous situation. To take precautionary measures.
Infavoidance	To avoid humiliation. To quit embarrassing situations or to avoid conditions which may lead to belittlement: the scorn, derision, or indifference of others. To refrain from action because of the fear of failure.
Nurturance	To give sympathy and gratify the needs of a helpless object: an infant or any object that is weak, disabled, tired, inexperienced, infirm, defeated, humiliated, lonely, dejected, sick, mentally confused. To assist an object in danger. To feed, help, support, console, protect, comfort, nurse, heal.
Order	To put things in order. To achieve cleanliness, arrangement, organization, balance, neatness, tidiness, and precision.
Play	To act for "fun" without further purpose. To like to laugh and make jokes. To seek enjoyable relaxation of stress. To participate in games, sports, dancing, drinking parties, cards.
Rejection	To separate oneself from a negatively cathected object. To exclude, abandon, expel, or remain indifferent to an inferior object. To snub or jilt an object.
Sentience	To seek and enjoy sensuous impressions.
Sex	To form and further an erotic relationship. To have sexual intercourse.
Succorance	To have one's needs gratified by the sympathetic aid of an allied object. To be nursed, supported, sustained, surrounded, protected, loved, advised, guided, indulged, forgiven, consoled. To remain close to a devoted protector. To always have a supporter.
Understanding	To ask or answer general questions. To be interested in theory. To speculate, formulate, analyze, and generalize.

Source: Calvin S. Hall and Gardner Lindzey, *Theories of Personality* (New York: Wiley, 1957), pp. 173–174. Adapted from *Explorations in Personality* by Henry A. Murray. Copyright 1938 by Oxford University Press, Inc.; renewed 1966 by Henry A. Murray. Used by permission.

Table 25.2—Abbreviated List of Press

Family insupport	Rejection, unconcern, scorn
Cultural discord	Rival, competing contemporary
Family discord	Birth of sibling
Capricious discipline	Aggression
Parental separation	Maltreatment by elder male,
Absence of parent: father, mother	elder female
Parental illness: father, mother	Maltreatment by contemporaries
Death of parent: father, mother	Quarrelsome contemporaries
Inferior parent: father, mother	Dominance, coercion, and prohibition
Dissimilar parent: father, mother	Discipline
Poverty	Religious training
Unsettled home	Nurturance, indulgence
Danger or misfortune	Succorance, demands for tenderness
Physical insupport, height	Deference, praise, recognition
Water	Affiliation, friendship
Aloneness, darkness	Sex
Inclement weather, lightning	Exposure
Fire	Seduction: homosexual, heterosexual
Accident	Parental intercourse
Animal	Deception or betrayal
Lack or loss	Inferiority
Of nourishment	Physical
Of possessions	Social
Of companionship	Intellectual
Of variety	
Retention, withholding objects	

Source: Calvin S. Hall and Gardner Lindzey, *Theories of Personality* (New York: Wiley, 1957), pp. 173–174. Adapted from *Explorations in Personality* by Henry A. Murray. Copyright 1938 by Oxford University Press, Inc.; renewed 1966 by Henry A. Murray. Used by permission.

for his variables. The result of these efforts is a set of concepts that makes a bold attempt to bridge the gap between clinical description and the demands of empirical research.

Need is the central concept in Murray's motivational theory. A need is defined as "a construct which stands for a force . . . in the brain region, a force which organizes perception, apperception, intellection, conation, and action in such a way as to transform in a certain direction an existing, unsatisfying situation." Following an intensive study of a small number of individuals, Murray arrived at a tentative list of twenty needs (see Table 25.1).

Needs are intimately linked with environmental events. Murray calls environmental events that act upon the individual *press*. A press is a property or attribute of an environmental object or person that facilitates or impedes the efforts of the individual to reach a given goal. A representative list of press is shown in Table 25.2.

The correlated concepts of need and press are represented by the term *thema*. For example, when a person has a need for affiliation and someone offers him his friendship, this correlation is called an affiliation thema.

A person's behavior is not, however, the product of a bundle of unrelated themas. There is unity to personality. Murray recognizes this in his concept of *unity thema*. The unity thema is essentially the single pattern of related needs and press, derived from infantile experiences, that gives meaning and coherence to the largest portion of the individual's behavior. For instance, a person's life may be dominated by a persistent striving for power.

Murray is probably best known for the Thematic Apperception Test (TAT), which he devised with the cooperation of Christiana Morgan. The test consists of a number of pictures shown one at a time to a person, who is asked to tell a story about each. The stories are then analyzed in order to determine the themes that are manifested. The test is widely used in clinical settings as well as for research on personality.

Organismic Theory

Ever since the philosopher-scientist Descartes in the seventeenth century split the individual into two separate yet interacting entities and Wundt, the founder of experimental psychology in the nineteenth century, atomized the mind by reducing it to the elementary particles of sensations, feelings, and images, there have been recurrent attempts to put the mind and body back together and to treat the organism as a unified, organized whole. One notable attempt, initiated by Kurt Goldstein, is known as the *organismic* or *holistic viewpoint*.

Abraham Maslow

Abraham Maslow has in his numerous writings (especially *Motivation and Personality* and *Toward a Psychology of Being*) espoused a holistic-dynamic point of view. Maslow considers his position to fall within the broad province of humanistic psychology, which he has characterized as a third force in American psychology, the other two being behaviorism and psychoanalysis. Maslow—unlike others who based their views on the study of brain-damaged and mentally disturbed persons—draws upon his investigations of healthy and creative persons (*self-actualized*) to arrive at certain formulations regarding personality.

Maslow upbraids psychology for its pessimistic, negative, and limited conception of man. He feels that psychology has dwelled more upon man's frailties than upon his strengths, that it has thoroughly explored his sins while neglecting his virtues. Where is the psychology, Maslow asks, that takes account of gaiety, exuberance, love, and well-being to the same extent that it deals with misery, conflict, alienation, shame, and hostility?

Maslow has devoted his energies to delineating the psychologically healthy man, for Maslow believes that man has an essential nature of his own that differentiates him from all other animals. He is a human being. His needs are good or neutral rather than evil. This inner nature of man is not strong like the instincts of animals but is weak and easily transformed by habit, cultural pressure, and wrong attitudes. Still, there is an active will toward health, an impulse toward the actualization of human potentialities. Maslow feels that many people are afraid of and draw back from becoming fully human.

Maslow has propounded a theory of human motivation that differentiates between *basic needs* and *metaneeds*. The basic needs are hunger, affection, security, self-esteem, and the like. Metaneeds are justice, goodness, beauty, order, unity, and so forth. The basic needs are deficiency needs, whereas the metaneeds are growth needs. The basic needs are prepotent, or preeminent, over the metaneeds in most cases, and the basic needs are arranged in a hierarchical order so that some are prepotent over others. The metaneeds have no hierarchy and consequently can be fairly easily substituted for one another. The metaneeds are as inherent in man as are the basic needs, and when they are not fulfilled the person may become sick. These metapathologies, as Maslow calls them, are such states as alienation, anguish, apathy, and cynicism.

Maslow has made intensive investigations of a group of self-actualized people—some famous people like Lincoln, Thoreau, Beethoven, Eleanor Roosevelt, and Einstein, and others who were friends and acquaintances of Maslow. These turned out to be their distinguishing personality characteristics: (1) they are realistically oriented; (2) they accept themselves, other people, and the natural world for what they are; (3) they have a great deal of spontaneity; (4)

they are problem-centered rather than self-centered; (5) they have an air of detachment and a need for privacy; (6) they are autonomous and independent; (7) their appreciation of people and things is fresh rather than stereotyped; (8) most of them have had profound mystical or spiritual experiences although not necessarily religious in character; (9) they identify with mankind; (10) their intimate relationships with a few specially loved people tend to be profound and deeply emotional rather than superficial; (11) their values and attitudes are democratic; (12) they do not confuse means with ends; (13) their sense of humor is philosophical rather than hostile; (14) they have a great fund of creativeness; (15) they resist conformity to the culture; and (16) they transcend the environment rather than just coping with it.

Maslow has also investigated the nature of what he calls peak experiences, the most wonderful experiences in one's life. It was found that when persons are undergoing peak experiences they feel more integrated, more in harmony with the world, more autonomous, more spontaneous, less aware of space and time, and more perceptive.

Rogers' Self-Theory

Carl Rogers, an American psychologist, has developed a theory of personality in which the self is the major concept. Rogers' theory, like those of Freud, Jung, Adler, and Sullivan, grew out of his experiences in working with individuals in the therapeutic relationship. From these experiences, Rogers initially developed a theory of therapy and change. The principal feature of this conceptualization of the therapeutic process is that when the client perceives that the therapist has unconditional positive regard for him and an empathic understanding of his (the patient's) internal frame of reference, then a process of change is set in motion. During this process, the client becomes increasingly more aware of his true feelings and experiences, and his self-concept becomes more congruent with the total experiences of the organism.

If complete congruence should be achieved, the client would then be a fully functioning person. This type of person has such characteristics as openness to experience, absence of defensiveness, accurate awareness, unconditional self-regard, and harmonious relations with others.

In recent years, Rogers has come to view the therapeutic process as just one instance of an interpersonal relationship with communication. This approach led him to formulate a general theory of interpersonal relationships. Rogers' theory of personality with which we are here concerned contains features of phenomenology, of holistic and organismic psychology, of Sullivan's interpersonal theory, and of self-theory. Rogers is closely identified with the new movement known as humanistic psychology.

There are two structural constructs in Rogers' theory, the *organism* and the *self*. The organism, psychologically conceived, is the location of all experience, of everything that is going on within the organism at any given moment that is potentially available to awareness. The totality of experience constitutes the *phenomenal field*, which is the individual's frame of reference and can be known only to the person himself. "The organism," Rogers writes, "is at all times a total organized system in which alteration of any part may produce changes in any other part."

A portion of the phenomenal field gradually becomes differentiated, and this portion is called the self. The self is an organized and consistent conceptual whole that comprises perceptions of the relationships of the individual to other people, things, and activities, and perceptions by the individual. The self may be

consciously viewed, though not necessarily. Though constantly changing, the self is specific at any given moment.

In addition to the self as it is, there is an *ideal self,* which is what the person would like to be. The greater the discrepancy between the real self and the ideal self, the greater the dissatisfaction of the person.

When the symbolized experiences that constitute the self faithfully mirror the experiences of the organism, the person is said to be adjusted, mature, and fully functioning. Such a person accepts the entire range of organismic experience without threat or anxiety. He is able to think realistically. Incongruence between self and organism makes the individual feel threatened and anxious.

Both the organism and the self strive to actualize themselves. If the actualizing of the organism is at cross purposes with the actualizing of the self, conflict will ensue.

Organism and self, although they possess the inherent tendency to actualize themselves, are subject to strong influences from the environment, especially from the social environment. Evaluations of an individual by others, particularly during childhood, tend to favor distancing between organism and self. If these evaluations were exclusively positive—that is, if the child received unconditional positive regard—then no incongruity between organism and self would occur. But because evaluations of the child's behavior by his parents and others are sometimes positive and sometimes negative, the child learns to differentiate between actions and feelings that are worthy and those that are unworthy. Unworthy experiences tend to become excluded from the self-concept even though they are valid for the organism, which results in a self-concept that is out of line with organismic experience. The child tries to be what others want him to be instead of trying to be what he really is. Gradually, then, throughout childhood these evaluations by others cause the self-concept to become more and more and more distorted. As a consequence, an organismic experience that is at variance with this distorted self-concept is felt as a threat and evokes anxiety. In order to protect the integrity of the self-concept, these threatening experiences are denied symbolization or are given a distorted symbolization.

Not only does the breach between self and organism result in defensiveness and distortion, but it also affects a person's relations with other people. A person is inclined to feel hostile toward other people whose behavior represents his own denied feelings.

How can this breach between self and organism be healed? Rogers proposes that this can take place during therapy in a nonthreatening situation where the therapist is accepting of everything the client says. The type of therapy that Rogers has evolved is called *nondirective* or *client-centered.* Under these conditions, the client is able to examine experiences that are inconsistent with the self-structure and assimilate them into the self. When this is done—that is, when the self-structure becomes more congruous with the experiences of the organism—the person is not only better adjusted and more fully functioning but also more understanding and accepting of others.

Allport's Psychology of the Individual

Gordon Allport (1897–1968) was for many years professor of psychology at Harvard University, and in many respects his orientation resembles that of his famous predecessor William James, perhaps the most illustrious name in American psychology. Allport was interested in understanding the personality of the normal human being. He felt that there was a discontinuity between the normal person and the abnormal one, between child and adult, and between animal and man, so that any model of personality based upon observations and studies of the mentally sick, of children, or of animals was inadequate for representing the personality of the normal adult. Furthermore, he tended to reject the concept of the unconscious, feeling that for the normal person, at least, conscious determinants of behavior are of overwhelming importance.

The most important concept in Allport's theory is that of *trait,* a predisposition to respond to many different kinds of stimuli in an equivalent manner. A trait not only initiates behavior but also guides how one will behave. Therefore, traits are not only structures of the personality but also motives.

Allport distinguished between several classes of traits. There are, for example, *individual* and *common traits.* In reality, no two individuals have exactly the same traits. Thus, in the most important sense, all traits are individual. But because of the common influences involved in a shared culture and a common biology, individuals do develop some roughly comparable traits.

There are also *cardinal traits, central traits,* and *secondary traits.* A cardinal trait is one that is so pervasive in the personality that few of the person's activities cannot be traced to it. Cardinal traits are relatively uncommon and are not to be found in every person—Tolstoy, it is said, had only one cardinal trait late in his life, that of simplification. More typical are the central traits, which represent tendencies that are characteristic of the individual, are often expressed, and are quite visible. Allport suggested that the number of central traits by which a personality can be described is surprisingly few, perhaps no more than five or ten. H. G. Wells asserted, for instance, that there were only two major themes in his life: interest in world government and sex. Secondary traits are more limited in their occurrence, less crucial in the personality, and more closely tied to specific responses and situations.

Do traits grow out of the basic organic drives of the person? Allport said no. Traits are *functionally autonomous* and have no connection, except perhaps a historical one, with the basic biological needs. According to this theory of functional autonomy, for which Allport is noted, a given form of behavior becomes an end in itself despite the fact that it may have been originally engaged in for some other reason. A trait that has become autonomous is capable of sustaining itself indefinitely in the absence of any biological reinforcement. For example, a child may originally want to achieve or produce something in order to please his mother, but as he grows up, achievement and production are sought for their own sake and have become independent of the functions they originally served. Thus, by functional autonomy the person is divorced from his past. Motives or traits, Allport asserted, are contemporary and are not bound to their historical origins. Adult motives supplant the motives of infancy. Personality development is discontinuous.

Allport, like Jung, placed great emphasis upon the forward-looking character of personality. What the person's intentions are is of greater importance than the past in determining his present behavior.

Sheldon's Constitutional Theory

That there is a fairly close correlation between physique and personality has always been a popular notion. Fat men are jolly and sociable, and lean ones are morose and moody. A number of attempts have been made to relate physique and character, but the most ambitious and rigorous one is associated with William Sheldon, who earned both a Ph.D. in psychology and an M.D. at the University of Chicago.

In Sheldon's theory, we find a clear and vigorous exposition of the crucial importance of the physical structure of the body as a primary determinant of behavior. Moreover, he has identified a set of objective variables that can be used as a bridgehead for describing physique and behavior.

Dimensions of Physique Sheldon's first task was to identify the primary components of physique. In order to do this, he took photographs of about 4,000 male college students, and by inspection of these pictures he teased out three primary components of physical variation. The first component is *endomorphy,* which is characterized by a soft and spherical appearance. The digestive viscera are highly developed and the bones and muscles are underdeveloped. The person high in this component is a fat person. The second component is *mesomorphy,* which is characterized by a hard and rectangular body, with a predominance of bone and muscle. The mesomorphic body is strong and tough. A person high in this component has an athletic build. The third component is *ectomorphy,* which is characterized by thinness, light muscles, fragility, and a large brain and central nervous system. A person high in this component is the skinny individual.

Few individuals are pure endomorphs, mesomorphs, or ectomorphs. Most people have some degree of all three. Sheldon developed a method called *somatotyping* for rating an individual on each of the primary components. The somatotype of the individual is expressed by three numbers, the first of which always refers to endomorphy, the second to mesomorphy, and the third to ectomorphy. The numerals range from 1 to 7, with 1 representing the absolute minimum of the component and 7 the highest possible amount. The rating of 4 is average. Thus, a person who has a somatotype represented by the numbers 462 is average in endomorphy, high in mesomorphy, and quite low in ectomorphy.

Figure 25.16
The appearance of the extreme endomorph, the extreme mesomorph, the extreme ectomorph, and a type having moderate degrees of all three components. (After Sheldon, 1954.)

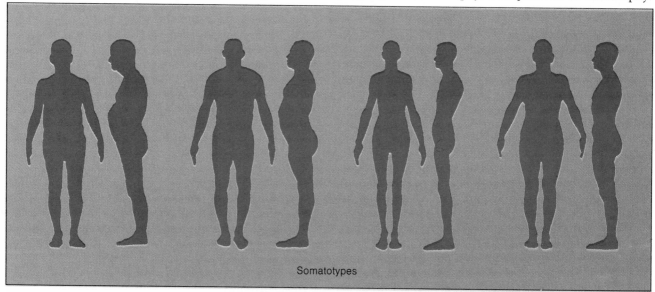

Somatotypes

Although there are 343 possible somatotypes, less than a 100 different ones have been found in a sample of 40,000 human physiques.

Dimensions of Temperament The next step was to identify the primary dimensions of personality, or temperament, as Sheldon prefers to call the behavior of a person. Starting with 650 traits, Sheldon reduced the list to 50 traits that seemed to represent all the specific phenomena dealt with by the original 650. He then observed a group of 33 young men for a period of a year. Each subject was rated on a 7-point scale for each of the 50 traits, and these ratings were then intercorrelated in order to find clusters of traits that correlated highly positive with each other and negatively with other clusters of traits. The results of the correlational analysis revealed three major clusters, to which Sheldon gave the names *viscerotonia,* *somatotonia,* and *cerebrotonia.* Viscerotonia is characterized by love of comfort, sociability, gluttony, relaxation, slow reactions, even temper, and tolerance. Somatotonia is characterized by aggressiveness, courage, vigorous activity, and domination. Among the cluster of traits under cerebrotonia are restraint, inhibition, secretiveness, self-consciousness, fear of people, overquick reactions, preference for solitude, and youthful appearance.

Temperamental typing yields three ratings on a 7-point scale for an individual. The first number stands for viscerotonia, the second for somatotonia, and the third for cerebrotonia. The next step was to find the relationship between the somatotype and the temperamental type. When this was done, a high correlation was obtained. That is, if a person had a somatotype of 462, he tended also to have a temperamental type of 462 or close to it.

What accounts for this close congruence between physique and temperament? Sheldon has considered four possible answers. First, the commonality may be due to genetic or inborn factors. Second, the congruence may be produced by common environmental determinants. The other two explanations are somewhat more complicated. One states that the relation is mediated by commonly accepted stereotypes existing in a given culture. A person with a mesomorphic build is expected to behave in a different manner than one with a predominantly ectomorphic build. The other explanation suggests that the success or reward that accompanies a particular way of behaving is a function not only of the environment but also of the kind of physique the person has. The person with a frail, ectomorphic body cannot successfully adopt an aggressive, dominant manner in relation to people, nor does a fat person get much pleasure from vigorous sports. Consequently, a person tends to form those habits and interests that are in keeping with his physique.

Trends for the Future

It is perhaps a truism that everyone living has his own theory of personality, of what people are really like. The psychological theories described above are more complete systems than those held by the average man, but even Freud's theory is inadequate and incomplete. Man is just beginning to study his own behavior objectively, to evaluate what he is like without passing judgment on what he is. As our theories of personality become more sophisticated, they must begin to include all the new experimental data on the biological underpinnings of man's behavior. The trend in the future will probably be away from the humanistic, almost literary descriptions of man as a spiritual entity toward man as a biosocial machine. A start in this direction has already come about with the rise to prominence of behavioristic psychology. Whether a mechanistic theory of personality will be more complete remains to be seen; that such an approach may lead to a reevaluation of psychotherapeutic techniques is explained in detail in Chapter 35.

26

ADJUSTMENT

IN HIS FAMOUS PLAY *The Admirable Crichton,* Sir James M. Barrie calls attention to a thorny problem of social injustice. A titled British family is shipwrecked on a desert island. Back home in England, these members of the upper class were waited on hand and foot; they would have thought it strange indeed if someone had suggested that they do something for themselves.

Work of any kind was anathema to them; hard labor was something you hired other people to do. They were perfectly adjusted to this life of ease and looked down on their butler, Crichton, as their social inferior. On the island, however, their money and their nobility were useless, and none of them was psychologically equipped to face such a changed situation. It was Crichton who saved them, who took over direction of their lives and forced them to put their past habits aside and face the realities of survival under primitive conditions. Crichton, the servitor, becomes the leader; the pretty daughter even falls in love with him. It is he, Barrie suggests, who has the true nobility, that of the quick mind that adapts to whatever surroundings it finds itself in. At the end of the play, however, when a ship rescues them, Crichton is demoted back to the position of a social inferior. But Barrie makes it clear that, even in this role, the admirable Crichton will survive and prosper, while the family he serves represents a kind of evolutionary blind alley.

The psychological evolution of society has been continuous invention and adjustment to meet the shifting demands and challenges of living. Thus, no one form of society is perfectly adapted to every era. Because society's structure is shaped to fit the temper of the times, in the face of catastrophe or cataclysm it

may change too slowly to survive the forces that would destroy it. In this sense, then, an individual discontented with the world as it is may be best able to survive its destruction and best able to adjust to the future.

The Meaning of Adjustment One can distinguish four phases of human adjustment: drive or instigation, seeking a solution, attaining a goal, and reducing tension. However, this view is a simplistic account of modern theory because it suggests that adjustment is best defined as any behavior that brings drive, need, motive, or instigation to a halt. For example, if you are cold and put on a sweater, this act is an adjustment, or if you avoid someone who angers you, this is an adjustment. Adjustment, in these terms, is nothing more or less than action that relieves tension and restores a previous equilibrium and sense of well-being. If we were to accept this definition, we need only ask how people learn to reduce tensions, satisfy needs, and restore balance to life to understand adjustment. This purely mechanical approach proposes that we learn to live with things as they are and not rebel against them. Many theorists emphatically reject such an interpretation. In their view, adjustment is neither bad nor good—it just is. What criteria, then, can be used to decide whether adjusting is an appropriate or inappropriate response?

Sheer survival is one measure; if adjusting results in the useless end of an individual's life, it might better be labeled maladjustment. Efficiency in getting along with society is another possible measure. But efficient social adjustment is costly if it means accepting a way of life that violates one's attitudes, beliefs, or fundamental values. There are also legal definitions of appropriate adjustment (obeying society's laws), statistical definitions (doing, on the average, what others do), and ethical definitions (acting consistently in terms of religious or philosophical views). Further, we can accept as appropriate those adjustments that reduce tension, do not interfere with other important motives in our life, and do not interfere with the attempt of other persons to adjust to the forces in their own lives.

Human beings have needs, urges, and impulses but live in a complicated society that sometimes makes adjustment by any definition almost impossible. College students, for example, well illustrate how social directions can take a wrong turn. College students have always run a little wild while out from under the parental thumb, but in the past they usually adjusted to the adult world in just enough time to worry about the irresponsible generation that followed them. Today's youth know that if they want a chunk of the good life in our society they must suffer being imprisoned in kidhood while supported financially by their parents until they graduate from college. As society becomes increasingly technological and computerized, technical training beyond the bachelor degree will extend this imprisonment for four or more additional years. Furthermore, whereas until recently relatively few attended universities, today increasing numbers of young people know they must attend, interested or not. Instead of adjusting quietly to college life not of their choosing, they are rebelling against being physical adults and social kids. They are tearing up a way of life that confuses them and makes them miserable. They are demanding change. Surprisingly, their descriptions of their maladjustment are frequently accurate. They demand changes in a university life that was designed to be appropriate fifty years ago. Thus, if these students were adjusting passively, they might be displaying the least mature of all possible responses.

Violent protest has become an outlet for some, but most people adjust by *accommodating* pressure—that is, by subordinating one set of urges in order to gratify another—or by *assimilating* pressure—that is, by mastering, eliminating, or rejecting one part of the conflicting demands.

The *accommodator* adjusts his feelings and pattern of behavior to fit the demands made on him and comes up with a compromise that he can live with.

This is not a perfect way to deal with the forces of his life, but it works and he gains enough in the way of gratification to be willing to pay the price it exacts.

The *assimilator* also adjusts to the demands social life makes on him, but he does so only if these demands do not dominate his personal life or dictate his every move. He remains his own person, resists group pressures that violate his beliefs, and tolerates disapproval of his way of life if he must. He believes that his view of life is accurate, even if others disagree. Being part of society yet his own person may cause him doubt and uncertainty, but he knows no other way to maintain his dignity. He may be an uncomfortable and reluctant member of the establishment, or he may paint himself some strange color, let his hair grow long, and visibly protest the direction the culture seems to be taking. In any case, he refuses to sell his self-respect to gain the approval of others. It is the assimilators of this world who are most likely to alter the direction of society. Although the alienated nonaccommodators and nonassimilators perform a vital function in provoking the apathetic majority, they burst brilliantly on the horizon only to vanish shortly, leaving the assimilators to convert dreams and hopes into a workable plan for society.

Components of Adjustment

We have considered generally the hopes, goals, and kinds of possible adjustment available to man, but we must now examine the complex problems that adjusting poses for the individual. Adjustment and maladjustment are customary terms for describing how frustration and anxiety are dealt with and how conflict is resolved. Frustration may generate conflict, cause anxiety, and destroy even the most vigorous attempts to adjust. When conflict is free of frustration and anxiety, it is no more significant in human life than the indecision of an engineer who must choose one of a number of equally acceptable alternatives for solving a complicated problem. His choice is rational rather than emotional, and his decision has little to do with how he leads his life or what pain or pleasure it brings him. In contrast, personal, psychological, and social decisions have consequences that are much more crucial to the satisfaction of our basic needs. To comprehend these complications, the notions of frustration and anxiety must be examined.

Frustration and Adjustment

There are several ways to view frustration. It may be treated as an exclusively internal state of the human organism (unsatisfied hunger), it can be described solely in terms of observable human behavior (someone appears frustrated), or it can be seen as an ideal or theoretical construct invented by researchers to explain human behavior by connecting what went before with what happened afterward.

One complication to any consideration of adjustment is that humans react in different ways to different sources of frustration. It makes a great deal of difference if frustration is due to physical obstacles rather than personal biological or psychological limitations. People are frustrated by other people more often than by physical obstacles or personal limitations, and their responses differ according to the source. Frustration is inevitable, and a measure of superior adjustment is a person's capacity to tolerate frustration, delay, and conflict without resorting to maladaptive responses. Because frustration is inevitable, an important aspect of growth and development lies in learning how to manage frustration in ways that are not destructive to the self or to others.

The frustration-aggression hypothesis of John Dollard and his colleagues at Yale suggests that frustration is produced when goals are interfered with and that aggression is a frequent (but not exclusive) response to frustration. The stronger

a person's drive toward a goal, of course, the greater the amount of frustration he experiences. In much the same fashion, the more times one is frustrated, the greater the anticipated response to frustration.

Aggression is not the only possible response to frustration. For example, Maier noted that *fixation* might be one response to frustration. In reporting his research with rats, he described a phenomenon called behavior without a goal—the recourse to a fixated and unproductive pattern of response to difficult situations. Maier forced rats to jump across an open space into small windows blocked by cardboard. If a rat chose the correct window, it landed safely and was fed; if it chose the wrong window, it bumped its nose against the unyielding surface and fell to a net below. When Maier rigged the experiment so that the rat could never solve the problem, the rat would choose one window and jump at it continuously even though it always hit its nose and fell into the net. In essence, the rat would stop trying to solve the problem and would adjust to an inappropriate pattern of response that no longer brought him closer to his goal. Humans, too, persist in making inappropriate responses to challenges cast by the culture.

Stress and Adjustment

Before conclusions can be reached about the basic adjustive stability of an individual, the element of stress must also be considered. Stress is most often defined as confrontation with an impending harmful event that will prove to be more than one can handle.

How one copes with stress is vital to adjustment. Primary coping is the attempt to deal with problems in the first place, and secondary coping is the attempt to manage problems caused by failure to cope adequately in the first place. Children are much freer than adults to choose to enter those situations they can manage or avoid those they cannot—the adult world is not nearly as permissive or willing to excuse selective participation. Grownups are allowed restricted latitude; that is, they can confront challenges reluctantly, and they can restructure life's situations. They can make life's pressures more comfortable and manageable by seeking advice and help from others or by limiting the risks they are willing to take. Thus, a fearful human being may cope with stress by turning down a new job opportunity (for good rather than real reasons) and protect himself from the emotional turmoil he fears will be its inevitable consequence.

Anxiety and Adjustment

Anxiety is a theoretical construct—an invention of scientists to explain observable behavior. The terms "stress" and "tension" are almost synonymous with "anxiety," but neither term is exactly fitting. Moreover, the words designed to depict degree (acute and chronic) are exceptionally inexact because anxiety is so much a function of the situation in which the individual finds himself.

Rank and Freud held that the original form of anxiety was an outcome of sudden, violent, diffuse stimulation produced by the separation of child from mother at birth. Later in life, when the behavior of other people resembled the threat of that separation, the child is reminded of the original trauma of birth. Thus, initial experience becomes the model for later reactions to interpersonal events.

Theorists of the 1930s and 1940s who went beyond Freud to build their image of the nature of man along social and cultural lines abandoned the concept of primary anxiety occasioned by the fact of birth and looked for an explanation of the relationship of the helpless infant to the all-powerful adults. To be helpless is to lack control over the source of gratifications of pressing needs and to be unprotected from danger. The child's developing awareness of his helplessness

and the concurrent anxiety he feels when his parents are angry and seem to withdraw support set the pattern of future anxiety.

Learning theorists believe that anxiety is formed in the process of seeking pleasure and avoiding pain. In the classic example, cats burned on hot stoves avoid not only hot stoves but cold stoves too; that is, pain avoidance becomes generalized to a host of objects barely related to the painful one. Thus, a child exposed to a great variety of intense fears will be made anxious by situations in adult life that resemble those of his youth. Learning theory, therefore, suggests that in the most perfect of all worlds it would be possible to raise a child almost completely free of anxiety. The science of child rearing is far from achieving such an objective, but it is working diligently to accomplish the reduction of child rearing to a science rather than an art.

Conflict and Adjustment

Conflict, an additional vital aspect of adjustment, results when a person must make a choice between possible alternatives. The conflict may be between incompatible internal and external pressures; between two or more clashing internal needs, wishes, or demands; or between external requirements that cannot simultaneously be satisfied.

All three kinds of conflict can be badly resolved if the level of personal stress is so high that an individual's normal judgment is distorted by anxiety and frustration. Anxiety, for example, interferes with one's ability to manage the complex elements of a problem. Anxiety narrows perception and slows down thinking (you may not get all the facts or understand the ones you have), limits attention and conversation (you are distracted and think in circles), and causes the problem solver to assign improper weight to various alternative solutions (gambling for high stakes to solve a financial problem). Further, stress is so painful that the easy way out may be chosen simply to escape from the pressure of the whole situation itself.

Changes in Adjustment

Everyone experiences different amounts of stress, frustration, anxiety, and conflict at different times in life, and the form and quality of adjustment differ accordingly. Most of the ups and downs of adjustment and maladjustment are self-corrective and do not destroy the individual. For more persons that we would care to count, however, unmanageable amounts of stress can have invisible but devastating consequences. The low points of adjustment may cripple the individual by shaking his basic confidence in his own ability and by killing his enthusiasm for the risk taking necessary for achievement. The victim may be unaware that he has quietly given up and decided to protect what he has rather than try for greater heights.

Maladjustment

The Hell's Angels—the band of leather-jacketed, bearded motorcyclists—are exceptionally well adjusted to the subsociety in which they live. They are free to drink, fight, race, drug themselves, riot, avoid work, and indulge their sexual whims. Their life is an odd mixture of the average man's nightmares and his secret fantasies. The Angels swagger through life speaking an alien jargon, feeling superior to the square citizens, and shocking the social establishment. If the members of the Hell's Angels were a primitive tribe bypassed by civilization, we would view their behavior with amusement and their exploits would be recounted in *National Geographic* rather than the front pages of our newspapers. The question this group poses is how we judge who is maladjusted. Such terms are strikingly relative. Definitions of adjustment or maladjustment in the United

States may be totally inappropriate for a Tokyo taxi driver, a rice farmer in Thailand, a hotel worker in Bombay, or a chambermaid in Paris. That is, judgment of adjustment or maladjustment is *culturally relative*. Furthermore, adjustmental criteria applied to a whole culture do not necessarily fit subgroups within that society (differing social classes, levels of occupation, education, ethnic origins, or religious persuasions). Thus, norms of adjusted behavior are difficult to establish and even more difficult to maintain intact over an extended period of time.

When we speak of adjustment, we must ask, "Adjustment to what?" Because man must adjust to such a multitude of social laws, rules, regulations, attitudes, beliefs, and common cultural practices, a productive way to study the concept of adjustment is to consider it from the vantage point of the primary motives that impel man to action—the drives that propel him out of the cocoon of childhood's dependency into the competitive jungle of people, things, and society. For this purpose, we can select from among the alternatives of sex, aggression, ambition, security, independence, and a host of other possibilities. Because it is so vital an aspect of human existence and so central a part of man's impulse life, aggression can serve as a model for our discussion of adjustment.

Aggression　It is beyond human capacity to reduce so complicated a condition as human aggression to a formula or philosophy adequate to encompass it. The study of aggression has always been a quicksand of words, hypotheses, and interpretations that tell us little. Rage, resentment, or anger may be the emotions that accompany or provoke aggression, but hostility is the enduring condition that makes all of them possible if not probable. The exploration of aggression, then, has always involved the study of human hostility.

In recent times, an ancient view of human aggression has reappeared. Simply put, the theory states that animals are instinctively aggressive; man is an animal (the only one that deliberately kills his own kind); human aggression is rooted in man's inherited instincts. This formula is depressing for the future of man in light of the frustration and stress of living in the complex cities and conflict-laden societies of this age.

In contradistinction to this pessimistic view, other theorists suggest that there is no adequate scientific proof that aggressive instincts really exist in human beings. They maintain that *Homo sapiens* learns to be hostile, to hate, to rage, and to attack—that bad teaching rather than bad gene is the culprit in human destruction. This is a philosophy of hope, not despair, for it suggests that man is not the victim of fixed, rigid inheritance. He is, rather, an improvable mortal in whom acts of violence and aggression will diminish when social injustices and inequalities are resolved, when the young learn to value peaceful ways, and when the problems of dealing peacefully with other nations are solved.

It would be comforting for man to be able to dismiss his violent behavior by blaming it on his animal nature, for such a theory would allow him to continue to transgress free of guilt. But no studies of animals have conclusively shown aggression to be a product of an instinctive urge in the organism. Rather, the

492

aggressiveness characteristic of every form of life seems to be fashioned from experience. In the study of aggression, the gap between human and animal research is narrowing rapidly enough that the information gained from work with animals can provide a model of cause and effect applicable to that brief period in human development before a child has acquired symbolic means of managing his strong emotions.

Infancy is the only period during which human beings are allowed to aggress as violently as possible against everyone and everything. The raging infant is impotent, of course, for he cannot do much damage and he rages most often with no idea of the cause of his frustration or pain. When he finally discovers what is irritating him, he begins to focus his aggressive behavior on the proper target and hits fewer innocent bystanders. Human targets, unfortunately, strike back. Learning to attack only an innocent, but less dangerous, object never quite works, because it is substantially less satisfying than exacting revenge from the real source of frustration.

The who, when, why, and how of individual aggressive choice are what we must consider. The target chosen and the kind of aggression expressed depend on the availability of targets, the amount of frustration experienced, and the amount of anxiety and guilt likely to accompany aggressiveness. When targets are arrayed for choice, the first choice is between anger directed toward the self and anger directed toward others.

Aggression Directed Outward

Aggression, to most people, means murder, assault, or rape, and many are convinced that our society is being made the victim of increasing violence. Yet a careful review of violent crime statistics suggests that, relatively speaking, there has been no substantial increase in aggressive crimes during recent years. It is true that robbery and forcible rape rates show moderate increases. Aggravated assault rates have increased the most but are far below the rate increases for property or nonviolent crime. In fact, it is quite likely that the changing form in which crime is reported is what has created a paper crime wave of staggering proportions. If simple categories of offense (assault and robbery, for example) are reported with no information about the *degree* of severity of the crime, then an assault is an assault, with no clear indication that we are or are not becoming more savage as a nation.

The ultimate in aggression—murder or assault—can most often be traced to the male of the species. Males assault others eight times more often than do females, and murder is seven times more often a masculine than a feminine act. Negroes commit a higher absolute and disproportionately higher relative rate of fatal crimes. Violence in the South—black or white—is greater than in the North, and the rate of violence in the inner city of large population centers is uniformly high. Homicide is most frequent among members of the lower socioeconomic classes, especially between the ages of twenty and thirty-nine. But these myriad facts of fatal encounter do not help much in solving the complicated jigsaw puzzle of murderous aggressive acts. Such acts can be understood only by examining the multiple factors involved and considering the acts as resolutions of forces both without and within the individual—a resolution of forces that produces a single act, which, in the case of murder, is so dramatic that it obscures the very forces that led to it.

Murder is so difficult to understand that the average person has many misconceptions about it. Scientific research on murderers, for example, has disproved one such notion, that the hostile ones among us form some kind of pool from which will come the murderers of the world. Those who have examined the issue objectively report that murderers tend to be the most docile, trustworthy, and least violent members of prison populations. In order to confirm these unusual conclusions, the aggressive behavior of delinquents in a detention home was studied. As predicted, those inmates who committed *extremely assaultive* crimes were the most cooperative, most self-controlled, and least aggressive inmates. These findings suggest that although murder is a highly visible measure of the violent individual, it need not reflect a lifelong pattern of assaultive behavior. Murder is often the desperate response of a normally unaggressive person who can no longer tolerate the pressures of life.

In addition, it has long been known that murderers are most often a friend, relative, or loved one of the victim. Those who live in terror of darkened streets might better examine their relationships with those closest to them.

Aggression Directed Inward

Aggression directed inward, with the self as a target, is an even more difficult theoretical tangle to unravel. Because it is not possible to study those who succeed in killing themselves, we must rely on the speculative reconstruction of what led to the act. The closer we look, the more evident it becomes that suicide is a complicated psychodynamic event in human life and that the distinction between murder and suicide may be misleading. Suicide is, of course, the most violent form of aggression directed to the self, but it is only one of the many forms of self-punishment.

In the United States, suicide rates vary with status in society. Those most socially favored have a higher relative rate than those lower on the socioeconomic scale. City residents kill themselves more often than do rural dwellers, and those living in the most crowded areas do so with highest frequency. Married people destroy themselves more frequently than do those who are single, widowed, or divorced. Suicide becomes more frequent with increasing age, and males are more likely than females to take their own lives. The male is not superior in this respect because women do not try (they do, more often) but because males are better at the task of ending their own lives.

How do we account for those who choose to destroy themselves? Among those who favor a purely social view of motivation, Durkheim suggests that there are three kinds of suicide: *egoistic suicide* (the individual is unable to integrate himself into society and chooses death rather than being without a meaningful place in the group), *altruistic suicide* (a cultural hero has become so involved in a social group that he sacrifices his life to assure the survival of the group), and *anomic suicide* (an individual kills himself in response to the feeling that the group or society from which he drew a sense of security has fallen apart and is no longer reliable).

In his modification of Freud's view of man's lingering wish for death, Menninger subdivided the aggressive drive into a series of elements to explain suicide. Suicide obviously contains the wish to kill, but in choosing himself as the victim, the individual is also expressing the wish to be killed. The need to suffer can take a lesser form and appear only in the passive placing of oneself in the path of a destructive force—under some circumstances, smoking, drinking, gambling, and provoking others may be a subtle way of saying, "Kill me, I want to die." Suicide is a quicker and cleaner solution to the problem of ending life than the slower and more prolonged forms of self-destruction in which one kills or cripples himself little by little. The ascetic, the martyr, the neurotic invalid, the hypochondriac, the alcoholic, the reckless driver, and the drug addict—all

may be turning aggression against the self in a subtle, unpredictable, slow-motion suicide.

Aggression turned on the self in the form of suicide is an unsolvable riddle. Suicide is logical and illogical at the same time. It is an unadjustive response to the pressures of life, just as murder is an inordinate response to its provocations.

Catharsis

Whether aggression is turned toward others or against the self, most people think that the best way to deal with an aggressive itch is to scratch it: it is "unhealthy" to be frustrated by holding in aggressive urges without blowing off steam once in a while. This justification for aggressive outbursts is as ancient as man, but it was given powerful impetus in years past by popular misinterpretations of Freudian theory. The belief that periodic catharsis, or releasing tensions, is healthy also implies acceptance of the notion that aggression is very much like hunger, thirst, sex, or some other biological drive. That is, relieving tension by aggressing reduces the urge to anger until the tension builds up again and explosion is once more necessary. Unfortunately, however, human beings are not quite this simple.

Venting hostile feelings would be absolutely effective if it could be done without the discomfort of guilt or anxiety. The script most often acted out, however, is as follows: Provocation or frustration again and again; a final frustration—the lash that drives the camel to his knees—then indulgence in an orgy of moral outrage, shouting, and abuse at the nearest and dearest; when the spasm has run its course, feeling drained of emotion and only then becoming aware of the steady squeeze of guilt and remorse for inability to control feelings. The victims did not deserve the outburst, and the unintentional regression to childish behavior produced the retribution of guilt feelings. Thus, the catharsis of aggressive feelings may reduce the probability of a similar outburst in the near future—not because internal, psychic pressure has been relieved but from shame that maturity disappeared so easily when it was most needed.

Someone seeking a superior means of aggressing against others—one that is freer of guilt, remorse, and anxiety—might better disguise hostility behind the mask of being open, honest, frank, and helpful to others. There is an unlimited range of hurtful items that can be passed on to others "for their own good." Under the guise of frankness and honesty, an enormous amount of hostility can be expressed openly, frequently, and with some pride. The most caustic, abrasive person may justify his style of life in terms of "straightening other people out" and thus feel good and be guilt-free about his aggression.

The Aggressive Person

It seems to be true that into each life a sprinkle of aggressive persons must fall, and we have difficulty understanding how they could possibly become so different from ourselves. Berkowitz's view of aggressive personalities offers a sociopsychological view of why such persons react as they do and how they became that type of person.

Berkowitz believes that aggressiveness is a habit learned via the rewards and punishments life metes out. The aggressive person is not continually angry or driven day and night by hostile urges. He has, rather, a "predisposition to be readily aroused" to anger and rage; that is, he is excessively quick to respond with anger to events that are neutral and nonprovocative to most people. When this habit is combined with an appropriate stimulus or provocation, the aggressive person frequently blows up. Cues or signals to aggression are not always present in the environment, and the habitually aggressive person has his quiet moments and resembles the rest of us at those times. He is rational and unaggressive during much of his daily life and thus tends to view himself as a calm, reasonable person when he is not being provoked beyond all human tolerance. Aggressive persons confirm their self-view by believing that the rest of the human race are sheep—passive, spineless, and too tolerant.

To become an aggressive person, one need only learn to associate certain internal feelings with threatening stimuli from the outside world. Someone with a rigidly negative attitude toward a wide range of persons and events will habitually respond in an aggressive fashion because one or another provocation is always present. A habitually aggressive person, according to Berkowitz, is someone who has developed a particular attitude toward large segments of the world about him and has learned to interpret (or categorize) a wide variety of situations and/or people as threatening or otherwise frustrating to him. This threat and frustration is reacted to habitually in an aggressive manner.

A truly aggressive person is consistent in his pattern of behavior. The results of one study suggest that this kind of consistency is learned early and practiced often. Extremely hostile boys between the ages of eight and eleven were studied and found to have substantially less variety in the ways they responded to different situations. Through the eyes of these aggressive boys, a great many situations seemed similar, and all evoked hostile rather than nonhostile responses. Most people like to believe that they judge situations objectively and do not attribute threat and frustration where it does not properly belong. The average person has a great variety of responses and employs raw aggressiveness only as a last resort. This is not the case with the aggressive personality.

What of the child-training and family interrelationships that contribute to the development of aggressive persons? When ratings of aggressive boys are compared with more acceptably socialized counterparts, aggressive boys express aggression in an uninhibited and direct fashion, have fewer positive feelings toward their peers, and are more openly antagonistic toward authority figures. They respect their mothers but feel rejected by both parents and are resentful and critical of their fathers. They seem markedly distrustful and fearful of situations that might force them to become emotionally dependent on others. Aggressive behavior, moreover, is often self-defeating, because it alienates the person from the affection he already feels deprived of and brings him under the more direct control of the authority figures whom he distrusts and resents. Aggressive young persons inevitably fall into a familiar trap in which the more they struggle to escape, the deeper they sink into the quagmire of a personal and social dilemma.

Psychologists, then, tend to think of aggression as a learned reaction to frustration brought about by parental and social reward and punishment. If a child learns to see personal frustration in every nook and cranny of life, each new frustration will reaffirm his expectation that things will always go wrong and readies him to respond aggressively. Sensitized to frustration and ever ready to respond aggressively, he has few other available forms of response; he becomes the familiar aggressive personality.

Adjustment and Maturity

Maturity and adjustment have long been confused because the terms were used interchangeably. A mature person was, by definition, well adjusted to people and life. Thus, Genghis Khan was beautifully adjusted to the task of laying Asia waste, Adolf Hitler was adjusted to the presence of concentration camp ovens, and the slum lords of today are remarkably well adjusted to the presence of rats in their profitable tenements. A closer look at what it means to be mature must be taken, for it is obvious that in many instances the most mature person in society may be the one who is least well adjusted to it.

Maturity is, of course, not something one has but rather is an ongoing striving toward a goal that is probably never reached in most lifetimes. No one knows exactly what a fully mature person would look like or how he would behave. Usually maturity is confounded with old age; younger leaders are said to have charisma; older leaders are said to be mature. Time, too, is a great eraser of immaturity. Most people think of Abraham Lincoln as a near-perfect example of maturity, but he was a president heavily abused in print in his day and seriously troubled as a person.

In defining what it means to be mature, experts and nonexperts at least agree that the mature person is realistic. He has developed a style of life that is not fixed or rigid, a way of living that allows him to grow as a person by keeping his mind open to change and new experience. They further agree that maturity is made up of compassion and tolerance for others that allow the mature person to establish sensitive, tender, loving relationships with his fellow human beings.

The mature person is certainly more than a simple collection of parts, traits, or characteristics; he must have managed a unique combination of the elements all of us possess, producing a pattern sought after by each of us. The most immature person among us can, at times, rise to exceptional maturity, just as his mature idol can buckle and warp under pressure or strain. Despite the seeming impossibility of putting maturity under the scientific microscope, we can agree that, at a minimum, the mature person ought to be one who is psychologically

healthy. This is not to say he is free of conflict or difficulties in adjustment, but he solves his problems in a consistently adaptive and productive way.

Psychological health implies that the mature individual must come to terms with what most of us believe to be real. Acceptance of common reality is a familiar measure of sanity in every society, but this does not mean blind acceptance of a reality based solely on what other people agree about. When mature citizens disagree bitterly with the popular view, the test of maturity then is how the individual deals with the differences between what he believes and what everyone else accepts as truth.

Becoming mature means discarding old beliefs and substituting new ones as more is learned about life. The beliefs of early childhood or adolescence are appropriate to their time but unworkable for the adult. Each stage of life demands a level of psychological response suited to its requirements. Adult truth is sometimes painful for the developing child to face because it intrudes with little regard for how the world ought to be. Yet facing what is real is the only path to maturity.

If man were without emotions, the task of becoming mature would be simpler indeed. Tempering emotions and channeling their focus become the prime accomplishments of maturity. Infantile, diffuse emotional expression must be tempered by a wise selection of which stimuli are to be responded to, which ignored. An adult whose pattern of emotional reactions remains infantile cannot be successfully integrated into the larger society. Emotional control implies postponing immediate gratification and learning to accept the necessity of work. It means selecting goals and laboring to achieve them.

Finally, maturity calls for a capacity to tolerate the inevitable frustrations of life and the ability to function in the face of fear. The immature person not only is unable to tolerate frustrations but is without the courage to continue to solve problems despite the anxiety they provoke in him. Maturity is a form of knowing oneself, of recognizing emotions and coping with them in a variety of life circumstances. Given these special qualifications, maturity and adjustment can be considered synonymous.

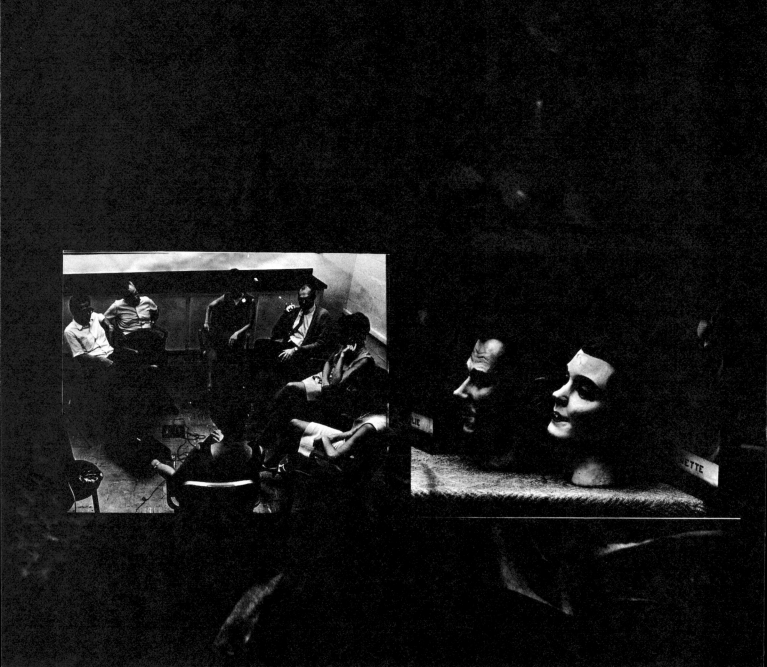

UNIT VII

DISORDER AND THERAPY

The greatest medical problem in the United States today is not cancer or heart attacks or even the common cold; rather, it is the problem of mental health. More than half the hospital beds in the United States are reserved for mental patients, and the money spent on and the pain suffered because of psychological illness are surely overwhelmingly greater than for all other forms of sickness combined. A hundred or so years ago, if your behavior became too aberrant or unusual, it was assumed that you were inhabited by devils, and you were locked up in a quasi-prison where you could do no one (save yourself) harm. Today, we know that "devils" are but a figure of speech and that merely hiding a person away in an insane asylum seldom helps. Mental illness occurs, for the most part, when a person is unable to adapt to the environment in which he finds himself. The only adequate therapy, then, is helping the person find new and better ways of adjusting to his world. Luckily, we are beginning to find ways of helping.

27

BEHAVIOR DISORDERS

IF ABNORMAL PERSONS DID NOT EXIST, our notions of normality would be meaningless, for we judge ourselves in terms of the behavior of others. Unfortunately, "normal" and "abnormal" are strikingly relative terms—terms that have no absolute meaning.

There is a statistical definition of normality and abnormality; normal is what is average or usual, and abnormal is what differs from this standard. Such a definition, however, is useless primarily because it does not tell us *how much* of *what* is too much for most of us to accept. Normality might better be described in terms of approximations to an ideal state of moderation, as defined by a particular culture at a particular time. This criterion implies that each of us needs to achieve a balance in life that is neither self-destructive nor socially destructive. We must, then, balance impulse and action, manage stress in constructive ways, become autonomous (independent of others), and face reality for what it is and become competent in managing it.

We may feel comfortable with our adjustment to life only to find that everyone else considers our actions, thoughts, and feelings to be bizarre, unusual, and socially deviant. The definition of what is or is not bizarre is relative to the society, the era, and the cultural mores of the moment. In the last decade, for example, our society has moved steadily in the direction of a less repressive attitude toward sex. The popular media have allowed freer access to sexual matters in writing, on the stage, and in films. Nudity, once forbidden, has become the vogue on stage and screen. The same degree of nakedness would have been considered bizarre not too long ago and those who participated in it would have been labeled deviant.

Finally, our production-oriented culture uses efficiency and inefficiency as a basis for assessment of normality and abnormality. We are each called upon to fulfill specific roles based on sex, age, vocation, and social status, and the adequacy with which such roles are managed determines who is and who is not normal. When one fails to perform such social tasks in an appropriate manner, he is labeled abnormal.

Thus, "abnormal" would be the term applied to an individual uncomfortable with his life, inefficient in performing the tasks required of him, and bizarre in his actions. Severe difficulty in any one of these three areas may be sufficient reason for society to label a person as being abnormal, as might a mild disorder in each of the three. One conclusion is evident: the notions of normality and abnormality are relative rather than absolute; they are useful abbreviations rather than statements of fact.

Neuroses   Everyone fears some things and takes steps to avoid them. A neurotic fears things inside himself—urges, thoughts, and feelings—whose expression may be punished. The steps the neurotic takes to avoid his fears merely hide rather than abolish them. He is continually anxious that they may reappear. As long as the anxiety is bearable, the neurotic may have no noticeable trouble with life and society. But if the anxiety increases, he must take increasingly severe steps to cope with it. As a result, the neurotic focuses too much on his own internal problems, and his social behavior suffers. His friends recognize that he is anxiously uptight, but they are unable to see inside him to the source of his fears. As the neurotic's social behavior becomes less and less satisfactory, he begins to worry about that, adding to his anxieties. Additional steps are taken to cope with both the internal and the external sources of anxiety. If they fail, a nervous breakdown may ensue; if they succeed, the neurotic lives on in society, but with a limited, anxious existence.

Certain basic theoretical premises are needed to explain the source of disordered human behaviors called neuroses. There is, first, the concept of *repression,* one step by which objectionable impulses are removed from consciousness in order to avoid the anxiety they evoke. We learn to be unaware of the thoughts that trouble us. If repression were always successful, there would be no reason for the emotional overreaction we call neurosis. It is when repression fails to be effective and forbidden thoughts and feelings threaten to return to consciousness that neurotic symptoms come into play as a kind of second line of defense against the threat of anxiety. Symptoms become tension-laden, last-ditch efforts that seem desperate maneuvers to normal persons but are the only defensive compromise the neurotic is capable of making.

Neurosis does not occur suddenly but requires time to develop. During the course of neurotic development, the continual repression of thoughts and impulses is costly. Some part of the psychic energy and attention usually applied to constructive work and managing interpersonal relationships is diverted by the neurotic to guarding the many caged impulses he has found necessary to repress throughout life. By adulthood the neurotic does not have as much free psychic energy as most of us and is thus crippled by limited resources in meeting the challenges of living. The neurotic does not deliberately choose this way of life; he is forced into it by his constant battle with internal and external sources of anxiety created by painful and negative experiences in the course of growing up.

The neurotic lives close to reality, but his is a troubled reality; his world is real but painful. He seldom acts in a totally bizarre fashion, but he is discomforted with life and deals with it in an inefficient manner. Not sick enough to seek treatment and not well enough to be happy, the neurotic may drift in a perpetual limbo of unrelieved emotional distress.

The anxiety the neurotic experiences may appear intellectually in the form of worry and concern, emotionally in the form of depression or mood swings, and physically in the form of any of a variety of bodily symptoms (headache, sweating, muscular tightness, feelings of weakness, heart palpitation). The neurotic's anxiety reaction makes him live a life marked by continuous upset and few periods of true tranquillity.

When this anxiety reaction is focused on a particular object or situation, it is called a *phobia*. Life has many dangers that realistically must be feared, but the victim of a phobia is frightened disproportionately by these aspects of existence. In addition, the phobic may be made anxious by objects or places that seem danger-free to most people (crowds, open spaces, closed areas, heights, germs).

Obsessions and Compulsions

When a neurotic's anxiety becomes unbearably painful, he may begin to display an *obsessive-compulsive* reaction. The obsessive neurotic is totally occupied with recurrent thoughts and actions that he cannot banish from his consciousness. The obsessive-compulsive behavior may be unpleasant and painful, such as a recurrent urge to murder one's family; or pleasant, such as sexual fantasies; or completely harmless, such as avoiding stepping on the cracks in the pavement.

The obsessive person is regularly heavy-laden with worry and doubt. He fears that he has failed to do something that is important to his welfare and to the well-being of his loved ones and may devote such an inordinate amount of time to an obsessive-compulsive double-checking of everything he does that he consequently accomplishes very little. He is even more threatened by being forced to make a decision about the future.

Obsessive-compulsive solutions to the problem of anxiety most frequently occur in intelligent persons with relatively high social status. This response to anxiety is intellectual—less direct and primitive than a neurosis such as hysteria.

Hysteria

The form of neurosis characterized by a collection of physical symptoms that exist without an actual organic basis is known as hysteria. The hysterical personality may experience a loss of hearing, speech, touch, or vision or may be the victim of severe pain or muscular weakness. These symptoms appear to be like those caused by organic illness—and indeed are difficult to differentiate—but they are not quite perfect imitations, for they tend to be greatly exaggerated. Nevertheless, they lessen the individual's anxiety.

The hysteric might awaken one morning paralyzed from the waist down or find himself deaf or blind. A normal reaction to such a traumatic event would be terror, agitation, and violent upset, but the hysteric may placidly lack anxiety about his condition—though this lack of concern is not characteristic of all hysterics. When a hysteric adapts well to such catastrophes, it is thought that the physical symptoms provide freedom from the nagging anxiety that had previously made life miserable for him. Subject to these symptoms, many hysterics live out their lives in the doctor's office, are frequently hospitalized, and experience more than an average number of fruitless surgical explorations.

Neurosis and Depression

When the neurotic fails to solve issues in his life, cope with the usual conflicts, or manage disturbed human relationships, the outcome may be an apathetic

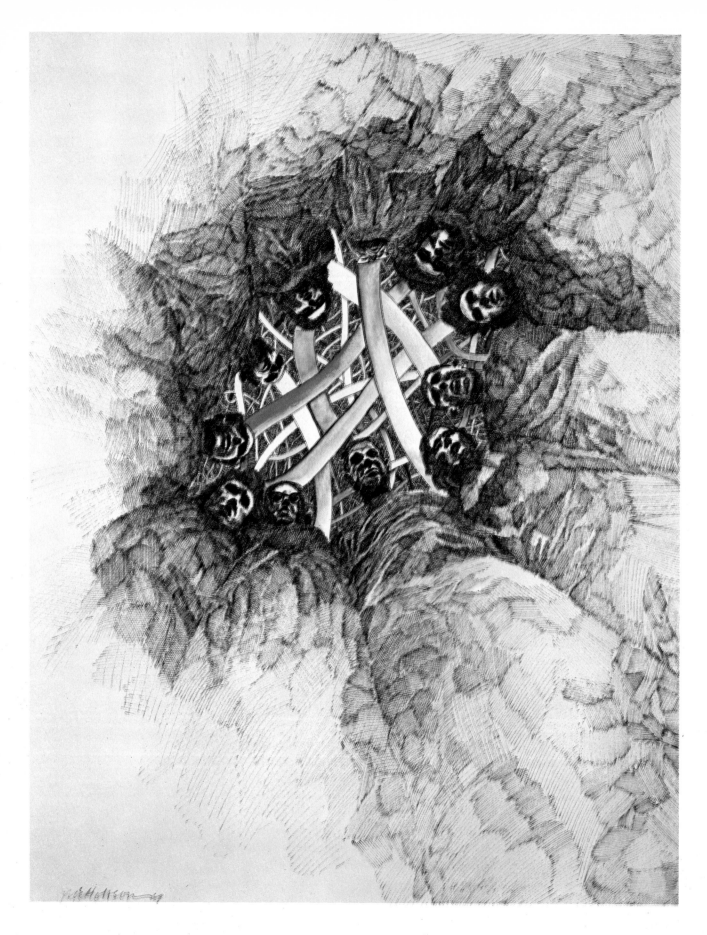

depression in which the individual ceases to function effectively. The "advantage" of depression is that it frees the individual from the pace of life, and this total withdrawal from conflict is a measure of the seriousness of the emotional disorder. Bodily movements slow down and become lethargic, a mood of hopelessness and helplessness pervades, and even mental and intellectual functions seem to drift in slow motion.

Reactive depressions of this kind may be a response to a severe personal loss such as losing a job or the death of a loved one. These depressions differ in intensity and duration from the mood changes that most people experience in such situations. Some neurotics seem moderately depressed throughout their lives, and this depression deepens in time of crisis. This generalized, daily depressive outlook on life may be coupled with an oppressive sense of fatigue, boredom, lassitude, and irritability.

Personality Disorders

Neurotic behavior comes about through attempts to control anxiety and is clearly abnormal. Other kinds of abnormality, not necessarily based on anxiety, include such personality disorders as psychopathy and sexual deviance. In each case, the person's life style is marked by a limited capacity to adapt to circumstances, with a consequent rigid and unsuccessful attempt to establish a rational, stable, rewarding relationship to the environment and the people who inhabit it. The behavior of such persons appears socially inappropriate and, on closer inspection, is found to be inflexible, self-defeating, unstable, and immature.

Most theorists believe that these disorders are based on anxious and painful childhood experiences that the developing person has not coped with successfully. The adult with a disordered personality acts out his conflicts in ways that bring rejection, censure, and punishment by the better-adjusted members of society. Those with personality disorders have failed to learn socially acceptable ways of resolving conflict and attaining gratification of their needs.

The Psychopath

The psychopath has been described as a person who misbehaves socially, is without guilt about his misbehavior, and is incapable of forming lasting affectionate bonds with other human beings. Thus, "sociopath" would be a more appropriate description.

Some sociopaths, or psychopaths, are irresponsible, emotionally shallow humans who cannot avoid getting into social trouble; some are in aggressive and open rebellion against society; some are criminals that prey on others as a way of life. Yet these types have certain common characteristics: each has failed to develop a conscience; is egocentric, impulsive, and irresponsible; cannot tolerate the normal frustrations usually taken for granted; and exercises poor judgment in seeking immediate gratification for his needs at the expense of more important and valuable long-term goals. The psychopath may be intelligent and charming, but his relationships to others are emotionless—without depth, love, or loyalty. He mimics human emotions that he cannot feel, and he cannot organize his life past the pleasures of the moment and the lure of immediate temptation. He is an indulged, spoiled child grown up; he has a child's maturity in an adult's body. Moreover, he has little insight about the kind of person he is and seems unable to profit from past errors in his style of life.

There are two schools of thought about how the psychopath developed. First, biologically oriented theorists have proposed that such a violent, impulsive lack of concern for the rules of social living must have a hereditary basis. These theorists, for example, point to the current discoveries of abnormal chromosomal structure in hardened criminals as evidence that these persons have never been quite normal and are not really responsible for the way they have developed. However, only a small percentage of known criminals and psychopaths display such physical indications of deviation, and other explanations are needed to complete the developmental picture of the psychopath.

The second and larger group of theorists assumes that parents' emotional deprivation and failure to instill an appropriate set of standards and values in the child produced the psychopath. Without proper guidance, the child does not learn to deal constructively with frustration, to have a conscience about his actions, or to model himself after socially successful persons. An absent father, a smotheringly indulgent mother, and a family setting that permits unrestricted self-gratification may encourage the development of an egocentric adult who recklessly and impulsively demands what he wants when he wants it.

Antisocial reactions can also be spawned in the poverty-stricken pockets of our culture in which prejudice, social injustice, and discrimination have taught the growing child to take what he can get today because there will be little opportunity for him to earn it honestly tomorrow. Juvenile delinquents learn early in life that there is little payoff to playing by the rules when obedience is so infrequently rewarding. Having learned the lesson of immediate gratification, even if it is at the expense of other people, they can hardly be expected to adopt the pale virtues of delay, hard work, and saving for a rainy day.

Psychopaths grow to adulthood free of anxiety and the need for acceptance and emotional support by other persons. People are like objects to them—something to be used for gratification and then cast coldly aside. Some psychopaths find this formula quite workable and rise to eminent positions. Their psychopathy is not recognized as an emotional disorder, and they are envied as ruthless businessmen or realistically tough and calculating politicians. Others, however, continue to get into trouble with social authority, to get divorced, and to be rejected by others until they finally seek help.

The Sexual Deviant   A deviant is one who departs from accepted standards of proper behavior. Yet it is common knowledge that private sexual behavior regularly differs from the public standards set for it. Normal sexual behavior is relative to what consenting adults agree to in private but popular opinion labels certain forms of sexual expression as sick or disordered. The professional clinician, in contrast, is concerned about sexual activity primarily when it is disordered by being compulsive, exclusive, destructive, accompanied by great anxiety and guilt, bizarre, inefficient, or the cause of discomfort.

Each of us has a biological sexual identity (we learn to feel, think, and act appropriate masculine or feminine roles). For some, however, the supposedly smooth road to mature sexual adjustment proves to be rocky; fears of normal sexual encounter develop, and socially forbidden sexual activities become more attractive. Thus, sexual satisfaction may be sought with such inappropriate objects as members of same sex (homosexuality), children (pedophilia), animals (bestiality), blood relatives (incest), or inanimate symbolic objects (fetishism).

Deviation can take the form of such variations in intensity and frequency of sexual urges as impotence or satyriasis in the male and frigidity or nymphomania in the female. Moreover, there are deviations in sexual gratification. Sexual gratification that can be attained only by means of oral-genital contact (fellatio, of the penis; cunnilingus, of the female genitalia), anal-genital contact (sodomy, between adult males; pederasty, between man and boy), manual or mechanical stimulation (masturbation), displaying the genitalia (exhibitionism), observation of the genitalia or sexual activity of others (voyeurism or scotophilia), or wearing the clothing of the opposite sex (transvestism) is labeled deviant. Further, to be considered normal, sexual pleasure should be attainable without inflicting mental or bodily pain (sadism) or being the victim of such pain (masochism).

■ FREQUENCY AND INTENSITY

Because sex is such a vital part of the total self, an impotent man or a frigid woman may experience more anxiety in our culture than he or she would as members of a less competitive, accomplishment-oriented society. There are several kinds of *impotence*. The male may be unable to achieve an erection, may be unable to maintain it long enough to accomplish the sexual act, or may come to orgasm too soon to satisfy the female. A male may be impotent because he fears that he will not perform in a creditable fashion or because he is inhibited and made anxious by intimate contact with a female. Frigidity may cause a woman to suffer a severe loss of self-esteem (she is not a complete woman) because she is repelled by male advances, is unusually difficult to arouse sexually, or has intercourse without full and satisfying response. These kinds of restricted responses to sexual experience may be based on such realistic fears as pregnancy or disease, or they may reflect an inhibiting guilt over sexuality.

Disorders of excess like *satyriasis* (male) and *nymphomania* (female) are judged to exist not because some persons are far more active sexually than the average but because sexual encounter with a variety of partners reflects a disorder of motivation and emotional involvement in the act. When the urge to sexual contact has a characteristically obsessive or compulsive quality to it, it becomes apparent that sex is being used to satisfy some nonsexual needs. Promiscuous sexual relations, for example, might be used to punish hated parents by flaunting the standards they taught.

■ DEVIANT MODES

Any method of achieving sexual gratification other than heterosexual contact of male and female genitalia used to be considered a perversion. Today it is considered normal for heterosexual activity to include a variety of modes of sexual stimulation, but when other than genital activity is the exclusive source of sexual pleasure, it is labeled deviant. Thus, exclusively oral-genital or anal-genital modes of sexual gratification are considered deviant because they fall short of full heterosexual expression.

For some persons, sexual satisfaction comes not from intercourse but from the act of looking at the naked sexual object. These persons, known as *voyeurs* or *Peeping Toms,* do not fill the seats of burlesque houses, movies promising nakedness, or cafes with topless waitresses. Nor are they the secret peekers at girlie magazines. The voyeur must spy on his object without her knowledge. He fears women and feels inadequate with them. This harmless, immature male gets his pleasure in part from spying on naked women *without their knowledge or permission.* It is this secret invasion of their privacy that fascinates him.

Deviant *exhibitionism* is primarily a male sexual activity. The male who exhibits his penis and masturbates when he has someone's attention is not inviting the female to have intercourse; he is, rather, trying to reassure himself of his maleness by demonstrating that his sex organ is so powerful and potent that it makes women run away frightened. The exhibitionist feels deeply guilty about his behavior but reports that he is unable to manage this impulse when the urge overtakes him.

Transvestism, another male preoccupation, is the donning of female clothing and acting out of the feminine side of an otherwise masculine personality. The transvestite feels like a woman, acts like a woman, and becomes a female version of himself. The sexual stimulation and gratification he experiences are produced both by genital contact with the female undergarments and by the sense of being fused into a woman-man. Contrary to popular belief, transvestites are not always active homosexuals.

Finally among the deviant modes of sexual gratification are *sadism* and *masochism*. Sexual pleasure achievable only when coupled with pain or humiliation is considered deviant. This is not to say that rough sexual play is abnormal; it is rather to underscore the fact that sexual and aggressive impulses and urges can become entangled in such a way that it is difficult to determine which is dominant in the sexual relationship. Some males can only be potent when using, abusing, or humiliating females; some females can only be aroused sexually when totally subservient to an abusive male. Male sadism in sexual encounter was once described as rape with permission, because the male seems incapable of relating to a female unless he has beaten her into submission and rendered her harmless.

■ DEVIANT OBJECTS

Homosexuality in males and *lesbianism* in females have always been a part of human existence, but the frequency has varied from era to era and from culture to culture. Although an estimated one-third to one-half of the male population has had at least some homosexual experience, only about 4 percent of the population is exclusively homosexual. Some latent homosexuals have powerful urges that never reach open expression in sexual encounter but appear only in such secondary forms as feminine interest hobbies and effeminate mannerisms.

Homosexuality is at least as complicated a sexual, interpersonal relationship as is heterosexuality. Thus, to describe homosexuality in grossly simple terms like masculine and feminine or active and passive is to pretend that some persons are not capable of enjoying both homosexual and heterosexual contacts. Homosexuals are more active than heterosexuals, more concerned with sexuality, and more adolescent in their relationships. They are aware early in life that they differ from social expectations, and although they try to excuse their condition on rational grounds, their confused problems of sexual identity indicate otherwise.

It is the choice of object that society labels as deviant, and theorists have attempted for years to account for this choice. As yet, there is no reliable evidence that there is any biological, glandular, or inherited basis for homosexuality. Theorists believe, rather, that the deviant choice of a sexual object is forced on the individual as a consequence of failure to learn the socially prescribed sexual roles or because of distortions introduced into the learning process.

Males selecting other males as sexual objects have been a prime concern in our society. Less attention is directed to lesbian relationships, in part because female homosexuality is less aggressive and such relationships are more easily disguised. After all, two women living together stimulate less gossip than the same living arrangement for two males. Moreover, females tend to establish longer-lasting homosexual relationships than do men. In this respect, males are more volatile, immature, and less reliable as partners.

Another deviation in choice of sexual object takes the form of *fetishism*—sexual stimulation provided by inanimate objects rather than people. Many fetish objects, such as female underclothing, have at least a symbolic relationship to conventional heterosexual objects; that is, they represent a heterosexual experience the fetishist is unable to manage. In a fetish, the part equals the whole, and sexual satisfaction is achieved when the object and fantasies of experience are combined.

The most censured sexual deviations are *pedophilia, incest,* and *bestiality*. As far as sex is concerned, children are sacrosanct. Adults choose children for sexual

molestation in great part because a child is less threatening, is easier to influence and control, and is less likely to reject the amorous pursuer. Children are safe, anxiety-free objects for sexuality. When sexual acts occur with such uncomprehending victims, it is most often a case of a totally or partially impotent male who gives in to his impulses, under the influence of alcohol, with a young female who is related or known to him. Most often, too, the sexual encounter involves masturbatory activity, exhibitionism, or sexual fondling.

Few sexual deviants voluntarily present themselves for therapeutic remedy. Deviants caught up in the coils of the law or anxious deviants perhaps with an overlay of severe personality disorder are those most likely to seek treatment. The sexual deviants whose problems are not personally annoying or publicly visible are reluctant to expose themselves because there are harsh social penalties for their way of life.

Psychoses

It has often been said that the better you get to know a mental patient, the less able you are to find a satisfactory label to describe him. The neurotic may be handicapped in interpersonal relations, but he continues to slug it out with life, emotionally crippled or not. His life is distorted by the persistence of unresolved problems. If these distortions and abnormalities of perception and behavior ever reach such an irrational, fantastic, and fear-laden level that the person withdraws completely from normal life, he is labeled *psychotic*. It has been said that the neurotic dreams in an unreal way about life, whereas the psychotic lives life as an unreal dream.

Both neurosis and psychosis appear to have a common base in tension, anxiety, and threat to the self. But the neurotic attempts to deal and cope with these issues with defenses; the psychotic, without the resources available to the neurotic, gives up and withdraws from life altogether.

The number of persons confined to mental institutions in the United States has risen steadily during this century. Since the 1880s, the population has expanded fourfold, but the number of mental patients has grown by eighteen times, and these statistics reflect only the smallest "official" portion of the emotionally disturbed. Estimates of those disturbed but not hospitalized exceed this total by untold numbers. Most of the increase in hospitalizations has come about because of an increase in facilities, a shift from home to hospital care, and the reduction of the stigma attached to mental illness.

The Nature of Psychosis

Psychosis is not a single disease; therefore, it has no single cause or single cure. It is, rather, a collection of symptoms that indicate that the ego or self is in serious trouble trying to meet the demands of life. In some yet unexplained way, biological and psychological forces combine to produce serious disorder. Either inherited genetic bases or biochemical imbalances can account for the disorder. Neither of these possibilities has been proven beyond scientific doubt.

Most theorists attribute serious disorder to early childhood experience in which the individual has reacted inadequately to stress, has failed to cope with it constructively, and has been forced to defend himself against the onslaught of anxiety. One must defend if coping has failed and defenses against anxiety are disruptive of normal motivation, perception, action, and thinking. This is to say that the psychotic reaches this state because he learns to respond in ways that deviate from the average but are sufficient to solve immediate problems.

Classifications of Psychosis

Classification of human disorder is a complicated endeavor, for diagnosticians disagree about which label best fits a patient. To be scientifically accurate, diagnostic pigeonholes should contain only one disease. Thus, when we call persons psychotic we assume that they are more alike than different, but this is not always true. In addition, human disorder is not a fixed event; the shape and frequency of its appearance change from time to time and differ according to the nature of each cultural group.

Finally, there has been a great deal of discussion among professionals about whether mental illness is really an illness like physical disease or is better seen as a disorder of interpersonal behavior. Because knowing a patient's diagnostic classification tells little about how he will behave, some theorists have insisted that there is no such thing as mental illness in the medical sense of the word "illness." For them, mental illness is an unsolved problem in living—a deformity of personality.

For peace of mind and orderliness—if for no other reason—man does classify and label, however, and psychotic disorders are usually classified as shown in the adjacent breakdown.

The individual severely disturbed in most of the dimensions of human existence may become psychotic, and this disorder may take the particular form generally called schizophrenia. All schizophrenics have in common severe disturbances in the cognitive, emotional, intellectual, and perceptual sense of the self and of others, but each differs from the other along specific dimensions, as can be noted in a brief examination of the subdivisions of schizophrenia.

■ SIMPLE SCHIZOPHRENIA

Simple schizophrenics are not usually subject to hallucinations or delusions, nor do they commonly act in bizarre ways. Rather, they are apathetic, seclusive human beings whose contact with others is minimal and restrictive. They are dull, unresponsive people who find an uncomplicated way of life most suited to them. The ranks of prisoners, hobos, tramps, bums, and prostitutes are swelled by such persons—persons who seem not quite able to make it in life.

■ HEBEPHRENIC SCHIZOPHRENIA

The popular stereotype of insanity stems from observing the bizarre behavior of those who undergo this most severe disintegration of personality. In the hebephrenic type of schizophrenia, speech may be incoherent or unintelligible. The hebephrenic may giggle or laugh inappropriately; he lives in a private world dominated by hallucination, delusion, and fantasy; and his behavior is nearly totally unpredictable. He may believe he is a famous person (Napoleon, God), he may be convinced that the world has come to an end and he is its only survivor, or he may lose bowel and bladder control and act like a very young child. It is this total departure from the real world that is so puzzling to the more normal members of society.

■ CATATONIC SCHIZOPHRENIA

In the catatonic type of schizophrenia, the patient lives in a stuporous state. The catatonic can hold himself in painful postures for hours on end and not show any response to physical discomfort that others would find impossible to bear. He may be mute and sit unmoving and unresponsive on the hospital ward. It is as if the catatonic is paralyzed by fear that any action or reaction on his part will jeopardize his already shaky, threatened security. While the patient inhibits his voluntary actions and resists responding to pressure by others, he may be preoccupied with a stream of hallucinations such as voices that whisper to him of plots against his life. Catatonia is a dramatic, emergency attempt to cope with

Schizophrenic Reactions
  Simple type
  Hebephrenic type
  Catatonic type
  Paranoid type

Affective Reactions
  Manic type
  Depressive type
  Agitated depression

Organic Psychosis
  Acute undifferentiated type
  Chronic undifferentiated type
  Residual type

Schizophrenic Reactions

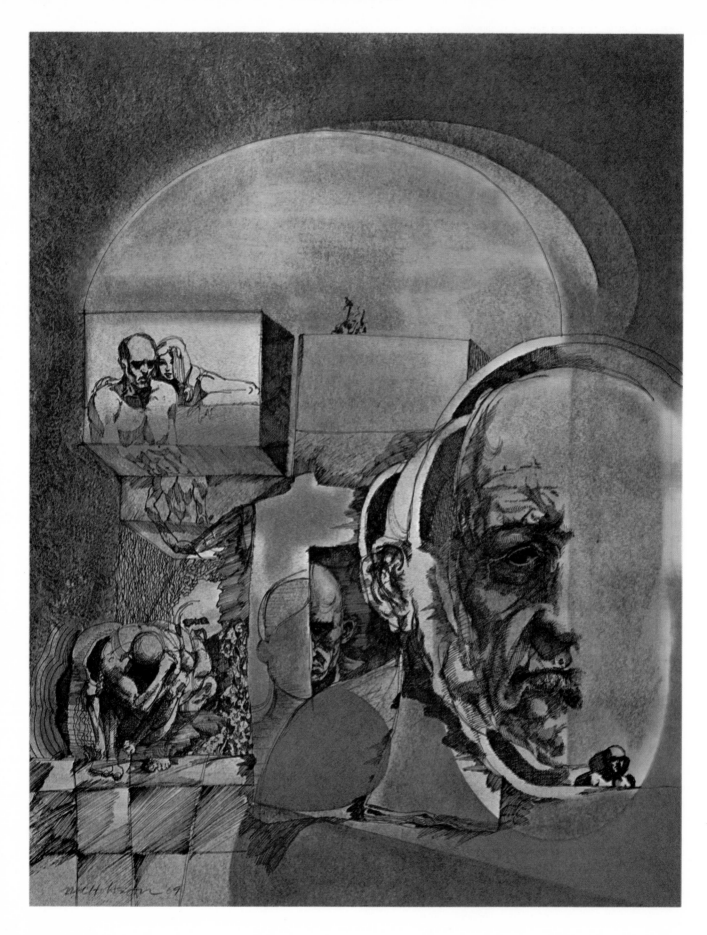

overwhelming, anxiety-laden experiences—seeing no escape, the patient immobilizes himself for fear of making a wrong move.

■ PARANOID SCHIZOPHRENIA

The symptoms of the paranoid schizophrenic are not as visible as the rigid withdrawal of the catatonic or the bizarre behavior of the hebephrenic; the paranoid schizophrenic's difficulty is in the way he views the world and the people in it. He trusts no one and is constantly watchful, for he is convinced others are plotting against him because they are jealous and envious of his superior ability. When to these grandiose paranoid delusions of persecution are added the emotional and mental disorganization of schizophrenia, the paranoid may become dangerous. He may seek to retaliate against his tormenters as he gathers "evidence" of a lifetime of suspicion. Each one of us draws erroneous conclusions about people and events, but we check the accuracy of our beliefs against the opinions and views of others. The mistrustful, resentful paranoid is isolated from such meaningful contact with others and thus systematically constructs a tangled, distorted view of life that warps his whole existence.

Affective Reactions

Typically, 14 percent of the patients admitted to mental hospitals each year are diagnosed as suffering from emotional or affective reactions. These are persons (usually female) suffering mood disorders in which they are excessively and inappropriately happy or unhappy, optimistic or pessimistic, depressed or manic. These emotional disorders may be further complicated by the disintegration and disorder of the schizophrenic process.

■ MANIC REACTIONS

About 30 percent of those with affective disorders are classified as manic. The manic patient displays symptoms of increasing agitation, excitement, and deteriorating judgment and relationships with others. The usual history of an expanding manic reaction describes a lightening of mood, a rising level of activity, a subjective sense of speeded-up thought processes, and increased alertness and perception. As the mania strengthens, speech and activity speed up, eating and sleeping become annoying interferences, and the victim becomes more agitated and easily irritated by attempts to slow him down. In the final stages of a full-blown manic reaction, the patient may be close to delirium, confused, disoriented, incoherent, and difficult to control. His world is very much like a movie that has been speeded up until the figures and events are no more than a blur of frantic, purposeless movement.

■ DEPRESSIVE REACTIONS

Depression and mania at first appear to be opposite sides of the same coin of human adjustment. But theorists have suggested that the frantic activity of the manic is a futile attempt to ward off an underlying depression. In some cases, depression and mania may alternate with one another over short or long periods in a person's life.

Depression, like mania, is an exaggeration of the moods that all of us experience for brief periods of time. The person sinking into a deepening depression begins to be preoccupied with feelings of failure, sinfulness, worthlessness, and despair. He cannot be reasoned with or told to cheer up, for his woe is an internal event that does not correspond to reality as others see it. Overcome with his personal hopelessness, the depressive cuts off communication with the outside world, abandons active attempts to help himself, and usually begins to contemplate ending it all by suicide. The depressive may not hallucinate but he may

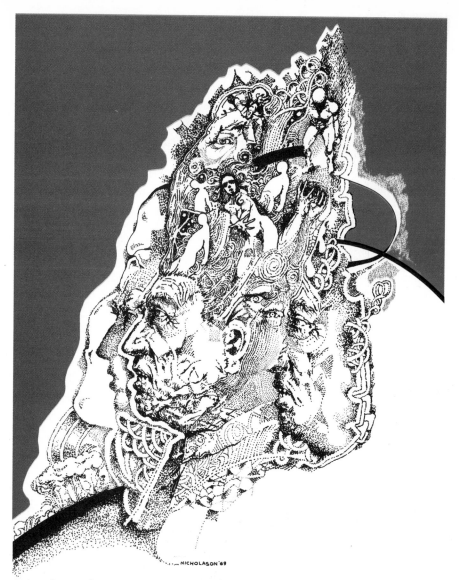

NICHOLASON '69

descend to such a stuporous level of mental and physical inactivity that he may be bedridden and require force-feeding.

■ AGITATED DEPRESSION

The depressed adult or the manic trying to avoid depression may merge in the combined picture of agitated depression. In this case, the predominant mood is one of sadness, but the activity level is agitated and excited. Such persons are usually convinced some catastrophe is imminent, and this delusion drives them restlessly to alert others of what lies just ahead. Worried, anxious, and harried, they scurry about wringing their hands and crying in despair about their fate. What the patient fears is about to occur in the outside world is a reflection of his chaotic, internal psychological condition.

Organic Psychosis

Psychoses resulting from acute or chronic brain disorders will become increasingly common as medical technology extends the average life span of human beings. The brain deterioration that may accompany growing old can distort memory, judgment, comprehension, and emotional control.

Patients in their seventies account for as much as 30 percent of all those admitted to mental hospitals each year. These patients not only have cerebral arteriosclerosis (hardening of the brain arteries) and other forms of senile brain disorder but display unmistakable evidence of psychotic disruption of their lives. Controls patients were once able to exert over their behavior, emotions, and thoughts now seem to deteriorate and become ineffective.

An important observation is that there is no necessary connection between the amount of damage to the central nervous system and the severity of the psychosis. Brain damage does not produce psychosis as much as it triggers the psychotic process in some persons. For some, past, present, and future are jumbled together, conscious and unconscious thoughts merge and mingle, the senses do not function properly, and these events create a psychological crisis great enough to tip the balance of rational adjustment.

Deterioration of the brain and central nervous system in an aging organism is only one of a number of causes of organic psychosis. Psychosis can be associated with infection, trauma, and faulty metabolism, nutrition, or growth. Of these, a significant contributor will continue to be accidental trauma to the brain. We kill more than 50,000 persons each year in automobile accidents and injure a great many more. When brain tissue is cut, torn, crushed, or penetrated in an accident, enough cells may be destroyed to produce a crisis in the person's life.

It is the patient's response to faulty psychological functioning that determines if he will become psychotic or manage to begin the long road back to a near normal existence. The psychological state of an individual before undergoing brain damage is a prime determinant of his response to this new event.

Bringing Order to Disorder

It is beyond the scope of this chapter to describe the variety of treatment methods in current use and specify the efficacy of each method with each disorder. We can, however, outline somatic therapies and psychotherapies.

Somatic Therapy

Somatic therapy covers a wide range of physical treatments known to alter the psychological state. These therapies include convulsions induced biochemically or electrically, brain surgery, and treatment with psychoactive chemicals (psychopharmacology) and are most used in the treatment of psychotic patients.

■ CONVULSIVE SHOCK THERAPY

In the 1930s, it was discovered that such chemicals as insulin or Metrazol would, when introduced into the bloodstream in sufficient quantity, induce a comalike state that relieved certain psychotic symptoms. Precise explanations of how and why this happened were then, and remain today, highly speculative.

Chemical methods of producing coma were quite erratic and unreliable. In addition, the initially exaggerated rates of "cure" were found to be less spectacular and less permanent as time wore on. In the late 1930s, chemical shock was replaced by a more practical, manageable, and equally effective means: electroshock. This method had widespread application and was particularly useful in improving depressive patients.

■ PSYCHOSURGERY

A brief but grisly chapter in therapy was written with a surgeon's knife. Difficult, agitated, long-term unimproved patients had prefrontal lobotomies—an operation on the brain to destroy some of the fibers that connect the frontal lobes with the rest of the brain. This method did quiet anxiety, but it did so by reducing the patient to a human vegetable without imagination, ambition, or insight. It ranked with the invention of primitive tribes who punched a hole in the top of the disordered person's skull to allow evil spirits to escape. For the unnumbered thousands of mental patients who were treated with psychosurgery there was no turning back, because brain cells once destroyed never grow again.

■ PSYCHOPHARMACOLOGY

The revolution in therapy for mental disorder came about in the 1950s with the discovery of psychoactive chemicals (tranquilizers and energizers). The spread of their application was astonishingly rapid, and life in mental hospitals and clinics was never the same. These drugs now make up an impressive percentage of all the prescriptions used by physicians in every kind of practice.

Major tranquilizers either are compounded from the rauwolfia alkaloids (Serpasil, Harmonyl, Moderil, and other trade names) or are phenothiazines (trade names such as Thorazine, Sparine, Mellacil, Stetazine). Compounds designated as *minor tranquilizers* are widely used and have such familiar trade names as Miltown, Equanil, and Librium. In general, major tranquilizers are administered to patients with acute or chronic psychoses, agitated depressions, or organic brain disorders. The rauwolfia compounds are used for acute and chronic schizophrenia and for the agitated states of manic psychoses or senile conditions. The minor tranquilizers are most often administered to neurotic rather than psychotic patients, but they have been used to complement major tranquilizers.

Energizers or antidepressants with such less familiar names as Ritalin, Nardil, and Marsilid are used most often to relieve depression by triggering the brain chemically to produce increased sensitivity to stimuli in hopes of reawakening the patient's interest in the outside world.

Scientific assessment of the effect of tranquilizers and energizers has most often failed to indicate that one drug is markedly better than the next for a specific disorder. All seem, in varying degrees, to produce the necessary stimulating, sedative, or tranquilizing effects. Experimentation in the future may find new combinations of drugs (as well as new drugs) that will spread their therapeutic effects to patients yet unresponsive to this chemical approach. The question of drugs and behavior is treated more fully in Chapter 22.

Psychotherapy

Psychotherapy is a verbal relationship between a professional and a client focused on the thoughts, feelings, and behavior of the troubled person. It is, essentially, two people talking about one person's problems. The aim of this exchange is to help the client to understand the nature of his problems and to assist him in designing a rewarding and less painful way of life. Beyond this common principle, psychotherapeutic ways and means differ depending upon one's theoretical view of the psychological nature of man, how he develops and learns, and how change is brought about in him.

Most modern methods of dynamic psychotherapy are derivatives of the original work in psychoanalysis done at the turn of the century by Sigmund Freud. Psychoanalysis relied on free association (saying whatever comes to mind) as a means of analyzing unconscious material (dreams, repressed urges and experiences, fantasies) in order to trace the root causes of current emotional problems. When unconscious urges and motives were made conscious for the patient, he was expected to be free to deal with them in a rational rather than irrational manner. Working together, the patient and the therapist hope to solve unresolved conflicts and emotions and feelings more appropriate to childhood rather than adult life.

Classic psychoanalytic methods have seldom been applied to psychotic patients; most analytic experience is with fairly affluent, well-educated members of the middle and upper classes. A more common form of psychotherapy is called

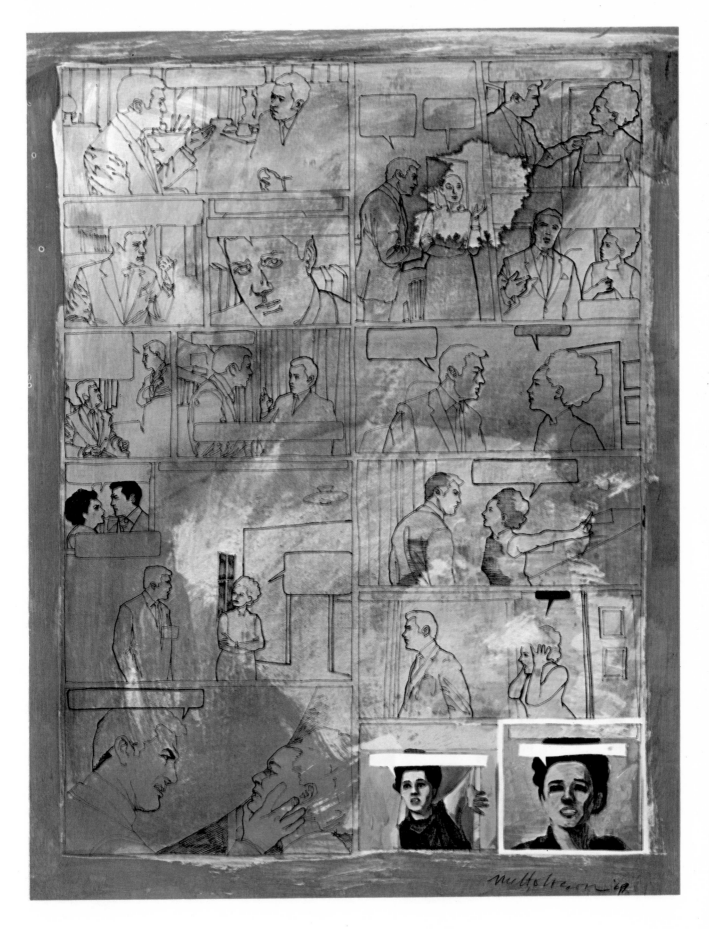

psychoanalytically oriented or dynamic. Currently it is often conducted in concert with the use of psychoactive drugs.

The goals of psychotherapy include insight into, and resolution of, handicapping or disabling conflicts, and improved sense of self and of one's identity, alteration of unacceptable patterns and habits of reaction, improved competence in interpersonal relationships, and the alteration of false assumptions about the self and the world.

Over the years, a number of theorists have raised questions about the effectiveness of individual psychotherapy. It is a costly, time-consuming process limited to too few trained professionals—a process that has little hope for solving the mass of emotional problems that exist in our society. Variations of this method have been tried to make it more effective and to extend its reach to greater numbers. The most prominent among these experiments has been group psychotherapy.

Because problems most often have their impact in terms of how one relates to others, it seems reasonable to conclude that problems might best be solved in company with others. It helps the troubled person just to be aware that others have similar problems and are equally laden with anxieties. There is a kind of social naturalness when persons with problems meet together to compare notes and discuss possible solutions. Scientific research designed to measure the effectiveness of group therapy and to compare it with one-to-one methods, unfortunately, has not been very adequate. In some instances, individual and group therapy have been combined to increase the effect of each.

Behavior Therapy   A new method of producing change in human behavior, behavioral psychotherapy consists of a process of social relearning in which the patient's behavior is the target the therapist must deal with and modify if treatment is to succeed. The treatment draws heavily on learning theory and modeling; reinforcement and extinction procedures are used to shape behavior and to reorganize or eliminate abnormal behavior. Reinforcement of certain patterns of behavior and extinction of less desirable ones can be done by a therapist without the extended training needed for traditional psychotherapy.

Behavior therapy holds concepts such as repression, the unconscious, defense mechanisms, and interpretation of symptoms to be unscientific. Behavior therapists care little for the historical origins of symptoms and are uninterested in probing unconscious dynamics. Emotional disorder, to them, is the outcome of a series of incorrect, undesirable, and unnecessary behavioral responses that must be unlearned by the patient.

Traditional psychotherapists cannot understand how permanent changes can be expected to occur without a close, intimate therapist-patient relationship and insist that the behavior therapists' "cures" can only be temporary and consist of symptomatic treatment that does not touch the basic causes.

The theoretical contest between traditional psychotherapy and behavioral therapy has yet to be decided. But it has begun a deepening reevaluation of current methods, and this inquiry promises hope for the future. The various methods of therapy will be examined in greater detail in following chapters.

Community Mental Health   Although we can earnestly hope that therapeutic methods will continue to improve and new discoveries will continue to occur, it is evident that we can only improve the state of mental health in our society if we learn to detect and prevent many of the problems before they escalate to serious proportions. With nearly half of the beds in our hospitals occupied by mental patients, the problem has assumed such serious proportions that more than one approach is needed. We know, for example, that we need a massive public-education program to change the public view of emotional disturbance. People fear and distrust those with psychological difficulties and, as a consequence, fail to provide financial support for adequate therapeutic facilities.

Moreover, mental illness is a long-neglected major social problem that is not solved by using the conventional doctor-patient, medical model. We need a redefinition of mental sickness and mental health, of who is sick and who is well. We must look to the structure of our society in order to detect the ways in which social evil and injustice produce environmental stress that, in turn, makes the individual incapable of meeting the challenges of life. We must know more of the reasons why some persons encounter frustration and grow stronger psychologically but others collapse under the strain.

It seems abundantly clear that we must look to new and perhaps radical ways of conceptualizing our problem and seeking remedies for it. At the moment, one hope for the future is to be found in the community mental health movement. With financial support from the federal government, an ambitious scheme has been undertaken to construct a minimum of 500 community mental health centers across the nation. The goal of these centers is to alter traditional patterns of treatment and extend therapy to segments of the population that have gone unserved in the past. In addition, taking psychological aid out of the mental hospital and bringing it into the community should erase some of the stigma that has long been attached to it.

Finally, it is likely that mental health must once again become everyone's business rather than the sole responsibility of the limited numbers of trained professionals. New mental health roles must be designed to care for disordered persons when they are young (and are more amenable to change and assistance), at times of crisis throughout critical periods in life, during periods of hospitalization, and in rehabilitation following treatment.

28

INDIVIDUAL THERAPIES

PEOPLE CHANGE. They change their attitudes, their ways of behaving and their relations with each other. Some of this change is natural learning, but some must be a relearning of attitudes. Attitudes that do not allow constructive functioning in the world and perhaps are also in conflict with other attitudes cry for change. As we saw in the preceding chapter, when this condition is relatively severe and the problems cannot be worked out through the natural channels of work, love, and social life, it is called neurosis. The neurotic person is his own worst enemy; he uses up so much of his concern and energy in an internal struggle that he has little left over for constructive achievement in life. When this condition is so severe that the person is so blocked by inner conflicts that he cannot perform useful work but has to be taken care of by others in hospitals, it is called *psychosis*. Various therapies try to help individuals overcome these blockages and utilize their potentialities. It is the task of the theories of therapy to see how people change and what facilitates their changing most effectively in desirable directions. This chapter focuses on individual therapies; group therapies are dealt with in Chapter 29 and behavior modifications in Chapter 35.

The goals of any treatment are fourfold: (1) to help the person recover from the debilitating effects of his symptoms; (2) to help him get over—if he chooses —badly maladaptive behavior patterns; (3) to help him make his actions consonant with the results—that is, to give him the freedom to choose, within limits, the kind of life he wishes; and (4) to help him establish enduring human relationships that lend him some security and his life meaning. Moreover, every form of psychotherapy presupposes (1) assumptions as to the nature of man, (2) some at least rudimentary personality theory, and (3) theoretical notions about psychopathology, that is, ideas about why people function inadequately. We shall consider classical psychoanalytic treatment first because of its historical primacy and its profound impact on all later forms of dynamic psychotherapy— "dynamic" in the sense that unconscious processes are considered important in the disruption of healthy functions.

Freudian Psychoanalysis

Almost all conventional forms of therapy go back to the explorations of the Viennese psychiatrist Sigmund Freud. In this chapter, we shall use the term *psychoanalysis* to refer to the Freudian theory of personality and psychopathology, to the classical Freudian technique of psychotherapy, and to the work of those who utilize Freud's basic ideas. Freud himself held that one could rightly call himself a psychoanalyst if, in theory and practice, he believed in and used the concepts of *repression* and *transference*. These doctrines imply belief in the function of the unconscious and the irrational transfer of problems onto the therapist, the patient's behaving as though the therapist were father or mother or lover. Classical psychoanalysis was developed to deal with neurotic disorders, that is, types of psychological disorders in which there are distressing symptoms but not the extreme disorganization of thinking or severe disruption of relatedness to others found in psychoses.

In his theory of personality (see Chapter 25), Freud assumed that human beings are driven by impulses derived from the biological demands of the body as represented, for example, by hunger, thirst, and sex. From infancy, the individual strives for a satisfaction of these needs and consequent tension reduction. The kinds and extent of the gratifications and frustrations he meets in his environment in his attempt to satisfy these needs are primarily responsible for his personality development.

Neurosis is considered by Freudian psychoanalysts first as representing a fixation in the neurotic's mental life at an early psychosexual level. Moreover, it is a condition in which unconscious processes tyrannize the personality, with conscious ideas, desires, and so on at their mercy. Neurotics have elaborate and extensive defenses against recognition of the psychic derivatives of their instinctual life, and consequently are seriously hampered in their freedom to act constructively and meaningfully. So much of the limited psychic energy of the neurotic individual is invested in the deadlocks between impulse and defense that he has little remaining energy to invest in objectively more consequential activities. Finally, in the Freudian scheme, the ego of the neurotic—being the agent of memory, judgment, perception, and other high-order mental functions—is inadequate and can neither effectively cope with external reality nor successfully deal with the urgent and threatening demands of the id and superego. This orientation to the understanding of neurotic problems is the underlying rationale of the classical psychoanalytic method.

Method

Patients are clinically evaluated before being accepted for psychoanalysis, because it is felt that only patients with relatively strong egos outside the area affected by their neurosis and patients who are psychologically minded are likely to benefit from this form of treatment. That is, patients with generally good judgment and reality testing and the ability to think in terms of human motivation and to understand somewhat the special logic of human emotions are amenable to this method.

The patient is usually expected to come for five visits per week, a schedule that motivates the patient in terms of both time and financial expense and permits the analyst to make careful and extensive observation of the patient's

life. He is asked to follow the basic rule of free association—always to say everything that enters his mind without censorship or attempts at social appropriateness, logical continuity, relevance, or avoidance of shame. The rule of free association is based on the notion that the id and repressed material are constantly seeking discharge and that whatever interferes with the free flow of associations is counterforce. By eliminating the social requirements of everyday conversation, the analyst permits a clearer observation of those deeper and more unconscious elements in the patient's personality that block this free flow. It is the analysis of these counterforces that is the chief work of the psychoanalytic treatment. During treatment, the patient lies on a couch, a posture that, because of its relationship to relaxation and sleep, is supposed to bring unconscious processes in the patient more readily to the surface.

Resistances Certain predictable reactions of the patient to the psychoanalytic situation are at the basis of the analytic method of treatment. While the patient is allied with the analyst in trying to get rid of his symptoms, gain more control over his own life, and gain more satisfaction from it, he also is opposed to the analyst in various ways—for example, in not wanting threatening and painful impulses and fantasies to be brought to consciousness. Any such opposition to the ultimate goal of the treatment, termed a *resistance*, represents a behavioral expression of the defenses the patient characteristically employs. The analyst's primary occupation then becomes the recognition of the patient's resistances to the analytic process. Eventually, the analysis aids in the dissolution of the unconscious conflicts between impulses and defenses, of which neurotic symptoms are an overt manifestation.

Primary among the resistances that inevitably develop in analytic treatment are *transference* resistances. Transference refers to inappropriate reactions to the analyst (or to any other person, for that matter) representing the expression of feelings toward significant major figures in the patient's childhood. These feelings are repressed and are unknowingly expressed by the patient in the analytic situation. The fact that the patient expresses these inappropriate feelings and fantasies, without being conscious of their nature and inappropriateness, is what makes them resistances. It is the analyst's task to help make these transference feelings and fantasies conscious, and hence expressed with awareness.

In the early months of the analytic treatment, various types of transferences are manifested toward the analyst. After this initial stage, there is typically the development of an elaborate system of related transference reactions to the analyst. These mirror the patient's childhood relationships to the critical figures of that time of his life as well as the feelings toward and fantasies about them that ultimately gave rise to the neurotic condition.

This system of transferences, which represents the central repressed neurotic conflicts of the individual, is termed the *transference neurosis*. The technical procedures of the analytic situation encourage a continuous regression in the patient's mental life. The interpretation by the analyst of each level of the transference neurosis also leads the patient to regress mentally, to become aware of thoughts and feelings that he had at early psychosexual stages of development. The resolution of this transference neurosis consists of acting out these early psychosexual conflicts in terms of reactions to the analyst and of rendering these conflicts conscious and hence under the control of the ego. In the course of this resolution, the patient's regression is reversed, and in successful treatment, the abnormalities of his psychosexual development are corrected. At this point, the termination phase of treatment begins. Here, various of the residual unconscious conflicts not touched on previously in the therapy are handled. In particular, the patient's reactions to separations are worked through so that leaving treatment will not precipitate a relapse.

Psychoanalytic treatment is very lengthy, typically on the order of three to five years. Defenses, or their manifestations (resistances) in the analysis, have usually proved their usefulness to the patient for years and years. Because they have protected him against pain, anxiety, and insecurity for nearly a lifetime, they are quite difficult to alter by the analytic method. They must be interpreted repeatedly and in various contexts before a lasting change in the patient's personality structure can be effected. This process of repeated interpretation of resistance in order to effect lasting change is termed *working through*.

Adlerian Approach

Several influential figures broke off from Freud's inner circle as the result of blind spots in Freudian doctrine. Each of these developed a point of view that had been slighted or overlooked by Freud. Alfred Adler was one of the first to develop his own approach to psychopathology and the technique of psychotherapy.

Every human being, according to Adler, begins life in a state of biological inferiority and insecurity. Each individual infant begins his existence in a state of helplessness and achieves security through progressively affirming his social relationships. In addition, an infantile inferiority may be augmented by *organic* weaknesses (of which even in adulthood he may be unaware); by *social discrimination* (for example, being born into a minority group or being a man in a culture that holds femininity to be superior); or by an *adverse position* in the family constellation (for Adler, being an only child was an example of this situation). Objective inferiority, however, can be adjusted to realistically despite the fact that it sets up hurdles to be surmounted in the individual's development. But subjective, imagined inferiority is the basis for neurosis.

Concerning methods of cure, Adler is very clear, albeit general. Neurosis can be dissolved only by affirming the bond that binds the individual to humanity. Only individuals who are conscious of belonging to the fellowship of man can go through life without anxiety. Thus, Adler's whole positive evaluation of the social nature of man has an emphasis radically different from Freud's and involves radically different implications for the overcoming of anxiety. Despite his oversimplifications and generalities, Adler has contributed lasting insights, particularly in the realms of the power struggles between persons and their social implications. Adler's understanding of freedom and creativity, as well as social interest, puts him in the line of existentialists and self-actualizing therapists.

Jungian Approach

Carl Jung met Freud in 1907 and with Adler became an early disciple. But Jung's gradual rejection of Freud's theory of the sexual etiology of neurosis led, with the publication of Jung's *Psychology of the Unconscious* in 1912, to a break between the two men. Jung then founded his own school, calling it *analytical psychology*. He introduced the words *complex*, *introvert*, and *extravert* into the psychoanalytical vocabulary (see Chapter 25). Jung postulated two dimensions of the unconscious. One is the *personal unconscious*, repressed events in the individual's life, represented by the *shadow*. The other is the *collective* (inherited) *memory*, represented by *archetypes*.

Jung believed that what makes a person ill psychologically is the invasion of his conscious mind by irrational forces and images from the collective unconscious. Anxiety is fear of the collective unconscious, fear of that residue of the functions of our animal ancestry and the archaic human functions that Jung conceived as still existing on subrational levels in the human personality. This possible upsurging of irrational material constitutes a threat to the orderly, stable existence of the individual. If the barriers within the individual to irrational tendencies and images in the collective unconscious are thin, there is the threat of psychosis, with its concomitant overpowering anxiety. But if, on the opposite extreme, the irrational tendencies are blocked off too completely, there is the experience of futility and lack of creativity. Both need treatment.

Jung believed that psychic health could be achieved through a recognition of the conflict between, and an acceptance of the tension inherent in, the opposition of the conscious and unconscious. The unifying factor, he maintained, was *symbol,* produced by the unconscious and understood through dreams. He considered man's ultimate psychological task—and the work of therapy—to be disaffiliation from a primitive identification *with* the collective unconscious so that he might establish a meaningful relationship *to* the collective unconscious. He thus could use its energy consciously rather than being controlled by it unconsciously. By establishing a relationship with his collective unconscious, man also identified with mankind as a whole, because all men share the same collective unconscious. In this sense, Jung was much like Adler in placing very un-Freudian emphasis on adult social interrelationships.

He called this process of relating to the unconscious *individuation,* believed that it properly belonged to the second half of life, and held that when it was set in motion it almost invariably came out of an almost religious yearning. Thus, he and his followers put great emphasis on the creative work of the patient.

Although sharing some views with both Freud and Adler, Jung was more intellectual and more mystical than either. Freud collected antique Egyptian statues, but Jung conducted a detailed exploration of myths and symbols. Adler saw the end of neurotic striving to overcome imagined inferiority in social relations, but Jung saw a religious attitude toward life as not only an essential but primarily an inherent characteristic of man.

Sullivan's Approach

Harry Stack Sullivan is the only American-born therapist, with the exception of Carl Rogers, to develop a special approach to therapy that has had the power to serve as the basis for a new school. Sullivan was very American in that he immersed himself in the pragmatism of philosophers like James and Dewey and in that he worked out the effects of the dynamic conceptualizations of twentieth-century social sciences. For this reason, his approach is called the *cultural school.*

Sullivan was energetically devoted to developing a successful method of treatment. He worked with schizophrenics, but his techniques contribute greatly to the treatment of neurotics, as well as to the whole science of interpersonal relationships in America. His central assumptions about man's nature hinge on the concept that man can only live, be understood, get sick, and be treated within an interpersonal context (see Chapter 25). For Sullivan, the role of the mother, particularly in early life, was central. If the mother's relation to the infant is relatively sound—that is, if she reduces the tensions of the infant—then this early basis for security allows the later feeling of interpersonal adequacy. But if the mother is frightened or anxious, the infant picks up this anxiety empathetically. If the self cannot avoid overwhelming anxiety from or of the parents, dissociation—the Sullivanian equivalent of Freudian repression—takes place: the infant simply blocks off, does not see, the things that would scare him too greatly.

In his therapy, Sullivan emphasized the *juvenile* and the *preadolescent* stages. The former, beginning with association with playmates (and incidentally

the entering of school), provides the child with the first period for allowing reflection on the nature of his family and the revision of his view of himself. Then comes the succeeding *preadolescent* period, which consists of getting to know another person very closely and learning how he experiences you. Sullivan became the founder of a new school that emphasized the chum period. He believed that if this period were omitted, the development of heterosexual love later became much more difficult. The other three stages are *early adolescence,* in which the lust dynamic first appears along with efforts to satisfy it; *late adolescence* up to the establishment of a love relationship; and finally *adulthood.*

Sullivan believed that we can describe a patient only as he manifests himself in his interpersonal field. The therapist is thus a participant-observer who influences the patient's responses as he listens to his communications; and the patient's behavior in the social environment of the therapy room particularly needs to be understood. Sullivan also believed that a careful case history has to be taken and that therapy did not begin until both the patient and the therapist had agreed on a goal, or goals, of treatment.

In the case history he tried to examine various developmental epochs in the patient's life, particularly with regard to the nature of the anxiety experienced and the kind of security operations employed against it; what developmental achievements were and were not made; and how these hindered later development. The essence of his treatment was the rediscovery of the self in its entirety, with the understanding elimination of experiences of faulty behavior and the acceptance of experiences that previously seemed to alienate the person.

Ego Analysts   The ego analysts are a group of psychoanalysts who maintain a basic allegiance to the Freudian theory of personality and psychopathology but have nevertheless sharply diverged from the Freudian conceptions. They stress the importance of human functioning that is not derived from internal physiological energies or instincts. Rather, the behavior of major interest to the ego analysts is learned in response to internal prompting other than sexual or aggressive energies or in response to the external environment. It is the behavior by which the individual consciously directs his activity and constructively deals with his environment. Among the major figures in this group is Anna Freud, Freud's daughter.

The term "ego analyst" refers to the fact that these theoreticians have primarily occupied themselves with a consideration of the ego, one of the three agencies included within Freud's structural theory of personality (see Chapter 25). They see many of the ego functions (for example, vision) as not developed out of the id, but rather developed as a result of innate tendencies to learn certain functions in interaction with the environment. These are autonomous ego functions, not encumbered with conflict from other parts of the personality (the id and superego). Although other ego functions, such as thought, perhaps originally developed because of pressure from the id, they have become relatively independent of the id and now exert control over it.

The ego analysts have noted and attempted to correct Freud's failure to study normal or healthy behavior in its own right. It is because of this failure, they argue, that Freud failed to appreciate the importance of functions within individuals that do not operate to reduce sexual or aggressive energies. Although the disordered aspects of the behavior of psychologically disturbed people often tend to develop and function in order to reduce imperative physiological emergencies, the ego functions of relatively healthy individuals tend to operate independently of these pressures. Moreover, the ego analysts argue, the mature individual is much less at the mercy of either his id or external situational events than is the maladjusted one. Thus, whereas Freud gave primary emphasis to the unconscious determination of behavior, the ego analysts have laid greater stress upon man's conscious planning and control of himself and his environment.

Typical of the ego analytical emphasis has been Robert White's remonstration that the operation of drive reduction is highly inadequate as an exclusive principle accounting for the development and maintenance of human behavior. He holds that *competence motivation*—man's pursuit of active contact with and mastery of his environment as an end in itself—can be viewed as one central motivation of human behavior.

The goal of ego therapy is to improve the functioning and organization of the ego so as to allow the individual greater control over himself than is exercised by either instinctual energies or situational events.

Existential Therapy

The existential therapies sprang from grave doubts about the adequacy of the theory of man in contemporary psychiatry, psychology, and specifically psychoanalysis. The older approaches apparently produced cures, but the therapist could not, as long as he confined himself to the generally accepted assumptions, arrive at any clear understanding of why these cures occurred or did not occur. The new existential therapists were unwilling to postulate unverifiable agents such as libido or censor, and they asked trenchant questions about what it really means when one says a patient projects or transfers something to someone else. They were particularly skeptical about the way the assumption of the unconscious is used as a carte blanche on which almost any causal explanation could be written. These explanatory devices, they argued, as often as not actually cover up rather than reveal precisely the empirical data they sought to understand. They shared the belief that the serious difficulties in the accepted theories of man, including psychoanalysis, not only would gravely limit research in the long run but also would seriously hamper the effectiveness and development of therapeutic techniques.

This movement has one feature in common with the other schools; namely, it was called forth by certain blind spots in the existing approaches to psychotherapy. It differs in that its attack is upon the underlying conception of man.

The basic contribution of existential psychiatry is its concept of man as *being*. Drives or dynamisms, by whatever name they may be called, can be understood only in the context of the existential structure of the particular person sitting before the therapist. Man is the being who can be self-conscious of, and therefore responsible for, his existence. It is this capacity to become aware of his own existence that distinguishes the *human* being from other organisms, and self-conscious responsibility must be presupposed in all psychiatric and psychological understanding of human beings as such.

In existential therapy, the patient comes in "building his world," as the existentialists put it, and the therapist seeks to understand the patient as a being in the world. The therapy is flexible, depending on what seems best for the patient; the couch may be used or the patient may sit up at various times. The therapist does not try to hide the fact that he is a real person.

The curative factor of the therapy lies in the impingement of the patient's world on the therapist, who represents the actual world. In this *encounter*, as it is called, the true meaning of transference comes out. Indeed, transference can be understood only as one aspect of encounter. The existentialists emphasize the *here and now* as the time dimension of therapy—not ignoring the past, but on the assumption that the past will come up in the context of what is going on now in the therapy sessions. The future will be real, by the same token, to the extent that the patient is genuinely experiencing it in the present. There is, also, the emphasis on the potential freedom of the patient: he would not be in therapy if he did not have some degree of freedom to change his way of life. For this reason, the existentialists emphasize will and decision.

One form of existential psychotherapy is Victor Frankl's *logotherapy*. After experience in a concentration camp, he developed logotherapy, which emphasizes man's search for meaning (*logos*). He bases this theory on the facts and presuppositions that people increasingly come to psychotherapists for help without any particular single symptom but with feelings of boredom, being "fed up," and lacking meaning in their lives. Logotherapy attempts to restore meaning and hence goals and involvement to the lives of the alienated.

Rogerian Therapy

Carl Rogers' conceptions of personality and psychopathology and his techniques of therapy have gained increasing acceptance in the United States. Chronologically, Rogers developed his technique of treatment first. Only considerably later did he begin to develop an integrated, inclusive theory about personality and psychopathology. Rogers assumed first that man's nature is innately good and that he will naturally become kind, concerned, friendly, and effective in the process of actualizing his nature (*self-actualization*) unless he is diverted from the course of his normal development (see Chapter 25).

Rogers sees psychopathology as rooted in the incongruence between a person's view of his own self and his actual experience. This incongruence generates anxiety, contradictory behavior, denial of certain thoughts or feelings, and feelings that his behavior is out of self-control, a condition in which the fundamental desire to actualize the self to its fullest potential has been deflected.

Rogerian treatment reduces conflicts within the individual by reducing the influence of the values of other people that have been incorporated into the self-concept. The reign of real self-centered experiencing is thereby reestablished and the basically fine and noble self is free to actualize itself once again.

Rogerian treatment was developed primarily with a college population and until recently was typically quite brief in duration (usually not exceeding forty weekly visits). In this treatment, the client's right of and capacity for self-determination is the basic working principle. The therapist's role is to reflect back to the client the feelings the client has expressed, so that they can be reevaluated, accepted, and integrated into the client's self. Therapy is a continual process of achieving self-awareness and of preparing for self-actualization.

The client experiences empathy and unconditional positive regard from the therapist, and in this free atmosphere gradually begins to symbolize experiences that have been out of awareness and to abandon secondhand values in favor of the self's own natural values. The self-actualization process is then reinitiated. The client is able to continue the process on his own momentum after the termination of the therapy.

Eclectic Approaches
Gestalt Therapy

Gestalt therapy is an approach developed by Frederick Perls, Ralph Hefferline, and Paul Goodman in which the principles of Gestalt psychology, originally applied to the study of perception, are generalized to the understanding of personality functioning in general and to the understanding and treatment of psychopathology. Gestalt psychology stresses that meaningful perception is based upon the apprehension of a configurational whole, in which a certain segment stands out as the figure and the remainder of the field is perceived as the background. The Gestalt therapists propose that healthy personality functioning

is generally dependent upon the individual's forming meaningful configurations in which there is a fluid alternation between those sets of experience that are in the focus of awareness and those in the background. This type of functioning is characterized by liveliness, attention, involvement, excitement, spontaneity, and grace. When, however, one's experience fails to form meaningful configurations (because critical elements are out of awareness—comparable to repression) or when an elastic alteration of figure and ground does not occur (fixation), the individual's experience becomes characterized by confusion, boredom, anxiety, compulsions, self-consciousness, and so on.

Gestalt treatment attempts to broaden the patient's awareness by the use of a series of graded experiments in remembering past experiences, trying to feel the sensations in his body, and so on that are designed to bring to his awareness such commonplaces as the way in which he walks, talks, dreams, fantasies, and remembers. During these experiments, the patient becomes aware of various inabilities (like Freudian resistances) to carry through the suggested experiments fully and successfully. Such experiments have the virtue of confronting the patient on his own with gaps in his experiences and awareness, rather than simply having them pointed out by his therapist, which lessens the patient's involvement in the experience. Hopefully, he is then able to reintegrate those missing aspects of awareness into a meaningfully configured whole.

Bruno Bettelheim

Bruno Bettelheim is a psychologist who since 1944 has been the director and major creative force behind the operation of the Sonia Shankman Orthogenic School at the University of Chicago. This is an institution for the long-term treatment of very seriously disturbed youngsters up to the age of fourteen who typically come from seriously destructive and chaotic home situations and have symptoms (frequent intense, hostile outbursts, profound withdrawal) of such severity as to preclude their treatment in outpatient settings.

With a deeply dedicated staff, Bettelheim has created at the school a highly tolerant atmosphere in which the doors are open for the children to leave if and when they like; the expression of asocial and aggressive tendencies is often temporarily encouraged at the expense of academic progress; emotional honesty takes precedence over polite conventions in respect to sex behavior, verbal expressions, orderliness, and cleanliness; and protection of property takes second place to the emotional needs of the children. The physical environment is so structured and the staff is chosen and trained to behave to these youngsters in an extremely tolerant and giving but honest way. Treatment at the school continues twenty-four hours a day.

Bettelheim has traced the principles underlying his creation of this particular type of therapeutic milieu to two major influences in his life. Before World War II in Europe, he received a thorough grounding in psychoanalysis. Although his faith in the heuristic value of psychoanalytic theory has remained strong, a period of internment in Nazi concentration camps in the late 1930s impressed upon him the enormous effect of situational structurings upon the course of personality changes, much out of keeping with psychoanalytic conceptions. For example, some apparently psychologically quite healthy individuals seemed to disintegrate readily under the impact of the excruciating concentration camp experiences, but others surprisingly seemed to gain an enduring strength from similar experiences. Bettelheim's treatment of the youngsters at the Sonia Shankman School, using the total environment of the school as the therapeutic lever, can thus be traced to his concentration camp experience. At the same time,

he continues to think of personality development in a way derivative of psycho-analytic theory and applies analytically derived ideas to the structuring and understanding of the interactions between his staff and the children.

As we have seen, there are so many different types of psychotherapy practiced today that one might think that the problem of mental health would soon be solved. It is true that people do get help from many types of therapy in the sense that they tend to feel better if they are paid attention to, are given a drug (even a placebo), or are afforded a boost in their self-esteem by becoming a part of a large movement that presumably has the prestige of science behind it. At what point this type of help leads to long-term cure, however, is unclear.

According to Rollo May, a noted American existential therapist, an increase in the need for therapy appears in human history whenever there is a breakdown in cultural values. In the classical period of ancient Greece, for example, there

The Future of Psychotherapy

535

was apparently little anxiety, depression, or despair among the populace, hence little psychotherapy practiced. But when the old Greek patterns of life—particularly the myths and symbols—began to disintegrate, as during the Hellenistic period of the third and second century B.C., there were psychological problems of many kinds and psychotherapists of all sorts abounded. The anteroom of every philosopher's and teacher's lecture room looked like an outpatient clinic. Likewise, according to May, in the Middle Ages psychotherapistlike functions burgeoned during that period of cultural decline characterized by a dramatic increase in sorcerers, witches, and other soul massagers.

May hypothesizes that when a culture is moving toward integration and unity, it has a system of symbols, myths, and values that give integration to the members of the society, and people are then relatively free from psychological breakdown. But when a culture is in the process of disintegration, it loses first of all its myths and symbols, then its system of values that have been based on these myths. Subsequently, people in large numbers come to seek psychological help. May believes that therapy will remain a critical part of our cultural scene until society discovers new myths and symbols to replace those we are currently losing.

That our times are turbulent is self-evident. The old humanistic myths and symbols are under attack on a number of fronts, but chiefly from those analysts of human behavior who insist that man's personality can be studied scientifically—that is, objectively and impartially. Systems of absolute values are giving way to a kind of cultural relativism that disturbs people brought up to believe that black is always black and white always white. As the behavioral sciences more and more embrace the relativistic viewpoint and value system of the physical sciences, they force man to take a new and disturbing look at himself. The more objective psychology becomes in its analysis of man, the more it destroys his prior myths and symbols.

There is little doubt that scientific psychology is a major contributor to many of the problems that trouble people today. But just as most of us are capable of adapting to the changing environment in which we find ourselves, so do psychotherapies change, develop, and evolve. And the social problems that behavioral science causes may best be resolved by wise use of behavioral science itself.

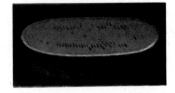

29

THE INTENSIVE-GROUP EXPERIENCE

ONE OF THE EXCITING SOCIAL INNOVATIONS of the past twenty years is the potent new development of the intensive-group experience. This innovation goes by many names: T-group, sensitivity group, encounter group, workshop in human relationships or in leadership, counseling, or education. In dealing with the drug addict, it is called a synanon. Intensive groups have functioned in a variety of settings, including industries, universities, church organizations, government agencies, educational institutions, and penitentiaries. Moreover, an astonishing range of individuals has been involved in these group experiences, from presidents of large corporations to adolescents.

The geographical spread of this rapidly expanding movement reaches from Bethel, Maine, to San Diego, California, and from Seattle, Washington, to Palm Beach, Florida. Intensive groups have also been conducted in a number of other countries, including France, England, Holland, Japan, and Australia.

One of the elements that makes this phenomenon well worth psychological study is the fact that it is truly a grass-roots movement that has grown out of personal, organizational, and social need. Unrecognized by any major university, without backing from foundations or government agencies until the last few years, it has nevertheless blossomed and grown until it has permeated every part of the United States and almost every social institution. It clearly has significant social implications. Part of the purpose of this chapter is to look into some of the reasons for its surprisingly rapid and spontaneous growth and development.

Some time prior to 1947, Kurt Lewin, a psychologist working at the Massachu- **Origin** setts Institute of Technology with his staff and students, developed the idea that training in human-relations skills was an important but overlooked type of education in modern society. The first so-called *T-group* ("T" standing for "train-

539

ing") was held in Bethel, Maine, in 1947, shortly after Lewin's death. The group that had worked with him continued to develop these training groups, both at MIT and later at the University of Michigan. The summer groups at Bethel came to be well known, and an outgrowth, the National Training Laboratories (NTL), whose primary thrust is in the industrial area, was formed.

The groups initially were training groups in human-relations skills in which the individuals were taught to observe the nature of their interactions with others and the nature of the group process. It was felt that in this way they would be better able to understand their own way of functioning and the impact they had on others and consequently would become more competent in dealing with difficult interpersonal situations.

In the T-groups organized by NTL for industry and gradually for groups outside of industry, it was found that individuals often had very deep personal experiences of change in the trusting, caring relationship that developed in the group itself.

Another aspect of the movement toward the intensive-group experience was taking place at about the same time at the University of Chicago, where, immediately after World War II, Rogers and his associates were asked by the Veterans Administration to create a brief but intensive course of training that would prepare men—all of whom had at least a master's degree—to become effective personal counselors in working with returning GIs. The staff felt that no amount of ordinary classroom training would prepare these men, so they experimented with an intensive-group experience in which the trainees met for several hours each day in order to understand themselves better, to become aware of attitudes that might be self-defeating in the counseling relationship, and to relate to each other in ways that would be helpful and that could carry over into their counseling work. This attempt to tie together experiential and cognitive learning in a process that had therapeutic value for the individual provided many deep and meaningful experiences for the trainees and was so successful in a sequence of groups that the staff continued to use this procedure in summer workshops thereafter.

Thus, the conceptual underpinnings of this whole movement were initially Lewinian thinking and Gestalt psychology on the one hand and Rogerian client-centered therapy (see Chapter 28) on the other. In recent years many other theories and influences have played a part.

Differing Emphases and Forms

As interest in and utilization of the intensive-group experience have grown, a wide diversity of forms and emphases has developed. Table 29.1 briefly indicates the broad spectrum of emphases involved in such group experiences.

In addition to a variety of emphases, a number of different forms can be found. There are stranger groups, composed of individuals who are not acquainted with each other. There are groups from one organization, people who are associated in their everyday life in industry, education, or other occupational settings. There are couples' groups, in which married couples meet with the hope of helping each other improve their marital relationships. A recent development is the family group, in which several families join in one group with parents learning from their own and others' children and vice versa.

Finally, there are differences in schedules. Most groups meet intensively for a weekend, a week, or several weeks. In some instances, group sessions are held once or twice a week. There are also marathon groups, which meet continuously for twenty-four hours or more. (The "nude marathons," in which people may or may not divest themselves of their clothes, have received an enormous amount of

Table 29.1—Intensive Groups

Group	Emphasis
T-group	Originally tended to emphasize human relations *skills* but has become much broader in its approach.
Encounter group (or basic encounter group)	Tends to emphasize personal growth and development and improvement in interpersonal communication through the experiencing of these things.
Sensitivity-training group Task-oriented group	May resemble either T-group or encounter group. Widely used in industry; focuses on the task of the group in its interpersonal context.
Sensory-awareness group, body-awareness group, body-movement group	Tends to emphasize physical awareness and physical expression through movement, spontaneous dance, and the like.
Creativity workshop	Focuses on creative expression through various art media.
Organizational-development group	Primarily aimed at leadership growth ability.
Team-building group	Used in industry to develop more closely knit and effective working teams.
Gestalt group	Emphasis on a Gestalt therapeutic approach where an expert therapist focuses on one individual at a time but from a diagnostic and therapeutic point of view.
Synanon group or "game"	Developed in the treatment of drug addicts by Synanon; tends to emphasize almost violent attack on the defenses of the participants.

publicity, although they certainly constitute less than one-tenth of 1 percent of intensive-group experiences.)

Threads of Commonality

Describing the diversity that exists in this field raises very properly the question of why these various developments should be considered as belonging together at all. Do any threads of commonality pervade all these widely divergent activities and emphases? They do seem to belong together and can be classed as focusing on the intensive-group experience in that they share certain similar external characteristics. The group in almost every case is small (from eight to eighteen members) and relatively unstructured, choosing its own goals and personal directions. The group experience often, though not always, includes some cognitive input, some content material presented to the group. In almost all instances, the leader's responsibility is primarily the facilitation of the expression of both feelings and thoughts on the part of the group members. Both in the leader and in the group members there is focus on the process and dynamics of the immediate personal interactions.

There are also certain practical hypotheses that tend to be held in common by all these groups. These might be formulated in quite different ways. Here is one such formulation.

A facilitator can develop, in a group that meets intensively, a psychological climate of safety in which freedom of expression and reduction of defensiveness gradually occur.

In such a psychological climate, many of the immediate feeling reactions of each member toward others, and of each member toward himself, tend to be expressed.

A climate of mutual trust develops out of this mutual freedom to express real

feelings, positive and negative. Each member moves toward greater acceptance of his total being, his emotional, intellectual, and physical being as it is, including its potential.

With individuals less inhibited by defensive rigidity, the possibility of change—in personal attitudes and behavior, in professional methods, in administrative procedures—becomes less threatening.

With the reduction of defensive rigidity, individuals can hear each other, can learn from each other, to a greater extent.

There is a development of feedback from one person to another so that each individual learns how he appears to others and what impact he has in interpersonal relationships.

With this greater freedom and improved communication, new ideas, new concepts, and new directions emerge. Innovation can become a desirable rather than a threatening possibility.

These learnings in the group experience tend to carry over, temporarily or more permanently, into the relationships with spouse, children, students, subordinates, peers, and even superiors.

Although this description of the basic aspects of group experience probably fits a majority of the groups, it would be less applicable in such situations as Gestalt therapy groups, where the leader is much more in charge and much more directly manipulative.

The Intensive-Group Process

In the present state of our knowledge, we can best speak of the group process in terms that are based on naturalistic observation. The descriptions that follow, as outlined by Carl Rogers in *Challenges of Humanistic Psychology,* are therefore based upon the observations of a limited number of facilitators, upon study of recorded group sessions, and upon diaries, comments, and letters from participants—obtained both during and after an encounter-group experience.

Certain threads weave in and out of the very complex interactions that arise in twenty, forty, sixty, or more hours of intensive sessions. Some of these trends are more likely to appear early, some more likely to appear later, but there is no clear-cut sequence in which one ends and another begins. The interaction is best thought of as a varied tapestry differing from group to group yet with certain kinds of trends evident in most of these intensive encounters and with certain patterns tending to precede and others to follow.

The following description of these process patterns applies primarily to groups in which interaction is basically verbal rather than physical. What follows would not be an accurate description of a task-oriented or team-building group, for example, both of which focus on external and specific problems. It does, however, constitute a rough description of a typical sequence in the great majority of T-groups, encounter groups, sensitivity-training groups, and the like.

Milling Around

As the leader or facilitator makes clear at the outset that this is a group with unusual freedom, that it is not one for which he will take directional responsibility, there tends to develop a period of initial confusion, awkward silence, polite surface interaction, mild to extreme frustration, lack of continuity.

Particularly striking to the observer is the lack of continuity between personal expressions. Individual A will present some proposal or concern, clearly looking for a response from the group. Individual B has obviously been waiting for his turn and starts out on some completely different tangent as though he did not hear A. One member makes a simple suggestion such as "I think we should introduce ourselves," and this opening may lead to several hours of highly involved discussion in which the underlying issues appear to be who the leader is, who is responsible for the group, who is a member of the group, and what the purpose of the group is. Not infrequently, a considerable amount of the frustration is directed toward the leader: "You're the expert, why don't you tell us what to do?" "You know what we are expected to do. What do you want from us?"

Resistance to Personal Expression or Exploration

During the milling period some individuals are likely to reveal some rather personal attitudes—toward themselves, toward others outside of the group, and sometimes toward members of the group or the experience of the group. Such revelations tend to develop very ambivalent reactions among the group participants. It is clear that many individuals feel frightened by emotional attitudes and feelings and tend to shut them out of awareness. Consequently, one of the most common sequences in an early group session is for someone to express something that has emotional significance for him and to find that his expression is completely disregarded by other members of the group. Sometimes this resistance extends to consciously warning people away from emotionalized material.

Description of Past Feelings

In spite of ambivalence about the trustworthiness of the group and the risk of exposing oneself, expression of feelings does begin to assume a larger proportion of the interactions. An executive tells how frustrated he feels because of certain situations in his industry. A housewife relates the problems she is experiencing with her children. A nun tells how angry she becomes at one of the individuals with whom she works.

For the most part, in the early portions of the group experience, these statements of feelings and self-revealing attitudes have to do with past situations or situations outside of the immediate group. The relationships within the group are not yet considered safe enough to discuss, and indeed many participants may hardly be aware of the reactions they are having toward the other members.

Expression of Negative Feelings

Curiously enough, the first expression of a genuinely significant "here and now" feeling is apt to come out in negative attitudes toward other group members or toward the group leader. In one group, in which members introduced themselves at some length, one woman refused, saying that she preferred to be known for what she was in the group and not in terms of her status outside. Very shortly afterward, one of the men in the group attacked her vigorously and angrily for this stand, accusing her of failing to cooperate with the group, of keeping herself aloof, of not being willing to be a member. It was the first personal, current feeling that had been brought into the open in the group.

What are the reasons that negatively toned expressions are the first current feelings to be expressed? Some theorists speculate that this is one of the best ways to test the freedom and trustworthiness of the group. Is it *really* a place where I can be and express myself, even negatively? Is this really a safe situation, or will I be punished? Another quite different reason is that deeply positive feelings are much more difficult and dangerous to express than negative ones. The person who expresses affection is vulnerable and open to rejection, which can be devastating. A person who attacks another is at best liable to *be* attacked, against which he can usually defend himself.

Exploration of Personally Meaningful Material

Following negative experiences, the event most likely to occur next is an individual's revealing himself to the group in a significant way. This puzzling se-

544

quence occurs, no doubt, because the individual member has come to realize that this is in part *his* group. He can help to make of it what he wishes. He has also had the experience of observing that negative feelings have been expressed and have usually been accepted or assimilated without any catastrophic results. He realizes that there is freedom here, albeit a risky freedom. A climate of trust is developing, so he risks letting the group know some deeper facet of himself.

If the beginnings of trust have developed in the group, then the individual finds that these expressions about himself are accepted by the group and that he himself is accepted more deeply because he has revealed them.

Expression of Immediate Interpersonal Feelings

Sometimes earlier, sometimes later, comes the explicit expression of feelings experienced in the immediate moment by one member toward another. These are reactions to the person as a person, not reactions to the category to which he belongs. Each of these attitudes can be and usually is explored in the increasing climate of trust.

Development of a Healing Capacity

A striking aspect of any intensive-group experience is the manner in which group members show a natural and spontaneous capacity for dealing in a helpful, facilitative, and therapeutic fashion with the pain and suffering of others. This kind of ability shows up so commonly in groups that it suggests that the ability to be healing or therapeutic is far more common in human life than we might suppose. Often it needs only the permission granted by a free-flowing group experience to become evident. Individuals who have had no training whatsoever in the helping relationship often exhibit a sensitive capacity to listen, an ability to understand the deeper significance of some of the attitudes expressed, and a warmth of caring that are truly helpful.

Self-Acceptance and the Beginning of Change

Many people feel that self-acceptance must stand in the way of change. Actually, in these group experiences, as in psychotherapy, it is a *beginning* of change.

Some examples of the acceptant attitudes expressed would include: "I *am* a dominating person who likes to control others. I do want to mold these individuals into the proper shape." "I really have a hurt and overburdened little boy inside of me who feels very sorry for himself. I *am* that little boy in addition to being a competent and responsible manager."

As might be expected, the acceptance of self leads to a feeling of greater realness and authenticity. It appears that the individual is learning both to accept and to *be* himself and thus is laying the foundation for change. Because he is closer to his own feelings, they are no longer so rigidly organized and are more open to change.

Cracking Façades

As the sessions continue, so many things tend to occur together that it is difficult to know which to describe first. It should be stressed again that these different threads and stages interweave and overlap. One of these threads is the increasing impatience with defenses. As time goes on, the group finds it unbearable that any member should live behind a mask or a front. Polite words, the intellectual understanding of each other and of relationships, the smooth coin of tact and cover-up—amply satisfactory for interactions outside—are just not good enough. The expression of self by some members of the group has made it very clear that a deeper and more basic encounter is possible, and the group appears to strive intuitively and unconsciously toward this goal. Gently at times, almost savagely at others, the group *demands* that the individual be himself, that his current feelings not be hidden, and that he remove the mask of ordinary social intercourse.

This refusal to accept a façade can lead the group to be mildly critical or sometimes violently attacking. This last characteristic is especially frequent in Synanon groups, where the drug-addicted person is often treated with much psychological violence, tearing his defenses to shreds. On the other hand, the group can also be sensitive and gentle.

Individual Feedback

In the process of freely expressive interaction, the individual rapidly acquires a great deal of data as to how he appears to others. The "hail fellow well met" discovers that others resent his exaggerated friendliness. The executive who weighs his words carefully and speaks with heavy precision may find that others regard him as stuffy. A woman who shows a somewhat excessive desire to help others is told in no uncertain terms that some group members do not want her for a mother. All these exchanges can be decidedly upsetting, but as long as these various bits of information are fed back in the context of caring that is developing in the group, they seem highly constructive.

Confrontation

There are times when the term "feedback" is far too mild to describe the interactions that take place, when it is better said that one individual *confronts* another, directly leveling with him. Such confrontations can be positive but frequently are decidedly negative, as the following example will make abundantly clear. In one of the last sessions of a group, Ann had made some quite vulgar and contemptuous remarks about Jack, who was entering religious work. The next morning, Louise, who had been a very quiet person in the group, took the floor, saying, "Well, I don't have *any* respect for you, Ann. None! First of all, if you wanted us to respect you, then why couldn't you respect Jack's feelings last night? Why have you been after him today? Why in the hell do you have to keep digging at him? Is it because of your weakness? You're not a real woman to me. Thank God you are not *my* mother! I'm just shaking, I'm so mad at you. I don't think you've been real once this week. I'm so infuriated that I want to come over and beat the hell out of you! I want to slap you across the mouth."

It may surprise or relieve the reader to know that these two women came to accept each other—not completely, but much more understandingly—before the end of the session. But this definitely *was* a confrontation.

Outside Helping Relationships

No account of the group process would be adequate if it did not mention the many ways in which group members are of assistance to each other not only in but outside of the group. Not infrequently, one member of the group spends hours listening to and talking to another member who is undergoing a painful new perception of himself. These helping relationships take many different forms and are a continuation of the healing capacity within the group.

The Basic Encounter

Running through some of the trends described is the fact that individuals come into much closer and much more direct contact with each other than is customary in ordinary life. This factor appears to be one of the most central, intense, and change-producing aspects of such a group experience.

A mother with several children who describes herself as "a loud, prickly, hyperactive individual" whose marriage was on the rocks and who felt that life was just not worth living told of how she had been "looking forward to the workshop with my last few crumbs of hope." She told of some of her experiences

in the group when she wrote to another participant: "The real turning point for me was a simple gesture on your part of putting your arm around my shoulder one afternoon after I had made some crack about the fact that no one could cry on *your* shoulder. In my notes I had written the night before, 'there is no man in the world who loves me.' You seemed so genuinely concerned that day that I was overwhelmed. I *received* the gesture as one of the first feelings of acceptance of *me,* just the dumb way I am—prickles and all—that I have ever experienced. I have felt needed, loving, competent, furious, frantic, everything and anything but just plain *loved.* You can imagine the flood of gratitude, humility, and release that swept over me. I wrote with considerable joy, 'I actually felt *loved.*'" Such "I-thou" relationships occur with some frequency in these group sessions and nearly always bring tears to the eyes of the participants. These encounters are so fully experiential that it is difficult to convey the oneness that is felt.

An inevitable part of the group process seems to be that when feelings are brought into the open and are accepted in a relationship, a great deal of closeness and positive feeling results. One person says, "The incredible fact experienced over and over by members of the group was that when a negative feeling was fully expressed to another the relationship grew and the negative feeling was replaced by a deep acceptance for the other. 'I can't *stand* the way you talk!' turned into a real understanding and affection for you, the *way* you talk." Thus, as the sessions proceed there is an increasing feeling of warmth and group spirit and trust built, not out of positive attitudes only but out of a realness that includes both positive and negative feeling.

Expression of Positive Feelings

Observation indicates that many changes in behavior occur in the group itself. Gestures change. The tone of voice changes, becoming sometimes stronger, sometimes softer—usually more spontaneous, less artificial, more feelingful. Individuals show an astonishing amount of thoughtfulness and helpfulness toward each other. Physical movements and postures become less stiff, more relaxed.

Behavior Changes in and After the Group

Our major concern, however, is with the behavior changes that occur following the group experience. One person gives a catalog that may seem too pat but is echoed in many other statements of the changes he sees in himself. "I am more open, spontaneous. I express myself more freely. I am more sympathetic, empathic, and tolerant. I am more confident. I am more religious in my own way. My relations with my family, friends, and co-workers are more honest and I express my likes and dislikes and true feelings more openly. I admit ignorance more readily. I am more cheerful. I want to help others more."

Following a satisfying experience in an encounter group, the participant's attitude toward *himself* is generally the element most likely to change. The attitude and behavior changes that come second are in the individual's close personal relationships. He tends to become more open and spontaneous with members of his family and with his close friends. Another area in which change is likely is in those situations in which the person feels potent. Thus, the teacher who feels in charge of and responsible for her class may change quite markedly in her relationship to the class and its members. Change appears a little less marked in peer relationships. Relationships with superiors may change, but this depends greatly upon the attitude and maturity of the superiors. Changes seem to come about most slowly in organizational structure and procedures, even when a number of members of the organization have engaged in encounter groups.

Gradations of Change

Research on Group Outcomes

Most of the studies of outcomes of the group process have found some changes in self-concept, in attitudes, and in behavior. Moreover, a reasonable number of these changes persist over time.

In one study, individuals (82 percent of those queried) responded to a simple questionnaire some three to six months after their experience in an encounter group. Only two felt that the experience had been mostly damaging and had changed their behavior in ways they did not like. A moderate number felt that the experience had been rather neutral or had made no perceptible change in their behavior, and another moderate number felt that it had changed their behavior but that this change had largely disappeared. The overwhelming majority felt that it had been constructive in its results or had been a deeply meaningful positive experience that had made a continuing positive difference in their behavior.

Research on the Group Process

There have been a number of studies of the process in encounter groups, but the best designed and most interesting is the study carried on by Meador. This study was based on a group that met for five sessions on one weekend for a total of sixteen hours. All sixteen hours were filmed. There were eight individuals in the group in addition to two facilitators. From the filmed account, Meador selected (in a standardized and unbiased way) ten two-minute segments for each individual—one from the first half and one from the second half of every session. Thus, she had ten two-minute film segments for each individual, or eighty such segments in all. The ten for each individual were spliced in random order, not sequentially. Thirteen raters then looked at each segment without knowing whether they were looking at an early or a late segment. (In fact, the raters had no knowledge whatever about the group.)

The instrument the raters used in their rating was Carl Rogers' process scale, a seven-stage scale representing a continuum of psychological activity ranging from a rigidity and fixity to a flow and changingness and spontaneity in the areas of feelings, of communication of self, of ways of construing experience, of relationships to people, of relationship to one's problems. The judges rated the eighty filmed segments according to this scale after a period of training in its use in which other filmed material was used. It was learned that although the judges thought they could distinguish early from late segments, they were quite mistaken in these judgments. Consequently, the ratings are truly unbiased and objective. It was not easy for them to make the ratings, because the process scale was designed originally as a measurement of process in individual therapy, and they did not feel at all secure in the ratings they were making. Analysis of their ratings showed, however, that there was a satisfactory degree of reliability; that is, they did tend to rate the segments in reasonably similar fashion. The findings were striking. Every one of the eight individuals in the group showed a significant degree of process movement toward greater flexibility and expressiveness. They became closer to their feelings, were beginning to express feelings as they occurred, and were more willing to risk relationships on a feeling basis, whereas these qualities had not been characteristic of the group initially. Meador noted that the individuals in the group, who were initially strangers, seemed to reach a level of relating to each other that was not characteristic of ordinary life. This study thus gives us a solid picture of at least one facet of the group process as it occurs in an encounter group.

Failures, Disadvantages, Risks

The intensive-group experience has been described thus far in positive terms. As

550

far as the evidence at hand indicates, it appears that it is nearly always a positive process for a majority of the participants. There are, nevertheless, negative aspects of the picture.

The most obvious deficiency of the intensive-group experience is that frequently the behavior changes that occur are not lasting. Ways are being discovered of extending such effects. If, for example, a number of people come from one organization or one community or one professional group working together, the likelihood of continued reinforcement from each other is enhanced.

A potential risk often mentioned is the possibility that an individual may become deeply involved in revealing himself but then be left with problems that are not worked through. There are also occasional accounts of an individual's having a psychotic episode during or immediately following an intensive-group experience. Again, steps are being taken to remedy or prevent this possibility. There is clearly a need for almost immediate follow-up of any encounter-group experience to give people the opportunity to work through further any unresolved conflicts. This may be done by drawing the group together for a follow-up experience or it may be through contacts with individual participants. In regard to the possibility of psychotic breaks, individuals have been observed living through what were clearly psychotic episodes and living these through very constructively in the context of an encounter group. The tentative clinical judgment has been made that the more positively the group process has been proceeding, the less likely it is that any individual will be psychologically damaged in any permanent way through membership in the group. However, this is a serious issue, and much more needs to be known.

Another deficiency often noted is that when only a husband or a wife is involved in an encounter group, the development of one spouse toward flexibility and growth may be quite threatening and disturbing to the other spouse. This effect is basic to the development of couples' groups.

Very closely related is the fact that in intensive workshops positive and loving feelings frequently develop between members of the group, and naturally these feelings sometimes occur between men and women. Inevitably, some of these feelings have a sexual component—a matter of great concern to the participants and a profound threat to their spouses if the feelings are not satisfactorily worked through. Again, in the long run a great growth experience seems to take place when individuals discover that they can have loving and even sexual feelings toward members of the opposite sex other than their own spouses and that these feelings do not lead to catastrophe.

Another negative potential sometimes observed is that some individuals who have participated in previous encounter groups may exert a stultifying influence on new groups that they attend. They sometimes exhibit what has been called the old-pro phenomenon. They feel they have learned the rules of the game and subtly or openly try to impose these rules on newcomers. Thus, they do quite the opposite of trying to promote true expressiveness and spontaneity. This phenomenon seems to develop most frequently when there has been a degree of phoniness in the initial groups they attended.

Another risk is the fact that all significant learning is to some degree painful and involves turbulence within the individual and within the system. There seems to be no way of avoiding this risk if constructive change is to come about, but it can be painful. Turbulence within an organization is particularly difficult to handle, especially when we take into account the fact that the higher the status of the individual and the more he has to defend, the more difficult it is for

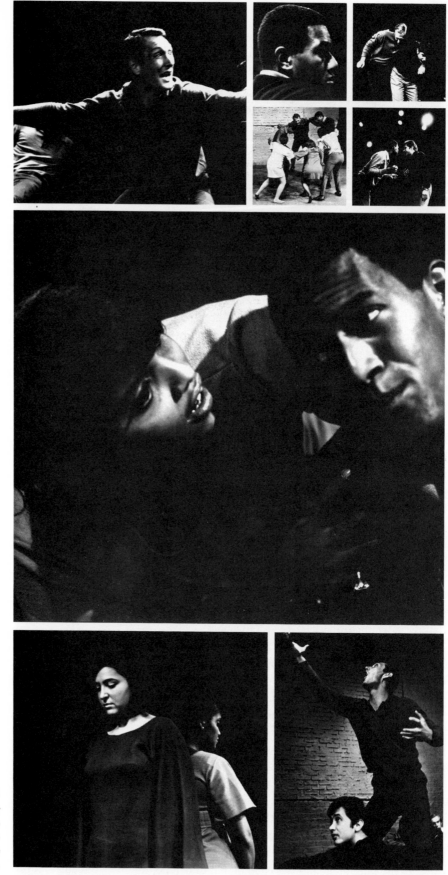

Figure 29.4
The play *The Concept* was improvised by people who had been narcotics users to show how their experience in group situations helped them overcome addiction to hard drugs.

him to be open with his colleagues and subordinates. Consequently, it is usually easier to reach the low-status people in an organization than it is the high-status. Thus, the turbulence tends to have a lid on it, and explosions can occur.

Areas of Application

Sensitivity training, or the intensive-group experience, has been more widely used in industry than in any other field—at every level, from executive development to training of foremen. In the field of organizational development or leadership training, it has been shown to create an open problem-solving climate throughout the organization; to build trust among individuals in groups throughout the organization; to make competition more relevant to work goals and to maximize collaborative efforts; to develop a reward system that recognizes both the achievement of the organization's mission (profits or service) and the organizational development (growth of people); and to increase self-control and self-direction for people within the organization.

In education, it has been used in different ways—to improve interpersonal communication between faculty and students, to assist administrative groups to work together more constructively, and to develop more innovative attitudes in teachers. Moreover, a plan to use the encounter group as an instrument to facilitate self-directed change was put into effect in a whole school system, involving a college, eight high schools, and fifty elementary schools. Many personal changes; considerable educational innovation; better communication between administrators, faculty, and students; and some changes in organizational procedures were among the results. A number of somewhat similar ventures are underway.

In religious organizations, encounter groups have been widely used to build, or to deepen, the sense of community and interpersonal trust.

In government, various departments and organizations have used encounter groups for the same purposes as in industry. Groups for diplomats, with the purpose of improving communication with other people and cultures, have been shown to be very effective.

In situations of racial tension, relatively little has been done, and then often too little and too late. Where tried, some modification of the intensive-group experience has been helpful.

Implications

There are a number of individual and social implications of the intensive-group experience. In one dimension, the intensive-group experience appears to be a cultural attempt to meet the isolation and alienation of contemporary life. The person who has entered into a basic encounter with another is no longer a completely isolated individual. Because alienation is one of the most disturbing aspects of our modern life, this factor is important.

A related implication is that the group experience is an avenue to fulfillment. When material needs are largely satisfied, individuals turn to the psychological world, groping for a greater degree of authenticity and fulfillment. In a culture that appears to be dehumanizing the individual, group experience can be in the opposite direction—working toward making relationships more meaningful and more personal in every area of life.

Another implication is that such groups can be an instrument for the handling of tensions. In a culture that is torn by racial explosions, student violence, and all types of conflict, it seems important that an instrument that improves basic gut-level communication be available. Like other social innovations, it has been tried all too infrequently in such tension situations; but when it

Figure 29.5
Carl Rogers in an encounter group.

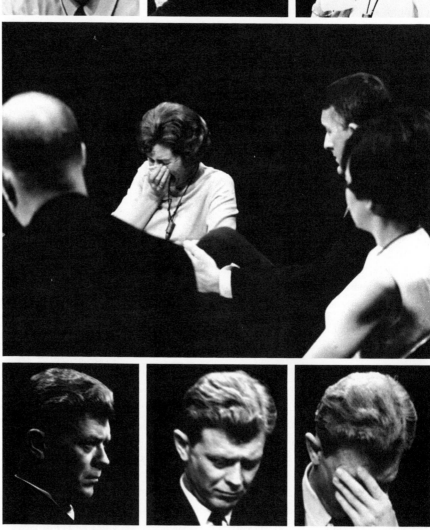

has been used, it has shown promise in reducing interracial conflict; conflict between students, faculty, and administration; and conflict in labor-management situations.

The intensive-group experience has an even more general philosophical implication: it is one expression of the existential point of view that is so pervasively evident in art and literature and modern life. The implicit goal of the group process seems to be to live life fully in the here and now of the relationship, obviously an existential point of view.

One of the unspoken problems of the modern age is the question of how rapidly the human organism can adapt to change. Can we leave the dogma and fixity of man's past approach to life and learn to live in a process manner, in a state of continual changingness? Clearly, the intensive-group experience can be of help in this regard.

A final issue that should be mentioned is the question raised by this experience as to our model of the human being. What is the goal of personality development? It seems evident from our review of the group process that in a climate of freedom and facilitation, group members move toward becoming more spontaneous, flexible, closely related to their feelings, open to their experience, and close and expressively intimate in their interpersonal relationships. This is the kind of human being we seem to be moving toward. Yet such a model goes directly contrary to many religious and cultural points of view and is not necessarily the ideal or goal toward which the average man in our society would wish to move. The issue, then, needs open consideration.

The use of the group experience as a psychological tool is still relatively new, and it is far too soon to predict what its final effect on the field of psychology will be. It does seem fairly certain that groups constitute a powerful stimulus for evoking the expression of deep-felt human emotions and for bringing about some types of behavioral and attitudinal changes in members of the group. As interesting as these effects are, however, they will not become a part of the science of psychology until much more work has been done to explain how these changes come about and what the factors are that facilitate or inhibit the behavioral changes described, and until the processes underlying these changes can be expressed in terms of human perception, learning, and motivation.

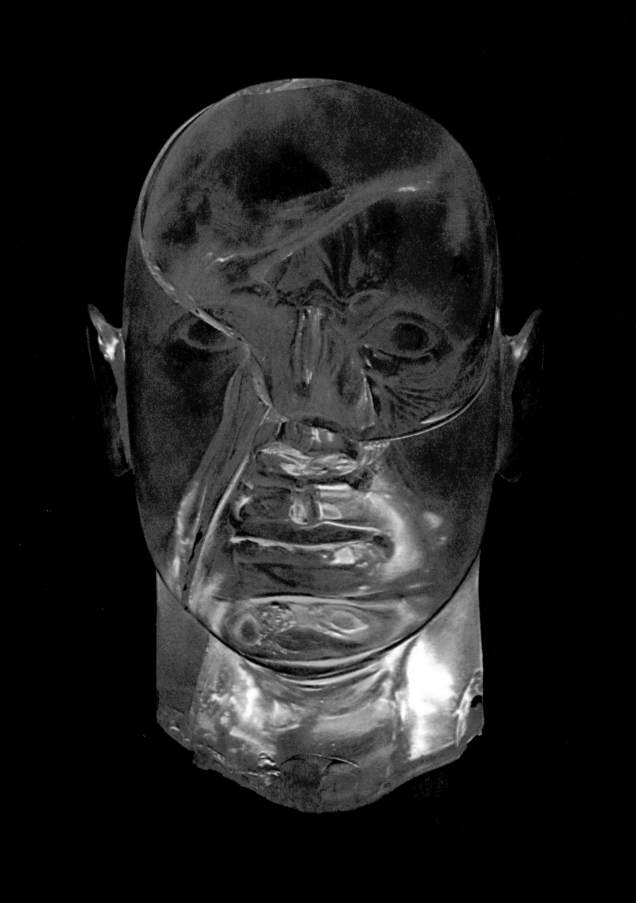

30

PSYCHIATRIC THERAPIES

PSYCHIATRISTS DIFFER FROM PSYCHOLOGISTS not in their interest in the mental and behavioral disorders of man but in their approach to them. Psychiatrists have taken the M.D. degree after a medical education, whereas most psychologists have taken a research degree, the Ph.D., after an education in academic psychology, which may or may not include some experience with clinical treatment. The clinical psychologist is likely to believe in a particular theory of personality and to practice therapy derived from it, and the psychiatrist, trained in the medical model of diagnosis and therapy, will select from the therapeutic possibilities the one that he feels is most likely to be beneficial to the particular patient under treatment, regardless of what psychological theory lies behind the therapy. Psychiatrists tend to be more biologically oriented than most psychologists, and because of their medical education, they are licensed by the community to administer drugs and somatic therapies to patients.

The relationship between psychiatry and psychology is synergistic, and as with all such relationships, there is a lag time in communication between the fields. Techniques of therapy—for example, those involved in behavior modification (see Chapter 35)—have evolved from a psychological background and have only later found their way into psychiatric practice; and techniques of drug therapy, for example, originated in psychiatry and only later made their impact on psychological theories of personality and behavioral abnormality. Skinner's behaviorism has had an impact via behavior therapy on psychiatry, and Freud's psychiatry has had an impact via his personality theory on psychology.

As a physician, the psychiatrist inherits the implicit social agreements regulating transactions between the community and patients and therapists. The identifica-

The Medical Model

tion of an instance of disturbed behavior and the appropriate broad response to it are institutionally programmed: the occasions for religious, police, or educative responses, as well as medical intervention, are established by social conventions. What is referred to as the professional or medical model of therapy comprises a class of humanistic interventions based in part on scientific knowledge and technical competence, in part on a certain pattern of personal responsibility, and in part on a routine of academic preparation. The institutionalized role of the healer as a physician determines in part the reciprocal roles and exemptions granted to the person who is sick and to his healer, as well as the mode of society's sanction of this relationship. The fact that a patient is referred or self-referred to the psychiatrist in itself involves a selection process involving many more criteria than those concerning the severity or mildness of the person's problem and this limits the populations of patients actually seen. The patient also comes with expectations that inevitably influence what is done. Psychiatric therapies take place within this general social framework.

Thus, the psychiatrist—whatever his private interests, aptitudes, aesthetic, or socializing ability—is first of all sanctioned as a medically trained practitioner. As a physician, he is expected to fulfill certain responsibilities, including scrutiny of the scientific rationale for his specific therapeutic interventions. It is not that a complete scientific rationale exists for most drug therapies of even the infectious diseases; but the trained physician is supposed to understand the extent to which such knowledge is available, the research by which such knowledge can possibly be attained, and the risks and gains that pragmatically can be identified for a specific use of a drug in a specific condition, in a specific patient.

Thus, the physician is trained to act on carefully garnered half-knowledge—and the mode for accomplishing this training has been called the acquisition of wisdom or clinical judgment. He has been trained to take a degree of personal responsibility for his task, which can be quite demanding—both of the physician and of the patient. The patient is an essential collaborator of the physician—while yielding autonomy in technical decisions, the patient expects technical competence to be exercised in his behalf. This orientation around personal responsibility is paramount and brings special problems to the social system in which the psychiatrist functions.

When the physician intervenes, his first task is to define the patient's problem. Diagnosis or recognition of the problem for which subsequent treatment may be designed can in itself be a time-consuming and extensive technical procedure. Having defined the problem, the physician assigns and plans the subsequent treatment, makes an ongoing assessment of the process, and watches out for the patient's welfare. The patient may be referred by the physician to special rehabilitation and educational experts or to social or public health agencies, whose specialists may or may not be required to have medical training. Such generalities obtain for tuberculosis, cerebral palsy, or poliomyelitis, as well as for a wide variety of behavioral disorders. As physicians, psychiatrists have particular problems, notably the extent to which the doctor-patient interaction itself may be emphasized as a therapeutic tool and the reluctance with which patients identify their behavioral as opposed to physiological problems.

The manifest psychoses have historically been the psychiatrist's focus. Yet, paradoxically, during the past thirty years psychiatric talent has been largely deployed to care for a minority of relatively rich people with neurotic and character problems. Currently, the demand is that this care be extended to a wide population of persons with a variety of complaints. If social values were the

criteria for this extension, arguments could be marshaled for any pattern of service delivery. If proof that therapy works is the criterion, then we have to deal with a number of issues, including the adequacy of research data. Where specific interventions for specific disorders are clearly efficacious—penicillin for syphilis —then the medical imperative clearly is dominant in dictating both social values and the deployment of professional functions. But it is not yet at all clear that specific therapies produce cures of the dramatic variety produced by penicillin.

Training in Psychiatric Therapies

Psychiatric training begins in the broad area of human biology and requires experience in the management of a number of human ills and ails. The training of the medical student begins with anatomy and cell biology and includes medicine, surgery, neurology, pharmacology, and, in varying degrees, exposure to the behavioral sciences, to general psychiatry, and to psychoanalysis. The specialist in psychiatry focuses on the latter group, with an emphasis on clinical experience guided by a trained psychiatrist.

What does a society expect of such training? The psychiatrist should be able to recognize among the patterns of disordered behavior referred to him those that have some identifiable organic cause, such as toxic psychoses or various chronic or acute brain syndromes. He, in fact, will have learned about a number of characteristic problems and their characteristic solutions as they are found in hospitals, clinics, and medical school environments. In order to identify problems and solutions, he should have an accurate sense of what disorganized people or people in trouble experience, how their environment characteristically reacts, and how such events influence the behavior in question. If he is very well trained, he should be able to select from among the array of available options the one that is specific to a particular case.

At the least, his preparation entails a firsthand experience with the severe psychoses and with a range of disordered behavior, from transient anxiety to severe symptomatic neuroses to character problems, and with its manifestations in specific situational conflicts. He should be sensitive to vicissitudes precipitated not only by different social classes and settings but also by the life cycle operating in them—the inherent problems, conflicts, and capacities of age groups such as the adolescent and the aged.

Most of all, he should learn to find, recognize, or elicit the potential for recovery—for organizing and adapting—which to varying degrees is present in all patients. He should appreciate transactional and biobehavioral factors that impede this process. In so doing, he will employ pharmaceuticals (commonly called drugs), direction, manipulation, persuasion—any *tested* procedure that might aid treatment. This is not a program advocating authoritarian arrogance but rather refers to quite realistic responses that an authentic expert—trained to be responsive, responsible, and comfortable in his expertise—must undertake. Psychiatric control of therapy refers to genuine expertness, technical competence, trustworthy experience, and capacity for explicitness on the part of the therapist or hospital environment, not to any paranoid or politicized version of coercive functions.

What the psychiatrist really gains in training (apart from specific knowledge about practices, theories, and methods) is a preceptor-guided experience in handling a wide variety of crises; he learns the criteria for self-confidence as he tries to achieve an acceptable level of competence. He learns something quite general about crisis management and, more importantly, something about himself as a party in it. Thus, it is in some self-mastery in the management of a range of brief or enduring crises affecting personality organization and personal and family life that the psychiatrist has some extensive experience if not expertise. Fully trained, he has acquired accountability and has learned how to relate these skills in a social system that requires and trusts in responsible conduct.

Today, the psychiatrist often diagnoses not only the level of organization and capacity for adaptation and response to therapy of a particular patient but also the various systems in which behavior disorder can be enhanced or diminished. He begins to understand families, office organizations, and all the various subcultures—occupational, avocational, and affectional—that bear upon specific instances of misbehavior. He will have seen adolescent children whose acting-up and acting-out behavior somehow serves to keep marital conflict between the parents contained, while they focus, displace, and agitate through their child. Similarly, the military psychiatrist will have learned that the frequency of behavior problems is often related to the practices and behavior of unit commanders. He will understand that what is deviance in the middle class may be a way of life for the upper or lower classes. Deviance does not necessarily mean disorganization of psychobiological functions any more than conformity means organization.

In dealing with such systems, the psychiatrist should maintain an open and candid relationship with his patient, siding with his patient's capacity to adapt and organize. He is a partisan to growth and development in the patient but not an advocate of various conflicting positions. He elicits, welcomes, and depends upon the patient's capacity and motives to participate and to direct energy and attention to the tasks of therapy. Therapy is a collaboration in which roles are assigned but personal responsibility—to the degree possible—by the patient is also important, if not crucial (whether he is taking medication or engaging in insight therapy). The psychiatrist attempts not to act out his own moral dilemmas, personal needs, ambitions, and political antagonisms. His job is to help the patient assume some effective control over his own destiny.

Psychoanalysis and Psychiatric Therapies

Although psychoanalysis has been interpreted in a variety of ways (see Chapter 28), its underlying bases have profoundly altered the general view of the nature of man and the meaning of his experience and behavior. The explanatory power of psychoanalysis in linking experience, bodily function, and behavior has been especially compelling, and many principles have emerged. Consciousness, for example, does not describe all that is directive in behavior. There is some link of early learning to contemporary thought, adaptations, and symptoms and a crucial role of affectional drives, bonds, and identifications as a part of all these processes. There is a construction of an inner world of private memories in the form of images, thoughts, words, and symbols—an internal coding and structuring of experience that may or may not be readily available to consciousness but acts as a guiding force. There is the exposition of two orders of thought—logical and goal-directed thought, and plastic, sensory, nonrational yet representational thought (as in dreams)—and the demonstration of a certain degree of only partially conscious coherence between these. Finally, there is the principle of the power of selective forgetting and displacement of thoughts, motives, and feelings or of partial perceptions or the restriction of motor and judgmental processes—internal mechanisms—in adapting to painful experiences.

Such notions could be brought to bear in explaining slips of the tongue, life goals and styles, or symptoms. It was demonstrated that talking and remembering with some vividness in the presence of a supportive relationship, structured by

special rules and boundaries, were therapeutic. The fact that pausing for self-knowledge in this context could be one of man's adaptive techniques apparently made a vast impression. A wide range of contemporary therapies either owe much to their psychoanalytic origins and do not admit it or call themselves psychoanalytic when they are actually quite derivative.

Psychoanalysis

The rule in classical psychoanalysis is that one does not gratify the patient—that when the analyst suspends the usual and expected response, the patient's thoughts and attention regress to the ongoing stream of consciousness and become expressive of private and repressed feelings and strivings. In this procedure, the analyst tries to make explicit what the patient's ongoing behavior is about by allowing it to emerge with vividness in the transference. This expression of narcissistic and affiliative demands, wishes, or fears of the analyst represents an inherent capacity to displace fundamental wishes and ambitions of childhood and to act them out in verbal expression or fantasies. In the therapeutic alliance, the analyst addresses himself to the observing and reasoning part of the patient, urging him to appreciate the goals and origins of his behavior and to question their current appropriateness. He discerns the pattern of persisting early adaptations and aids the patient in gaining control of them by demonstrating their action and origins. He does not use technical jargon but addresses himself to what is observably reproduced in the session and provides clearly labeled reconstructions for missing gaps in the story. Properly conducted, there is nothing inexplicit about a well-run psychoanalysis.

Transference and Suggestion

It is clear that the discovery of transference has been important to the training of psychiatrists. This phenomenon brought a new focus upon the whole problem of the psychology of suggestion. The reality-distorting force of needs for affiliation and the directive force of such needs in motivating goal- and person-related behavior are immense. Psychoanalysis asks the patient to scrutinize and, as much as possible, to resolve the irrational (but not necessarily the positive) components of the transference. It was discovered that the analyst, too, had characteristic needs that might motivate his response and that he, too, could treat the present transaction as if it represented a past one.

Theory and Goals

So many fundamental psychological dimensions were described through psychoanalytic theory and techniques that most psychiatrists have been exposed to them. Familiarity with a variety of affective intensities and personal intimacies, with the ethical and emotional problems that arise in their management, and with the dangers of therapeutic zeal and of not approaching the patient as a particular person with a need for hope are now part of training experiences.

It is sad but fair to say that many grandiose and unrealistic therapeutic promises have been made in the name of these intellectual and methodological developments. Where therapeutic goals are not explicit and realistic, it is possible for therapists—drawing on their own and every human's hope for transcendence and perfection—to claim that salvation really lies in their system and not in others. Only their system can "really" guarantee "solid" personality change. Thus, a number of foolish and unsubstantiated notions until recently permeated psychiatry. One finds shallow therapies and truly deep therapies that strike at real causes. The referent for "deep" generally is that the arrangement be long, expensive, intense, probing, intimate, and highly personalized (criteria that could easily apply to many exploitative as well as therapeutic enterprises).

Whether the unconscious is deep or extensive—whether it has vertical or horizontal coordinates—might well be a matter for debate; such metaphors do not lead to the devising of specific responses adequate for a specific problem. Nor do they substitute for evaluations of therapeutic techniques, processes, and outcomes in specific populations. Such sloganeering in psychiatry has diverted attention from realizable accomplishments. The extension of the term "psychoanalysis" to almost any technique that utilizes a fifty-minute time span several times a week (if not a couch) for almost any disorder has further clouded definition and progress in understanding and advancing psychiatric therapies.

The investigative intent of classical psychoanalysis is often forgotten by practicing psychoanalysts, some of whom treat the theoretically desired outcome as a real and proven achievement. The facts are that profound therapeutic consequences often can ensue with brief interventions and that profound experiences occur in many therapeutic settings, from groups to hypnosis. The overwhelmingly challenging fact is that we still lack evaluations that give us scientifically sound bases for classifying different therapies. Finally, the real hope for highly differentiated and specific therapies lies in identifying different subgroups of patients, in finding distinctive dimensions differentiating apparently similar behaviors.

New Directions and Applications

This goal has been approached during the past hundred years in such advances as differentiating the psychoses from all toxic conditions and CNS syphilis or pellegra from all psychoses. New biochemical definitions are beginning to be more clearly articulated, and attempts at dissecting the different modes of intake, modulation, and processing of sensory input show the possibility of distinguishing subpopulations among the schizophrenic psychoses. The regulation of sleep through certain brain "centers" is under investigation, and distinct "phases" in the course of a psychosis may possibly be delineated. Whether or not drugs are useful or harmful for certain of these subgroups is now being tested. This thrust in research points to the new directions from which genuine progress toward therapeutic control can rapidly advance.

Today, we can recognize a common brand of talking therapy known as *dynamic psychotherapy*, or psychoanalytically oriented psychotherapy. The dynamic therapist has cognizance of the characteristics of behavior that the classical psychoanalytic investigations described, but no matter how he comprehends the anatomy of psychological forces, he tends to focus on assets and on explicit and soluble problems. He encourages less regression, less free-floating associations, and a more circumscribed program of focusing upon immediate problems as a paradigm of important personality issues. He has thus learned principles—only some of which he applies—from classical procedures.

The psychiatrist, then, should have had the experience of knowing a variety of people—both like himself and dissimilar—who present themselves with severe troubles, with mistrust, with hope or despair; he should have seen some quick and some long-term resolutions of these situations into outcomes useful to the patient; and he should have encountered striking failures in his ability to influence behavior. Having dealt with death and disorder in both medical and psychiatric patients, he should have some appreciation of the possible real outcomes of psychiatric (or *any* well-intentioned) interventions undertaken. He may even have found each individual's unique way of organizing experience (and experiencing those modes of being) an education in psychology—but he will not tax the patient unduly for such education.

Whether he orients his activities around notions of self-actualization, the learning of preferred behaviors, intervention in social systems influencing the patient, or the dampening of intensity in behavior by pharmacological agents, the psychiatrist develops a keen appreciation of his own limits, the limits the situation offers, the patient's assets and resources, and the pragmatic outcome useful to the patient. He does not expect to "cure" aggression or instincts or any other given fact of life but rather aims for diminished suffering or new learning that can help the patient to develop or to get around previously aggravating and disorganizing obstacles. He will have learned from the experience of the psychoanalyst that one diagnoses or assesses a situation in an ongoing fashion, just as in medicine, and that in having a sequence of specific goals, an open-ended and expectant view of the unfolding relation is a possible and useful attitude. But he will not prescribe psychoanalysis for every disorder or mistake it for a really deep therapy striking at true causes (rather than a really broad theory, which it is). After all, the physiology of fever indicates that temperature regulation occurs in the hypothalamus; but physicians do not employ surgery or depth electrodes in treating a fever—mistaking basic anatomy for proximal causes and effects.

Evaluation and Choice of Therapy

Jerome Frank has commented that all therapies must do some good, or they would disappear. In the past decade, there have been serious efforts to establish the appropriate criteria for evaluating therapies. This trend was accentuated with the advent of psychopharmacological agents. Studies of their efficacy employ highly sophisticated methodologies comparing various drugs in specified patient populations or a single drug in an appropriate range of dosage in different therapeutic settings. The development of reliable rating scales for a variety of simple or complex behaviors has advanced. Criteria for outcomes are intrinsically difficult to establish and global ratings still remain useful, but use of discharge rates from the hospital or clinic as end points appears crude because they may be dependent only on social interactions in these settings and assets in the community. Other dimensions center around the actual kind of psychotherapy undertaken, for the actual behavior and interventions of therapists belonging to the same school might differ vastly. Moreover, the therapist's level of experience, accurate empathy, and nonpossessive warmth and genuineness are characteristics recently indicated to be important.

More differentiated criteria have to do with evaluating the status of the patient; these include his self-evaluations and those of others. The patient's comfort, self-awareness, and social effectiveness are important outcome variables. More ambitious research might well provide a description of the neurotic patient, his setting, the phase of his dysfunction, and his specific modes of successful and unsuccessful adaptation and might evaluate, in terms of these, what has happened after the period of therapy.

The appreciation of subjective changes as an outcome variable is important. In many neurotic dysfunctions, only certain negative features attest to successful therapy. The patient, for example, may no longer pay the same kind of attention to persistent symptoms or may feel more optimistic about coping. In any event, a catalog of complaints may not be sufficiently precise and a generalized psychodynamic inventory of defenses may be too general to be useful. Objective behavioral test situations provide another (though not comprehensive) arena for defining outcome of therapy.

Psychiatry is thus emerging from the stage of taking either the patient's or the doctor's word for its successes as sufficient data.

For the psychoses, sophisticated studies consistently tend to show pharmacotherapy generally more useful than any other approach. The situation is less clear (but the trend is the same) for depressions and anxiety states. Psychotherapy combined with pharmacotherapy has been investigated in such studies; this combination may be useful, but, used alone, psychotherapies do not show superiority for such conditions.

Factors Influencing Choice

We can look forward to more realistic and sophisticated evaluations, and the search for predictors (what will be the best drug or therapy for a patient) is in the process of objectifying the field. Yet it must be recognized that the choice of therapy today is frequently dependent upon what the therapist is comfortable in doing. Thus, most therapists see a wide variety of problems in different phases of development and intensity. If the response is that the patient needs therapy, this statement frequently means that the patient needs what the therapist knows how to do. In situations in which a wide range of talent is scarce, it is difficult to argue with this approach, but one need not be satisfied with it.

The patient, on the other hand, must take what he can get, but he tends to bring to any therapy his intrinsic capacity for recovery of function. Any therapist does well if he can quickly recognize the extent to which his approach and capacity can meet the needs of the patient and, at the very least, can be alert not to put obstacles in the patient's way. Every therapist can—if trained and willing—have a clear conception of his realistic limits and resources. When this potentiality is comprehended by both the patient and the doctor, the patient is able to orient toward the realistic resources that are authentically available to him—an auspicious beginning phase of therapy. Patients establish a relationship and invest their sense of security in even the clinic building or the administrative arrangements of the help-giving resource. This relationship is evident although they may be seen only once a month, primarily for medication (as the case must be with many chronic schizophrenics); patients get some orienting anchors and frames of reference in even brief interactions. Thus, the need to be recognized, visible, respected, looked after, or even rescued is basic to bringing doctor and patient together, and some realistic regard *and* limits with respect to these needs are helpful.

Nonrational and rational needs for personal attention and the wish for competence make up the dominating motivational dimensions of the doctor-patient relationship. The patient's willingness to concur with the doctor's regimen or to rebel can be influenced, in both the somatic and the psychosocial therapies, by the physician's attitudes and approach. In successful therapy, many patients have followed the doctor's orders in one sense: they identify their wishes with his wishes to foster some solution to a current or chronic condition or problem. For some patients, the therapy is experienced as a competitive and antagonistic venture, and yet even though full of turmoil, they may well show improvement in spite of—in order to spite—the therapy or therapist.

Therapeutic Mechanisms

There are many explanations of the mode of action in successful therapy. Probably each of the popular explanations contains some truth. Whether insight, catharsis, the practice of communicating significant experiences, or other factors form the therapeutic basis is a question that requires much more research. The amazing fact is that many therapies can be helpful even though one or another of these dynamics may be emphasized. All therapies involve learning and management, whether we speak of the psychoanalytic or the behavior therapies (which take place in the context of a personal relationship). All therapies are, if not directive, at least structured; at some juncture in the relationship some

programming is generated and rules of conduct are implicitly or explicitly followed.

The most useful fact to bear in mind is that procedures inducing behavior change and etiological factors that produce the disorder need not at all be directly related. Digitalis affects the force of the failing heart, whatever the cause of cardiac decompensation, and the mode of action of that drug does not reveal the causal sequences or mechanisms of heart failure. If we understand the biological principles of organization, integration, and homeostasis, we cannot expect to find an exact replica of the past in the ongoing equilibria of the present. Instead, we deal with a construction of the past and with consequences of such constructions as they operate in the present. For example, we may hear of a terrible conflict between mother and child and observe that the patient presents and reacts to problems modeled on this relationship; but if we search for etiological factors, it may well be that the patient's immaturity or inability to integrate (which could be biologically or experientially determined, or both) may be the critical element that made the interpersonal events appear central. When psychiatrists speak of regression, they are observing not only the loss of efficient and recently consolidated controls but the current impact and current representation of past events and modes of adaptation. Similarly, drugs may repair certain ongoing neurochemical and neurobehavioral malfunctioning, but they do not necessarily reverse the sequences that led to the malfunction.

Thus, the organism's psychological or organic responses to deficit or injury are attempts at adjustment or repair. They are often attempts to establish a new equilibrium. They may bring consequences that are painful—such as scar formation, or, in psychiatry, such as ego restrictions and neurotic symptoms that represent attempts to bring some order in the presence of psychological dysfunction. Similarly, successful therapies may not be without pain and constraints—some cost to the patient's ambitions and preferences. But in growth and development, we cannot run the film backward, so to speak. In general, we can attempt to remove obstacles to what may be thought of as deferred or inhibited growth.

Therapeutic Regimens

These various comments on the orientation, training, and culture of psychiatry should not be construed as indicating that there are not empirical grounds and data for preferring one or another therapeutic regimen for specific disorders. There are a number of specific tools available.

Drugs

As was discussed in detail in Chapter 22, drugs are widely used in treatment. Drugs may be classified as antipsychotic, antidepressive, and sedative antianxiety agents. A wide number of such agents are available, and current research is directed toward predicting what constellation of symptoms or behavioral attributes responds best to the many available compounds. Generally, drugs such as the antipsychotics are not well tolerated by normal people but are by people who suffer from serious disorganization, often even after recovery. The objective data on their efficacy are impressive, and although it is clear that they do not specifically cure, they have broad utility in the psychoses—whether behavior is excited and agitated or simply withdrawn and disorganized.

Convulsive Therapies

Since the 1930s, a number of convulsive therapies have been available, including insulin, metrazol, carbon dioxide, and electroconvulsive therapy (ECT). Their mode of action is not clear, but it seems that generally they produce a lapse in consciousness that is followed by a more primitive organization of mental functions for a period of time and a subsequent reorganization with a dampening of the pathogenic function. The major convulsive therapy still used today is electro-convulsive therapy, and a variety of forms of it (including nonconvulsive electric treatment) are employed. It is not, in itself, subjectively painful. Just as anti-psychotic drugs may reduce overanticipation and response in the psychotic, ECT may reduce certain mental functions that are dominant, overactive, and patho-genic. The lack of an explicit mechanism of action—in spite of empirical relief—is troublesome to the scientifically trained therapist.

Other Somatic Therapies

Somatic therapies range from massage and hydrotherapies to psychosurgery, which today has fairly specific indications and limited use. For some of the behaviorally significant psychomotor epilepsies, which often resemble schizo-phrenic and dissociated states where lesions of the temporal lobe are accountable, depth electrodes and cauterization or chemical treatments delivered directly to the epileptogenic foci have been employed.

Hospitalization

The major form of treatment for people who require some special control for a period of time has been hospitalization. Whether or not this is a preferred or adequate treatment depends upon the services and therapies that can be articu-lated in a hospital environment. It has been clear that "hospitalization" can often be a brutalizing experience and that the patient can become institutionalized, removed from his family and community and entrenched in a pattern of sick behavior. In well-run hospitals, this phenomenon is avoidable, and the aim is for prompt and relevant treatment. For many individuals, however, separation and distance from provoking and precipitating familial, occupational, and social stimuli can be a humane and needed arrangement.

Many practices abound today—such as revolving-door policies—in which the patient is kept for a minimum period of time, discharged, then readmitted as needed. Psychiatric patients do not so much need beds as environments in which they can attain a level of organization required for socialization. There are numerous methods by which the staff and the patients are in intense communi-cation and by which this living experience becomes a learning experience. What is critical is that grossly sensational and short-sighted generalizations about the abuses of hospitalization not be translated into policy that could deprive those populations who for diagnostic or therapeutic purposes, or both, require a con-trolled environment. The use of rehabilitation training, halfway houses, day hospitals, night hospitals, and various clubs and groups to support the patient as he finds a way to participate in the larger community has been an important step. The impact of the currently popular community psychiatry movement is really to make an array of facilities readily available, so that the patient has at his disposal those services that will best help him with the phases of his problem. A useful trend has been the use of general hospitals for prompt or emergency care. The tendency for hospitalization to be very brief—too short—may represent an overreaction to the era in which a hospital was a citadel of insanity, located far from home and community.

Some studies show that the cost to the family who must, in the current climate, live with a seriously disturbed person may be overwhelming, especially to developing children. The community has been forced in contemporary movements to face its responsibilities and participate in rather than ignore the treatment and prevention programs. The definition of subpopulations and of appropriate choice of treatment will depend on the extent to which evaluation

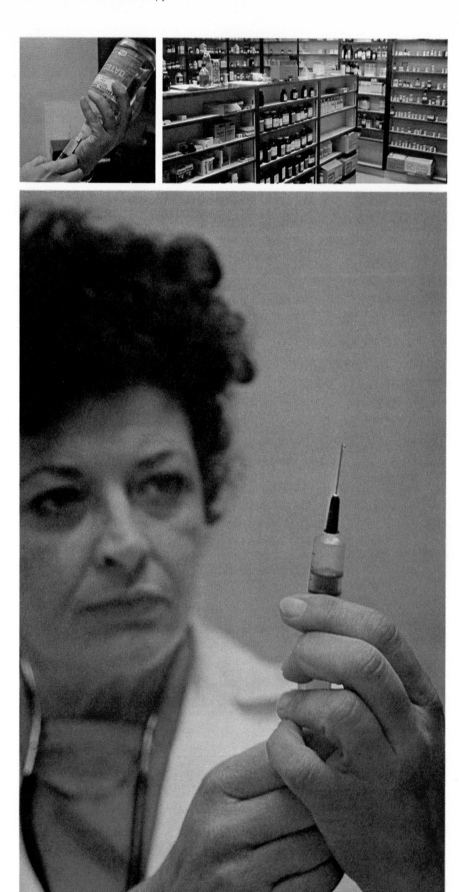

can proceed. In the evangelical mood of the moment, this may be forgotten, and humanizing impulses may lead to chaotic, disappointing therapeutic outcomes.

For the severe and psychotic depressions, it is clear that antidepressant medication may be useful. A variety of other treatments, including psychotherapy and hospitalization, may be required, and several months of treatment are to be expected. For suicidal depressions and for the depressions of middle life, electric shock therapy has been shown to be more rapid and efficacious than other therapies, and at times life saving. There is some tendency, however, for relapses to occur more frequently.

For mania and perhaps for hypomania conditions, a new and still investigational therapy—the drug lithium—has apparently had excellent effects in preventing recurrence in about two-thirds of the cases. Lithium is an ion related to the sodium series and can be quite toxic if dosage is not appropriately controlled. It currently is being investigated for periodic depressions, and there is research on its effects on periodicity as a general phenomenon in mental dysfunction.

For the severe psychoses and schizophrenias, there is not only overwhelming evidence of the efficacy of antipsychotic drugs but strong evidence that maintenance on phenothiazine therapy can help prevent relapse. These drugs are superior to the electroconvulsive and the insulin shock therapies. Drugs combined with good social work and milieu therapy, or even drug therapy without specific additional therapies, have been shown in objective studies to be superior to psychotherapy alone. There are undoubtedly subpopulations—for example, schizophreniform psychoses (acute psychotic breaks, usually in the young, usually without recurring breaks)—for which the drugs may not be required. Generally, their use facilitates milieu or psychotherapy. Electroconvulsive shock is still used to sedate uncontrollable, wild, destructive, life-threatening psychotic behavior.

It should be clear from the discussion in Chapter 27 that there are several schizophrenias, determined probably by the relative weighting of genetic, neonatal, experiential, psychosocial, and biochemical factors. In the treatment of schizophrenia, therefore, those forces that can help in the specific situation must be brought to bear. The aim is to mobilize the patient's intrinsic potential for recovery. Many psychoanalytically trained psychiatrists combine drug therapy either with occasional brief interviews or with occasional intensive psychotherapies. Often, it is effective to involve the family in some phase of the therapy, either conjointly with the patient or separately. This involvement in no way implies blame of the family or the patient but is used to help diagnose what can be done to stop vicious cycles of familial interactions, which usually compound the patient's problems. The patient may reside in the parental home, with a foster family, or in a halfway house, apartment, or hospital, as circumstances require. As the patient recovers his capacity for more organized behavior, various rehabilitative procedures involving group living or special training are useful. It has generally been shown that intensive and prompt treatment, whether brief or prolonged—with the use of isolation only as the patient requires it in order to keep his world less confusing—can prevent the entrenchment of the patient into a hospital system.

For the psychotic states associated with organic brain syndromes, phenothiazine therapy can be effective. Evaluation of efficacy in both young and geriatric patients is quite difficult and tentative. Special training and education in boarding schools or day schools are important procedures with severely disturbed

Indications for Treatment
Psychoses

children, and stimulant drugs possibly have a place for certain subgroups. Prevention of isolation, contact with the familiar, and good general physical treatment aid in the senile disorders where nursing homes may sometimes be essential for all concerned.

Neuroses The neuroses and various anxiety states can be treated with a number of sedative antianxiety agents, but the treatment of choice here generally is one of the many forms of individual or group psychotherapy (see Chapters 28 and 29). Psychotherapy combined with drugs has objectively been shown in most studies to be useful, but the problems of measurement of efficacy here are quite difficult. In general, clinic patients are better off if a regimen of drug therapy is available to them. There are, of course, numerous problems in the psychology of managing drug therapy that have to be taken into account. Most skilled clinicians find that neurotic dysfunctions require pharmacotherapies less frequently than do the psychoses.

The behavior therapies are being advanced based on conditioning and learning theories. Whether or not they sufficiently account for motivational and transference factors, certain clear-cut target symptoms—such as phobias, stuttering, and frigidity—that are quite easily demonstrated to the patient lend themselves readily to these approaches. Psychiatrists are acquiring some skill with them. The psychosocial therapies have much to learn from those approaches that involve programming of behavior, because this requires explicit steps. For example, the therapist must learn what the patient requires in order to respond and put this to a systematic test. The various approaches to such behavior modification will be discussed in detail in Chapter 35.

Societal Implications In general, we may be seeing fewer symptomatic neuroses and many more characterological problems. Social unrest and movements can mobilize certain conformist traits and serve to structure, absorb, or mask pathological drives and trends. Adherence to a single belief system or apparently similar social behaviors undertaken by groups does not mean that the involved individuals have lost their individuality. The same social behavior can be oriented around quite different personal histories and symbols just as the same symptom (say, depression) can have many different pathogenic histories. Psychiatric experience with the low and the mighty, the dull and the gifted, indicates that underlying the meaning of manifest social behaviors and values is an idiosyncratic and quite personal rendition that may or may not be in harmony with public behaviors. Although this observation too often leads to unwarranted psychologizing and reductionism of social accomplishments and goals, the facts are that fervor, rigidity, and utopianism on the public scene are empirically frequently found to represent distortions of ego control, reality testing, and pleasure integration at the level of private life and affectional relationships. The point is that groups can reinforce pathological trends, as well as growth and development.

As we enter an era in which individual destinies are more and more manipulated by group phenomena, we do not thereby abolish the psychology that describes individual growth organization. Rather, the task is to steadfastly enlarge understanding of individual and group psychology, to identify specific biobehavioral deficits and pathologies, and to refine and evaluate the treatments that may be required. These therapies require a sound understanding of social processes, their value, and their limitations. They require a better grasp of principles of training and learning. Yet psychiatric treatments are not to be designed (and

could not be) for total societies but rather for individuals whose psychobiological integrity requires some sense of personal coherence in meaningful transactions with others.

Study of the growth of knowledge of behavior disorders and their treatment brings increasing evidence that developmental processes are influenced by complex but definable biosocial factors that can be controlled. Accordingly, we should anticipate that, for some major dysfunctions, specific causes and treatments will be discovered; for others, treatments will advance in ignorance of causes. Whatever research brings, those who treat behavior disorders should remember the medical adage that describes the destiny of good therapists: to cure where possible, improve many, comfort most—and first of all, not to harm.

UNIT VIII

SOCIAL PSYCHOLOGY

As John Donne said, no man be an island unto itself. We are never alone in our lifetimes, for even in the womb we exist as a part of our mother, and even a hermit on a desert island carries in his mind the voices of yesteryear. Man is a social animal; he cannot exist without others like him. Other people set our standards, give us the language we use, teach us the roles we are to play in life, reward us when we do well, and punish us when we fail. Indeed, the very meaning of our lives comes from the relationships that we have with others. We live in groups, communities, and nations. For the most part, we live in harmony. But no group is perfect, and no community or nation exists without conflict. The study of the psychology of social interactions is, in no small part, the study of how these groups and nations are formed, how conflicts arise and how best they can be resolved, and how members of these groups can shape their own behavior to make for a better life.

31

GROUPS AND GROUP CONFLICT

THIS IS YOUR CHANCE to save the world. It is some time in the 1970s. The prospects of nuclear war have become so frighteningly real that both Russia and the United States have made one last-ditch effort at negotiation. For a variety of reasons, the Russians have insisted that preliminary talks take place between students selected at random from the two countries; you are chosen in a lottery as one of five students to represent the United States.

The meeting takes place in Geneva. For weeks you and four other young Americans have sat across a large table from your five Russian counterparts. You have been briefed daily by people from our Department of State as to what you should say, what you can offer, what you must demand. But ultimately, the decision on what to say rests with you and your colleagues. Until a day or so ago, it seemed as if the meeting must end indecisively, for the Russians have categorically turned down each suggestion of good faith you have made and have offered little or nothing acceptable in return. But at the last moment the Russians come up with the following daring proposal: Both countries will, in the next six months, destroy all their nuclear weapons and will promise not to manufacture new ones for at least five years. At the end of the six months, the heads of both governments will meet here to discuss the next step in the negotiations.

Two of your American colleagues (whom you have nicknamed the liberals) are much in favor of agreeing to the proposal. They point out that a nuclear war is almost inevitable unless both sides make some kind of show of good faith and that the destruction of all nuclear arms by the two countries will ease the immediate threat sufficiently for calm and reason to prevail. The other two

American students (whom you call the conservatives) are totally opposed. They point out that Russia has a history of not living up to her international agreements and that we would have no effective means of inspecting the destruction of her weapons. The Soviets might well decide to hold back a sizable number of nuclear bombs and warheads and then, six months from now, be in a position to threaten the entire free world with complete destruction if we did not capitulate. The liberal students offer as a counterargument the fact that if we do not negotiate in some way, the present situation will surely escalate and the free world will probably be destroyed anyway. The conservatives remark that at least if we retain our arms, we can also destroy Russia.

After considerable heated debate, the conservatives make a new suggestion. They propose that we make a great show of accepting the Russian offer, but then secretly hold back a sizable number of nuclear arms ourselves, "just in case." The liberals insist that the Russians will surely get wind of this and, taking it as proof of their prior fear that Americans cannot be trusted, will attack at once.

It is obvious that you will cast the deciding ballot. What do you think is the best way to make sure that the United States is not destroyed? Should the Russian proposal be accepted or rejected? If accepted, should we really destroy all our nuclear arms, or should we fudge a little and hold a number of bombs ready "just in case"? While trying to make up your mind, you ask yourself if such situations always are so structured that if one country gains something, the other must necessarily lose. What is there about human nature that has made conflicts like this so prevalent in the past? Why do the Russians see the Americans in such a different light than that in which the Americans see themselves? What is there about a group that makes its members behave so differently than they do as isolated individuals? And you ask yourself further if social scientists have discovered anything about groups in conflict that will help you come to the wisest decision in this case or, at the very least, help you to structure the situation better in your own mind? But to whom could you turn for information?

The Study of Group Behavior

The field of social psychology is primarily devoted to an attempt to understand and explain basic psychological processes—thinking, striving, perceiving, and learning—as they occur in a social environment. Social psychology may be viewed as an interdisciplinary field overlapping several social sciences, especially sociology and cultural anthropology. Cultural anthropology is primarily concerned with norms—customs, traditions, attitudes, and other learned behaviors—with socialization, or the process by which norms are learned; and with how norms are transmitted from generation to generation in a given society. Sociology, on the other hand, is primarily concerned with social groups, organizations, and institutions and how they are interwoven into a *social structure*—the complex system of relations between individuals, groups, and classes of people and the status hierarchy between such units in a given society.

The norms of a society and the place of the individual in the larger context of the society significantly influence his behavior. There is, moreover, considerable evidence that differences in child-rearing practices and other aspects of the socialization process produce significant differences in personality patterns. Even differences in the grammar and syntax of language, an essential aspect of culture, may affect the processes of thinking and perceiving (see Chapter 12).

The Individual in the Group

Each individual in a given society is a member of many groups—for example, the family group, the work group, the church group, and the social club. Within each of these groups, he assumes a title or *position*, such as father, daughter, foreman, minister, or friend; and for each of these positions there is an associated set of behaviors, attitudes, and beliefs expected of an individual occupying the position. Such a set of expectations is called a *role*. Some investigators have further differentiated between role expectation and role behavior: role expectation comprises expectations associated with a given role, whereas role behavior is the actual behavior of a person in a role category. The distinction is drawn because role behaviors may or may not agree with or conform to the expectations.

A collection of people—such as all elementary schoolteachers in the United States, members of the Republican Party, or members of the Catholic Church—is usually referred to as a *category* of people. As used by social psychologists, the term "group" is restricted to a collection of individuals who are in a cooperative interdependent relationship with one another. Some theorists use the term

Figure 31.1
Quite different sets of behavior are expected of the same man as a researcher and as a father.

579

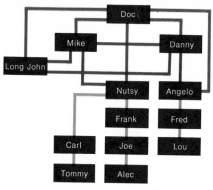

Figure 31.2
Among groups of children, status structure is influenced strongly by the relative ages of the members.
(After Whyte, 1943.)

"interdependent" to mean interaction; others, however, specify two criteria for interdependence: (1) the members must share some common norms with regard to certain behaviors, attitudes, and beliefs; and (2) there must be a system of interlocking roles such that each member has certain expectations regarding how others will behave toward him and, in turn, how he ought to behave toward others in the group.

Groups vary in many ways—in size, goals, characteristics of its members, type of leadership. An important property of groups—one that especially affects the pattern of interaction of its members—is the *group structure,* or differentiation of roles and role relationships within a group. A highly organized group in which each member's role and function is rigidly specified, such as a baseball team, is said to have a high degree of structure. Structure—especially in informal groups —is frequently described in terms of status and role in the group and in terms of the communication and decision-making structure. Figure 31.2 illustrates the status structure (or hierarchy) of a street-corner gang in Boston. It can be seen

that Doc is the leader of the group and that Mike and Danny are the two subleaders or lieutenants, each with several followers under their "command."

Figure 31.2 also illustrates the communication and decision-making structure of a group. In most informal groups, there is some correspondence between the status, communication, and decision-making structure, and the lines connecting the various members in Figure 31.2 may be used to describe the frequency of the interaction and communication between the members of the group, as well as the status structure of the group. It should be noted, however, that in formal groups and organizations—where there are clearly defined and formalized rules regarding the lines of communication and patterns of authority, such as in the military or in industry—other methods of describing structure may be more appropriate and important. Moreover, group structure—especially the communication structure—not only determines the pattern of interaction in the group but affects the problem-solving efficiency of the group.

Another important property of a group is its *cohesiveness,* or strength of the forces that keep the group together. Cohesiveness literally means sticking together, and if a group such as a family is highly cohesive, the members would be expected to remain together even under extremely adverse conditions. Several indices of group cohesiveness have been used. A commonly used technique called the *sociometric method* requires each member of the group to choose or name individuals he likes inside or outside the group. The extent to which ingroup choices outnumber outgroup choices (the proportion of ingroup to outgroup choices) is then used as an index of cohesiveness.

There are many reasons or motives for remaining in a group, including need for affiliation, achieving group goals, and need for power and status. No single motive, however, is likely to reflect the primary motive of all members of the group, and for this reason most of the single indices used in the past have been criticized. On the other hand, in an experiment conducted by Back, pairs of strangers were instructed to write a story based upon three photographs presented to them individually. After each member of the pair had written his story, they were brought together and allowed to discuss each other's story. After the discussion, each member was again individually asked to write the story. These stories were then analyzed to determine the extent of the partner's social influence as measured by the change from the first to the second story. Within this context, Back used three methods of varying the bases of mutual attraction (cohesiveness) of the pairs. His results indicated that the stronger the mutual attraction, the more the partners influenced each other *regardless of the basis of attraction.*

One of the most significant effects of cohesiveness is that it sets limits on the power of the group to demand conformity to its norms. If the forces to remain in a group are compared with the opposing forces to resist conformity, it is easily seen that the degree to which the group can influence its members is directly related to its cohesiveness. In one study, for example, it was hypothesized that the cohesiveness of a group would be related to the ability of the group to enforce conformity to a given standard of productivity. In a laboratory situation in which subjects were asked to cut out checkerboards, it was found that cohesiveness was related to productivity when the standard was for low production, with high cohesive groups restricting output more than low cohesive groups. However, when the standard was set for high production, high cohesive groups did not produce significantly more than low cohesive groups. Thus, the hypothe-

Group Cohesiveness

Figure 31.4
Sets of pictures used in Back's experiment. Slight differences between the sets given to each member of a pair of subjects induced differences in interpretation although none of the subjects ever realized that his set was not identical to his partner's.

sis was supported in only one direction—in the tendency for conformity to restrict output. In addition to the power of the group to influence its members, other consequences of cohesiveness that have some empirical support include the ability of the group to retain its members and their loyalty and to impart feelings of security.

Festinger has defined cohesiveness as the resultant of all forces acting on members to remain in the group. This definition implies that there are mutually opposing forces—to leave the group as well as to remain in the group—and that cohesiveness is the positive composite or balance of these forces. There is no reason to believe, however, that the underlying motives to leave the group are any different from those that motivate members to remain in the group. If, for a given individual, the need for status and power happens to be the primary reason for wanting to remain in the group and over a period of time his expectations are not fulfilled, he may turn to another group as a source of need satisfaction. This example illustrates the concept of *comparison level for alternatives* proposed by Thibaut and Kelley, in which an individual is assumed to evaluate the need satisfaction he might obtain if he switched to another group. Consequently, the cohesiveness of a group, according to Thibaut and Kelley, would be a function of not only need satisfaction from group membership but also need satisfaction anticipated from alternatives open to him.

Another important variable that affects cohesiveness is the interpersonal attraction between members of the group; but because belonging to a group is, in turn, one of the bases of interpersonal attraction, we defer discussion of this point until Chapter 34.

The processes of conformity and deviation have been studied in some detail by social psychologists. When pressures toward uniformity in a group become ineffective—especially with regard to relevant behaviors, attitudes, and beliefs—and deviate subgroups emerge, there is a tendency for deviates to be rejected by the majority. It is reasonable to assume, moreover, that if the number of deviates is sizable, cohesiveness may be strained to the point that a minority subgroup might break off and the composition of the entire group change.

Conflict

Conflict, at the interpersonal, intergroup, and international level, has been interpreted by many theorists as being dysfunctional and viewed as something that should be eliminated. Several theorists, however, have emphasized that human conflict is not necessarily destructive but can serve some useful function. According to the latter view, the problem of conflict is not its elimination but how to control and channel it for the benefit of society. That is, conflict is not intrinsically good or bad. It is, rather, a fact of life that can be destructive or productive, depending upon how it is channeled.

When social conflict results in violence and disorder, there is justifiable concern among many people that some mechanism be found to *reduce* rather than channel the tension and hostility resulting from such conflict. Within a given society, there are established norms and sanctions that attempt to prevent violent modes of resolving conflict, and if such attempts fail, there are legal procedures to resolve the conflict. At the international level, however, such legal procedures seem to have been less than successful. It behooves the social scientist, therefore, to study and determine the relevant variables that result in violence and disorder.

Several approaches have been employed by social scientists for the study of conflict and modes of conflict resolution. One of the major contributions of the

psychologist derives, in part, from research at the individual, psychological level, with emphasis on the individual as a biological organism. Several theorists have emphasized the hereditary basis of aggression, whereas others have postulated an environmental, learned basis of aggression.

Prejudice as Displaced Aggression

The frustration-aggression hypothesis, combined with a mechanism for displacing aggression, has been one of the dominant theories of racial conflict and prejudice. The first basis of this theory is that frustration produces aggression. Imagine an obese Southern planter, of the type frequently portrayed by Faulkner, harassed by flies, sweat, indolent employees, his health, and his own incompetence in breaking out of the unproductive rural-agrarian economic and intellectual morass that he inherited from his ancestors. These conditions breed frustration, which in turn leads to a large reserve of aggression.

The second basis of the theory, the notion of displacement, now takes over. Rationally, the planter should attack the flies, the heat, the motivation of his

Figure 31.6
Zimbardo's subjects pounding on a car.

584

employees, his doctor, his own incapacity, and the ignorance of his ancestors. But because none of these is psychologically possible for him, he instead turns his aggression irrationally toward other people, usually easily distinguishable groups of people. Such groups have historically included the financial Jews of Wall Street, the railroad, carpetbagging politicians, communists, and the most recognizable and omnipresent group in the proximal environment, the Negro. All the pent-up wrath of external and internal origin is vented on the Negro as a group. The Negro stands as the scapegoat, not at all because he is rationally at the base of the frustrations, but only because he is a handy distinguishable scapegoat.

Once released, violent aggression tends to perpetuate itself. Zimbardo has pointed out that aggressive behavior may be intrinsically enjoyable. He has shown that white, middle-class graduate students of social psychology, once encouraged to act violently, may continue in a veritable frenzy of destructive behavior. He encouraged students to damage a new automobile a little, so that it would make good bait for car strippers on a lonely street in California. The students, reluctant to damage the car at first, eventually struck it a couple of times with a sledge hammer. They continued until they beat the car into unrecognizability with a continual series of blows. Once released onto an object, however inappropriate and for whatever reason, the violent behavior of which we are all capable is not only difficult to stop but may be self-perpetuating. It is a fair guess that the car once dented, like the Negro once suppressed, appeared to deserve further damage and punishment as an inferior object. This may have provided the continuing destructive motivation for the graduate students.

Most social psychologists now recognize, however, that the displaced-aggression or scapegoat theory of prejudice is oversimplified and that the problem of prejudice is much too complex to be explained by a single-factor theory.

Although various definitions of prejudice have been proposed, there is general agreement that it involves an attitude toward some group or class of individuals. Gordon Allport indicates the essential ingredients of prejudice: an attitude of favor or disfavor that is based on overgeneralized beliefs held without sufficient reason. There is little reason to believe that the variables and mechanisms underlying the development of prejudice—and therefore the principles and procedures for the reduction of prejudice—should be any different from those underlying the development of attitudes and of attitude change. Such principles, theory, and research involving attitude formation and change will be discussed in detail in Chapter 33.

Intergroup Conflict

Another approach to the study of social conflict—based primarily on laboratory studies—attempts to abstract, rigorously control, and systematically vary the basic elements underlying conflict. Some theories of social psychology have interpreted social interaction in terms of the costs and rewards to the participants. In trying to manipulate costs and rewards experimentally, many investigators have turned to two-person games as a research paradigm for the study of conflict and conflict resolution.

Although many types of games can be used to study conflict, the game that has been most extensively studied is the prisoner's dilemma game, illustrated in Figure 31.7, which shows the number of dollars won by each player for each of the four possible combinations of choices. The players choose simultaneously and without knowing what the other player will do. If both players choose D, then neither wins anything. Note that if both choose C, then each gets $10. This turns out to be the best choice for maximizing mutual gain and is thus coopera-

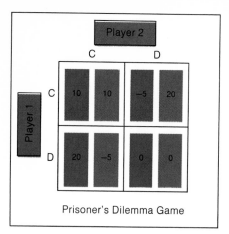

Prisoner's Dilemma Game

Figure 31.7

The prisoner's dilemma: the outcomes of the four possible combinations of the players' choices are shown in the four cells.

tive. The dilemma arises because a C choice is risky in that one can lose $5 if the other person does not cooperate by reciprocating a C choice. The gamble on choosing D is a gain of $20 if the other player chooses C. Because the game requires mutual trust between the two persons, several investigators have used it to study the variables underlying the development of trust, as well as to study cooperation.

The players are in fairly good shape if only they know the chances that their opponent will choose C or D. Obviously, if you know that your opponent will always choose C, you must choose C also because that gives you $10, whereas a choice of D will lose $5. Because the difference between $10 and $5 is $5, the strategy of choosing C all the time has for you an *expected gain* of $5 per play. Now, if you know that your opponent always chooses D, you must choose D also because, although that amounts to nothing for you, a choice of C means a negative expected gain for you, a certain loss of $5 on each play.

The game becomes a little more interesting when we consider known uncertainties of choice on the part of your opponent. Suppose that it is known that he chooses D three-fourths of the time and C only one-fourth and that you will both play the game several hundred times. What are the expected gains or losses from a consistent C or D choice on your part under these circumstances? Your expected gain from choosing C all the time turns out to be an expected loss of $1.25 for each play of the game. This comes about because you win an average of $1.50 per play from those one-fourth of the plays on which your opponent chooses C (one-fourth times $10), but you lose $3.75 per play on those three-fourths of the plays on which your opponent chooses D (three-fourths times $5). But what happens if you choose D consistently? When your opponent chooses C, one-fourth of the time, you win $20, or an average expected gain of $5 per play. When he also chooses D, you lose nothing. Thus, the expected gain of choosing D consistently is $5 per play, which is considerably better than the expected loss incurred by consistently choosing C. Thus, the best strategy to employ, if you are a prisoner and must play the game, is to consistently choose D, provided of course that you are certain that your opponent will in fact choose C only one-fourth of the time and that you will continue playing for quite a while.

One of the reasons the prisoner game has been used extensively in research is that it represents a situation in which there is a mixture of mutual and divergent interests—a tendency to maximize mutual gain and a tendency to maximize personal gain through competition. Accordingly, this game has been referred to as a mixed-motive game.

A second type of game, called the zero-sum game, illustrated in Figure 31.8, also has been studied. Unlike the mixed-motive game, what one player wins, the other must lose (and the gains and losses of the two sum to zero). Because it is a strictly competitive game, there is no basis for cooperation, and the only strategy open to each player is to overcome and beat the other. From a social psychological point of view, therefore, this game is of little interest empirically. It has great theoretical relevance, however, for representing the manner in which many individuals, groups of individuals, and representatives of nations perceive a conflict situation. Schelling, in a critique of game theory and its applicability to deeper insights into international conflict resolution, has argued that most real-life political, military, and diplomatic situations are representative of mixed-motive games. Indeed, several theorists have claimed that one of the basic reasons for the state of the world—of escalation, threat-counterthreat sequences, and the resulting violence and disorder—is that the protagonists view the conflict situa-

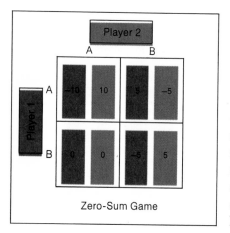

Zero-Sum Game

Figure 31.8

A set of outcomes yielding a zero-sum game.

586

tion as a zero-sum game and attempt to achieve complete and total victory over the opposition, rather than viewing the situation as a mixed-motive game and seeking a solution through mutual accommodation and cooperation.

Conciliation through negotiation is one way to manage and regulate conflict. Osgood's model of graduated reciprocation in tension reduction (GRIT), for example, assumes that concessions by one party to a conflict will be reciprocated and that in order to reduce tensions, one party must initiate a small concession to induce the other to reciprocate. In subsequent negotiations, these reciprocated

Bargaining and Negotiation Models

concessions are assumed to become progressively larger. Given two basically friendly parties who really want to reduce tension, this approach often works.

Another theory, proposed by Siegel and Fouraker, based upon the negotiators' level of aspiration, assumes that concessions by one party have the effect of raising the other's level of aspiration and thereby increasing his demands. Their model, therefore, predicts that concessions will not be reciprocated and that if one wishes to maximize gain, one should make very small concessions, if any. Under appropriate circumstances, this approach works very well indeed.

Because the two models of bargaining imply opposing strategies and both have some empirical support, it seems reasonable to ask under what specific conditions one or the other is valid. One clue to this inconsistency is the context in which the two theories were proposed. Osgood's theory was proposed in the context of international conflict, whereas Siegel and Fouraker's theory was proposed in the context of a laboratory-type experiment with college students as subjects. It is plausible, therefore, that Osgood's theory would be valid when the costs of not reaching agreement are high and that Siegel and Fouraker's theory would be valid when such costs are minimal. Only extensive tests of both theories under a wide variety of conditions will tell.

Social Perception and Attribution

A critical factor affecting the nature and process of conflict resolution is the perception of the participants involved in the conflict. The process of perception is subjective and selective, and perception does not always correspond to reality. Our motives have strong influences on perception, and we tend to perceive what we expect to perceive.

In the context of intergroup and international conflict, there is a tendency to distort and to exaggerate characteristics. This tendency to perceive individuals, groups, and nations in a black-white, good-bad picture, with one's own group seen as good and the other side as bad, has been referred to as the mirror-image phenomenon. Moreover, this process of distortion—assuming, of course, that both parties to a conflict are rarely entirely correct in their perceptions—seems to apply not only to the perception of individuals and groups but also to the process of attributing motives and placing blame. Thus, a benevolent act may not necessarily be perceived with trust, and a conciliatory act or a concession that may weaken one's military or bargaining advantage may be viewed with suspicion—the recipient of such acts may infer some ulterior motive. If both parties to a conflict wish to resolve the conflict through negotiations, one of the most important problems in conflict resolution is therefore to determine the effective means of communicating one's intentions so that the other party will not misperceive the intent behind such conciliatory acts.

The significance of perceptual processes in group conflict is illustrated in Stagner's definition of conflict as a situation in which two or more human beings desire goals that they perceive as attainable by one or the other *but not both*. Note that in this definition there is no implication that these goals must be incompatible—rather they must be *perceived* as incompatible—and that each party perceives the other as a threat to goal attainment.

Resolution of Conflict

One of the most critical problems of the world today is the problem of managing and controlling conflicts—conflicts between labor and management, between various ethnic groups, and between nations. To the extent that we can generalize from the research in interpersonal and intergroup conflict—and with due regard to the possible risk and consequences of overgeneralizing—what principles can

be derived and employed for the purpose of facilitating conflict resolution? What can we generalize or conclude about the variables underlying a cultural climate that might facilitate constructive resolutions of conflict? In this context, Deutsch claims that conflicts can be constructive or destructive and that the nature and form of its resolution is contingent upon two processes: a competitive (zero-sum) and a cooperative (mixed-motive) process.

Cooperation

A cooperative process, according to Deutsch, is characterized by (1) open and honest communication between the parties to the extent that each is interested in informing as well as being informed by the other; (2) sensitivity to similarities and common interests; (3) trusting and friendly attitudes toward one another; and (4) defining the conflict situation as a mutual problem to be solved by collaborative effort. These characteristics, of course, are highly interdependent—if two groups or nations have trusting and friendly attitudes toward one another, they will tend to have open and honest communication, perceive common interests, and define the situation as a mutual problem.

Friendly attitudes between the people of two nations, hopefully, will inhibit suspicious and hostile responses between the two groups, and open communication and interaction between the individuals in these groups may lead to such friendly attitudes. Prior relations between two or more nations is another factor. If two nations have a history of mutual cooperation and assistance, acts by one nation that might normally be interpreted as hostile by the other may be perceived not as a threat but with trust. Trusting and cooperative relations between countries may also be aided by such common goals as pursuit of science, avoidance of nuclear war, international trade, and common tariffs.

The present conflict between East and West may be viewed as a mixed-motive situation in which the two parties have a common predicament, namely, the possibility of total nuclear war. Our common adversary is not another nation but a hostile environment. This situation can be viewed as a class of mixed-motive game—similar to the prisoner's dilemma game—called the game of chicken, illustrated in Figure 31.11. It can be seen that if both parties escalate by using force and threats, the final outcome—through a spiraling process of force-counterforce—may be total nuclear war represented by the −100 for both parties. On the other hand, if both parties can convince each other that mutual escalation is intolerable and can reach a mutual agreement to compromise and negotiate, they can each obtain a positive outcome represented by 10. The dilemma still remains, however, in that if one party can bluff the other into believing that he is not "chicken," he can gain a larger outcome (20) while the other will lose a small amount (−5).

In the process of attempting to bluff the other (brinksmanship might be considered such an attempt), one frequently resorts to the use of threats. The use of threat, however, not only has the effect of reducing trust and friendly attitudes, if they existed in the first place, but is typically met with counterthreats and counteraggression.

It is reasonable to assume, therefore, that one of the crucial problems in arriving at a constructive, cooperative solution is for the parties to define the conflict situation as a mixed-motive rather than a zero-sum (win-lose) game. Under a mixed-motive definition of the situation, the parties would perceive that they could reach a mutually agreeable, satisfactory outcome—and would be more likely to approach the situation with a problem-solving orientation—and that neither need fear that what one won the other must lose. The role of the initial

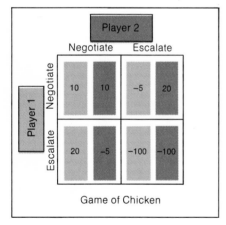

Figure 31.11
Game of chicken.

orientation toward one another has also been emphasized by many theorists and, as was noted earlier, will affect how one perceives the actions of the other—with trust or suspicion, as friendly or hostile—and whether there is benevolent or malevolent intent.

Several theorists have also emphasized the effects of norms and regulations for resolving disputes. Deutsch, for example, has noted that conflict within industry has been progressively institutionalized through various bargaining procedures and consequently not only is the likelihood of destructive conflict reduced, but the parties have developed a common interest in maintaining the functioning system.

The problem remains, however, that despite the development of procedures for regulating conflict, if one party violates mutually accepted rules and regulations, the other party is likely to reciprocate such acts. When such outbreaks occur, the use of third parties may be an effective means of inducing the parties to terminate hostilities—at least temporarily—and to abide by the rules and negotiate the dispute. For third parties to be effective, however, both sides must trust them, or they must be strong enough to compel an ending of combat.

Reduction of Tension and Hostility

Once the spiraling escalation process has begun, how can the process be reversed so as to reduce tensions? Osgood's GRIT model, as we have seen, is directly applicable. However, there seem to be two major problems in Osgood's proposal: (1) how to induce one party to take a unilateral initiative so as to reduce tension and increase trust; and (2) once such a concession is made, how to induce the other to reciprocate such concessions.

Regarding international tensions, there have been several interesting proposals. One that makes sense consists of making such demarcations as the DEW line, our early warning system, bidirectional, so that the Russians would be warned of an attack from the United States just as the United States would be warned of a Russian attack. This type of unilateral initiative not only might be interpreted as a concession but would reduce tension and fear of a surprise attack and thereby increase the security level of both countries. Indeed, if such warning systems could be administered and supervised by a neutral third party, such as a United Nations force agreeable to both parties, and implemented in strategic locations throughout the world, it is plausible that tensions would be reduced considerably. Moreover, the likelihood of an accidental nuclear attack on the United States or Russia would also be reduced, and with it the specter of war between the two countries.

SMALL GROUPS

IMAGINE THAT YOU ARE an astronaut headed for the Moon. You and two other men are cooped up in a tiny metal bubble no larger than many ordinary elevators here on Earth. Your movements are tremendously restricted. The air you breathe is recycled over and over again, as is the water you drink. All your bodily functions must be taken care of in public; you have no privacy. Worst of all, perhaps, you are absolutely dependent on the other two men with you for your very survival. All that stands between you and the near vacuum of space are the walls of the spaceship. If any one of your colleagues in this venture makes a mistake, it is your hard luck as well as his. For days, perhaps weeks on end, you *live* with these other two whether you like it or not.

What would it be like to make a trip to the Moon under these conditions with complete strangers? What would it be like with two of your best friends? What can psychology tell us that might make the trip more tenable?

Oddly enough, although we think of our lunar landings as being tremendous engineering achievements, the National Aeronautics and Space Administration

(NASA) employs not only engineers and physical scientists but psychologists and psychiatrists as well. For NASA has learned that in order to conquer the outer space of the planets and stars, man must first learn a great deal more about his inner, psychological space.

What do three men in a spaceship, an assembly room of industrial workers, a surgical team, a graduate seminar, a therapy group, a family, and a boys' gang have in common? The answer is that they are all comparatively small groups—that is, they are small enough so that each individual can make a critical difference. Personalities are important, as well as the way that particular personalities fit together. Thus, the ability to cooperate effectively, safely, and with enthusiasm is generally sought in such groups, and good leadership is prized.

Some groups claim to be leaderless. One would never find a leaderless group of astronauts, but one might hear such a claim at a meeting of the Students for a Democratic Society or in a therapy group. The facts of life tend to produce, even to require, some degree of leadership and some degree of structure in groups—some inequalities in power, in authority, in affection given and received—but an established structure exacts a price. It may not fit present needs. In a task-oriented group, such as the astronauts or a surgical team, personal dissatisfactions and interpersonal conflicts can be very damaging. In a personality-oriented group like a family, dissatisfactions and conflicts may put some individuals in a very poor situation, perhaps interfere with their adjustment and personal development. Psychologists are interested in small groups because most of us spend most of our time living and working with just a handful of other people at any given time (though seldom in such tight conditions as aboard a spaceship).

What is a group? How does one come into being? What kinds of groups are there, and what external conditions favor the formation of one kind or another? What kinds of information does the psychologist have, what kinds of experiments have psychologists performed, that would tell you—or the astronauts—how better to live together with other people even under the worst of conditions?

Cooperation and Competition

Basically, cooperation or competition is a result of the way members define their relationship to the situation from which they get their rewards. If they feel that the rewards are limited so that what one gets the others must lose, they define the situation as one of competition. On the other hand, if they believe that no one will get rewards unless they all work together, they define the situation as one of cooperation.

Very often in a work group, an external authority sets up the way in which pay, recognition, grades, or other forms of reward are distributed among the members. In this case, the members are under strong pressure to define the situation in the way authority defines it, and cooperation or competition will prevail in the group as determined by the conditions set by authority.

In other cases—for example, in a boys' gang—the members themselves define the situation. A single member, by acting in a threatening manner, monopolizing the time and attention of the group, regarding others contemptuously, or inciting others, can permeate the group with competition, especially if he insists on taking something scarce but valuable to all the members—such as talking time, attention, space, physical goods, or resources. If the resource is limited, he can make competition inevitable just by taking more than his share.

Most groups are partly cooperative, partly competitive. Members may be forced to cooperate in order to succeed in some task, but they still have to deal with differing degrees of interpersonal dominance and compete to some extent

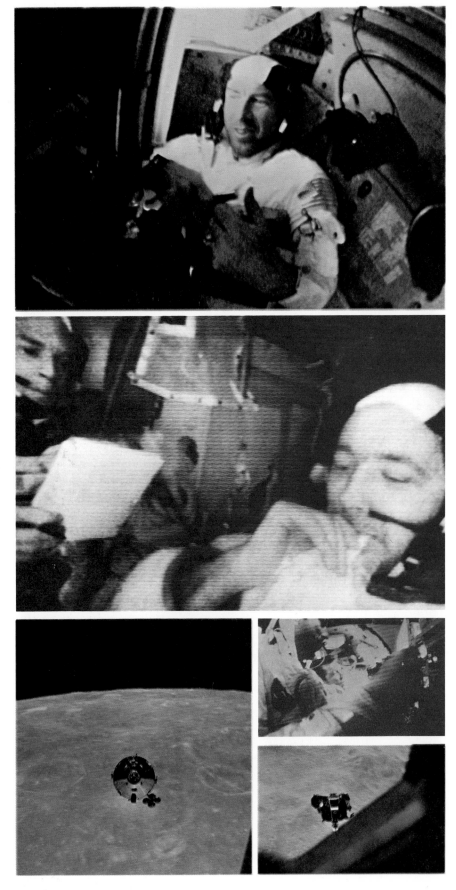

Figure 32.1
The breakdown of cooperation between men in a space capsule could easily result in their deaths.

for the rewards. These they are able to give each other directly through their attitudes: affection, love, admiration, approval. Equal distribution of rewards, or equality in the power to give or withhold rewards or punishments, though often idealized, is probably never very completely realized. A dimension of relative dominance, a pecking order or power structure of some kind, is characteristic of all groups. In cooperative behavior, the differences in personal dominance are tolerated. In competitive behavior, they are contested. The pecking order may change under protest, but usually only partially, and only by degrees.

Experimental studies show general damaging effects on group processes when members define their relationship to each other as highly competitive. It has been found that on tasks requiring cooperation for completion, if members are forced to feel they must compete with each other for the final distribution of rewards for task success, they pay less attention to the content of what individual members say, comprehend less well, are less interested in task achievement, tend not to help each other, have more difficulty in coordinating their task efforts, are more likely to duplicate others' efforts, tend to be more inefficient per unit time on the task, and turn out a poorer job. Moreover, they tend not to like what they have produced, not to like the group, and not to like each other as individuals.

On the other hand, not all kinds of jobs require the same kind or degree of cooperation. It may be that some kinds of inventive, intellectual, or creative tasks that a single individual with high ability can do alone receive some helpful impetus from competition for final rewards and less idealization of harmonious group processes. The optimum degree of competition versus cooperation is an ideological issue on which different persons, to say nothing of different societies and cultures, are apt to differ. The nature of the task or type of group problem is not usually sufficiently considered in discussions of this ideological issue.

The Formation of Small Groups

One of the most important conditions in the formation of natural groups is that the members be able to interact with each other easily and frequently, or even that they be forced to do so by some external circumstance. Geographic proximity in urban areas is such an important factor in the choice of marriage partners, for example, that the probability of marriage can be shown to fall off in a regular gradient with the distance separating the potential partners. Occupants of dormitories or apartment buildings who live close to each other or whose paths cross naturally in their daily activities tend to form groups and begin to show the

typical earmarks of group formation—emotional involvement with each other, usually a preponderance of liking or attraction over disliking, the tendency toward greater uniformity in opinions, and the formation of group norms. They become increasingly similar to each other in some attitudes, opinions, and values, though not in all (see Chapter 34).

Muzifer Sherif and his collaborators in an ingenious experiment showed that if a group of preadolescent boys is divided into two smaller groups so that the pairs of boys who have begun to like each other are separated and the two smaller groups are then physically separated, the interaction within each of the groups results in new attachments of liking within each group. When the two groups are put in a competitive situation, dislikes in each group become focused on the other group (even though it contains former friends). When the two groups are then put in a situation where they must cooperate and interact, the dislikes tend to dissolve and to be replaced by liking.

Studies of race relations in the military have shown that interaction between blacks and whites under battle conditions tends to result in mutual acceptance, though prior attitudes may have been prejudiced. Moreover, industrial workers in the same room tend to form cohesive groups as they interact, though the structure is not always quite that of one big happy family.

The relationship between interaction and liking is not completely straight-forward and simple. Interaction apparently tends to result in mounting emotional involvement, which includes both liking and disliking, in some proportion depending upon many other conditions. Either liking or disliking may be repressed in the relationship with a given person or diverted to another target. In any group held together in continued interaction by external factors, a few of the members are apt to be disliked, to some extent, by the others. One or a few are apt to be the focus of liking of many of the members.

The majority of members in most natural groups are usually more liked than disliked, and consequently the level of liking within a group generally tends to increase gradually up to some point in a way correlated with the amount of interaction. For some few individuals, however, disliking increases as interaction continues, again up to some point. It is also true that a group may split into two groups in conflict with each other under competitive conditions, in which case the dislikes within each of the groups may tend to be suppressed to some extent. Not much is known about these complicated adjustments, but the theory that a scapegoat makes it possible to displace dislikes to it and thus to intensify the feeling of liking for those in the group seems plausible and is commonly held.

Leadership in Small Groups

When members of a small group are asked to rate each other on leadership, they generally seem to take three factors into account. First, they pick a person who is at least moderately *powerful* in the group—one who is active physically and verbally, one who possesses abilities and resources that make it possible for him to influence others, against their will if necessary, by giving or denying them opportunities, rewards, or punishments. All the components of personal power do not necessarily go together, however. An individual having high verbal output, for example, will not necessarily also have money or intelligence, but the components of personal power are synergistic in that by superior access to resources the person with power can force others to submit.

It is not simply the most powerful or dominant person in the group who is generally thought to exercise the most leadership, however. The second factor that group members seem to take into account is *likability*. The person chosen as leader is generally more liked and admired than not. Members' feelings about him are somewhat on the positive side, though not always very far. In his behavior, he gives reason for their positive feelings toward him. One way or another, he gives more opportunities to others than he denies and rewards them more than he punishes. He is, in fact, usually the main social means by which the resources distributed unevenly within the group are put in the service of others, so that after some redistribution, the majority of members of the group receive a positive balance of rewards over punishments. An extremely well-liked person can distribute some rewards simply through his liking of others and through his symbolization of the affectionate ties that bind members to each other. But without personal power of other sorts, his ability to reward others is too limited to maintain him in a position of leadership. Typically, there are a number of negative members, sometimes subgroups, who do not respond positively to him. If they are powerful, the person regarded as exercising effective leadership must be powerful enough to deal with them. Leadership thus involves both power and likability to some extent.

But even the combination of dominance and likability is normally not enough for leadership. Group members typically take one further factor into account: the ability of the leader to bring about the success of the group in their main instrumental tasks. *Task success* to some degree is a must if rewards are to be obtained from the external environment, and many groups are heavily dependent upon task success.

The person regarded as exercising the most leadership in a group may himself directly exercise the abilities needed to perform the task, or he may coordinate the efforts of others on the direct work. In this coordination, his relation to whatever norms the group may have defining authority is crucial. Authority is the presumed legitimate right to decide how others should act. It is distinct from personal dominance in that it is conferred by the group in some form. Some groups work on tasks defined by a powerful external authority and under a designated head to whom authority has been delegated. Other groups elect a head, and still others refuse to recognize any one person as holding authority, even though informally they may respond to a leader who is also given some of the attributes of legitimate authority. The norms of an established and stable group nearly always define some kind of legitimacy, and if a given person possesses legitimate authority, he is in a critical position to affect the task success of the group.

Although the components of leadership should be regarded as separable, they may have implications for each other over various time spans. The degree of task success, for example, may go up and down over rather short time spans, from hour to hour or day to day, according to the kind of task. Legitimate authority is usually conferred with some degree of insulation from short-term fluctuations of task success, but if task failure persists over a long enough time, legitimate authority is likely to be undermined. Similarly, liking for an individual tends to persist through short-term failures in his ability to reward, but liking can be worn out in time by repeated actions that arouse bad feeling. Personal dominance built on possession of multiple resources tends to be rather durable in most small groups. It does not depend on the way others feel to the same extent as legitimacy and liking, but it yields to a sufficient combination of the power of others organized in opposition.

Position in Group   The position of any member in a group can be located in terms of the same

Figure 32.3
Although the coxswain directs, the real leader in a rowing team is the stroke, the first rower in the stern.

components as leadership, for these turn out to be dimensions of group structure as well. For many purposes, a simplified version of these components that recognizes three dimensions is useful. As other members perceive and evaluate a given member, he can be located somewhere on a scale of personal dominance ranging from ascendant to submissive, on another independent dimension ranging from likable to unlikable, and on a third independent dimension ranging from task-oriented to nontask-oriented. The person other members usually think of as exercising the most leadership is usually moderately dominant, moderately well liked, and moderately task-oriented. Not infrequently the leadership in a group is divided between two persons—one, perhaps the formally appointed head, who is dominant and task-oriented, neither much liked nor disliked; and another, sometimes called the natural leader, who is primarily well liked, less dominant, and less task-oriented than the other but who supports him and in turn is supported by him.

As the task-oriented leader leans in his behavior toward the negative direction and employs punishments, he approximates the organizational type sometimes called the hatchet man. As the well-liked natural leader swings in his behavior away from the task-oriented direction, he approximates a kind of "group mother." In an industrial organization, the supervisor and the shop steward sometimes have these two roles. In a military unit, the noncommissioned officer (often the sergeant) is more apt to take the role of the hatchet man and the commissioned officer (the captain or lieutenant) that of the group mother.

If two such partial or specialized leaders cooperate, they may be able substantially to unify quite disparate factions in the group and between them provide all the main components of successful leadership. If they are unable to cooperate, however, the group may split and even undergo a kind of revolution, with the hatchet man heading the "party of the right," concerned with authority, discipline, punishment, external problems, and enemies, while the group mother heads the "party of the left," opposed to authority and concerned with greater equality of rewards, emotional supportiveness and warmth, and social change to solve internal problems. This is only one of many possible types of group split, however. Presumably a group may polarize into two or more conflicting subgroups along any of the three dimensions mentioned, or any combination of them, depending upon the personalities of the particular group members and many other circumstances.

Verbal ideologies or groups of values justify all the directions or positions in the three-dimensional space. The set of social attitudes that Hans Eysenck calls tough-minded, after the description given by William James, tends to be characteristic of those who are in positions of dominance and simultaneously disliked. Those who answer the description of James' tender-minded type are seen as somewhat submissive and simultaneously liked.

In general, traits of extraversion, physical activity, high verbal output, high demand for attention, and energetic expressions of both sexual and aggressive drives tend to restrict the opportunities of others and are regarded as dominant. The repression or concealment of these same tendencies is seen as submissive.

Traits of alienation, feelings of anxiety, hostility, suspicion, and many kinds of neurotic symptoms tend to arouse the dislike of others. Absence of these feelings and, instead, feelings of psychological health, calm acceptance of self and others, liking, respect, spontaneous warmth, and admiration for others tend to arouse their liking in return.

Members with the personality traits of perseverance and obsessive or compulsive striving for order are usually perceived by others as conservative and conforming, concerned with task achievement, whereas active exhibitionism, egocentricity, provocativeness, passive dependence, pessimism, and withdrawal are generally seen as nontask-oriented and negative. Not all nontask-oriented traits are negative, however. Active, spontaneous emotional warmth is usually seen as dominant, nontask-oriented, and positive.

Any person in a group may at one time or another exercise leadership in the limited sense of becoming a focal point of attention. A group generally saturated with work may welcome the relief provided by an active exhibitionist. A group in which hostility has long been suppressed may at first react negatively to the suspicious irritability of a negative group member but then begin to unravel with relief into an outbreak of hostility. A group in which participation has been too highly concentrated among a few nonstop talkers may suddenly fasten upon a silent member and, even though they may get only a few words out of him, may have the opportunity to define their problem with the overdominant members. There is hardly any personality trait that may not have its limited usefulness in this way, because emotional conditions in the group may vary tremendously over

Figure 32.4 *(opposite)*
Group members' attitudes toward each other create a three-dimensional group space within which each can be located. The relationships of the members of a typical small group in this space often take on a spiral shape corresponding to the "social pyramids" of large organizations.

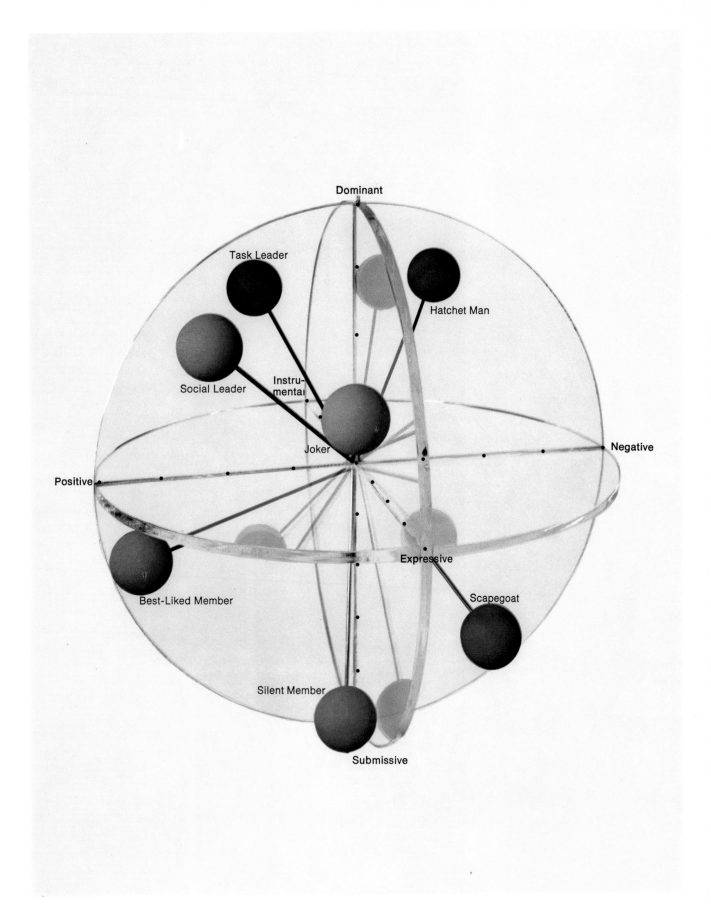

time. This does not mean, however, that there is no need for a generalized and durable leadership or that the rewards of successful leadership are very likely to be spread equally among all members. Although the ideology of equality holds this to be desirable, most groups, by their actual evaluation, disperse their members in positions over all three of the dimensions described, according to the behavior of each individual and the effect of that behavior on other members.

Dyadic Groups

Dyadic groups (groups of two) constitute a special class. Many institutionally defined and regulated relationships fall in this class: doctor and patient, lawyer and client, teacher and student, for example, as well as such important family relationships as husband and wife, parent and child, and brother and sister.

When experimentally formed dyadic groups with no clear definition of their relationship are asked to come to a common decision on a problem, they show features not common to similar groups of larger sizes. Groups of two are markedly low on showing disagreement and unfriendly behavior but markedly high on showing tension and asking for information. They appear to take extra care to avoid conflict and to persuade each other gently. In such a group, either member may exercise a complete veto by withdrawal, refusal of cooperation, or the like. In groups of larger sizes, either of two conflicting members can appeal to other persons in the group to combine with them or act as impartial judges. The pressure of a coalition or the pressure of somewhat impersonal group norms can be brought to bear. But in an isolated group of two, each member of the pair is unusually vulnerable to the other.

The social and legal regulation of common sorts of dyadic relationships probably helps to ease this problem. Society specifies within broad limits how each person in these institutionalized pair relations should act and what the rights and responsibilities of each are. The less powerful member is usually protected to some extent against the more powerful, but the latter is often given some authority vis-à-vis the less powerful, as well as some responsibility for protecting his welfare. This system works reasonably well in our society for doctor and patient, less well, at the present time, for teacher and student, and quite miserably for husband and wife.

The general tendencies toward equality of the sexes in our society, the long and close interactive contact between husband and wife, and the high degree of emotional involvement make the quality of their relationship very problematic and varied from pair to pair. Very much depends upon their unique personalities and the way they fit together. They may polarize in conflict along any of the dimensions described earlier, and if they do, they have very little leverage for getting out of their predicament. They sometimes try to use a child as an ally, a mediator, or a scapegoat, but usually without much success and with a high probability of damaging the development of the child.

The family is a highly charged group situation, and most other small groups bear traces of its major problems. Group members under emotional stress are generally prone to construe important features of their present situation—such as a struggle over leadership or hostility toward authority—in terms reminiscent of their earlier family experiences. The same is true, in fact, of husbands and wives. It's a wise man who knows, in the heat of marital conflict, whether his wife is his father or mother. He may, unconsciously, treat her as either—or both.

Group Problem Solving

When we speak of group problem solving, we usually have in mind the solution of problems calling for action and decision. There are other kinds of problems,

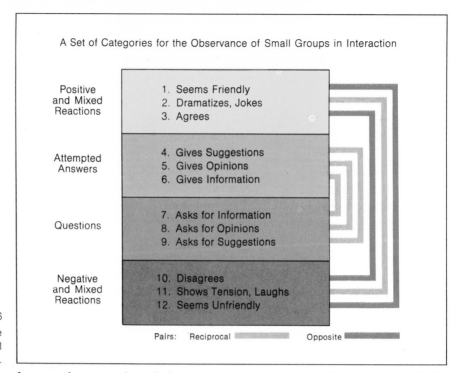

A Set of Categories for the Observance of Small Groups in Interaction

Positive and Mixed Reactions	1. Seems Friendly 2. Dramatizes, Jokes 3. Agrees
Attempted Answers	4. Gives Suggestions 5. Gives Opinions 6. Gives Information
Questions	7. Asks for Information 8. Asks for Opinions 9. Asks for Suggestions
Negative and Mixed Reactions	10. Disagrees 11. Shows Tension, Laughs 12. Seems Unfriendly

Pairs: Reciprocal   Opposite

Figure 32.6

These categories are used to make measurements of the behavior of small groups engaged in problem solving.

however, having to do with the expression of emotions and feelings and with the organization of people relative to each other.

Task-oriented work is meant to serve a purpose that is in turn related to more general purposes and eventually to quite abstract attitudes, values, or convictions as to what is good. Play, as well as work, is related to general values, though it is generally more spontaneous and expressive, less planned and instrumental, than work. Nevertheless, it has effects, and the effects are evaluated in terms of more general convictions as to what is good. Virtually nothing that occurs in any small group, work or play, is meaningless, though it may be presented as nonsense. In a very general way, every act has significance in terms of motives or of problems to be solved or of values realized (or not) after its completion.

Both instrumental and socioemotional problems are solved, or at least affected, through overt behavior of some kind. The work performed on physical aspects of the environment, as well as the expression of feelings and the change of social relationships, takes place in a context of verbal intercommunication or social interaction. It is possible to observe and record some of the most important distinctions between types of social interaction in terms of a rather simple set of categories. The set of twelve shown in Figure 32.6 perhaps seems so simple as to be nearly self-evident.

Suggestions and opinions are clearly related to commonsense ideas as to what has to be done to try to solve the instrumental task problems of the group and to monitor and evaluate the success of such efforts. When one person gives opinions or suggestions, others evaluate his efforts in terms of their general attitudes and values, then agree or disagree. The more ascendant members may disagree and continue with their own opinions and suggestions; the more submissive may simply agree or say nothing.

It is hard, perhaps impossible, to agree or disagree with another person's opinions and suggestions without making him feel that you either like him or dislike him as a person. What a person does or says is usually an extension or manifestation of his conception of *himself,* and if you disagree with what he says, he will probably think that, to some extent, you do not like *him.* Thus, work on instrumental tasks tends to create *social problems.*

The categories of friendly and unfriendly behavior (1 and 12 in Figure 32.6) are directly relevant to the social problems of dislike among members. When all members like each other, their social problems are minimized, and most of them may not be conscious of any. But when unfriendly behavior appears, they feel a problem and may consciously try to remove the dislike by friendly behavior. Some friendly behavior is also probably an attempt to forestall negative reactions on the part of others. However, one should not be cynical about the overly rational nature of friendly behavior in general. The sexual motives and their sublimated derivatives presumably give rise to much genuine friendly behavior, not narrowly egocentric and calculating, and these drives are very strong in man generally.

On the other hand, one cannot assume that all persons prefer friendliness to be maximized among all members of a group to which they belong. Jealousy, envy, and resentment are also very real. Friendliness has the consequence of binding the members of a group together, of making them feel similar to each other and "identified" with each other. It increases their ability to influence each other. All of this makes some persons very nervous. They feel hostility toward others, and as the bonds between others tighten, they feel threatened, left out, and at the same time forced to suppress their hostile feelings.

Aggression, in the sense of the possession of all the physiological underpinnings of animal attack and self-defense, is presumably as widespread and fundamental as the sexual drive in the human species, though it may not generally be so strong and perhaps is aroused more intermittently. There is little agreement among psychologists about these matters; there never has been any among philosophers. But there is little doubt that in some personalities, hostile feelings on the average outweigh friendly feelings. For such persons, the maximizing of friendly bonds within a group is felt as a social problem, and they react to it with increased hostility. Their unfriendly behavior is an attempt to solve the social problem as they feel it.

The suppressing of unfriendly feelings, or of friendly feelings, for that matter, creates an emotional condition often called tension. Work on the group task may to a certain degree provide a sublimated way of expressing friendly as well as unfriendly feelings. It is also a common way of dealing with, or anchoring, feelings of anxiety. But, depending upon the difficulties of the task and the underlying differences in basic attitudes and values of the group members, continued hard work on the group task may raise the level of tension or suppressed feelings. The high level of suppressed feelings may in time come to be a more important problem than the instrumental tasks of the group. The problems of dealing with underlying feelings (anxious, aggressive, sexual, or other) may be called the *expressive problems* of the group. At mild levels, presumably, these feelings may be fused into instrumental work; at higher levels, their expression loses its coordination with the work, and they begin to interfere with and supplant the work. This happens in a cyclical way in much group problem solving. Instrumental and expressive activity alternate over time, each giving way to the other, as suggested by Figure 32.8.

The early signs of the rise of tension in a group are often a rise in the rate of disagreement. A tone of unfriendliness begins to creep into previously neutral opinions and suggestions. Sometimes there are attempts to counteract the rising negative feeling by an increase in the rate of agreement and friendly behavior. If

Figure 32.7
In the process of a business meeting,
discussion of the problems of production
periodically gives way to more
emotional expression.

the tension continues to rise, one begins to see more explicit signs of it—faltering silences, sighs, uneasy tics in the facial expressions and bodily attitudes of members, lapses in attention, slouching, doodling, and turning away, both voluntary and involuntary. These and other similar indications are referred to in Figure 32.6 as showing tension, category 11.

At some point, perhaps prior to the resolution of the disagreement in a group decision, perhaps after, the focus of the group is likely to shift suddenly, with the introduction of a joke, a quick remark, or an anecdote on some vague parallel to the group predicament that captures everyone's attention. They laugh, and the tempo of interaction picks up, as one after another dashes in to try changes on the joke or embroider the anecdote. The laughter continues, the general noise level is high, the physical movement of 'members is animated. Acts of joking or somehow dramatizing in fantasy the emotional problems of the group alternate rapidly with laughing and other signs of previously existing tension, now in the explosive process of release. These activities are mostly subsumed in categories 2 and 11 of Figure 32.6, and when their rates are high, the rates of serious task activities, particularly giving opinion and suggestion, are apt to be low, as the chart implies.

Eventually, the joking and the laughing die down, sometimes an uncomfortably suggestive fantasy or dramatization is squelched, and a slightly guilty or bemused silence sets in. One of the more submissive task-oriented members may turn toward some one or more of those he regards as task leaders and ask for suggestions (category 9). Or some more personally oriented member may ask for an opinion or for information (categories 8 and 7). And then, perhaps with a false start or two, the focus of the group is likely to turn again to some instrumental task, thus beginning a new cycle.

Giving information (category 6) is necessary to the accomplishment of most instrumental tasks, though it is sometimes skipped over and neglected by members who are more eager to get on to the giving of opinions and suggestions. But giving information is also the external form of much of what we call social activity—graceful or polite smalltalk that helps the members to warm up to each other. As a consequence of these various uses, giving information is primarily neither task-oriented nor expressively oriented. Similarly, in its time relations to these two directions of activity, it tends to occur after an expressively oriented phase and preliminary to the more directly task-oriented phase.

Figure 32.8 shows a smoothed and somewhat idealized conception of the rise and fall in rates of the various categories of interaction as they often occur within the course of a meeting of a group or, more exactly, in a single cycle of problem-solving activity when the problem is one that makes a balanced demand on the exchange of information, opinion, and suggestion, leading to a binding group decision. The categories have been grouped into related pairs to simplify the illustration.

It will be noted in Figure 32.8 that the rate of each pair of categories peaks at a different time, the successive phases constituting a complete cycle that ends with all the rates in the same relation as at the beginning of the cycle. Actually, most groups, dealing with a number of problems, go through a number of such cycles in the course of a single meeting and depart from the idealized conception in many ways, depending upon the nature of the group, its temporary condition, and the task.

In spite of infinite variations in detail and magnitude, however, the overt interaction of individuals in a group tends to show certain uniformities, along the

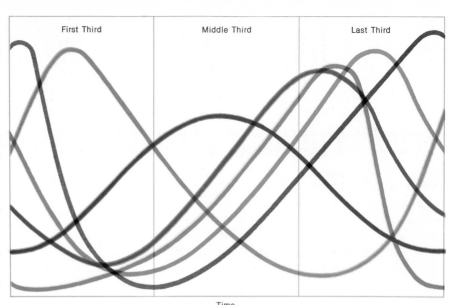

First Third | Middle Third | Last Third

Showing Tension, Dramatizing, Joking, Laughing

Agreeing, Seeming Friendly
Asking for and Giving Information

Asking for and Giving Suggestions

Asking for and Giving Opinions

Disagreeing, Seeming Unfriendly

Time
Idealized Phasing of Interaction Over Time in a Single Problem Cycle

Figure 32.8

An idealized representation of the changes in frequency of the kinds of interaction that take place during a cycle of problem-solving activity.
(After Berkowitz, 1956.)

lines suggested by the idealized problem-solving cycle. If people are to make themselves understood to each other, reach any goals at all, and experience any satisfaction from successful task performance, someone must express opinions and suggestions, there must be some minimum of agreement (usually more than disagreement) to the opinions and suggestions, questions must be answered, there must be some pauses for relaxation and recovery, and so on. These are the steps by which progress in *any* direction must be made. They are analogous to putting one foot in front of the other and shifting the weight in walking.

Categories 11 and 2, groupings that bring together showing tension, dramatizing, joking, and laughing, are shown as high at both the beginning and the end of the idealized average meeting. At the beginning, this is the familiar warm-up activity often considered preliminary to, and not really a part of, the meeting. A businesslike meeting is usually considered actually to get under way at the point just following that, when asking for information and giving it rise to a peak, as the minutes of the last meeting are read and the explanation of the problem is given.

About a third of the way through the total time of the average meeting, however, the rising rate of asking for opinion and giving it crosses over the falling rate of exchange of simple information, and the phase of analysis and evaluation of the various facets of the problem sets in. This phase ordinarily lasts almost through the middle third of the meeting and sometimes is quite prolonged if the problem is difficult.

Meanwhile, the rate of asking for suggestions and giving them has been rising and at some point crosses over and becomes the most salient type of activity, as the group closes in toward a decision.

Perhaps unnoticed all this time, through the middle third of the meeting, the rate of disagreement and seeming unfriendliness has probably been rising, closely related to the rising rate of suggestions but trailing it by a short time lapse. At some point, not long after the rate of suggestions reaches its peak, the rate of disagreement and unfriendly behavior is likely to cross over and become highly salient. This may be called the crisis point in the decision-making cycle. The question is whether any suggestion can command sufficient agreement to be adopted, or alternatively, whether the desire for agreement and friendly relations

will finally result in the acceptance of some suggestion even though it is not fully satisfactory. Much evidence suggests that persons who like each other tend to change their opinions toward agreement with each other. The so-called *balance theories* in social psychology deal with this kind of dilemma or crisis of decision.

All during the rise in the rate of disagreement and unfriendly behavior, the rate of agreement and friendly behavior has also been rising, following at a small lapse in time. The rise probably occurs partly in response to the general pressure for decision and partly as an attempt to counteract the negative reactions and negative feelings. If the crisis is passed successfully, the rate of agreement and friendly behavior is likely to cross over and become the most salient activity. If not, the phase of disagreement and unfriendly behavior may be prolonged and exaggerated.

Sooner or later, in either event, the tension indicators attending the decision-making efforts are likely to rise to a cross-over point, and a period of expressively oriented activity and recovery sets in. Often this is a period of joking and laughing, particularly if a decision has been made and agreement and friendly behavior have been relatively high or are rising.

If a decision has not been made and disagreement and unfriendly feelings are evidently high, sometimes the conflict seems to escalate by transformation into a kind of fantasy realm, where metaphorical figures and situations replace the actual group and its problems, truth loses its binding meaning, and feelings are exaggerated and dramatized. Often this substitution of a group fantasy for the intractable group reality takes place without the explicit awareness of the members and vaults along with considerable excitement to some point where the repressed problems of the group or some of its members become painfully evident. At this point, a silence may fall, the topic may be quashed or abandoned, and the members remobilize their repressions, perhaps with some joking and laughing if they are unable to deal otherwise with the problem.

Thus, either successfully or unsuccessfully, a cycle of problem-solving effort comes to an end, and the group is ready to disband for the time being or to begin another cycle.

Helping Relationships

Helping others, either in a one-to-one relationship or in larger groups, involves a specialized kind of leadership. Often the aim is not just to help temporarily but to change the other person so that he becomes independent of the relationship in the future, as in education or in psychotherapy. This kind of leadership is based, ideally, on a sensitive and comprehensive understanding of the stage, state, and condition of the person to be helped and on the providing of what he needs to help him grow to a new stage. Probably this ideal is seldom realized. Helping relationships, like all others, are tied up with ideologies, basic values, interpersonal preferences, and the personality traits of those who desire to help, as well as those they try to help.

Therapeutic Dyadic Groups

In the nondirective therapy of Carl Rogers (see Chapter 28), the therapist concentrates most of his activity in the very early phases of the group problem-solving cycle. Once the relationship is settled, he gives information about what the patient has just indicated to him about feelings—this is called the reflection of feeling. The therapist maintains an equalitarian relationship with the patient, basically very positive and supportive, with agreement and friendly behavior. The patient is helped to see himself more clearly, and his self-picture often becomes more positive. He tends to feel very positive about the therapist also, because he is constantly accepted and reinforced in his attempts to express his feelings and to work toward a decision for himself. The therapist seldom gives opinions or suggestions, disagrees, seems unfriendly, jokes, or laughs but rather keeps bringing the process back to the early phases of the problem-solving cycle where friendly behavior and exchange of information predominate. The patient does most of the talking, but the therapist talks a moderated amount and also maintains a sensitive, positive feedback on every remark of the patient.

In the classical Freudian procedure of psychoanalysis, the picture is different. The patient does nearly all the talking, under the requirement to say whatever comes into his mind—that is, to free-associate. The analyst is silent most of the time, and when he does speak (very sensitively timed), he tends to concentrate on interpretation or analysis of the underlying defenses of the patient—a specialized variety of giving opinion. The patient gives a good deal of information, expresses many negative as well as positive feelings, reports his dreams and fantasies, and catches them on the wing—in fact, carries on most or all of the other functions of the problem-solving cycle. But the analyst specializes in the phase of giving opinion or analysis. He seldom either agrees or disagrees and is neither friendly nor unfriendly. He maintains a neutral position in the expectation that the patient will place on him both negative and positive feelings, transferred from other emotionally important relationships, particularly those concerning his former and present families. The analysis centers on the feelings and associations so produced, and in time the patient learns to analyze his emerging feelings along the model presented by the analyst. His attitude toward the analyst is hopefully basically positive but in the course of the analysis usually fluctuates markedly.

Other varieties of psychological treatment specialize in still other ways that may be located as special phases in the problem-solving cycle. So-called inspirational-repressive therapy tends to concentrate on opinion and suggestion on the part of the therapist, who (unlike the psychoanalyst) is very active in persuading. Hypnotic suggestion (seldom used for therapy today) concentrates almost exclusively on the nonstop giving of monotonous suggestion, with only passive, generally nonverbal compliance from the patient. Behavior therapy, which attempts to apply experimental findings in learning theory, involves many direct suggestions designed to activate specific feelings or tendencies of the patient and to bring reward or punishment directly to bear upon the emerging behavior. In these forms of therapy the therapist usually appears to the patient as very dominant, but dominant by previous agreement. The therapist usually tends to minimize or ignore the positive or negative feelings that the patient may have about him as a person. Sometimes sound recordings or machines are used in the attempt to avert these more personally oriented feelings.

It might be thought that there would be no form of psychological treatment in which the therapist concentrates on the crisis phase of the problem-solving cycle, where disagreement and unfriendly behavior are most salient, along with a high rate of suggestions. This is not true, however. "Direct confrontation," as used in some forms of individual psychotherapy, tends to have this character and is increasingly used in certain forms of group therapy for drug addiction and similar problems. The use of experiences in groups for many different kinds of psychologically oriented purposes is growing rapidly and has far outstripped research. It is no longer within the control of professional psychologists but is part of a general social movement.

Finally, there are forms of stimulated group experience intended for therapy or self-improvement in which the kinds of behavior characteristic of the final phase of the problem-solving cycle are utilized. In this phase, there is much eliciting of explosive feeling through means that circumvent the ordinary defenses of the individual personality. In ordinary social interaction, these means are joking or informal fantasy and dramatization. Increasingly, as a part of the general social movement that is exploiting the potentials of group experience, more direct and forcible methods of breaking down defenses are being employed. We need to know more about the possible dangers of these forcible methods.

Therapeutic efforts, and helping relationships in a more general sense, need to be based upon a higher degree of understanding of personalities and groups than psychology yet possesses. But the fact that so many people are turning to specialized group procedures for so many different purposes reminds us that group experiences are powerful indeed and promises that the rewards of better psychological understanding will be great.

33

ATTITUDES AND THEIR CHANGE

LOVE IS A FOUR-LETTER WORD. It is also a hypothetical construct, that is, a term that psychologists use to describe or explain consistent patterns of human behavior. Love, hate, thirst, learning, intelligence—all of these are hypothetical constructs. They are hypothetical in that they do not exist as physical entities; therefore, they cannot be seen, heard, felt, or measured directly. There is no love center in the brain that, if removed, would leave a person incapable of responding positively and affectionately toward other people and things. Love and hate are constructs in that we invent these terms to explain why, for instance, a young man spends all his time with one young girl while completely avoiding another. From a scientific point of view, we might be better off if we said that this young man's behavior suggested that he had a relatively enduring, positive-approach attitude toward the first girl, a negative-avoidance attitude toward the second.

Attitudes are hypothetical constructs that have cognitive, affective, and conative components. If we are interested in a white man's attitude toward blacks, for instance, we would want to find out how much he actually knows about blacks (the cognitive component), whether he likes or dislikes them (the affective or emotional component), and whether his feelings are expressed overtly or covertly (the conative or action component). Using such tools as questionnaires, social psychologists can measure (indirectly) a person's attitude toward any task, object, group, institution, or other person. And once the person's attitude is known in quantitative terms, the psychologist can perform experiments to determine how the attitude was formed and what factors might cause it to change.

Determinants of Attitudes Any human tendencies as basic and pervasive as attitudes are likely to derive from many sources and to be affected by many factors. In trying to account for the origin and change of attitudes in any exhaustive manner, we must consider genetic factors, the person's physiological state, his direct experience with the object of the attitude, the social institutions of which he is a member, and the specific persuasive communications to which he is exposed. Because we are discussing attitudes from the standpoint of the social psychologist, the social formative agents will be stressed in this chapter. But a brief discussion, at least, of the more biological factors will help to put the social determinants of attitudes in proper perspective.

Genetic Factors Some theorists hold that a person's attitudes are acquired entirely during his own lifetime and are in no way inherited. However, because an important component of attitudes is a person's favorableness toward the object, there is at least one respect in which genetic factors seem to play some role in the transmission of attitudes, namely, in affecting the person's general level of hostility toward others. For example, people differ in their hostility to certain national groups, in part, because they differ in general hostility levels. General hostility level does have a genetic basis in that one can breed aggressive or placid strains of dogs by appropriate selection of the parents.

The further question arises whether attitudes are inherited in the more specific sense that not only general hostility level but also the specific target of the hostility is transmitted genetically. For example, there was the notion of racial unconsciousness in the theorizing of Jung and, to a lesser extent, of Freud. Data are utterly lacking for any such process and it is hard to imagine a genetic mechanism that could account for it.

Physiological States Although they derive primarily from social influences, our attitudes are also affected by a variety of physiological states. The adolescent period is often associated with altruistic and optimistic attitudes toward society and our fellow man, and old age is often associated with conservative attitudes. It could be argued, of course, that these relationships, insofar as they exist, reflect the social characteristics of the given time of life rather than the strictly physiological aspects of the aging process. States of health and illness also may affect attitudes, though evidence for such relationships seems to come more from the artist's intuition than from hard scientific evidence. For example, it has been suggested that tuberculosis has been associated with an optimistic attitude toward life and one's fellow man, and such an implication can be found in Thomas Mann's *Magic Mountain*; in the writings of Dostoevsky, we find suggestions that epilepsy is associated with a suspicious attitude regarding others. Clinicians suggest that victims of encephalitis, even after recovery, tend to be somewhat more hostile and aggressive than before.

Not all the physiological conditions that affect attitudes are due to natural causes. Psychosurgery and administration of pharmaceutical agents can affect a person's attitudes in a general way at least. A few years ago, a drastic but technically simple procedure called lobotomy was widely used in treating patients diagnosed as psychotic. The procedure involves severing the neural path connecting the frontal lobes of the cerebrum with other areas of the brain.

Evaluations of the procedure called its efficacy into question, and its popularity as a treatment for psychosis has gone down considerably in the past several years. One of the often reported transient effects was an attitudinal one characterized by a more casual and irresponsible attitude toward other persons and one's obligations.

The possibility of changing attitudes by surgical procedures involving lesions, implanted chemical agents, electrical stimulation, and so on are already technologically feasible. It has been shown in animal research and to lesser extent in man that an individual can be made placid or enraged on a persisting or moment-to-moment basis by direct intervention at the proper site in the hypothalamus or in other brain areas (see Chapter 7). Aside from ethical and legal restraints, it will soon be possible to prepare a person surgically so that he becomes more hostile or docile on an enduring basis.

Further opportunities for attitude change through surgical intervention are provided by the discovery of certain reinforcement or reward areas in the brain, through the stimulation of which a person could be pretrained to respond on later occasions favorably or unfavorably toward any group of persons, symbols, or other attitude objects. The possibilities opened by these techniques already seem awesome, and we may not yet have recognized their most important ultimate uses. As with other innovations that bear dramatically on the human condition, the prospect arouses anxiety, and one wonders if it might have been better had

Figure 33.1
Tiny amounts of chemicals can be introduced at a particular point in this monkey's brain through a permanently implanted fine tube called a cannula.

615

the discovery never been made. But it seems unlikely that the researchers (or even mankind in general) would opt to erase such discoveries. The mental effort would better be put into maximizing their benefits and minimizing their evil.

Still another high-growth area regarding possible manipulation of attitudes by physiological means involves the use of psychopharmacological agents (see Chapter 22). A salient feature of our time is the use of drugs to alter the states of consciousness. Drugs are widely used to relax and to perk up, to go to sleep and to stay awake, to deaden our sensitivities to the thoughts and experiences that beset us, and to enliven our thoughts by enhancing our awareness of obscure realms of experience. Advances in psychopharmacology parallel those in direct manipulation of the brain in the importance of their implications for human potentiality and quality of life. Each can be used to manipulate the attitude system by varying the person's overall hostility level, by affecting his openness to outside influence, by enhancing his readiness to respond in certain directions,

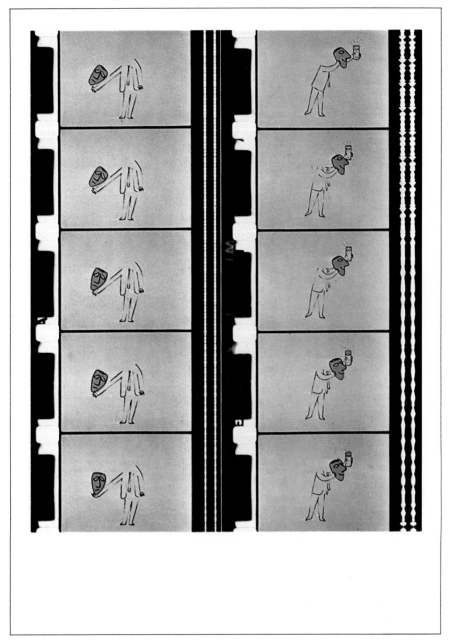

and by rewarding the attitudinal responses he makes. Perhaps direct brain stimulation is more manageable as a reinforcer of specific attitudes than are the more generically working pharmaceutical agents, but the latter have the compensating advantage that they are more accessible to use and administration. Both types of physiological manipulation open up wide areas of potential benefit or harm.

Direct Experience

One factor that underlies a person's attitude toward a particular target or class of events is the person's own experience with it. Indeed, it appears that people like to think of their attitudes as deriving mainly from such direct experience rather than from indirect communication about the targets received from other people in face-to-face conversation or through print or electronic media. Though the importance of direct experience may be exaggerated, direct experience both in the form of single salient incidents and in the form of cumulative contact of a more ordinary sort does play some role in the determination of certain attitudes.

The role of a single traumatic incident in producing a basic change in attitude is famous in song and story though difficult to demonstrate in actual life and completely elusive in the laboratory. Religious conversions seem to be a particularly fertile field for the dramatic belief changes occasioned by a single event, so that even an André Gide does not hesitate, perhaps with tongue in cheek, to recount how the village atheist becomes an avid believer overnight on the basis of a relatively trivial incident. So many have seen the light in a vivid moment since Saint Paul was struck by the truth on the road to Damascus that William James invented the concept of the *twice born* to handle a considerable proportion of religious conversions. Although the devotional literature reveals many cases of those who acquired a love of God on the basis of a sudden experience, clinical literature recounts numerous cases of those who discovered fear in a similarly privileged moment, as in cases of war neuroses. How prevalent such sudden basic changes in attitude are, whether or not they do occur, and whether or not they represent merely a seeming discontinuity in what is actually a gradual unconscious development are not at all certain. But we are all reluctant to come out against the possibility of love at first sight.

More prosaic is the development of attitudes gradually through prolonged or repeated direct experience with the object. Most of the research on this topic has involved interpersonal attitudes as they develop in face-to-face contact. This research asks if to know a man is to love him—for example, whether or not racially integrated living reduces ethnic hostilities. Behind this research lies a preconception that interracial hostility stems from ignorance and that when people are brought into contact with one another they develop a greater appreciation for their common humanity and more positive affective bonds to one another. It has even been taken as a theorem of interpersonal relationships that liking is positively related to familiarity (see Chapter 34).

KILL FOR PEACE

Help kill disease, ignorance, superstition, poverty, malnutrition.

Write the Peace Corps, Washington, D.C. 20525
□ Please send me information.
□ Please send me an application.
Name_____
Address_____
City_____
State_____ Zip Code_____
Published as a public service in cooperation with The Advertising Council and the International Newspaper Advertising Executives.

Institutions as Determinants

From birth, the human is enmeshed in social institutions that constitute his environment in as real a sense as does the physical world about him. Primary social units, such as one's childhood home, constitute an almost totally programmed environment in which one's personality and ideology are formed. Even after a person reaches the school years and begins to live in a richer institutional context, including playgrounds of his peers and the school systems in which he is placed, he does occasionally fall into a narrow total institution only slightly less overwhelming than his childhood home. This happens, for example, should he enter military service or be declared a deviant by society and placed in a prison or in a mental institution, both of which aim at total behavioral and even ideological control over their members.

Our attitudes are also formed through social influence, that is, through the way other people behave toward the attitude object and what they say about these objects. Such persuasive communication has received more research attention than any other determinant of attitudes, and we shall devote the remainder of this chapter to the resulting knowledge of the psychology of persuasion.

The Nature of Persuasion

Every persuasion experience is unique. Influence is exerted in a wide variety of styles, ranging from the more obvious techniques used by the unskilled or powerful to the more subtle procedures by which some are able even to dominate through weakness. On the receiving side, some people are influenced by communications that leave others unmoved. Despite this wide diversity among social-influence situations, it is instructive to group them into five types, each of which has been subjected to a considerable amount of research. These five are suggestions, conformity, group discussion, persuasion, intensive indoctrination.

One type of social-influence situation, rather mechanical and devoid of intellectual content, is what we refer to as *suggestion*. By suggestion we mean exerting influence simply by constant reiteration that one do or believe something, often without any insistence that one is expected actually to comply or that one will experience any particular reward for doing so. Faith in the effectiveness of suggestion is exhibited by those who entrust life and fortune to presenting us with repetitious billboard advertisements: "Impeach Earl Warren," "Drive Slowly."

In *conformity situations,* the person changes his attitude or behavior toward that espoused by others. Here the persuasive communication is simply an implicit or explicit statement of a belief by another person, without any arguments given to support it or even any insistence that the other agree with it. Conformity distortion of what one sees, or at least reports, in a situation has been demonstrated in the Asch experiment, where a person is asked to judge the longest line of three presented, among which one is clearly longer than the other two. It can be shown that although the respondent hardly ever makes an error in judging these lines by himself, if the experimenter enlists the aid of some confederates and has them all report an incorrect judgment first, in many cases the respondent will also begin to report an erroneous judgment that agrees with the confederates'.

A more forceful and direct form of social influence than that involved in suggestion and conformity comes in face-to-face *group discussion*. Here a person not only states a point of view and endorses it as his own but also tends to urge it actively upon the listeners with supportive arguments tailored to the receivers' objections and sympathies. Usually in group discussions there are social pressures that incline one to accommodate one's own opinion toward that of another person in order to reach a consensus of views.

The social influence situation that has attracted the most attention by researchers, critics, governmental agencies, and the general public is that involving *mass communication*. Here we refer to those situations in which people are presented with argumentative messages explicitly designed to produce attitude change, as in advertising and public relations, religious and ideological proselytizing, and political campaigning. With the development of the mass media of newspapers and magazines, and more recently of radio and television, the amount of such social influence to which the average individual in the United

States is exposed has grown vastly. Much of the research results that will be discussed in the remainder of this chapter refer most directly to these mass-media type of influence situations.

Intensive indoctrination situations are, finally, the more exotic and drastic situations in which the individual's total environment is programmed in order to force upon him a basic ideological reorientation. Here the situation is designed to instill in the person some basic beliefs, often diametrically opposed to his initial ones. The social influence is typically exerted monopolistically and in a highly emotional context.

An adequate depiction of the persuasive communication process, that is, how

Persuasive Communication

communications received from other people change one's attitudes and behavior, requires that we analyze both the independent variable involved in the communication situation and the dependent variable involved in the attitude change.

Components of Social Communication

It would be hard to think of a more succinct specific definition of man than that he is an animal with language, and our discussion here will focus on this distinctive feature of man. However, we should mention also that some social communication occurs on the nonverbal level. There has been a revival of interest in communication through such nonverbal mechanisms as facial expression, posture, eye contact, and touching by both psychological researchers and practitioners of sensitivity training and encounter groups who are exploring possible therapeutic functions of nonverbal communication during interpersonal encounters (see Chapter 29).

The components of the communication process, terms borrowed from communications engineering, include source, message, channel, receiver, and destination. Source variables have to do with the characteristics of the speaker or writer of the communication. Message factors include what is said in the message, its contents, organization, and style. Channel variables include the way the message is transmitted, for example, through which sensory modality, whether directly or through one of the mass media. Receiver variables comprise the characteristics of the person who receives the message as they affect its impact—for example, his ability level, personality characteristics, and initial position on the issue. Destination factors are the specific targets in terms of which message effectiveness is measured—for example, whether immediate or delayed impact is under study, whether the impact is being evaluated in terms of verbalized attitude or more gross behavior, and so on. Later in this chapter, we shall consider the influence over attitude change of variables falling under each of these five headings.

Components of Attitude Change

The consequence side of the communication-persuasion process is the series of steps into which the persuasion or attitude-change response can be analyzed. The whole process, from presentation of the communication to the ultimate changed attitude or behavior in which we are interested, can be divided into successive behavioral steps, each depending upon the previous one, as follows. If a communication is to have an attitude-change impact, it is necessary first of all that the person attend to it. If he pays attention to it, there is the further necessity that he comprehend its content. It is then necessary that he yield to its conclusion. The effect over any appreciable amount of time is a question of whether or not this yielding will be retained until the impact is measured. If we are interested in some gross behavior beyond the attitudinal yielding, then there is the further question of whether or not the verbalized attitude change eventuates in the gross behavior of interest, such as buying the product, voting for the candidate, going for a medical checkup, or whatever is the target behavior at which the persuasive communication is aimed. We can measure the persuasive effectiveness of a communication campaign at any one of these five stages.

Research Findings

The amount of research on attitude change is immense. In this chapter, we shall present only isolated studies that indicate the nature and scope of this research and provide some specific results of interest, without describing the total field.

■SOURCE VARIABLES

Kelman has viewed attitude change in terms of three aspects of the source of the communication that affect its attitude-change impact, namely, the source's credibility, its attractiveness, and its power. Each of the three involves different underlying psychodynamics in producing attitude change.

By the term "credibility" is meant the source's attitude-change potential, insofar as it satisfies the receiver's need to arrive at true and accurate beliefs; thus, the source has credibility insofar as it is perceived as expert and as trustworthy. Credibility is a function of perceived intelligence, education, level, or even social class. For example, members of a jury panel who have more prestigious jobs tend to have greater impact on the verdict reached.

The source's attractiveness in no small part determines its effectiveness in changing attitudes. Source attractiveness produces attitude change insofar as the target person desires to establish community with the source at least in his own fantasy. The source's expertise is only incidental, as is the convincingness of its

If the people of New Hampshire can't run a successful gambling business, maybe they should hire someone who can.

New Hampshire thought gambling was a sure thing. Start a lottery and make big money fast. But in three years government operated lottery earnings dropped from $2.77 million to $1.84 million.

Forbes Magazine ran a piece on the lottery business because it was a business. And one that could mean lower taxes in lottery states.

(New York's lottery is just getting started. Other states are interested.)

But for New Hampshire the big payoff never came off. Federal laws kept out-of-state consumers from buying tickets. Illegal competition — the pros — siphoned off consumer dollars.

The gambling business, then, is much like any other business, a gamble. With marketing, merchandising and consequently, profit problems.

Forbes is always poking its nose into other people's business, reporting what it finds to the business community — warts and all. In New Hampshire we found management trying to bump up lottery sales with all sorts of business techniques. With one exception.

Bringing in the outside expert.

Forbes: capitalist tool

arguments; the important factor is whether or not the target wishes to identify ideologically with it. A new attitude established on the basis of source attractiveness will persist so long as the source remains attractive to the recipient.

The source's attractiveness derives from a number of factors, including its similarity to the target, its familiarity to him, or its general admirability as derived from the target's liking or reverence for it. For example, Byrne and his co-workers have shown in numerous experiments that one's liking for a source increases as a straight-line function of the source's similarity to oneself, and with increased liking there is increased attitude change.

In addition to credibility and attractiveness, a factor that determines the source's attitude-change impact is its power—that is, the extent to which it has control over the rewards and punishments of the target person. The attitude change produced by source power tends to be somewhat more transient and superficial than that produced by source credibility or source attractiveness. For one thing, it tends to be on the overt level rather than internalized (though overt compliance tends in the long run to lead to internalized belief change). Also, power-induced change tends to persist only as long as the source's power over the recipient continues.

Source power sometimes conflicts with source attractiveness. Is it better to be feared or loved? There is an interesting methodological specificity in that the answer to this question seems to be different depending upon whether it is obtained in the laboratory or in the natural environment. When one contrasts a powerful (or expert) but disliked source against a source who is neither powerful nor expert, the laboratory results suggest that the former has greater attitude-change impact; but in field research, people are more influenced by those who share their own relative powerlessness. For example, an extensive field study on attitude determinants was conducted among the housewives of a city with practically no distinguishing characteristics that would make it nonrepresentative of other cities. The researchers discovered that the ladies' decisions about fashions,

movie attendance, purchases of consumer goods, and attitudes on public affairs were most influenced by others who were rather similar to themselves—roughly the same age, the same sex, the same socioeconomic level, and so on. The basic difference here is between an effective force exposure in the laboratory and exposure to one's peers without salient power figures in the natural environment.

■ MESSAGE FACTORS

We here turn from variables having to do with who said it to those involving what is said and how it is said. The attitude-change effects of several classes of message variables have been studied. For example, there has been much research on the relative persuasive impact of what is included or omitted from the message, of the ordering of the included content, of the discrepancy of the position urged from the receiver's own initial position, and so on.

The persuasive use of fear has received considerable attention. Fear has been used to induce the public to get periodic checkups for cancer, to use seat belts in automobiles, and to give up smoking to avoid heart attacks or lung diseases. Such campaigns are motivated by the assumption that if a person is threatened by loss of life or health if he does not carry out these preventive measures, he will change his attitudes and practices in the urged direction.

"When I'm all tensed up, driving relaxes me."

Mobil
We want you to live.

The outcome of fear arousal is an upside-down U-shaped relationship between the amount of change in attitude and the amount of fear aroused: the greatest amount of attitude change is produced by a moderately strong fear appeal—one that is not so weak as to fail to motivate the person to take action but not so strong as to cause him to repress the whole matter. Just where the optimal intermediate level of fear arousal lies depends on a number of variables in the situation, such as the person's chronic anxiety level, his feeling of vulnerability to the danger mentioned, the availability of the preventive measure, and the complexity of the advice.

Another class of message factors is inclusions and omissions from the message. One question is whether the conclusion is explicitly drawn within the message or left for the recipient to draw for himself. Various experiments suggest that the persuasive message is more convincing if only the evidence leading to the conclusion is presented; nondirective therapists have long claimed that people resist new insights less if the therapist maneuvers the person to drawing them for himself. But in actual studies of persuasion, the message has been found to make more impact when the conclusion is explicitly drawn rather than left to the recipient. The intelligence of the receiver is also important. In general, the more intelligent the audience, the less effective it is to draw explicit conclusions for them. However, the more confusing the situation, the more necessary it is to point out what the audience's conclusion should be. As Krech and Crutchfield have shown, the propagandist fishes best in muddy waters.

Another inclusion variable studied in persuasion research is whether opposition arguments are mentioned and refuted or simply ignored. Political studies suggest that it is best to ignore the opposition's arguments, ignore his existence, and mention neither him nor his arguments.

This variable was explored as part of the U.S. Army's attempt to prepare soldiers in Europe during World War II for the likelihood that they would not be released from service soon after the surrender of Germany but that the war with Japan would continue for a considerable time after the German surrender. Persuasive programs arguing that the war with Japan would continue for a long time were prepared in alternate forms, one ignoring arguments to the contrary and the other considering these arguments and refuting or at least down-rating them. Neither program turned out to be absolutely superior to the other; the mention and refutation approach proved to be the more efficacious with soldiers of high intelligence or those opposed to the position; the version that ignored the opposition arguments proved more effective with the less intelligent soldiers and those who initially tended to agree with the conclusion being urged. Subsequent research has shown that mentioning and refuting the opposition arguments does have the clear-cut advantage of preparing the person to resist strong counter-attacks against the position being urged. If we wish to immunize the person against subsequent attacks against the belief, it is better to expose him to the counterarguments weakened by refutation rather than ignoring the existence of the opposition.

Still another type of message variable has to do with the size of the discrepancy between the position being urged in the message and the receiver's own initial position. For example, assume that the receiver has a preconception that eight hours of sleep per night is ideal and suppose that the source wishes to lower this estimate of the ideal as far as possible. Should he argue for an extremely discrepant position—say, that three hours of sleep per night is ideal—or should he advocate a less discrepant position by arguing that, say, six or seven hours of sleep per night is ideal? If he does the former, then there is the possibility of a great change due to the great discrepancy, but there is also a worry that the claim might be too incredible to be taken seriously and the message might even boomerang. If one makes the more conservative claim, then there is less chance that the communication will be rejected as incredible; but even if the recipient yields completely, his total change will be rather small.

This discrepancy question illustrates the importance of considering each of the steps in the attitude-change process, including attention, comprehension, and yielding. Regarding attention, one must take into account the *selective-exposure hypothesis,* which has been called the most important finding of communication research. This hypothesis states that people tend to seek out information that confirms their preconceptions and to avoid information that is discrepant from their prior beliefs. This hypothesis thus implies that as the message position becomes increasingly discrepant from the believer's preconception, he will tend more and more to avoid attending to it, so that its attitude-change effect would be attenuated. A considerable amount of laboratory and field research has been done on this hypothesis, and its validity has been often assumed and asserted, but the data bearing on this hypothesis indicate that it has very limited generality.

A perennial topic in psychology is how a person's perception of a communication is distorted to suit his own need and value system. *Assimilation-and-contrast theory* states that messages with a moderate degree of discrepancy are perceived fairly accurately but that those close to a person's own position are subject to assimilation errors—they are distorted toward the person's own position. The theory further defines the three ranges in which the three classes of perceptual response occur as follows. Around the person's most preferred position there is an ascertainable range of other positions with which he will in general agree, and it is in this latitude of acceptance that assimilation distortion occurs. For example, the person might choose eight hours of sleep per night as his most preferred position but include anything between six and a half hours and nine hours as acceptable. Outside the latitude of acceptance, there is a zone of indifference (in this case an hour or so on either side of his latitude of acceptance) that includes the position about which the individual feels somewhat ambivalent. It is communications that argue for positions within the zone of indifference that are accurately perceived, according to the assimilation-and-contrast theory. Outside the zone of indifference in both directions, there is the rest of the response continuum containing positions that invite the positive disagreement of the believer, and positions in these latitudes of rejection are subject to contrast errors—they are distorted farther away from the person's own position. The evidence for these relationships between discrepancy and distortion has moderate empirical support.

In the attitude-change process, the overall relationship between size of discrepancy and amount of yielding seems to be nonmonotonic, that is, to have an upside-down U-shaped relationship with maximum yielding occurring at the midranges of discrepancy. In general, though up to surprisingly large discrepancies, increasing discrepancy produces increasing attitude change, and the falling off occurs only at extreme discrepancies.

■CHANNEL FACTORS

The different media through which the persuasive communication reaches the receiver hold considerable interest. They have generally been studied by practitioners interested in answering a specific question rather than by basic researchers seeking general principles. The research on channel variables can be illustrated by examining the relative persuasive effectiveness of the written versus the spoken word and the effectiveness of the mass media as compared to face-to-face communication.

A considerable amount of research has been done on the relative effectiveness of the written versus spoken word, but much of this work has been done by educators. In general, they found that comprehension is greater for a given educational message with reading than with hearing. But when we trace the process further to include the actual change of an attitude, spoken words have a

If your son is old enough to shave, he's old enough to get syphilis.

You know that wide-eyed, clean cut kid of yours. The one who's tops in his class and plays basketball on Saturdays.

The last thing on earth you'd expect him to get, is syphilis.

Well, what makes your son so special?

What makes him any different from the hundreds of nice kids who are coming down with syphilis and gonorrhea every week?

The fact is: New York City is in the midst of a V.D. epidemic. And no matter what kind of a home your son comes from, he's not immune.

In the last ten years the number of V.D. cases has gone up 500%.

But, what's more unbelievable is that over half of these victims are teenagers.

WINS felt the way to fight this growing problem was by telling people just what was going on.

We told that, in New York City schools, almost every child is taught what causes beri-beri, rickets and malaria. But rarely, V.D. And that's found much closer to home.

We told how V.D. can cause blindness, make you sterile, and even kill. How, ironically enough, if it's spotted in its early stages, V.D. may be cured with a few shots of penicillin. And how, at any one of the twelve New York City Public Health Centers, these injections are free.

In every broadcast WINS made this point: V.D. isn't a dirty word. It's a disease, and should be treated like one.

In every editorial we made our position clear: The answer is education. Our children must be made aware of the dangers, even before they become teenagers.

Since WINS brought this problem out into the open, twice as many people have requested information and educational material from City Public Health Centers.

Many people requesting a V.D. examination from local health clinics, gave the WINS V.D. campaign as their reason.

But our broadcasts go beyond New York City.

A member of the Connecticut Assembly, after hearing our campaign, introduced a bill to make treatment more easily available to teenagers who've contracted venereal disease.

WINS feels it's important to take action on problems that affect the health and well being of the community.

But, we feel it's even more important to get the community to take action for itself. When that happens, we know we've done our job.

WINS RADIO 1010 GROUP WESTINGHOUSE BROADCASTING COMPANY

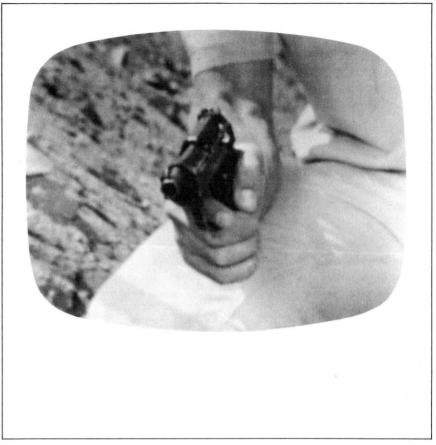

somewhat more persuasive impact. The written word is more effective in producing comprehension, and the spoken word, attitude change. It would appear that one feels much more compelled to agree with a person—even though he may not be as thoroughly understood—if he speaks his message aloud than when he presents it in writing.

Radio, television, newspapers, and magazines are financed almost entirely by advertisers who spend billions of dollars per year to change people's attitudes and behavior regarding certain products. But there appears to be a remarkable lack of real attitude change as a result of exposure to the mass media.

On the other hand, the impact of mass media, especially television, is often underestimated. The entertainment part of a TV program, lacking the persuasive intent of the advertisements, does seem to affect attitudes and behavior, often in undesirable ways. For example, laboratory research strongly suggests that watching aggression of the type common on television does incite children to aggressive behavior. The high level of violence in television shows (and some of the other entertainment media) is at least suspect as a contributing factor to violent behavior in society today.

There are cases of real increase in the public's acceptance of a product directly following extensive and expert exposure or reexposure of the product via mass media. Such a correlation does not prove a relation of cause and effect, and an increased tendency to patronize a particular airline or buy a special deodorant may not indicate a real positive change in the attitude toward the product, but it would be dangerous indeed to overlook the very real potentiality for attitude change inherent in the mass media. On the other hand, most of us have had the experience of humming a particularly clever advertising jingle while ordering the competitor's product. What these seeming contradictions mean is that the complex business of attitude change has only begun to be explored scientifically.

■RECEIVER FACTORS

Receiver factors in attitude change include the characteristics of the target person that affect his susceptibility to influence. Relevant factors are such demographic characteristics as age and sex, ability factors, such personal characteristics as general intelligence, and such personality characteristics as self-esteem and anxiety level, as well as more transitory and specific variables having to do with the recipient, such as how actively he participates in the communications situation.

There is fairly conclusive evidence over a wide range of social-influence situations that women are more persuasible than men. The evidence is weaker for the early years of life, but by adolescence the greater persuasibility of women appears as a slight but consistent difference. A second general finding regarding sex differences is of a more complex nature: a man's persuasibility can be predicted from his personality characteristics more accurately than can a woman's.

Both of these findings raise questions as to whether sex differences are due to genetic factors or to the different socialization practices to which men and women are exposed. The current consensus of students of the topic leans toward socialization. It is argued that our child-rearing practices and social structure are such that more pressure is put on women than on men to be obedient and subservient, and women's greater susceptibility to social influence could be due to this socialization difference. The fact that the persuasibility differential is more sizable in adulthood than during the earlier years is suggestive evidence. It also may be true that in our culture men have greater freedom in determining in what ways and under what conditions they will be subservient. Even so, the operation of a genetic factor cannot be ruled out; cross-cultural research suggests

LOVE   PEACE   PARAPHERNALIA

that women are more susceptible to social influence than are men in a wide variety of cultural settings.

There is a common oversimplification regarding how an individual's intelligence or personality characteristics relate to his susceptibility to social influence: the misconception is the belief that intelligence and persuasibility are negatively related because a more intelligent person is better able to detect the flaws in the arguments presented to him, to back up his own belief, and to sustain a discrepancy between his own beliefs and that of the source.

All these assumptions underlying the oversimplification might indeed be true, but they concentrate exclusively on the yielding step of the persuasion process, neglecting completely the attention and comprehension steps. When we note that a person's persuasibility is also influenced by the extent to which he attends to and comprehends the arguments presented to him, we see that the relationship of variables such as intelligence to persuasibility is more complex. Intelligence may protect the individual from being persuaded by making him less yielding, but it also enhances his susceptibility by making him a better attender and comprehender of the messages. The point becomes more obvious when one considers extreme cases of receivers very low in capacity for attention and comprehending, such as young children or schizophrenics, two categories of people who are notoriously difficult to influence by ordinary persuasive communications. It may well be that if one could get past the reception barrier with such people, their lack of effective intelligence and high dependency would make them prone to yield. But the resistance to persuasion that they have through their low attention and comprehension more than compensates for any higher yieldingness.

In this case, as in so many others considered in this chapter, our two variables of intelligence and persuasibility are related in opposite directions by the two mediating processes, the comprehension step and the yielding step in the attitude-change process. As before, the resultant overall relationships between intelligence and persuasibility will thus tend to be of the inverted-U shape, with those of intermediate levels of intelligence being the most susceptible to social influence.

Many other personality variables have a relationship to persuasibility similar to that described for intelligence. For example, anxiety level and self-esteem, two very popular personality variables in psychological research, tend to be related to persuasibility in opposite directions depending upon whether we consider attention and comprehension or yielding. People of moderate levels of anxiety or moderate self-esteem tend to be more influenceable than those who are either quite high or quite low in these characteristics. Hypnotic induction uses persuasive messages of a very simple and repetitious type so that very little strain is put on attention and comprehension. Thus, the relationship between a personality characteristic and attitude change will be mostly determined by the yielding step. Because intelligence is negatively related to yielding, the less intelligent a person is, the greater his susceptibility to hypnosis—at least, until we get to the extremely low levels of effective intelligence as in schoolchildren and schizophrenics, who are practically impossible to hypnotize. At the other extreme, in social-influence situations involving very complex messages, where attention and comprehension of the arguments are difficult, those with high intelligence are relatively more influenceable than those with low intelligence.

How is the persuasive impact of a communication affected by the extent to which the receiver participates actively in the process? Early research on this topic indicated that passively reading a persuasive communication produced less attitude change than participating actively by reading it aloud and especially by

The heir to American business.

The children who are bored with the world will soon be Congressmen.

The girls in go-go cages will soon climb out and join the PTA.

And the world, believe it or not, will be ready to accept them.

Because the attitudes from the past fifty years, which changed these teddy bears into iconoclasts, are molding the future of the rest of the world, too.

Sometimes, outrageously.

Which is why the past fifty years is the subject of Forbes Fiftieth Anniversary Issue. (It will be published this coming September 15, 1967.)

We will dissect this fifty-year chunk of history to help businessmen find ideas and directions.

Strangely enough, some of the direction will come from the advertisements that you will be running in our special Fiftieth Anniversary Issue.

When Forbes writes about how a business grew, your advertisement can tell businessmen how your own company has developed.

When we write about the possible paths an industry might take, your ad can discuss your company's own potentials.

This, it seems to Forbes, makes the ads as important as the editorials.

But that should be expected from a magazine that only talks about business.

Ideally, of course, some of the kids who are about to take over the world should also read this special issue.

Or have it read to them.

Forbes: capitalist tool

improvising arguments as one went along. It appears that active self-indoctrination is more effective than passively reading the persuasive material, although the extent to which the difference is due to better attention, better comprehension, or more yielding in the active-participant condition is unclear. Later research has investigated conditions under which active participation will produce the greatest amount of internalized opinion change. A popular source of ideas in this research is Festinger's *dissonance* theory. According to this formulation, if a person is made to act overtly as if he had a certain belief (for example, by publicly advocating a position that he does not really hold), then the overt compliance will result in internal opinion change *to the extent that the pressures put on him to comply are minimal*. This notion yields predictions somewhat contrary, at least on a superficial level, to common sense. For example, it is predicted that maximum internal opinion change will result if the active participation in the defense of a position contrary to one's own belief is undertaken with minimum promise of reward; also, maximum internalization is predicted when the overt compliance is undertaken at the insistence of the least-attractive source. The current state of the question in each of these areas is less clear-cut than we would like but is at least suggestive in its support.

The dissonance prediction states that the amount of internalized opinion change that results from overcompliance in advocating a position contrary to one's own will increase as the amount of promised reward decreases. A straightforward incentive theory would predict the opposite, namely, that the greater the promised reward, the greater the induced compliance from advocating the assigned position. The contrary prediction from the dissonance viewpoint stems from the notion that if one has agreed to defend publicly a position opposite to one's own for the promise of a great reward (or to avoid a great punishment), then the sanctions themselves would justify to a large extent the overcompliance.

But where the attitudinal advocacy is induced under rather low-reward or low-threat conditions, then the believer is left in the awkward position of justifying to himself why he behaved in a manner so at variance with his beliefs for so little reward or to avoid so little punishment. He can reduce the unpleasant *dissonance* of perceiving that he believes one thing and says another (or maintain his self-esteem under these conditions) if he shifts his private belief in the direction of that which he overtly advocated. Then he can justify to himself his overt advocacy by saying that the position he publicly espoused represents the way he actually feels and was not undertaken for the relatively trivial reward. There is some evidence for this mildly paradoxical position; however, the effect is rather delicate and the opposite result occurs under many test conditions.

A somewhat analogous controversy exists regarding the role of source attractiveness in affecting a belief change. Here again, incentive theory would predict that the more attractive the source, the more self-indoctrination would result from overt compliance. The dissonance formulation, on the other hand, predicts that the less attractive the source, the more the internalization. The underlying reasoning is that if one complies with a very pleasant source, then one can justify advocating a position at variance with one's own as a favor to the attractive person; but if the person is quite unpleasant, then there is much less self-justification in such an explanation. The person can then better live with himself only by deciding that he actually believed what he said all the time, and he does this by shifting his private beliefs in the direction of his public advocacy. There is some fairly convincing evidence for the paradoxical dissonance prediction in the "grasshopper" experiments. Zimbardo carried out research in which Army personnel were induced to eat grasshoppers by pleasant and unpleasant officers and then asked to indicate their own attitudes regarding the palatability of the ini-

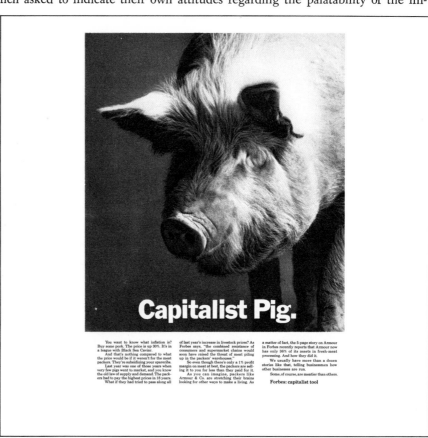

tially disliked insects. It was found that when the grasshoppers were eaten at the insistence of the unpleasant officer, more internalized liking of the unusual food resulted, as required by the dissonance explanation of an internal shift to justify one's overt compliance with the unpleasant source.

■DESTINATION FACTORS

Destination factors include the kinds of behavioral targets at which the persuasive communication is aimed. Typical variables include whether we are interested in the immediate persuasive impact or the long-term persistence of induced attitude change; whether we are interested in the direct attitude change produced or in the extent to which the person is made more resistant to subsequent counterarguments; and whether the arguments are aimed at changing verbal attitudes or purchasing behavior or voting. As with the other classes of factors affecting attitude change, a few variables will be used to illustrate work on destination factors.

Attitude change depends in large part on the acquisition or learning of new information. Typically, as studies on human learning have shown, we tend to forget much of this new information rapidly. But do we forget the attitude change rapidly as well? What few studies have been done on this problem suggest that the attitude change often persists even when the subject is no longer aware of the information that induced it.

A related phenomenon is the *sleeper effect,* in which the immediate effects of attitude change are shown to be quite different from the long-term effects. Suppose that we have two groups of people who, to begin with, are fairly neutral toward a topic like sex education in public schools. We present to the first group a strong argument in favor of sex education and state that this material appeared in some high-credibility source, such as *The New York Times.* We present the same argument to the second group but tell them that it appeared in some low-credibility source, such as the Russian newspaper *Pravda.* What kind of attitude change would you predict?

Experiments have shown that, immediately after reading the material, the first group tends to be strongly influenced in a favorable direction but that the second group is influenced negatively. Obviously, because both groups read the same argument, the *source* attributed to the material is of critical importance. People tend to reject information coming from a low-credibility source but to accept the same information if it comes from a high-credibility source.

But what if we measure the groups' attitude toward sex education a month afterward? What changes would you expect then, if any? The answer is an interesting one. As Figure 33.14 shows, the first group is no longer as favorably impressed as they were immediately after being exposed to the argumentative material—they have dropped back toward their originally neutral position. The second group, however, shows a more dramatic shift. Although they were influenced negatively immediately after first exposure, a month later they show a fairly strong shift in a positive direction; in fact, they end up being just as positively influenced by the material as is the first group. This sleeper effect suggests that the credibility of the source has a strong but evanescent influence on attitude change because, in the long run, we remember the material itself but not the source from which it came.

Resistance to Persuasion

At least four general approaches have been used to make people resistant to persuasion. One approach involves making the person's belief firmer by anchoring it to other cognitions. The belief can be linked to the person's goals by having him rehearse ways in which the attitude is conducive to goals he seeks, or

Figure 33.14

The sleeper effect. Source credibility does not have a lasting effect on attitudes.

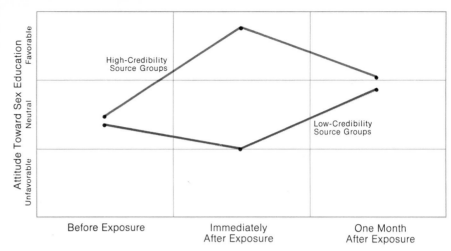

it can be linked to reference groups that the person admires by convincing him that these groups endorse the beliefs.

A second approach for conferring resistance to persuasion is to put a person in a resistant motivational state. For example, manipulating the person's anxiety level by threats or reassurances to his self-esteem has an impact on his general and specific susceptibility to persuasion. However, arousing anxiety might either increase or decrease his susceptibility to social influence, depending on his initial level of anxiety and the complexity of the persuasive attack to which he is exposed. These complexities arise from the inverted U-shaped relationship between anxiety (and many other personality variables) and attitude change, as described previously. It is also possible to make the person resistant to persuasion by training him in an evasive technique, such as how to depress his attention level or to distort messages toward his own position. These are in some sense unhealthy ways of immunizing against persuasion. Attempts have also been made to train people in general critical ability so that they will resist persuasion, but the success of this method has been rather limited.

A third general approach for increasing a person's resistance to persuasive onslaughts is to enhance his commitment to his own belief. Commitment can be aired in a number of ways, for example, by having the person behave overtly in a way that makes it more painful and costly for him to change his beliefs subsequently. More subtle commitments also reduce subsequent persuasibility, including having a person simply announce his belief without any further action on the basis of it or even having him think about his position on the issue privately without any public statement. All these procedures have been found to increase subsequent resistance to persuasive attack. Indeed, resistance to subsequent attack is enhanced even by simply telling the person that other people believe he has the contrary belief before the attack comes.

One line of work on immunization against persuasion that has received considerable research attention involves inoculation. The analogy is to biological inoculation, where an individual is protected against disease by first inoculating him with a weakened form of the disease, which stimulates without overwhelming his biological defenses. In the case of ideological health, the situation is often analogous to the health of someone who has been brought up in a germ-free environment, for one's ideological environment is quite often monolithic, at least regarding certain beliefs that are taken as truisms within one's culture. In these cases, it has been found that the person is made resistant to subsequent strong attacks on these truisms by preexposing him to weakened forms of the attacking arguments. In fact, this preexposure to the opposition argument is more efficacious in conferring resistance than is giving the person strong arguments in support of his own belief.

A great deal has been learned about attitude change and the psychology of persuasion during the years of concentrated research that began during World War II. In this chapter, we have been able to describe only illustrative results rather than provide an exhaustive review. The experimental research has put our knowledge of attitude change on a much sounder and more useful basis than was the case a quarter-century ago. It has given us a firmer grasp of the relationships involved in persuasion by revealing empirically valid general principles and theoretical formulations of meaningful relationships for these principles.

Still, despite considerable empirical and conceptual advance, the attitude-change area has not come to a set of mechanically applicable principles or theoretical formulations from which can be derived specific answers to questions about effective persuasion in concrete situations. Even if practitioners of persuasion—the public-opinion manipulators, the merchandisers, the public health professionals, the engineers of consent, and so on—were to become fully acquainted with this body of research regarding attitude change, there would still remain a large area in which they would have to proceed by art and craft rather than by the mechanical utilization of this scientific knowledge.

To design a persuasion campaign in any specific situation requires an insightful analysis of the concrete conditions that obtain in that situation, as well as knowledge of the principles emerging from scientific research on persuasion. The latter indicate some of the relevant variables that must be looked for, but additional variables remain to be taken into account on the basis of the creative intuition of the practitioner. Even the application of known principles requires this artistic judgment. Thus, when we are faced with a decision regarding persuading our fellow men, we are compelled to act as both scientists and artists if our attempts are to be successful.

But there is a third role that we must also take upon ourselves whenever we seek to influence our fellow men, namely, the role of moralist. Any attempts to change the attitudes and behavior of other people seem inevitably to raise moral issues about both the means used and the ends advanced. It is not our intention or right to play the role of judge and lay down guidelines for what is permissible in exerting intentional or unintentional social influence on those with whom we come into contact. At least where this influence is exerted intentionally, it is incumbent upon us to evaluate the means and ends, not just as regards their effectiveness, but also as regards their morality.

State of the Art

34

INTERPERSONAL ATTRACTION

To UNDERSTAND THE NATURE of interpersonal attraction—why people seek out and want to be with particular other people—we can best begin by taking a step backward and asking a more general question: Why is man a gregarious animal? What is the basis for his tendency to affiliate? Before we can properly understand why one person chooses a particular other person, we need a notion of why anyone at all is chosen.

Isolation and Anxiety

Some insight into the kinds of things that make people affiliate can be gained by observing what happens to a person who is deprived of human contact. This situation is difficult to study experimentally, but shipwrecked sailors, monks in certain religious orders, and prisoners in solitary confinement, for example, are all isolated for extended periods of time. Reports of what happens to a person under these conditions indicate that one common phenomenon is an emergence of overwhelming anxiety. This anxiety is not in response to any of the realistic dangers that the isolate faces but seems to consist of a total, uncontrollable, anxious flooding of the individual. If this anxiety is the result of isolation, then perhaps the prevention of this anxiety is one of the functions of affiliation. Stated experimentally, we might therefore hypothesize that if a person were made more anxious by some extraneous technique, he would be more likely to seek out and affiliate with others. Stanley Schachter, a pioneer researcher in the area, tested this notion by setting up a simple experiment, upon which much subsequent research was based.

Each subject, all of whom were female undergraduates, was to take part in an experiment of unknown nature. They found themselves in a room faced by a rather ominous-looking gentleman in a white coat with a stethoscope in his pocket. A rather impressive array of electric equipment was spaced around the

Figure 34.2
Which of these people do you think you would like most?

room. The experimenter introduced himself as Dr. Gregor Zilstein of the medical school and explained that he had asked them to come in to serve as subjects in an experiment with the effects of electric shock. He added that the subject would receive a number of electric shocks, which would indeed be painful. After further explanation of the experiment, he repeated that the shocks would hurt, that they would be quite intense, but that they would cause no permanent physical tissue damage. This description constituted the experimental manipulation that we shall call *high anxiety*. We assume that subjects who were given this description of what they were about to undergo were somewhat frightened and apprehensive.

Each of another group of subjects came into the same room and were met by the same experimenter, but the equipment was absent. They were told that they would be receiving electric shocks but that the word "shock" was really almost a misnomer, for the shocks would be very mild, producing ticklish, tingling sensations that would certainly not be unpleasant. These subjects constitute what we shall call the *low-anxiety* condition.

Each group was then told that before the experiment began, there would be a ten-minute delay while the experiment was set up, and the subjects were told that they would have to wait down the hall. The experimenter told them that there were a number of rooms and that if they wished to wait by themselves, each could have a room, but there was also a larger room for any subjects who wished to wait together. He then asked each girl in the experiment to indicate whether she would prefer to wait alone or to wait with some of the other subjects. The answer to this question constitutes the main dependent variable of interest in the experiment. Thus, it could be determined if subjects in the high-anxiety condition were more likely to prefer to wait with other people than were subjects experiencing low anxiety. The results can be seen in Table 34.1.

Subjects who have been frightened are more likely to choose to wait with other subjects, a basic result that has been repeated in a large number of experiments. It provides a beginning solution to our question as to why people want to affiliate, because it gives us at least one set of conditions under which people are more likely to want to be with other people. On the other hand, it raises as many questions as it answers. Why do the frightened subjects want to wait with other people? Do they hope that the other people will somehow relieve this fear? Would they like to be with anyone else or only subjects in this experiment? Do they hope that the other subjects will tell them about what will happen?

Probably the most adequate explanation for why subjects want to affiliate in this particular situation—and in a wide variety of similar situations—was developed by Leon Festinger. In his theory of social comparison, Festinger points out that there are two kinds of information in the world, two kinds of ways in which we

Table 34.1—Anxiety Level and Affiliation

Level	Choose to Affiliate	Choose to Be Alone or Do Not Care
High	20	12
Low	10	20

Source: S. Schachter, *The Psychology of Affiliation* (Stanford: Stanford University Press, 1959), p. 18.

Social-Comparison Theory

can verify certain of our beliefs. Some beliefs can be verified objectively by looking at the world around us. You may believe, for example, that if you take a hammer and smash it against a window, the window will break. You can check that belief objectively by simply taking the hammer, smashing it against the window, and seeing if the glass breaks. You have a belief about the nature of glass and the nature of blows with hammers, and you can verify that belief in an objective fashion. In contrast, if you believe that you can run fast, how can you verify that belief? If you were to proceed again in an objective fashion, you might time how long it takes you to run a hundred yards. Although a stopwatch may indicate that your time was 14.2 seconds, you still do not know if you can run *fast* unless you compare your time to that of other people. This notion is the core of Festinger's theory: we cannot verify a large number of beliefs, attitudes, and values except by comparing ourselves with others—hence the phrase "social-comparison theory." The necessity for comparison in no way implies that human nature is conformist but rather that some factors cannot be evaluated except in terms of other people.

Let us examine the experiment that Schachter set up in terms of social-comparison theory. We have assumed that the student faced with high anxiety, anticipating this rather poorly defined, frightening shock, is afraid. But she does not know how much fear she should have—or, in fact, what she should be feeling. Should she be frightened, interested, or apprehensive? What is the appropriate feeling in this situation? The argument, based on the social-comparison theory, is that she wants to know how she should be feeling. She has been thrust into a situation in which she does not know what is going to happen, but more importantly, she does not know what the most appropriate feelings are.

Consider the basic provisions of the Schachter experiment. One of the clearest predictions of the social-comparison notion that we have described is the subjects' preference for waiting with other people who are in the same psycho-

logical state—for only a person who is in an identical psychological situation can serve as a good source, a good reference, a good comparison for how one should feel. Subjects who have finished the experiment, for example, may be an excellent source of information as to what the experiment was about, but as a comparison group they provide no information about how one should be feeling at the moment. Similarly, people who have not been subjects in the experiment might provide an excellent diversion, but again they cannot provide any information as to the appropriateness of the feelings while anticipating the experiment.

These possibilities, and others, led Schachter to carry out a second experiment, in which he presented subjects with the same high-anxiety instructions. Half were then given the choice of waiting with other subjects who were about to participate in the experiment, and the other half were offered the option of waiting alone or waiting with a group of girls who were sitting down the hall, waiting to see their adviser. As the social-comparison theory would predict, subjects were far more likely to choose to affiliate when they were able to affiliate with other people waiting to be in the experiment.

This experiment, unfortunately, is subject to a variety of interpretations. The most obvious focuses on the kind of people who might be waiting to talk to their adviser—perhaps they are dull, uninteresting, or otherwise unattractive persons. A far more sophisticated test of the hypotheses was carried out by Zimbardo and Formica. Using the same basic paradigm, they gave some subjects the choice of waiting alone or waiting with other subjects in the identical situation. Other subjects had the choice of waiting alone or waiting with people who had been in the same experiment but who had completed it. This latter group is presumably of far more use from an informational point of view: having completed the experiment, they could describe what was involved, how severe the shocks were, what the whole thing was like. The critical factor they lack is being in the same state as the subject. They cannot tell the subject how they feel and thus can provide no information as to what the appropriate feelings are.

This experiment provided strong support for the social-comparison theory. Subjects who were frightened chose to affiliate with the other subjects who were in the same state. In sharp contrast, subjects who were offered the alternative of waiting with people who had completed the experiment did not choose to affiliate: they were just as likely to wish to wait alone. Apparently the objective information about the experiment was not critical in the subjects' minds. What they wanted was the opportunity to be with people who were in the same psychological state as they were. They evidently wished to find what feelings were appropriate in this ambiguous psychological situation.

Relevant Comparisons

A recent set of experiments by Gerard provides more direct evidence of this theory. Gerard used the same basic paradigm as Schachter, but he added one intriguing variation: he presented each subject with a large dial attached to a number of electrodes placed at presumably strategic places on the subject's body and explained that the dial would provide him with evidence of his internal state. The dial was calibrated from 0 to 100, and presumably the higher the number, the more aroused the subject was internally. In the first experiment, Gerard compared three different conditions. In one case, the subject was presented with information about his own presumed internal state; in another, he was provided with no information; and in the third, he was provided with information about not only his personal internal state but also the internal states—that is, the dials—of three other subjects in the experiment with him.

639

The dials, in fact, were not linked to the subjects' internal state but were controlled by the experimenter.

The condition in which no information is presented to the subject is parallel to Schachter's basic paradigm. Gerard found that subjects were more likely to choose to affiliate when they were frightened than when they were not. When subjects were presented information supposedly about their own internal state, there was no reduction in the tendency to affiliate. This information is similar to the timing of the hundred-yard dash; subjects who were told only that they were in a state of 65 had no idea what that meant without comparing themselves to others. The tendency to affiliate, however, was reduced in the third experimental condition. Subjects presented with information not only about their own internal state but also about that of three other subjects had something to compare themselves with and presumably could find out whether their own feelings were appropriate. Consequently, the tendency to affiliate was reduced sharply.

Homogenization   Another social-comparison study was conducted by Wrightsman, who began with the same basic Schachter paradigm. However, rather than merely asking people if they wanted to affiliate, he allowed them to affiliate and observed what happened to them after a few minutes of sitting together with other subjects in the same psychological state. If subjects are really choosing to be with other people in order to alleviate their anxieties, one would predict that the anxiety levels in the group that affiliated and talked would go down. Wrightsman therefore asked subjects at the end of this period how anxious they felt. He compared their feelings at the end of the session with their feelings after they had heard the description of the frightening stimulus but before they had participated in any group.

His findings were complicated, yet fascinating. On the average, the groups allowed to affiliate did not become less anxious or more anxious. The only clear result in his data is the phenomenon he referred to as *homogenization*—that is, the various members of the groups became more similar in their anxiety level than they had been before taking part in the group. Thus, in some groups most members became more anxious; the anxiety level of the group went up and the members of the group uniformly reported a high level of anxiety. On the other hand, when the average level of anxiety went down, most members became less anxious and all the members of the group became very similar in the level of anxiety. Although the factor that determined whether the group went up or down or remained the same is not known, whenever a group moved in one direction, all the members of the group moved in that direction and thus became very similar in their feelings as a result of the affiliative experience. This result is exactly what we would expect from a social-comparison kind of notion. The subjects, all unsure as to exactly what the appropriate feeling was for the situation, were looking around them, trying to compare themselves to others, trying to find out how they should feel. After a period of interaction, their feelings homogenized, and they all tended to move toward some common norm defined in some way that is not yet totally understood.

Taken together, then, these experiments suggest strong support for the theory that one important reason for seeking out other people and for being attracted to other people is that they provide us with information about how we do or should feel in an ambiguous psychological situation. Some of the implications of this conclusion for interpersonal attraction are obvious. We seek out people who are in some sense similar or comparable to us, for we find appropriate information

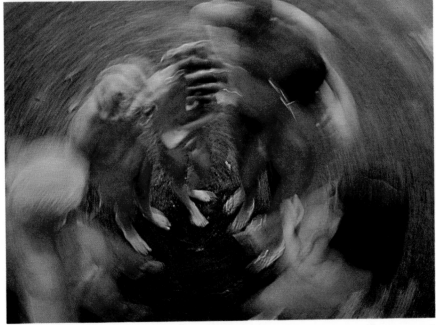

about how we should feel only from people who are basically similar to us. A second implication is that we prefer to be with people who are in a psychological state similar to our own. Both of these notions are borne out when we examine the variables that determine which people are especially attractive to us.

The general question of affiliation was examined in a further experiment that serves to refine our conceptions about fear, anxiety, or the general nature of stimuli that trigger social-comparison motivations. Sarnoff and Zimbardo initially questioned the feeling aroused by the stimulus "you are about to receive a strong electric shock." Freud made an extremely important distinction between realistic fear, or a person's apprehension about a real danger that exists in his environment, and neurotic anxiety, or a feeling of apprehension that may flood the individual but has no realistic object in the external world. Typically, according to Freud, this anxiety arises from the presence of certain unconscious impulses that are not acceptable to the conscious ego. The person is anxious about the presence of the impulses and does not know the source of his anxiety because the impulses are unconscious; the phenomenological result is a feeling often called an anxiety attack. The individual describes himself as being terribly anxious but is unable to explain what frightens him.

Sarnoff and Zimbardo suggest that affiliation will indeed be the result of presenting a subject with realistic fear. In this case, the subject wonders what he should feel, and it is quite appropriate to seek out and converse with other people about the nature of the appropriate response. On the other hand, when a

Stimuli to Comparison

person is faced with neurotic anxiety, he will not want to seek out others. He is frightened of the impulses unknown to him. He does not want to expose the very existence of those impulses to other people. Indeed, he does not even wish to expose them to himself, so the possibility that other people will expose them to him is doubly frightening.

In an ingenious experiment, Sarnoff and Zimbardo presented half their subjects with essentially the Schachter paradigm. In two groups, subjects were either frightened or not frightened. Some of the subjects were told that they were going to experience severe shocks to the tongue; other subjects were told that they would experience mild, prickly sorts of shocks to the tongue. These two conditions were described as high fear and low fear. The other half of the subjects were exposed to a manipulation intended to create neurotic anxiety. The

Figure 34.5
In solitude, anxiety may be hard to control.

experimenters reasoned that all of us have a certain number of unconscious oral impulses—in Freud's terms, everyone has certain strong, unconscious impulses toward oral gratification that are residual from infancy and unacceptable to the conscious ego. Accordingly, in order to make their subjects anxious, Sarnoff and Zimbardo offered them the opportunity for gratification of these impulses. They told the subjects who were in the so-called high-anxiety condition that they would be asked to suck on pacifiers, chew nibble shields, and engage in a variety of infantile, oral-gratifying behavior. In the low-anxiety condition, subjects were

642

also told that they would have to mouth various objects, but the objects were innocuous sorts of things not calculated to arouse strong anxiety.

The results show that subjects who were frightened in a manner analogous to that used by Schachter were far more likely to choose to affiliate than subjects who were not frightened. The interesting comparison is between those subjects offered infantile, oral gratification and those presented with the low-anxiety condition. In this case, the desire to affiliate was exactly the opposite of that characteristic of fear. Subjects who were made anxious did not desire to affiliate. They strongly preferred to be alone.

The implications of these results are straightforward. When a person is put into a strong emotional state that he defines as psychologically acceptable but in which he is not quite sure of the appropriate response, he will choose to affiliate. On the other hand, in certain emotional states—states that presumably are unacceptable to the individual—he strongly desires to be alone.

Why Friends Are Chosen

Let us turn now from the more general question of why people want to be with any other person to the more specific question of why people choose particular other people to associate with. What are the basic variables that determine interpersonal attraction? Why do we like one person and not like another? Why do some people like us and others not like us? These are questions, typical of social psychology, about which most people have strong, intuitive notions and about which there is a great deal of folklore and popular literature. As the question has been investigated scientifically, however, the major determinants of interpersonal attraction have turned out to be rather different from those popular in folklore. In one sense, they are less exciting, for they turn out to be things that we have very little control over and appear, at least at first glance, somewhat mundane. However, they seem to be extremely powerful determinants of the extent to which any given person will like or be attracted to another.

Nearness

The variable that is by far the most powerful in predicting interpersonal attraction is *propinquity*, or nearness. People tend to like people who are physically close to them. They like people who live near them, whom they meet often, with whom they have a great deal of interaction. This phenomenon is related to a simple but powerful sociological observation sometimes referred to as *Dodd's law*. Dodd's law addresses itself to the question of the amount of communication between any two population centers. For example, we might ask how many telephone calls there will be on a given Wednesday between Denver and San Francisco, or we could ask the number of letters sent in the month of March between New York and New Orleans, or we could ask about the number of airline tickets from San Francisco to Vancouver sold on a given Friday. Dodd's law, in a form analogous to the law of gravitation, states that the number of communicative acts between any two population centers will be directly proportional to the product of the two populations and inversely proportional to the distance between them. Stated formally, $C = k (P_1 \times P_2)/D$, where C equals the number of communications, P_1 and P_2 are the populations of the two cities involved, D is the number of miles between them, and k is the constant of proportionality. The critical element for our purposes is that the amount of communication is exactly inversely proportional to the distance between the two population centers.

Perhaps the most extensive examination of the effects of physical proximity on liking was carried out by Festinger, Schachter, and Back, who studied the

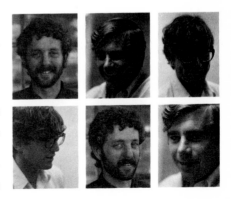

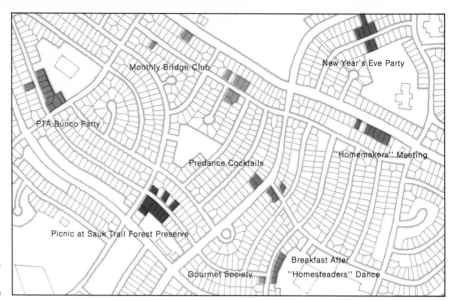

New Year's Eve Party

Monthly Bridge Club

PTA Bunco Party

"Homemakers" Meeting

Predance Cocktails

Picnic at Sauk Trail Forest Preserve

Breakfast After
"Homesteaders" Dance

Gourmet Society

Figure 34.6
Friendship patterns in Chicago.
(After Whyte, 1956.)

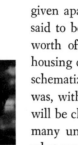

development of social interaction in married-student housing units at MIT just after World War II. The availability of housing was extremely limited, and the students were assigned, almost at random, to housing units as they became available. Almost none of the students in any of the housing patterns had known each other prior to moving into the housing. Figure 34.7 is a schematic diagram of the typical housing unit in this pattern. It contains apartments on two floors, with stairs at each end. We can measure, very crudely, how far it is from any given apartment to any other apartment; thus, two adjacent apartments may be said to be one unit of physical distance apart, and so on. We can add a unit's worth of distance for having to go up or down stairs. Each member of this housing complex, which actually consisted of many apartment units like the one schematized, was asked to list his best friends in the project. A basic question was, within the same apartment building, what is the probability that a person will be chosen as one of the close friends of another person as a function of how many units of physical distance away from the first person he lives? That is, what proportion of people listed as one of their close friends the person who lives next door to them, what proportion listed the person who lives two doors away, and so on? Partial results are shown in Table 34.2.

As can be seen, even within these very narrow limits the closer one lives to another person, the more likely one is to list him as a close friend. People who live next door to the subject are more likely to be listed as his close friend than are people who live two doors away. These people, in turn, are more likely to be listed than people who live three or four doors away. It is reasonable to assume that large physical distances make a difference in who our friends are—after all, we all know that when a formerly close friend moves to another town some distance away, the friendship tends to diminish. But should it make a difference whether a person lives six feet away instead of fifteen feet? This result does indeed seem surprising, but it has been repeated many times.

In Festinger, Schachter, and Back's study, the result was consistent not only within apartment houses but between apartment houses. People were more likely to have friends in apartment houses adjacent to theirs, much less likely to have friends in apartment houses two units away, and still less likely to have friends in apartment houses three, four, or five units away. Thus, it appears that over a wide range of distances, the actual physical distance between your home and the

644

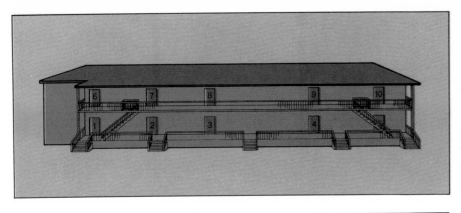

Figure 34.7

The type of housing unit in which the effects of physical proximity on social interaction were studied at MIT. (After Festinger, et al., 1950.)

Table 34.2—Sociometric Choice and Physical Distance

Units of Distance	Number of Choices Given	Possible Number of Choices	Percentage Choosing
1	112	8 × 34	41.2
2	46	6 × 34	22.5
3	22	4 × 34	16.2
4	7	2 × 34	10.3
Source: L. Festinger, et al., Social Pressures in Informal Groups (New York: Harper & Row, 1950), p. 38.			

home of another person is very important in determining whether you will list him as a friend. The difference between his living only 6 feet away and 15 feet away is important, but so is the difference between living 60 feet or 6,000 feet away. Before we leave this study, one small anomaly might be noted. There were certain subjects who tended to be chosen somewhat more frequently than would be expected by chance. These were the people who lived in the apartment adjacent to the foot of the stairs. The garbage can was behind the stairs, and it appears that perhaps more people passed by their door (and thus saw them) than passed by the doors of people living in other apartments. We shall see below why it would be expected that these subjects would tend to be chosen more frequently as friends.

One final study of the effects of proximity on liking should be noted. In order to be sure that there were no chance factors that might have affected earlier findings, Newcomb set up his own experimental dormitory at the University of Michigan. Entering students were offered an opportunity to live rent-free in a special dormitory in return for their cooperation in filling out various questionnaires. He assigned subjects to rooms in the dormitory at random, then observed the development of friendship patterns. Just as in previous experiments, after subjects had lived in this dormitory for several months, they were far more likely to list as their friends those people who lived in rooms that were physically close to theirs. For example, people were far more likely to have friends living on the same floor in the dormitory than on a different floor.

How are we to explain this simple finding? One portion of the explanation has already been alluded to. Availability is certainly a necessary precondition of friendship. We can only have as friends people whom we know or whom we have access to. We are more likely to meet and have an opportunity to become friends with someone who lives close to us. Although this is certainly a partial explanation of the phenomenon, it seems unlikely that it is a sufficient one. After living for six months in a dormitory, we are certainly likely to have had a chance to meet the person who lives two doors away. Moreover, it is unlikely that we have had more chances to meet the person who lives next door to us than the

Figure 34.8
Which of these people do you think you
would like most?

person who lives two doors away or, for that matter, a person who lives down-stairs. An explanation simply in terms of meeting does not seem sufficient to explain the generality of the phenomenon.

An additional explanation is derived from an application of something like Dodd's law. The closer two people live together, the more likely they are to have interaction. If we could show that the more frequent the interaction people had, the more likely they were to like each other, we would have gone a long way toward understanding this phenomenon. Such a result is suggested by recent experiments. In these experiments, subjects were simply exposed to photographs of various other people once, twice, four times, eight times, or sixteen times. After being exposed to each photograph for varying numbers of times, they were asked to guess how much they thought they would like the people in the photographs. The relationship was just what we would expect: the more frequently a person had seen a photograph, the more likely he was to like the person.

In an attempt to make this experience more realistic, Freedman and Carlsmith had subjects come in for an experiment, ostensibly to study the effects of various kinds of music on aesthetic appreciations. Subjects sat in chairs and listened to music on earphones. The chairs were set up so that two of the subjects faced each other across the table so that they would see each other for the period of time they were listening to the music. Another pair of subjects sat behind a partition, also facing each other, but unable to see the first two. After one minute of listening to music, all subjects stood up and changed chairs in such a pattern that each subject saw one of the other three subjects only once during the course of the experiment, saw a second subject three times, and saw the third subject six times. Again, subjects were asked at the end of the experiment how much they liked each of the other people who had taken part in the experiment. The result was the same as before. The more frequently they had seen another person—even though in this case they had not actually interacted with him but only sat opposite him, looking over the table at him for one minute while listening to music—the more likely they were to say that they thought they would like him.

It appears that simple, continued exposure to another person is likely to make you like him better. This, then, would be an explanation for the proximity data. Recall also that in the Festinger, Schachter, and Back study, students who lived in apartments at the foot of the stairs were more likely to be chosen as friends. This result is consistent with that just reported; they were more likely to be seen by the other people in the dormitory as the other people came down the stairs to go to class, empty their garbage, or whatever. It is perhaps worth repeating that although the fact that increased proximity leads to increased liking may not seem to have the glamour of a do-it-yourself program for becoming popular, the evidence is overwhelming that it is one of the most important determinants of friendship formation and of interpersonal attraction. Despite all the other characteristics that must have been present in the students in these various studies, it is the case that physical proximity was a terribly important, if not *the* most important, determinant of who their friends were. To be popular, be seen often—a tried and true political adage.

Similarity

The second major factor known to affect liking can be most simply summarized as the similarity between the person who is being liked and the person who is doing the liking. We like people who are very similar to us. This similarity can be along a number of dimensions, although it most typically has to do with attitudes, background, values, and so on. There is not much evidence that we tend to prefer people who are the same height as we are (although it might well turn out to be true), but there is a tremendous amount of evidence that we tend to choose people for our friends who are very similar to ourselves and to our basic attitudes toward the world. One strong counterexample to basic findings that parties tend to consist of people who live close together is the special-interest group, for example, a gourmet society. The members of a gourmet society are presumably all very similar in their attitudes about food. They believe in the importance of especially well cooked and flavored food, and this shared frame of reference may be the basis for their friendship.

This basic phenomenon has been replicated in an almost endless series of experiments. Byrne has shown in a large number of studies that people will expect to like another person more the more similar he is to them on a wide variety of attitudes, beliefs, values, or whatever. When Newcomb set up an experimental dormitory to see how friendship patterns developed, he was able to show that having similar backgrounds, similar interests, and similar values was a very strong predictor of who a person's friends would be. One example of his data would be instructive. When students in his dormitory were asked to estimate which other people were most similar to themselves in terms of attitudes about basic values and to rate the other people in terms of how much they liked them, nineteen of the people who were rated as especially liked were also rated as highest or second highest in agreement with the subject on his own basic values, whereas only two of the people who were basically disliked were rated as being close to the subject or similar to the subject on basic values.

This result leaves us with an ambiguity as to whether the subjects liked other people because they were similar to them or whether they assumed that other people were similar to them because they liked them for some other reason. We can nevertheless gain some confidence in our assumption that similarity produces liking by noticing that the same relationship holds after two weeks of acquaintance as holds after three months of acquaintance. Thus, it seems that a person living in a close continuous interpersonal interaction would eventually find out whether other people did hold similar attitudes. The fact that this relationship between similar values and liking holds over a long period suggests that it is the similarity of the other person's attitudes to one's own that produces liking.

All the recent fads on computer dating are based essentially on this principle. Computer dating services are in fact successful because they work on the basic assumption that people who have very similar attitudes or beliefs will tend to like each other. Thus, if a large number of people are asked for their attitudes on a large number of different things and people are paired on the basis of their similar attitudes, such services will indeed be successful in producing pairs of people who will like each other. This fact is obvious when we consider such major similarities as color of skin and social or economic class, but it is also true for a wide variety of more psychological variables such as beliefs, attitudes, and values. This fact probably underlies much of the proximity results in the sociological literature. That is, people tend to an overwhelming extent to marry people who live near them—which could be explained by the effect of proximity on liking but also probably reflects the fact that people who live close together tend to come from similar backgrounds and thus to hold similar beliefs.

Other reasons underlying this phenomenon are not hard to find. If people hold similar attitudes, they tend to want to engage in similar behavior. This desire to engage in similar behavior is critical in reducing conflict. If, for example, a boy and girl hold similar attitudes about what are fun things to do on a date, they will agree easily on what to do and will end up liking each other.

Another reason for expecting similarity to lead to liking may be found if we recall the data on the reasons for affiliation in general. One of the basic reasons for desiring to affiliate with other people was social comparison—the desire to

Figure 34.9
Items from the questionnaire of a computer dating service.

compare oneself with others to find out how one was or should be feeling. The only people who are effective for comparisons are people who are very similar to oneself. Thus, we will tend to seek similar people as friends so that we can consistently and continually, whenever we are uncertain about our beliefs or internal state, compare ourselves and our feelings with them.

One paradox, or apparent paradox, extending from this finding should be mentioned briefly. There is in the folklore and indeed in sociological literature the statement that opposites attract, that people tend to be attracted to people who are the opposite of themselves. This proclamation is noted most in literature describing how people find marriage partners; it is assumed that very often there is a domineering husband and a submissive wife, or some other sort of complementary pair of attributes. This assumption would seem to go against our whole similarity notion; it suggests that rather than liking people who are similar to us, we would like people who are exactly the opposite. The paradox can easily be resolved, however, if we consider what is meant by these opposites. When we say that people like people who are similar to themselves, we specify that we mean people who hold similar attitudes or beliefs. The primary instance in which the notion of similarity seems to fail is the marriage relationship. When we analyze it closely, however, it becomes apparent that the supposedly opposite members of the marriage partnership in fact are very similar in their attitudes about the nature of appropriate role relationships. Thus, they share the belief that the husband in the marriage should be domineering and the wife should be submissive, as is reflected in the husband's engaging in domineering behavior and the wife's engaging in submissive behavior. In terms of their basic attitudes about the world—about the nature of appropriate behavior for husband and wife, in this case—they are very similar.

Rewardingness

The final major variable affecting whom we like is a conglomeration of a number of little things that can be lumped together under the general title of rewardingness. We tend to like other people when they either reward us directly or are in some way rewarding to be with. In its simplest form, this variable explains such findings as the fact that we like people who are physically attractive. We like people who are funny. We like people who are interesting. We like people who have various sorts of virtues. Although there are exceptions, each of these types of people is in some way rewarding to us directly or rewarding to be with. Although the phenomenon may seem trivial, it takes on a little interest when we explore in more detail just how it works.

One of the clearest ways in which we can imagine someone being rewarding is to picture him saying nice things to us or about us. We tend to like a person who says that we look very nice that day. This generalization is usually true, but some of the subtler cases in which it dramatically fails give us a great deal of insight into why it usually works. When would we expect someone who says something nice to us not to be liked? One example that comes readily to mind is walking into a used-car lot and having a somewhat sleazy-looking salesman tell us that we certainly do have awfully good taste in clothes and that he can tell right off that we are the kind of perceptive person that he would like. Here we might imagine that we would not like this person even though he had said nice things to us. Why not? Presumably we would not like him because we would mistrust his motives for being nice.

This general class of events has been investigated by Edward Jones. He reasoned that although in general we will like people who say nice things to us,

649

we will not like ingratiators—people we believe to be saying nice things in order to obtain some gain for themselves. Jones has carried out numerous experiments on this phenomenon, and two facts seem to emerge from the research. First, when another person is perceived as attempting to ingratiate himself by saying nice things or doing nice things for us, we tend to like him less than we would have if we had not perceived those ingratiatory motives. The second and perhaps more fascinating conclusion, found in almost all research, is that although we like him less when he is ingratiating, we like him more than we would have had he not done the nice thing. That is to say, we do not like the used-car salesman as much as we would like someone whose motives we had no reason to suspect, but we like him more than a person of pure motives who does not say the nice things. Thus, ingratiation, although not as good a technique as sincere flattery, is still not ineffective. It is better than saying nothing or than saying something unpleasant.

A somewhat similar line of reasoning was followed by Deutsch and Solomon, who hypothesized that you would like a person who said something nice about you, but only if the something nice was in some sense deserved. They therefore set up an experimental situation in which the subject's performance was either quite good or quite bad. His teammate, who was actually a confederate in the experiment, then sent him a note telling him what he thought of the performance. For half of each original group of subjects, the note said very flattering things—for example, "You did an awfully good job" and "I hope we can be on the same team together again." For the other half of the subjects, the note was quite unflattering—for example, "Your performance wasn't really very good there" and "I think if you had tried a little harder you might have done better." Deutsch and Solomon predicted that subjects would like confederates who had sent them notes that were consistent with their performance. Thus, subjects who had in fact performed well would like someone who had said nice things. But subjects who had performed badly would like people who had said the honest but somewhat unflattering truth.

The results were in part consistent with this theory. A subject who had performed well did indeed like the confederate who had said nice things about him much more than the confederate who had said nasty things. A subject who had performed badly did not like the person who had said nice things about him as much as a comparable subject who had performed well. However, as with ingratiation, even subjects who had performed badly tended to like confederates who had said nice things about them, but only slightly more than confederates who had said nasty things about them. Again, we like people who say nice things about us even if we mistrust their motives or know that they are inaccurate. This phenomenon, which Deutsch and Solomon called a positivity effect, seems to be widespread.

Why did Deutsch and Solomon get the results they did? The most obvious explanation is that the confederate who says nice things is not believed when the subject has performed badly. If his remarks are not believable, then they are not rewarding. Alternatively, in line with the ingratiation research, we might suspect the motivation of the confederate. We might suspect that he was going to manipulate us in some way. These explanations were tested in a very ingenious experiment by Aronson and Linder. In their experiment, the subject was again exposed to a series of remarks by a confederate. The subject interacted with the confederate for five minutes, then, through an elaborate guise, listened to the confederate's impressions of him for five minutes, then interacted again for five minutes, then listened to impressions for five minutes, and so on over an extended sequence of trials.

For some of the subjects, the confederate made positive remarks throughout the session. Another group of subjects heard the confederate make negative remarks about them throughout the session. In the final two groups, the nature of the confederate's remarks changed drastically throughout the session. In one of these, the subject started off by making very negative remarks and ended by making positive comments; in the final group, the confederate began by making positive remarks but ended in a negative fashion. The results were consistent with what we have been arguing, although perhaps inconsistent with our intuition. Confederates who were uniformly positive were not the most well liked, even though they had said many positive things. The best-liked confederates were those who began by saying negative things and ended by saying positive things. By the same token, it was not as bad to say consistently negative things as it was to begin by saying some positive things and end with a series of negative remarks. Apparently, the early remarks served to establish the credibility of the confederate. When he began by saying negative things and ended with positive statements, the subject in effect said to himself, "This is a very perceptive guy. He's not easy to impress. He began by saying some negative things, but then he had some insight into my true character and ended by liking me." In the comparable positive-to-negative condition, the subject evidently let down all his defenses when the confederate began by saying positive things and was devastated when the confederate suddenly started making all sorts of nasty remarks. Thus, it is not just how often or how strongly the person says rewarding things about you. Although in general we do tend to like people who do rewarding things for us, the extent to which we like them can be strongly modified by our interpretation of their motivation, their credibility, and their expertise.

These three classes of variables do not totally exhaust what is known about what makes people like other people. There exist a host of very small findings about conditions under which people will be liked slightly better than under other conditions, but the remarkable thing about interpersonal attraction is that, although there may be other minor variables that affect attraction, these three large classes determine almost entirely who likes whom. Although we can contrive a situation in which some other variable will have some little effect, in the real world interpersonal attraction will be primarily determined by the combination of nearness, similarity, and rewardingness. To win friends, get close to similar people—and smile sincerely.

35

BEHAVIOR MODIFICATION

THE SCENE IS A MENTAL HOSPITAL. A nurse hands a small plastic token to a patient, an elderly gentleman who has been hospitalized for more than twenty years. He puts the token into a slot of a turnstile. He is then able to enter the room on the other side of the turnstile. It is a dining room. He picks up the tray, selects his food, sits down, eats fairly well, and leaves. The unusual thing about this scene is that for fifteen years prior to this week, the man had been force-fed three times a day because the hospital staff had been certain that he was unable to feed himself and would starve unless he were force-fed.

The scene is a schoolroom. Children enter as the class is about to begin. One boy who is about ten takes out a large watch, places it in front of him, and selects material from a nearby table. The material is a series of problems in addition. He works on it slowly; when he has completed it, he notes the time and summons the teacher. She corrects the material, smiles, and says, "Very good. You get ten tokens for this. I'll mark it on this piece of paper." He then selects other material to work on, and the same scene with the teacher is repeated four times in the space of two hours. At the end of this period, he is given a slip that indicates his total tally for the session. He goes across the hall to another room, where a smiling woman offers him a selection of small toys or candy in return for his scorecard. He selects a candy bar, smiles happily, and skips off back to his ward in this hospital for the mentally retarded. The boy's IQ when he came to the hospital was about 25, but the director of the hospital says the staff has been shaping his ability to learn to the extent that he is performing things of which no one thought him capable.

These are recently reported examples of an approach to working with people's problems called *behavior modification* or *behavior therapy*. In recent years, this approach has developed to the point that it is used in mental hospitals, clinics, group therapy, schoolrooms, and homes. Its origin, growth, and development illustrate an important point about applied psychology: although the applications grow out of basic laboratory research, they may take unique directions. In this chapter, we shall describe the history, rationale, and techniques of behavior modifications that involve the application of the basic science of psychology to the very real, everyday problems of people.

Origins and Rationale

A number of streams in the history of psychology have served as the source of inspiration for behavior modification. First, there was the development of the professional clinical psychologist as an assessor of human behavior and capacities. The devising of standard test situations to observe and measure individual performance may be traced back to the investigations of several psychologists in the laboratories of Columbia University in the late nineteenth century. As we saw in Chapter 24, the intelligence test, an old and favorite standby of the modern psychologist, was developed in the early years of this century by the French psychologist Alfred Binet to meet the needs of Paris schools in identifying children with learning disabilities. Terman translated these tests to meet the needs of American schools, and the classic Stanford-Binet test resulted. World War I was the impetus for the development of paper-and-pencil personality tests to see whether or not poor-risk individuals could be screened out of the Army in advance. These performance, intelligence, and personality tests illustrate one kind of practical application of psychology, that of screening, identifying, and predicting human behavior. These applications focus on observing and classifying rather than on changing behavior.

The other important stream, which leads more directly to modern applied psychology, involves the changing of human behavior. One group of investigators and professional psychologists who were strongly influenced by their psychiatric colleagues, particularly Sigmund Freud, argued that human behavior is determined to a large extent by intrapsychic forces, or events that take place within the mind, and that each of us therefore struggles to obtain some level of balance of the forces and conflicts within our own psyche. Thus, if a change in behavior is to be brought about, something must first be changed internally—the conflict must be resolved, the individual must achieve an insight into his difficulties, or his ego must be strengthened. This type of psychotherapy may be called *evocative* because it seeks to evoke an internal change to bring about external change. It is based on a model of man's behavior sometimes referred to as the disease model because of its analogy to physical illness. The proponents of this approach argue that you must get at the underlying roots or causes of abnormal behavior within the psyche in order to bring about any meaningful change. Changing a person's behavior without having affected the underlying cause will result only in its replacement by some other undesirable behavior or symptom.

The contrasting approach is a behavioral or social-learning one, which argues that the goal in helping people is to work directly on the behavior that is now a problem to them or to others. Human beings have learned their current behavior and therefore can relearn or modify it so that they can do the things that will make their environment more rewarding and less aversive to them. In the twentieth century, such investigators as John B. Watson, Ivan Pavlov, and B. F. Skinner have had major impact in the application of behavioral psychology to the clinical problems of human beings. Current investigators and practitioners who identify with this approach are apt to call themselves *behavior therapists.*

The more general term for those investigations that attempt to link the basic laboratory work to its application with human problems is *behavior modification.*

The works of B. F. Skinner and of the investigators who were influenced by him are a good example of how psychologists progress from basic laboratory work to applied clinical work. In the mid-1930s, Skinner reported his early research with rats in laboratory experiments. His most important observation was that the behavior of the rat was determined by its consequences; that is, if the animal were to perform a certain act (pressing a bar in a cage was a typical response worked with by Skinner), the probability of this act's being repeated in the future was enhanced by the animal's being reinforced immediately by a pellet of food. This procedure of reinforcing a' behavior that was operating upon its environment is termed *operant conditioning* (see Chapter 6).

It is a far cry from a lonely rat in Skinner's box to a nurse handing out tokens to a patient who has just shaved, but the ward program developed, more or less directly, from the earlier experimental study. There were a number of highlights in this development. Although Skinner's first book on operant conditioning was published in 1938, not until 1949 did the first report of the deliberate application of Skinner's conditioning procedure in a clinical setting appear. In that year, Fuller reported working with an eighteen-year-old vegetative idiot, a boy so mentally retarded that if it had been possible to measure his IQ, it would probably have been close to zero. Fuller shaped the movement of the boy's right arm by squirting a warm sugar-milk solution into his mouth every time there was a random movement of his arm in an upward direction. Every little step of the way in the desired direction resulted in a reinforcement (the boy was fed). Very quickly, the boy learned to move his arm upward, perhaps as a signal that he wanted food. This technique of rewarding small bits of behavior on the way to a larger desired behavior is called, appropriately enough, *successive approximation* (see Chapter 6). Although Fuller's accomplishment may seem small, this simple experiment opened the way for further "learning" on the part of the boy, even though the physicians in the institution had thought that it would be impossible for this boy to learn anything. Fuller demonstrated that, in only four sessions, an important addition could be made to the boy's very limited repertoire of behavior.

A major step forward in the development of behavior modification was made by Lindsley and Skinner in their studies at Metropolitan State Hospital in Boston. They worked with fourteen male psychotic patients, who averaged thirty-eight years of age and seventeen years of hospitalization. Each was placed in a small experimental room—in effect, a large version of Skinner's box, designed for human beings. The response being measured was pulling a lever like the one on a vending machine. Candy, cigarettes, or colored pictures were used as reinforcing stimuli or rewards consequent to the lever pulling. Lindsley and Skinner used a variation based on Skinner's earlier studies with rats; they used a *schedule* of reinforcement rather than reinforcing *each* lever pull. Thus, the individual might receive a reinforcement at an average of one a minute (a variable-interval schedule), or he might receive a reinforcement for every tenth lever pull (a fixed-ratio schedule). The results obtained by Lindsley and Skinner indicated that the performance of the psychotic patients was determined by the reinforcement program in much the same way as the performance of animals had been. Further, there were differences in performance that were related to the particular schedule of reinforcement the individual received. The authors con-

Clinical Applications

cluded that the behavior of the psychotic patient could be successfully studied with operant conditioning procedures. The behavior generated was stable and predictable and thus could provide a uniform baseline for studying variables involved in changing human behavior. This finding was important because previously it had been believed that the behavior of the psychotic was, almost by definition, unpredictable.

The Token Economy

The next major step involved the substitution of a token for such specific reinforcers as food or cigarettes. Physically a token could be a piece of plastic, a poker chip, a check mark on a piece of paper, or even green stamps. A token is essentially an object that stands for something else having back-up reinforcers behind it. The most obvious token in real life is money. The advantage of a token over a specific reinforcer is that it is a generalized reinforcer (see Chapter 6)—there need be no concern about whether the individual likes a *specific* food or is satiated with it or will consume it on the spot. The token gives him freedom of choice. The use of the token represented a major breakthrough in the application of operant conditioning to clinical problems. It paved the way for the *token economy,* which represents one method of behavioral modification, but not the only one that has been used.

■HOSPITAL TOKEN USE

A token-economy program involves the setting up of a *contingent reinforcement program* in an institution such as a hospital or a school. The first step is to select the behaviors of patients that the staff deem desirable, behaviors that simply help the individual adjust to life in the institution and make things easier for the staff—such as getting out of bed in the morning, dressing oneself, shaving, or running errands. It may involve behaviors expected to increase the patient's likelihood of leaving the hospital—such as attending group therapy or occupational therapy or going out on a two-hour pass. The behaviors may enhance the patient's chance of maintaining himself in the community after he leaves the hospital—such as cooking a meal for himself, wearing a tie, or doing gardening. The desired behaviors may not be immediately available or apparent. At first, it may seem a long way from the patient's dressing himself to his painting the wall in the ward a bright green. Yet the method of shaping described in the Fuller study opens the way to doing this. Thus, in an active token program, new, desirable behaviors are continually being added. After these behaviors have been determined, the reinforcement is given by the staff contingent upon the patient's appropriate behavior or approximation of it.

It is at this point that the token comes into its own. As we have seen, it is unnecessary for an aide to carry food around with him when he wants to reinforce a desired behavior. He can merely hand the patient a token and tell him why he is receiving it. The patient can then spend the token for any of the good things in life that may be available, including extra food, a choice location for a bed, a chance to watch television, an opportunity to leave the ward in the evening, or even a weekend pass. The *economy* part refers to the complex laws of supply and demand that determine the changing token values. In effect, economic principles are involved in much the same manner as with money in real life.

The goals of a token program are to develop behaviors that will lead to social reinforcement from others in a natural setting, such as an office or a home, and thus to enhance the skills necessary for the individual to take a responsible social role in the institution and eventually to enable him to live outside the hospital.

Figure 35.2
The token economy set up by Atthowe and Krasner has produced activity and interest in patients who had been living virtually featureless lives for years.

Basically, the individual learns that he can control his own environment in such a way that he will obtain positive reinforcement from others.

Although operant conditioning had been used previously in mental hospitals, the first systematic attempt totally to control the environment on a ward in terms of a token economy was initiated by Ayllon and Azrin in the early 1960s in Illinois' Anna State Hospital. Not only was theirs an effective program, but it was so designed as to offer experimental evidence that the token program was actually changing behavior. Ayllon and Azrin reported a series of experiments in each of which they demonstrated that target behavior *systematically* changed as a function of the token reinforcement. One experiment is typical of the procedures developed by these investigators. The behavior they were interested in was the choice of off-ward work assignments. A patient was given a list of available jobs, such as clerical or kitchen work, and was told that he would receive tokens for working. He then selected the job he preferred. After ten days, he was told that he could continue working on his job but that there would be *no* tokens for the work. Of the eight patients involved, seven immediately selected another job that had previously been nonpreferred but for which they would now receive tokens. The eighth patient switched a few days later. In the third phase of the experiment, the contingencies were reversed and the preferred jobs once more would lead to tokens. All eight immediately switched back to their original jobs.

The results of the various experiments demonstrated that the reinforcement procedure was effective in maintaining desired performance. In each experiment, the performance fell to a near-zero level when the established response-reinforcement relation was discontinued. On the other hand, reintroduction of the reinforcement procedure restored performance almost immediately and maintained it at a high level. There seemed to be a clear relationship between the likelihood of the particular behavior and the receiving of the token.

Another token-economy program was set up by Atthowe and Krasner in a Veterans Administration hospital in California with male patients averaging fifty-

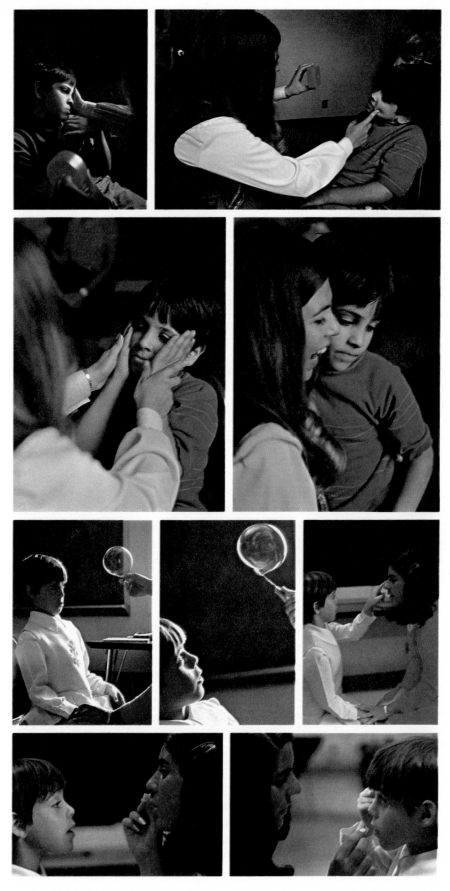

Figure 35.3
Reinforcing outward-directed behavior
in autistic children.

eight years of age and a median length of twenty-four years of hospitalization. Most of these patients had been labeled at some point in their lives as chronic schizophrenics, and the rest had a label indicating organic brain damage of some kind. As a group, their behavior was apathetic and indifferent. They were inactive, dependent, and socially isolated. The procedures used by Atthowe and Krasner were similar to those developed by Ayllon and Azrin; however, one major difference was in the amount of total control exerted by the experimenters. The program was designed to be used on an open ward on which patients could come and go *if* they had the right number of tokens for the gatekeeper. The token economy had to compete with the economy outside the ward, which used dollars and cents as its tokens. Many kinds of economic problems had to be faced, so such special procedures had to be developed as a banking system to foster savings, a monthly discount rate to cut down hoarding, and the use of specially designed tokens to prevent stealing.

Prior to the introduction of tokens, most of these patients had refused to go to any of the hospital activities available to them and had showed little interest in their environment. The patients sat or slept on the ward during the day. In effect, their behavior represented the end point of years of shaping compliant and apathetic institutional behavior. It is important to note that after an individual has been hospitalized for a long time, the original problems that resulted in his hospitalization lose relevance, and the influence of the institution increasingly fosters this apathy. The reports of this study and subsequent reports from a large number of hospitals indicate very promising results. The target behaviors change significantly; apathy is sharply reduced; the patients become more responsible, active, and usefully employed; they are more likely to leave the hospital (although whether or not they will be able to stay out longer is still to be determined by follow-up studies); staff morale improves enormously because they are actually doing something that directly affects the patients' behavior, and they have more time to respond to the patients as human beings rather than as objects needing custodial care. The token programs are still in an early developmental stage and must be carefully evaluated by controlled studies, but at this point they do seem to be an application of basic psychology that offers considerable hope for helping individuals who have had such major problems in living that society has had to hospitalize them.

■ SCHOOL TOKEN USE

A major extension of the token system was its movement into the classroom. Bijou and his collaborators were the first to introduce the principles of token economy into a classroom, working with retarded children at Rainier State Hospital in the state of Washington. The schoolroom scene described in the opening paragraphs of this chapter was a part of this program. An even more recent development has been the extension of the token-economy approach into a normal school whose students have some specific problem behaviors. A study reported by O'Leary and Becker is the prototype of token programs in the classroom. The teacher was faced with the problem of coping with a class of seventeen children, most of whose behavior was disruptive. Observers were sent into the classroom to rate the specific behaviors.

Observations were focused on the eight most disruptive children. Two observers recorded behaviors labeled deviant (for example, pushing, talking, making a noise, and chewing gum) every thirty seconds for an hour and a half on three days in a week. Behaviors manifested during the observation periods were classified as either disruptive or nondisruptive. On the first day of training, the experimenter put the following words on the blackboard: "In seat, face front, raise hand, working, pay attention, desk clear." The experimenter then explained that tokens would be given for these behaviors and that the tokens could be exchanged for candy, comics, perfume, and so on. The teacher, during several brief class interludes, rated the extent to which each child had met the criteria. For the first three days, tokens were exchanged at the end of each period; tokens were then accumulated before being cashed in, first for two days, then three days, and finally four days. The process was designed to fade out the back-up reinforcers gradually so that the more traditional, acquired reinforcer of teacher's praise would take over. In addition, group points (exchanged for ice cream) were awarded for quietness of the group during the rating period. Verbal praise and ignoring disruptive behavior (extinction) were also used, as appropriate. During the baseline observation period, the disruptive (deviant) behavior ranged from 66 to 91 percent of the observations. The daily mean of observed disruptive behavior dropped to a range of from 4 to 32 percent during the period of token training.

Other programs in the school situation have included work with ghetto children, delinquent children, and normal children suffering from a variety of other specific problems. One illustration of recent applications of behavioral principles to modifying the behavior of juvenile delinquents is Project CASE (Contingencies Applicable for Special Education) at the National Training School for Boys. The target behavior was studying, using programmed instruction. For example, if a student completed a unit of the program with a score of at least 90 percent, he was eligible to take an examination on which he could earn reinforcement in the form of points, each worth one cent. These could be used to buy soft drinks, potato chips, or department store items; to gain entrance into a lounge where friends were; to register for a new program; to rent books; or to get time in the library or in a private office with a telephone. These points, unlike the tokens previously described, were not transferable. The only way the student could obtain points was by manifesting the desired behavior—namely, studying. This study also illustrated that the systematic contingent application of reinforcement was most effective when it took place within an environment programmed so that the likelihood of desirable behavior was *enhanced* and that of undesirable behavior lowered. Thus, the investigators built a special environment, including classrooms, study booths, control rooms, library, store, and lounge. They also used the principle of gradually incorporating newer and more relevant payoffs. The students gradually switched from working for soft drinks to working for the more educationally relevant behavior of library time or new programs.

■HOME TOKEN USE

Examples of the behavior-modification approach to the home and to working with individuals in noninstitutional settings are numerous. Variations include the training of parents to work with their children (described below), the use of role-taking techniques in the office, and even the introduction of token-economy principles into the home.

Stuart reported his work with four couples who sought assistance for their marital problems. Stuart assumed that the exact pattern of interaction between a husband and wife at any point in time is the most rewarding of all the currently available alternatives. According to Stuart, most married adults expect to enjoy reciprocal relations with their partners. In order to modify an unsuccessful marital interaction, he believes that it is essential to develop the power of each partner to mediate rewards for the other. Based upon this formulation, his ap-

Figure 35.4
A token system has been set up in Mimosa
Cottage, a community of mentally
retarded girls at Parson State Hospital and
Training Center in Kansas.

proach sought to construct a situation in which the frequency and intensity of mutual positive reinforcement were increased.

The first step was to train the couple seeking help in the logic of the approach. The next was to ask each of the partners to list the three behaviors that he would like to see increased in the other. This phase involves training people in the ways of observing each other and conceptualizing just what a behavioral sequence is, that is, behavior *and* its consequences. Each individual was trained in transferring the observed data onto a graph, to keep a record of the other's positive behavior. This record keeping helped them keep track of their observations and was a way of checking to see if there really were changes. The last step consisted of working out a series of exchanges of desired behaviors. Because the couples usually complained of a lack of communication, which is a euphemism for a failure to reinforce each other, the task of the therapist was to offer a technique to foster communication between husband and wife.

At this point, the therapist introduced a token system into the home situations of the four couples who had sought treatment in a last effort to avoid divorce. The one behavior that was much desired by each of the wives was to have her husband converse with her more. Each wife was instructed to purchase a timer and to give her husband a token after each hour in which he talked with her for sufficient time and in sufficient depth to meet her criterion. However, an important part of the procedure was that the wife had to feed back cues to her husband within the first thirty minutes of each hour if she felt that his performance was unsatisfactory. If she failed to do so, he had to be given a token at the end of the hour even if he did not perform adequately. Tokens were redeemable at the husband's request from a menu of behaviors stressing physical affection. A different menu was constructed for each couple that took into account the baseline level of sexual activity, the desired level of activity, and the number of hours available for nonsexual (conversational) interchange. On this basis, husbands were charged three tokens for kissing or for light petting with their wives, five tokens for heavy petting, and fifteen tokens for intercourse. The results indicated that, compared with baseline measures, the rates of conversation and sex increased sharply after the start of treatment and continued through follow-ups after twenty-four and forty-eight weeks. The participants were asked to fill out inventories about their own satisfaction and their perception of their spouse's satisfaction in marriage. These reports showed that satisfaction increased dramatically as the behaviors changed.

Only seven sessions were held with the therapist (by each individual couple). The therapist did not introduce anything new in terms of behavior but rather suggested behaviors that doubtless had been requested, cajoled, and demanded by each party many times in the past. He clarified and spelled out the contingencies involved, introduced the clear expectation of change in the partners, and, most important, removed the situation from that of a coercive context. Requests had been put in the form of demands in these families, so that adherence to the request involved the reinforcing of demands, something usually held to be undesirable by most people. The importance of the gamelike qualities the therapist gave the treatment should not be ignored. Because all games should have names, he called this one prostitution because it appealed to all concerned.

Other Behavior-Therapy Techniques

The focus of this book is on the functioning of contemporary psychology, so it is good to point out that it is the *clinical* psychologist who is primarily involved in devising methods of helping other individuals. The clinical psychologist who employs the techniques of behavior therapy is actually applying the implications derived from the research of the experimental psychologist. A series of procedures involving such other behavioral techniques as modeling, desensitization, and parental training can show how he works.

Modeling

To illustrate the modeling procedure, which is based on early experimental studies of how children learn by imitation, we shall describe a recent study by a group of investigators at Stanford under the direction of Bandura, who worked with individuals suffering from acute fear of snakes. The thirty-two subjects were persons for whom fear of snakes represented a real interference in their day-to-day life; they answered a newspaper advertisement offering to help them with snake phobia. Some were unable to go hunting, hiking, and camping for fear of snakes; some were real estate salesmen who encountered snakes in showing homes in a beautiful but snake-ridden part of town. Others were individuals anticipating Peace Corps assignments in foreign countries, a museum official who was fearful of the snake room in his museum, and schoolteachers whose children would bring in pet snakes for fondling. One woman had a neighbor who kept a boa constrictor, fear of which had almost given her a heart attack—her physician had recommended that she seek a cure for her response to snakes.

The experimenters set up four groups, with different conditions in each. In the first, the subjects were treated by a procedure called systematic desensitization (described in detail later in this chapter). The second group watched films of children and adults playing with snakes. The third group first watched through a one-way mirror as the therapist played with a snake, then entered the room, and, through gradual steps, touched the snake and eventually held it. The therapist modeled the snake handling for each person and told him to imitate the behavior when he felt comfortable enough. As the subject increased his snake-handling behavior, the therapist gradually faded out his activity. The fourth group of subjects served as a control group; they received the same pretreatment and posttreatment tests (involving approach-avoidance behavior toward a live snake) as the other three groups but received no intervening treatment. Each of the three experimental groups received ten treatment sessions. At the end of the treatment, each subject was retested on the same behavioral task they had been given at the beginning of the study.

The results were clear and unequivocal. The live-modeling and guided-participation procedure was significantly more effective than either the film model or the desensitization procedure, both of which were significantly better than no treatment. In fact, each of the subjects in the live-model procedure reached the last item in the confrontation task: he was able to sit in a chair with his hands at his side and allow a snake to be placed in his lap and to crawl on him for thirty seconds.

The investigators next took an unusual and important step. They were convinced by pilot work and their results that the live-model procedure would be overwhelmingly effective, so to each subject in the desensitization and film-model procedures who had not been cured, that is, who was unable to achieve the final task, they gave retraining by means of the live-model and guided-participation task. They succeeded in generating cures in 100 percent of the subjects.

Systematic Desensitization

In systematic desensitization, a person is taught to relax, and this state of relaxation is associated with the gradual visualization of potentially threatening situations. The situations are arranged in a series, or *hierarchy*, which moves from the

Figure 35.5
The live-modeling procedure is highly effective in helping people to overcome extreme fear of snakes.

least to the most threatening situation. As each situation in the hierarchy is successively associated with the response of relaxation, all other items in the hierarchy are affected, and the person progresses to items that originally were difficult for him to handle. Generalizations to the extratherapy situation parallel progress on the visualized hierarchy.

Applications to Child Behavior

It is in work with children that some of the more exciting new applications of behavior modification have developed. The most interesting of these procedures is the training of parents in general principles of psychology in much the same way that the nurse is trained on the token-economy ward, the teacher in the schoolroom, or the sexual partner as in the Stuart study previously described. The parents are trained to observe behavior and its consequences, that of both their child and themselves. They are then trained to select desired behaviors and to respond systematically and contingently.

Training may include watching films and reading manuals. It is the recent movement of such training into the home that is most exciting. In traditional psychotherapy, the child's behavior is rarely observed in the situation in which his behavior is disturbing others, specifically in the home or classroom. Nor is the most important element, the behavior of the parent toward the child. Moreover, usually no objective record of behavioral change is kept to measure the efficacy of treatment.

One of the first reports on helping a child by working with his parents at home was by Hawkins and his colleagues, who performed a study that can be considered prototypical of this kind of clinical application. A child named Peter was brought to the clinic because he was difficult to manage. The Stanford-Binet test had indicated Peter to be of borderline intelligence, and he was described as hyperactive.

The first task of the behavior therapist was to help determine the specific hyperactive or disruptive behaviors. In Peter's case, these included hitting others, calling them names, removing his clothing, and throwing objects. The frequency of these behaviors was observed *in the home* for successive ten-second intervals during each hour session. The observation of his behaviors and the mother's reactions to them were recorded for sixteen baseline sessions, which make up the first phase of the study. In the second phase, which included the first experimental sessions, the mother was told about the objectionable target behaviors. The therapist arranged with the mother three sets of hand signals: The first signal was given when Peter emitted an objectionable behavior. The second was given if Peter did not stop or if he repeated the objectionable behavior. The third was given if he did a particularly desirable thing. She was requested to tell Peter to *stop* what he was doing, or to *place him in his room*, or to give him *praise, attention*, and *affection*. This new set of contingencies for Peter's mother was in sharp contrast with her previous behavior, which was to respond to objectionable behavior by an explanation of what he was doing wrong or by offering toys or food to distract him. In effect, she had previously been doing the very things that reinforce the undesirable behavior.

The notion of a *time-out room* has become an important one in behavior therapy with children. The room is usually empty of distracting or attractive stimuli, and the child is not let out until he is calm or quiet, so the reinforcement of being released from the room is contingent upon this desirable behavior. After six experimental treatment sessions, the mother was told to behave as she had previously. Fourteen such sessions were followed by a second experimental period of six sessions. Finally, there was a period of three sessions in which Peter's mother used any technique she wanted. These last three sessions represented a follow-up twenty-four days after the study. At this point, the rate of Peter's objectionable behavior was approximately one-sixth what it had been in the initial baseline period (see Figure 35.6).

The use of the repeated baseline periods should be explained. At first, it looks as if the parent or teacher or nurse is being asked to return to a system that will invoke the previous, undesired behavior, but actually the person being trained gets an opportunity to compare his new behavioral contingencies with the old. It is a dramatic demonstration to the parent that he is doing something that is actually affecting the child's behavior. The undesirable behavior temporarily increases but does not return to its original frequency. (It is interesting that the graphed data generated by such studies with children are very similar to those recorded in earlier studies with animals.)

Figure 35.6

The reduction of Peter's objectionable behaviors when contingencies appropriate to objectionable and to desirable behaviors were imposed. (After Hawkins, *et al.*, 1966.)

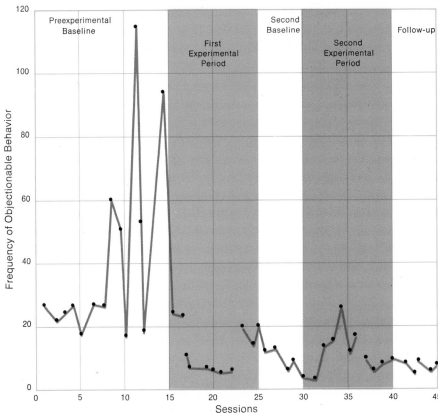

Behavior Therapy Versus Traditional Methods

The studies described in this chapter have focused on a behavioral approach to helping people. This approach is gaining considerable attention and interest in American psychology—from the clinic and hospital to the schoolroom and home. It would be hard to estimate how many practicing therapists use behavioral techniques, but their use has increased for several reasons. Traditional, psychoanalytically oriented procedures necessitate treatment over a long period of time and often fail to demonstrate their effectiveness. The shorter time needed to apply the behavioral techniques does not affect their efficacy, which may sometimes be dramatic. The effectiveness can, in fact, be measured, because objective data are used. Also, in some basic formulations, the behavioral approach is more palatable than the psychoanalytic one. Instead of being viewed as a sick, irresponsible individual—with the pessimistic corollary that his behavior is determined by uncontrollable, instinctual, aggressive drives and conflicts—the client is considered a person who has some problems in living that can be affected by environmental change. There is simplicity and parsimony in working directly with human behavior.

Where does behavior modification go from here? The seeds of the future are always in the present, but can they be recognized? Behavior modification places major emphasis upon environmental planning; it follows that the direction of this approach to helping human beings lies in social and economic planning that can modify social institutions in such a way that individual suffering—emotional, interpersonal, and economic—is minimized and that human dignity and human qualities are maximized. For example, the token-economy program offers many opportunities to test out such social and economic questions as the effects of a guaranteed annual wage on individual behavior.

Skinner was the first to foresee the long-range consequences of his reinforcement approach to modifying human behavior. In writing *Walden Two*, a novel within a utopian framework, Skinner correctly guessed that the direction such an approach would eventually take would be in social, educational, and environmental planning of society. The psychology of tomorrow will involve the development of clear and explicit *value* judgments as to what kinds of human behavior are most desirable under specific sets of circumstances and will offer technical recommendations about how to effect these behaviors. For example, if a society places greater value on altruistic than on aggressive behavior, it is quite likely that its social institutions can be modified to support the behavior it wants and to extinguish the other. The technology of achieving this type of change through environmental control is probably far closer to realization than the ability of our society to make the kinds of value decisions that are a necessary prerequisite. The goal of the behavior therapist is to help the individual who seeks help to gain some measure of control over his environment and his own behavior. It will be the eventual goal of the behavior therapist to demonstrate to society at large that it can control its own social institutions and that even war, crime, and poverty can be extinguished in the same manner as any other learned maladaptive behavior.

Behavior Therapy in a Social Context

CONTRIBUTING CONSULTANTS

J. Aronoff

J. Carlsmith

R. Bales

M. Deutsch

R. Dominowski

E. Fantino

J. Fentress

D. Fiske

D. Freedman

S. Glickman

JOEL ARONOFF is assistant professor of psychology at Michigan State University. He received both the B.A. (in history) and the Ph.D. (in psychology) from Brandeis University and has taught at Harvard and Cornell Universities. His contributions to the psychological literature range from studies of human motivation to studies of the influence of motives on the social structure of natural and experimental groups.

R. FREED BALES, a professor of social relations at Harvard University, has devoted his research effort to the understanding of the processes inherent in the functioning of small groups of individuals. He took the Ph.D. at Harvard in 1945 and, with brief excursions to Yale, RAND Corporation, and Salzburg Summer Seminars, has been there ever since. In addition to innumerable scientific papers over the last twenty-five years, Bales has published several books, two in collaboration with the eminent sociologist Talcott Parsons.

J. MERRILL CARLSMITH, fellow of Stanford University, received his Ph.D. from Harvard after a B.A. from Stanford. He was influential in the early days of the development of dissonance theory in social psychology with Leon Festinger, but his interests now center on more general theories of, and experiments on, interpersonal attraction and attractiveness. Before joining the faculty at his alma mater, he taught for two years at Yale University. Carlsmith is internationally recognized as an authority on experimental social psychology.

MORTON DEUTSCH, professor at Teachers College, Columbia University, has a Ph.D. from MIT. He taught at New York Univer-

sity and spent seven years with the Bell Telephone Laboratories before moving to Columbia. He is a social psychologist with broad interests in human groups, their dynamics, and their reconciliation at the personal, national, and international levels.

ROGER L. DOMINOWSKI, associate professor of psychology at the Chicago Circle campus of the University of Illinois, holds the Ph.D. from Northwestern University, where he worked with Carl Duncan. His major interests are in problem solving and thinking, among the most rewarding and productive areas of modern experimental psychology. He is particularly concerned with factors that facilitate or inhibit successful problem solving.

EDMUND J. FANTINO, assistant professor of psychology at the University of California, San Diego, has the Ph.D. from Harvard and has taught at Yale. His interests are in animal learning and motivation, and he contributes regularly to the psychological literature on choice, conditioned reinforcement, and aversive control.

JOHN C. FENTRESS, assistant professor of psychology and biology at the University of Oregon, holds the Ph.D. from Cambridge University, where he worked under the direction of W. H. Thorpe and R. A. Hinde. His interests are both ethological and physiologically psychological. He has published extensively on ethological problems of animal behavior and motivation, both here and abroad. Among his ethological works has been the taming of a wolf, who, with its wife, lives with him and his wife.

DONALD W. FISKE, professor of psychology

at the University of Chicago, received the M.A. from Harvard University and the Ph.D. from the University of Michigan. A lifelong interest in the validity and reliability of human inventories and tests has distinguished his career at Wellesley College, Michigan, and Chicago. He has been active in psychological associations, as well as in the production of four books and numerous articles on the theory and practice of measuring the characteristics of people.

DANIEL X. FREEDMAN, chairman and professor of psychiatry at the University of Chicago, holds a B.A. from Harvard and an M.D. from the Yale University School of Medicine (with the Keese Prize for research). He has taught at both Yale and Chicago. His primary interest within psychiatry—apart from schizophrenia, which he believes every psychiatrist sees as primary—is in neuropsychopharmacology, an area almost as intricate as its name is long. A devotee of the experimental method, Freedman has published more than seventy articles of scientific content, as well as a text on psychiatry and a handbook of psychopharmacology.

STEPHEN E. GLICKMAN, professor of psychology at the University of California, Berkeley, followed a Ph.D. from McGill University with teaching and research positions at New Mexico, Northwestern, and Berkeley. His interests are in physiological psychology and in comparative psychology. His primary research thrust is aimed at untangling the brain mechanisms involved in learning, motivation, and emotion.

RICHARD L. GREGORY is currently director of the Bionics Research Laboratory and chair-

R. Gregory

J. Hirsch

R. Isaacson

C. Hall

D. Jackson

S. Komorita

L. Krasner

D. Lindsley

J. Langer

man of the Department of Machine Intelligence and Perception at the University of Edinburgh. He has received the CIBA Foundation Prize for work on aging; the very prestigious Craik Prize in physiological psychology from St. John's, Cambridge; and the Waverley Prize and gold medal for his solid-image microscope. He taught at Cambridge, UCLA, MIT, and NYU, before taking up his duties at Edinburgh. He holds a dozen patents for optical and other devices, including a three-dimensional drawing machine. He is a prolific scientific contributor in both apparatus and perception, and his book *Eye and Brain* has appeared in ten languages.

CALVIN S. HALL, the director of the Institute of Dream Research and senior lecturer at the University of California, Santa Cruz, has had a long and distinguished career in teaching and writing. He is coauthor of the widely admired *Theories of Personality* and author of the popular *Primer of Freudian Psychology*. He has taught at Berkeley, the University of Oregon, Western Reserve, Syracuse, and Miami and has held a Fulbright professorship at Nijmegen University, Holland. His abiding interests are in the theory of personality and in the meaning of dreams, about which he has written extensively.

JERRY HIRSCH, professor of psychology and of zoology at the University of Illinois, Urbana, holds a Berkeley Ph.D., taught at Columbia, and was fellow at the Center for Advanced Study in the Behavioral Sciences before taking up his present position. His field is behavior-genetic analysis, about which he writes comprehensively and comprehensibly. He has been concerned particu-

larly with geotropism in fruit flies and has successfully demonstrated that tropisms can be transferred genetically and analyzed chromosomally. His broad field of interest is the relations between heredity and behavior in animals and men. He is the editor of *Animal Behavior*.

ROBERT L. ISAACSON, professor of psychology at the University of Florida, has also taught at the University of Michigan, where he took the Ph.D. in 1958. His interests are physiological psychology, with particular emphasis on the contribution of phyletically older brain structures to behavior and the developing nervous system. He has written some sixty technical articles, edited two books, and coauthored two introductory psychology texts.

DOUGLAS N. JACKSON, senior professor of psychology at the University of Western Ontario, has a Ph.D. from Purdue in clinical psychology. He has been associated with the Menninger Foundation, where he pursued research, and with the Veterans Administration, where he pursued clinical work. Jackson taught at the Pennsylvania State University and at Stanford before taking on his current position. He has edited, with Sam Messick, *Problems in Human Assessment* and is a frequent contributor to the scientific literature on the assessment of human characteristics. A major contribution is the Personality Research Form, which brings to bear on assessment problems all the sophistication of both the computer age and the history and experience of assessment tests.

SAMUEL S. KOMORITA, professor of psychology at Indiana University, holds the Ph.D. from the University of Michigan and has

been associated with the RAND Corporation, Vanderbilt University, and Wayne State University. He has been primarily involved with game theory and decision processes. His most recent interest is in the area of bargaining, with particular emphasis on the psychological processes underlying conflict resolution.

LEONARD KRASNER, professor of psychology and director of clinical training at the State University of New York, Stony Brook, obtained the Ph.D. at Columbia University in 1950. His main interest is in clinical psychology, and within the field of psychotherapy, he has become quite closely identified with behavior therapy. He has taught at Massachusetts, Colorado, and Stanford, as well as at SUNY.

JONAS LANGER, associate professor of psychology at the University of California, Berkeley, has expressed his abiding interest in *Theories of Development* and has participated in the editing and writing of a collection of original chapters on developmental problems. He holds a classical developmental Ph.D. from Clark University, where he collaborated with Heinz Werner and Seymour Wapner, two of the most distinguished, developmentally oriented psychologists of recent history. His research efforts have spanned the field of development from cognitive considerations to the general theory of the processes of individual development.

DONALD B. LINDSLEY, professor of psychology at the University of California, Los Angeles, holds a Ph.D. from the University of Iowa. His interests are in the electroencephalogram and in physiological processes within psychology. He has held the presti-

A. Maslow

R. May

J. McConnell

W. McGuire

E. McNeil

N. Miller

E. Murray

H. Murray

C. Mueller

gious William James Lectureship in Psychology at Harvard and has taught at the University of Illinois, Brown, Western Reserve, and Northwestern, as well as at UCLA.

ABRAHAM H. MASLOW, professor of psychology at Brandeis University and resident fellow, W. P. Laughlin Foundation, received his Ph.D. from Wisconsin and went on to teach there, at Columbia, and at Brooklyn College before joining the Brandeis faculty. He numbers among his major contributions to the field of psychology numerous books, innumerable articles, a large number of students of renown, and considerable lecturing. Maslow is identified with the concept of self-actualization and holds an honorary degree from Xavier University. Currently, he is a member of the board of editors of no fewer than nine journals. He is, last but not least, a major figure in the theory of the human personality, one of the two or three this country has produced in this century.

ROLLO MAY, a practicing psychotherapist affiliated with the William Alanson White Institute in New York, holds the Ph.D. from Columbia and has taught and counseled in Greece, at Harvard, and at Princeton. He is also adjunct professor in the graduate school of New York University and lecturer at the New School. His interests are in therapy and personality theory. He is one of the prime American authorities on existential psychotherapy.

JAMES V. MCCONNELL, professor of psychology at the University of Michigan, is best known for his studies of memory transfer at the physiological level and for his

abiding interest in the theory and composition of science fiction. With a Ph.D. under Dallenbach at the University of Texas, he has taught at both Texas and Michigan. He is also a research psychologist with the Mental Health Research Institute at Michigan. He has consulted the Departments of Defense and Commerce and the Smithsonian Institution on a variety of problems connected with his interests in motivation and learning. A frequent contributor to the scientific journals, McConnell also edits *The Journal of Biological Psychology* and the popular, though humorously serious, *Worm Runner's Digest*.

WILLIAM J. MCGUIRE, professor of psychology at the University of California, San Diego, is a Yale Ph.D. who taught at Yale, Illinois, and Columbia before undertaking his present post. He is a social psychologist, primarily concerned with attitude change, selective perception, and psychological implication. Possessed of an extraordinarily classical as well as modern, analytical mind, McGuire has consistently been in the forefront of social psychological debates and issues, not to mention empirical work, for the past decade. He is currently editor of the *Journal of Personality and Social Psychology*.

ELTON B. MCNEIL, professor of psychology at the University of Michigan, received his Ph.D. from there in clinical psychology. His interests are too numerous to elaborate upon, for they span the fields of consumer behavior, introspection, mental health, adjustment, education of the gifted, human conflict, sex, subliminal stimulation, and psychosis. He is a frequent contributor to scholarly journals and is the author of numerous books, including *Human Socialization*.

NEAL E. MILLER, professor and head of a laboratory of physiological psychology at the Rockefeller University, holds a Ph.D. from Yale, with which he was affiliated for a number of years. From 1952 until assuming his present post, Miller held the James Rowland Angell Professorship. His interests are in learning and motivation and in their physiological basis. He has conducted numerous incisive experiments on motivational mechanisms and continually contributes to the theory of the application of animal studies to the human condition.

CONRAD G. MUELLER, professor of psychology and chairman of the Psychology Department at Indiana University, took his Ph.D. in 1948 at Columbia, where he also served as chairman of the Psychology Department. He has been visiting professor in biophysics at the Rockefeller Institute. His interests are in sensory processes, particularly visual ones, and in the theory and treatment of data.

EDWARD J. MURRAY, professor of psychology at the University of Miami, has pursued his interest in feelings and emotions both with animals and with people since taking a Yale Ph.D. in 1955. He taught at Syracuse before taking up his present post. His interests also include sleep deprivation, and he is now working with emotionally disturbed children and their families.

HARRY G. MURRAY, assistant professor of psychology at the University of Western Ontario, took his Ph.D. at the University of Illinois, where he worked on research projects in both behavior genetics and human learning. His primary field of interest is general experimental psychology. An expert in both learning theory and genetics, Murray

D. Norman

R. Ornstein

H. Pick, Jr.

G. Reynolds

B. Scharf

D. Slobin

C. Rogers

S. Stevens

L. Tyler

R. Watson

attempts in his research to study processes of learning and to show how these combine with hereditary mechanisms in the determination of human and animal behavior.

DONALD A. NORMAN, associate professor of psychology at the University of California, San Diego, received an M.S. in electrical engineering and the Ph.D. in mathematical psychology from the University of Pennsylvania. He has taught at Harvard, where he was affiliated with the Center for Cognitive Studies. His interests are in understanding computers and human memory, and perhaps simulating one with the other.

ROBERT E. ORNSTEIN, research psychologist at the Langley Porter Neuropsychiatric Institute in San Francisco, has a Stanford Ph.D. He has written *On the Experience of Time* and is currently interested in sleep, dreaming, and states of consciousness in general.

HERBERT L. PICK, JR., professor of psychology at the University of Minnesota (Institute of Child Development), took the Ph.D. at Cornell University. In 1959–1960, he studied in Russia at the Moscow State University and has visited there since. Pick's interests are in perception generally and in the development of perceptual experience in children.

G. S. REYNOLDS, professor of psychology at the University of California, San Diego, holds the Ph.D. from Harvard University in experimental psychology. His interests are reflected in his *A Primer of Operant Conditioning*. He taught at Harvard and the University of Chicago before taking his present post. As consulting editor to *Psychology To-*

day, he has contributed surreptitiously to several areas of psychology and has himself published papers in the areas of operant conditioning, human responses to stress, psychoacoustics, psychopharmacology, and physiological psychology. His current interests are schedules of reinforcement and personality theory.

CARL R. ROGERS, resident fellow at the Center for Studies of the Person, La Jolla, California, is internationally known as the originator of client-centered psychotherapy, which he developed while head of the Counseling Center at the University of Chicago. For twenty years his research and writing has been in the fields of psychotherapy, personality theory, and education, and increasingly in the last five years he has been involved in both the theory and the practice of encounter groups (sensitivity training). His most recent books indicate something of his interest—*On Becoming a Person*, and *Freedom to Learn: A View of What Education Might Become*. He is the only psychologist in the United States to receive from the American Psychological Association both its Scientific Contribution Award and its Award for Professional Contribution. Rogers, the author of many books and articles, has been a professor at Ohio State University, the University of Chicago, and the University of Wisconsin.

BERTRAM SCHARF, associate professor of psychology at Northeastern University, holds a Ph.D. from Harvard University. His interests are in sensory processes and in psychoacoustics. His particular interests are in masking and in loudness summation. He has served as visiting research associate at both the Technische Hochschule Stuttgart and

the Laboratory of Sensory Communication, Syracuse University.

DAN I. SLOBIN, associate professor of psychology at Berkeley, holds a Ph.D. from Harvard, where he worked with Roger Brown, Jerome Bruner, and George A. Miller on problems of developmental psycholinguistics. His interests cover sociological and anthropological subjects as well as psychology. He edits the translation journal *Soviet Psychology* and is a frequent translator of foreign psychological literature.

S. S. STEVENS, professor of psychophysics at Harvard University, took a Harvard Ph.D. in psychology under E. G. Boring after flirting with both medicine and education. In 1938, he coauthored *Hearing*, a book so thorough in its coverage that it is standard today. Stevens is best known for his recent work on the power law of sensory magnitude.

LEONA E. TYLER, professor of psychology and dean of the Graduate School, University of Oregon, received the Ph.D. from the University of Minnesota and has taught at Minnesota, Oregon, Berkeley, and the University of Amsterdam. Her interests are in tests and measurements of the human potential and achievement, areas in which she has published many books and articles.

ROBERT I. WATSON, professor of psychology at the University of New Hampshire, took the Ph.D. at Columbia University. He has served at Dana College, Newark, and Northwestern as well as at New Hampshire, and also Carnegie Institute of Technology and Washington University School of Medicine. His interests are in clinical psychology and particularly the history of psychology.

SELECTED BIBLIOGRAPHY

I. Introduction

2. The Biological Organism

BRAZIER, M. A. *Electrical Activity of the Nervous System.* 3rd ed. Baltimore: Williams & Wilkins, 1968.

BUTTER, C. N. *Neuropsychology: The Study of Brain and Behavior.* Belmont, Calif.: Brooks/Cole, 1965.

ECCLES, J. C. *The Physiology of Nerve Cells.* Baltimore: Johns Hopkins, 1957.

GARDNER, E. *Fundamentals of Neurology.* 4th ed. Philadelphia: Saunders, 1963.

GROSSMAN, S. P. *A Textbook of Physiological Psychology.* New York: Wiley, 1967.

ISAACSON, R. L. (ed.). *Basic Readings in Neuropsychology.* New York: Harper & Row, 1964.

KATZ, B. "The Nerve Impulse," *Scientific American,* 187 (1952), 55–64.

KRIEG, W. J. S. *Functional Neuroanatomy.* New York: McGraw-Hill, 1942.

McCLEARY, R. A., and R. Y. MOORE. *Subcortical Mechanisms of Behavior.* New York: Basic Books, 1965.

SHERRINGTON, C. S. *The Integrative Action of the Nervous System.* New Haven, Conn.: Yale University Press, 1906.

STEVENS, C. F. *Neurophysiology: A Primer.* New York: Wiley, 1966.

TALBOT, N. B., *et al. Functional Endocrinology, From Birth Through Adolescence.* Cambridge, Mass.: Harvard University Press, 1952.

WALTER, W. G. *The Living Brain.* New York: Norton, 1953.

3. Measurement and Methods

ALLPORT, G. W. *The Use of Personal Documents in Psychological Science.* New York: Social Sciences Research Council, Bulletin No. 49, 1942.

BLOOM, B. S., and F. PETERS. *The Use of Academic Prediction Scales for Counseling and Selecting College Entrants.* New York: Free Press, 1961.

COURTS, F. A. *Psychological Statistics: An Introduction.* Homewood, Ill.: Dorsey, 1966.

HAYS, W. L. *Statistics for Psychologists.* New York: Holt, Rinehart and Winston, 1963.

HESS, E. H. "Attitude and Pupil Size," *Scientific American,* 212 (1965), 46–54.

ROSENTHAL, R. *Experimenter Effects in Behavioral Research.* New York: Appleton-Century-Crofts, 1966.

II. Learning and Motivation

4. Kinds and Nature of Learning

DALLENBACH, K. M. "Twitmyer and the Conditioned Response," *American Journal of Psychology,* 72 (1959), 633–638.

KÖHLER, W. *The Mentality of Apes.* New York: Harcourt, Brace & World, 1925.

PAVLOV, I. P. *Conditioned Reflexes.* G. V. Anrep (tr.). New York: Dover, 1927.

REYNOLDS, G. S. *A Primer of Operant Conditioning.* Glenview, Ill.: Scott, Foresman, 1968.

SKINNER, B. F. *The Behavior of Organisms.* New York: Appleton-Century-Crofts, 1938.

SOLOMON, R. L., and L. H. TURNER. "Discriminative Classical Conditioning in Dogs Paralyzed by Curare Can Later Control Discriminative Avoidance Responses in the Normal State," *Psychological Review,* 69 (1962), 202–219.

5. Animal Behavior and Instinct

DARWIN, C. *Expression of the Emotions in Man and Animals.* Chicago: University of Chicago Press, 1965.

FRAENKEL, G. S., and D. L. GUNN. *The Orientation of Animals.* New York: Dover, 1961.

FRISCH, K. VON. *The Dancing Bees.* London: Methuen, 1953.

JENNINGS, H. S. *Behavior of the Lower Organisms.* New York: Columbia University Press, 1906.

LORENZ, K. *Evolution and Modification of Behavior.* Chicago: University of Chicago Press, 1965.

———. *King Solomon's Ring.* New York: Crowell, 1952.

MARLER, P. R., and W. J. HAMILTON. *Mechanisms of Animal Behavior.* New York: Wiley, 1966.

MATTHEWS, G. V. T. *Bird Navigation.* London: Cambridge University Press, 1955.

ROE, A., and G. SIMPSON (eds.). *Behavior and Evolution.* New Haven, Conn.: Yale University Press, 1958.

THORPE, W. H. *Bird-Song.* London: Cambridge University Press, 1961.

———. *Learning and Instinct in Animals.* 1st ed. London: Methuen, 1956.

TINBERGEN, N. *The Study of Instinct.* Fair Lawn, N.J.: Oxford University Press, 1951.

6. Operant Conditioning

CORNING, W. C., and S. C. RATNER (eds.). *The Chemistry of Learning.* New York: Plenum Press, 1967.

FANTINO, E. "Of Mice and Misers," *Psychology Today,* 2 (1968), 40–43, 62.

HANSON, H. M. "Effects of Discrimination Training on Stimulus Generalization," *Journal of Experimental Psychology,* 58 (1959), 321–334.

HEBB, D. O. *The Organization of Behavior.* New York: Wiley, 1949.

HONIG, W. H. (ed.). *Operant Behavior: Areas of Research and Application.* New York: Appleton-Century-Crofts, 1966.

McCONNELL, J. V. "Comparative Physiology: Learning in Invertebrates," *Annual Review of Physiology,* 28 (1966), 107–136.

REYNOLDS, G. S. *A Primer of Operant Conditioning.* Glenview, Ill.: Scott, Foresman, 1968.

SKINNER, B. F. "Are Theories of Learning Necessary?" *Psychological Review,* 57 (1950), 193–216.

———. *The Behavior of Organisms.* New York: Appleton-Century-Crofts, 1938.

7. Fundamentals of Motivation

BERLYNE, D. E. *Conflict, Arousal, and Curiosity.* New York: McGraw-Hill, 1960.

COFER, C. N., and M. H. APPLEY. *Motivation: Theory and Research.* New York: Wiley, 1964.

DOUGLAS, R. J. "The Hippocampus and Behavior," *Psychological Bulletin,* 67 (1967), 416–442.

GELLHORN, E. *Principles of Autonomic-Somatic Integrations.* Minneapolis: University of Minnesota Press, 1967.

GROSSMAN, S. P. "Eating or Drinking Elicited by Direct Adrenergic or Cholinergic Stimulation of the Hypothalamus," *Science,* 136 (1960), 301–302.

HESS, W. R. *The Functional Organization of the Diencephalon.* New York: Grune & Stratton, 1957.

MILLER, N. E. "Behavioral and Physiological Techniques: Rationale and Experimental Designs for Combining Their Use," in C. F. Code and W. Heidel (eds.), *Handbook of Physiology—Section 6: Alimentary Canal.* Washington, D.C.: American Physiological Society, 1967, I, 51–61.

———. "Experiments on Motivation: Studies Combining Psychological, Physiological, and Pharmacological Techniques," *Science,* 126 (1957), 1271–1278.

———, L. V. DiCARA, and G. WOLF. "Homeostasis and Reward: T-maze Learning Induced by Manipulating Antidiuretic Hormone," *American Journal of Physiology,* 215 (1968), 684–686.

OLDS, J., and P. MILNER. "Positive Reinforcement Produced by Electrical Stimulation of Septal Area and Other Regions of Rat Brain," *Journal of Comparative and Physiological Psychology,* 47 (1954), 419–427.

SHEFFIELD, F. D., J. J. WULFF, and R. BACKER. "Reward Value of Copulation Without Sex Drive Reduction," *Journal of Comparative and Physiological Psychology,* 44 (1951), 3–8.

SOLOMON, R. L., and L. C. WYNN. "Traumatic Avoidance Learning: The Principles of Anxiety Conservation and Partial Irreversibility," *Psychological Review,* 61 (1954), 353–385.

TEITELBAUM, P., and A. N. EPSTEIN. "The Lateral Hypothalamic Syndrome: Recovery of Feeding and Drinking After Lateral Hypothalamic Lesions," *Psychological Review,* 69 (1962), 74–90.

8. Human Motivation

ARONOFF, J. *Psychological Needs and Cultural Systems.* Princeton, N.J.: Van Nostrand, 1967.

FISKE, D. W., and S. R. MADDI. *Functions of Varied Experience.* Homewood, Ill.: Dorsey, 1961.

MADDI, S. R. *Personality Theories.* Homewood, Ill.: Dorsey, 1968.

MASLOW, A. H. *Motivation and Personality.* New York: Harper & Row, 1954.

———. *Toward a Psychology of Being.* Princeton, N.J.: Van Nostrand, 1962.

McCLELLAND, D. C., J. W. ATKINSON, R. A. CLARK, and E. L. LOWELL. *The Achievement Motive.* New York: Appleton-Century-Crofts, 1953.

McGREGOR, D. *The Human Side of Enterprise.* New York: McGraw-Hill, 1960.

WYLIE, R. C. *The Self Concept.* Lincoln: University of Nebraska Press, 1961.

III. Psychological Development

9. Behavior Genetics

CRICK, F. H. C. "The Genetic Code," *Scientific American,* 207 (1962), 66–74.

DOBZHANSKY, T. *Genetics and the Origin of Species.* 3rd ed. New York: Columbia University Press, 1951.

EYSENCK, H. J., and D. B. PRELL. "The Inheritance of Neuroticism: An Experimental Study," *Journal of Mental Science,* 97 (1951), 441–465.

FULLER, J. L., and W. R. THOMPSON. *Behavior Genetics.* New York: Wiley, 1960.

GOTTESMAN, I. I. "Heritability of Personality: A Demonstration," *Psychological Monographs,* Vol. 77, No. 9 (1963).

HIRSCH, J. (ed.). *Behavior-Genetic Analysis.* New York: McGraw-Hill, 1967.

KALLMAN, F. J. *Heredity in Health and Mental Disorder.* New York: Norton, 1953.

MURRAY, H. G., and J. HIRSCH. "Heredity, Individual Differences and Psychopathology," in S. C. Plog, R. B. Edgerton, and W. C. Beckwith (eds.), *Changing Perspectives in Mental Illness.* New York: Holt, Rinehart and Winston, 1969.

10. The Development of the Individual

BOWER, T. G. R. "The Visual World of Infants," *Scientific American,* 215 (1966), 80–92.

ERIKSON, E. H. *Childhood and Society.* 2nd ed. New York: Norton, 1963.

GESELL, A. *First Five Years of Life.* New York: Harper & Row, 1940.

KAGAN, J., and H. A. MOSS. *Birth to Maturity.* New York: Wiley, 1962.

MUSSEN, P. H. *The Psychological Development of the Child.* Englewood Cliffs, N.J.: Prentice-Hall, 1963.

PIAGET, J. *The Child's Conception of the World.* New York: Humanities, 1929.

———. *Construction of Reality in the Child.* M. Cook (tr.). New York: Basic Books, 1954.

———. *Judgment and Reasoning in the Child.* New York: Humanities, 1947.

———. *Language and Thought of the Child.* Cleveland: World Publishing, 1955.

———, and B. INHELDER. *The Child's Conception of Space.* New York: Humanities, 1948.

SCOTT, J. P. *Early Experience and the Organization of Behavior.* Belmont, Calif.: Brooks/Cole, 1968.

SIGEL, I. E., and F. H. HOOPER (eds.). *Logical Thinking in Children: Re-*

search Based on Piaget's Theory. New York: Holt, Rinehart and Winston, 1968.

WERNER, H. *Comparative Psychology of Mental Development.* Rev. ed. New York: International Universities Press, 1966.

———, and B. KAPLAN. *Symbol Formation: An Organismic-Developmental Approach.* New York: Wiley, 1963.

11. Perceptual Development

BOWER, T. G. R. "The Visual World of Infants," *Scientific American,* 215 (1966), 80–92.

GHENT, L. "Form and Its Orientation: A Child's Eye View," *American Journal of Psychology,* 74 (1961), 177–190.

GIBSON, E. J., et al. "A Developmental Study of the Discrimination of Letter-Like Forms," *Journal of Comparative and Physiological Psychology,* 55 (1962), 897–906.

GREGORY, R. L., and J. G. WALLACE. "Recovery From Early Blindness: A Case Study," *Experimental Psychological Society Monograph.*

HELD, R., and A. HEIN. "Movement-Produced Stimulation in the Development of Visually Guided Behavior," *Journal of Comparative and Physiological Psychology,* 56 (1963), 872–876.

WALK, R. D., and E. J. GIBSON. "A Comparative and Analytic Study of Visual Depth Perception," *Psychological Monographs,* Vol. 75, No. 15 (1961).

12. Linguistic and Cognitive Development

BROWN, R. *Words and Things.* New York: Free Press, 1958.

BRUNER, J. S., et al. *Studies in Cognitive Growth.* New York: Wiley, 1966.

CHOMSKY, N. *Language and Mind.* New York: Harcourt, Brace & World, 1968.

FURTH, H. G. *Thinking Without Language: Psychological Implications of Deafness.* New York: Free Press, 1966.

JAKOBOVITS, L. A., and M. S. MIRON. *Readings in the Psychology of Language.* Englewood Cliffs, N.J.: Prentice-Hall, 1967.

SMITH, F., and G. A. MILLER. *The Genesis of Language: A Psycholinguistic Approach.* Cambridge, Mass.: MIT Press, 1966.

VYGOTSKY, L. S. *Thought and Language.* E. Hanfmann and G. Vakar (tr.). Cambridge, Mass.: MIT Press, 1962.

WHORF, B. L. *Language, Thought and Reality.* New York: Wiley, 1956.

IV. The Sensory World
13. Consciousness and Awareness

BRUNER, J. S. "On Perceptual Readiness," *Psychological Review,* Vol. 64 (1957).

DEMENT, W. C. "A New Look at the Third State of Existence," *Stanford M.D.,* 8 (1968–1969), 2–8.

———, and N. KLEITMAN. "The Relation of Eye Movements During Sleep to Dream Activity: An Objective Method for the Study of Dreaming," *Journal of Experimental Psychology,* 53 (1957), 339–346.

GAZZANIGA, M. S. "The Split Brain in Man," *Scientific American,* Vol. 217 (1967).

KAMIYA, J. "Conscious Control of Brain Waves," *Psychology Today,* 1 (1968), 56–60.

MASTERS, R. E. L., and J. HOUSTON. *The Varieties of Psychedelic Experience.* New York: Holt, Rinehart and Winston, 1966.

ORNSTEIN, R. *On the Experience of Time.* Baltimore: Penguin, 1969.

SOLOMON, P., et al. *Sensory Deprivation.* Cambridge, Mass.: Harvard University Press, 1961.

14. Stimulation and Sensation

BORING, E. G. *Sensation and Perception in the History of Experimental Psychology.* 2nd ed. New York: Appleton-Century-Crofts, 1950.

STEVENS, S. S. "The Surprising Simplicity of Sensory Metrics," *American Psychologist,* 17 (1962), 29–39.

15. Auditory, Chemical, and Other Senses

AMOORE, J. E., J. W. JOHNSTON, JR., and M. RUBIN. "The Stereochemical Theory of Odor," *Scientific American,* 210 (1964), 42–49.

BÉKÉSY, G. VON. "Current Status of Theories of Hearing," *Science,* 123 (1956), 779–783.

———. *Sensory Inhibition.* Princeton, N.J.: Princeton University Press, 1967.

GELDARD, F. A. *The Human Senses.* New York: Wiley, 1953.

HELMHOLTZ, H. *On the Sensations of Tone.* New York: Dover, 1954.

JENKINS, W. L. "Somesthesis," in S. S. Stevens (ed.), *Handbook of Experimental Psychology.* New York: Wiley, 1951.

LOWENSTEIN, O. *The Senses.* Baltimore: Penguin, 1966.

PFAFFMANN, C. "Taste and Smell," in S. S. Stevens (ed.), *Handbook of Experimental Psychology.* New York: Wiley, 1951.

ROSENBLITH, W. A. (ed.). *Sensory Communication.* Cambridge, Mass.: MIT Press, 1961.

WEVER, E. G. *Theory of Hearing.* New York: Wiley, 1949.

16. Visual Sensations

BORING, E. G. *Sensation and Perception in the History of Experimental Psychology.* 2nd ed. New York: Appleton-Century-Crofts, 1950.

DETWILER, S. R. "The Eye and Its Structural Adaptations," *American Scientist,* 53 (1965), 327–346.

GRAHAM, C. H. (ed.). *Vision and Visual Perception.* New York: Wiley, 1966.

GREGORY, R. L. *Eye and Brain: The Psychology of Seeing.* New York: McGraw-Hill, 1966.

HUBEL, D. H., and T. N. WIESEL. "Receptive Fields and Functional Architecture in Two Nonstriate Visual Areas (18 and 19) of the Cat," *Journal of Neurophysiology,* 28 (1965), 229–289.

PRITCHARD, R. M. "Stabilizing Images of the Retina," *Scientific American,* 204 (1961), 72–78.

RATLIFF, F. *Mach Bands.* San Francisco: Holden-Day, 1965.

SHEPPARD, J. J. *Human Color Perception.* New York: American Elsevier, 1968.

VALOIS, R. L. DE. "Behavioral and Electrophysiological Studies of Primate Vision," in W. D. Neff (ed.), *Contributions to Sensory Physiology.* New York: Academic Press, 1965, I, 137–178.

WALD, G. "The Photoreceptor Process in Vision," in J. Field (ed.), *Handbook of Physiology—Section 1: Neurophysiology.* Washington, D.C.: American Physiological Society, 1959, Vol. I.

17. Problems of Perception

ALLPORT, G. W., and T. F. PETTIGREW. "Cultural Influence on the Perception of Movement: The Trapezoid Illusion Among Zulus," *Journal of Abnormal and Social Psychology,* 55 (1957), 104–113.

BEELER, N. F., and F. M. BRANLEY. *Experiments in Optical Illusion.* New York: Crowell, 1951.

BORING, E. G. *Sensation and Perception in the History of Experimental Psychology.* 2nd ed. New York: Appleton-Century-Crofts, 1950.

GIBSON, J. J. *The Perception of the Visual World.* Boston: Houghton Mifflin, 1950.

GREGORY, R. L. *Eye and Brain: The Psychology of Seeing.* New York: McGraw-Hill, 1966.

HELD, R., and J. BOSSON. "Neo-Natal Deprivation and Adult Rearrangement: Complementary Techniques for Analyzing Plastic Sensory Motor Coordinations," *Journal of Comparative and Physiological Psychology,* 54 (1961), 33–37.

674

Hoch, P. H., and J. Zubin (eds.). *Psychopathology of Perception.* New York: Grune & Stratton, 1965.

Holway, A. H., and E. G. Boring. "Determinants of Apparent Visual Size with Distance Variant," *American Journal of Psychology,* 54 (1941), 21–37.

Ittelson, W. H., and F. P. Kilpatrick. "Experiments in Perception," *Scientific American,* 185 (1951), 50–55.

Julesz, B. "Experiment in Perception," *Psychology Today,* 2 (1968), 16–23.

Kaufman, L., and I. Rock. "The Moon Illusion," *Scientific American,* 207 (1962), 120–130.

Kohler, I. "Experiment With Goggles," *Scientific American,* 206 (1962), 62–86.

Köhler, W. *Gestalt Psychology.* 2nd ed. New York: Liveright, 1947.

Michotte, A. *The Perception of Causality.* New York: Basic Books, 1963.

Rock, I. *Nature of Perceptual Adaptation.* New York: Basic Books, 1966.

———, and C. Harris. "Vision and Touch," *Scientific American,* 216 (1967), 96–104.

Solomon, P., *et al. Sensory Deprivation.* Cambridge, Mass.: Harvard University Press, 1961.

V. Human Function
18. Human Information Processing

Fitts, P., and M. I. Posner. *Human Performance.* Belmont, Calif.: Brooks/Cole, 1967.

Kolers, P., and M. Edan (eds.). *Pattern Recognition.* Cambridge, Mass.: MIT Press, 1968.

Neisser, U. *Cognitive Psychology.* New York: Appleton-Century-Crofts, 1967.

Norman, D. A. *Memory and Attention: An Introduction to Human Information Processing.* New York: Wiley, 1969.

Wooldridge, D. E. *The Machinery of the Brain.* New York: McGraw-Hill, 1963.

19. Human Learning and Memory

Adams, J. A. *Human Memory.* New York: McGraw-Hill, 1967.

Bartlett, F. C. *Remembering: An Experimental and Social Study.* London: Cambridge University Press, 1932.

Ebbinghaus, H. *Memory: A Contribution to Experimental Psychology.* H. A. Ruger and C. E. Bussenius (tr.). New York: Teachers College, Columbia University, 1913.

Peterson, L. R., and M. J. Peterson. "Short-term Retention of Individual Verbal Items," *Journal of Experimental Psychology,* 58 (1959), 193–198.

20. Problem Solving

Bruner, J. S., J. J. Goodnow, and G. A. Austin. *A Study of Thinking.* New York: Wiley, 1956.

Freedman, J. L. "Increasing Creativity by Free-Association Training," *Journal of Experimental Psychology,* 69 (1965), 89–91.

Harlow, H. F. "The Formation of Learning Sets," *Psychological Review,* 56 (1949), 51–65.

Maltzman, I. "On the Training of Originality," *Psychological Review,* 67 (1960), 229–242.

Mednick, S. A. "The Associative Basis of the Creative Process," *Psychological Review,* 69 (1962), 220–232.

Polya, G. *Mathematics and Plausible Reasoning.* Princeton, N.J.: Princeton University Press, 1954, Vols. I and II.

Scheerer, M. "Problem Solving," *Scientific American,* 208 (1963), 118–128.

21. Emotion and Feeling

Arnold, M. B. *Emotion and Personality.* New York: Columbia University Press, 1960, Vols. I and II.

Berlyne, D. E. *Conflict, Arousal, and Curiosity.* New York: McGraw-Hill, 1960.

Brady, J. V. "Ulcers in 'Executive' Monkeys," *Scientific American,* 199 (1958), 95–100.

Buss, A. H. *The Psychology of Aggression.* New York: Wiley, 1961.

Dollard, J., *et al. Frustration and Aggression.* New Haven, Conn.: Yale University Press, 1939.

Harlow, H. F. "The Nature of Love," *American Psychologist,* 13 (1958), 673–685.

Murray, E. J. *Motivation and Emotion.* Englewood Cliffs, N.J.: Prentice-Hall, 1964.

———. *Sleep, Dreams and Arousal.* New York: Appleton-Century-Crofts, 1965.

Schachter, S., and J. E. Singer. "Cognitive, Social and Physiological Determinants of Emotional State," *Psychological Review,* 69 (1962), 379–399.

Selye, H. *The Stress of Life.* New York: McGraw-Hill, 1956.

Watson, J. B., and R. Rayner. "Conditioned Emotional Reactions," *Journal of Experimental Psychology,* 3 (1920), 1–14.

22. Drugs and Behavior

Alpert, R., S. Cohen, and L. Schiller. *LSD.* New York: New American Library, 1966.

Barron, F., M. E. Jarvik, and S. Bunnell, Jr. "The Hallucinogenic Drugs," *Scientific American,* 210 (1964), 29–37.

Jarvik, M. E. "The Psychopharmacological Revolution," *Psychology Today,* 1 (1967), 51–59.

Jellinek, E. M. *The Disease Concept of Alcoholism.* New Haven, Conn.: Hillhouse Press, 1960.

Leary, T. *High Priest.* New York: New American Library, 1967.

Mann, M. *New Primer on Alcoholism.* New York: Holt, Rinehart and Winston, 1958.

Uhr, L. M., and J. G. Miller. *Drugs and Behavior.* New York: Wiley, 1960.

Weil, T., E. Zinberg, and J. M. Nelsen. "Clinical and Psychological Effects of Marihuana in Man," *Science,* 162 (1968), 1234–1242.

VI. Personality
23. Individual Differences and Their Measurement

American Psychological Association. *Standards for Educational and Psychological Tests and Manuals.* Washington, D.C.: American Psychological Association, 1966.

Bayley, N. "On the Growth of Intelligence," *American Psychologist,* 10 (1955), 805–818.

Campbell, D. P. *Manual for the Strong Vocational Interest Blank.* Stanford, Calif.: Stanford University Press, 1966.

Cattell, J. McK. "Mental Tests and Measurements," *Mind,* 15 (1890), 373–380.

Ghiselli, E. E. *The Validity of Occupational Aptitude Tests.* New York: Wiley, 1966.

Tyler, L. E. *The Psychology of Human Differences.* New York: Appleton-Century-Crofts, 1965.

24. Measurement of Personality

Allport, G. W., P. E. Vernon, and G. Lindzey. *Study of Values: Manual.* Boston: Houghton Mifflin, 1960.

Atkinson, J. W. *Motives in Fantasy, Action and Society.* Princeton, N.J.: Van Nostrand, 1958.

Calvin, A. D., and J. V. McConnell. "Ellison Personality Inventories," *Journal of Consulting Psychology,* 17 (1953), 462–464.

Dahlstrom, W. G., and G. S. Welsh. *An MMPI Handbook.* Minneapolis: University of Minnesota Press, 1960.

Holtzman, W. H., *et al. Inkblot Perception and Personality.* Austin: University of Texas Press, 1961.

Jackson, D. N. *Manual for the Personality Research Form.* Goshen, N.Y.: Research Psychologists Press, 1967.

MACHOVER, K. *Personality Projection in the Drawing of the Human Figure: A Method of Personality Investigation.* Springfield, Ill.: Charles C Thomas, 1949.

MEEHL, P. E. "Wanted—A Good Cookbook," *American Psychologist,* 11 (1956), 263–272.

MESSICK, S., and D. N. JACKSON (eds.). *Problems in Human Assessment.* New York: McGraw-Hill, 1967.

MURRAY, H. A., *et al. Explorations in Personality.* Fair Lawn, N.J.: Oxford University Press, 1938.

ROHDE, A. R. *The Sentence Completion Method.* New York: Ronald, 1957.

25. Theories of Personality

ALLPORT, G. W. *Patterns and Growth in Personality.* New York: Holt, Rinehart and Winston, 1961.

ANSBACHER, H. L., and R. R. ANSBACHER (eds.). *The Individual Psychology of Alfred Adler.* New York: Basic Books, 1956.

FORDHAM, F. *An Introduction to Jung's Psychology.* Baltimore: Penguin, 1953.

FROMM, E. *Escape From Freedom.* New York: Holt, Rinehart and Winston, 1941.

HALL, C. S., and G. LINDZEY. *Theories of Personality.* New York: Wiley, 1957.

JONES, E. *The Life and Work of Sigmund Freud.* New York: Basic Books, Vol. I, 1953; Vol. II, 1955; Vol. III, 1957.

MASLOW, A. *Toward a Psychology of Being.* Princeton, N.J.: Van Nostrand, 1968.

MURRAY, H. A., *et al. Explorations in Personality.* Fair Lawn, N.J.: Oxford University Press, 1938.

ROGERS, C. R. *On Becoming a Person.* Boston: Houghton Mifflin, 1961.

SHELDON, W. H. *Varieties of Delinquent Youth: An Introduction to Constitutional Psychiatry.* New York: Harper & Row, 1949.

SULLIVAN, H. S. *The Interpersonal Theory of Psychiatry.* New York: Norton, 1953.

26. Adjustment

BANDURA, A., and R. H. WALTERS. *Adolescent Aggression.* New York: Ronald, 1959.

BERKOWITZ, L. *Aggression: A Social Psychological Analysis.* New York: McGraw-Hill, 1962.

BETTELHEIM, B., and M. JANOWITZ. *Social Changes and Prejudice.* New York: Free Press, 1964.

DURKHEIM, E. *Suicide.* New York: Free Press, 1951.

LEVITT, E. E. *The Psychology of Anxiety.* New York: Bobbs-Merrill, 1967.

LORENZ, K. *On Aggression.* New York: Harcourt, Brace & World, 1966.

McNEIL, E. B. (ed.). *The Nature of Human Conflict.* Englewood Cliffs, N.J.: Prentice-Hall, 1965.

VII. Disorder and Therapy
27. Behavior Disorders

BELLAK, L. *Schizophrenia: A Review of the Syndrome.* New York: Lozos Press, 1958.

BIEBER, I. *Homosexuality.* New York: Basic Books, 1962.

BUSS, A. H. *Psychopathology.* New York: Wiley, 1966.

GREENBLATT, M. "Psychosurgery," in A. M. Freedman and H. I. Kaplan (eds.), *Psychiatry.* Baltimore: Williams & Wilkins, 1967, pp. 1291–1295.

KINSEY, A. C., W. B. POMEROY, and C. E. MARTIN. "Concepts of Normality and Abnormality in Sexual Behavior," in P. H. Hoch and J. Zubin (eds.), *Psychosexual Development in Health and Disease.* New York: Grune & Stratton, 1949, pp. 11–32.

MONTAGU, A. "Chromosomes and Crime," *Psychology Today,* 2 (1968), 42–49.

WHITE, R. W. *The Abnormal Personality.* 3rd ed. New York: Ronald, 1964.

28. Individual Therapies

ADLER, A. *The Neurotic Constitution.* New York: Humanities, 1926.

ERIKSON, E. H. *Childhood and Society.* 2nd ed. New York: Norton, 1963.

FREUD, S. *A General Introduction to Psychoanalysis.* Garden City, N.Y.: Doubleday, 1938.

KRASNER, L., and L. P. ULLMAN. *Case Studies in Behavior Modification.* New York: Holt, Rinehart and Winston, 1965.

MAY, R., *et al. Existential Psychology.* Rev. ed. New York: Random House, 1969.

ROGERS, C. R. *Counseling and Psychotherapy.* Boston: Houghton Mifflin, 1942.

SULLIVAN, H. S. *Clinical Studies in Psychiatry.* New York: Norton, 1956.

———. *Conceptions of Modern Psychiatry.* Washington, D.C.: William Alanson White Psychiatric Foundation, 1947.

WHITE, R. W. "Motivation Reconsidered: The Concept of Competence," *Psychological Review,* 66 (1959), 297–333.

29. The Intensive-Group Experience

BRADFORD, L. P., J. R. GIBB, and K. D. BENNE (eds.). *T-Group Theory and Laboratory Method.* New York: Wiley, 1964.

BUGENTAL, J. F. T. (ed.). *Challenges of Humanistic Psychology.* New York: McGraw-Hill, 1967.

GORDON, T. *Group-Centered Leadership.* Boston: Houghton Mifflin, 1955.

ROGERS, C. R. *Freedom to Learn.* Columbus, Ohio: Merrill, 1969.

30. Psychiatric Therapies

ALEXANDER, F., and H. ROSS (eds.). *Dynamic Psychiatry.* Chicago: University of Chicago Press, 1952.

ENGLISH, O. S., and S. M. FINCH. *Introduction to Psychiatry.* 3rd ed. New York: Norton, 1964.

FARNSWORTH, D. L. *Psychiatry, Education, and the Young Adult.* Springfield, Ill.: Charles C Thomas, 1966.

HALLECK, S. L. *Psychiatry and the Dilemma of Crime.* New York: Harper & Row, 1967.

HOCH, P. H., and J. ZUBIN (eds.). *Future of Psychiatry.* New York: Grune & Stratton, 1962.

REDLICH, F. C., and D. X. FREEDMAN. *Theory and Practice of Psychiatry.* New York: Basic Books, 1966.

VIII. Social Psychology
31. Groups and Group Conflict

ALLPORT, G. W. *The Nature of Prejudice.* Reading, Mass.: Addison-Wesley, 1954.

BERKOWITZ, L. *Aggression: A Social Psychological Analysis.* New York: McGraw-Hill, 1962.

FESTINGER, L., S. SCHACHTER, and K. BACK. *Social Pressures in Informal Groups.* New York: Harper & Row, 1950.

GUETZKOW, H. (ed.). *Groups, Leadership and Men.* Pittsburgh: Carnegie Press, 1951.

HOMANS, G. C. *Social Behavior: Its Elementary Forms.* New York: Harcourt, Brace & World, 1961.

KELMAN, H. (ed.). *International Behavior: A Social Psychological Analysis.* New York: Holt, Rinehart and Winston, 1965.

NEWCOMB, T. M., R. H. TURNER, and P. E. CONVERSE. *Social Psychology: The Study of Human Interaction.* New York: Holt, Rinehart and Winston, 1965.

OSGOOD, C. E. *An Alternative to War or Surrender.* Urbana: University of Illinois Press, 1962.

SHERIF, M., *et al. Intergroup Conflict and Cooperation.* Norman: University of Oklahoma Press, 1961.

THIBAUT, J. W., and H. H. KELLEY. *The Social Psychology of Groups.* New York: Wiley, 1959.

32. Small Groups

BALES, R. F. *Interaction Process Analysis, A Method for the Study of Small Groups.* Reading, Mass.: Addison-Wesley, 1950.

———. *Personality and Interpersonal Behavior.* New York: Holt, Rinehart and Winston, 1969.

EYSENCK, H. J. *The Psychology of Politics.* London: Routledge and Kegan Paul, 1954.

FESTINGER, L., S. SCHACHTER, and K. BACK. *Social Pressures in Informal Groups.* New York: Harper & Row, 1950.

HEIDER, F. *The Psychology of Interpersonal Relations.* New York: Wiley, 1958.

STOUFFER, S. A., *et al. The American Soldier.* Princeton, N.J.: Princeton University Press, 1949, Vol. I.

33. Attitudes and Their Change

ABELSON, R. P., *et al.* (eds.). *Theories of Cognitive Consistency: A Sourcebook.* Chicago: Rand McNally, 1968.

ASCH, S. E. "Studies of Independence and Conformity: A Minority of One Against a Unanimous Majority," *Psychological Monographs,* Vol. 70, No. 9 (1956).

BECHAM, J., and A. R. COHEN. *Explorations in Cognitive Dissonance.* New York: Wiley, 1962.

BERKOWITZ, L. (ed.). *Advances in Experimental Social Psychology.* New York: Academic Press, 1967, Vol. III.

FESTINGER, L. *A Theory of Cognitive Dissonance.* New York: Harper & Row, 1957.

GREENWALD, A. G. (ed.). *Psychological*

Foundations of Attitudes. New York: Academic Press, 1968.

HILGARD, E. R. *Hypnotic Susceptibility.* New York: Harcourt, Brace & World, 1965.

HOVLAND, C. I., I. L. JANIS, and H. H. KELLEY. *Communication and Persuasion.* New Haven, Conn.: Yale University Press, 1953.

JANIS, I. L., and C. I. HOVLAND (eds.). *Personality and Persuasibility.* New Haven, Conn.: Yale University Press, 1969.

ROSENBERG, M. J., *et al. Cognitive Organization and Change.* New Haven, Conn.: Yale University Press, 1960.

SCHEIN, E. H. *Coercive Persuasion.* New York: Norton, 1961.

SHERIF, C. W., M. SHERIF, and R. E. NEBERGALL. *Attitude and Attitude Change.* Philadelphia: Saunders, 1965.

34. Interpersonal Attraction

BYRNE, D. "Attitudes and Attraction," in L. Berkowitz (ed.), *Advances in Experimental Social Psychology.* New York: Academic Press (in press), Vol. IV.

FESTINGER, L. "A Theory of Social Comparison Processes," *Human Relations,* 7 (1954), 117–140.

———, S. SCHACHTER, and K. BACK. *Social Pressures in Informal Groups.* New York: Harper & Row, 1950.

JONES, E. E. *Ingratiation: A Social Psychological Analysis.* New York: Appleton-Century-Crofts, 1964.

NEWCOMB, T. M. *The Acquaintance Process.* New York: Holt, Rinehart and Winston, 1961.

SCHACHTER, S. *The Psychology of Affiliation.* Stanford, Calif.: Stanford University Press, 1959.

ZIMBARDO, P. G., and R. FORMICA.

"Emotional Comparison and Self-Esteem as Determinants of Affiliation," *Journal of Personality,* 31 (1963), 141–162.

35. Behavior Modification

AYLLON, T., and N. H. AZRIN. *The Token Economy.* New York: Appleton-Century-Crofts, 1968.

BIJOU, S. W. "The Mentally Retarded Child," *Psychology Today,* 2 (1968), 46–51.

EYSENCK, H. J. *Experiments in Behavior Therapy.* New York: Pergamon, 1963.

FERSTER, C. B. "Positive Reinforcement and Behavior Deficits of Autistic Children," *Child Development,* 32 (1961), 437–456.

HAWKINS, R. P., *et al.* "Behavior Therapy in the Home: Amelioration of Problem Parent-Child Relations With the Parent in a Therapeutic Role," *Journal of Experimental Child Psychology,* 4 (1966), 99–107.

LAZARUS, A. A., and J. WOLPE. *Behavior Therapy Techniques.* New York: Pergamon, 1966.

LENT, J. R. "Mimosa Cottage: An Experiment in Hope," *Psychology Today,* 2 (1968), 51–58.

LINDSLEY, O. R. "Operant Conditioning Methods Applied to Research in Chronic Schizophrenia," *Psychiatric Research Report,* 5 (1956), 118–139.

SKINNER, B. F. "Freedom and Control of Men," *American Scholar,* 25 (1955–1956), 45–65.

———. *Walden Two.* New York: Macmillan, 1948.

ULRICH, R., T. STACHNIK, and J. MABRY. *Control of Human Behavior.* Glenview, Ill.: Scott, Foresman, Vol. I, 1966; Vol. II, 1970.

677

GLOSSARY

aberration. Any departure from that which is normal.

ability. The capacity for skillful performance, usually on an already learned task. See also aptitude.

abnormal psychology. The branch of psychology that studies the causes and treatment of behavioral disorders.

abreaction. See catharsis.

abscissa. The horizontal axis of a graph. Usually used to plot the measure of the independent variable. See also ordinate.

absolute judgment. Judgment made in the absence of any standard of comparison.

absolute refractory phase. The brief period following transmission of a nerve impulse when the neuron is completely unresponsive to stimulation.

absolute threshold. The minimum amount of stimulus energy that can be detected.

absolute zero point. The point on a ratio scale at which the variable being measured ceases to exist.

absorption. The retaining of energy such as light, heat, or sound.

accommodation. The changes in the shape of the lens that regulate the focus of the image of an object on the retina.

accommodator. One who adjusts his feelings and pattern of behavior to fit the demands made on him. See also assimilator.

acetylcholine (ACh). A chemical believed to be the agent by which a nerve impulse crosses the synapse.

acetylcholinesterase. An enzyme involved in the inactivation of acetylcholine.

ACh. See acetylcholine.

achievement. Accomplishment or attainment of a goal.

achievement motive. The motive to achieve for its own sake rather than for the benefits of the achievement.

achievement test. A test used to evaluate what a person knows or can do at a given time. See also aptitude test.

achromatic colors. Black, gray, and white.

achromatism. Total color blindness.

acoustics. The scientific study of the properties of sound.

acquisition. The process whereby a learned response becomes more probable.

ACTH. See adrenocorticotrophic hormone.

action potential. Electric potential changes that accompany a nerve impulse.

activator. A drug used to increase level of activity.

active stretch. Muscle activity involved in bodily movement.

adaptation. The adjustment of sensory apparatus in response to the raising or lowering of stimulation.

adaptation level. The theory holding that context sets the standard against which events or objects are perceived.

addiction. Psychological or physiological overdependence on drugs.

additive mixture. The mixture of lights, in vision.

adenine. A component of DNA.

ADH. See antidiuretic hormone.

adjustment. The achievement of harmony between an individual and his environment.

adrenal cortex. The outer portion of an adrenal gland.

adrenal glands. A pair of endocrine glands located above the kidneys. They are the sources of epinephrine, norepinephrine, and cortin.

adrenal medulla. The inner portion of an adrenal gland.

adrenaline. See epinephrine.

adrenergic-cholinergic system. The part of the nervous system activated by both adrenalinlike and acetylcholine transmitter substances. See also cholinergic system.

adrenocorticotrophic hormone (ACTH). A hormone secreted by the anterior pituitary gland. Its functions include influencing the adrenal cortex to release steroid hormones, which help to regulate water balance and energy expenditure.

aerial perspective. A monocular clue to depth perception, based upon the fact that distant objects appear less distinct and less brilliant than nearby objects.

affect. Liking or disliking of a given stimulus.

affective reactions. Psychotic reactions characterized by extremes of mood such as depression or manic elation.

afferent. Conducting nerve impulses toward the brain or spinal cord. See also *efferent.*

afterdischarge. The continued discharge of nervous impulses after stimulation has ceased.

afterimage. In vision, the image that remains after the original stimulus has been removed. It is similar in shape but of a complementary color to the original stimulus.

AGCT. See *Army General Classification Test.*

aggression. A general term describing feelings and behavior of anger or hostility.

aggression anxiety. Anxiety caused by one's own aggressive tendencies.

agitated depression. A depressed state in which the predominant mood is one of sadness but the activity level is agitated and excited.

agnosia. Inability to recognize objects and their meaning, usually stemming from brain damage.

agoraphobia. Irrational fear of open places.

aha experience. Sudden insight into the solution of a problem.

alarm reaction. The first stage of the general adaptation syndrome. See also *general adaptation syndrome.*

alcoholism. Compulsive consumption of and dependence on alcohol.

algorithm. A problem-solving method in which all possibilities in a situation are systematically considered. See also *heuristic method.*

allele. One of two or more alternative forms of the gene that represent differences in the chemical effects of the gene.

all-or-none law. The property of a neuron to respond to a stimulus completely or not at all.

Allport-Vernon Study of Values. A personality inventory designed to discover the relative strengths of interest in such value areas as politics, economics, religion, and aesthetics.

alpha waves. Waves from the occipital region of the cortex, measured on an electroencephalogram. The average frequency is about ten cycles per second.

altruistic suicide. According to Durkheim, one of the three kinds of suicide. It occurs when an individual becomes so involved in a social group that he

sacrifices his life to assure survival of the group. See also *anomic suicide; egoistic suicide.*

ambivalence. Simultaneously holding conflicting reactions toward a person or object.

Ames room. A demonstration in depth illusion designed by Adelbert Ames. It is a distorted room that looks normal from a certain vantage point but in which objects and people appear distorted in size.

amnesia. A partial or total loss of memory that can be caused by physical injury or can occur as the result of repression.

amphetamine. A drug that produces a psychologically stimulating effect by releasing epinephrine in the brain.

amplitude. The height of a wave from a zero point. The amplitude of sound waves corresponds to loudness; the amplitude of light waves corresponds to brightness. See also *sound pressure.*

ampulla. In the ear, the enlarged portion of the semicircular canals that contains the receptor cells that signal rotational acceleration and deceleration.

amygdala. A structure of the forebrain connected to the hypothalamus and involved in emotional behavior.

anagram. An apparently random group of letters that, when rearranged, form a meaningful word or phrase.

anal stage. According to Freud, the second stage of psychosexual development, during which the child's interest centers on anal activities.

analeptic. A stimulant that works on the central nervous system.

analgesic. A drug that works as a pain reliever.

analogue. A system that is similar enough in structure to another system so that data about the first can be applied to the second.

analytical psychology. A school of psychology founded by Carl Jung. The term can be applied to any school of psychology that reduces phenomena to their constituent elements.

androgen. The collective term for the male sex hormones.

anechoic room. An echo-free room.

anesthetic. A drug that acts either generally to induce unconsciousness or locally to deaden sensation.

anger. The emotional state arising from frustration.

animistic reasoning. Reasoning based on natural coincidences, such as when the observation that washing the car precedes a storm leads to the conclusion that the washing caused the storm.

anion. A negatively charged ion.

anomic suicide. According to Durkheim, one of the three kinds of suicide. It

occurs when an individual kills himself because of the feeling that the group or society from which he drew a sense of security has fallen apart and is no longer reliable. See also *altruistic suicide; egoistic suicide.*

anthropomorphism. Interpreting animal behavior in terms of human experiences.

antianxiety drugs. Psychotherapeutic drugs used chiefly to treat anxiety and neurotic conditions and to reduce stress.

antidepressant drugs. Psychotherapeutic drugs used chiefly to treat depression and phobic-anxiety states.

antidiuretic hormone (ADH). A hormone secreted by the posterior pituitary that enhances the retention of body water.

antipsychotic drugs. Psychotherapeutic drugs used chiefly to treat schizophrenia, manic-depressive states, and senile psychosis.

anxiety. Fear or apprehension.

anxiety, moral. According to Freud, anxiety that arises when one does something or thinks of doing something that is contrary to the moral code he learned from his parents.

anxiety, neurotic. According to Freud, the fear that the instincts will get out of control and cause the person to do something for which he will be punished.

anxiety, reality. According to Freud, anxiety caused by environmental threats.

anxiety reaction. A class of psychoneurosis characterized by acute anxiety.

apathy. Indifferent and listless behavior.

aphasia. Impaired or lost ability to speak resulting from brain damage.

apparent motion. Perception of motion in situations where no actual motion occurs.

apperception. Understanding of relationships between a presented object and the existing body of knowledge.

appetitive behavior. Seeking behavior.

applied psychology. The utilization of psychological discoveries and principles for practical ends.

approach-approach conflict. Conflict arising from the necessity to choose between two desirable but incompatible actions or objects.

approach-avoidance conflict. Conflict arising when a single action or object is simultaneously desirable and repellent.

apraxia. Impaired or lost ability to perform skilled movements, resulting from brain damage.

aptitude. Capacity for skillful performance on an as yet unlearned task. See also *ability.*

aptitude test. A test used to predict a

person's capacity to perform. See also *achievement test.*

aqueous humor. The fluid filling the interior chamber of the eye.

archetype. For Jung, the primeval content of the racial unconscious consisting of inherited predispositions and ideas.

arithmetic mean. The sum of all scores divided by the number of scores.

Army Alpha. A group intelligence test developed during World War I for classifying soldiers.

Army Beta. A group intelligence test developed during World War I for classifying soldiers.

Army General Classification Test (AGCT). A group intelligence test developed during World War II for classifying soldiers. Areas covered by the test include numerical, verbal, reasoning, and perceptual relations.

articulation. In speaking, the production of consonants.

assimilator. One who adjusts to the social demands made on him only insofar as they do not dominate his personal life and convictions. See also *accommodator.*

association areas. Areas of the brain not related directly to motor or sensory functions. They are believed to be the areas where sensations are associated to motor functions.

associative cells. Cells that intervene between sense perception and motor activities.

assortative mating. The tendency of either similar or dissimilar phenotypes to mate together.

asymptote. The limit that a graphic or mathematical function approaches but never reaches.

atmosphere effect. The tendency to reach a wrong conclusion in reasoning because of an impression created by the premises. For example, negative premises will tend to produce negative conclusions.

atrophy. A wasting away, as may occur in paralyzed muscles.

attention. The focusing of perception on a certain stimulus or stimuli while ignoring others.

attitude. A predisposition to respond positively or negatively to particular objects or issues.

attribute. A characteristic or fundamental property of a stimulus.

audiogram. A graph representing an individual's auditory sensitivity.

auditory canal. The canal connecting the outer ear with the eardrum. Also called the external auditory meatus.

auditory nerve. The nerve connecting the brain and the cochlea.

autism. A schizophrenic symptom characterized by absorption in fantasy to the exclusion of interest in reality.

autoerotic. Sexual activity involving only oneself, as in masturbation.

autogenic. Self-generated; having origins within the self.

autonomic nervous system. A network of nerve fibers that regulate the action of the smooth muscles and endocrine glands.

autonomous. Independent of others.

autonomous ego functions. According to ego analysts, ego functions that develop as a result of innate tendencies to learn certain functions in interaction with the environment.

aversive control. Negative reinforcement; achieved by using stimuli whose withdrawal reinforces behavior.

avoidance-avoidance conflict. Conflict arising from the necessity to choose between two undesirable actions or objects.

avoidance conditioning. A form of operant conditioning in which the introduction of a noxious stimulus is avoided by the correct response.

awareness. Consciousness; cognizance of one's surroundings.

axon. The portion of a neuron that transmits impulses from the cell body to adjacent neurons or to an effector.

azimuth. The angle between a location in space and a line passing forward through the center of the head, perpendicular to an imaginary line connecting the ears.

balance theory. The theory that when a person holds conflicting attitudes he ignores the problem, changes one of the attitudes, or redefines one of the attitudes.

basilar membrane. The membrane in the cochlea that supports the organ of Corti.

behavior. Any activity of an organism.

behavior disorders. A general term referring to all forms of disordered activities.

behavior genetics. The study of genetic influences on behavior.

behavior modification. See *behavior therapy.*

behavior therapy. A type of psychotherapy based on classical and operant conditioning methods.

behaviorism. The school of psychology that holds that the proper object of study in psychology is behavior alone, without reference to consciousness.

belongingness. Identification with a group and the feeling of being accepted by that group.

bestiality. Sexual intercourse between humans and animals.

binaural. Referring to the simultaneous use of two ears.

binaural differences. The small differences between the sounds reaching the two ears.

binaural interaction. The way in which the two ears influence what is heard.

binocular parallax. The incongruent views the two eyes receive because of their different positions in space.

bipolar cell. In the retina, a cell connecting the rods and cones with ganglion cells.

blind spot. The area in the retina that is insensitive to light.

blood sugar level. The proportion of glucose in the blood. Normally between 0.08 and 0.11 percent.

brain. The forward extension of the spinal cord encased in the skull. It is the center for sensory experience, learning, and thinking.

brightness. The psychological dimension of light dependent upon intensity.

brightness constancy. The tendency for objects to retain their relative brightness under various levels of illumination.

Broca's area. An area of the left cerebral hemisphere thought to be responsible for speech.

butyric acid. A chemical found in rancid butter and perspiration; responsible in part for body odor.

candle problem. A reasoning test requiring the subject to affix a candle to a cardboard wall in such a way that it does not drip wax on the floor. He is given matches and a box of tacks. The solution requires that he use an object or objects in an untypical way.

Cannabis sativa. A weed, sometimes known as Indian hemp, from which marijuana comes.

cardinal trait. A personality trait that is so pervasive that few of the person's activities are not influenced by it.

carotid artery. An artery feeding the brain.

castration complex. According to Freud, the infantile fear of losing the genitals in retaliation for forbidden sexual desires toward the parent of the opposite sex.

catatonic schizophrenia. A type of schizophrenia characterized by extreme lack of movement and maintained postures.

catch trial. In signal detection, a trial during which no signal is presented. It is used to aid in estimating an individual's response criterion.

catharsis. The release of tensions through

the expression of pent-up emotions or through the reliving of traumatic experiences.

cation. A positively charged ion.

Cattell 16 PF Inventory. A personality test that attempts to measure personality traits through factor analysis.

CCC. A group of three unrelated consonants (such as CFT and RGJ) used in studying memory and rote learning. See also *CVC syllables; nonsense syllables.*

central nervous system (CNS). The brain and the spinal cord. See also *peripheral nervous system.*

central sulcus. See *fissure of Rolando.*

central traits. Personality traits that represent tendencies characteristic of the individual.

cerebellum. A structure in the hindbrain regulating the coordination of bodily movements and balance.

cerebral arteriosclerosis. Hardening of the brain arteries.

cerebral cortex. The surface layer of the cerebrum.

cerebral hemispheres. The two symmetrical halves of the cerebrum that constitute the bulk of the brain in man.

cerebrum. The largest portion of the brain, consisting of two hemispheres. It contains centers that mediate sensory, motor, and conceptual activities.

chaffinch. An Old World finch, used by Hinde in motivation experiments.

channeling. Finding a new goal object for a drive.

character disorder. A behavioral disorder characterized by immaturity and antisocial reactions.

chemical senses. Smell and taste.

chemical transmitters. Chemicals released from the terminal points of axon filaments that diffuse across a fluid-filled space and induce electrical changes in the dendrite and cell bodies of the neurons with which they come in contact. See also *acetylcholine.*

chemotherapy. The treatment of mental disorders with drugs.

chinking. The characteristic cry of the chaffinch. See also *chaffinch.*

chlorpromazine. A tranquilizing drug.

choleric. A personality type characterized by a low threshold for outbursts of rage or anger.

cholinergic system. The part of the nervous system activated by acetylcholine transmitter substances. See also *adrenergic-cholinergic system.*

cholinesterase. An enzyme involved in the inactivation of acetylcholine.

choroid layer. The middle layer of the wall of the eyeball.

chromatic aberration. The failure of light rays to come to a single focal point because the various wavelengths are refracted differently as they pass through the lens of the eye.

chromatic colors. All colors other than black, white, and gray. See also *achromatic colors.*

chromosomal loci. Specific spots on a chromosome corresponding to genes.

chromosome trisomy. The carrying of a particular chromosome in triplicate rather than in duplicate, as in Down's syndrome (mongolism).

chromosomes. The chainlike structures within the nucleus of the cell that contain genes, the transmitters of hereditary traits.

chronological age. Age in years.

chunking. The process in human memory that groups items of information.

ciliary muscles. Muscles controlling the shape of the lens of the eye.

cingulate cortex. A portion of the limbic system that lies in the longitudinal fissure above the corpus callosum.

class. A collection of people having something in common, such as members of the Democratic Party, college students, or farmers.

classical conditioning. An experimental method in which a conditioned stimulus and an unconditioned stimulus are paired.

claustrophobia. An irrational fear of closed places.

client-centered therapy. A type of psychotherapy developed by Carl Rogers in which the therapist displays warmth and acceptance toward the patient, thus enabling the patient to take the initiative in resolving his problems.

clinical psychology. The branch of psychology concerned with the treatment of personality problems and mental disorders.

closure. The tendency for gaps to be perceived as filled in.

CNS. See *central nervous system.*

cochlea. The coiled cavity of the inner ear containing receptors for hearing.

codability, problem of. The notion that in some languages it may be easier to think or talk about certain phenomena because there are handy linguistic expressions with which to do so.

coding. The process whereby the nervous system transforms information about the environment into a particular pattern of nervous discharge.

cognition. An idea or thought.

cognitive dissonance. The inconsistency between the various thoughts and attitudes held by an individual. The desire to resolve cognitive differences is thought by some to be an important factor in human motivation.

cognitive map. Tolman's term for an or-

ganism's grasp of spatial relationships in the environment.

cohesiveness. The quality of grouping together or being mutually attracted.

cold spot. An area on the skin that is sensitive to cold stimuli.

collective unconscious. According to Jung, that part of the unconscious that is inherited and that predisposes mankind to behave as it has throughout history.

color blindness. A defect in vision characterized by partial or total inability to discriminate colors.

common fate. The principle that elements that are perceived to function, move, or change in the same way tend to be perceived as belonging together.

comparative psychology. The study of lower organisms in their relationships with each other and with man.

compensation. Counterbalancing failure in one area by excelling in another.

competence motivation. An individual's pursuit of active contact with, and mastery of, his environment as an end in itself.

complex. The form in which the contents of the collective unconscious are organized, according to Jung. Complexes are universal thought forms containing a large element of feeling.

compulsion. An irrational and irresistible impulse to perform some act repeatedly.

conation. Willing, acting, or striving.

concept formation. Initially, the mental process by which individual concretes are grouped into units on the basis of commensurable characteristics. In higher stages, already formed concepts take the place of concretes, and the process is repeated.

concordance rate. In genetics, the proportion of cases in which both members of a pair of relatives show the same expression of a trait, for example, color blindness or blood type.

conditioned reinforcing stimuli. See *secondary reinforcing stimuli.*

conditioning. See *classical conditioning; operant conditioning.*

conduction velocity. The speed with which an action potential moves along an axon. The minimum velocity is approximately 3 meters per second. The maximum is 100 meters per second.

conductive impairment. A cause of deafness involving pathology of the conductive mechanisms of the external or middle ear. See also *sensorineural impairment.*

cone. Visual receptors of the retina, found chiefly in the fovea. They are the receptors for color as well as achromatic sensations.

confabulation. The improvisation of

stories to compensate for lapse of memory.

conflict. The simultaneous arousal of two or more incompatible motives.

conformity. Response governed by prevailing attitudes and opinions.

consanguineous marriage. Marriage between blood relatives, usually cousins.

conscious awareness. Cognizance of the immediate environment.

consciousness. Conscious awareness.

constancy. The fact that an object perceived from different points of view still looks like the same object.

consummatory behavior. Behavior that fulfills a motive.

contact comfort. An emotional reaction based upon contact (usually with a mother or mother surrogate) that is reciprocally related to fear. As contact comfort rises, fear declines.

content-addressable storage system. A memory storage system in which the features of the items to be stored themselves determine where they will be stored. Human memory is probably a content-addressable storage system. See also pigeon-hole memories.

content validity. The success of a test in sampling the concepts and skills involved in a particular area.

contingent reinforcement system. A therapeutic program in which patients are rewarded for particular actions. See also token economy.

continuity. The quality of being without interruption in duration.

continuous reinforcement. Reinforcement of every occurrence of a response.

control group. A group used for comparison with an experimental group. It undergoes the same experiences as the experimental group, with the exception that the independent variable is not applied to the control group.

convergence. Turning the eyes inward as the object viewed is brought closer to the viewer.

convergent and discriminant validity. See validity.

conversion reaction. A form of hysteria characterized by physical symptoms in the absence of any organic pathology.

convulsive therapies. Any form of somatic therapy that utilizes induced convulsions.

core elements (of the individual). The central motivational properties of the individual.

cornea. The transparent bulge in the outer layer of the eyeball through which light waves enter.

corpus callosum. A band of nerve fibers connecting the two cerebral hemispheres.

correlation. The relationship between two variables as measured by the correlation coefficient.

correlation coefficient. A statistical index for measuring correspondence in changes occurring in two variables. Perfect correspondence is +1.00; no correspondence is 0.00; perfect correspondence in opposite directions is −1.00.

correlational method. A type of psychological investigation in which the interrelationships among response measures are sought.

cortex. A layer of cells near the surface of any organ; an outer covering.

counterconditioning. The replacement of a particular response to a stimulus by the establishment of an incompatible response to the same stimulus.

counterforce. In psychoanalytic theory, that which interferes with the free flow of associations.

covert behavior. Unobservable behavior.

cranial nerves. The peripheral nerves running to and from the brain stem.

creative self. Adler's conception of the self. It is a personalized subjective system that meaningfully interprets the experiences of the organism. Adler's self searches for experiences that will aid in fulfilling a person's unique style of life, and if these cannot be found, the self tries to create them.

creativity. The seeking and discovering of new relationships and new solutions to problems.

credibility. Believability.

crista. The structure of the inner ear that supports the ampulla and contains the receptor hair cells.

criterion. The indicator of performance in real life against which a psychological test is evaluated.

critical band. The band of noise at a given frequency that contributes to masking. The band is narrow at low frequencies but widens at higher frequencies.

crossing over. During meiosis, the breaking, exchanging of parts, and recombining of chromosomes.

crucial stage. The third of the three stages of alcoholism, according to Jellinek. In this stage the subject drinks compulsively, often for days or weeks at a time. He feels a powerful need for alcohol when deprived of it. See also prealcoholic stage; prodromal stage.

cultural anthropology. The branch of anthropology that studies the structure and function of societies.

cumulative record. In operant conditioning, a graphic record of the responses of a subject.

cunnilingus. Oral stimulation, of the female genitals.

cupula. In the inner ear, a gelatinous mass inside the ampulla. Its movement bends the endings of the receptor hair cells.

curare. A drug that immobilizes the organism. It is used in experiments in perceptual learning.

curiosity. The tendency to explore, seek, and investigate.

cutaneous. Pertaining to the skin or skin sensation.

CVC syllables. Nonsense syllables formed with a vowel between two consonants. Also known as trigrams. See also CCC; nonsense syllable.

cytogenetics. The direct microscopic study of chromosomes.

cytoplasm. The substance of a cell outside the nucleus.

cytosine. A component of DNA.

dark adaptation. Adjustment of the eye to low levels of illumination.

daughter cell. Either of the two new cells that remain after cell division.

dB. See decibel.

death instinct. According to Freud, a basic instinct of an aggressive-destructive nature, originating from the unconscious wish to return to the inorganic.

decibel (dB). A measure of the intensity of sound, having a logarithmic relation to amplitude.

defense mechanism. A reaction to frustration or conflict in which the individual deceives himself about his real motives and goals to avoid anxiety or loss of self-esteem.

déjà vu. The feeling that what is now happening has happened before.

delayed-reaction method. An experimental technique in which the subject is required to respond to a stimulus some time after it has been removed.

delusion. A false belief, often a symptom of paranoid schizophrenia.

dendrite. The extension of a neuron that serves to receive impulses from other neurons.

denial. A defense mechanism in which the subject rejects those events or aspects of events that he finds unpleasant.

deoxyribonucleic acid (DNA). The complex molecules of which genes are composed. DNA is thought to be the mechanism for genetic inheritance.

dependent variables. Variables that change in response to the independent variable. In psychology, the dependent variable is behavior.

depressive reaction. A psychoneurotic reaction resulting from severe loss. It is characterized by extreme unhappiness and depression.

depth perception. The perception of the distance of objects from the observer.

dermatome. The area of skin served by a particular sensory nerve.

dermis. The inner layer of the skin.

descriptive statistics. A simplified method of summarizing measurements. Descriptive statistics include the number of subjects; measurements of the average, including the mean, median, and mode; and measurements of variability, including range and standard deviation.

desensitization. A weakening of a response with repeated exposure to a situation. In psychotherapy, a method used to enable a person to become comfortable in a situation that previously evoked fear or anxiety.

design error. An error that occurs when the experimenter measures something that does not exactly coincide with what he wants to measure, as with a psychologist who studies dreams by using reports of the dreams written after they have occurred.

detour problem. See *Umweg problem.*

developmental psychology. The psychological study of the development and maturation of the individual from conception to adulthood.

deviation. A departure from normal.

diabetogenic hormone. A hormone secreted by the anterior pituitary that acts upon the pancreas.

diadic group. See *dyad.*

difference threshold. See *just-noticeable difference.*

diffraction. The bending of a sound or light wave by a lens or obstacle.

diphthong. Two vowels combined to make one sound.

discrimination training. Training an organism to respond differently to each of two similar but distinct stimuli.

displacement. The transference of an emotional attachment from its proper object to a replacement.

displacement activity. Inappropriate behavior when instinctive reactions are in conflict.

dissociation. A neurotic reaction in which the individual dissociates himself from the conflicts troubling him. It often takes the form of amnesia or multiple personality.

dissonance. See *cognitive dissonance.*

distribution of practice. The way in which practice is distributed over time.

dizygote twins. Twins that develop from two separate eggs; fraternal twins.

DNA. See *deoxyribonucleic acid.*

Dodd's law. The law stating that the number of communicative acts between any two centers with populations P_1 and P_2 and D miles apart is equal to k $(P_1 \times P_2)/D$, where k is the constant of proportionality.

dominance hierarchy. The hierarchy into which social animals usually organize themselves in a natural situation, the more dominant animals controlling the less dominant ones by mere threats.

dominant gene. A gene whose hereditary characteristics always prevail. See also *recessive gene.*

dorsal surface. The back surface of an organism.

double blind. An experimental design used primarily in drug research in which neither the investigator nor the patients know which group is drugged and which is not, or which drug is being administered.

double helix. The form in which the chemical components of DNA are arranged.

Down's syndrome. A congenital physical condition associated with mental retardation and characterized by such morphological features as thickness and fissuring of the tongue, flattening of the face, and slanting of the eyes (mongolism). See also *chromosome trisomy.*

Draw-a-Person test. An expressive test of personality popularized by Machover. It requires simply that the subject draw a person and afterward draw a second person of the opposite sex.

drive. An aroused condition in which the organism's behavior is directed toward eliminating deprivation or escaping a noxious stimulus.

drive-reduction theory. The theory that all motivated behavior arises out of drives and that the satisfaction of a drive promotes learning.

drosophila. A genus of small two-winged flies used extensively in genetic experiments.

duodenum. The upper portion of the small intestine that connects with the stomach.

dyad. A two-person group.

eardrum. A membrane between the outer ear and the inner ear that vibrates when sound waves reach it.

eccentric cells. In the visual nervous system, neurons whose axons form the optic nerve.

echolocation. The process used by bats to orient themselves while flying. It involves emitting high-frequency sounds that bounce back from obstacles, thus locating them for the bat.

ecology. The study of organisms in relation to their natural environments.

ectomorphy. One of the three body types identified by Sheldon; typically tall, thin, and fragile. See also *endomorphy; mesomorphy.*

educational psychology. The application of psychological methodology to the problems of education.

EEG. Electroencephalogram or electroencephalograph.

effectors. Muscles and glands.

efferent. Conducting nerve impulses away from the brain or spinal cord.

ego. According to Freud, that part of the personality that corresponds most closely to the perceived self. It functions by reconciling the conflicting forces of the id and superego.

egocentricity. Irrational and excessive preoccupation with the self.

egoistic suicide. According to Durkheim, one of the three kinds of suicide. It occurs when an individual is unable to integrate himself into society and chooses death rather than being without a meaningful place in the group. See also *altruistic suicide; anomic suicide.*

electroconvulsive shock therapy (EST). A form of therapy used chiefly with depressed patients in which high-voltage current is passed through the head, producing convulsions and unconsciousness.

electrodes. Conductors used to establish electric contact.

electroencephalogram (EEG). A graphic record of the electric activity of the brain obtained by placing electrodes on the skull.

electrolyte. A substance such as salt that, when dissolved in water, becomes an ionic conductor.

electromagnetic radiation. Light, radio waves, X rays, and cosmic rays.

electromagnetic spectrum. The entire frequency range of electromagnetic radiation.

electron microscope. A microscope that uses a beam of electrons to enlarge the image.

electroretinogram (ERG). A graphic record of the electrical activity of the eye when it is exposed to light.

electroshock therapy. See *electroconvulsive shock therapy.*

elicited behavior. Behavior produced by known stimuli in a reflex manner. See also *emitted behavior.*

emergency reactions. The visceral changes accompanying states of intense emotional excitement. Cannon views these changes as preparations for concerted action, either flight or fight.

emitted behavior. Behavior with no known eliciting stimuli. See also *elicited behavior.*

Emmert's law. The law that states that the perceived size of an afterimage

683

varies directly with the distance at which it is seen.

emotion. Visceral changes (chiefly in the autonomic nervous system and the endocrine system) that result from the subject's value-response to a given stimulus. Emotions are the physiological forms in which men experience their estimate of the harmful or beneficial effects of stimuli.

empathy. The realization, understanding, and vicarious participation in another person's feelings and attitudes.

enactive representation. According to Bruner, one of the three modes of representation. It is representation by action, "muscle imagery." See also *ikonic representation; symbolic representation.*

encounter. In existential theory, the impingement of the patient's world on the therapist.

encounter group. An intensive group that emphasizes development and improvement in interpersonal communication.

endocrine gland. A ductless gland that secretes hormones into the bloodstream or lymph system.

endogenous factors. Factors affecting an organism's behavior originating within the organism or biological group to which it belongs. See also *exogenous factors.*

endolymph. A liquid within the membranous canal in the semicircular canals of the inner ear.

endomorphy. One of the three body types identified by Sheldon; typically round, corpulent, and obese. See also *ectomorphy; mesomorphy.*

engram. The physiological change that occurs in the nervous system after an experience and that is responsible for memory. Also known as a memory trace.

environmental planning. Social and economic planning with the goal of modifying social institutions in such a way that human suffering is minimized.

enzyme. An organic catalyst that regulates chemical steps in metabolism.

epidermis. The outer layer of the skin.

epigenesis. The theory that in embryonic development properties are developed out of intracellular interaction and prenatal environmental influences.

epiglottis. An elastic cartilage projecting upward between the tongue and glottis.

epinephrine. A hormone secreted by the adrenal medulla that stimulates the sympathetic nervous system.

epithelium. Thin cell layers covering the body, organs, and inner surfaces.

EPSP. See *excitatory postsynaptic potential.*

ERG. See *electroretinogram.*

ergotism. A disease characterized in its early stages by psychological disorientation and malaise. It progresses to serious physical disorders and, finally, death.

erogenous zones. Those areas of the body particularly responsive to sexual stimulation.

eros. In Freudian theory, the sexual instinct, comprising the instincts for self-preservation and reproduction. Its energy is called libido.

error of expectation. An error in psychophysical testing, involving ascending or descending series, in which the subject reports receiving a stimulus before he actually does because he has been warned it is coming.

error of habituation. An error in psychophysical testing, involving ascending and descending series, in which the subject continues to report receiving stimulation after it is no longer present.

escape conditioning. A form of operant conditioning in which a noxious stimulus is removed after the correct response. See also *avoidance conditioning.*

ESP. See *extrasensory perception.*

EST. See *electroconvulsive shock therapy.*

esteem need. According to Maslow, an organismically based need that includes the desires for achievement, independence, freedom, reputation, and prestige.

ethogram. A descriptive study of the component parts and interrelationships of the behavior patterns of animals.

ethology. The branch of zoology concerned with the study of animal behavior.

Euler's circles. See *Venn diagrams.*

euphoria. A psychological state of extreme optimism and well-being, physically characterized by heightened motor activity.

evocative psychotherapy. Therapy that seeks to evoke an internal change in order to bring about external change.

evoked potential. Electric activity in some area of the nervous system produced by stimulation elsewhere.

excitatory postsynaptic potential (EPSP). Electric potential in the second of two cells at a synapse caused by depolarization.

exhaustion. The third stage of the general adaptation syndrome. See also *general adaptation syndrome.*

exhibitionism. The compulsive tendency to achieve sexual gratification from the exposure of the sex organs or other parts of the body.

existential psychology. A psychological system that emphasizes being rather than essence and freedom rather than determinism.

exocrine gland. A gland that secretes fluids through a duct upon a selected body surface.

exogenous factors. Factors affecting an organism's behavior but originating outside of the organism or biological group to which it belongs. See also *endogenous factors.*

experimental extinction. The gradual waning of the conditioned response achieved by repeated presentation of the conditioned stimulus without the unconditioned stimulus.

experimental group. In experimentation, a group subjected to an independent variable whose effect is under investigation. See also *control group.*

experimental method. A scientific method characterized by discovering information by means of controlled experiments.

experimental psychology. The study, using controlled, systematic, scientific methodology, of an organism's interaction with its environment.

expressive problems. Problems dealing with underlying feelings, such as anxiety and aggression.

extinction. The experimental procedure of no longer reinforcing responses previously reinforced. The responses decrease in frequency.

extinction curve. A graph showing the gradual decrease of no longer reinforced responding over time.

extrasensory perception (ESP). Perception supposedly not mediated by known sensory channels.

extravert. An outward-oriented personality. One who prefers the company of others. See also *introvert.*

facilitator. The leader of a group whose responsibility is the facilitation of the expression of both feelings and thoughts on the part of group members.

factor analysis. A statistical method used in test construction and in interpreting scores of such tests, designed to reveal patterns of correlation and to isolate the factors that contribute to a complex trait.

false alarm. Mistaken detection.

false negative. In lie detection, the tendency for some individuals to show almost no reaction even when it is known that they have been involved in a crime.

false positive. In lie detection, the tendency of some individuals to show a heightened activity when there is little cause for concern.

family group. A type of intensive-group experience in which several different families join in one group, with parents learning from their own and others' children and vice versa.

fantasy. Daydreaming and imagining a world of one's own, often as a defense mechanism.

feature extraction. In sensory analysis, the process of isolating important features of the physical signals.

feedback system. A system that uses return information to regulate its own activity (as a thermostat).

feeling. A term often used to indicate an emotion of low intensity.

fellatio. Oral stimulation of the male genitals.

fetishism. A form of sexual deviation in which stimulation is derived from inanimate objects rather than from other people.

fibril. A filament running through the cell body of a neuron and outward through the peripheral processes.

figure-ground perception. Perception of objects, patterns, or events as standing out clearly from a background.

firing. The triggering of electric impulses through a nerve cell.

fissure. A crevice in the cerebral cortex. See also *sulcus.*

fissure of Rolando. The central fissure of each cerebral hemisphere, situated between the frontal and parietal lobes.

fissure of Sylvius. A deep fissure in the side of each cerebral hemisphere and above the temporal lobe.

fixation. Stereotyped repetitive responding.

fixed-action pattern. In ethology, a stereotyped, consistently similar act.

fixed-interval schedule. A reinforcement schedule in which a response is reinforced after a fixed time interval.

fixed-ratio schedule. A reinforcement schedule in which a response is reinforced after a fixed number of responses have occurred.

follicle-stimulating hormone (FSH). A hormone secreted by the anterior pituitary.

following response. The response developed in the young of many species to follow the first large moving object they see.

foot-candle. The amount of illumination produced by a candle at a distance of one foot.

forced choice. A memory-searching procedure in which the subject is shown several items but told that only one is the correct choice.

forebrain. The forward part of the brain, comprising the thalamus, hypothalamus, and cerebrum.

forgetting. A loss of retention of previously learned materials.

fovea. The central area of the retina containing only cones. It is the point of highest visual acuity.

frame of reference. A background or context against which judgments are made.

fraternal twins. See *dizygotic twins.*

free association. A test in which the subject responds to a stimulus word with the first word that comes to mind.

frequency. The number of cycles per second of a wave.

frequency distribution. A distribution showing the frequency with which each particular score occurs in a population of scores.

frequency polygon. A graphic representation of a frequency distribution.

frigidity. In the female, inability to experience sexual arousal or gratification.

frontal lobe. The portion of each cerebral hemisphere located in front of the central fissure.

frustration. The state resulting from the blocking of an ongoing, goal-directed sequence of behavior.

frustration-aggression hypothesis. The theory that frustration produces a tendency toward aggression and that aggression is traceable to frustration.

FSH. See *follicle-stimulating hormone.*

functional autonomy. The theory that behavior that has often led to reward may become rewarding in itself, even though it no longer produces the original reward.

functional fixedness. The inability to perceive familiar objects in unfamiliar uses. See also *candle problem; two-string problem.*

GABA. See *gammaaminobutyric acid.*

galvanic skin resistance. Electrical resistance in the skin. The change of this resistance (detected by a galvanometer) serves as an emotional indicator.

galvanic skin response (GSR). A change in the electrical resistance of the skin.

gamete. A sex cell; an egg or sperm.

gammaaminobutyric acid (GABA). A substance found in mammalian brains that may serve as an inhibitory transmitter.

ganglion. A group of nerve cells whose cell bodies are located outside the central nervous system.

ganglion cell. In the retina, nerve cells whose axons are the fibers of the optic nerve.

Ganzfeld. A completely homogenous visual field.

GATB. See *General Aptitude Test Battery.*

gating. See *sensory gating.*

gene. The elementary unit of heredity, carried on the chromosomes. See also *dominant gene; recessive gene.*

gene pool. The totality of alleles carried by members of a breeding population; the population genotype.

gene transmission. The mechanisms by which genes are transmitted from parent to offspring.

general adaptation syndrome. Selye's phrase describing the generalized reaction of the body to a large number of specific stimuli causing emotional stress. The stages of the reaction are alarm, resistance, and exhaustion.

General Aptitude Test Battery (GATB). A set of aptitude tests developed by the U.S. Employment Service designed to make it possible for a client to find out whether or not he meets minimum standards for a number of occupations.

general paresis. A condition associated with syphilitic damage to the central nervous system. Among the symptoms is a loss of recent memory.

generalized reinforcer. A stimulus that is paired with several different primary reinforcers.

generic. Having wide application.

genetic code. The means by which DNA molecules record genetic patterns.

genetics. The branch of biology concerned with the transmission of hereditary characteristics.

genital stage. In Freudian theory, a stage of psychosexual development characterized by heterosexual interest.

genotype. In genetics, the characteristics of an organism that are hereditarily determined and can be transmitted to offspring. Also, the traits or characteristics common to a biological group.

geotaxis. A preference for movement with or against the pull of gravity.

Gestalt psychology. The school of psychology that holds that the proper subject matter for psychology is behavior and experience as wholes. In perception, the study of the tendency of objects to be perceived as wholes or perceptual units.

Gestalt therapy. A therapeutic approach based on the principles of Gestalt psychology. It attempts to help patients form "meaningful configurations" by broadening their awareness of themselves and the world around them.

gland. An organ that secretes. See also *endocrine gland; exocrine gland.*

goal. The object or event toward which an organism strives.

gradient of generalization. The decrease

in strength of response that corresponds to the decrease in similarity to the original stimulus of the stimulus presented. Usually plotted on a curve. See also *stimulus generalization*.

graduated reciprocation in tension reduction (GRIT). Osgood's model of bargaining and negotiation that assumes that concessions by one party to a conflict will be reciprocated, to which gradually larger concessions and reciprocations are added until the conflict is resolved.

GRIT. See *graduated reciprocation in tension reduction*.

group. A collection of individuals who are in an interdependent relationship with one another. "Interdependent" can mean either interaction or the sharing of common norms of behavior and attitude coupled with certain expectations regarding behavior toward others in the group.

group structure. The differentiation of roles and role relations within a group.

group test. A test that can be administered to many persons at the same time.

group therapy. Treatment of several patients simultaneously.

grouping. The tendency to perceive objects in groups.

GSR. See *galvanic skin response*.

guanine. A component of DNA.

gustation. The sense of taste.

gyrus. A ridge in the cerebral cortex. See also *sulcus*.

habituation. The process of becoming accustomed to a particular set of circumstances.

hair cell. Any of the pressure-sensitive cells located in the organ of Corti that convert sound waves to nerve impulses.

hallucination. Sensory experience for which there is no external stimulus.

hallucinogen. A drug that produces hallucinations.

handedness. The tendency to use either the right or the left hand predominantly.

Hardy-Weinberg law. The principle that, within a given gene pool, as long as matings occur at random, the relative frequencies of particular alleles and genotypes will remain constant in succeeding generations.

hashish. See *marijuana*.

hebephrenic schizophrenia. A type of schizophrenia characterized by immature and regressive, agitated behavior.

hedonic theory of motivation. The theory that all behavior is either directed toward approaching stimuli associated with pleasure or avoiding stimuli associated with unpleasant emotions. This theory holds that emotion is the key to understanding human motivation.

hemispheric dominance. The tendency for one half of the brain to have greater control over the body than the other half.

Henning's smell prism. A method of classifying odors based upon six supposedly pure qualities.

heroin. An addictive narcotic derived from morphine.

hertz (Hz). Cycles per second; the measure of the frequency of sound waves.

heterogeneous summation. The combined effects of different stimulus components.

heterozygous. A gene pair containing a dominant and a recessive gene.

heuristic method. A limited problem-solving method in which a solution may be reached through broad generalizations, trial and error, analogies, and other procedures. See also *algorithm*.

hierarchy. The arrangement of objects, persons, values, or elements in an order based upon criteria such as importance, dominance, or ability.

high. The euphoric state usually associated with the intake of such drugs as marijuana.

hindbrain. That portion of the brain that includes the medulla, cerebellum, and pons.

hippocampus. A curved nerve tract located in the forebrain believed to function in olfactory and visceral processes, which may play a part in memory-storage processes.

holism. The theory that behavior of an organism cannot be explained solely in terms of the behavior of the parts.

Holtzman inkblot technique. A personality test derived from the Rorschach. It combines careful standardization with highly reliable scoring.

homeostasis. The condition of physiological equilibrium within an individual.

homogenization. The term Wrightsman used to describe the tendency of members of a group to become more similar in their anxiety level than they had been before taking part in the group.

homologous pairs. Relating to chromosomes, the fact that pairs of chromosomes are similar in structure but different in the genes they carry.

homosexuality. Sexual intercourse with or attraction toward a member of the same sex.

homozygous. A gene pair containing either two dominant or two recessive genes.

hormone. A substance produced and secreted by any of the endocrine glands.

House-Tree-Person projective technique. An expressive test devised by Buck requiring the subject to a draw a house, tree, and person, in that order.

hue. The scientific term for color. It is determined mainly by the wavelength of light.

human nature. The innate characteristics of all mankind.

hybridization. The production of offspring by parents belonging to two different species or genotypes.

hydrotherapy. Therapeutic treatment by means of water packs, baths, and hot-water bottles.

hyperthyroid. An accelerated metabolic rate caused by excessive secretion of the thyroid gland.

hypnosis. A dreamlike state in which a person is extremely susceptible to suggestion.

hypnotic age regression. A hypnotic technique in which the subject is instructed to "go back" to early childhood in memory.

hypnotic drugs. Drugs used to treat insomnia and anxiety by inducing depression and sleep.

hypophysis. See *pituitary gland*.

hypothalamus. The portion of the forebrain below the thalamus that serves as a mediator between the brain and the body, helping control many motivational and emotional processes, including hunger, sleep, thirst, body temperature, and sexual behavior.

hypothyroid. A subnormal metabolic rate caused by undersecretion of the thyroid gland.

hysteria. A form of psychoneurosis that includes conversion reaction and dissociative reactions.

Hz. See *hertz*.

id. According to Freud, that part of the personality consisting of primitive instincts toward sexuality and aggression. The id seeks immediate gratification regardless of the consequences but is held in check by the superego.

ideal self. That which the person would like to be.

identical twins. See *monozygotic twins*.

identification. The process by which a person takes over the features of another person and incorporates them into his own personality.

idiosyncratic. Peculiar to the individual.

ikonic representation. One of Bruner's three modes of representation. Ikonic representation utilizes visual imagery, as with maps.

illuminance. The intensity of light falling on a surface, measured in foot-candles.

illusion. A distorted or incorrect perception, as distinguished from hallucination, which is false perception.

impotence. In the male, inability to perform the sex act.

imprinting. Behavior attached to stimuli very early in life and generally not reversible. It occurs at critical stages of development.

incentive. The promise or hope of a goal object that will reduce or eliminate a drive.

incidental learning. Casual learning that takes place without incentive or reinforcement.

incus. One of the three bones of the middle ear. See also *malleus; stapes.*

independent variable. The variable that is controlled by the experimenter in order to determine its effect on the dependent variable.

individual difference. A difference in traits between an individual organism and other members of its species.

individual test. A psychological test designed to be given to only one person at a time.

individuation. Jung's term for the development of all parts of the personality.

indoctrination. Training with a goal of inducing complete, uncritical acceptance.

industrial psychology. The application of psychological methodology to industrial problems. Also called organizational psychology.

inferential statistics. Statistics used to make generalizations from measurements. See also *level of confidence; level of significance.*

inferiority complex. According to Adler, the characteristic feeling of inadequacy and insignificance that develops out of frustration in striving for superiority.

informal group. A group that is not highly organized.

information processing. The flow of information through a system.

infrared rays. Wavelengths lying outside the visible spectrum at the red end.

inhibition. The suppression of behavior.

innate releasing mechanism. In ethology, the mechanism that releases species-characteristic responses in the presence of the appropriate stimulus.

inner ear. The internal portion of the ear containing the cochlea, vestibular sacs, and semicircular canals.

innervation. The excitation of a motor unit by a nerve.

insight. In learning, the sudden grasping of the solution of a problem after much unfruitful thought and trial-and-error behavior.

instinct. Unlearned, biologically based behavior. In ethology, the term applies to complex, repetitive behavior specific to a species.

instinct derivative. A behavior that occurs when the energy of an instinct is diverted toward an object different than the one innately determined for that instinct.

instrumental conditioning. See *operant conditioning.*

insulin. A hormone secreted by the pancreas and involved in repleting blood sugar.

insult condition. A frustration test in which, upon completion of a purported intelligence test, subjects are chided and insulted as to their low intelligence. The subjects are then asked to report their reactions on a questionnaire. See also *personal frustration condition; task-frustration condition.*

intellectualization. A defense mechanism in which the individual analyzes his problem in purely intellectual terms without reference to emotions.

intelligence. The ability to conceptualize effectively and to grasp relationships.

intelligence quotient (IQ). An index to the rate of mental growth of a child obtained by dividing chronological age into a mental-age score achieved on a test, then multiplying by 100.

intelligence test. A test designed to measure intelligence.

intensity. A quantitative measure of strength or degree of a sensory experience.

intensive-group experience. A general term that encompasses groups in which individuals are taught to observe their interactions with others and the nature of the group process. See also *encounter group; sensitivity group; synanon; T-group.*

internal clock. The idea that each organism has some kind of internal representation of temporal durations.

interneuron. A neuron that connects sensory and motor neurons within the spinal cord.

interposition. A cue to depth perception occurring when a near object interrupts vision of a second object.

intervening variable. A hypothetical variable postulated to account for responses to stimuli.

intrapsychic forces. Forces within the mind.

introspection. The process of observing and reporting the content of one's own consciousness.

introvert. An inward-oriented personality; one who prefers his own thoughts and activities to associations with others. See also *extravert.*

intrusion. False recall.

inventory. A test for assessing the presence or absence of certain traits, behaviors, interests, attitudes, or values.

ion. An electrically charged particle.

IQ. See *intelligence quotient.*

IQ scale. A scale of IQ scores of which 100 is the average. See also *intelligence quotient.*

IQ score. See *intelligence quotient.*

iris. The set of autonomically controlled muscles that varies the amount of light entering the eye.

isogenic state. In inbreeding, the state in which all members of a strain are genetically identical.

isomorphism. In Gestalt psychology, the hypothesis that there is a point-for-point correspondence between a stimulus and excitatory fields in the cerebral cortex.

isotonic. A muscle contraction in which the muscle shortens.

James-Lange theory of emotion. A theory of emotion holding that emotional experience results from the physiological reaction to a stimulus.

jnd. See *just-noticeable difference.*

jump stand. An experimental device developed by Karl Lashley used in learning experiments; it consists of a platform from which the subject (usually a rat) must jump toward doors, each outfitted with distinctive stimuli.

just-noticeable difference (jnd). The smallest difference between two stimuli that can be detected dependably.

key-word system. A mnemonic system in which certain words (often rhymes) are associated with the items to be remembered.

kinesis. Behavior that is elicited, accelerated, and decelerated by experimental stimuli but that is not directly guided by these stimuli.

kinesthesis. Sensory impressions arising from tendons, muscles, and joints that provide information about the positions and movements of the body.

klinotaxis. A response in which the organism's behavior is guided by successive comparisons of two stimuli.

knee jerk. The involuntary response that occurs when the patellar tendon is tapped.

knowledge of results. A subject's knowledge of how well he has done in a learning situation. It generally aids performance.

koan. In Zen, a single question that may be the focus of concentration of an individual for years.

Korsakoff's syndrome. Symptoms associated with vitamin deficiency in chronic alcoholics. Persons suffering from this condition suffer loss of recent memory.

Krause bulbs. Sensory receptors thought to respond to cold.

labyrinth. The inner ear, particularly the vestibulary structures.

language. An abstract system of word meanings and syntactic structures that facilitate communication.

larynx. The upper part of the windpipe containing the vocal cords.

latency period. According to Freud, the stage in psychosexual development that follows the phallic stage and during which the sexual drives become temporarily dormant.

latent learning. Learning that is not evident until a situation arises in which it can be used.

lateral geniculate. An area of the brain to the rear of the thalamus related to vision.

lateral hypothalamic feeding-drinking area. An area of the brain near the ventromedial nucleus related to feeding and drinking processes. Destruction of this area will cause an animal to stop drinking and eating completely.

lateral inhibition. In the limulus eye, inhibition via lateral neural connections among the eccentric cells, causing an analogue of Mach bands. See also *Mach bands.*

law of effect. The law that holds that if behavior is reinforced it will tend to repeat itself.

law of independent assortment. Mendel's second law of inheritance, which describes the simultaneous inheritance of two or more traits.

law of segregation. Mendel's first law of inheritance. It maintains that each phenotype trait is governed by a separate pair of elements that divide and recombine when producing offspring.

learning. A relatively permanent modification of behavior resulting from reinforced practice.

learning to learn. Harlow's term for the cumulative effect of previous learning on the ease of subsequent learning of the same type.

lens. The structure in the eye that changes shape to focus images sharply on the retina.

lesbianism. Female homosexuality.

level of activation. The dimension in an emotion-rating scale that reflects the intensity of emotions (rated on a seven-point scale from active to passive). See also *pleasantness-unpleasantness dimension.*

level of confidence. In the *t* test, expression of the assurance with which a null hypothesis can be rejected, often expressed as a percentage. If the desired result could occur by chance one in twenty times, the level of confidence is 5 percent.

level of significance. In the *t* test, expression of the confidence with which a null hypothesis can be rejected, usually expressed as a decimal fraction. If the desired result could occur by chance one in twenty times, the level of significance is .05.

lexical. Pertaining to words and word formation.

LH. See *lutenizing hormone.*

libido. According to Freud, the energy of the sexual, life instincts.

lie detector. A device for detecting emotional responses during lies. It measures rate of breathing, heart rate, blood pressure, and galvanic skin response.

life instinct. According to Freud, those instincts such as hunger, thirst, and sex that maintain individual survival and propagation of the race. The form of energy by which they work is called libido.

light. The visible spectrum of electromagnetic radiation.

light adaptation. Adjustment of the eye to moderate or high levels of illumination.

limbic system. The central areas of the brain, including the hypothalamus, amygdala, septal area, and cingulate gyrus. The limbic system is related to the activities of the visceral organs and to emotional-motivational behavior.

limulus. Horseshoe crab.

linear perspective. A clue to depth perception based on the apparent convergence of lines and decrease in size of objects as the distance from the viewer increases.

linguistic determinism. The notion, closely related to linguistic relativity, that states that the structure of the individual's language determines, to some degree, his patterns of thought. See also *linguistic relativity.*

linguistic relativity. The notion, closely related to linguistic determinism, that holds that different languages have different effects upon thought. See also *linguistic determinism.*

linguistics. The investigation of the origin, structure, and effects of language.

lobotomy. See *prefrontal lobotomy.*

localization. In audition, the localization of sounds in space by means of the physical and temporal differences between the sounds arriving at the two ears.

locus. A specific place on an organ or the body's surface.

logotherapy. Frankl's form of existential psychology, which emphasizes man's search for meaning.

long-term memory (LTM). The "permanent" information-storage system of the human mind, as opposed to short-term memory.

loudness. A psychological dimension of sound related to sound pressure. See also *sound pressure.*

love needs. According to Maslow, the needs to possess affectionate relationships with other people and to belong to a wider group.

LSD (lysergic acid diethylamide). A psychedelic drug chemically derived from lysergic acid. It causes quasi-psychotic symptoms that may be similar to those of schizophrenia.

LSD trip. The state following intake of the drug LSD.

LTM. See *long-term memory.*

lumbar region. The center of the back.

luminance. Light energy from a given source.

lutenizing hormone (LH). A hormone secreted by the anterior pituitary that acts on the ovaries in the female.

lymphatic system. A system, similar to the blood system, that carries lymph, a plasma fluid, to the various parts of the body.

lysergic acid. $C_{15}H_{15}N_2COOH$. A crystalline tetracyclic acid obtained by hydrolysis from ergotic alkaloids. See also *LSD.*

Mach bands. In vision, the bands that appear along the border of two areas of different intensity. A bright band appears on the lighter side and a dark band on the darker side. They are thought to result from lateral inhibition. See also *lateral inhibition.*

macula acustica. The hair cells and supporting cells of the utricle and saccule.

macula lutea. The central retinal area, containing the fovea, where visual acuity is best.

magicophenomenalistic stage. According to Piaget, a stage in the child's development in which he thinks he is the sole cause of certain physical events.

magnitude estimation. A sensation-measurement procedure in which subjects assign numbers to stimuli proportional to one of their attributes, such as loudness.

maladjustment. Inability to behave in a manner harmonious with the environment.

malevolent transformation. According to Sullivan, a stage in childhood during which one feels that he is living among enemies.

Tell us what you think

All over the country today students are taking an active role in the quality of their education. They're telling administrators what they like and what they don't like about their campus communities. They're telling teachers what they like and what they don't like about their courses.

This response card offers you a unique opportunity as a student to tell a publisher what you like and what you don't like about his book.

Student Response Card

We care about your opinion of *Psychology Today: An Introduction*. It took us a lot of time and effort to produce, and the best we could do at the time went into it. But we know it can be improved. Any textbook can be improved. What we don't know is where you think the improvements should be made. What are your general impressions?

May we get back to you for more specific comments? We'd like to send you a detailed questionnaire that will take about half an hour to fill out. We need your guidance, and if you'll serve us through our questionnaire as a consultant in the evaluation of *Psychology Today: An Introduction*, we'd like to offer you a choice of books—free—from the Psychology Today Book Club in return.

Name_____ Date _____

Address *(good for the next three months)*:

_____

_____

City_____State_____Zip_____

Thanks. We'll try to get the questionnaire to you by return mail.   Q108

THIS FLAP IS GUMMED | JUST FOLD, SEAL, AND MAIL | NO STAMP NECESSARY *malleus.* One of the three bones of the middle ear. See also *incus; stapes.*

mandala. A symbol taken from Hindu writings by Jung. It is a circle representing the unity of the self and is used as an object for meditation.

manic-depressive psychosis. A psychotic reaction characterized by extreme variation in mood, from a highly elated state to depression and back and forth.

manic reactions. Violent, uncontrollable excitement and impulsiveness.

mantra. A sonorous word repeated over and over. Used in some forms of Yoga for meditation.

marathon groups. Intensive therapy groups that meet continually for twenty-four hours or more.

marijuana. A drug derived from the hemp plant Cannabis sativa. Intake may tend to enhance sensory input and produces a state of euphoria.

masking. The effect of one sound's raising the threshold of another sound.

masochism. A pathological state in which the individual derives sexual gratification from having pain inflicted upon himself.

masturbation. Achievement of sexual gratification by manual stimulation.

maturation. The completion of growth processes in the body and the accompanying behavioral changes.

maze. An experimental device used in the study of learning. It consists of a correct path and blind alleys.

mean. See *arithmetic mean.*

measure of central tendency. In testing, the measure of the average performance—usually the median, the mode, or the arithmetic mean.

measurement. The assignment of units of numbers to events, objects, or traits.

medial geniculate. One of the "relay stations" for sound between the ear and the auditory cortex.

median. The middle score when all the scores are arranged from highest to lowest.

meditation. Sustained, contemplative thinking.

medulla. The hindmost portion of the brain, connected to the spinal cord. It is concerned with regulating breathing, heartbeat, and blood pressure.

meiosis. The splitting of somatic cells, which forms gametes.

Meissner corpuscle. An organ found primarily on the surface of the skin, thought to mediate the sense of touch.

mel. The unit of pitch.

melancholia. Temperament characterized by depression and pessimism.

memory banks. A general term referring to that body of information that has been learned and retained.

memory trace. Believed by some to be a physical change in the nervous system that accompanies learning. It is thought to fade with time and lack of use.

memory transfer. The apparent transfer of learning by injecting untrained planaria with RNA from trained planaria. The untrained planaria subsequently exhibit the behavior learned by the trained worms.

Mendelian population. A community of interbreeding organisms that is reproductively isolated from other organisms of the same species.

mental age. A summary evaluation of an individual's mental attainment based upon testing. One who scores as well as the average twelve-year-old does is said to have a mental age of twelve, regardless of his actual age.

mental test. Any test designed to measure a psychological trait such as attention or intelligence.

mesomorphy. One of the three body types identified by Sheldon; typically muscular and well developed. See also *ectomorphy; endomorphy.*

messenger RNA. The RNA that determines which type of proteins the cell will produce at a given moment. See also *ribonucleic acid.*

metaneeds. According to Maslow, growth needs, including justice, goodness, beauty, order, and unity.

metapathologies. According to Maslow, pathologies that arise when metaneeds are not fulfilled. They include alienation, anguish, apathy, and cynicism. See also *metaneeds.*

methadone. A depressant drug used to reduce pain.

method of limits. A method for determining sensory thresholds in which stimuli are presented in increasing and decreasing orders of intensity.

midbrain. The middle section of the brain.

middle ear. That portion of the ear between the eardrum and the inner ear that contains the malleus, incus, and stapes.

millilambert. A unit of luminance.

minimum separable acuity. In vision, a term referring to an individual's ability to resolve lines at the greatest possible distance.

minimum visible acuity. In vision, a term referring to an individual's ability to detect a dark line against a light background at the greatest possible distance.

Minnesota Multiphasic Personality Inventory (MMPI). A widely used personality questionnaire.

mirror-image phenomenon. The tendency to identify with individuals and groups in a black and white picture, with oneself or one's group seen as good and the other side seen as bad.

miss. Complete failure of detection or recall in a psychological or memory experiment.

mitosis. A process of cell division involving the duplication of chromosomes and the production of two daughter cells.

MMPI. See *Minnesota Multiphasic Personality Inventory.*

mnemonic system of loci. A mnemonic system involving the formation of a pictorial image of that which is to be remembered.

mnemonics. A technique for remembering involving a set of memorized symbols that serve as attachment units for new stimuli. See also *key-word system; mnemonic system of loci; number-consonant alphabet.*

mode. A measure of central tendency. The most frequent score in a frequency distribution.

model. An object or area similar in structure to the object or area being investigated. Information about the model will yield information about the object of study.

mongolism. See *Down's syndrome.*

monozygotic twins. Twins that develop from the same egg. Identical twins.

mother archetype. According to Jung, an archetype of the mother that is inherited by everyone.

mother surrogate. A person or object that functions for the subject as though it were his mother.

motion parallax. The different relative motions that objects at different distances appear to have as a person moves his head.

motivation. A general term referring to factors within an organism that arouse and maintain behavior directed toward satisfying needs and drives.

motor area. The area of the cerebral cortex in front of the fissure of Rolando. Electrical stimulation of this area elicits bodily movement.

motor cells. Cells involved in the activation of the muscles and the glands.

motor skill. Any skill, such as walking or following a pursuit rotor, that requires muscular coordination.

Müller-Lyer illusion. A visual illusion utilizing two lines of equal length, the ends of one enclosed in acute angles and the ends of the other enclosed in obtuse angles. The obtuse angles make the second line appear longer.

multiple determination. The fact that specific behavioral responses often have more than one cause.

multivariate. Involving many nondependent variables.

mutation. Genetic inaccuracy.

myelin sheath. A white fatty covering on many neuron fibers.

myopia. Nearsightedness; the inability to clearly distinguish distant objects.

nAch. See *need for achievement.*

narcissism. In psychoanalytic theory, a developmental stage characterized by extreme concern with the self and little or no concern for others.

National Training Laboratories (NTL). A pioneer T-group whose thrust was in industrial areas. See also *T-group.*

natural leader. A well-liked member of a group who works with the formally appointed, more task-oriented leader.

naturalistic observation. Observation of naturally occurring events and situations in which the observer tries to remain inconspicuous.

Necker cube. An ambiguous graphic representation of a cube.

need. Physiologically, a lack or deficit within an organism.

need for achievement (nAch). The need to accomplish or attain goals for the sake of achieving.

negative correlation. A relationship between two variables in which high values in the first correspond to low values in the second and vice versa. See also *positive correlation.*

negative reinforcement. See *escape conditioning.*

negative transfer. The interfering effect of previous learning on learning in a new situation. See also *positive transfer.*

neonate. A newborn infant.

nerve cell. See *neuron.*

neuroglia. A class of cells in the brain whose function is unknown but believed to be that of supporting nerve cells.

neurohumors. Chemical substances that serve as transmitters of nervous activity.

neurohypophysis. The posterior pituitary.

neuromuscular junction. The point at which a motor neuron synapses with a muscle.

neurons. Specialized cells that transmit electrical activity from one region of the nervous system to another and to the muscles or glands.

neurosis. A mental disorder that prevents the victim from dealing effectively with reality. It is characterized by anxiety and partial impairment of functioning.

night blindness. Subnormal visual acuity in conditions of dim illumination. Often due to lack of vitamin A.

nominal scale. A scale in which numbers are simply assigned to persons or objects, as in numbering members of athletic teams.

nondirective therapy. See *client-centered therapy.*

nondisjunction. The failure of a pair of chromosome homologues to separate and be distributed to different gametes during meiosis.

nonsense syllable. Syllables constructed so as to resemble meaningful language as little as possible. They are used chiefly in studies of memory and rote learning. See also *CCC; CVC syllable.*

nonverbal communication. Communication by means other than language.

noradrenalin. See *norepinephrine.*

norepinephrine. A hormone believed to be the transmitter in some sympathetic synapses.

norm. An average score on a test, obtained after many persons have taken it. It provides a standard by which to compare later scores.

normal curve. The graphically plotted form of a normal frequency distribution.

noxious stimulus. An unpleasant stimulus or one that functions as a negative reinforcer.

NTL. See *National Training Laboratories.*

nucleotide bases. Four components of DNA (adenine, guanine, thymine, and cytosine).

nucleus. The differentiated, central portion of the cell.

number-consonant alphabet. A mnemonic system involving the translation of numbers into letters of the alphabet and the subsequent formation of words or phrases from the letters.

nymphomania. Pathologically extreme sexual desire in the female.

nystagmus. Involuntary back-and-forth movement of the eyes.

observer effects. Effects associated with a particular perspective or set of conditions.

obsession. A persistently recurring, disturbing thought.

obsessive-compulsive reaction. A neurotic reaction characterized by persistent repetition of some thought or act.

occipital lobe. The back portion of the cerebral hemisphere, containing the visual sensory areas.

octave. A pitch interval between two tones, the top tone having twice the frequency of the lower.

Oedipus complex. According to Freud, a complex that appears during the phallic stage. It consists of sexual attraction to the parent of the opposite sex and

hostility for the parent of the same sex.

Ohm's law. In audition, the law stating that the individual components of any complex sound can be heard.

olfaction. The sense of smell.

olfactory bulbs. Protrusions of the forebrain under the cerebrum that mediate the sense of smell.

olfactory epithelium. The membrane in the nasal cavity containing smell receptors.

ommatidia. The small visual receptors that make up compound eyes, such as those of the limulus.

ontogenetic development. Development of the individual from conception to death. See also *phylogenetic development.*

operant conditioning. The form of conditioning in which the organism's response is instrumental in obtaining reinforcement.

operators. See *pivot words.*

opiates. Drugs of the opium family. They usually work by depressing higher nervous centers and inducing a state of euphoria.

optics. The scientific study of the properties of light.

optokinetic nystagmus. See *nystagmus.*

oral stage. In psychoanalytic theory, the first stage of psychosexual development. In this stage gratification centers around the mouth and oral activities.

ordinal scale. A scale in which objects or qualities are ranked with ordinal numbers: first, second, third, and so forth.

ordinate. The vertical axis of a graph; usually used to plot the dependent variable. See also *abscissa.*

organ of Corti. The structure of the ear in the basilar membrane of the cochlea containing the receptors for hearing.

organic psychosis. A psychosis with a known physiological cause.

organismic psychology. The school of psychology that rejects the mind-body dichotomy and views psychology as the study of the organism as a unified, organized whole. See also *holism.*

organismically based needs. According to Maslow, those needs that men must satisfy in order eventually to reach self-actualization. He identified five levels of needs arranged in hierarchical order. See also *esteem needs; love needs; physiological needs; safety needs; self-actualization.*

organizational psychology. See *industrial psychology.*

originality. The ability to respond in previously untried manners.

osmolarity. The relative amount of salt contained in bodily fluids.

osmoreceptors. Areas in the brain sensitive to osmolarity and responsible in part for regulating water intake.

ossicles. Three bones in the middle ear through which sound is conducted from the eardrum to the cochlea.

otoliths. Stonelike particles contained above the macula in the inner ear; part of the vestibular sense.

otosclerosis. In the ear, a conductive impairment that occurs when bone forms around the stapes, resulting in deafness.

outer ear. That part of the ear that consists of the pinna and the external auditory canal.

oval window. The membrane through which sound waves are transmitted to the cochlea from the bones of the middle ear.

ovariectomy. Surgical removal of the ovaries.

overlearning. The process of continued practice after mastery in learning a set of materials.

overt behavior. Behavior observable by others.

oxytocin. A hormone secreted by the posterior pituitary; it is released during pregnancy to induce uterine contractions in the female mammal.

Pacinian corpuscle. A specialized nerve structure believed to be a receptor for pressure.

paired-associate learning. The learning of pairs of items, as tested by later presenting one of the items and asking the subject to recall the other.

pancreas. An endocrine gland that secretes insulin. It is located along the lower wall of the stomach.

papillae. Small bumplike structures such as those found covering the surface of the human tongue.

parabiotic twins. Siamese twin animals that are created artificially by surgery for experimental purposes.

paradoxical cold. The response of cold receptors in the skin to a warm stimulus.

parallax. The apparent movements of two objects in the field of vision, one closer than the other, which occurs when the head is moved from side to side.

paralytic drugs. Drugs that produce motor paralysis by acting at the neuromuscular junction.

paramecium. A protozoan.

paranoia. Psychotic behavior characterized by delusions of either grandeur or persecution.

paranoid schizophrenia. A form of schizophrenia characterized by paranoid reactions.

parasympathetic nervous system. A division of the autonomic nervous system that conserves body resources and controls many of the visceral organs.

parietal lobe. The portion of the cerebral hemisphere located behind the central fissure and between the occipital and frontal lobes.

part learning. Learning a task in small sections rather than as a whole unit.

passive stretch. Muscle tension as opposed to actual muscle movement.

patellar reflex. The involuntary response that occurs when the patellar tendon is tapped. Commonly known as the knee-jerk reflex.

patellar tendon. The tendon just below the kneecap that, when tapped, produces the knee-jerk reflex.

Pavlovian conditioning. See *classical conditioning.*

payoff matrix. In signal detection, the gains for reporting a signal correctly and the losses for reporting it incorrectly.

peak experiences. According to Maslow, the most wonderful experiences in one's life.

peak shift. The shift, due to discrimination training, of the peak of the gradient of generalization away from the stimulus associated with nonreinforcement.

pederasty. Oral-genital contact between a man and a boy.

pedophilia. Sexual attraction for children.

Peeping Tomism. See *voyeurism.*

peg system. See *key-word system.*

penis envy. In psychoanalytic theory, the point in the phallic stage of development at which the girl is envious of the more visible sexual organs of the boy.

percentile. A percentage indicating the level of scoring equaled or excelled.

perception. The awareness of one's environment obtained through interpreting sense data.

perceptual learning. Learning that occurs without overt responses.

perceptual readiness. Bruner's term for the tendency of an individual to see what he expects to see.

performance. Learning translated into action or behavior.

peripheral elements of the individual. Those characteristics acquired in the course of life.

peripheral nervous system. That part of the nervous system lying outside of the central nervous system.

periphery. In the eye, the retina, excluding the fovea.

personal equation. The time required for each specific person to react to something he observes.

personal frustration condition. A frustration test in which subjects are given a time limit in which to solve a jigsaw puzzle and are then purposely interfered with and prevented from reaching a solution within the time limit. See also *insult condition; task-frustration condition.*

personal unconscious. According to Jung, that part of the unconscious unique to the individual. It results from the repression of individual experience.

personality. An individual's characteristic pattern of behavior and thought.

personality adjustment tests. Tests that measure interests, aptitudes, values, and other areas of personality.

personality inventory. A questionnaire that measures an individual's appraisal of his own personality.

Personality Research Form (PRF). A personality questionnaire developed by Jackson that makes use of the digital computer in scale development.

perspective. A frame of reference from which a problem is viewed.

phallic stage. In psychoanalytic theory, the third stage of psychosexual development, during which gratification centers on the sex organs. The Oedipus complex also manifests itself during this stage.

phase. In sound, the point in a cycle of sinusoidal motion at a given instant, relative to some arbitrary reference point.

phenomenal field. That which is being experienced by an individual at a given moment.

phenomenology. The study of phenomena.

phenotype. In genetics, the observable characteristics of an organism.

phenylthiocarbamide (PTC). A chemical that, due to hereditary differences, can be tasted by some individuals and not by others.

phi phenomenon. See *apparent motion.*

phlegmatic. A personality type, characteristically sluggish and apathetic.

phobia. An irrational, strong fear.

phobic reaction. An anxiety state characterized by irrational fears.

phosphenes. Luminous sensations produced by pressure on the eyeball or electrical stimulation of the cornea.

photic driving. The application, by use of visual stimuli, of rhythmic stimulation to the brain and the synchronization of brain response with the frequency of the flashes.

photochemicals. Light-sensitive chemicals found in visual receptors.

photon. A measure of amount of light energy. Also, a "particle" of light.

photopic vision. Vision at normal intensity levels mediated by cones.

phylogenetic development. The psychological and physiological changes that occur as one moves from simple to complex organisms.

physiological needs. According to Maslow, needs that fill some physical deficit in the body, such as hunger, thirst, and sleep.

pigeon-hole memories. Memory storage systems in which material is compartmentalized in a system similar to post office pigeon holes.

pinna. The commonly visible portion of the outer ear.

pitch. The psychological attribute of sound correlated with frequency. High frequencies yield high pitch; low frequencies, low pitch.

pituitary gland. The endocrine gland located centrally in the head and consisting of anterior and posterior parts. Also known as the hypophysis.

pivot words. In the development of speech in children, the first or second word of a two-word sentence that the child is able to combine with a variety of other words.

placebo. An inert preparation often used as a control in experiments.

planarian. A flatworm.

play therapy. A type of psychotherapy for children utilizing play and fantasy construction.

pleasantness-unpleasantness dimension. The evaluative dimension of an emotion-rating scale. It involves rating various emotions on a seven-point scale from "good" to "bad." See also *level of activation.*

pleasure principle. In Freudian theory, the tendency to satisfy id impulses.

polarization. The treatment of light so that all waves oscillate parallel to a single axis.

polygenic traits. Traits that depend on the combined effect of many genes acting together.

pons. The upper portion of the hindbrain.

Ponzo illusion. A visual illusion utilizing linear perspective.

population. In statistics, the total group from which a sample of scores is drawn.

population genetics. The study of the relations between the distribution of genes and the distribution of individual differences in trait expression in Mendelian populations.

positive correlation. A relationship between two variables in which high values in the first correspond to high values in the second and low values in the first correspond to low values in the second. See also *negative correlation.*

positive transfer. The positive effect of previous learning on learning in a new situation. See also *negative transfer.*

positivity effect. Deutsch and Solomon's term for the tendency to like people who say nice things about us.

postcentral gyrus. A ridge located behind the fissure of Rolando. It is the primary receiving area for the skin senses.

prealcoholic stage. The first of the three stages of alcoholism, according to Jellinek. The subject discovers that alcohol eases psychological pressure and induces self-confidence. See also *crucial stage; prodromal stage.*

precedence effect. The suppression of the numerous echoes and reverberations that usually accompany a sound.

predictive ability. The ability of a test to predict performance on a later task.

prefrontal area. The anterior portion of the frontal lobe of the brain.

prefrontal lobotomy. The surgical severing of the pathways leading from the frontal association areas.

pregenital stages. In psychoanalytic theory, the oral, anal, and phallic stages of psychosexual development.

premises. Basic assumptions from which one begins reasoning about a given subject.

prenatal environment. The environment before birth.

press. H. A. Murray's term for an object or demand in the environment that bears on the individual.

pressures toward uniformity. Pressures encountered in a group that tend to make the members conform.

PRF. See *Personality Research Form.*

primacy effect. In learning, the fact that the items near the beginning of a series are easier to learn than those near the center. See also *recency effect.*

primary coping. The initial attempt to deal with problems. See also *secondary coping.*

primary social units. The basic small groups of which a person is a part, such as family and peers.

principle of successive approximations. In shaping, the selection for reinforcement of successively closer approximations to the desired behavior.

proactive interference. The interfering effect of previous learning upon the recall of newly learned material. See also *negative transfer; retroactive interference.*

problem solving. Thinking directed toward the goal of solving a problem.

prodromal stage. The second of the three stages of alcoholism, according to Jellinek. In this stage, alcohol becomes a drug upon which the drinker relies heavily. It may cause memory blackouts. See also *crucial stage; prealcoholic stage.*

progesterone. One of the hormones secreted by the female gonads.

projection. Seeing one's own traits and motives in others.

projective technique. A test in which the subject is expected to project his own traits into fabricated stories. See also *Holtzman inkblot technique; Rorschach test; Thematic Apperception Test.*

prolactin. A pituitary hormone that induces the secretion of milk.

propinquity. The physical nearness of other people; there is a tendency for an individual to like people physically close to him.

proprioception. The sense of body position and movement.

Protozoa. The phyllum of animals having an acellular structure. They range from single-celled organisms such as amoeba to more complex cell colonies such as volvox.

proximity. The principle in Gestalt psychology that states that perceptual objects near each other will be perceived as units.

psilocybin. A psychedelic drug.

psychedelic drugs. Complex drugs (including LSD and psilocybin) that sometimes produce excitement, agitation, pleasurable sensations, and hallucinations, but at other times produce deep depression.

psychiatrist. An M.D. who is a specialist in the diagnosis and treatment of mental illness.

psychiatry. The branch of medicine that specializes in the diagnosis and treatment of mental illness.

psychic energizers. Antidepressant and excitement-inducing drugs.

psychic energy. According to Freud, energy obtained from the instincts.

psychoacoustics. The scientific study of sound as related to hearing.

psychoanalysis. A method of psychotherapy developed by Freud. It emphasizes the techniques of free association and transference and seeks to give the patient insight into his unconscious conflicts and motives.

psychoanalyst. A practitioner of the psychoanalytic method of therapy developed by Freud. See also *psychoanalysis.*

psychodrama. Spontaneous playacting used in psychotherapy.

psycholinguistics. Study of the underlying knowledge and abilities necessary to learn and use language.

psychological dependence. A term generally referring to an excessively strong craving for a given substance but with no real physiological need.

psychologist. A specialist in the field of psychology, usually holding a master's degree or Ph.D. in psychology.

psychology. The science of behavior and mental phenomena.

psychopath. An individual suffering from a mental disorder.

psychopharmacology. The study of the psychological effects of drugs.

psychophysics. Fechner's term for the study of the relation between sensation and stimulus.

psychosexual development. In Freudian theory, the sequence of stages through which the child progresses. See also *anal stage; genital stage; oral stage; phallic stage.*

psychosis. Severe mental disorder.

psychosomatic illness. A physical disorder attributable to emotional or other psychological causes.

psychosurgery. Brain surgery sometimes used for the alleviation of mental disorders.

psychotherapeutic drugs. Drugs used in the treatment of psychological and psychiatric disorders.

psychotherapy. The treatment of mental and emotional disorders by the application of psychological methods.

psychotogenic drugs. Drugs that produce psychosislike changes in mood, thinking, and behavior. See also *psychotherapeutic drugs.*

PTC. See *phenylthiocarbamide.*

puberty rites. The rites that serve to initiate a young man into adult status.

public opinion poll. A survey of the general trend of opinion in a population segment; obtained by selective sampling.

punishers. Consequences of behavior that result in the suppression of the behavior that produces them. See also *reinforcers.*

punishment. The application of unpleasant stimulation in response to undesirable behavior.

pupil. The opening in the iris through which light waves are admitted into the eye.

Purkinje effect. A shift in color perception that accompanies the change from cone to rod vision. The colors at the red end of the spectrum seem to lose brilliance in relation to those at the blue end.

pursuit rotor. An experimental device consisting of a rotating disc on the surface of a rectangular box. It tests motor skill by requiring the subject to keep a stylus in contact with the disc.

quadragram. A four-letter nonsense syllable. See also *nonsense syllable.*

radiant energy. See *electromagnetic radiation.*

range. A measurement of variability in a frequency distribution. It is obtained by subtracting the lowest score from the highest.

rapid eye movement (REM). During sleep, eye movement that usually occurs during dreaming.

rarefaction. A state of minimum compression in a sound wave.

rating. An estimation of an individual made by another.

ratio production. An experimental technique in the investigation of sensation in which subjects are given control of the intensity of a sound and asked to make it twice as loud, half as loud, three times as loud, and so forth, as another sound.

ratio scale. A measurement scale composed of equal units and having an absolute zero point. The measurements of length in feet and of weight in pounds are examples of ratio scales.

rationalization. The process of justifying one's impulsive or irrational behavior by presenting false but acceptable reasons to oneself or to others.

reaction formation. A defense mechanism involving the replacement in consciousness of an anxiety-producing impulse or feeling by its opposite.

reaction time. The time from the presentation of a stimulus until the onset of a response.

read-only system. A memory system in which information cannot be deleted or erased at will.

reality principle. In psychoanalytic theory, the action of the ego as it tries to cope with the realities of the environment.

recall. The form of remembering in which previously learned material is reproduced with a minimum of cues.

receiver-operating characteristic curve (ROC curve). In signal detection, a graphic representation of the shifts in the relationship between hits and false alarms that accompany shifts in the criterion for detection.

recency effect. In learning, the fact that items near the end of a series are easier to learn than those near the center. See also *primacy effect.*

recessive gene. A gene whose hereditary characteristics will not prevail when paired with a dominant gene. See also *dominant gene.*

reciprocal inhibition. A psychotherapeutic technique developed by Wolpe in which new, more desirable responses are substituted for the previous

undesirable responses that had been characteristic of the individual.

reciprocal translocation. The exchange of parts between chromosomes during meiosis.

recognition. The form of remembering in which the previously learned material is recognized as such.

reductionistic theory. The theory that holds that the proper method of explaining phenomena is to reduce them to the smallest possible parts and principles.

reflection of feeling. In client-centered therapy, the technique of restating what the client has said in such a way as to bring out the emotional significance of the statement.

regenerative process. The restoration by growth of a damaged or lost part of the body.

regression. Currently immature behavior appropriate only to an earlier stage of development.

rehearsal. Repeating or reviewing information to be learned. Rehearsal prolongs the retention of material in short-term memory and aids in transferring it to long-term memory.

reinforcement. In operant conditioning, the experimental procedure of immediately following a response with a reinforcer.

reinforcement schedule. See *schedule of reinforcement.*

reinforcers. Consequences of behavior that result in the repetition of the behavior that produces them. See also *punishers.*

relative refractory period. The brief period following the absolute refractory period in which a nerve fiber is responsive only to stimuli somewhat stronger than normal.

reliability. The self-consistency of a psychological test as a measure of behavior.

REM. See *rapid eye movement.*

reminiscence. The phenomenon in which a subject performs better after a delay than he did immediately after learning.

replication. Repetition of an experiment in order to test its validity.

repression. In psychoanalytic theory, the defense mechanism of forcefully ejecting unpleasant memories or impulses from conscious awareness.

reserpine. A tranquilizing drug often used to lower high blood pressure in hypersensitive patients.

resistance. The second stage of the general adaptation syndrome. See also *general adaptation syndrome.*

respiratory rate. Rate of breathing.

respondent conditioning. See *classical conditioning.*

response. A bit of an organism's behavior, either operant or elicited by a stimulus.

resting potential. The electric charge maintained by a cell between its interior surface and the body fluids just outside its cell membrane.

retention. The amount of previously learned material that can be remembered.

reticular activating system. A network of cells extending from the upper spinal cord, through the medulla and pons. It serves as an indirect sensory pathway to the cerebral cortex and is believed to be an important center for the regulation of activation and alertness.

retina. The light-sensitive portion of the eye containing the rods and cones, the receptors for vision.

retinal disparity. The difference between the images an object projects on each of the retinas. This difference serves as a cue to depth.

retinene. A chemical material in the retina instrumental in the formation of rhodopsin.

retrieval. The process of bringing a previously learned item to the level of conscious awareness.

retroactive interference. The interfering effect of new learning upon the recall of previously learned material. See also *proactive interference.*

reverberation time. The time required for a sound in a room to diminish to one-millionth of its original intensity.

reward areas. Areas of the brain in which the application of electricity is reinforcing.

rhodopsin. The light-sensitive material in the rods of the eye.

ribonucleic acid (RNA). Complex molecules that are believed to act as transfer agents and messengers in genetic development. They are also believed by some to be involved in memory storage.

ribosomes. The bodies in the cytoplasm of a cell that synthesize proteins.

RNA. See *ribonucleic acid.*

ROC. See *receiver-operating characteristic curve.*

rods. Receptors for vision located in the retina. They function primarily for peripheral and nighttime vision. See also *cones; retina.*

Rogers' process scale. A seven-stage rating scale developed by Carl Rogers, representing a continuum of psychological activity from rigidity and fixity to flow and spontaneity.

role. The pattern of behavior usually exhibited by a person in a particular social position.

role behavior. The actual behavior of a person functioning in his role.

role expectation. The behavioral expectations associated with a particular role.

Rorschach test. A projective test in which inkblots are used as stimuli.

rote learning. Memorization of meaningless verbal material.

Rotter Incomplete Sentences Blank. A projective test for personality assessment that employs a rating for maladjustment on each of forty completions of incomplete statements.

round window. One of two membrane-covered openings between the cochlea and the middle ear.

Ruffini endings. Receptors thought to respond to warmth.

saccule. A saclike swelling in the inner ear; part of the vestibular apparatus.

sacral division. The lower parts of the autonomic nervous system, located in the region of the sacrum.

sadism. The infliction of pain upon another for the purpose of sexual gratification.

safety needs. According to Maslow, needs that are centered around the human requirement for an orderly and predictable world. They include the needs for stability and security.

sanguine. A personality type characteristically anxiety-free and optimistic.

saturation. The dimension of color that describes its purity or richness.

satyriasis. Pathologically excessive sexual desire in men.

savings. A method of measuring retention. Measurement is made of the number of trials required for relearning as compared with the number of trials required for original learning.

Scanlon plan. A program for the application of theory Y to industry. See also *theory Y.*

scapegoating. The displacement of hostility to a convenient person or group.

schedule of reinforcement. The program for choosing from among the many occurrences of a response those that will be reinforced. See also *fixed-interval schedule; fixed-ratio schedule; variable-interval schedule; variable-ratio schedule.*

schizophrenia. A form of psychosis in which the patient becomes withdrawn and apathetic. Hallucinations and delusions are common.

scopolamine. A chemical that acts to depress transmission at synaptic junctions.

scotopic vision. Rod vision.

secondary appraisal. During an emotional reaction, the point at which a person perceives and evaluates his own bodily reactions.

secondary coping. The attempt to manage problems required by the failure of primary coping. See also *primary coping.*

secondary reinforcement. Reinforcement provided by a stimulus that has gained reward value by being paired with a primary reinforcing stimulus.

secondary reinforcing stimuli. Stimuli that accompany presentation of a primary reinforcer.

secondary traits. Limited personality traits closely tied to specific responses and situations.

selection. In genetics, the correlation between genotype and reproductive capacity.

selection differential. In genetics, the average trait score of selected parents minus the average trait score of the original population.

self-acceptance. Satisfaction with one's qualities and aptitudes and recognition of one's limitations.

self-actualization. According to Maslow, the highest of man's needs. It consists of developing one's own true nature and fulfilling one's potentialities.

semantics. The scientific study of the meaning of words.

semicircular canals. Three canals in the inner ear containing receptors for the vestibular sense.

senile psychosis. A form of psychosis caused in part by the physiological changes due to aging. It is characterized by delusions, memory defects, and general disorientation.

sensation. That which is experienced when a sense receptor is stimulated.

sensitivity group. A training group that may resemble either a T-group or an encounter group. See also *encounter group; T-group.*

sensitization. The phenomenon of becoming more than usually sensitive to a stimulus.

sensorimotor stage. The first stage in the mental development of the child, during which the purely biological organization of his personality is gradually changed into a biopsychological organization through his contacts with the world.

sensorineural impairment. A cause of deafness involving pathology of the cochlea or the auditory nervous system.

sensory-awareness group. An intensive group that tends to emphasize physical awareness and physical expression through movement, spontaneous dance, and so forth.

sensory deprivation. An experimental

situation in which the subject receives extremely restricted sensory input.

sensory gating. Focusing selectively upon one set of sensations while holding the others in the background.

sensory-information store (SIS). The momentary storage of sensory information, primarily at the level of the sensory receptors themselves.

sensory neuron. A neuron that transmits impulses from sense organs to the central nervous system.

sensory transducing systems. Systems, such as the visual and auditory, that change incoming stimuli into physiological energy patterns to be sent to the brain.

sentence-completion technique. A projective technique for personality assessment in which the subject is asked to complete sentences without being given any clearly formulated guidelines.

septal area. A portion of the limbic system that is thought to be involved with the emotions.

serial-position effect. In memorization, the tendency to remember those items nearest the beginning and end of the material to be learned.

serotonin. A brain amine thought to be important in emotional, perceptual, and cognitive functions.

set. In problem solving, a tendency to try a particular method of solution or to seek a certain kind of solution.

shadow. According to Jung, the unconsciously held opposite of what is consciously stressed by the individual.

shadowing. An experimental procedure for studying attentional capacity in which the subject must listen to a series of words or numbers and repeat each, as soon as he can, after it is said.

shape constancy. The tendency to perceive familiar objects as always having the same shape, regardless of the viewing angle.

shaping. Modifying behavior by reinforcing successive steps that lead to the desired final behavior.

short-term memory (STM). Memory with limited capacity and short duration. See also *long-term memory.*

shuttlebox. An experimental device, used to study learning, in which an animal must run or climb to a special compartment in order to escape shock.

sign stimuli. Particular features in the environment that elicit fixed action patterns.

sinusoidal. Relating to a wave whose coordinates are proportional to the sines of the abscissas, with the equation $y = a \sin x$.

SIS. See *sensory-information store.*

size constancy. The tendency to perceive familiar objects as always having the same size, regardless of the distance from which they are viewed.

Skinner's box. An experimental device designed by B. F. Skinner. It consists of a box with a mechanism at one end that, if operated, will automatically reinforce the subject's behavior.

small groups. Groups with such a small number of members that each one can make a critical difference to the group, such as a family.

social adjustment inventory. A test that measures how a person views his own relationships with other people.

social-comparison theory. Festinger's theory that there are a number of beliefs, attitudes, and values that cannot be verified or evaluated except by comparison with others.

social pressures. Coercion on the part of a group to make individuals conform to the standards of the group.

social psychology. The study of the members of a society in relation to that society.

social structure. The network of relationships among individuals and groups in a society.

socialization. The process of learning the values and customs of the culture in which one exists.

sociology. The scientific study of the structure and functions of social groups.

sociometric method. An index of group cohesiveness that requires each member of the group to indicate names of individuals he likes either inside or outside the group. The relationship between the ingroup and outgroup choices serves as the index.

sociopath. A person who is hostile and aggressive toward society or social institutions.

sodomy. Anal-genital contact between males.

soma. The cell body of a neuron.

somatype. Body typology. See also *ectomorphy; endomorphy; mesomorphy.*

sound pressure. The effective amount of mechanical pressure that a given sound actually exerts. Sound pressure is correlated with loudness.

sound pressure level (SPL). A measure of sound pressure expressed in the logarithmic unit known as the decibel.

sound spectrographs. Charts that plot the frequency and intensity of sound against time.

species-specific behavior. In ethology, components of behavior that are characteristic of a species.

spherical aberration. The failure of light

rays to come to a single focal point because of differential refraction at different locations of the curved lens.

spike. The wave of electrical energy that sweeps across the cell body when a neuron fires.

spinal cord. The bundle of neurons running through the spinal column.

SPL. See *sound pressure level.*

spontaneous discharge. The rhythmic discharge of spike potentials not dependent on external stimuli.

spontaneous recovery. The reappearance, after a lapse of time following extinction, of a conditioned response.

sprouting. The phenomenon in which fibrils from nearby neurons grow into areas from which the original input area to the spinal cord has been removed.

stabilized image. An image that always stimulates the same part of the retina.

stage of alarm. The first stage of the general adaptation syndrome, characterized by the swelling of the adrenal glands and the release of hormones.

stage of exhaustion. The third stage of the general adaptation syndrome, characterized by an exhaustion of the organism's capacity to resist stress.

stage of resistance. The second stage of the general adaptation syndrome, characterized by an increase in the organism's reaction to stress.

standard deviation. The square root of the variance in a frequency distribution.

standard score. A derived score based on the number of standard deviations between the original score and the average score.

Stanford-Binet scale. An intelligence scale that delineates the mental age for scores achieved on Stanford-Binet tests.

stapes. One of the bones in the middle ear. See also *incus; malleus.*

stereoscopic depth. Depth perception based on the fusion of images of objects seen by each eye from a different angle.

steroid hormones. A variety of hormones secreted by the adrenal cortex that regulate water balance and energy expenditure.

stimulants. Drugs that elevate mood, increase alertness, and prevent fatigue.

stimulus. Any form of environmental energy capable of affecting the organism.

stimulus control. The control of behavior by stimuli that have previously set the occasion for the reinforcement of the behavior.

stimulus error. A problem in experimentation that occurs when an observer knows something about the actual stimulus, so that his knowledge may influence and distort the report of his experience.

stimulus generalization. The tendency of an organism to respond less and less to stimuli as they become less similar to the original conditioned stimulus.

STM. See *short-term memory.*

storage. The actual physical retention of information in long-term memory.

Strong Vocational Interest Blank. An inventory that gives an index of the strength of the subject's interest in a vocational field compared with that of persons already in the field.

sublimation. The substitution of a socially acceptable activity for an unacceptable one.

suggestion. The exertion of influence by constant reiteration that one do something or believe something.

sulcus. A shallow fissure in the cerebral cortex.

Summerhill School. A school in England based on the principle that it is essential to trust students to find out what activities are appropriate for them.

superego. According to Freud, that part of the personality that restrains the activity of the ego and the id.

superior olive. One of the "relay stations" for sound between the ear and the auditory cortex.

supernormal stimulus. An exaggerated stimulus used in studies of species-characteristic behavior.

suppression. Intentional exclusion of unpleasant thoughts from consciousness.

survey methods. Methods of collecting information by questioning a large selection of people.

syllogism. A three-part reasoning process developed by Aristotle. It consists of major and minor premises and a conclusion that must follow from them.

syllogistic reasoning. Reasoning by means of the syllogism. See also *syllogism.*

symbolic operational stage. The stage of mental development in which the child begins to make symbolic representations about his world.

sympathetic nervous system. A section of the autonomic nervous system composed of long chains of ganglia lying along the sides of the spinal column. It prepares the organism for emergency situations.

synanon. A general term for any group therapy for drug addicts.

synapse. The meeting of two neurons.

synaptic junction. See *synapse.*

T-group. An intensive group that emphasizes human-relations skills.

t test. A statistical test used to calculate whether a difference in scores is significant or due to chance.

tachistoscope. An apparatus for presenting stimuli for brief, controllable periods of time.

task-frustration condition. A frustration test in which subjects are required to do an insoluble jigsaw puzzle as an "intelligence test." See also *insult condition; personal-frustration condition.*

taste bud. The receptor for taste.

TAT. See *Thematic Apperception Test.*

taxis. Behavior of an organism involving movement toward or away from the source of stimulation. See also *klinotaxis; telotaxis; tropotaxis.*

tectorial membrane. The membrane in the organ of Corti in which the hair cells are embedded.

telekinesis. In parapsychology, the movement of objects by other than physical means.

telepathy. Thought transference from one person to another.

telotaxis. Response in which the organism moves toward or away from the stimulus without successive or simultaneous comparisons of stimulus strength. See also *klinotaxis; tropotaxis.*

template. In information processing, a single, specific, stored item of information against which others may be compared for identity.

temporal lobe. A portion of each cerebral hemisphere located below the lateral fissure and in front of the occipital lobe.

tender-minded. According to James, the class of people who are idealistic, optimistic, and rationalistic. See also *tough-minded.*

test. A set of questions and/or tasks used to measure individual differences.

testosterone. A male sex hormone.

tetrahydrocannabinol (THC). The active ingredient in marijuana.

thalamus. The area of the forebrain that relays impulses to the cerebral cortex.

THC. See *tetrahydrocannabinol.*

thema. H. A. Murray's term representing the correlated concepts of need and press.

Thematic Apperception Test (TAT). A projective test in which the subject is required to make up stories about pictures.

theory. A set of assumptions and deductions used to explain observed events.

theory X. According to McGregor, the set of assumptions that (1) an individual dislikes his work; (2) the job of the industrialist is to coerce people to work; and (3) the average person prefers to be directed. See also *theory Y.*

theory Y. According to McGregor, the set of assumptions that (1) the expenditure of energy is natural; (2) external control is not the only way to ensure good performance; (3) the commitment to objectives in work is related directly to the goals sought; (4) people like responsibility; (5) many people are creative. See also *theory X.*

thinking. The active process of conceptualization, involving integrating percepts, grasping relationships, and asking further questions.

thirst. A drive stemming from water deprivation.

threshold. The minimum stimulation required for response.

thymine. A component of DNA.

thyroid-stimulating hormone (TSH). A hormone secreted by the anterior pituitary.

thyroxin. A hormone of the thyroid gland. It is a regulator of metabolism.

timbre. The quality of sound dependent upon the overtones that accompany the fundamental tone.

tinnitus. Ringing in the ears caused by pathological conditions in the receptors.

token economy. A method of applying operant conditioning to clinical problems. It uses tokens as secondary reinforcers that can be exchanged for primary reinforcers.

tonotopic organization. In audition, the correlation between place and sound frequency noted on the basilar membrane and in the auditory nervous system.

tough-minded. According to James, the class of people who are materialistic, pessimistic, and fatalistic. See also *tender-minded.*

tracking. A variation of the method of limits in which the subject controls the intensity of the sound himself. See also *method of limits.*

trait. Allport's term for a predisposition to respond to many kinds of stimuli in an equivalent manner.

tranquilizer. A drug used to reduce anxiety, tension, and depression and to induce relaxation.

transactionalists. Those scientists who emphasize the assumptive aspect of awareness.

transduction. The process of converting one type of energy into another. See also *sensory transduction.*

transference. In psychoanalytic theory, the tendency for the patient to respond to the analyst as he did to persons important in his life history (such as his mother and father).

transpositional errors. A long-term-memory error in which the order of stored items is transposed, as in transposing two digits of a telephone number.

transvestism. Sexual gratification from wearing the clothes of the opposite sex.

tree of possibilities. An expanding problem-solving situation in which each decision creates others to be made.

trichromatic theory of color vision. The theory that all hues are detected by the action of only three primary color receptors.

trigram. A three-letter nonsense syllable.

tropotaxis. A response in which bilaterally symmetrical organisms make simultaneous comparisons of stimuli falling on either side of the body.

TSH. See *thyroid-stimulating hormone.*

two-string problem. A reasoning test requiring the subject to tie together two suspended strings that he cannot bring together unaided. The solution requires that he use an object or objects in an untypical way. See also *functional fixedness.*

ultraviolet rays. Light rays beyond the visible spectrum on the violet end.

Umweg problem. An experiment revised by Köhler in which the subject must momentarily move away from the reward in order to obtain it. Also known as the detour problem.

unconditioned response. The response given naturally to an unconditioned stimulus.

unconditioned stimulus. A stimulus that, without training, elicits a response.

unconscious inference. A nonverbalized judgment acted upon without awareness.

unconscious processes. Psychological events not in conscious awareness.

unity thema. The single pattern of related needs and press, derived from infantile experiences, that gives meaning and coherence to the largest portion of the individual's behavior.

utricle. The structure of the inner ear containing receptors for change in head position.

Uznadze illusion. A visual illusion in which two concentric circles are shown successively, the outer first. The inner circle appears smaller than it really is.

vacuum activity. Species-characteristic behavior that is observed in the absence of appropriate releasing stimuli.

validity. The extent to which a measuring device is successful in measuring what it is supposed to measure.

variable-interval schedule. A reinforcement schedule in which a response is reinforced after a variable time interval. The schedule is described in terms of the average of these periods of time.

variable-ratio schedule. A reinforcement schedule in which a response is reinforced after a variable number of responses has occurred. The schedule is described in terms of the average number of responses required.

variance. The square of a standard deviation.

vasoconstriction. The constricting or closing of a blood vessel.

Venn diagram. A graphic representational system that aids in reasoning. Circles or ellipses are used to demonstrate inclusion, exclusion, or intersection of propositions.

ventral surface. The front surface of an organism.

ventromedial nucleus. An area of the hypothalamus related to hunger. Its destruction leads to overeating and obesity.

verbatim. Word for word.

vertebrate. Any animal with a backbone.

vestibular apparatus. The labyrinth, utricle, and saccule, which contain receptors for acceleration, deceleration, and changes in head position.

vestibular sense. The sense of balance.

visceral organs. The internal organs.

visual angle. The angle formed by the lines connecting the outer extremes of the object viewed and the eye.

visual projection area. The area of the occipital lobe elicited by visually perceived stimuli.

visual purple. Rhodopsin.

vitreous humor. The transparent material in the eye filling the space between the retina and the lens.

vocational aptitude test. A test that measures the ability to perform specialized skills required in various types of jobs.

volley theory. Wever and Bray's theory of hearing that states that the neurons of the auditory system fire in "volleys" rather than in unison in order to follow high frequencies.

volume. An attribute of sound related to both intensity and frequency.

voyeurism. Sexual gratification achieved by watching persons disrobe and/or engage in the sex act.

WAIS. See *Wechsler Adult Intelligence Scale.*

warm spots. Areas on the skin that are sensitive to warm stimuli.

warm-up. The tendency for performance to increase rapidly at the beginning of a period of work.

Weber's law. A law stating that the difference threshold is a fixed percentage of the stimulus magnitude at which it is measured.

Wechsler Adult Intelligence Scale (WAIS). An individual intelligence test for adults.

Wechsler Intelligence Scale for Children (WISC). An individual intelligence test for children.

wedge prism. A triangular-shaped prism.

white noise. Noise composed of sounds of all frequencies.

whole learning. Learning a task as a whole unit rather than in sections. See also *part learning.*

Whorf hypothesis. The hypothesis that linguistic differences cause cognitive, perceptual, and behavioral differences.

WISC. See *Wechsler Intelligence Scale for Children.*

word-association test. See *free association.*

working through. In psychoanalytic theory, the process of taking the patient through the same conflicts repeatedly in order for him to master them.

X chromosome. A chromosome that, when paired with another X chromosome, determines that the individual will be female.

Y chromosome. The chromosome that, combined with an X chromosome, determines that the individual will be male.

Young-Helmholtz theory. A theory of color vision that holds that there are three types of cones, which are responsive to red, green, and blue, respectively.

Zener cards. Cards, plain on one side with a symbol on the other, used in ESP experiments.

zygote. The product of the union of a sperm cell and an egg cell.

697

PICTURE CREDITS AND ACKNOWLEDGMENTS

We wish to thank the following persons and organizations for their contributions:

Dr. Marion White McPherson, Archive of History of American Psychology; Mr. Ward C. Edwards, University of Michigan; Circus-Circus Casino, Las Vegas, Nevada; Dr. James J. Jenkins, University of Minnesota; Mr. John Ponticello, Four Queens Casino, Las Vegas, Nevada; Dr. Stephen E. Glickman, University of California, Berkeley; Dr. Frank Beach, University of California, Berkeley; Dr. Herbert Pick, University of Minnesota; Dr. Harry Harlow, University of Wisconsin; Dr. Sebastian P. Grossman, University of Chicago; Dr. Eckhard H. Hess, University of Chicago; Dr. Robert McCleary, University of Chicago; Dr. James McConnell, University of Michigan; Dr. Harlan Lane, University of Michigan; Dr. Peter Marler, Rockefeller University; Dr. Neal E. Miller, Rockefeller University; Dr. Karl Pfaffman, Rockefeller University; Colonel Joseph Brady, Walter Reed Hospital; Dr. Tom Bower, Harvard University; Dr. John Smith, San Diego State College; Dr. David Kenny, Mr. Rusty White, and Mr. Jim Richards, Sea World; Dr. Henry F. Taylor, Naval Electronics Laboratory; Dr. Donald A. Norman, University of California, San Diego; Dr. George S. Reynolds, University of California, San Diego; Mr. Wayne Wykoff, Mesa Vista Hospital; Mr. Charles Shaw, San Diego Zoo; Dr. O. Ivor Lovaas, University of California, Los Angeles; Dr. John M. Atthowe, Palo Alto Veterans Administration Hospital; and Dr. Leonard Krasner, State University of New York, Stony Brook.

ILLUSTRATIONS

THE BETTMANN ARCHIVE: 4, 6, 7, 8 (left, top), 9, 10 (top), 11 (top center right).
GERRIE BLAKE: 8 (bottom), 27, 51, 68, 148, 149, 151, 211, 224 (bottom), 225 (top), 235 (bottom), 243 (top), 359, 371, 376, 596, 611.
JOHN DAWSON: 6 (top left, right), 7 (top far left, bottom far left, center, bottom center), 8 (bottom right), 9 (top left, top center right), 10 (top center left, top right), 11 (top center left, center, top center right, bottom center, bottom left), 12 (left, top center), 13 (center left, center, bottom center right), 14 (far left, bottom left), 15 (bottom center), 16 (bottom left), 69, 74 (center), 89, 95, 99, 103, 108, 109, 129 (bottom), 138 (bottom), 150, 176, 217, 252 (bottom), 399 (top).
JOYCE FITZGERALD: 156, 159.
MARTY GUNSAULLUS: 19 (left center), 414, 416, 419, 420 (foldout).
PHILIP KIRKLAND: 9 (bottom center), 525, 529, 533, 535, 536.
MILLSAP AND KINYON: 8 (center), 16 (bottom right), 17 (top left, top center left, center, center far left), 24, 25, 27, 29, 30, 32, 34, 36, 37, 39, 134, 137, 138 (top), 167, 241, 272–275, 278, 281, 283 (left), 285, 289–291, 297, 301 (bottom), 347, 400.
PAMELA MOREHOUSE: 11 (bottom far left), 12 (right), 250, 251, 442, 445, 447, 449, 451, 452, 454, 458, 459, 469.
KARL NICHOLASON: 11 (top right), 12 (top right), 13 (top left), 17 (bottom left), 18 (bottom left, far left), 51, 154, 240, 345–417 (flip drawing), 453, 475, 495, 506, 511, 514, 516, 519, 669–672.

PHOTOGRAPHS

STEVE MCCARROLL: 6 (far left, top center), 10 (top center right, bottom center), 11 (top bottom left), 12 (bottom center left), 13 (bottom left, bottom right), 14 (top left, center right), 15 (top center, far left, bottom left), 16 (far left, center far left, top center left, center bottom, bottom), 17 (bottom right), 18 (top center, center, center left), 19 (far left, top and bottom; top center; right and far right, bottom center; far right, bottom), 42, 44, 47, 53 (bottom), 57–59, 61, 64, 67, 72 (top), 73 (bottom left and right), 75, 79–81, 83, 90, 102 (top), 104, 107, 110, 112, 115, 119 (top), 120 (top), 130, 134, 139, 142,

158, 162, 184, 185 (top), 195, 197, 203, 204, 218, 223, 224 (top), 226, 235 (top), 242, 253 (top), 270, 312, 322 (bottom), 323, 324, 326, 331 (bottom), 335 (bottom right), 340, 355 (top), 360, 372–375, 384, 393, 395, 396, 398, 401, 404 (top), 405, 421, 424, 433 (top), 437, 456, 457, 462, 466, 468, 489, 498, 538, 559, 562, 567, 570, 579, 602 (top, center far right, bottom), 606, 609, 615, 619 (bottom right), 626, 639–641, 643–645, 650, 651, 655, 658, 664, 666.
JOHN OLDENKAMP: 9 (bottom right), 12 (bottom center), 14 (top), 16, 19 (top right, far right), 66, 73, 146, 182, 185 (bottom), 220, 336 (bottom), 350, 356, 421, 440, 460, 465, 467, 468, 470, 471, 477–479, 481, 482, 502, 522, 548, 556, 573, 576, 589, 591, 619, 622, 636, 642, 652, 657, 661.

TOM SUZUKI: 2, 18 (center bottom), 45, 48, 200, 207, 238, 294, 348, 355, 406, 592, 602, 612, 637, 646.
SCIENCE SERVICES: 9, 12, 13, 14, 15, 16, 19.

In addition to the citations in the text we wish to acknowledge the following:

UNIT I: 5 (right), 9 (top center and right), 10 (bottom)—Culver Pictures; 7 (center far right), 15 (top right), 16 (top right), 17 (center left)—H. Lee Pratt; 14 (right), 15 (top left)—T. Polumbaum; 15 (left), 16 (top center left)—Harvard University News Service; 15 (top center)—Brown University; 15 (center)—Nancy Bayley; 16 (bottom center)—Eugene H. Kone; 16 (top)—Courtesy of Karl Menninger; 17 (far left)—Dellenback; 17 (right)—Bar Photography, Ltd.; 18 (bottom left)—Ed James; 18 (bottom center right)—Photo File; 18 (bottom right)—Frank Ross Photography; 19 (bottom center)—Janie Cowles; 20—Rowland Sherman; 53 (top)—Charlie Aqua Viva; 60—Bob Fountain.

UNIT II: 84, 91 (bottom)—George Leavens; 85—Lajoux: Tassili, Rapho Guillumette Pictures; 87, 88—John C. Fentress; 91 (top left)—Tony Florio, National Audubon Society; 91 (center)—John H. Gerard, National Audubon Society; 91 (right)—Roy Pinner, National Audubon Society; 96—Thomas McAvoy, Life Magazine © Time Inc.; 98—So Excellent a Fishe by Archie Carr © 1957 by Archie Carr. Reprinted by permission of Doubleday and Company; 117 (top)—Bill Bridges; 123—Wilder Penfield; 127—James McConnell; 129 (center)—Jack Griffith, Courtesy of Genes in Action, The Upjohn Company, Kalamazoo, Michigan; 136, 144 (bottom)—Neal E. Miller; 144 (top)—Valentin Scheglowski; 145 (top)—Jose M. R. Delgado; 152, 153—Bill Noonan.

UNIT III: 181—Dr. James L. German; 187–189, 191–193, 199—George S. Zimbel, Monkmeyer Press.

UNIT IV: 246, 335 (bottom left)—Reprinted with permission. Science Digest © The Hearst Corporation; 252 (top)—Yale Joel, Life Magazine © Time Inc.; 254—Rowland Sherman; 265—Bell Laboratories; 274—National Aeronautics and Space Administration; 283—J. Rhodin, An Atlas of Ultra Structure, Saunders, 1963; 302—Floyd Ratcliff, Holden Day Publishers; 312, 313—Gordon Menzie; 316, 337 (bottom)—Bill Noonan; 333—Philip Clark.

UNIT V: 357—© 1968 Metro-Goldwyn-Mayer, Inc.; 390—National Aeronautics and Space Administration; 420—Robert and Krys Black.

UNIT VI: 433—Psychological Corporation; 463—Culver Pictures; 484—Rowland Sherman; 485, 487—Art Shay; 486—Janie Cowles; 488, 491—Jim Kay; 492—William G. Macdonald.

UNIT VII: 542, 545—Michael Alexander; 552—Raimondo R. Borea; 554—H. Lee Pratt.

UNIT VIII: 580—Nancy Chase; 581—Dr. Kurt W. Back; 583—Art Shay; 587 (color)—Paul Ganster; 587 (black and white)—Wide World Photos; 595—National Aeronautics and Space Administration; 599—Elliot Erwitt, Magnum Photos; 617 (33.3)—Courtesy of Young and Rubicam, Inc., and the Peace Corps; 619 (33.4)—advertisement for

McCall's Magazine courtesy of Doyle Dane Bernbach, Inc.; 621, 629, 630— Reprinted by permission of Forbes Magazine; 623—Photo courtesy of Mobil Oil Corporation; 625—Advertisement for WINS Radio, produced by Delehanty, Kurnit, and Geller, Inc.; 627—Bill Silano; 632, 633—Miles Laboratory and Jack Tinker and Partners; 634—Don Peterson; 638— James F. Flores; 641—Location, "The Swallows"; 648— Image Analysis.

GRAPHS AND DIAGRAMS

UNIT I: 8 (bottom left)—Hilgard and Atkinson, Introduction to Psychology, 4th edition, 1967, Harcourt, Brace and World, Inc., publishers; 10 (far right)—H. Mysiak and V. Sexton, History of Psychology, 1966, Grune and Stratton, Inc.; 11 (top right)—Courtesy of R. J. Reynolds Tobacco Company; 14, 15—R. G. Carraher and J. B. Thurston, Optical Illusions and the Visual Arts, © 1966 by Reinhold Book Corporation, by permission of Van Nostrand Reinhold Company; 18 (center left)—L. Festinger, S. Schachter, and K. Back, Social Pressures in Informal Groups, 1950, © 1950 by Harper & Row, Publishers; 18 (top left)—E. Zwicker and B. Scharf, "A Model of Loudness Summation," Psychological Review, 1965, Vol. 72, p. 7, © 1965 by the American Psychological Association, and reproduced by permission; 18 (top left, bottom)—S. S. Stevens, "The Surprising Simplicity of Sensory Metrics," American Psychologist, 1962, Vol. 17, pp. 29–39, © 1962 by the American Psychological Association, and reproduced by permission; 19 (top center)—H. M. Hanson, "Effects of Discrimination Training on Stimulus Generalization," Journal of Experimental Psychology, 1959, Vol. 58, pp. 321–334, © 1959 by the American Psychological Association, and reproduced by permission; 25 (2.3)—B. Katz, "The Nerve Impulse," Scientific American, 1952, Vol. 185, pp. 55–64, © 1952 by Scientific American; 26 (2.4)—C. T. Morgan, Psychological Psychology, 1943, reproduced by permission of McGraw-Hill Book Company; 29 (2.8, 2.9)—W. S. J. Krieg, Functional Neuroanatomy, 1966, © Brain Books, reproduced by permission of McGraw-Hill Book Company; 31 (2.12)—Wilder Penfield and Lamar Roberts, Speech and Brain-Mechanisms, © 1959, reprinted by permission of the Princeton University Press; 32 (2.14)—Penfield and Rasmussen, The Cerebral Cortex of Man, 1950, © The Macmillan Company; 34 (2.15)—after Frank H. Netter, M.D., from The CIBA Collection of Medical Illustrations; 36 (2.16)—H. Gray, Anatomy of the Human Body, 1966, © 1966 by Lea & Febiger; 38 (2.19)—after Frank H. Netter, M.D., from The CIBA Collection of Medical Illustrations; 39 (2.20)—The Body, p. 170, © 1964 Time Inc.

UNIT II: 69 (4.4, 4.5)—The Psychological Bulletin, 1909, Vol. 6, pp. 257–273, © 1909 by the American Psychological Association, and reproduced by permission; 70 (4.6, 4.7)—Hilgard and Atkinson, Introduction to Psychology, 4th edition, 1967, Harcourt, Brace and World, Inc., publishers; 73 (4.11)—R. S. Woodworth, Psychology, 1921, © by Holt, Rinehart and Winston, Inc.; 76 (4.16)—E. A. Bilodeau, I. McD. Bilodeau, and D. A. Schumsky, "Some Effects of Introducing and Withdrawing Knowledge of Results Early and Late in Practice," Journal of Experimental Psychology, 1959, Vol. 58, p. 143, © 1959 by the American Psychological Association, and reproduced by permission; 76 (4.17)—from Introduction to Psychology by Morgan and King. Copyright © 1966 by McGraw-Hill. Used by permission of McGraw-Hill Book Company; 78 (4.18)—reproduced by permission of Ronald Press Company; 78 (4.19)—Ballard, "Oblivescence and Reminiscence," British Journal of Psychology, 1913, No. 2, p. 5; 82 (4.23)—E. C. Tolman and C. H. Honzik, "Introduction and Removal of Reward, and Maze Performance in Rats," University of California Publications in Psychology, 1930, Vol. 4, pp. 257–275, used by permission of the University of California Press at Berkeley; 86 (5.5)—from Harlow and Woolsey, Biological and Biochemical Bases of Behavior, 1958; 90 (5.11), 96 (5.16)—R. A. Hinde, 1954, The Royal Society; 94 (5.12)—N. Tinbergen, The Study of

Instinct, 1951, the Clarendon Press, Oxford; 97 (5.17)—P. Ullyott, *Journal of Experimental Biology,* Vol. 13, 1936; 100 (5.20)—W. H. Thorpe, *Bird-Song,* 1961, by the Cambridge University Press; 102 (5.22)—from E. H. Hess in D. Robert and Gerald Handel, *Family Worlds: A Psychological Approach to Family Life,* © 1959, the University of Chicago Press; 113 (6.8)—H. M. Hanson, "Effects of Discrimination Training on Stimulus Generalization," *Journal of Experimental Psychology,* 1959, Vol. 58, pp. 321–334, © 1959 by the American Psychological Association, and reproduced by permission; 120 (6.17)—E. Fantino, D. Sharp, and M. Cole, "Factors Facilitating Lever-press Avoidance," *Journal of Comparative and Physiological Psychology,* 1966, Vol. 62, No. 2, pp. 214–217, © 1966, by the American Psychological Association, and reproduced by permission; 123 (6.19)—Wilder Penfield and Lamar Roberts, *Speech and Brain-Mechanisms,* © 1959, reprinted by permission of the Princeton University Press; 126 (6.21)—C. H. Hamlyn, "An Electric Microscope Study of Pyramidal Neurons in the Ammon's Horn of the Rabbit," *Journal of Anatomy,* 1963, used by permission of the Cambridge University Press; 135 (7.4)—D. Novin, "The Relation Between Electrical Conductivity of Brain Tissue and Thirst in the Rat," *Journal of Comparative Physiological Psychology,* 1962, Vol. 55, pp. 145–154, © 1962 by the American Psychological Association, and reproduced by permission.

Unit III: 164 (9.1), 174 (9.7)—Calvin P. Stone (ed.), *Comparative Psychology,* © 1951, reprinted by permission of Prentice-Hall, Inc., Englewood Cliffs, New Jersey; 176 (9.8)—J. Hirsch, "Studies in Experimental Behavior Genetics: II," *Journal of Comparative and Physiological Psychology,* 1959, Vol. 52, pp. 304–308, © 1959 by the American Psychological Association, and reproduced by permission; 176 (9.9)—L. Erlenmeyer-Kimling, J. Hirsch, and J. Weiss, "Studies in Experimental Behavior Genetics: III," *Journal of Comparative Physiological Psychology,* 1962, Vol. 55, pp. 722–731, © 1962 by the American Psychological Association, and reproduced by permission; 181 (9.11) – J. Hirsch and L. Erlenmeyer-Kimling, *Contemporary Approach to Psychology,* 1967, used by permission of the Van Nostrand Reinhold Company, © Reinhold Publishing Company; 205 (11.4)—T. G. R. Bower, "The Visual World of Infants," *Scientific American,* 1966, 215(6), 80–92, p. 4, © 1966 by Scientific American; 208 (11.8)—H. Thomas, "Preferences for Random Shapes: Ages Six Through Nineteen Years," *Child Development,* Vol. 37, pp. 843–859, The Society for Research in Child Development, Inc., © 1966, University of Chicago Press Journals; 208 (11.9), 209 (11.10)—Gibson, Gibson, Pick, and Ossen, *Journal of Comparative and Physiological Psychology,* 1962, Vol. 55, pp. 897–906, © 1959 by the American Psychological Association, and reproduced by permission; 213 (11.12)—R. G. Carraher and J. B. Thurston, *Optical Illusions and the Visual Arts,* © 1966 by Reinhold Book Corporation, by permission of Van Nostrand Reinhold Company; 215 (11.13)—M. Parish, R. Lundy, and H. Leibowitz, "Hypnotic Age-regression Magnitudes of the Ponzo and Poggendorf Illusions," *Science,* 1968, Vol. 159, pp. 1375–1376, © 1968 by the American Association for the Advancement of Science; 217 (11.15)—R. Held and A. Hein, "Movement Produced Stimulation in the Development of Visually Guided Behavior," *Journal of Comparative and Physiological Psychology,* 1963, Vol. 56, pp. 872–876, © 1963 by the American Psychological Association, and reproduced by permission; 228 (12.7)—H. A. Gleason, Jr., *An Introduction to Descriptive Linguistics,* Revised Edition, 1961, © Holt, Rinehart and Winston, Inc.; 233 (12.11, 12.12)—D. I. Slobin (ed.), *The Ontogenesis of Grammar,* 1969, used by permission of the Academic Press.

Unit IV: 247 (13.11)—D. N. Spinelli and K. H. Pribram, *Electroencephalography and Clinical Neurophysiology,* 1966, Elsevier Publishing Company; 248 (3.12, top)—P. Naitoh and L. C. Johnson, "Sleep Patterns of Aquanauts During Tektite I," Navy Medical Neuropsychiatric Research Unit Report; 259 (14.4)—H. Fletcher, *American Journal of Physics,* 1946, Vol. 14, pp. 215–225; 262 (14.6, 14.7)—S. S. Stevens, "The Surprising Simplicity of Sensory Metrics," *American Psychologist,* 1962, Vol. 17, pp. 29–39, © 1962 by the American Psychological Association, and reproduced by permission; 263 (14.8)—R. S. Woodworth and H. Schlosberg, *Experimental Psychology,* Revised Edition, 1954, p. 197, © Holt, Rinehart and Winston, Inc.; 264 (14.9)—S. Hecht and J. Jsia, *Journal of the Optical Society of America,* 1945, Vol. 35, pp. 261–267; 264 (14.10)—J. Steinhardt, "Intensity Discrimination in the Human Eye," *Journal of General Physiology,* 1936, Vol. 20, pp. 185–209, © 1936 by the Rockefeller University Press; 264 (14.11)—D. B. Judd, "Chromaticity Sensibility to Stimulus Differences," *Journal of the Optical Society of America,* 1932, Vol. 22, pp. 72–108; 265 (14.12)—H. Davis and S. Z. Silverman (eds.), *Hearing and Deafness,* Revised Edition, 1960, Chap. 2, © Holt, Rinehart and Winston, Inc.; 266 (14.14)—E. Zwicker and B. Scharf, "A Model of Loudness Summation," *Psychological Review,* 1965, Vol. 72, p. 7, © 1965 by the American Psychological Association, and reprinted by permission; 267 (14.16)—E. Zwicker, G. Flottorp, and S. S. Stevens, *Journal of Acoustical Society of America,* 1957, Vol. 29, p. 556; 269 (14.18)—J. A. Swets, "Is There a Sensory Threshold," *Science,* 1961, Vol. 134, pp. 168–178, © 1961 by the American Association for the Advancement of Science; 272 (15.1, 15.2)—H. Davis and S. R. Silverman (eds.), *Hearing and Deafness,* Revised Edition, 1960, Chap. 3, © Holt, Rinehart and Winston, Inc.; 277 (15.7)—ISO Recommendation R 226, 1st Edition, December 1961, "Normal Equal Loudness Contours for Pure Tones and Normal Threshold of Hearing Under Free Field Listening Conditions"; 279 (15.10)—W. E. Fedderson, T. T. Sandel, D. C. Teas, and L. A. Jeffress, "Localization of High Frequency Tones," *Journal of Acoustical Society of America,* 1957, Vol. 29, pp. 988–991; 282 (15.14)—R. Hinchcliffe, "The Threshold of Hearing as a Function of Age," *Journal of the Acoustical Society of America,* 1959, Vol. 9, p. 303; 289 (15.20)—After Frank H. Netter, M.D., from *The CIBA Collections of Medical Illustrations;* 291 (15.22)—After Frank H. Netter, M.D., from *The CIBA Collections of Medical Illustrations;* 291 (15.24)—R. S. Woodworth, *Experimental Psychology,* 1938, © Holt, Rinehart and Winston, Inc.; 298 (16.4, top)—L. A. Riggs, F. Ratliff, J. C. Cornsweet, and T. N. Cornsweet, "The Disappearance of Steadily Fixated Test Objects," *Journal of the Optical Society of America,* 1953, Vol. 43, pp. 495–501; 300 (16.8)—S. Hecht, C. Haig, and G. Wald, "The Dark Adaptation of Retinal Fields of Different Size and Location," *Journal of General Physiology,* 1935, Vol. 19, pp. 321–339, used by permission of Rockefeller University Press Journals; 302, 303 (16.10, 16.13, 16.14)—R. L. de Valois, "Neural Processing of Visual Information," Chapter 3 in R. W. Russell (ed.), *Frontiers in Physiological Psychology,* 1966, pp. 51–91, used by permission of Academic Press; 303 (16.12)—G. von Békésy, "Funneling in the Nervous System and Its Role in Loudness and Sensation Intensity on the Skin," *Journal of Acoustical Society of America,* 1958, Vol. 30, pp. 399–412; 305, 306 (16.15, 16.16)—S. Hecht, *et al.,* "The Dark Adaptation of Retinal Fields of Different Size and Location," *Journal of General Physiology,* 1935, Vol. 19, pp. 321–339; 321 (17.5, top left)—Josef Albers, "Structural Constellations," *Despite Straight Lines,* 1953–1958, pp. 63, 79. Courtesy of the artist. 311 (16.22)—reproduced by permission of the author of the Dvorine Pseudo-Isochromatic Plates, published by the Scientific Publishing Company, Baltimore, Maryland 21207; 320, 321 (17.4, 17.5)—R. G. Carraher and J. B. Thurston, *Optical Illusions and the Visual Arts,* © 1966 by Reinhold Book Corporation, by permission of Van Nostrand Reinhold Company; 320 (17.5)—B. R. Bugelski and D. A. Alampay, *Canadian Journal of Psychology,* 1961, Vol. 15, p. 206, used by permission of University of Toronto Press; 333 (17.20)—R. M. Lundy, *et al.,* "Hypnotic Age Regression Magnitudes of the Ponzo and Poggendorf Illusions," *Science,* March 22, 1968, Vol. 159, pp. 1375–1376, © 1968 by the American Association for the Advancement of Science.

Unit V: 367 (19.6)—From H. Ebbinghaus, *Memory: A Contribution to Experimental Psychology,* Dover Publications, Inc., New York, 1913, reprinted through permission of the publisher; 369 (19.8) — Osgood, *Psychological Review,* 1949, Vol. 56, p. 140, © 1949 by the American Psychological Association, and reproduced by permission; 370 (19.10)—L. R. Peterson and M. J. Peterson, "Short Term Retention of Individual Verbal Items," *Journal of Experimental Psychology,* 1959, Vol. 58, pp. 193–198, © 1959 by the American Psychological Association, and reproduced by permission; 386 (20.7)—Lyle E. Bourne, Jr., *Human Conceptual Behavior,* p. 7, © 1966 by Allyn and Bacon, Inc., Boston, used with the permission of the publisher; 389 (20.9)— B. R. Corman, "The Effect of Varying Amounts and Kinds of Information as Guidance in Problem-Solving, *Psychological Monographs,* 1957, Vol. 71, © 1957 by the American Psychological Association; C. P. Duncan, "Attempts to Influence Performance on an Insight Problem," *Psychological Reports,* 1961, Vol. 9, pp. 35–42, © 1961 by the American Psychological Association; F. Restle and J. Davis, "Success of Speed of Problem Solving by Individuals and Groups," *Psychological Review,* 1962, Vol. 62, pp. 520–536, © 1962 by the American Psychological Association; E. R. Hilgard, R. D. Edgren, and R. P. Irvine, "Errors in Transfer Following Learning With Understanding," *Journal of Experimental Psychology,* 1954, Vol. 47, pp. 457–464, © 1954 by the American Psychological Association; R. M. Gayne and E. C. Smith, Jr., "A Study of the Effects of Verbalization on Problem Solving," *Journal of Experimental Psychology,* 1962, Vol. 63, pp. 12–18, © 1962 by the American Psychological Association; F. Restle and G. A. Davis, "Success and Speed of Problem Solving by Individuals and Groups," *Psychological Review,* 1962, Vol. 69, pp. 520–536, © 1962 by the American Psychological Association, and all reproduced by permission; 399 (21.6)—K. Lorenz, *On Aggression,* © 1966, Harcourt, Brace and World, Inc.; 399 (21.7)—Edward J. Murray, *Motivation and Emotion,* © 1964, Prentice-Hall, Inc., Englewood Cliffs, New Jersey, used by permission. Originally from K. M. B. Bridges, "Emotional Development in Early Infancy," *Child Development,* 1932, Vol. 3, pp. 324–341, The Society for Research in Child Development, Inc., © 1932, University of Chicago Press Journals.

Unit VI: 431 (23.3)—L. M. Terman and M. A. Merrill, *I.Q. Distribution Revised Stanford-Binet Intelligence Scale,* © 1937 by Houghton Mifflin Company; 433 (23.7)—*Wechsler Intelligence Scale For Children Maze Test,* © 1949 by the Psychological Corporation, all rights reserved; 432 (23.4)—from the *Wechsler Adult Intelligence Scale Record Form* reproduced by permission and © by the Psychological Corporation; 434 (23.8)—L. E. Tyler, *The Psychology of Human Differences,* 1965, p. 130, Appleton-Century-Crofts, Educational Division, Meredith Corporation, and also from "Psychological Activities in the Training Command, Fort Worth, Texas," by the Army Air Force Psychological Section, *Psychological Bulletin,* © 1945 by the American Psychological Association, and reproduced by permission; 438 (23.10)—reprinted from Strong Vocational Interest Blank for Men, Form T399, by Edward K. Strong, Jr., revised by Edward K. Strong, Jr., David P. Campbell, Ralph F. Berdie, and Kenneth E. Clark, with the permission of the publishers, Stanford University Press. Copyright © 1938, 1945, 1964, 1965, and 1966, by the Board of Trustees of the Leland Stanford Junior University; 443 (24.2)—W. G. Dahlstrom and G. S. Welsh, *MMPI Handbook: A Guide to Use in Clinical Practice and Research,* 1960, used by permission of the University of Minnesota Press; 449 (24.8)—Douglas N. Jackson, © 1967 by Research Psychologists Press, Inc., Goshen, New York.; 469 (25.8) – C. G. Jung, translated by R. F. C. Hull, *Archetypes and the Collective Unconscious,* 1959, Bollingen Foundation; 473 (25.11)—adapted from Henry A. Murray, *Explorations in Personality,* © 1938 by Oxford University Press, Inc., renewed 1966 by Henry A. Murray. Used by permission; 480 (25.16)—W. H. Sheldon, *Atlas of Men: A Guide for Somatotyping Men of All Ages,* 1954.

Unit VIII: 580 (31.2)—W. F. Whyte, *Street Corner Society: The Social Structure of an Italian Slum,* 1943, p. 8, © 1943, the University of Chicago Press; 589 (31.10)—copyright by Rand McNally & Company, R.L. 69–S–82; 591 (31.12)—copyright by Rand McNally & Company, R.L. 69–SF–18; 608 (32.8)—Leonard Berkowitz, "Personality and Group Position," *Sociometry,* 1956, Vol. 19, pp. 210–222, the American Sociological Association, and also Murray Glanzer and Robert Glaser, "Techniques for the Study of Group Structure in Small Groups," *Psychological Bulletin,* 1961, Vol. 58, pp. 1–27, © by the American Psychological Association, and reproduced by permission; 644 (34.6)—copyright, 1956 by William H. Whyte. Reprinted by permission of Simon and Schuster, Inc.; 645 (34.7)—L. Festinger, S. Schachter, and K. Back, *Social Pressures in Informal Groups,* 1950, © 1950 by Harper & Row Publishers; 666 (35.6)—R. Hawkins, R. Peterson, E. Schweid, and S. Bijou, "Behavior Therapy in the Home: Amelioration of Problem Parent-Child Relations With the Parent in a Therapeutic Role," *Journal of Experimental Child Psychology,* 1966, Vol. 4, p. 105, © 1966 by the American Psychological Association, and reproduced by permission.

This book was set in Fairfield, Helvetica, and Goudy Old Style typefaces by American Book–Stratford Press, Inc., New York, New York.

Transparencies were processed and assembled by Robert Crandall Associates, New York, New York.

The text was printed in web offset lithography by Rand McNally & Co., Chicago, Illinois.

The insert was printed in offset lithography by Rand McNally & Co.

Text paper is Glatcotext Web, furnished by Perkins & Squier Company, New York, New York.

Insert paper is Old Forge Offset Enamel Gloss, furnished by Perkins & Squier Company, New York, New York.

Endsheets are Schlosser Multicolor.

The book was bound in Bancroft cloth by Rand McNally & Co.

David A. Dushkin, *President and Publisher, CRM BOOKS*

Richard L. Roe, *Vice-President, CRM BOOKS, and Director, College Department*
Sales Manager, College Department: Richard M. Connelly
Fulfillment Manager, College Department: Nancy Le Clere
College Staff: Elaine Kleiss, Carol A. Walnum, La Delle M. Willett

Jean Smith, *Vice-President and Managing Editor, CRM BOOKS*
Editors: Gloria Joyce, Arlyne Lazerson, Cecie Starr, Betsy H. Wyckoff
Editorial Assistants: Susan Ellenbogen, Jacquelyn Estrada, Ann Scales
Rights and Permissions: Donna L. Taylor

Jo Ann Gilberg, *Vice-President, CRM BOOKS, and Director, Manufacturing and Production*
Production Manager: Eugene G. Schwartz
Production Supervisors: Barbara Blum, E. Cecile Mayer
Production Assistants: Georgene L. Martina, Patricia Perkins
Production Staff: Mona F. Drury, Margaret M. Mesec

Tom Suzuki, *Vice-President, CRM BOOKS, and Director of Design*
Art Director: Leon Bolognese
Designers: Reynold Hernandez, John Isely, George Price
Associate Designer: Catherine Flanders
Assistant Designers: Robert Fountain, Pamela Morehouse
Art Staff: Jacqueline McLoughlin

Paul Lapolla, *Vice-President, CRM BOOKS, and Director, Psychology Today Book Club*
Assistant: Karen De Laria

Controller: Robert Geiserman
Assistant: Maryann Errichetti

Office Manager: Lynn D. Crosby
Assistants: Phyllis J. Trout, Janie Fredericks, Drew Reeves